Congress and Its Members

15th Edition

For Nancy; Douglas, Victoria, Elizabeth, Thomas, James, Alexander; Chris, Theo, Emily, and Olivia

—R. H. D.

For Janet, Mark, and Eric

—W. J. O.

For Emery and Beverly

—F. E. L.

For Terri, Sam, and Lea

—E. S.

Congress and Its Members

15th Edition

Roger H. Davidson

University of Maryland

Walter J. Oleszek

Congressional Research Service

Frances E. Lee

University of Maryland

Eric Schickler

University of California, Berkeley

Los Angeles | London | New Delhi
Singapore | Washington DC

Los Angeles | London | New Delhi
Singapore | Washington DC

FOR INFORMATION:

CQ Press

An Imprint of SAGE Publications, Inc.

2455 Teller Road

Thousand Oaks, California 91320

E-mail: order@sagepub.com

SAGE Publications Ltd.

1 Oliver's Yard

55 City Road

London EC1Y 1SP

United Kingdom

SAGE Publications India Pvt. Ltd.

B 1/I 1 Mohan Cooperative Industrial Area

Mathura Road, New Delhi 110 044

India

SAGE Publications Asia-Pacific Pte. Ltd.

3 Church Street

#10-04 Samsung Hub

Singapore 049483

Printed in the United States of America

ISBN 978-1-4833-8888-5

This book is printed on acid-free paper.

Acquisitions Editor: Sarah Calabi

eLearning Editor: Robert Higgins

Editorial Assistant: Raquel Christie

Production Editor: David C. Felts

Copy Editor: Talia Greenberg

Typesetter: C&M Digitals (P) Ltd

Proofreader: Alison Syring

Indexer: Will Ragsdale

Cover Designer: Scott Van Atta

Marketing Manager: Amy Whitaker

SUSTAINABLE FORESTRY INITIATIVE

Certified Chain of Custody
Promoting Sustainable Forestry
www.sfiprogram.org
SFI-01268

SFI label applies to text stock

15 16 17 18 19 10 9 8 7 6 5 4 3 2 1

BRIEF CONTENTS

Reference Materials

CONTENTS

Reference Materials

TABLES, FIGURES, AND BOXES

Tables

Figures

Boxes

SOUTHERN CHIVALRY — ARGUMENT versus CLUB'S.

*F*our Pivotal Events in Congressional History. British troops burn the Capitol and capture Washington, D.C., in 1814 (top left). Inflamed sectional passions caused violence on the Senate floor in 1856 (top right): An enraged representative Preston Brooks, S.C., right, raises his cane against an unsuspecting senator Charles Sumner, Mass. Laurence M. Keitt, a fellow South Carolinian (center), raises his cane and holds a pistol behind his back to keep other Northerners from interfering. In the televised Army-McCarthy hearings of 1954 (bottom), Sen. Joseph McCarthy, R-Wis., is chastened by U.S. Army counsel Joseph Welsh (left) during the Senate inquiry into McCarthy's reckless charges about communists in government. "At long last, sir, have you no sense of decency?" Welsh exclaimed after McCarthy attacked one of the lawyer's young aides. The dramatic exchange was a turning point in McCarthy's career; eventually he was censured by his Senate colleagues. Finally (center), Senate Majority Leader Lyndon B. Johnson, D-Tex., gives "the treatment"—prolonged persuasion at very close range—to Sen. Theodore Francis Green, D-R.I.

PREFACE

As authors of the fifteenth edition of a book that first appeared in 1981, we are perforce believers in the maxim that in politics six months is a long time and four years practically a lifetime. Events of recent years surely bear out this wisdom. The roller-coaster reversals of government and politics require frequent updates of any text on the U.S. Congress that aims to be both current and comprehensive.

Presidents typically suffer steep declines in public support during their tenures in office. Three postwar presidents—Gerald R. Ford, Jimmy Carter, and George H. W. Bush—were denied a second term. A fourth, Lyndon Johnson, withdrew from his reelection race after losing the support of critical factions in his own party. George W. Bush's approval ratings declined from some of the highest ever recorded for any president to some of the lowest. Entering office during a financial crisis and the worst recession since the Great Depression, Barack Obama has never enjoyed particularly high approval ratings. Even so, he saw his public support drop sharply during his first term. Six months before election day in 2012, it appeared quite possible that Obama would lose his reelection bid. In the end, he survived to grapple with a second term just as challenging as his first.

Nearly every president since World War II has faced a Congress controlled wholly or in part by the opposition party. Each of the last three presidents has endured midterm backlashes that cost their party control of Congress. After an exceptionally productive Congress under unified government in his first two years of office, Obama received what he termed a "shellacking" in the 2010 elections, in which Republicans gained a historic sixty-three seats to retake control of the House of Representatives. In 2014 Republicans padded their House majority, the largest since 1947 and gained the largest number of Senate seats for any party since 1980, recapturing the Senate majority. Since 2011 the president's relations with Congress have lurched from crisis to crisis, with impasses threatening to halt federal agency operations or send the government into default. The current Congress, mired in the depths of public disapproval, will be asked to address a multitude of difficult issues left outstanding from previous years.

The precarious fortunes of recent presidents and congressional majorities are a reminder of the pervasive pluralism of the American political system, with its diverse viewpoints and interests. Presidents and congressional leaders see their perceived mandates collide with the founders' intricate "auxiliary precautions" for preventing majorities from winning quick or total victories. Not the least of the system's attributes is what we call the "two Congresses": Congress is both a conduit for localized interests and a maker of national policy.

In this edition, we discuss new developments and fresh research on nearly every aspect of Congress. When the first edition of this book came out, political scientists were still seeking to explain the decline of party unity in Congress. Today, the strength of partisanship and party leaders is the most salient reality of Capitol Hill. Congress is a vortex of the so-called permanent campaign, in which electioneering is interlocked with the process and content of lawmaking. We record shifts in party leaders, the committee system, floor procedures, and the Capitol Hill community. Complex, interdependent relationships with presidents, bureaucrats, and the courts put Congress at the center of the entire federal government.

In the midst of fundamental political change, there remain underlying constants in Congress's character and behavior. Most important is the dual nature of Congress as a collection of career-minded politicians and as a forum for shaping national policy. We employ the two-Congresses theme to explain the details of congressional life as well as scholarly findings about legislators' behavior. Colorful personalities and interesting events are never in short supply when examining Capitol Hill. We strive to describe recent developments and trends; more important, we try to place them in broader historical and conceptual context.

These are troubling times for those of us who believe in representative democracy. True, Congress has, with varying levels of success, absorbed astonishing changes in its membership, partisan control, structural and procedural arrangements, and policy agendas. Yet Congress has all too often retreated from its constitutional mandate to initiate national policy and oversee government operations. Its prerogatives are under siege from executive decision makers, federal judges, and elite opinion makers, who constantly belittle its capacities, ignore its authority, and evade its scrutiny. Lawmakers themselves are to blame for failing to address pressing policy problems, for reinforcing disdain of the institution, and for substituting partisan allegiance for independent judgment and critical thinking. Today's Congress all too often falls short of the founders' vision as the "first branch of government"—for reasons that this book explains.

This edition, like its predecessors, is written for general readers seeking an introduction to the modern Congress as well as for college or university students taking courses on the legislative process or national policy making. We try to present accurate, timely, and readable information, along with insights from scholars and practitioners. Although wrapped around our core theme, the book's chapters are long on analysis. We make no apologies for this. Lawmaking is an arduous, complicated business; those who would understand it must master its details and nuances. At the same time, we hope to convey the energy and excitement of the place. After all, our journalist friends are right: Capitol Hill is the best beat in town.

ACKNOWLEDGMENTS

We have incurred more debts to friends and fellow scholars than we could ever recount. We thank especially our colleagues at the Congressional Research

Service and elsewhere: Richard Beth, Ida Brudnick, Maeve Carey, Royce Crocker, Christopher Davis, C. Lawrence Evans, Louis Fisher, Sam Garrett, Valerie Heitshusen, William Heniff Jr., Henry Hogue, Michael Koempel, Emery Lee, Mindy Levit, Megan Lynch, Jennifer Manning, Elizabeth Rybicki, James Saturno, Judy Schneider, Barbara Schwemle, Stephen W. Stathis, Jacob Strauss, Kenneth Thomas, Jim Thurber, Jessica Tollestrup, and Donald Wolfensberger. The views and interpretations expressed in this book are in no way attributable to the Congressional Research Service. Kelsey Hinchliffe and Emily Hertz provided valuable research assistance. We wish to thank our reviewers: Ross Baker, Rutgers University; Roger Byrd, Brewton-Parker College; Kenneth Cosgrove, Suffolk University; Rick Henderson, Texas State University; Ed Miller, University of Wisconsin, Stevens Point; Elizabeth Palmer, University of Arizona; and Norman Rodriguez, John Wood Community College. The comments of these valued colleagues prompted us to consider new questions and undertake improvements for the current edition.

Our friends at CQ Press deserve special appreciation. We thank Sarah Calabi, our editor, for keeping us on track as we revised the book to reflect the most recent developments. Charisse Kiino offered much guidance as we worked out the division of responsibilities for this and future editions. Talia Greenberg offered skilled and probing editorial assistance. David C. Felts supervised the book's production. And we thank Raquel Christie for providing photo research.

Our deep appreciation for our families, for their love and support, cannot be fully expressed in words. As a measure of our affection, this book is dedicated to them.

—Roger H. Davidson
Santa Barbara, California

—Walter J. Oleszek
Fairfax, Virginia

—Frances E. Lee
Washington, D.C.

—Eric Schickler
Berkeley, California

April 2015

Roger H. Davidson is professor emeritus of government and politics at the University of Maryland, and has served as visiting professor of political science at the University of California, Santa Barbara. He is a Senior Fellow of the National Academy of Public Administration. During the 1970s, he served on the staffs of reform efforts in both the House (Bolling-Martin Committee) and the Senate (Stevenson-Brock Committee). For the 2001–2002 academic year, he served as the John Marshall Chair in political science at the University of Debrecen, Hungary. His books include *Remaking Congress: Change and Stability in the 1990s,* co-edited with James A. Thurber (1995), and *Understanding the Presidency,* 7th ed., co-edited with James P. Pfiffner (2013). Davidson is co-editor with Donald C. Bacon and Morton Keller of *The Encyclopedia of the United States Congress* (1995).

Walter J. Oleszek is a senior specialist in the legislative process at the Congressional Research Service. He has served as either a full-time professional staff aide or consultant to every major House and Senate congressional reorganization effort beginning with passage of the Legislative Reorganization Act of 1970. In 1993 he served as Policy Director of the Joint Committee on the Organization of Congress. A longtime adjunct faculty member at American University, Oleszek is a frequent lecturer to various academic, governmental, and business groups. He is the author or co-author of several books, including *Congressional Procedures and the Policy Process,* 9th ed. (2014), and *Congress under Fire: Reform Politics and the Republican Majority,* with C. Lawrence Evans (1997).

Frances E. Lee is professor of government and politics at the University of Maryland. She has been a Research Fellow at the Brookings Institution and an APSA Congressional Fellow. She is the author of *Beyond Ideology: Politics, Principles, and Partisanship in the U.S. Senate* (2009), which received the Richard F. Fenno Jr. Prize for the best book on legislative politics in 2010 and the D. B. Hardeman Prize for the best book on the U.S. Congress published in 2009. She is also co-author, with Bruce I. Oppenheimer, of *Sizing Up the Senate: The Unequal Consequences of Equal Representation* (1999). Her articles have appeared in the *American Political Science Review, Journal of Politics, Legislative Studies Quarterly,* and *American Journal of Political Science,* among others.

Eric Schickler is Jeffrey & Ashley McDermott Professor of Political Science at the University of California, Berkeley. He is the author of *Disjointed Pluralism: Institutional Innovation and the Development of the U.S. Congress* (2001), which won the Richard F. Fenno Jr. Prize for the best book on legislative politics in 2002. He is the co-author, with Donald Green and Bradley Palmquist, of *Partisan Hearts and Minds* (2002) and, with Gregory Wawro, of *Filibuster: Obstruction and Lawmaking in the U.S. Senate* (2006), which won the Fenno Prize in 2007. His articles have appeared in the *American Political Science Review*, *American Journal of Political Science*, *Legislative Studies Quarterly*, and *Studies in American Political Development*, among others.

FIFTEENTH EDITION

Congress and Its Members

AP Photo/Susan Walsh

AP Photo/Steve Helber

Rep. Dave Brat, R-Va., poses with John Boehner, R-Ohio, shortly after having voted against him for another term as Speaker of the House. Majority Leader Eric Cantor, R-Va., concedes after his stunning primary defeat in June 2014. College economics professor and Republican candidate for Congress David Brat is pictured on the campus of Randolph-Macon College in April 2014.

Jay Paul/Getty Images

The Two Congresses

"I mean, it's a miracle," marveled economics professor Dave Brat.[1] In one of the most stunning congressional upsets in a generation, Brat had just defeated House Majority Leader Eric Cantor, R-Va., in a Republican primary. Never before had a House majority leader been unseated in a primary.

The outcome surprised almost everyone. Cantor enjoyed some seemingly unassailable advantages. A skilled political leader who had risen through the ranks to top Republican Party leadership, Cantor was likely next in line for Speaker of the House. After more than a decade in Congress, Cantor's was also a household name in his conservative, strongly Republican Richmond-area district. Meanwhile, Brat was a professor in a small liberal arts college who had never before held elective office. Cantor was one of Capitol Hill's top fund-raisers, and his campaign outspent Brat's by 26 to 1. Cantor had spent nearly as much on fund-raising dinners at steakhouses as Brat had raised in total for his whole campaign.[2] In the lead-up to the election, every poll had shown Cantor with a solid lead.[3] Nevertheless, in the end, Brat defeated Cantor—and by a lopsided margin of 11 percentage points. "Can you believe it? Unbelievable!" said Brat to his daughter as the Associated Press called the race in his favor.[4]

Although surprising and extraordinary, the outcome of the 2014 Brat–Cantor primary highlights fundamental truths about political representation. The work of Congress is conducted not only on Capitol Hill but also in states and districts hundreds or thousands of miles away. There is no question that Cantor had distinguished himself as a power broker and party leader in Washington. "He's a tier-one talent," said Rep. Peter Roskam, R-Ill. "He uniquely brought us together . . . at a time when the president was at a 70 percent approval, and he saw the weakness of [President Barack Obama's economic] stimulus, rallied against it, and that was the beginning of the GOP comeback."[5]

But Cantor's ties to his home constituency had frayed. The fund-raising expected of party leaders required him to spend a lot of time traveling to meet with prospective donors all over the country. Even when he was in his district, Cantor wasn't "one to slap backs, kiss babies, knock on doors, or work the room."[6] Cantor preferred to hold invitation-only events. One of his aides was quoted telling a local Tea Party activist, "Eric Cantor will never hold a town hall meeting. Over my dead body! You hear me?"[7] Over time, Cantor's popularity among constituents had declined. A local reporter for the *Chesterfield Observer* described the changing mood in the district: "You could tell wherever you went that Cantor was incredibly unpopular, that people saw him as arrogant."[8] "He was a lot more in touch when he first ran 14 years ago," remarked a local drugstore manager.[9]

Brat was able to take advantage of Cantor's underappreciated vulnerabilities. With Cantor's support already softened, Brat identified issues with strong local appeal in the district. He found populist themes to capitalize on voter discontent with Congress and Washington insiders. "I am running against Cantor," he wrote in an op-ed a week before the primary, "because he does not represent the citizens of the 7th District, but rather large corporations seeking insider deals, crony bailouts and a constant supply of low-wage workers."[10] The reference to "low-wage workers" was aimed at Cantor's support for some immigration reforms. Brat, with considerable exaggeration, lambasted Cantor as "the leading force in the House pushing for amnesty for illegal immigrants."[11] The immigration issue touched a nerve among conservative voters in the district. It also attracted national attention. A variety of prominent conservative media personalities embraced Brat and began to promote his campaign, including Laura Ingraham, Ann Coulter, Matt Drudge, and Mark Levin.[12] "Every [talk radio] newscast was talking about [Cantor's] support for immigration," observed a national Tea Party activist. "Dollars can't buy an advertisement like that."[13]

The Brat–Cantor race illustrates central themes of this book. No matter how much members of Congress distinguish themselves as lawmakers or Beltway insiders, they also have to distinguish themselves in the eyes of local constituents. There is no question that Cantor had an illustrious and accomplished career in Congress, but a successful representative cannot rest on laurels won in Washington. Ambitious potential challengers, back in the district, are always watching for early signs of weakness. For this reason, lawmakers must win and continually renew bonds of trust with their constituents. These bonds rest on constituents' sense of connection to their representatives. Members must maintain personal relationships and open lines of communication. Constituents may not always understand the details of national policy debates, but they know whom they trust—and whom they doubt.

THE DUAL NATURE OF CONGRESS

Eric Cantor's political experiences underscore the dual nature of Congress. Like all members, Cantor inhabited two very different but closely linked worlds. There is the world of Virginia's expansive 7th Congressional District, where representatives must connect with voters in suburbs, exurbs, and small towns sprawling across more than one hundred miles. Then there is the world of Washington policy making, where Cantor had cultivated a reputation as one of the Republican Party's up-and-coming "young guns." "I was in my district every week," Cantor said at a news conference after his defeat. "There is a balance between holding a leadership position and serving constituents back home."[14] The balance is often difficult to strike. Cantor's first political mentor, former representative Tom Bliley Jr., R-Va. (1981–2001), observed, "One of the major problems for him: He was involved in the leadership, but he wasn't spending time in the district, particularly in New Kent, Culpeper, and Orange, in the outer part of the district."[15] Such tensions highlight the dual character of the national legislature—Congress as a lawmaking institution and Congress as an assembly of local representatives.

In this sense, there are two Congresses. One is the Congress of textbooks, of "how a bill becomes a law." It is Congress acting as a collegial body, performing constitutional duties, and debating legislative issues that affect the entire nation. This Congress is a fascinating arena in which all the forces of American political life converge—presidents, cabinet members, career bureaucrats, activists, lobbyists, policy wonks, military leaders, and ambitious political entrepreneurs of every stripe. This Congress is more than a collection of its members at any given time. It is a mature institution with a complex network of rules, organizations, and traditions. Norms mark the boundaries of the legislative playing field and define the rules of the game. Individual members generally must accept Congress on its own terms and conform to its established ways of doing things.

A second Congress exists as well, and it is every bit as important as the Congress portrayed in textbooks. This is the representative assembly of 541 individuals (100 senators, 435 representatives, 5 delegates, and 1 resident commissioner). This Congress includes men and women of many different ages, backgrounds, and routes to office, all doing what is necessary to maintain political support in their local constituencies. Their electoral fortunes depend less on what Congress produces as a national institution than on the policy positions they take individually and the local ties they build and maintain. "As locally elected officials who make national policy," observes Paul S. Herrnson, "members of Congress almost lead double lives."[16]

The two Congresses are in many ways separated by a wide gulf. The complex, often insular world of Capitol Hill is far removed from most constituencies, in perspective and outlook, as well as in miles. Lawmaking and representing are separate tasks, and members of Congress recognize them as such. Yet these two Congresses are bound together. What affects one affects the other—sooner or later.

Legislators' Tasks

The duality between institutional and individual duties permeates legislators' daily activities and roles. As Speaker Sam Rayburn, D-Tex., once remarked: "A congressman has two constituencies—he has his constituents at home, and his colleagues here in the House. To serve his constituents at home, he must also serve his colleagues here in the House."[17]

No problem vexes members more than that of juggling constituency and legislative tasks. The pull of constituency business is relentless. To maintain their local connections, congressional calendars allow for lengthy recesses, termed "district work periods," and most legislative weeks are scheduled from Tuesday to Thursday. "I can tell you based on my experience that the number of days Congress spends in Washington should not be correlated with the quality of the work that is accomplished. . . . I can also tell you that time spent in our districts is not 'time off,'" observed Rep. Rob Bishop, R-Utah. "There is much more to effective representation than just voting in Washington."[18] On average, between 2000 and 2014, Congress was in session for 137 days a year, about one out of every three days. Members spend much of the rest of their time at home in their constituencies.

Reelection is the paramount operational goal of members of Congress. As a former representative put it, "All members of Congress have a primary interest in getting reelected. Some members have no other interest."[19] After all, politicians must win elections before they can achieve any long-range political goals. "[Reelection] has to be the *proximate* goal of everyone, the goal that must be achieved over and over if other ends are to be entertained," David R. Mayhew observed in *Congress: The Electoral Connection.*[20]

Individual legislators vary in how they balance the twin roles of legislator and representative. Some legislators devote more time and resources to lawmaking, while others focus almost entirely on constituency tending. With their longer terms, some senators stress voter outreach and fence mending during the two years before reelection and focus on legislative activities at other times. Yet senatorial contests normally are more competitive and costlier than House races, and many senators now run for reelection all the time—like most of their House colleagues.[21] Most senators and representatives would like to devote more time to lawmaking and other Capitol Hill duties, but the press of constituency business is relentless.[22]

Popular Images

The notion of two Congresses also conforms to the average citizen's perceptions. The public views the U.S. Congress differently from the way it sees individual senators and representatives. Congress as an institution is perceived primarily as a lawmaking body. It is judged mainly on the basis of citizens' overall attitudes toward politics, policy processes, and the state of the Union. Do people like the way things are going or not? Do they feel that Congress is carrying out its duties equitably and efficiently? Are they optimistic or pessimistic about the nation's future?

In contrast with their expectations of Congress as a whole, citizens view their own legislators largely as agents of local concerns. People judge individual legislators by yardsticks such as communication with constituents, their positions on prominent issues, service to the district, and home style (the way officeholders present themselves in their districts or states). In judging their senators or representatives, voters ponder questions such as: Is the legislator trustworthy? Does the legislator communicate well with the state (or district) by answering mail promptly and offering timely help to constituents? Does the legislator listen to the state (or district) and its concerns?[23]

The public's divergent expectations of Congress and its members send conflicting signals to senators and representatives. Congress as a whole is judged by the processes it uses and the policies it adopts (or fails to adopt), however vaguely voters understand them.[24] But individual legislators are regularly elected and returned to office because of their personal qualities, the positions they take, and their constituency service. In response to this incongruity, officeholders adopt a strategy of opening as much space as possible between themselves and those other politicians back in Washington.

The Constitutional Basis

Congress's dual nature—the dichotomy between its lawmaking and representative functions—is dictated by the U.S. Constitution. Congress's mandate to write the nation's laws is found in Article I of the Constitution. By contrast, Congress's representational functions are not specified in the Constitution, although these duties flow from the constitutional provisions for electing senators and House members.

It is no accident that the Constitution's drafters devoted the first article to establishing the legislature and enumerating most of the government's powers. Familiar with the British Parliament's prolonged struggles with the Crown, the authors assumed the legislature would be the chief policy-making body and the bulwark against arbitrary executives. "In republican government, the legislative authority necessarily predominates," observed James Madison in *The Federalist Papers*.[25]

Although in the ensuing years the initiative for policy making has shifted many times between the legislative and executive branches, the U.S. Congress remains virtually the only national assembly in the world that drafts in detail the laws it passes instead of simply debating and ratifying measures prepared by the government in power.

The House of Representatives was intended to be the most representative element of the U.S. government. House members are elected directly by the people for two-year terms to ensure that they do not stray too far from popular opinion. As Madison explained, the House should have "an immediate dependence on, and an intimate sympathy with, the people."[26] For most representatives, this two-year cycle means nonstop campaigning, visiting, and looking after constituents.

The Senate was initially one step removed from popular voting. Some of the Constitution's framers hoped the Senate would temper the popular passions expressed in the House, so under the original Constitution, state legislatures selected senators. But this original vision was ultimately overruled in favor of a Senate that, like the House, directly expresses the people's voice. In 1913 the Seventeenth Amendment to the Constitution was adopted, providing for direct popular election of senators. Although elected for six-year terms, senators must stay in close touch with the electorate. Like their House colleagues, senators typically regard themselves as constituency servants. Most have transformed their office staffs into veritable cottage industries for generating publicity and handling constituents' inquiries.

Thus the Constitution and subsequent historical developments affirm Congress's dual functions of lawmaker and representative assembly. Although the roles are tightly bound together, they nonetheless impose separate duties and functions.

Back to Burke

On November 3, 1774, in Bristol, England, the British statesman and philosopher Edmund Burke set forth in a speech the dual character of a national legislature. The constituent-oriented parliament, or Congress, he described as

a Congress of ambassadors from different and hostile interests, which interests each must maintain, as an agent and advocate, against other agents and advocates.

The parliament of substantive lawmaking he portrayed in different terms. It was

a deliberative assembly of one nation, with one interest, that of the whole—where not local purposes, not local prejudices, ought to guide, but the general good, resulting from the general reason of the whole.[27]

Burke preferred the second concept and did not hesitate to let his voters know it. He would give local opinion a hearing, but his judgment and conscience would prevail in all cases. "Your faithful friend, your devoted servant, I shall be to the end of my life," he declared; "a flatterer you do not wish for."[28]

Burke's Bristol speech is an enduring statement of the dilemma legislators face in balancing their two roles. Burke was a brilliant lawmaker. (He even sympathized with the cause of the American colonists.) But, as might be said today, he suffered from an inept home style. His candor earned him no thanks from his constituents, who turned him out of office at the first opportunity.

Burke's dilemma applies equally on this side of the Atlantic. American voters tend to prefer their lawmakers to be delegates who listen carefully to constituents and follow their guidance. During an encounter in Borger, Texas, an irate Baptist minister shouted at then-representative Bill Sarpalius, D-Tex., "We didn't send you to Washington to make intelligent decisions. We sent you to represent us."[29] Sarpalius was later defeated for reelection.

Representing local constituents is not the whole story, of course. Burke's idea that legislators are trustees of the nation's common good is still extolled. In a 1995 decision, U.S. Supreme Court justice John Paul Stevens noted that, once elected, members of Congress become "servants of the people of the United States. They are not merely delegates appointed by separate states; they occupy offices that are integral and essential components of a single national Government."[30]

Many talented individuals seek public office, often forgoing more lucrative opportunities in the private sector, precisely because they believe strongly in a vision of what government should do and how it should do it. For such legislators, winning office is a means to a larger end. It is reasonable to assume that elected officials "make an honest effort to achieve good public policy."[31]

Burke posed the tension between the two Congresses so vividly that we have adopted his language to describe the conceptual distinction that forms the crux of this book. From Burke, we have also drawn the titles for Part II, "A Congress of Ambassadors," and Part III, "A Deliberative Assembly of One Nation." Every member of Congress sooner or later must come to terms with Burke's dichotomy; citizens and voters will have to form their own answers.

THE TWO CONGRESSES IN COMPARATIVE CONTEXT

A look around the world reveals that most democracies differ from the United States in how they elect legislators. Members of Congress are selected by means of the oldest form of elected democratic representation: a plurality vote within geographic constituencies. By contrast, most other advanced democracies elect legislative representatives under systems of proportional representation (PR), a more recent innovation in democratic institutions. Many varieties of PR are in use, but compared with the U.S. electoral system, these systems tend to tie legislators more closely to their political parties than to local constituencies. In this way, PR systems somewhat alleviate the difficult trade-offs that members of Congress face as they attempt to balance national lawmaking with attention to local constituencies.

PR systems rest on the basic principle that the number of seats a political party wins in the legislature should be proportional to the level of support it receives from voters. If a political party wins 40 percent of the vote overall, then it should receive about 40 percent of the seats. In other words, these systems explicitly assume that political parties are more important than geographic locales to voters' values and political interests.[32] Most commonly in these systems, the parties put lists of candidates before the electorate. The number of a party's candidates to be seated in the legislature from those lists then depends on the percentage of voters supporting that party in legislative elections. To a greater extent than is true of members of the U.S. Congress, candidates elected in PR systems thus serve as representatives of their party's policy goals and ideological commitments.

Legislators in PR systems face fewer dilemmas about how to balance local constituency politics with national party platforms. Indeed, some PR systems, such as those in Israel and the Netherlands, do not tie representatives to local geographic constituencies at all; legislators represent the entire nation. Other countries, such as Austria and Sweden, elect multiple representatives from regional districts. Such districts are not captured by a single party on a winner-take-all basis (this is the system used in the United States, where each constituency has only one representative). Districts in which more than one political party enjoys a meaningful level of voter support will elect representatives from more than one party, with each legislator representing those voters who supported his or her party. Some countries, such as Germany, Italy, and New Zealand, use a mixed system, with some representatives elected in individual geographic constituencies and others drawn from party lists to ensure proportionality. In all cases, citizens and legislators alike recognize that the system is primarily designed to ensure that voters' party preferences are proportionally represented.

Members of the U.S. Congress, by contrast, officially represent all residents of their geographic constituency—a difficult task. The constituents grouped together within congressional districts often have little in common. Indeed, constituencies can be very diverse in terms of race, class, ethnicity, religion, economic interests, and urbanization. The largest states are often microcosms of the nation. Some constituencies are narrowly divided in terms of partisanship and ideology, forcing representatives to cope with continual local controversy about their stances on national issues. Some constituencies even present a member with the challenge of representing constituents who lean toward the opposing party.

In attempting to represent their whole state or district, some senators and House members attempt a "lowest common denominator" form of representation, de-emphasizing their party affiliation and their opinions on controversial national issues. Instead, they advertise their personal accessibility to constituents; focus on narrow, localized concerns; and dodge hot-button questions whenever they can.[33] This strategy is most appealing to members representing swing or cross-pressured states and districts. But, to an important extent, the U.S. system of representation encourages a focus on parochial matters among lawmakers generally. Members see themselves, at least to some degree, as attorneys for their constituencies.

Even though the U.S. system of representation does not recognize the importance of political parties in the way that PR systems do, members of Congress have nevertheless become far more closely tied to their parties since the 1970s. Lawmakers vote with their parties much more reliably than they did in the 1950s and 1960s. The sources of this increased partisanship are many, but it has corresponded with an increasingly partisan-ideological polarization in the activist base of both political parties. "The American public has become more consistent and polarized in its policy preferences over the past several decades," writes Alan I. Abramowitz, "and this increase in consistency and polarization has been concentrated among the most politically engaged citizens."[34] At the same time, the politically engaged public has also sorted itself into more ideologically coherent political parties, with fewer liberals identifying with the Republican Party and fewer conservatives identifying with the Democratic Party.[35] Consequently, relatively few voters split their tickets today by voting for one party's presidential candidate and another party's congressional candidate. These trends have reduced the cross-pressures that members face as they attempt to balance their roles as constituency representatives and national policy makers. More members are able to cooperate with their national party leaders without endangering the support of an electoral majority in their constituency. At the same time, a body of members responding to this more polarized activist base may have a harder time engaging in genuine deliberation and crafting workable legislative compromises.

All members must constantly cultivate the local roots of their power as national legislators. Yet Congress is one body, not two. The same members who attempt to forge national legislation in committee and on the floor must rush to catch planes back to their districts, where they are plunged into a different world of local problems and personalities. The same candidates who sell themselves at shopping centers also shape the federal budget or military weapons systems in the nation's capital. The unique character of Congress arises directly from its dual role as a representative assembly and a lawmaking body.

DIVERGENT VIEWS OF CONGRESS

Congress is subject to intense scrutiny, as the huge array of books, monographs, blogs, and articles devoted to it attest. Many of its features make Congress a favorite object of scholarly attention. For one thing, it is relatively open and accessible, so it can be approached by traditional means—journalistic stories, case studies, normative assessments, and historical accounts. It is also amenable to the analytic techniques of social science. Indeed, the availability of quantitative indicators of congressional work (floor votes, for example) permits elaborate statistical analyses. Its rule-governed processes allow it to be studied with sophisticated formal models. And Congress is, above all, a fascinating place—the very best location from which to view the varied actors in the American political drama.

Writers of an interpretive book on the U.S. Congress thus can draw on a multitude of sources, an embarrassment of riches. In fact, studies of Congress constitute a vast literature. This is a mixed blessing because all this information must be integrated into a coherent whole. Moreover, the scholarly writing is often highly detailed, technical, and theoretical. We have tried to put such material in perspective, make it accessible to all interested readers, and use illustrative examples wherever possible.

Meanwhile, a gaping chasm exists between this rich scholarly literature and the caricature of Congress prevalent in the popular culture. Humorists from Mark Twain and Will Rogers to Jay Leno, Bill Maher, Stephen Colbert, and Jon Stewart have found Congress an inexhaustible source of raw material. Citizens tend to share this disdain toward the legislative branch—especially at moments of furor over, say, ethics scandals or difficult legislative fights. When legislators are at home with constituents, they themselves often reinforce Congress's poor image by portraying themselves as escapees from the funny farm on Capitol Hill. As Richard F. Fenno puts it, members "run *for* Congress by running *against* Congress."[36]

The picture of Congress conveyed by the media is scarcely more flattering. Journalistic hit-and-run specialists perpetuate a cartoon-like stereotype of

Congress as "a place where good ideas go to die in a maelstrom of bureaucratic hedging and rank favor-trading."[37] News magazines, editorial writers, and nightly news broadcasts regularly portray Congress as an irresponsible and somewhat disreputable gang, reminiscent of Woodrow Wilson's caustic description of the House as "a disintegrated mass of jarring elements."[38]

To comprehend how the two Congresses function—both the institution and individual members—popular stereotypes must be abandoned and the complex realities examined. Citizens' ambivalence toward the popular branch of government—which goes back to the beginnings of the Republic—says something about the milieu in which public policy is made. We believe we know our subject well enough to appreciate Congress's foibles and understand why it works the way it does, yet we try to maintain a professional, scholarly distance from it.

According to an old saying, two things should never be viewed up close: making sausages and making laws. Despite this warning, we urge readers to take a serious look at the workings of Congress and form their own opinions about Congress's effectiveness. Some may recoil from what they discover. Numerous flaws can be identified in members' personal or public behavior, in their priorities and incentive structures, and in lawmaking processes generally. Recent Congresses especially have displayed troubling tendencies, including rushed legislation, extreme partisanship, frequent gridlock, and abdication of legislative power to the executive branch.[39]

Yet careful observers will also discover much behavior in Congress that is purposeful and principled, many policies that are reasonable and workable. We invite students and colleagues to examine with us what Congress does and why, and to ponder its values and its prospects.

SECTION THROUGH DOME OF U.S. CAPITOL

Refreshing Congress. The United States Capitol Dome was constructed more than 150 years ago from a design by architect Thomas U. Walter. The Dome is undergoing a major renovation today to restore its original grandeur, which has been gradually eroded by age and weather. Just as the physical appearance of the Capitol has undergone many changes over the years, the institutions of Congress have developed over many decades as members have adapted to new challenges and opportunities.

chapter 2

Evolution of the Modern Congress

T he first Congress met in New York City in the spring of 1789. Business couldn't begin until April 1, when a majority of the fifty-nine House members finally arrived to make a quorum. Members then chose Frederick A. C. Muhlenberg of Pennsylvania as Speaker of the House. Five days later, the Senate achieved its first quorum, although its presiding officer, Vice President John Adams, did not arrive for another two weeks.

New York City, the seat of government, was then a bustling port on the southern tip of Manhattan Island. Congress met in Federal Hall at the corner of Broad and Wall Streets. The House of Representatives occupied a large chamber on the first floor and the Senate a more intimate chamber upstairs. The new chief executive, George Washington, was still en route from Mount Vernon, his plantation in Virginia; his trip had become a triumphal procession with crowds and celebrations at every stop. To most of his countrymen, Washington—austere, dignified, the soul of propriety—embodied a government that otherwise was no more than a plan on paper.

The two houses of Congress did not wait for Washington's arrival. The House began debating tariffs, a perennial legislative topic. In the Senate, Vice President Adams, a brilliant but self-important man, prodded his colleagues to decide on proper titles for addressing the president and himself. Adams was dubbed "His Rotundity" by a colleague who thought the whole discussion absurd.

On inaugural day, April 30, Adams was still worrying about how to address the president when the representatives, led by Speaker Muhlenberg, burst into the Senate chamber and seated themselves. Meanwhile, a special committee was dispatched to escort Washington to the chamber for the ceremony. The swearing-in was conducted on an outside balcony in front of thousands of assembled citizens.[1] Then the nervous Washington reentered the Senate chamber and haltingly read his inaugural address. After the speech, everyone adjourned to nearby St. Paul's Chapel for a special prayer service. Thus the U.S. Congress became part of a functioning government.[2]

ANTECEDENTS OF CONGRESS

The legislative branch of the new government was untried and unknown, searching for procedures and precedents. And yet it grew out of a rich history of development—stretching back more than five hundred years in Great Britain and no less than a century and a half in North America. If the architects of the U.S. Constitution of 1787 were unsure of how well their new design would work, they had firm ideas about what they intended.

The English Heritage

The evolution of representative institutions on a national scale began in medieval Europe. Monarchs gained power over large territories where inhabitants were divided into social groupings, called "estates of the realm"—among them, the nobility, clergy, landed gentry, and town officials. The monarchs brought together the leaders of these estates, not to create representative government but to fill the royal coffers.

These assemblies later came to be called parliaments, from the French *parler,* "to speak." Historians and political scientists have identified four distinct stages in the evolution of the assemblies of estates into the representative legislatures of today. The first stage saw the assemblies representing the various estates gathering merely to vote taxes for the royal treasury; they engaged in little discussion. During the second stage, these tax-voting bodies evolved into bodies that presented the king with petitions for redressing grievances. In the third stage, by a gradual process that culminated in the revolutions of the seventeenth and eighteenth centuries, parliaments wrested lawmaking and tax-levying powers from the king. In the fourth and final stage, during the nineteenth and twentieth centuries, parliamentary representation expanded beyond the older privileged groups to embrace all adult men and women.[3]

By the time the New World colonies were founded in the 1600s, the struggle for parliamentary rights was well advanced into the third stage, at least in England. Bloody conflicts, culminating in the beheading of Charles I in 1649 and the dethroning of James II in the Glorious Revolution of 1688, established parliamentary influence over the Crown.

Out of the struggles between the Crown and Parliament flowed a remarkable body of political and philosophic writings. By the eighteenth century, works by James Harrington (1611–1677), John Locke (1632–1704), William Blackstone (1723–1780), and the Frenchman Baron de Montesquieu (1689–1755) were the common heritage of educated leaders in North America as well as in Europe.

The Colonial Experience

European settlers in the New World brought this tradition of representative government with them. As early as 1619, the thousand or so Virginia colonists elected twenty-two burgesses, or delegates, to a general assembly. In 1630 the Massachusetts Bay Company established itself as the governing body for the Bay Colony, subject to annual elections. The other colonies followed suit.

Representative government took firm root in the colonies. The broad expanse of ocean shielding America from its European masters fostered autonomy on the part of the colonial assemblies. Claiming prerogatives similar to those of the British House of Commons, these assemblies exercised the full range of lawmaking powers—levying taxes, issuing money, and providing for colonial defense.[4] Legislation could be vetoed by colonial governors (appointed by the Crown in the eight royal colonies); but the governors, cut off from the home government and dependent on local assemblies for revenues and even for their own salaries, usually preferred to reach agreement with the locals. Royal vetoes could emanate from London, but these took time and were infrequent.[5]

Other elements nourished the growth of democratic institutions. Many of the colonists were free-spirited dissidents set on resisting traditional forms of authority, especially that of the Crown. Their self-confidence was bolstered by the readily available land, the harsh frontier life, and—by the eighteenth century—a robust economy. The town meeting form of government in New England and the separatists' church assemblies helped cultivate habits of self-government. Newspapers, unfettered by royal licenses or government taxes, stimulated lively exchanges of opinions.

When Britain decided in the 1760s, following the ruinous French and Indian War, to tighten its rein on the American colonies, it met with stubborn opposition. Colonists asked: Why don't we enjoy the same rights as Englishmen? Why aren't our colonial assemblies legitimate governments, with authority derived from popular elections? As British enactments grew increasingly unpopular, along with the governors who tried to enforce them, the locally based legislatures took up the cause of their constituents.

The colonists especially resented the Stamp Act of 1765, which provoked delegates from nine colonies to meet in New York City. There, the Stamp Act Congress adopted a fourteen-point *Declaration of Rights and Grievances.* Although the Stamp Act was later repealed, new import duties levied in 1767 increased customs receipts and enabled the Crown to begin directly paying the salaries of royal governors and other officials, thereby freeing those officials from the influence of colonial assemblies. The crisis worsened in the winter of 1773–1774, when a group of colonists staged a revolt, the Boston Tea Party, to protest the taxes imposed by the Tea Act. In retaliation, the House of Commons closed the port of Boston and passed a series of so-called Intolerable Acts, further tightening royal control.

National representative assemblies in America were born on September 5, 1774, when the First Continental Congress convened in Philadelphia. Every colony except Georgia sent delegates—a varied group that included peaceable souls loyal to the Crown, moderates such as Pennsylvania's John Dickinson, and firebrands such as Samuel Adams and Paul Revere. Gradually, anti-British sentiment congealed, and Congress passed a series of declarations and resolutions (each colony casting one vote) amounting to a declaration of war against the mother country.[6] After Congress adjourned on October 22, King George III declared that the colonies were "now in a state of rebellion; blows must decide whether they are to be subject to this country or independent."[7]

If the First Continental Congress gave colonists a taste of collective decision making, the Second Continental Congress proclaimed their independence from Britain. When this second Congress convened on May 10, 1775, many colonists had still believed war might be avoided. A petition to King George asking for "happy and permanent reconciliation" was even approved. The British responded by proclaiming a state of rebellion and launching efforts to crush it. Sentiment in the colonies swung increasingly toward independence, and by the middle of 1776 Congress was debating Thomas Jefferson's draft resolution that "these united colonies are, and of right ought to be, free and independent states."[8]

The two Continental Congresses gave birth to national politics in America. Riding the wave of patriotism unleashed by the British actions of 1773–1774, the Congresses succeeded in pushing the sentiments of leaders and much of the general public toward confrontation and away from reconciliation with the mother country. They did so by defining issues one by one and by reaching compromises acceptable to both moderates and radicals— no small accomplishment. Shared legislative experience, in other words, moved the delegates to the threshold of independence. Their achievement was all the more remarkable in light of what historian Jack N. Rakove describes as the "peculiar status" of the Continental Congress, "an extra-legal body whose authority would obviously depend on its ability to maintain a broad range of support."[9]

Eight years of bloody conflict ensued before the colonies won their independence. Meanwhile, the former colonies hastened to form new governments and draft constitutions. Unlike the English constitution, these charters were written documents. All included some sort of bill of rights, and all paid lip service to the doctrine of separating powers among legislative, executive, and judicial branches of government. But past conflicts with the Crown and the royal governors had instilled a fear of all forms of executive authority. So nearly all the constitutions gave the bulk of powers to their legislatures, effectively creating what one historian termed "legislative omnipotence."[10]

The national government was likewise, as James Sterling Young put it, "born with a legislative body and no head."[11] Strictly speaking, no national executive existed between 1775 and 1789—the years of the Revolutionary War and the Articles of Confederation (adopted in 1781). On its own, Congress struggled to wage war against the world's most powerful nation, enlist diplomatic allies, and manage internal affairs. As the war progressed and legislative direction proved unwieldy, Congress tended to delegate authority to its own committees and to permanent (executive) agencies. Strictly military affairs were placed in the hands of Commander in Chief George Washington, who at the war's end returned his commission to Congress in a public ceremony. Considering the obstacles it faced, congressional government was far from a failure. Yet the mounting inability of the all-powerful legislative bodies, state and national, to deal with the postwar problems spurred demands for change.

At the state level, Massachusetts and New York rewrote their constitutions, adding provisions for stronger executives. At the national level, the Confederation's frailty led many to advocate what Alexander Hamilton called a more "energetic" government—one with enough authority to implement laws, control currency, levy taxes, dispose of war debts, and, if necessary, put down rebellion. Legislative prerogatives, Hamilton and others argued, should be counterbalanced with a vigorous, independent executive.

In this spirit, delegates from the states convened in Philadelphia on May 25, 1787, intending to strengthen the Articles of Confederation. Instead, they drew up a wholly new governmental charter.

CONGRESS IN THE CONSTITUTION

The structure and powers of Congress formed the core of the Constitutional Convention's deliberations. The delegates broadly agreed that a stronger central government was needed.[12] But the fifty-five delegates who met in the summer of 1787 in Philadelphia were deeply divided on issues of representation, and more than three months passed before they completed their work. The plan, agreed to and signed on September 17, 1787, was a bundle of compromises. Divergent interests—those of large and small states, land-locked states and those with ports, Northern and Southern (that is, slave-holding) states—had to be placated in structuring the representational system. The final result was an energetic central government that could function independently of the states, but with limited, enumerated powers divided among the three branches.

Powers of Congress

The federal government's powers are shared by three separate branches: legislative, executive, and judicial. Separation of powers was not a new idea. Philosophers admired by the framers of the Constitution, including Harrington, Locke, and especially Montesquieu, had advocated the principle. But the U.S. Constitution's elaborate system of checks and balances is considered one of its most innovative features. The failure of the Articles of Confederation to separate governmental functions was widely regarded as a serious defect, as were the all-powerful legislatures created by the first state constitutions. Thus the framers sought to create a federal government that would avoid the excesses and instabilities that had marked policy making at both the national and state levels.

Article I of the Constitution embraces many provisions to buttress congressional authority and independence. Legislators have unfettered authority to organize the chambers as they see fit, and are accorded latitude in performing their duties. To prevent intimidation, they cannot be arrested during sessions or while traveling to and from sessions (except for treason, felony, or breach of the peace). In their deliberations, members enjoy immunity from any punitive action; for their speech and debate, "they shall not be questioned in any other place" (Article I, section 6).

Despite their worries over all-powerful legislatures, the framers laid down an expansive mandate for the new Congress. Mindful of the achievements of New World assemblies, not to mention the British Parliament's struggles with the Crown, the framers viewed the legislature as the chief repository of the government's powers. Locke had observed that "the legislative is not only the supreme power, but is sacred and unalterable in the hands where the community have placed it."[13] Locke's doctrine found expression in Article I, section 8, which enumerates Congress's impressive array of powers and sets out virtually the entire scope of governmental authority as the eighteenth-century founders understood it. This portion of the Constitution clearly envisions a vigorous legislature as the engine of a powerful government.

Raising and spending money for governmental purposes stand at the heart of Congress's prerogatives. The "power of the purse" was historically the lever by which parliaments gained bargaining advantages over kings and queens. The Constitution's authors, well aware of this lever, gave Congress full powers over taxing and spending.

Financing the government is carried out under Congress's broad mandate to "lay and collect taxes, duties, imposts and excises, to pay the debts and provide for the common defense and general welfare of the United States" (Article I, section 8). Although this wording covered almost all known forms of taxation, there were limitations. Taxes had to be uniform throughout the country; duties could not be levied on goods traveling between states; and "capitation or other direct" taxes were prohibited, unless levied according to population (Article I, section 9). This last provision proved troublesome when the U.S. Supreme Court held in 1895 (*Pollock v. Farmers' Loan and Trust Co.*) that it precluded taxes on incomes. To overcome this obstacle, the Sixteenth Amendment, ratified eighteen years later, explicitly conferred on Congress the power to levy income taxes.

Congressional power over government spending is no less sweeping. Congress is to provide for the "common defense and general welfare" of the country (Article I, section 8). Furthermore, "No money shall be drawn from the Treasury, but in consequence of appropriations made by law" (Article I, section 9). This funding provision is one of the legislature's most potent weapons in overseeing the executive branch.

Congress possesses broad powers to promote the nation's economic well-being and political security. It has the power to regulate interstate and foreign commerce, which it has used to regulate not only trade, but also transportation, communications, and such disparate subjects as civil rights and violent crime. The exact limits of the commerce power have been the subject of numerous political and legal battles. In 2012 this issue was at the center of the dispute over the constitutionality of the individual mandate, a key provision of the Patient Protection and Affordable Care Act ("Obamacare"). The individual mandate requires every person to obtain health insurance or suffer a (relatively minor) sanction. Five justices held that the individual mandate exceeded Congress's commerce power because it was a regulation of commercial *inactivity*, as opposed to commercial activity. Nevertheless, Chief Justice John Roberts and four other justices upheld the individual mandate as a valid exercise of Congress's power to tax.[14] Congress may also coin money, incur debts, establish post offices, build post roads, issue patents and copyrights, provide for the armed forces, and call forth the militia to repel invasions or suppress rebellions.

Although the three branches supposedly are coequal, the legislature is empowered to define the structure and duties of the other two. The Constitution mentions executive departments and officers, but it does not specify their organization or functions, aside from those of the president. Thus the design of the executive branch, including cabinet departments and other agencies, is spelled out in laws passed by Congress and signed by the president.

The judiciary, too, is a statutory creation. The Constitution provides for a federal judicial system consisting of "one supreme Court, and . . . such inferior courts as the Congress may from time to time ordain and establish" (Article III, section 1). Congress determines the number of justices on the Supreme Court, and the number and types of lower federal courts. The outer limits of the federal courts' jurisdiction are delineated in Article III, but Congress must also define their jurisdictions through statute. Moreover, the Supreme Court's appellate jurisdiction is subject to "such exceptions" and "such regulations as the Congress shall make" (Article III, section 2). Congress can also limit the federal courts' discretion in ways other than altering their jurisdiction. Mandatory minimum sentences imposed by statute, for example, limit judges' discretion in imposing prison sentences.

Congress's powers within the federal system were greatly enlarged by the Civil War constitutional amendments—the Thirteenth (ratified in 1865), Fourteenth (ratified in 1868), and Fifteenth (ratified in 1870). The Radical Republicans, who had supported the war and controlled Congress in its aftermath, feared that former Confederate states would ignore the rights of former slaves—the cause over which the war had ultimately been waged. The Civil War amendments were primarily intended to ensure that former slaves would have the rights to vote, to be accorded due process, and to receive equal protection of the laws. Nevertheless, the language of the Fourteenth Amendment was cast broadly, referring to "all persons" rather than only to "former slaves." These amendments also authorized Congress to enforce these rights with "appropriate legislation." As a result, these amendments (and subsequent legislation) greatly expanded the federal government's role relative to the states. Over time, the Civil War amendments effectively nationalized the key rights of citizenship throughout the United States. Through a long series of Court rulings, state governments were eventually required to respect many of the Bill of Rights guarantees that originally applied only to the federal government.

Congress can also be an active partner in foreign relations and national defense. It has the power to declare war, ratify treaties, raise and support armies, provide and maintain a navy, and make rules governing the military forces—including those governing "captures on land and water." Finally, Congress is vested with the power "to make all laws which shall be necessary and proper for carrying into execution the foregoing powers" (Article I, section 8).

Limits on Legislative Power

The very act of enumerating these powers was intended to limit government, for by implication those powers not listed were prohibited. The Tenth Amendment reserves to the states or to the people all those powers neither delegated nor prohibited by the Constitution. This guarantee has long been a rallying point for those who take exception to particular federal policies or who wish broadly to curtail federal powers.

Eight specific limitations on Congress's powers are noted in Article I, section 9. The most important bans are against bills of attainder, which pronounce a particular individual guilty of a crime without trial or conviction and impose a sentence, and ex post facto laws, which make an action a crime after it has been committed or otherwise alter the legal consequences of some past action. Such laws are traditional tools of authoritarian regimes.

The original Constitution contained no bill of rights. Pressed by opponents during the ratification debate, supporters of the Constitution promised early enactment of amendments to remedy this omission. The resulting ten amendments, drawn up by the First Congress (James Madison was their main author) and ratified December 15, 1791, are a basic charter of liberties that limit the reach of government. The First Amendment prohibits Congress from establishing a national religion, preventing the free exercise of religion, or abridging the freedoms of speech, press, peaceable assembly, and petition. Other amendments secure the rights of personal property and fair trials and prohibit arbitrary arrest, questioning, or punishment.

Rights not enumerated in the Bill of Rights are not necessarily denied (Ninth Amendment). In fact, subsequent amendments, legislative enactments, judicial rulings, and states' actions have enlarged citizens' rights to include the rights of citizenship, of voting, of privacy, and of "equal protection of the laws."

It should also be noted that the political process itself is a significant limit on the use of government powers, even those clearly granted in Article I, section 8. As Madison noted in *Federalist* No. 51, "A dependence on the people is, no doubt, the primary control on the government."[15]

Separate Branches, Shared Powers

The Constitution not only lists Congress's powers but also sets them apart from those of the other two branches. Senators and representatives, while in office, are prohibited from serving in other federal posts; those who serve in such posts are, in turn, forbidden from serving in Congress (Article I, section 6). This restriction forecloses any form of parliamentary government in which leading members of the dominant party or coalition form a cabinet to direct the ministries and other executive agencies.

Because the branches are separated, some people presume that their powers should be clearly distinct as well. In practice, however, governmental powers are interwoven. Madison explained that the Constitution created not a system of separate institutions performing separate functions but separate institutions that share functions, so that "these departments be so far connected and blended as to give each a constitutional control over the others."[16]

Historically, presidents, Congress, and the courts have reached accommodations to exercise the powers they share. As Justice Robert Jackson noted in 1952, "while the Constitution diffuses power the better to secure liberty, it also contemplates that practice will integrate the dispersed powers into a workable government."[17]

Legislative–Executive Interdependence. Each branch of American government needs cooperation from its counterparts. Although the Constitution vests Congress with "all legislative powers," these powers cannot be exercised without the involvement of the president and the courts. This same interdependency applies to executive and judicial powers.

The president is a key figure in lawmaking. According to Article II, the president "shall from time to time give to the Congress information on the state of the Union, and recommend to their consideration such measures as he shall judge necessary and expedient." Although Congress is not required to consider the president's legislative initiatives, the president's State of the Union address profoundly shapes the nation's political agenda. In the modern era, Congress has "enacted in some form roughly six in ten presidential initiatives."[18] The Constitution also grants the president the power to convene one or both houses of Congress in a special session.

The president's ability to veto congressional enactments influences both the outcome and content of legislation. After a bill or resolution has passed both houses of Congress and has been delivered to the White House, the president must sign it or return it within ten days (excluding Sundays). Overruling a presidential veto requires a two-thirds vote in each house. Presidential review might seem to be an all-or-nothing affair. In the words of George Washington, a president "must approve all the parts of a bill, or reject it in toto." Veto messages, however, often suggest revisions that would make the measure more likely to win the president's approval. Furthermore, veto threats allow the president to intervene earlier in the legislative process by letting members of Congress know in advance what measures or provisions will or will not receive presidential support. Considering the extreme difficulty of overriding a president's veto, members of Congress know that White House support for legislation is almost always necessary and so will often incorporate presidential preferences into early drafts of legislation.

Carrying out laws is the duty of the president, who is directed by the Constitution to "take care that the laws be faithfully executed" (Article II, section 3). To this end, as chief executive the president has the power to appoint "officers of the United States." However, the president's appointment power is limited by the requirement to obtain the Senate's advice and consent for nominees, which has been interpreted as requiring a majority vote in the Senate.[19] The president's executive power is further constrained by Congress's role in establishing and overseeing executive departments and agencies. Because these agencies are subject to Congress's broad-ranging influence, modern presidents have struggled to force them to march to a common cadence.

Even in the realms of diplomacy and national defense—the traditional domains of royal prerogative—the Constitution apportions powers between the executive and legislative branches. Following tradition, presidents are given wide discretion in such matters. They appoint ambassadors and other envoys, negotiate treaties, and command the country's armed forces. However, like other high-ranking presidential appointees, ambassadors and envoys must be approved by the Senate. Treaties do not become the law of the land until they are ratified by a two-thirds vote of the Senate. Although the president may dispatch troops on his own, only Congress may formally declare war. Even in time of war, Congress still wields formidable powers if it chooses to employ them. Congress can refuse to provide continued funding for military actions, engage in vigorous oversight of the executive branch's military operations, and influence public opinion regarding the president's leadership.[20]

Impeachment. Congress has the power to impeach and remove the president, the vice president, and other "civil officers of the United States" for serious breaches of the public trust: treason, bribery, or "other high crimes and misdemeanors." The House of Representatives has the sole authority to draw up and adopt (by majority vote) articles of impeachment, which are specific charges that the individual has engaged in one of the named forms of misconduct. The Senate is the final judge of whether to convict on any of the articles of impeachment. A two-thirds majority is required to remove the individual from office, or to remove and also bar the individual from any future "offices of public trust."

Three attributes of impeachment fix it within the separation of powers framework. First, it is exclusively the domain of Congress. (The chief justice of the United States presides over Senate trials of the president, but rulings by the chief justice may be overturned by majority vote.) The two chambers are also free to devise their own procedures for reaching their decisions.[21]

Second, impeachment is essentially political in character. The structure may appear judicial—with the House resembling a grand jury and the Senate a trial court—but lawmakers decide whether and how to proceed, which evidence to consider, and even what constitutes an impeachable offense. Treason is defined by the Constitution and bribery is defined by statute, but the words "high crimes and misdemeanors" are open to interpretation. They are usually defined (in Alexander Hamilton's words) as "abuse or violation of some public trust"—on-the-job offenses against the state, the political order, or the society at large.[22] According to this definition, they could be either more or less than garden-variety criminal offenses. Both presidential impeachment trials (Andrew Johnson, 1868; Bill Clinton, 1998–1999) were fiercely partisan affairs, in which combatants disputed not only the facts but also the appropriate grounds for impeachment.

Finally, impeachment is a blunt instrument for punishing officials for the gravest of offenses. Congress has many lesser ways of reining in wayward officials. As for presidents and vice presidents, their terms are already limited. Although impeachments are often threatened, only sixteen Senate trials have taken place, and only eight individuals have been convicted. Significantly, all eight who were removed from office were judges—who, unlike executive officers, enjoy open-ended terms of office.[23]

Interbranch "No-Fly Zones." Although the constitutional system requires that the separate branches share powers, each branch normally honors the integrity of the others' internal operations. Communications between the president and his advisers are mostly (though not entirely) exempt from legislative or judicial review under the doctrine of "executive privilege." Similarly, Article I places congressional organization and procedures beyond the scrutiny of the other branches. This provision was given new meaning in 2007 when the courts determined that an FBI search of the office of Rep. William J. Jefferson, D-La., who was under investigation for bribery, had been unconstitutional under the Constitution's speech and debate clause.[24] The case established a precedent that members of Congress be provided advance notice and the right to review materials before the execution of a search warrant on their congressional offices.

Judicial Review

The third branch, the judiciary, interprets and applies laws in particular cases, when called upon to resolve disputes. In rare instances, this requires the judiciary to adjudicate a claim that a particular law or regulation violates the Constitution. This is called "judicial review." Whether the framers anticipated judicial review is open to question. Perhaps they expected each branch to reach its own judgments on constitutional questions, especially those pertaining to its own powers. Whatever the original intent, Chief Justice John Marshall soon preempted the other two branches with his Supreme Court's unanimous assertion of judicial review in *Marbury v. Madison* (1803). Judicial review involves both interpretation and judgment. First, "It is emphatically the province and duty of the judicial department to say what the law is." Second, the Supreme Court has the duty of weighing laws against the Constitution, the "supreme law of the land," and invalidating those that are inconsistent—in *Marbury,* a minor provision of the Judiciary Act of 1789.[25]

Despite the *Marbury* precedent, Congress—not the Court—was the primary forum for weighty constitutional debates until the Civil War. Before 1860, only one other federal law (the Missouri Compromise of 1820) had been declared unconstitutional by the Court (in *Dred Scott v. Sandford,* 1857). Since the Civil War, the Court has been more aggressive in interpreting and judging congressional handiwork. For the record, the Supreme Court has invalidated 177 congressional statutes in whole or in part—the vast majority of these during the twentieth century.[26] This count does not include lower-court holdings that have not been reviewed by the Supreme Court. Nor does it include laws whose validity has been impaired because a similar law was struck down.

Who Is the Final Arbiter? Congress's two most common reactions to judicial review of its enactments are not responding at all or amending the statute to comply with the Court's holding.[27] Other responses are repealing the law, repealing the law to pass new legislation, or even seeking a constitutional amendment.

Reconstruction laws and constitutional amendments after the Civil War explicitly nullified the Court's 1857 holding in *Dred Scott v. Sandford*.[28] More recently, a great deal of legislative ferment has followed the Supreme Court's ruling in *Citizens United v. Federal Election Commission* (2010),[29] a 5–4 decision that held that the First Amendment protects corporate, union, and nonprofit funding of independent political speech. Even though legislation has not yet been passed in response to *Citizens United*, many members of Congress want to find ways to undo or mitigate the Court's holding in this case.

In some cases, Congress reacts to Supreme Court rulings by simply ignoring them. For example, even though legislative veto provisions were largely outlawed by the Court's decision in *Immigration and Naturalization Service v. Chadha* (1983),[30] Congress continues to enact them, and administrators nevertheless feel obliged to honor them out of political prudence.

The Supreme Court does not necessarily have the last word in saying what the law is. Its interpretations of laws may be questioned and even reversed. One study found that 121 of the Court's interpretive decisions were overridden between 1967 and 1990, an average of 10 per Congress. The author of the study concluded that "congressional committees in fact carefully monitor Supreme Court decisions."[31] However, as Congress has become increasingly polarized, forging agreement to override important Court decisions has proven increasingly elusive.[32]

Nor are the courts the sole judges of what is or is not constitutional. Courts routinely accept customs and practices developed by the other two branches. Likewise, they usually decline to decide sensitive political questions within the province of Congress and the executive.

In summary, the courts play a leading but not exclusive role in interpreting laws and the regulations implementing them. When Congress passes a law, the policy-making process has just begun. Courts and administrative agencies then assume the task of refining the policy, but they do so under Congress's watchful eye. "What is 'final' at one stage of our political development," Louis Fisher observes, "may be reopened at some later date, leading to revisions, fresh interpretations, and reversals of Court doctrines."[33]

Bicameralism

Although "the Congress" is discussed as if it were a single entity, Congress is divided internally into two very different, virtually autonomous chambers—that is, it is bicameral. Following the pattern that originated with the British Parliament and was then imitated by most of the states, the Constitution created a bicameral legislature. If tradition recommended the two-house formula, the politics of the early Republic commanded it. The larger states preferred population-based representation, but the smaller states insisted on retaining the equal representation they enjoyed under the Articles of Confederation.

The first branch—as the House was called by framers James Madison and Gouverneur Morris, among others—rests on the idea that the legislature should represent "the many," the people of the United States. As George Mason, another framer, put it, the House "was to be the grand depository of the democratic principles of the government."[34]

By contrast, the composition of the Senate reflected the framers' concerns about controlling excessive popular pressures. Senators were chosen by the state legislatures and not by popular vote. This, in theory, would curb the excesses of popular government. "The use of the Senate," explained Madison, "is to consist in its proceeding with more coolness, with more system, and with more wisdom, than the popular branch."[35]

Senate behavior did not necessarily match up with the framers' theories, however. Even though senators were chosen by state legislatures, they were not insulated from democratic pressures. To be selected, Senate candidates "had to cultivate local party officials in different parts of the state and appeal directly to constituents."[36] Once in office, senators voiced their state's dominant economic interests. They also sponsored private bills for pensions and other relief for individual constituents, doled out federal patronage, and sought committee assignments that would enable them to bring home their state's share of federal money. Recent research has shown that senators selected by state legislators were not substantially different from modern, directly elected senators.[37]

Historical evolution finally overran the framers' intentions. Direct election of senators was ushered in with the Seventeenth Amendment, ratified in 1913. A by-product of the Progressive movement, the new arrangement was designed to broaden citizens' participation and blunt the power of shadowy special interests such as party bosses and business trusts. Thus the Senate became directly subject to popular will.

Bicameralism is the most obvious organizational feature of the U.S. Congress. Each chamber has distinct processes for handling legislation. According to the Constitution, each house sets its own rules, keeps a journal of its proceedings, and serves as final judge of its members' elections and qualifications. In addition, the Constitution assigns unique duties to each of the two chambers. The Senate ratifies treaties and approves presidential appointments. The House must originate all revenue measures; by tradition, it also originates appropriations bills.

The two houses jealously guard their prerogatives and resist intrusions by the other body. Despite claims that one or the other chamber is more important—for example, that the Senate has more prestige or that the House pays more attention to legislative details—the two houses staunchly defend their equal places. On Capitol Hill, there is no "upper" or "lower" chamber.

INSTITUTIONAL EVOLUTION

Written constitutions go only a short way toward explaining how real-life governmental institutions work. On many questions such documents are inevitably silent or ambiguous. Important issues of both power and process emerge and develop only in the course of later events. Political institutions continually change under pressures from public demands, shifting political contexts, and the needs and goals of officeholders.

Congress has evolved dramatically over time. "Reconstitutive change" is what Elaine K. Swift calls instances of "rapid, marked, and enduring shift[s] in the fundamental dimensions of the institution."[38] During one such period—1809–1829—Swift argues, the Senate was transformed from an elitist, insulated "American House of Lords" into an active, powerful institution whose debates stirred the public and attracted the most talented politicians of the time. Major reform efforts in Congress have also periodically resulted in bold new departures in process and structure.

Yet much of Congress's institutional development has occurred gradually. Early on, Congress had little formal structure. When the first Congress convened, there were no standing committees. Deliberation about policy issues occurred directly on the floors of the House and Senate, where any interested members could participate. After chamber-wide debate had taken place on a broad issue, members would create temporary ad hoc committees to draft bills. The early Congress also had no formal party leadership organization.[39] Prior to the 1830s, the Federalist and Republican coalitions that existed in Congress were "no more than proto-parties."[40]

Today's Congress is a mature institution characterized by complex internal structures and procedures. It is led by a well-defined party apparatus, with each party organized according to its established rules and headed by a hierarchy of leaders and whips, elected and appointed. Party organization extends to policy committees, campaign committees, research committees, and numerous task forces. Minority and majority party leaders command considerable resources in terms of budgets and staff. Taken together, they employ some four hundred staff aides, and the various party committees employ about an equal number.[41]

The contemporary Congress also has an elaborate committee system bolstered by a vast body of rules and precedents regulating committee jurisdictions and operations.[42] In the 113th Congress (2013–2015), the Senate has sixteen standing committees and the House has twenty. But these committees are only the tip of the iceberg. House committees have about one hundred subcommittees; Senate committees, nearly seventy subcommittees. Four joint House–Senate committees have been retained. All this adds up to some two hundred work groups, plus an abundance of informal caucuses.

A basic concept scholars use to analyze the development of Congress's growth and adaptation is *institutionalization*. Political scientist Nelson W. Polsby applied this concept to track the institution's professionalization of the legislative career; its increasing organizational complexity—the growth of more component parts within the institution (committees, subcommittees, caucuses, leadership organizations); and its elaboration and observance of formal rules governing internal business.[43] Scholars have identified some important factors that have driven institutional development. Among these are legislative workload, institutional size, conflict with the executive branch, and members' partisan interests.

Workload

Congress's workload—once limited in scope, small in volume, and simple in content—has burgeoned since 1789. Today's Congress grapples with many issues that were once considered entirely outside the purview of governmental activity or were left to states or localities. From five to seven thousand bills and joint resolutions are introduced in the span of each two-year Congress; from three to six hundred of them are enacted into law.[44] By most measures—hours in session, committee meetings, floor votes—the congressional workload doubled between the 1950s and the late 1970s. Legislative business expanded in scope and complexity as well as in sheer volume. The average public bill of the late 1940s was two-and-a-half pages long; by the first decade of the 2000s, it ran to more than fifteen pages.[45]

Changes in workload have been an important driver of institutional change over the course of congressional history. Many of the earliest committees were established to help Congress manage a growing volume of constituent requests. When the nineteenth-century Congress was deluged with petitions requesting benefits, members created committees such as Claims, Pensions, and Public Lands to process requests.[46] Similarly, the creation and, occasionally, the abolition of committees reflect shifting perceptions of public problems. As novel policy problems arose, new committees were added.[47] The House, for example, established Commerce and Manufactures in 1795, Public Lands in 1805, Freedmen's Affairs in 1866, Roads in 1913, Science and Astronautics in 1958, Standards of Official Conduct in 1967, Small Business in 1975, and Homeland Security in 2005. An extensive system of committees allows the contemporary Congress to benefit from a division of labor as it strives to manage a far-reaching governmental agenda.

Congress's growing workload does not come only from outside the institution. From the earliest days to the present, members themselves have contributed to their collective burden. Seeking to make names for themselves, members champion causes, deliver speeches on various subjects, offer floor amendments, refer matters to committees for consideration, and engage in much policy entrepreneurship. All these activities raise the congressional workload.

At regular intervals over congressional history, the crush of business, combined with a widespread sense that Congress is unable to manage its responsibilities, prompts members to experiment with institutional reforms.[48] In 2010, for example, Congress created a short-lived institutional mechanism to negotiate an agreement on the pressing problem of long-term deficit reduction:

a joint select committee, known generally as the "Super Committee."[49] In the end, the committee could not break the partisan deadlock on fiscal policy, and the effort is now widely regarded as an institutional failure. Under workload pressure, Congress has repeatedly adopted measures to streamline procedures. Like the Super Committee, many such reforms are not successful. Nevertheless, pressure for change is ongoing, with congressional innovators devising new "unorthodox" procedures to cope with today's institutional challenges.[50]

The Size of Congress

Like workload, the size of a legislative institution profoundly affects its organization. Legislatures with more members face greater problems of agenda control and time management, unless they adopt mechanisms to manage the participation of their members.[51] The U.S. Congress grew dramatically over time, and this growth created pressure for institutional adaptation.

Looking at the government of 1789 through modern lenses, one is struck by the relatively small circles of people involved. The House of Representatives, that "impetuous council," was composed of sixty-five members—when all of them showed up. The aristocratic Senate boasted only twenty-six members, two from each of the thirteen original states.

As new states were added, the Senate grew, from thirty-two senators in 1800 to sixty-two in 1850; ninety by 1900; and, since 1959, one hundred.

For much of the nation's history, the House grew alongside the nation's population. The House membership was raised to 104 after the first census, and it steadily enlarged throughout the nineteenth century. The 1910 census, which counted 92 million people, led to an expansion to 435 members. After the 1920 census, Congress declined to enlarge the House further. And that is the way things stand to this day.

Growth impelled House members to empower strong leaders, to rely on committees, to impose strict limits on floor debate, and to devise elaborate ways of channeling the flow of floor business. It is no accident that strong leaders emerged during the periods the House experienced the most rapid growth. After the initial growth spurt in the first two decades of the Republic, vigorous leadership appeared in the person of Henry Clay (1811–1814, 1815–1820, and 1823–1825). Similarly, the post–Civil War expansion of the House was met with an era of forceful Speakers that lasted from the 1870s until 1910.

In the smaller and more intimate Senate, vigorous leadership has been the exception rather than the rule. The relative informality of Senate procedures and the long-cherished right of unlimited debate testify to the looser reins of leadership. Compared with the House's complex rules and voluminous precedents, the Senate's rules are relatively brief and simple, putting a premium on informal negotiations among senators interested in a given measure.

Conflict with the Executive Branch

Conflict with the president is a perennial impetus for institutional reform. When Congress cannot collaborate on policy with the executive branch, members seek out ways to increase their capacity for independent action. During such confrontations, Congress creates new institutions and procedures that often endure long beyond the specific contexts that gave rise to them.

One of the most important standing House committees, Ways and Means, was first established to provide a source of financial information independent of the controversial and divisive Treasury secretary at the time, Alexander Hamilton.[52] Similarly, the landmark Legislative Reorganization Act of 1946 was adopted amid members' growing concerns about congressional power. Following the massive growth of the administrative state during the New Deal and World War II, members feared that Congress could simply no longer compete with the executive branch. Reformers saw "a reorganized Congress as a way to redress the imbalance of power that had developed between the branches."[53] The act streamlined the legislative process by dramatically reducing the number of committees and regularizing their jurisdictions. Sen. Owen Brewster, R-Maine, argued at the time that the reforms were necessary "to retain any semblance of the ancient division of functions under our constitution."[54] The act was adopted by a sizable bipartisan majority, with both Republicans and Democrats expressing hope that reform would strengthen Congress's power and prestige.

Another major institutional innovation, Congress's budget process, was fashioned in an environment of intense interbranch warfare between President Richard Nixon and a Democratic Congress.[55] President Nixon's unprecedented assertion of authority to withhold funds that Congress had appropriated was a major stimulus for passage of the Congressional Budget and Impoundment Control Act of 1974. Without the power of the purse, Sen. John Tunney, D-Calif., remarked, "we may as well go out of business."[56] However, the act addressed an array of structural issues that went far beyond the particulars of the dispute over the president's impoundment powers. It established a new internal congressional budget process; new budget committees in both chambers; and a new congressional agency, the nonpartisan Congressional Budget Office (CBO). The goal was to allow Congress to formulate a comprehensive national budget on its own, backed by appropriate estimates and forecasts, without relying on the president's budget or the executive branch's Office of Management and Budget.

In *Federalist* No. 51, Madison justified the Constitution as a system to "divide and arrange the several offices in such a manner as that each may be a check on the other." Congress's institutional development bears the indelible stamp of this checking and balancing, as Congress has repeatedly reformed itself to meet challenges from the executive branch.

Partisan Interests

Political parties had no place in the original constitutional blueprint. However, no account of institutional development in Congress can ignore their vital role. Everything about the organization and operation of Congress is shaped by political parties. Indeed, the first thing a visitor to the House or Senate chamber notices is that the seats or desks are divided along partisan lines—Democrats to the left facing the dais, Republicans to the right. Although today's congressional parties are remarkably cohesive and energetic, the goals and capacities of the political parties have been a major engine of change throughout congressional history.

Parties began to develop in Congress during the first presidential administration. When Treasury secretary Alexander Hamilton unveiled his financial program in 1790, a genuine partisan spirit swept the capital. The Federalists, with Hamilton as their intellectual leader, espoused energetic government to deal forcefully with national problems and foster economic growth. The rival Republicans, who looked to Thomas Jefferson and James Madison for leadership, rallied opponents of Federalist policies and championed local autonomy, a weaker national government, and programs favoring agricultural or debtor interests. By 1794 Sen. John Taylor of Virginia could write:

> The existence of two parties in Congress is apparent. The fact is disclosed almost upon every important question. Whether the subject be foreign or domestic—relative to war or peace—navigation or commerce—the magnetism of opposite views draws them wide as the poles asunder.[57]

Parties also flourished throughout the nineteenth century. Regional conflicts, along with economic upheavals produced by rapid industrialization, nurtured partisan differences. At the grassroots level, the parties were differentiated along class, occupational, and regional lines. Grassroots party organizations were massive and militant. In the context of this vibrant nineteenth-century party system, the majority party gained organizational control over the House of Representatives. Ever since the Civil War, the leader of the House majority party has served as Speaker.[58] By the end of the nineteenth century, strong Speakers had tamed the unruly House, and a coterie of state party bosses dominated the Senate.

Even though parties were weaker during the Progressive era and throughout the middle of the twentieth century, they never became irrelevant. Despite the demise of the strong Speakership (1910), the direct election of senators (1913), and profound divisions in the Democratic majority party between the late 1930s and the 1970s, the parties continued to organize Congress down to the present day.[59] All contemporary House and Senate members receive and retain their committee assignments through their parties. Likewise, members of the majority party chair all the standing committees of Congress.

Party politics has impelled the development of floor procedure, members' parliamentary rights, leaders' prerogatives, and agenda-control devices. The rules of the legislative process at any given time are, in Sarah A. Binder's words, a "result of hard-nosed partisan battles—fought, of course, under a particular set of inherited institutional rules."[60]

A watershed moment in the development of the House of Representatives, the adoption of Reed's Rules in 1890, offers one of the clearest examples of partisan influence on institutional procedure. Prior to 1890, the minority party in the House of Representatives possessed an arsenal of dilatory tactics to obstruct the majority party's agenda.[61] Reed's Rules, named for then–House Speaker Thomas Brackett Reed, R-Maine, revolutionized House procedure by granting the Speaker secure control over the order of business and strictly curbing the minority party's ability to obstruct the majority party's floor agenda. Majority party Republicans fought for the adoption of Reed's Rules over strong opposition from the Democrats. At that time, Republicans had just won unified party control of the government for the first time in nearly a decade, and they had an ambitious and controversial agenda. Knowing that Democrats would use their resources to obstruct their agenda, Republicans changed the rules of the House to permit majority party control over the institution, a fact of life in the House of Representatives since. In procedural terms, Reed's Rules permanently transformed the House of Representatives.

The circumstances surrounding the adoption of Reed's Rules offers a blueprint for many partisan rules changes over the course of House history. Based on a study of all procedural rules changes that benefited the majority party at the expense of the minority party between 1789 and 1990, Binder finds that "crucial procedural choices have been shaped not by members' collective concerns about the institution, but by calculations of partisan advantage."[62] When necessary to overcome minority party obstruction, unified majority parties have repeatedly shown themselves willing to alter the institution's rules to ensure the passage of their agenda.

Members' Individual Interests

Institutional development has been driven by more than members' partisan and institutional goals; members also have individual goals. As individuals, members want to build a reputation as effective lawmakers and representatives. To do so, they must be able to point to achievements of their own. When congressional rules or structures inhibit their ability to do so, pressure builds for institutional reform.

In addition to its value as an institutional division of labor, the elaborate committee system in Congress serves members' individual political needs and policy goals. Because of the multitude of leadership positions created by the numerous committees and subcommittees, nearly every member has an opportunity to make an individual contribution. "Whatever else it may be, the quest for specialization in Congress is a quest for credit," observes David R. Mayhew. "Every member can aspire to occupy a part of at least one piece of policy turf small enough that he can claim personal responsibility for some of the things that happen on it."[63]

The congressional reforms of the 1970s are one example of the ways in which members' individual goals have affected institutional development.

Over that decade, the two chambers revamped their committee systems to allow more input from rank-and-file members. The streamlined committee systems that had been put in place after the Legislative Reorganization Act of 1946 offered relatively few committee leadership positions, and those were gained on the basis of seniority. Every committee was led by its longest-serving members, who retained their positions until death, defeat, or retirement. The large classes of new members elected in the 1970s, feeling thwarted by this system, began to press for change.[64] Out of this ferment emerged a variety of reforms that opened up new opportunities for junior members. Among these reforms, the seniority system was weakened as committee chairs were forced to stand for election in their party caucus, making them accountable to the party's rank and file.

The persistence of Senate rules that permit unlimited debate is another example of the ways in which individual goals shape institutional rules.[65] Despite the many frustrations unlimited debate has caused for Senate majority parties over the years, senators have generally been unwilling to embrace changes that would allow for simple majority rule. Senators realize that a great part of their own institutional power derives from their ability to take advantage of unlimited debate to block votes on matters that have majority support. Senate leaders are forced to negotiate with senators who threaten to obstruct Senate action via unlimited debate.

Reforms that would make it possible for a Senate majority to force a vote have long been in the interest of the Senate's majority party. But such reforms come at a direct, substantial cost to senators' individual power. Not surprisingly, senators have proven very reluctant to trade off so much of their individual influence in favor of collective party goals. In November 2013, majority party Democrats grew sufficiently frustrated with Republican filibusters of judicial and executive branch nominations to make a substantial change. The Democratic majority imposed a new precedent allowing a simple majority to end debate on all confirmations for offices other than the Supreme Court. Even so, Democratic senators proved loath to establish simple majority rule for legislation, suggesting that senators continue to value their individual prerogatives.

Like everything else about Congress, the institution's rules and procedures can only be fully understood in the context of the two Congresses. Members want rules and processes to serve them as individual lawmakers and representatives, as well as to facilitate the functioning of the legislature as a whole.

Changing pressures on the institution, congressional–executive conflicts, partisan agendas, and members' individual goals have all been important drivers of Congress's institutional development. Indeed, significant reforms are almost always the result of several of these forces simultaneously buffeting the institution. One broad-ranging study of forty-two major institutional innovations concludes that institutional reforms are typically brought about through "common carriers," reform initiatives that are at once supported by several different groups of legislators for different sets of reasons.[66] The Legislative Reorganization Act of 1946, for example, was espoused by many legislators who wanted to enhance the power and effectiveness of the legislative branch, but it was also supported by members who valued the new pay and pension benefits included in the legislation.[67] Similarly, many members favored the 1970s reforms reducing the power of committee chairs because they wanted access to more policy turf of their own. At the same time, many liberal members backed the reforms because they wanted to reduce the influence of the disproportionately conservative committee chairs.[68]

Because the same reforms are so often backed for several different reasons, no single theory can explain congressional change. Legislative institutions incorporate internal tensions and contradictions, rather than maximize the attainment of any particular goal.[69] Furthermore, reforms inevitably fall short of their sponsors' objectives. Instead of achieving stable, effective arrangements, reforms frequently produce "a set of institutions that often work at cross-purposes."[70] At the same time, innovations usually have unanticipated consequences, which may lead to yet another round of reform.

EVOLUTION OF THE LEGISLATOR'S JOB

What is it like to be a member of Congress? The legislator's job, like the institution of Congress, has evolved since 1789. During the early Congresses, being a senator or representative was a part-time occupation. Few members regarded congressional service as a career, and according to most accounts the rewards were slim. Since then, lawmakers' exposure to constituents' demands and their career expectations have changed dramatically. Electoral units, too, have grown very large. With the nation's population estimated at some 320 million citizens, the average House constituency since the 2010 reapportionment consists of more than 713,000 people, and the average state of more than 6 million.

The Congressional Career

During its early years, Congress was an institution composed of transients. The nation's capital was an unsightly place, and its culture was provincial. Members remained in Washington only a few months, spending their unpleasant sojourns in boardinghouses.[71]

The early Congresses failed to command the loyalty needed to keep members in office. Congressional service was regarded more as odious duty than as rewarding work. "My dear friend," a North Carolina representative wrote to a constituent in 1796, "there is nothing in this service, exclusive of the confidence and gratitude of my constituents, worth the sacrifice."[72] Of the ninety-four senators who served between 1789 and 1801, thirty-three resigned before completing their terms, only six to take other federal posts.[73] In the House, almost 6 percent of all early-nineteenth-century members resigned during each Congress.

Careerism mounted toward the end of the nineteenth century. As late as the 1870s, more than half the House members at any given time were freshmen, and the mean length of service was barely two terms. By the end of the century, however, the proportion of newcomers had fallen to 30 percent, and average House tenure had reached three terms, or six years. About the same time, senators' mean term of service topped seven years, in excess of one full term.[74]

Today, the average senator has served nearly ten years, the average House member nine. Table 2-1 shows changes since 1789 in the percentages of new and veteran members and the mean number of terms claimed by incumbents. In both the House and Senate, members' average length of service has increased over time, and the proportion of first-termers is substantially lower than it was during the first hundred years of the nation's history.

Rising careerism has a number of causes. The increase in one-party states and districts following the Civil War, and especially after 1896, enabled repeated reelection of a dominant party's candidates—Democrats in the South, Republicans in the Midwest and the rural Northeast. Members themselves also began to find congressional service more rewarding. The growth of national government during the twentieth century enhanced the excitement and glamour of the Washington political scene, especially when compared with state or local renown.

The prerogatives accorded to seniority further rewarded lengthy service. Beginning in the late nineteenth century in the Senate and in the early twentieth century in the House, members with the longest tenure in office began to dominate positions of power in Congress. However, seniority norms have been considerably eroded since the 1990s. After taking over the House in 1995, Republican leaders passed over several senior members in naming committee chairs. At the same time, the GOP majority won adoption of a House rule that also limited chairs' terms to six years—a provision again enforced when Republicans selected committee chairs after reclaiming a House majority in the 2010 elections.[75] Although seniority is no longer the unquestioned norm it once was, extended service generally remains a prerequisite for top party and committee posts. The benefits accruing to seniority continue to compound the returns on long service in the contemporary Congress.

Professionalization

During the Republic's early days, lawmaking was not a full-time occupation. As President John F. Kennedy was fond of remarking, the Clays, Calhouns, and Websters of the nineteenth century could afford to devote a whole generation or more to debating and refining the few great controversies at hand. Rep. Joseph W. Martin, R-Mass., who entered the House in 1925 and went on to become Speaker (1947–1949, 1953–1955), described the leisurely atmosphere of earlier days and the workload changes during his service:

> From one end of a session to another Congress would scarcely have three or four issues of consequence besides appropriations bills. And the issues themselves were fundamentally simpler than those that surge in upon us today in such a torrent that the individual member cannot analyze all of them adequately before he is compelled to vote.

TABLE 2-1 **Length of Service in House and Senate, 1789–2015**				
	Congress			
Chamber and terms	1st–56th (1789–1901)	57th–103rd (1901–1995)	104th–113th (1995–2015)	114th (2015–2017)
House				
One (up to 2 years)	44.0%	23.3%	14.3%	12.9%
Two to six (3–12 years)	53.4	49.7	50.7	55.1
Seven or more (12+ years)	2.6	27.0	35.0	32.0
Mean number of terms[1]	2.1	4.8	5.2	5.5
Senate				
One (up to 6 years)	65.6%	45.6%	33.0%	45.0%
Two (7–12 years)	23.4	22.4	26.6	24.0
Three or more (12+ years)	11.0	32.0	40.8	31.0
Mean number of terms[1]	1.5	2.2	2.3	2.3

Sources: Adapted from David C. Huckabee, "Length of Service for Representatives and Senators: 1st–103rd Congresses," Congressional Research Service Report 95-426GOV, March 27, 1995. Authors' calculations for the 104th through 114th Congresses. See also Mildred Amer, "Average Years of Service for Members of the Senate and House of Representatives, First–109th Congresses," Congressional Research Service Report RL32648, November 9, 2005.

[1] Figures are derived from the total number of terms claimed by members whether or not those terms were served out. For example, members in their initial year of service are counted as having one full term, and so on. Thus the figures cannot be equated precisely with years of service.

In my early years in Congress the main issues were few enough so that almost any conscientious member could with application make himself a quasi-expert at least. In the complexity and volume of today's legislation, however, most members have to trust somebody else's word or the recommendation of a committee. Nowadays bills, which thirty years ago would have been thrashed out for hours or days, go through in ten minutes.[76]

In recent decades, legislative business has kept the House and Senate almost perpetually in session—punctuated by constituency work periods. Members of the contemporary Congress are—and must be—full-time professional politicians.

Congress has also professionalized in that members now direct a large staff of aides. Until recent decades, members of Congress had access to very limited staff. In the 1890s, only 142 clerks (62 for the House and 80 for the Senate) were on hand to serve members of Congress. Many senators and all representatives handled their own correspondence. It was not until 1946 that

Congress began to develop professional staffing. Every member now has employees to handle mail and phone calls, appointments, policy research, speechwriting, and constituent service. With each member directing his or her own staff "enterprise," Congress now sustains a distinct Washington subculture.[77] All told, the legislative branch employs more than twenty-five thousand people housed in nearly a dozen Capitol Hill buildings.[78]

Constituency Demands

Since the beginning, American legislators have been expected to remain close to voters. Early representatives reported to their constituents through circular letters, communications passed around throughout their districts.[79] But the volume of those demands has increased many times over. Before the Civil War, a member's business on behalf of constituents was confined mainly to awarding rural mail routes, arranging for Mexican War pensions, sending out free seed, and only occasionally explaining legislation. This unhurried pace has long since vanished.

Reflecting on his forty years of congressional service concluding in 1967, Representative Martin remarked on the dramatic upsurge of constituent awareness:

> Today the federal government is far more complex, as is every phase of national life. People have to turn to their Representative for aid. I used to think ten letters a day was a big batch; now I get several hundred a day. In earlier times, constituents didn't know their Congressman's views. With better communications, their knowledge has increased along with their expectations of what he must know.[80]

People of Martin's era would be astonished at the volume of constituency work now handled by House and Senate offices. The advent of new communications technologies has increased the volume of congressional mail by an order of magnitude. In 1997, the last year before e-mail use became widespread, members of Congress received 30.5 million pieces of posted mail; by 2007 the volume of mail, e-mail included, had surged to 491 million pieces.[81] Not only are constituents more numerous than ever before, but they are also better educated, served by faster communication and transportation, and mobilized by lobby organizations. Public opinion surveys reveal that voters expect legislators to dispense federal services and to communicate frequently with the home folks. Even though the more flagrant forms of pork-barrel politics are denounced, constituents' demands are unlikely to ebb in the future.

CONCLUSION

While the founders understood the guiding principles of representative assemblies, they could not have foreseen what sort of institution they had created. They wrote into the Constitution legislative powers as they understood them and left the details to future generations.

Just as the Earth's history is marked by periods of intense, even cataclysmic, change—punctuated equilibrium—so historians of Congress have identified several eras of intensive institutional change, such as the advent of Reed's Rules or the early-nineteenth-century transformation of the Senate described by Elaine Swift. But institutional change is not necessarily dramatic. Incremental changes of one kind or another are also always unfolding.

Over time, as a result of changes large and small, Congress became the mature institution of today. The contemporary Congress abounds with norms and traditions, rules and procedures, committees and subcommittees. In short, the modern Congress is highly institutionalized. How different it is from the First Congress, personified by fussy John Adams worrying about what forms of address to use.

This institutionalization has a number of important consequences, some good and some bad. It enables Congress to cope with its extensive workload. A division of labor, primarily through standing committees, permits the two houses to process a wide variety of issues simultaneously. Careerism encourages legislators to develop skills and expertise in specific areas. In tandem with staff resources, this specialization allows Congress to compete with the executive branch in absorbing information and applying expertise to public issues. The danger of institutionalization is organizational rigidity. Institutions that are too rigid can frustrate policy making, especially in periods of rapid social or political change. Structures that are too complex can tie people in knots, producing inaction, delays, and confusion.

The institutionalization of the contemporary Congress must be taken into account by anyone who seeks to understand it today. Capitol Hill newcomers—even those who vow to shake things up—confront not an unformed, pliable institution but an established, traditional one that must be approached largely on its own terms.

Electoral Process. A former mayor and city councilwoman, Rep. Mia Love of Utah—the first black Republican woman elected to Congress—reaches into a box to draw a number as newly elected House lawmakers take their chances in a traditional lottery to determine who gets priority in choosing office assignments. A former Maryland state senator, Rep. Alex Mooney, R-W.Va., reacts after drawing the eighth pick in the lottery. Rep. Tom MacArthur, R-N.J., rubs his head for good luck before drawing. He was previously an insurance executive and mayor of the North Jersey town of Randolph. Numbered chips are placed in order before the start of the lottery.

chapter 3

Going for It:
Recruitment and Candidacy

At the start of the 114th Congress in January 2015, seventy-four new members of Congress took the oath of office. Among the thirteen new senators (12R, 1 ID) were two business executives, a college president, a former governor, a state house Speaker, and five former U.S. House members. Among the sixty-one new House members (44R, 17D) were a school administrator, a pastor, a union leader, a dentist, a farmer, an engineer, and an economics professor.

How did these people get to Congress? This question has no simple answer. In the broadest sense, all legislators are products of recruitment—the social and political process through which people seek and win leadership posts. Recruitment is a key to the effective performance of all institutions, including legislatures. Ideally, the recruitment process should secure the ablest individuals to lead their community, a subject addressed in the first great book about politics, Plato's *Republic*. Sociologists have long observed, however, that recruitment reflects a society's class structure: privileged members of society are overrepresented in the power structure. Political scientists, whatever their normative concerns, have charted the paths that individuals travel to gain positions in Congress and other institutions of government.

Any recruitment process has both formal and informal elements. For Congress, the formal elements include the Constitution and state and federal laws governing nominations and elections. Equally important are the informal, often unwritten, rules of the game. Ambitions, skills, and resources favor certain aspirants over others; popular moods and attitudes—which are changeable—induce citizens to support some candidates and reject others. Taken together, such elements add up to a series of filters or screens. The recruitment process is a mix of rules, probabilities, chance events, and timing. Its biases, both overt and hidden, affect the quality of representation and decision making in the House and Senate.

FORMAL RULES OF THE GAME

The formal gateways to congressional office are wide. There are only three constitutional qualifications for holding congressional office: age (twenty-five years of age for the House, thirty for the Senate); citizenship (seven years for the House, nine years for the Senate); and residency (in the state from which the officeholder is elected).

These qualifications cannot be augmented by the states or by Congress. For example, the Supreme Court has held that states cannot limit the number of terms their members of Congress can serve. A change of this kind can only be made through constitutional amendment.[1] Notably, the drafters of the Constitution considered but rejected term limits. According to *The Federalist Papers,* officeholders' desire for reelection was thought a powerful incentive for faithful service. In addition, the framers valued the expertise that experienced lawmakers—people like themselves—could bring to legislative deliberations.

The residency requirement is traditionally stricter in practice than the Constitution prescribes. Voters tend to prefer candidates with long-standing ties to their states or districts and to shun outsiders who move into a state primarily to seek public office (so-called "carpetbaggers"). Nevertheless, Americans' geographical mobility has swollen the "carpetbagger caucus" on Capitol Hill. About a third of the members of both chambers in recent Congresses were born outside the states they represent. Especially in the more populous, faster-growing areas, shrewd candidates can overcome objections to their outsider status. Barely a year after he settled in Arizona, Republican senator John McCain, a career navy officer and six-year prisoner of war in North Vietnam, beat three established politicians for a congressional nomination. He stifled carpetbagging charges by explaining that, as the son of a navy officer and one himself, he had never been able to put down roots: "The longest place I ever lived was Hanoi."

Senate Apportionment

At the 1789 Constitutional Convention, delegates from small states demanded equal representation in the Senate as the price for their support of the Constitution. This arrangement is virtually unamendable, because Article V assures that no state can be deprived of its equal voice in the Senate without its own consent. As a result, the Senate is the one legislative body in the nation in which "one person, one vote" emphatically does not apply. By this standard, the Senate is one of the most malapportioned legislatures in the democratic world.[2] The nine most populous states are home to 51 percent of the population but control only 18 percent of the Senate; the twenty-six least populous states elect 52 percent of the Senate but hold only 18 percent of the population.[3]

Over time, widening disparities in state population eroded the Senate's representative character. After the first census in 1790, the spread between the most populous state (Virginia) and the least populous (Delaware) was nineteen to one. Today, the spread between the most populous state (California) and the least populous (Wyoming) is sixty-six to one.

Populous states complain that they are shortchanged in the federal bargain. Compared with lightly populated states, they contribute more revenue and receive fewer benefits.[4] One study using survey, electoral, and demographic data concludes that the Senate's malapportionment "has increasingly come to underweight the preferences of liberals, Democrats, African Americans, and Latinos."[5]

House Apportionment

The 435 House seats are apportioned among the states by population, with districts averaging more than 713,000 people each. This apportionment process excludes the five delegates (American Samoa, the District of Columbia, Guam, the Virgin Islands, and the Northern Mariana Islands) and one resident commissioner (Puerto Rico). These nonapportioned seats represent populations ranging from 55,519 (American Samoa) to 3.7 million (Puerto Rico).

Role of the Census. To allocate House seats among the states, the Constitution requires a census of the population every ten years. Once the figures are gathered by the Commerce Department's Census Bureau, House apportionment is derived by a mathematical formula called the method of equal proportions.[6] However, reapportionment does not fully guarantee equality of district population because of two additional requirements: (1) every state must receive one House member, and (2) congressional districts cannot cross state lines.[7] After the 2010 apportionment, for example, the entire state of Montana, with one representative-at-large for nearly a million people, was the nation's most populous district. Neighboring Wyoming, with slightly over half a million represented by its single seat, was the least populous.

Because the size of the House has remained unchanged since 1911, one state's gain now means another state's loss.[8] This reality provoked sharp controversy in the aftermath of the 1920 census. For the first time ever, the results indicated that more Americans lived in urban than in rural areas. With the nation's cities and rural towns sharply at odds over the burning issue of the enforcement of Prohibition, the power struggle over representation was so intractable that Congress failed to pass a reapportionment bill after the 1920 census.[9] Finally, in 1929 a law was enacted that "established a permanent system for apportioning the 435 House seats following each census."[10] Thus the reapportionment of House seats occurred after the 1930 census and every census since (see Figure 3-1).

For some decades now, older industrial and farm states of the Northeast and Midwest have lost ground to fast-growing states in the South and West— the declining Rust Belt versus the booming Sun Belt. After the 1940 census, states in the East and Midwest commanded 58 percent of all House seats, compared with 42 percent for states in the South and West. With the 2000 census, the ratio was exactly reversed. Over two generations, then, "a huge shift in political power" occurred between the geographic regions.[11] The trend continued with the results of the 2010 census, after which the northeastern and midwestern states once again lost seats to the Sun Belt. Most dramatically, Texas and Florida increased their congressional representation by four and two seats, respectively, while Ohio and New York each lost two seats.

FIGURE 3-1 House Apportionment in the 114th Congress

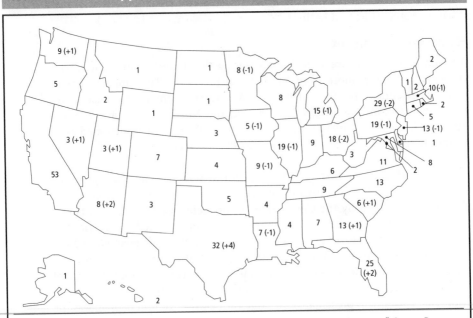

Source: "Apportionment Population and Number of Representatives, By State: 2010 Census," Census Bureau, U.S. Department of Commerce, December 21, 2010, http://2010.census.gov/news/pdf/apport2010_table1.pdf.

Note: Entries show the total number of House seats held by each state. Numbers in parentheses show the seats each state gained or lost after the post-2010 reapportionment.

Census Politics. The Constitution describes the decennial census as an "actual enumeration" of persons (Article I, section 2). The Fourteenth Amendment adds: "Representatives shall be apportioned among the several States according to their respective numbers, counting the whole number of persons in each State, excluding Indians not taxed." Because population figures determine seats and affect power, including each state's share of the Electoral College vote for president and vice president, controversy surrounds nearly every aspect of apportionment and districting.

First, counting such a large and diverse population is logistically and methodologically daunting. Certain hard-to-contact groups—transients, the homeless, renters, immigrants (legal or not), children, and poorer people generally—elude census takers and are undercounted. College students or others temporarily living away from home are sometimes double-counted (an overcount, in effect).[12] The so-called "tri-caucus" in the House—the Black Caucus, the Hispanic Caucus, and the Asian Caucus—has long been concerned about getting accurate counts of hard-to-reach minorities.[13]

Second, the issue of statistical sampling has been a subject of considerable controversy. For the 2000 census, the Census Bureau had planned to use statistical sampling to augment its traditional methods for counting people so as to minimize the undercount of minority populations. But, because minorities tend to vote Democratic, congressional Republicans feared that "sampling would overestimate minority populations and thereby cause Republicans to lose seats to Democrats."[14] Legal challenges to the sampling plan eventually ended up in the Supreme Court, which held that sampling could not be used to apportion seats among the states, but kept open the possibility that it could be used for other purposes, such as the redistricting of House seats within a state.[15]

Third, the immigration issue adds yet another dimension to census politics. Because the Fourteenth Amendment refers to "persons" rather than "citizens," states with large numbers of undocumented immigrants (such as Arizona, California, Nevada, and Texas) gain House seats at the expense of states with fewer undocumented immigrants (such as Michigan and Pennsylvania). "It's one thing if we lose seats simply because of population loss," complained Rep. Candice Miller, R-Mich., "but it's another thing if we lose this seat because of illegal immigration, and that's exactly what is happening."[16] However, the Supreme Court in 2013 declined to review lower-court rulings on an Irving, Texas, case—in which the complainants argued that any count that included noncitizens diluted their votes and deprived them of the Fourteenth Amendment's guarantee of equal protection of the laws. Thus the census embraces all residents—whether they are citizens or noncitizens, or whether or not they are qualified to vote.[17]

DISTRICTING IN THE HOUSE

Redistricting is fundamentally a state responsibility, but the federal courts increasingly govern the process. Congressional districting is regulated by two federal statutes. The first is a 1967 statute that mandates that all states entitled to more than one seat create districts, each represented by a single member. At-large or multimember districts are prohibited. The second statute is the Voting Rights Act of 1965, which requires that districts not dilute the representation of racial minorities. In addition to interpreting these statutes, the courts have construed the Constitution to require that districts be nearly equal in population, a standard that they rigorously enforce.

Redistricting is a fiercely political process that affects the fortunes of many people—state legislators, governors, incumbent House members, the congressional leadership, lobbyists, and the leaders of racial and ethnic groups.[18] To insulate the process from politics, a handful of states have turned the job over to some form of independent commission.[19] In most states, however, redistricting is carried out by the legislature, with the governor able to approve or veto the plan. If a state's politicians become deadlocked on redistricting, or if they fail to observe legal guidelines, judges may finish the job—sometimes awarding victory to parties that lost out earlier in the political fracas.

In the redistricting wars no weapons are left sheathed. Both political parties pour money into state legislative and gubernatorial elections and into postcensus lobbying efforts so they can control the map-making process. The shift of only a few seats in a state legislature can thereby determine not only which party dominates its congressional delegation, but potentially which party achieves majority control of the House itself. As a GOP consultant said about his role in drawing House seats, "As a mapmaker, I can have more of an impact on an election than a campaign, than a candidate."[20]

Because congressional seats are political prizes, districting is a tool by which politicians seek partisan, factional, and even personal advantage. Two perennial problems of districting are malapportionment and gerrymandering.

Malapportionment

Before 1964, districts of grossly unequal populations often existed side by side in the same state. As metropolitan areas grew in population, rurally dominated legislatures simply refused to redistrict, holding on to power regardless of population movements and demographic trends—the "silent gerrymander." The courts were slow to venture into this "political thicket." By the 1960s, however, the problem of unequal representation was crying out for resolution.[21]

In a series of landmark rulings in the 1960s, the Supreme Court held that districting schemes that fell short of standards of population equality violated the Constitution. In *Reynolds v. Sims* (1964), the Court ruled that the Fourteenth Amendment's equal protection clause requires that all state legislative seats be apportioned "substantially on population." That same year, the Court also applied the "one person, one vote" principle to the U.S. House of Representatives. In *Wesberry v. Sanders* (1964), the Court based its decision not on the Fourteenth Amendment but on Article I, section 2, of the Constitution, which directs that House representatives be apportioned among the states according to their respective numbers and chosen by the people of the several states. This language, argued Justice Hugo Black, means that "as nearly as is practicable, one person's vote in a congressional election is to be worth as much as another's."

How much equality of population is "practicable" within the states? The Supreme Court has adopted rigid mathematical equality as the underlying standard. In a 1983 case (*Karcher v. Daggett*), a 5–4 majority voided a New Jersey plan in which districts varied by no more than one-seventh of 1 percent. "Adopting any standard other than population equality would subtly erode the Constitution's ideal of equal representation," wrote Justice William J. Brennan for the majority.

Other goals must sometimes be sacrificed to achieve population equality. It is often not feasible to follow other economic, social, or geographic boundaries in drawing districts of equal population. The congressional district, therefore, tends to be an artificial creation, often bearing little relationship to real communities of interest—economic, geographic, or political. "The main

casualty of the tortuous redistricting process now under way," remarked journalist Alan Ehrenhalt, "is the erosion of geographical community—of place—
as the basis of political representation."[22]

Gerrymandering

The term *gerrymander* refers to district line-drawing that purposefully maximizes
seats for one party or voting bloc. The gerrymander takes its name from Gov.
Elbridge Gerry of Massachusetts, who in 1812 created a peculiar, salamander-
shaped district north of Boston to benefit his Democratic Party (see Box 3-1).
Gerrymandering is used not only to gain partisan advantage but also to shape the
political prospects of incumbents, particular aspiring politicians, or racial or ethnic groups. For most of its history, Congress has regarded gerrymandering as part
of the spoils of partisan warfare.

Two common gerrymandering techniques are *cracking* and *packing*.
Cracking splits a party's or a group's strength between two or more districts,
thereby diluting its voting leverage. A Republican cracking strategy, for example, might call for dividing a Democratic-leaning university town across two
districts, combining each with the surrounding Republican-leaning rural areas,
ensuring that Democrats will have difficulty winning either seat. A *packing*
strategy draws districts dominated by voters of one party or group. Obviously,
packing will likely make a district safe for a particular party, group, or incumbent. But it is also a way to waste votes. If a party's or ethnic group's voters are
systematically concentrated in a small number of districts, it will win those seats
with more votes than it needs, reducing its chances of winning nearby seats.

Today, gerrymandering is much more easily carried out than it was in the
past. With computer technology and software, knowledgeable individuals and
groups can use census and other data to match people's voting patterns to
where they live, even street by street. Political leaders are able to consider various alternative plans until they identify a redistricting map that achieves their
objectives.

Partisan Gerrymandering. The most common form of gerrymandering
is aimed at partisan advantage. This type of gerrymandering occurs in states in
which one political party controls the process. A noteworthy and unusual
example involved the Texas legislature after the 2002 elections. Texas
Republicans—controlling both legislative chambers and the state house for the
first time since Reconstruction—pushed through a new districting plan even
though an earlier postcensus districting scheme was already in place. When
the plan was used for the 2004 balloting, the GOP gained five seats, four of
them from defeated Democratic incumbents. Subsequently, the U.S. Supreme
Court upheld the 2003 Texas redistricting scheme by a 7–2 margin (*League of
United Latin American Citizens v. Perry*, 2006).[23] Despite finding that the Texas
GOP appeared to have acted "with the sole purpose of achieving a Republican
majority," Justice Anthony M. Kennedy—speaking for the Court—found that
the case did not provide a "workable test" for deciding "how much partisan
dominance is too much."

BOX 3-1   Origins of the Gerrymander

The practice of "gerrymandering"—the excessive manipulation of the shape of a legislative district to benefit certain persons or groups—is probably as old as the Republic, but the name for the practice originated in 1812.

In that year, the Massachusetts legislature carved out of Essex County a district that historian John Fiske described as having a "dragon-like contour." When the artist Elkana Tisdale saw the misshapen district at a dinner party, he penciled in a head, wings, and claws. Richard Alsop, a poet, then termed the district a "Gerry-mander" —after Elbridge Gerry, then-governor of Massachusetts. Federalists reprinted the image widely in newspapers, and the term "gerrymander" gained brief currency as slang for being deceived.

By the 1990s, the term had broadened to include the modern-day practice of drawing maps to benefit racial and ethnic groups. In the past, the term was applied largely to districts drawn to benefit incumbents or political parties.

Source: Michael P. McDonald, "State Legislative Districting," *Guide to State Politics and Policy,* ed. Richard Niemi and Joshua Dyck (Washington, DC: CQ Press, 2013).

On the issue of partisan gerrymandering, the Supreme Court, like Congress, has largely chosen to look the other way. In a 1986 case involving Indiana state legislative districts, a Court majority held that gerrymandering was a justiciable issue—that is, it could be properly raised in court (*Davis v. Bandemer*).[24] If the gerrymandering were substantial, long-standing, and truly harmful to a political minority, it could violate the Constitution's equal protection clause. At the same time, the Court's majority was not convinced that the Indiana gerrymander met those tests. Indeed, the Court has never overturned a districting scheme on the grounds of partisan gerrymandering. Despite a number of cases dealing with the issue, the Court has neglected to set out any standard for distinguishing permissible from impermissible partisan gerrymandering.[25]

Because of their large gains in state legislatures and gubernatorial seats in the 2010 elections, Republicans enjoyed substantial advantages over Democrats in redrawing House district boundaries after the most recent reapportionment. Republicans held the governor's mansion and both chambers of the state legislature in seventeen states, which allowed them to redistrict four times as many seats as Democrats.[26] Favorable district lines helped Republicans retain their House majority in 2012, when President Barack Obama won reelection and Democrats received 1.1 million more votes than Republicans in House elections nationally.[27] District lines undoubtedly affect party fortunes. According to a Brennan Center analysis of the 2012 elections, in states where Republicans had controlled the redistricting process, Republican candidates won 53 percent of the vote and 72 percent of the seats. By comparison, in the states where Democrats were in control, Democratic candidates won around 56 percent of the vote and 71 percent of the seats.[28]

Many pundits and politicians complain that the prevalence of partisan gerrymandering inhibits the construction of cross-party coalitions. As former representative John Tanner, D-Tenn., stated:

> When Members come here from these [partisan] districts that have been gerrymandered, they have little incentive really to work across party lines in order to reach solutions. As a matter of fact, they have a disincentive because if their district is skewed so heavily one way or the other, then the election is really in the party primaries, where . . . the highly charged partisans, either Democrat or Republican, [dominate]. And so if one comes here wanting to work across the aisle, one has to watch one's back, because the highly charged partisans don't like that.[29]

Scholarly research, however, provides little support for the claim that gerrymandering is an important cause of party polarization in Congress. Political scientist Sean M. Theriault reports that redistricting is responsible for between 10 and 20 percent of the party polarization that has occurred.[30] Other scholars dispute even this relatively modest effect. A study by Nolan McCarty, Keith T. Poole, and Howard Rosenthal concludes that gerrymandering has not contributed to the rise of partisanship to any meaningful extent: "Polarization is not primarily a phenomenon of how voters are sorted into districts. It is mainly the consequence of the different ways Democrats and Republicans would represent the same districts."[31] Changes in congressional districts over time simply cannot account for party polarization in Congress. Republicans who represent swing districts are little different in their voting behavior than Republicans who represent seats that are safe for their party. The same is true for Democrats.

Pro-Incumbent Gerrymandering. Bipartisan or "sweetheart" gerrymanders are those with lines drawn to protect incumbents. These gerrymanders are often by-products of divided party control—either between the two chambers of the legislature or between the legislature and the governor. In the wake of the 2000 census, the dominant parties in several populous states—California, Illinois, Michigan, and New York—chose to hoard their existing assets. In New York, which lost two seats in the reapportionment, two pairs of incumbents (one from each party) were thrown into the same districts, and the remaining twenty-seven districts were drawn for incumbents. "Neither party [wanted] to lose its hard-won gains," election analyst Rhodes Cook explained.[32]

The case of California, home of 12 percent of all House members, illustrates how districting affects the fate of incumbents. After the 2000 census California's ascendant Democrats opted to play it safe and adopted an incumbent-friendly districting plan. Under this map, only one California congressional incumbent was defeated over the course of the five election cycles between 2002 and 2010.[33] All this changed after California voters took the job of redistricting away from the state legislature and gave it to a bipartisan citizens' commission. After the 2010 census, the commission drew contiguous and compact districts without regard for the fate of incumbents or political parties. In conjunction with California's new primary system, in which the top two vote getters advance to the general election regardless of party affiliation, competition in California House races intensified after 2010. There was considerable turnover in California's congressional delegation in 2012, when eight House members opted not to run for reelection and seven incumbents lost their seats. No California House members were defeated in 2014, but eight incumbents were reelected with narrow margins of less than 55 percent of the vote.

Some commentators blame incumbent-protective line-drawing for producing noncompetitive elections.[34] However, the prevalence of partisan gerrymandering (parties' efforts to boost their number of seats) tends to counteract the effect on competition. When parties seek to maximize the number of seats they can win, they cannot afford to create many "safe" seats without wasting votes.[35] Parties expose their incumbents to greater electoral competition when they spread out their party's voters across more districts in an effort to win more seats. In Florida's post-2010 redistricting, for example, Republicans sought to pad their large majority of the state's House seats. Their goal was to craft a plan that would allow Republicans to win both of the new seats Florida received as a result of reapportionment, as well as to hold onto their current seats. With Florida a swing state, they could not do so without endangering some of their incumbents.[36] In the end, Florida Republicans lost

House seats after 2010, going from controlling 76 percent of the state's House delegation in 2011 to only 63 percent in 2013 and 2015.

The competitiveness of congressional elections is shaped by demography as well as by gerrymandering. "The problem is not who draws the legislative lines, it's where people live," notes one observer.[37] As Bruce Oppenheimer of Vanderbilt University explains, "Democrats tend to live next to Democrats. Republicans tend to live next to Republicans."[38] Urban Democrats, in particular, may be victims of what political scientists Jowei Chen and Jonathan Rodden call "unintentional gerrymandering": natural geographic patterns in which Democrats live in "dense, urban areas . . . effectively packing themselves into fewer districts."[39]

Combating partisan and incumbent-friendly districting could nevertheless become the next big voting reform cause. "The reason that people push for taking this out of the hands of the Legislature is there is really an inherent conflict of interest here where politicians are getting to custom-design which voters they want in their districts," one reform advocate explained.[40] A number of reform initiatives were considered in the lead-up to the post-2010 redistricting, with California reformers having the most success. Whether such remedies will sufficiently address the root causes of safe districts is another matter.

Majority-Minority Districts

Another form of gerrymandering involves the districting of racial minorities. There is a long history of racial gerrymandering in the United States, meaning "the deliberate and arbitrary distortion of district boundaries for racial purposes."[41]

The earliest forms of racial gerrymandering were designed to disempower African Americans. After the Fifteenth Amendment was ratified to grant former slaves the right to vote, southern states adopted a variety of measures to thwart the law. One of those was the racial gerrymander. In the 1870s, for example, Mississippi opponents of Reconstruction concentrated the bulk of their state's black population in one long, narrow congressional district running along the Mississippi River, leaving five other districts with white majorities. As another example, Alabama lawmakers scattered black voters over six different congressional districts to dilute their influence.[42] In other words, blacks were systematically "packed" into or "cracked" across congressional districts in order to weaken their electoral influence. In addition to racial gerrymandering, a variety of tools, such as literacy tests and poll taxes, were instituted to disenfranchise African Americans across the South, largely denying blacks the right to participate in elections until the civil rights reforms of the 1960s.

The Voting Rights Act (VRA) of 1965 is arguably the most effective civil rights law ever enacted. It did away with the whole panoply of legal impediments that had been erected to limit minority electoral participation and influence. It simply abolished all voting qualifications or prerequisites that stood in the way of the franchise.

A further requirement of the VRA, invalidated by the Supreme Court in 2013, imposed "preclearance" procedures on specific states (mainly southern) that historically had discriminated against minorities. Preclearance meant that these states had to receive advance approval from either the U.S. District Court for the District of Columbia or the U.S. attorney general for any changes in election rules to ensure that those changes would not deny or abridge the right to vote on account of race or color. Changes to election rules were precleared only if they would not lead to "a retrogression in the position of racial minorities."[43] With respect to districting, this requirement meant that changes could not lessen the likelihood that minorities would be elected. In *Shelby County* v. *Holder* (2013), the Supreme Court overturned the preclearance requirements for specific states.[44] Chief Justice John Roberts wrote that the requirements wrongly singled out particular states "based on 40-year-old facts having no logical relationship to the present day."[45] Districting and other changes to voting laws are still subject to judicial oversight and the Voting Rights Act, but only as a consequence of legal challenges after the fact, rather than via a preclearance process.

In more recent decades, race-conscious districting has been employed to help minorities elect candidates of their choice. Unlike in previous eras when districts had been manipulated to limit minority influence, states after 1990 began to deliberately create "majority-minority" districts to enhance the probability that minorities would be elected to Congress. The George H. W. Bush Justice Department used the preclearance process to require states to maximize the number of majority-minority districts. "As the plans were redrawn to obtain preclearance, some districts took on bizarre shapes," noted a National Conference of State Legislatures report.[46] During this time, fifteen new majority African American districts were created, thirteen of them in the South, along with nine new majority Latino districts. Many of these districts were so oddly shaped they made Governor Gerry's 1812 creation look amateurish.

The Supreme Court Enters the Quagmire. Some of these newly created majority-minority districts were later attacked in federal court. Plaintiffs charged that the districts violated white voters' Fourteenth Amendment right to equal protection of the law. The legal battles that resulted progressively deepened the Court's involvement in congressional districting. In a long series of complex, sometimes contradictory cases, the Court has attempted to balance two competing values: first, the Fourteenth Amendment's requirement that states not discriminate on the basis of race, and second, the VRA's protection against racial discrimination in the electoral process.

At the center of one controversy was North Carolina's shoestring Twelfth District, which remained under a legal cloud after four remappings (see Figure 3-2). As first drawn, this district was 160 miles long, in many places no wider than a two-lane highway, winding back and forth to capture pockets of black voters. Examining the North Carolina map, Justice Sandra Day O'Connor questioned "districting so highly irregular that, on its face, it rationally cannot be understood as anything other than an effort to segregate voters . . . on the basis of race."[47] In the 1993 case reviewing the North Carolina districting scheme (*Shaw v. Reno*), a narrowly divided Supreme Court recognized a claim of "racial gerrymandering" and held that districts could be challenged under the Fourteenth Amendment's equal protection clause.

In cases dealing with racial gerrymandering, the Court has indicated that it will apply a standard of "strict scrutiny" to any district in which race was the "predominant factor" in its creation.[48] To prove racial predominance, it must be shown that "the legislature subordinated to racial considerations traditional race-neutral districting principles, including but not limited to compactness, contiguity, and respect for political subdivisions of communities defined by actual shared interests."[49]

"Strict scrutiny" sets a very high bar that requires a state to demonstrate that its districting plan is, in the language of the legal test, "narrowly tailored to achieve a compelling state interest." For a districting scheme to survive this test, states must show that the challenged districts were drawn specifically to satisfy the requirements of the VRA. According to the Court's reading of the law, a districting scheme is not narrowly tailored to avoid discrimination when there is not a population of minority voters "sufficiently large and geographically compact to constitute a majority in a single-member district."[50] Majority-minority districts that are not "reasonably compact" have been unable to withstand strict scrutiny.[51] The Court has also adopted "nonretrogression" as a standard in judging whether a plan is narrowly tailored to avoid discrimination, meaning that the new map must not cause fewer minority representatives to be elected than before.[52] Most districting schemes subjected to the strict scrutiny standard have been overturned.[53]

Subsequent cases have clarified the law, although considerable uncertainty remains about precisely what majority-minority districting schemes will stand or fall upon judicial review. One important clarification is that such plans will be sustained unless race was the "predominant factor" in the creation of the district.[54] Writing for the Court in *Easley v. Cromartie* (2001), Justice Clarence Thomas declared:

> A jurisdiction may engage in constitutional political gerrymandering, even if it so happens that the most loyal Democrats happen to be black Democrats and even if the state were conscious of that fact.[55]

Because of the close correlation between race and partisanship, lawmakers may use race as a way to engage in partisan gerrymandering. Unlike racial discrimination, partisan gerrymandering does not trigger strict scrutiny. Thus a challenge to a districting scheme will not be upheld even if race was a factor in the districting if it was not the predominant factor.[56]

The Supreme Court has not, however, given carte blanche to the use of race as a factor in partisan gerrymandering. Instead, it has demonstrated that it will continue to scrutinize race-conscious districts, even when they are created as part of a broader partisan gerrymander. In 2015, the Court overturned the post-2010 congressional districts in both Alabama and North Carolina, ruling in favor of black officeholders and Democrats who argued that the districting schemes placed too much emphasis on race. In both cases, the Court remanded the cases for further proceedings, enjoining lower courts to reconsider whether race, in fact, had been the "predominant" factor in drawing the districts and to evaluate whether the new districts harmed black voters' ability to "elect a candidate of their choice."[57] At this writing, it is not yet known what these rulings will mean for the districts in those states or for the state of the law going forward. The Court has still not laid down clear standards. "We have somehow arrived at a place where the parties agree that Alabama's legislative districts should be fine-tuned to achieve some 'optimal' result with respect to black voting power; the only disagreement is about what percentage of blacks should be placed in those optimized districts," said Justice Thomas in a dissenting opinion. Still, these 2015 cases have established that the claim of racial gerrymandering can now be used to advance minority voting rights, rather than only as a challenge to majority-minority districts.[58]

In the end, the key question is whether the Supreme Court will provide clear guidelines as to what racial (and partisan) redistricting the Constitution will permit. In the quest for a workable standard, the justices seem to adhere to a version of Justice Potter Stewart's 1964 test for defining obscenity: "I know it when I see it." And in view of the closeness of its past decisions on majority-minority districts—nearly every major case on this question has turned on a 5–4 vote—the Court could again shift its direction as its membership changes.

Consequences of Majority-Minority Districts. Proponents of majority-minority districts view them as "the political equivalent to the ethnically homogeneous neighborhood," in the words of law professor Lani Guinier. "They are a safe haven for members of that group, a bit of turf that one ethnic grouping controls, a place where their voice is pre-eminent."[59] The growing numbers of majority-minority districts have unquestionably made the House of Representatives more racially and ethnically diverse. Most minority legislators are elected in districts where minority groups make up the majority of the population. Indeed, a recent study confirms that a district's racial composition is by far the most important factor in determining the race of the representative it elects: "Race-conscious redistricting and the creation of effective minority districts remain the basis upon which most African American and Latino officials gain election."[60] Over time, representatives of majority-minority districts have built up a great deal of seniority and institutional clout within the Democratic Party in the House.

Nevertheless, the creation of majority-minority districts comes at some cost to minority voters. Concentrating minorities into districts where they constitute a majority wastes their votes by producing outsized electoral majorities for the winning candidates. Relatedly, the way districting plans pack minority voters together has arguably slowed the diversification of Congress. Minority populations have grown faster than the share of House districts that elect minority representatives. A *National Journal* analysis after the 2010

FIGURE 3-2   **Racial Gerrymandering in the 1990s and 2000s: North Carolina's First and Twelfth Congressional Districts**

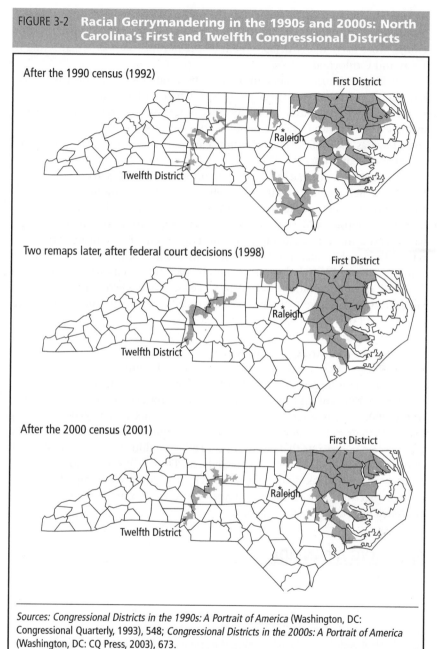

After the 1990 census (1992)

Two remaps later, after federal court decisions (1998)

After the 2000 census (2001)

Sources: Congressional Districts in the 1990s: A Portrait of America (Washington, DC: Congressional Quarterly, 1993), 548; *Congressional Districts in the 2000s: A Portrait of America* (Washington, DC: CQ Press, 2003), 673.

Note: North Carolina's First and Twelfth Congressional Districts were drawn to give the state its first black representatives in ninety-three years. First elected in 1992, the two African American representatives were subsequently reelected. Twenty years later, these two geographically equivalent districts were still electing blacks by overwhelming majorities.

redistricting determined that minority voters were more concentrated in fewer House districts than they were after the 2000 redistricting."[61] Latino groups were particularly disappointed by the latest rounds of redistricting in Texas and California.

Packing minority voters into districts simultaneously "bleaches" surrounding nonminority districts, along with whatever leverage minority voters might wield. Even if the share of minority officeholders rises, "the number of white legislators who have any political need to respond to minority concerns goes down as their minority constituents are peeled off to form the new black and Hispanic districts."[62]

There is evidence that racial redistricting has contributed to the Democratic Party's southern meltdown since the 1990s.[63] Concentrating minority (mostly Democratic) voters in safe (mainly urban) districts strengthened the GOP in outlying suburban and rural areas. The combination of African Americans, who wanted more representation in the House, and Republicans, who supported that goal because it served their political purposes, has been dubbed an "unholy alliance."[64] Scholar David Lublin has described the outcome as a "paradox of representation" in which packed districts yielded more minority lawmakers but also led to a more conservative House that reduced minorities' leverage and influence over legislative outcomes.[65]

Many doubt that packing districts is the best way to advance minorities' interests. Another strategy for enhancing the political influence of minorities is to maintain substantial minorities of racial and ethnic voters—say, 40 percent or so—in a larger number of districts (so-called "influence districts") to expand the ranks of officeholders responsive to minority needs.[66] In the wake of the 2000 census, many Democrats concluded that racial gerrymandering had hurt their party. "For 20 years I've been arguing against the stacking of black voters in districts that has the overall effect of diluting the voting strength of black people," said Rep. James E. Clyburn, D-S.C. "It's better to maintain a 35 to 40 percent black district where [blacks] would have a tremendous influence on elections. I don't think you need 75 percent in order for a black to be elected. That's kind of insulting to me."[67]

BECOMING A CANDIDATE

Very few of those who are eligible to serve in Congress vie for a seat. Candidates who meet the legal qualifications must weigh a variety of considerations—some practical and rational, others personal and emotional. Candidacy decisions are often the pivotal moments in the entire recruitment process, although students of politics have only recently given them the attention they deserve. "The decision to run obviously structures everything else that goes on in the primary process," writes political scientist L. Sandy Maisel. "Who runs, who does not run, how many candidates run. These questions set the stage for the campaigns themselves."[68]

Called or Chosen?

From their Jacksonian heyday in the 1830s to the decline of big-city machines in the 1960s, local party organizations customarily enlisted and sponsored candidates. When these organizations withered, the initiative passed to the candidates themselves: self-starters who pulled their own bandwagons. "The skills that work in American politics at this point in history," writes Alan Ehrenhalt, "are those of entrepreneurship.... People nominate themselves."[69]

Congressional aspirants, however, quickly encounter national networks of party committees and their allied interest groups. At the heart of these networks are the two major parties' House and Senate campaign committees, now active in nearly all phases of congressional elections.[70] They seek out and encourage promising candidates at the local level, sometimes even taking sides to help ensure their nomination. They assist promising candidates with filing deadlines, lining up supporters, and handling finances. In fact, recent research reveals that "recruitment from party leaders, elected officials, and political activists is one of the most important predictors" of who will consider a candidacy for political office.[71]

During the recruiting season (generally beginning in early 2015 for the 2016 contests, for example), the leaders and campaign committee staffs of the two major parties "reach out across the country in search of political talent. Like college football coaching staffs in hot pursuit of high-school prospects, they are putting together the lineups of the future."[72] Prospects can expect calls from the president, former presidents, governors, high-profile financial backers, and other notables. The run-ups to recent elections all began with fierce recruiting seasons, as both parties sought lineups that could win House and Senate majorities. Just a few days after the 2014 elections, the Democratic Congressional Campaign Committee was actively recruiting five recently defeated candidates to mount rematches in 2016.[73]

Not all recruiting takes place outside Washington. Open seats—those in newly created districts or those in which incumbents have died or retired—are less secure. So, to the extent they can, party leaders try to discourage their incumbent colleagues from retiring. If members are going to retire, however, party leaders encourage them to announce their retirement early so that they have time to make preparations to hold the seat.[74]

Most would-be officeholders seek advancement within the two major parties, which boast not only the brand loyalties of a huge majority of voters but also extensive financial and logistical resources. Still, independents and minor-party candidates enter congressional contests. Seldom do these contenders win a sizable number of votes, but they do provide alternatives where only one major party fields a candidate. Only two independents served in Congress in 2015: Vermont senator Bernard Sanders, a self-styled "democratic socialist," and Maine senator Angus King.

Amateurs and Professionals

How do would-be candidates, whether self-starters or recruited by party leaders, make up their minds to run? The answer often depends on whether the individual is a political amateur or a professional.

Amateurs. Amateur candidates are defined by their lack of previous political experience. Despite inexperience and nonexistent name recognition, many amateurs run for Congress. A few run to bring a specific issue to public attention and are less interested in winning than in advancing their cause. Most amateurs are what David T. Canon calls "hopeless amateurs"—people with little or no chance of winning.[75] Nevertheless, political amateurs regularly compete, and almost every congressional election brings a few amateurs to Capitol Hill. About a quarter of the new members elected to Congress in 2014 had no prior experience of elected office.[76]

Amateurs are more willing than experienced politicians to make a long-shot bid for office. They are frequently the only candidates who will take on seemingly invulnerable incumbents. Amateurs often find that an uncompetitive primary offers their only chance to win a major-party nomination. More attractive political opportunities will generally entice more politically experienced competitors. "I think his chances have gone from absolutely out of the question to extremely remote," remarked the wife of one hopeless contender. "But he's learning a lot, and I think he has enjoyed it."[77] Many such amateurs nevertheless indulge in self-delusion about their prospects. Maisel, a political scientist who wrote candidly about his own unsuccessful congressional primary campaign, described politicians as possessing an "incredible ability to delude themselves about their own chances."[78]

One group of amateurs, however, sometimes proves to be the exception—those with highly visible nonpolitical careers. Astronauts, war heroes, entertainers, and athletes are in big demand as candidates. Local or statewide television personalities also make attractive contenders. Al Franken's status as a nationally known comedian, writer, and commentator helped to launch his political career as a candidate in 2008 for Minnesota's U.S. Senate seat.

Professionals. Professionals are more cautious than amateurs about the races they enter. Those who seek to make a career in politics must consider carefully not just whether to run for a particular political office but when to do so. Political careerists often have more to lose than amateurs from an unsuccessful bid for office, because entering one race often means forgoing the office they already hold. An experienced state legislator is unlikely to gamble a safe seat in the state house or senate on a remote chance that he or she might defeat a popular congressional incumbent. Such a candidate will wait for a better opening, when an incumbent retires or is clearly vulnerable. Similarly, a sitting House member will usually wait for an open seat or an exceptional opportunity before attempting to move up to the Senate. In the end, such decisions hinge on "the not-so-simple calculus of winning."[79]

Strategic contenders evaluate their own personal strengths and weaknesses in campaigning, voter appeal, and fund-raising. They consider how well they would personally fit in with the ideological bent of their party in Congress.[80] They weigh the chances of getting the party's nomination in view of the party's ideological bent, leadership, and nominating procedures. They also consider what it will cost to succeed. If there is an incumbent, they identify the incumbent's weaknesses. And they take a look at the broader political environment, including the condition of the economy, the president's standing, and public dissatisfaction with the status quo.

Most successful congressional candidates are professionals—seasoned politicians—before they run for Congress. Grassroots organizations and movements are a breeding ground for candidates—for example, environmental activists in the 1970s, religious conservatives in the 1990s, antiwar activists during the George W. Bush presidency, and Tea Party activists after 2008. But more often, elective office is the immediate springboard: mayors, district attorneys, or state legislators for the House; governors, lieutenant governors, and attorneys general—who have already faced a statewide electorate—for the Senate. Service in the House has become an increasingly common path to the Senate since the 1980s.[81] An outright majority of senators in the 114th Congress had "moved up" from the House.

The circle of people pondering a candidacy (the challenger pool) may be large or small, depending on the office and the circumstances.[82] Any number of elected officials—state legislators (especially if subject to term limits), county officers, mayors, city council members, even governors—are weighing a race for Congress at any given time. "The people who have been successful in the political world are people who know when to strike at the right time," remarked one veteran state legislator contemplating a run against a House incumbent.[83]

Finding Quality Candidates

Candidate quality and campaign strength are critical factors in many battles for congressional seats.[84] A party's success in November hinges on its efforts during the recruitment season. Often, races turn on bids that are not made. An election outcome frequently becomes a *fait accompli* when a strong potential candidate chooses whether to run.

According to Maisel and his colleagues, candidate quality is measured in strategic resources and personal attributes.[85] Quality candidates are skilled in presenting themselves as candidates and are attractive to voters. Previous experience in public office—and the accompanying visibility and credibility—is one of the most important attributes of a quality candidate. Simply having a familiar political name can also be a ticket to candidacy. In particular, candidates from famous political families have a "brand-name" advantage.[86] Fame or notoriety can sometimes overcome lack of relevant background or experience. Other characteristics of quality candidates include physical appearance, personality, speaking ability, and a talent for organizing or motivating others. Fund-raising ability or potential is essential as well. Overall, likely candidates have ambition and a keen desire for public life, both of which will help them to succeed in their attempt to gain public office.[87]

Stamina is also important. No matter how talented, principled, or well funded, aspirants for public office must be ready, physically and emotionally, to face the rigors of campaigning. They must be willing to hit the road nonstop, meet new people, attend gatherings, sell themselves, ask for money, and endure verbal abuse—all the while appearing to enjoy it. "People who do not like to knock on strangers' doors or who find it tedious to repeat the same 30-second introduction thousands of times," explains Alan Ehrenhalt, "are at a severe disadvantage in running for office."[88]

The Incumbency Factor. Of all the inducements for launching a candidacy, the odds of winning stand at the top. A clearly winnable seat seldom lacks for eager quality candidates. Open seats—those without an incumbent running—are especially attractive. As a result, open-seat races are more likely to be competitive and to shift party control than those with an incumbent. Party strategists thus concentrate on these races.

In most House and Senate contests, however, incumbents will be running, and most of them will be reelected. As Gary C. Jacobson writes, "Nearly everything pertaining to candidates and campaigns for Congress is profoundly influenced by whether the candidate is an incumbent, challenging an incumbent, or pursuing an open seat."[89] Less forcibly, the same can be said of the Senate. Since World War II, on average 94 percent of all incumbent representatives and 82 percent of all incumbent senators running for reelection have been returned to office. In 2014, 95 percent of House members and 82 percent of senators seeking reelection were returned to Congress.

Because any savvy politician contemplating a bid for Congress recognizes the difficulty of defeating an incumbent, incumbents often face only low-quality opponents. Challengers are often weak fund-raisers, poorly qualified, and unknown to voters. Party leaders sometimes struggle to rouse any candidate at all willing to run against an incumbent. In 2014, thirty incumbent House members and one senator ran for reelection unopposed.[90] Democrats had so much difficulty finding a challenger for Sen. Bob Corker, R-Tenn., in 2012 that the state's Democratic primary victor, Mark Clayton, prevailed despite raising no money, having no website, and being a member of a known hate group.[91]

An incumbent's most effective electoral strategy is to scare off serious opposition. "If an incumbent can convince potentially formidable opponents and people who control campaign resources that he or she is invincible," says Jacobson, "he or she is very likely to avoid a serious challenge and so will be invincible—as long as the impression lasts."[92] Any sign of weakness is likely to encourage opponents in the next election.[93] For that reason, incumbents try to sustain wide electoral margins, show unbroken strength, keep up constituency ties, and build giant war chests of reelection money.

Incumbents are hardly invincible, even if their high reelection rates make them seem so. Indeed, in view of the prevalence of strategic retirement—the tendency of incumbents to retire when they perceive themselves to be politically vulnerable—reelection rates are a misleading indicator of incumbent safety. Incumbents keep close tabs on political developments in their constituencies, and many prefer to retire rather than suffer the rebuke of voters. These strategic considerations lurk behind many incumbents' retirements, even when they cite other reasons for their decisions. In 2014, for example, Democratic senators Max Baucus of Montana, Tim Johnson of South Dakota, and Jay Rockefeller of West Virginia all opted to retire rather than face the voters of their Republican-leaning states in an unfavorable political climate. In short, the chances of success are equally important for incumbents as for challengers when considering future career options.[94]

No-Shows. High-caliber potential candidates apparently abound in America's communities—even in minority party circles within noncompetitive districts.[95] But all too often these individuals prefer to remain on the sidelines. The road to public office is increasingly arduous and costly. And the odds are often long, especially when running against a dominant party or an entrenched incumbent. Therefore, quality challengers often fail to step forward. Poor-quality challengers raise less money and are less successful than the handful of blue-ribbon contenders. This dynamic depresses competition in congressional elections across the board.

Raising the money needed to run an effective race is a major deterrent to would-be candidates. Twenty-five percent of potential candidates in one survey designated fund-raising as a major obstacle to running; they described the prospect of soliciting campaign funds with words such as "daunting," "petrifying," "disgusting," "off-putting," and "more painful than a root canal without anesthesia."[96] Other candidates reject campaigns because of the high costs for their personal lives, incomes, careers, and families. The benefits side of the ledger may not outweigh the costs of gaining and holding public office. All too often, prospective candidates decide that their destinies lie elsewhere—in state or local politics, in nonprofit community service, or in family and profession.

Women are especially likely to forgo opportunities to run for political office, even when they have been highly successful in the professions that usually precede public office. Research by political scientists Jennifer L. Lawless and Richard L. Fox reports that prominent female lawyers, business people, educators, and political activists are less likely than similarly situated males to see themselves as good candidates for political office.[97] U.S. political institutions are more male-dominated than those in most other advanced democracies, but the cause appears to lie more with the calculations of prospective candidates than with voters. Women are not less likely than men to win races they enter, but they are less likely to consider a candidacy in the first place. In part, this difference reflects the fact that party leaders, elected officials, and advocacy groups are less likely to recruit women to run. But it also reflects broader societal norms and socialization processes that make it more difficult for women to promote themselves and seek political leadership positions.

NOMINATING POLITICS

Nominating procedures, set forth in state laws and conditioned by party customs, further shape the potential pool of candidates. Historically, these procedures have expanded to ever wider circles of participants—a development that has diminished the power of party leaders and thrust more initiative upon the candidates themselves. In most states, the direct primary—allowing party voters to choose their party's nominees—is the formal mechanism for selecting congressional candidates.

Rules of the Nominating Game

Every state has election laws that provide for primary elections for House and Senate candidates, but these laws vary widely.[98] The critical question is who should be permitted to vote in a party's primary. The states have adopted varying answers. Party leaders naturally prefer strict rules that reward party loyalty, discourage outsider candidates, and maximize their own influence on the outcome. States with strong party traditions therefore tend to have closed primaries. This arrangement, found in twenty-three states, requires voters to declare party affiliation in order to vote in the primary. (Their affiliation is considered permanent until they take steps to change it.) In open primaries, conducted in twenty states, voters can vote in the primary of either party (but not in both) simply by requesting the party's ballot at the polling place.

Few primaries are competitive races. Primary winners typically prevail in lopsided victories, and incumbents are almost always renominated. According to a recent study, only about 1 percent of incumbents in the post–World War II period were defeated in a primary.[99] Despite a number of high-profile primary challenges in recent congressional elections, contested primaries are not becoming more frequent. Instead, recent primary challenges tend to be more nationally visible, because they are funded by more outside groups and centered around larger, ideological controversies.[100] Nominations for open-seat races, however, are virtually certain to feature contested primaries. "If a district party is without an incumbent, and has a fighting chance in November," Harvey L. Schantz writes, "there is a strong possibility of a public contest for the U.S. House nomination."[101] But even including primaries for open seats, the typical primary winner's share is more than 60 percent of the vote.[102]

Parties and Nominations

Despite the prevalence of primaries, party organizations at all levels are hardly without leverage in nominations. Although party organizations play no formal role in the primary process in the majority of states, in nine states parties have conventions that influence candidates' access to the primary ballot.[103] More important, party organizations influence nominations indirectly—by contacting promising prospects, linking them with campaign contributors, endorsing them, and assisting in other ways.

Parties are centrally involved in candidate recruitment. Parties are most active in districts regarded as winnable, and the people they seek out are the "usual suspects"—officeholders, prominent figures, and the wealthy.[104] The obvious candidate also may be someone who has run for the seat before. For example, at least ten House races in 2014 were rematches of the same candidates from a previous election.[105]

Party leaders tend to be pragmatists—above all, bent on finding winners. Democrats deliberately seek to recruit anti-abortion, pro–gun rights candidates in conservative areas such as the South. Republicans have historically recruited moderates for swing states and districts, though the strategy has been more difficult to execute since the emergence of the Tea Party movement, which has successfully resisted the nomination of moderate Republicans in many cases.

Intraparty rivalries often mark nominating contests. The Tea Party movement, in particular, fueled an unusually high level of internal ideological contention within the Republican Party between 2009 and 2014. In 2010, for example, candidates endorsed by the Tea Party unseated eighteen-year veteran senator Bob Bennett, R-Utah, and declined to renominate Sen. Lisa Murkowski, R-Alaska—who, remarkably, retained her seat as a write-in candidate. In 2012 a Tea Party favorite, Richard Mourdock, defeated longtime senator Richard G. Lugar, R-Ind., for the Republican nomination. Mourdock then went on to lose the seat in a year when the Republican nominee for president carried Indiana by 10 percentage points. In 2014 mainstream Republicans largely fended off primary challenges from Tea Party and other conservative candidates, with the exception of the high-profile primary defeat of Rep. Eric Cantor, R-Va. In most primary contests involving conservative insurgents, Republican incumbents or candidates favored by the party's mainstream prevailed, including in the races for Senate nominations in Mississippi, North Carolina, and Kentucky.

Sizing Up the Primary System

The direct primary was one of the reforms adopted early in the twentieth century to overcome corrupt, boss-dominated nominating conventions. It has permitted more participation in selecting candidates, and yet primaries normally attract a narrower segment of voters than do general elections. Primary contests in recent years have drawn less than 25 percent of eligible voters—or less than half the number who voted in the general elections. Less publicized than general elections, primaries tend to attract voters who are somewhat older, wealthier, better educated, more politically aware, and more ideologically committed than the electorate as a whole.[106]

Primaries also have hampered the political parties by encouraging would-be officeholders to appeal directly to the public and construct support networks apart from the party machinery. Still, leaders strive to influence who enters their primaries and who wins them. Displaying impressive resilience and adaptability, party organizations have recast themselves as organizations "'in service' to [their] candidates and officeholders but not in control of them."[107]

Finally, primaries are a costly way of choosing candidates. Unless candidates begin with overwhelming advantages (such as incumbency), they must mount virtually the same kind of campaign in the primary that they will repeat later in the general election.

CONCLUSION

The rules of the game that narrow the potential field of congressional contenders can be thought of as a series of gates, each narrower than the one before. First are the constitutional qualifications for holding office. Far more restrictive are the personal attributes associated with a successful public career. Next are the complex rules of apportionment and districting. Beyond these are the nominating procedures (usually primaries). These successive gates sharply reduce the number of people who are likely to become real contenders.

Equally important, individuals must make up their own minds about running for the House or Senate. Such choices embrace a range of considerations—many personal and emotional, but all based on some estimate of the likely benefits and costs of the candidacy. This winnowing process presents voters with a limited choice on election day: two, occasionally more, preselected (or self-selected) candidates. From this tiny circle, senators and representatives are chosen.

Winners and Losers. Newly minted senator Joni Ernst celebrates her election with constituents in Des Moines, Iowa. Ernst is the first woman to represent Iowa in Congress and the first female combat veteran to serve in the U.S. Senate. The same night, Democratic candidate Bruce Braley waves to supporters after losing the race to Ernst. Republican Alex Mooney speaks at a victory celebration in West Virginia, where he is the state's first Hispanic congressman. Elise Stefanik, at age thirty the youngest woman ever elected to Congress, cheers with supporters in New York.

Making It: The Electoral Game

"It is very edgy. I will admit that," candidate Joni Ernst observed when asked about the campaign advertisement that helped cata-pult her into the lead for the Republican nomination in the 2014 Iowa Senate race. Ernst, who had grown up on a farm in southwest Iowa, joined ROTC, and served in combat during the Iraq war, had spent $9,000 to air an advertisement that highlighted her unique qualifications: "I grew up castrating hogs on an Iowa farm, so when I get to Washington, I'll know how to cut pork. . . . Washington is full of big spenders, let's make 'em squeal." Within three days, the ad had been viewed nearly 400,000 times on YouTube, and Ernst gained an edge in fund-raising and name recognition that soon translated into a lead in the primary polls.[1]

Ernst went on to win the GOP nomination, facing off against four-term Democratic representative Bruce Braley in November. Braley had long been seen as the frontrunner to succeed retiring Democratic senator Tom Harkin, who had served in the Senate for three decades. Braley's experience seemed to make him a strong candidate, and he led in all nine general election polls held before June 2014.[2] But Braley committed a series of missteps that played into Ernst's claim that she was the better fit with Iowa traditions. The first danger sign for Braley was when a video emerged from a Texas fund-raiser in which Braley warned that Iowa's longtime incumbent Republican senator, Charles Grassley, would become chair of the Judiciary Committee if the GOP won the Senate majority: "A farmer from Iowa who never went to law school, never practiced law" should not chair Judiciary, suggested Braley.[3] A few months later, Braley was accused of threatening to sue a neighbor for allowing his chickens to cross onto Braley's property. Although the Democrat denied that he had threatened to sue, the episode reinforced the sense that Braley was out of touch with ordinary Iowans.

Ernst, meanwhile, proved to be an effective campaigner. Democrats had hoped that Ernst's staunch conservatism would damage her chances in the closely divided swing state. For example, Ernst was on record in support of a "Personhood" amendment that declared life begins at conception and aimed to protect "the inalienable right to life of every person at any stage of develop-ment."[4] But Ernst downplayed divisive social issues during the campaign, focusing instead on wasteful spending, the problems implementing Obamacare, and foreign policy. Accusing Braley of failing to fund American troops, Ernst declared that "You don't play politics when American lives are at stake."[5] Ernst capped her campaign with a round-the-clock bus tour through all ninety-nine Iowa counties, referred to as "the full Grassley" in tribute to the senior Republican senator's annual tour through the state. The bus, festooned with images of Ernst, the American flag, a cornfield, and the slogan "Mother. Soldier. Independent leader," brought home Ernst's message that she represents "the Iowa way."[6] On election day, Ernst triumphed easily over Braley, winning by a 52 percent to 44 percent margin.

Idiosyncratic in so many respects, the 2014 Iowa Senate battle underscores several elements of congressional elections. Ernst's campaign was buoyed by a national environment favoring Republicans: President Obama's low approval ratings made life difficult for Democratic candidates across the country in 2014. But Ernst's substantial margin—which had seemed unimaginable just a few months earlier—also reflected her personal skills and campaign message. Even in an era when relatively few voters split their tickets, Americans' party preferences are not so rigid that skilled candidates cannot sometimes overcome them. Ernst's persona and message were tailored to her Iowa constituents. Advertisements about making hogs squeal might not work in most parts of the country, but they were part of a broader strategy designed to show that Ernst— far more than the experienced lawmaker Braley—was the true Iowan. Congressional campaigns are ultimately a matter of candidates persuading voters that they are suited to represent their interests and values, that they "fit" their constituency better than their opponent. Ernst's success attests to the continued importance of individual candidates, even in a political context in which party allegiances have become more important both in Washington and to voters.

CAMPAIGN STRATEGIES

Campaigns are volatile mixtures of personal contacts, fund-raising, speech-making, advertising, and symbolic appeals. As acts of communication, campaigns are designed to convey messages to potential voters. The goal is to win over a plurality of those who cast ballots on election day.

Asking the Right Questions

Whether incumbents or challengers, candidates for Congress strive to map out a successful campaign strategy. To that end, each potential candidate must consider the following questions: What sort of constituency do I seek to represent? Are my name, face, and career familiar to voters? What resources—money, group support, volunteers—can I attract? What leaders and groups are pivotal to a winning campaign? What issues are uppermost in potential voters' minds? How can I reach those voters most effectively? When should my campaign begin, and how should it be paced? And, perhaps most important, what are my chances for victory? The answers to such questions define campaign strategy.

The constituency itself shapes a candidate's campaign. In populous states, Senate aspirants must appeal to diverse economic and social groups scattered over wide areas and many media markets. In fast-growing states, even Senate incumbents must introduce themselves to new voters who have arrived since the last election. Only small-state Senate candidates are able to know their constituents as well as House candidates know theirs. But unlike states, House districts often fit within no natural geographic community, media market, or existing political division.[7] In such situations, candidates and their managers must find the most suitable forums, media outlets, and organizations to reach voters who may have little in common other than being enclosed within the same district boundaries.

Because incumbents are typically hard to defeat, the incumbent's decision to seek reelection colors the entire electoral undertaking. The partisan leanings of the electorate are also critical. The dominant party's candidates stress party loyalty, underscore long-standing partisan values, and sponsor get-out-the-vote (GOTV) drives, because high voter turnout usually aids their cause. Minority party campaigns highlight personalities, downplay partisan differences, and exploit factional splits within the majority party, perhaps by invoking "wedge issues" designed to pry voters away from their usual party home. As voters' partisan attachments have hardened amid rising polarization, it has become more and more difficult for candidates to win over enough "defectors" to triumph in a district that tilts toward the other party.

Finally, the perceptions and attitudes of voters must be reflected in campaign planning. Through surveys, focus groups, or old-fashioned informal pulse taking, strategists take account of what is on voters' minds and what, if anything, they know or think about the candidate. Well-known candidates try to capitalize on their visibility; lesser-known ones run ads that repeat their names over and over again. Candidates with a reputation for openness and geniality highlight those qualities in ads. Those who are more introverted (yes, there are such politicians) stress experience and competence. Candidates who are young emphasize their vigor, energy, and new ideas. Candidates who have made tough, unpopular decisions are touted as courageous leaders. In the wake of scandals, honesty and openness are on display.

Choosing the Message

The average citizen is barraged with media messages of all kinds—an hour of television commercials per day, among other things. The candidate's overarching challenge is to project an image through this cacophony of media appeals, including those from other candidates. "The only way to cut through this communication clutter," a political marketing executive points out, "is to adopt the strategy proven effective by successful businesses. Create a brand. And manage the message with discipline and impact."[8] In other words, forge a message that will stand out from all the competing messages in the media marketplace.

A candidate's message is usually distilled into a single theme or slogan that is repeated on radio, TV, billboards, websites, and in campaign literature. "A good message . . . is a credible statement that can be summed up in a few sentences and frequently ends with a kicker slogan."[9]

Strategists use these messages to frame the campaign: to set the election's agenda—not by changing people's attitudes, but by shifting their attention to issues that favor their candidate or diminish the opponent. "There's only three or four plots," explained Carter Eskew, a Democratic consultant. "Plots for incumbents are Representative X is different from the rest; X can deliver; X stands with you. And the perennial plot for challengers is (fill in the blank) years are long enough; it's time for a change."[10]

As challengers seek lines of attack, officeholders often find that incumbency has its liabilities. An extensive public record gives enterprising opponents many potential openings to exploit. Past votes or positions may be highlighted to discredit the officeholder, sometimes fairly and sometimes unfairly. Incumbents may be shackled to unpopular issues, such as Medicare premium hikes, ongoing wars, economic crises, or unpopular presidents. Sometimes incumbents become complacent and take voters' support for granted, a major political mistake. One campaign consultant summed up the lesson of such races: "You have to earn that support every two years. A lot of members of Congress forget how to run."[11]

CAMPAIGN RESOURCES

Even the best campaign strategy will fail if the candidate cannot muster the resources necessary to implement it. The chief resources in congressional elections are money and organization.

"Money is the mother's milk of politics," declared California's legendary Assembly Speaker Jess Unruh. Money is not everything in politics, but many candidates falter for lack of it, and nearly all expend valuable time and energy struggling to get it. Every candidate, writes Paul S. Herrnson, wages not one but two campaigns—a campaign for resources (the so-called money primary) that precedes, and underwrites, the more visible campaign for votes.[12]

Campaigns in the United States are very costly. In the 2013–2014 electoral cycle, congressional candidates raised $1.6 billion and spent most of it. The average Senate race cost over $7 million for each of the two major-party nominees. The average House contest cost $1 million per nominee.[13] When modern record-keeping began some forty years ago, no House candidate spent one-third that much.[14] Even controlling for inflation, expenditures for congressional campaigns have nearly tripled over the last forty years.

No mystery surrounds these skyrocketing costs. Population growth and new campaign technologies—electronic media, polling, and consultants of all kinds—account for much of the increase. To be sure, old-fashioned campaigns based on armies of volunteers canvassing door to door can be effective in some contests. But candidates raise as much money as they can for good reason.

Fund-raising consumes tremendous amounts of time. In January 2013, the Democratic Congressional Campaign Committee (DCCC) gave a presentation for incoming freshmen about the time they should expect to dedicate to raising money. Figure 4-1 displays a slide from the PowerPoint presentation these new members received. The DCCC prescribed a ten-hour day for members while they are in Washington, D.C. Out of each day, four hours should be spent on "call time" and another hour set aside for "strategic outreach," which includes fund-raising as well as media relations. By comparison, three to four hours are set aside for doing the regular work of Congress, including hearings, votes, and meetings with constituents. A subsequent slide specified that members should expect to devote three hours for fund-raising out of every eight-hour work day while they are in their districts during congressional recesses. Former representative Tom Periello, D-Va., commented that the time the DCCC recommended for fund-raising may even be "low balling the figure so as not to scare the new members too much."[15] To be sure, fund-raising practices vary; members from safe districts often raise less money than their party committees request. There is no question, however, that fund-raising puts intense year-round pressure on members' daily schedules.[16]

Campaign Finance Regulations

The regulation of campaign finance in the United States is a dauntingly complicated subject. Congress's regulatory efforts have led to a proliferation of entities, many with the sole purpose of raising and spending money in political campaigns, each with its own rules and regulations. In addition, campaign finance law in the United States has been greatly complicated by a variety of Supreme Court rulings. In the landmark case of *Buckley v. Valeo* (1976),[17] the Supreme Court held that campaign contributions and spending are free speech

FIGURE 4-1   **The Democratic Congressional Campaign Committee's Recommended Daily Schedule for New Members, 2013**

☑	4 hours	Call Time
☑	1–2 hours	Constituent Visits
☑	2 hours	Committee/Floor
☑	1 hour	Strategic Outreach Breakfasts, Meet & Greets, Press
☑	1 hour	Recharge Time

Source: Ryan Grim and Sabrina Siddiqui, "Call Time for Congress Shows How Fundraising Dominates Bleak Work," *Huffington Post,* politics blog, January 8, 2013, www.huffingtonpost.com/2013/01/08/call-time-congressional-fudraising_n_2427291.html?ncid=edlinkusaolp00000003.

protected by the First Amendment of the Constitution. The Court ruled that Congress may legitimately regulate campaign contributions—to prevent corruption or the appearance of corruption. But the Court held that most campaign spending could not be regulated. Other recent Supreme Court cases have had far-reaching effects on the state of the law in this area.

We must distinguish between (1) the rules governing how candidates can raise money for their own campaigns, and (2) the rules governing the electioneering activities of organized entities not controlled by candidates. So-called "outside money"—campaign expenditures made by party committees and other organized groups not under candidates' control—has become a much more important feature of campaign financing.

Candidates' Campaigns. Congressional candidates may raise funds from four sources: individual contributors, political action committees (PACs), party committees, and themselves and their families. More than half of the money raised by House and Senate candidates comes from individuals. In the 2013–2014 election cycle, congressional candidates (or their campaign committees) could receive up to $2,600 from each individual contributor for each election (primary, general, run-off). Individual contributions of more than $200 must identify the contributor's name and employer—information reported to the Federal Election Commission (FEC), the federal agency charged with regulating campaign finance. Prior to April 2014, an individual's overall contribution to federal candidates for the entire cycle was capped at $46,200, but the Supreme Court invalidated this limitation in the *McCutcheon v. FEC* case. Writing for the 5–4 majority, Chief Justice John Roberts declared that "Congress may not regulate contributions simply to reduce the amount of money in politics, or to restrict the political participation of some in order to enhance the relative influence of others."[18]

PACs may also contribute directly to congressional candidates. Under current regulations, multicandidate PACs are defined as those registered for more than six months, having fifty or more contributors, and making contributions to five or more candidates for federal office. In the 2013–2014 election cycle, multicandidate PACs could contribute up to $5,000 to a congressional candidate (or the candidate's campaign committee) for each election. For PACs not meeting the definition of multicandidate PACs, contributions to congressional candidates were capped at $2,600 per election. Neither type of PAC is subject to an overall cap on contributions for the election cycle. In the 2013–2014 election cycle, PAC contributions topped $440 million. PACs are key players in House races: they accounted for more than a third of House candidates' campaign receipts in 2014 and just slightly more than 15 percent for Senate candidates.

In the 2013–2014 election cycle, party committees—national, state, congressional, and local—could contribute up to $5,000 per election to congressional candidates. National party committees could not exceed a total of $45,400 to any Senate candidate per campaign. As these amounts make clear, party funds cannot begin to cover the costs of today's campaigns. Party organizations of all types account for a relatively small portion of individual candidates' direct funding, even though in recent years they have greatly increased their efforts and fund-raising capacities. Parties may also use additional funds to pay for services requested by a candidate such as polling, advertisements, and media time. But these "coordinated expenditures" are also subject to limits set by the FEC.

Another source of campaign money for congressional candidates is the candidate's own funds. Candidates and their families may spend as much of their own money in a campaign as they wish. Self-financing is no guarantee of success, however. In the 2012 elections, extraordinary sums were personally spent by Senate candidates Linda McMahon in Connecticut ($48.8 million), David Dewhurst in Texas ($20.4 million), and Tom Smith in Pennsylvania ($16.8 million)—and they all lost.

Independent Expenditures. Parties and organized groups also seek to influence elections, separate from candidates' own campaigns. They develop campaigns, run media ads, and support get-out-the-vote drives—that is, underwriting independent activities formally unconnected to candidates' own efforts. Such independent expenditures are not subject to any limits.

There are several types of organized groups, each typically identified by the sections of the Internal Revenue Code that govern their structure and activities. Tax-exempt 527s, for example, must register with the Internal Revenue Service (IRS) and disclose expenses and contributors. Subject to those requirements, they may raise unlimited funds from individuals, labor unions, and corporations. In the 2013–2014 election cycle, for example, 527s spent about $170 million on congressional races.

A wide array of new organized groups operating outside the control of federal candidates have emerged in the wake of two 2010 court rulings, *Citizens United v. FEC*[19] and *Speechnow.org v. Federal Election Commission*.[20] Exploiting the opportunities opened up by these cases, hundreds of new, big-spending organizations known as "Super PACs" have been formed. Super PACs are defined by the FEC as "non-connected political action committees." Such PACs cannot contribute directly to federal candidates' campaigns and cannot spend money in coordination with their campaigns. But they are permitted to make unlimited expenditures to influence the outcome of elections. Before 2010, corporations, nonprofits, and labor unions could not spend funds out of their general treasuries for pro-candidate advertisements. In *Citizens United*, the Supreme Court struck down that limitation as a form of censorship of protected political speech.

The Court expected, however, that such independent expenditures would be subject to the disclaimer and disclosure requirements imposed by existing campaign finance law. In the Court's opinion, Justice Anthony Kennedy wrote, "A campaign finance system that pairs corporate independent expenditures with effective disclosure has not existed before today. . . . With the advent of the Internet, prompt disclosure of expenditures can provide shareholders and citizens with the information needed to hold corporations and elected officials accountable."[21]

In practice, however, campaign finance law does not provide for the information that Justice Kennedy assumed would be available. Under the current FEC interpretation, a contribution of $1,000 or more to a group making an electioneering communication—that is, a pro-candidate advertisement in close proximity to an election—is reportable only if the contributor designated it to be used for a particular electioneering communication.[22] In other words, a contributor may avoid disclosure merely by not directing the contribution toward any particular advertisement.

Certain types of groups are wholly exempted from disclosure laws. The 2010 midterm elections saw the emergence of groups organized under section 501(c)(4) of the Internal Revenue Code.[23] These groups are generally civic organizations, with no more than half of their activities classed as political. Organized as a 501(c)(4), Karl Rove's Crossroads Grassroots Policy Strategies, for example, is not required to disclose its funders. American Crossroads/Crossroads GPS spent $104.7 million in the 2012 election and another $48 million in 2014. The U.S. Chamber of Commerce, which is organized as a 501(c)(6), does not identify its donors, even though it spent $35 million in 2013–2014, largely to assist Republican candidates. In the 2013–14 cycle, a total of $154 million in outside money was spent with no disclosure of the donors, and another $121 million was subject to only partial disclosure.

The upshot of these developments is that the fund-raising efforts of outside groups are far less stringently regulated than those of both candidates and political parties. "Super PACs can raise and spend money relatively easily," writes campaign finance expert Ray LaRaja. "For example, a Super PAC called 'Winning Our Future' in support of GOP presidential candidate Newt Gingrich, received most of its $17 million financing from one mega-donor."[24] Thus expenditures by outside groups have surged since 2010. These groups went from being a negligible factor in congressional elections as recently as 2004 to providing $534 million of the $3.67 billion (15 percent) spent on congressional campaigns in 2014.[25]

Unlike contributions to Super PACs, contributions to the parties are subject to caps, though higher ones than permitted as direct contributions to the candidates themselves.[26] In the 2013–2014 election cycle, the national parties' entities, including the House and Senate campaign committees, raised and spent more than $1.1 billion, accounting for 30 percent of all congressional campaign spending.[27] The vast majority of this money was spent as independent expenditures in targeted races. This is a staggering figure, considering that the parties face an array of contribution limits that don't apply to outside groups.[28]

The combined effect of independent spending by outside groups and parties is that "candidates are no longer directly in control of financing of their campaigns."[29] Individual candidates accounted for just 43 percent of all campaign spending in the 2014 cycle.[30] Outside spending is especially important in the most expensive, hotly contested races: for example, independent expenditures accounted for $81 million of the $116 million spent in the November 2014 North Carolina Senate race in which Republican Thom Tillis defeated Democratic incumbent Kay Hagan.

As one former FEC commissioner put it, then, "the money's flowing."[31] When the last major campaign finance reform law (the Bipartisan Campaign Reform Act, BCRA) was enacted in 2002, skeptics argued that the new law would do little to halt the overall flow of money into political campaigns. "This law will not remove one dime from politics," predicted Sen. Mitch McConnell, R-Ky., the measure's leading GOP foe. McConnell's skepticism has certainly been borne out, both by innovations in campaign finance and by Supreme Court rulings limiting the scope of regulatory restrictions. In the end, campaign finance laws have failed to limit the influence of money in politics. Big money is alive and well in U.S. elections. Furthermore, it increasingly flows through organized groups and party channels that operate independently of individual candidates.

Incumbents versus Challengers

Although incumbents need less money than do challengers, they receive more—a double-barreled financial advantage (see Figure 4-2). Incumbents are both better known than challengers and enjoy government-subsidized ways of reaching constituents. Nevertheless, incumbents are able to raise substantially more money. In 2014 House incumbents spent $1.5 million on average to defend their seats—three times what their opponents could muster. Senate incumbents spent an average of $10.9 million in 2014, outpacing their general election foes by a two to one ratio.[32]

Challengers' first hurdle is to raise enough money to make their names and faces known to voters. Because most of them start from a low baseline of name recognition, their campaign dollars tend to be more cost-effective than those of incumbents. Nevertheless, they must raise a great deal of money to defeat an incumbent. As Gary C. Jacobson points out, "The minimum price tag for a competitive House campaign under average conditions today is probably [around] $800,000; 125 of the 136 challengers who defeated incumbents from 1996 through 2010 spent more than that amount."[33]

Incumbents of both parties are able to raise money far more easily than challengers because contributors see them as better investments. Many donors to congressional campaigns seek to cultivate closer relationships with people in positions of power. Donors know that incumbents usually win reelection, so they do not usually waste their money on challengers, even when those challengers might be more appealing in their policy stances or party affiliation. Indeed, "access-oriented" giving follows the shifts in party control of Congress, as donors curry favor with committee chairs and other leaders regardless of party.[34] Challengers obviously cannot attract this type of campaign donation, which gives incumbents a substantial fund-raising advantage.

Challengers have a difficult time convincing donors that they have any reasonable chance of winning. In this arena, as in so many others, nothing succeeds like success. "Failure to raise enough money creates a vicious spiral," explains political analyst Thomas B. Edsall. "Some donors become reluctant to invest their cash, and then state and national parties are less likely to target . . . party building and get out the vote drives in those races."[35]

FIGURE 4-2   **Average Campaign Expenditures for Incumbents, Challengers, and Open-Seat Candidates: House and Senate, 1974–2014**

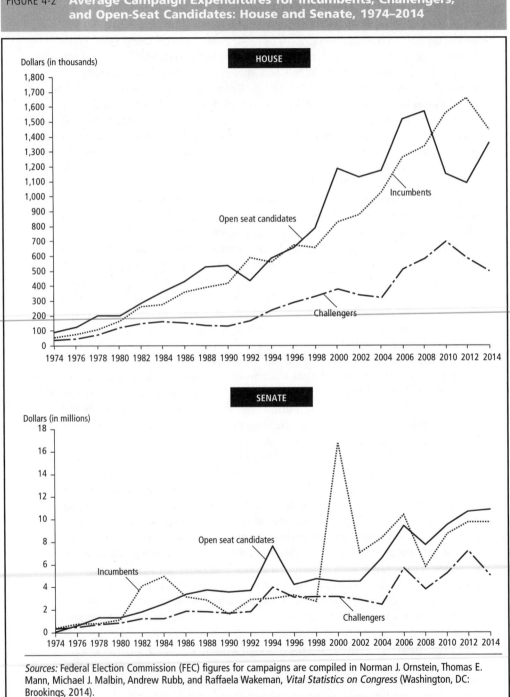

Sources: Federal Election Commission (FEC) figures for campaigns are compiled in Norman J. Ornstein, Thomas E. Mann, Michael J. Malbin, Andrew Rubb, and Raffaela Wakeman, *Vital Statistics on Congress* (Washington, DC: Brookings, 2014).

When challengers are successful in raising money, they typically find that the funds make a significant difference in their electoral chances. Generally speaking, the more challengers spend, the more votes they are likely to attract.[36] The same is not true of incumbents. In fact, for incumbents there is actually a negative correlation between campaign expenditures and electoral success. Vulnerable incumbents tend to speed up their fund-raising. As Jacobson points out, "Incumbents can raise whatever they think they need."[37] Endangered incumbents thus raise prodigious sums as they seek to hold onto their seats. Meanwhile, safe incumbents—especially senior members who infrequently face significant electoral challenges—spend much less. Despite the negative correlation, incumbents are unquestionably better off with more campaign money than less. But compared to challengers, incumbents' success or failure is much less tied to their fund-raising totals.

Many incumbents raise and spend far more than is necessary. Incumbents' overspending is frequently motivated by a sense of uncertainty and risk. "Because of uncertainty," Jacobson explains, "members tend to exaggerate electoral threats and overreact to them. They are inspired by worst-case scenarios— what would they have to do to win if everything went wrong?—rather than objective probabilities."[38]

Not all incumbent fund-raising is actually aimed at the race at hand. Incumbents often have strategic purposes for fund-raising beyond campaign finance. Preemptive fund-raising is aimed at dissuading serious opponents. "If you look like a 900-pound gorilla, people won't want to take you on," remarked a GOP campaign aide.[39] Some members, especially those with party leadership ambitions, raise money so they can impress colleagues by distributing funds to needier candidates. Sometimes longtime incumbents deliberately overspend in pursuit of decisive electoral victories that might establish their claims for higher office.

Allocating Resources

As exercises in communication, campaigns are driven by the need to find a cost-effective way of reaching citizens and getting them to vote. Candidates and their managers face many different trade-offs as they make decisions about allocating resources, depending on the context.

As a rule, statewide Senate races are mass media contests with messages conveyed mainly through radio and television. Costs are especially high in densely populated states with large metropolitan media markets. Senate candidates typically spend far more on media advertising and fund-raising than do their House counterparts, who spend more on traditional means of voter contact.

Despite its astronomical costs, television advertising is popular because candidates believe it works. Almost all households in the United States own at least one television, and the average adult watches five hours of television a day.[40] The 2014 congressional elections saw nearly unprecedented expenditures for television advertising. Between January 1, 2014, and election day, over 1.57 million election-related spots aired on television for House and Senate candidates, at a total estimated cost of $814 million.[41] This level of spending on television advertisements was nearly double the amount spent for the 2008 congressional races.

Candidates tailor their use of media to their political circumstances. Confident incumbents can channel their money into telephone, Internet and e-mail, or door-to-door appeals that direct their messages to activists, partisans, and supporters. Lesser-known candidates must turn to broad-scale media, such as television, radio, newsletters, and billboards, to promote name recognition.

Candidates also have to make decisions about their pace of spending. Especially useful is early money—that is, having funds on hand to organize a campaign at the outset. EMILY's List—Early Money Is Like Yeast ("It makes the 'dough' rise")—a group begun in 1985, was formed on this premise. This group collects (bundles) individuals' donations for Democratic women candidates who support abortion rights. The Republican counterpart is Women in the Senate and House (WISH).

Late-blitz money also can turn the tide, although money alone rarely makes the difference at the end of a race. In the final weeks of a hard-fought race, both sides are trying to reach undecided voters. "You've got to move that 10 or 15 percent, many of whom are not paying much attention," a Democratic consultant explained. "Unfortunately, the way to do that is with negative or comparative ads."[42] Late in a competitive race, opponents frantically attack and—despite the scant time—counterattack.

Another question of timing involves candidates facing tough contests in both the primary and general elections. In this situation, candidates lacking personal wealth find themselves in an especially vexing dilemma. Should they ration their outflow of funds and risk losing the primary, or should they wage an expensive primary campaign and risk running out of money later on?

Organizing the Campaign

Implementing a campaign strategy is the job of the candidates and their organizations. Waging a campaign is not for the fainthearted. Take the case of psychology professor Brian Baird, a Democrat who won Washington's Third District (comprising Olympia and southwest Washington State) seat in 1998. Having lost to the incumbent by a mere 887 votes two years earlier, Baird vowed to run full tilt the second time. As a result, he spent almost all of his waking hours campaigning during the peak months (July–October)—more than ten hours a day for 123 days. Travel alone consumed many hours in his average-sized district.[43]

Few localities today boast tight party organizations. In some strong party areas, voter contact is the job of ward, precinct, and block captains. Candidates in some such areas still dispense "walking-around money" to encourage precinct captains to get out the vote and provide small financial rewards for voting. But in most places today the traditional local parties have been replaced by hybrid organizations that partner with state and national parties and their allied interest groups.

When they can pay the price, today's candidates purchase campaign services from political consulting firms, most of them operating within partisan networks. Consulting firms account for roughly 15 percent to 20 percent of congressional campaign spending.[44] Some firms offer a wide array of services; others specialize in polling, direct mail, phone banks, advertising, purchasing media time, coordinating volunteer efforts, fund-raising, or financial management and accounting. Despite the hype they often receive, consultants by themselves rarely turn a campaign around. At best, they can make the most of a candidate's resources and help combat opponents' attacks. They cannot compensate for an unskilled or lazy candidate or for a candidate's staff who do not follow through on details.

CAMPAIGN TECHNIQUES

Campaigns are designed to convey the candidate's messages to people who will lend support and vote in the election. Campaigns are not necessarily directed at all voters. Often, narrower groups are targeted—most notably, the political party's core supporters.

The Air War: Media and Other Mass Appeals

Candidates reach the largest numbers of voters by running broadcast ads and making televised appearances. Television is the broadest spectrum medium, and its costs eat up the bulk of most campaign budgets.

Candidates obviously cannot fully control their media coverage. Some of the most effective appeals—news coverage and endorsements, for example—are determined by persons other than the candidate. Because journalists can raise unwanted or hostile questions, many politicians seek out the friendlier environments of talk shows hosted by nonjournalists. Even more congenial are appeals the candidates themselves buy and pay for—newsletters, websites, media ads, and direct mail. The drawback is that self-promotion is seen as less credible than information from independent sources.

Nearly half of all voters rely primarily on television for their campaign news—network, cable, or local. About a quarter turn to the Internet as their primary campaign news source, and 8 percent rely on newspapers.[45] And yet local news programming largely ignores congressional campaign coverage. In the weeks preceding the 2012 elections, for example, 83 percent of the scheduled half-hour local news programs in a diverse sample of media markets offered no coverage at all of the U.S. House races in the area. For those media markets with a statewide Senate race, the "blackout rate" was also over 80 percent.[46] Most candidates must therefore pay to reach the voters.

Positive Themes. Most campaign themes call for promotions that evoke positive responses from citizens. Positive ads present candidates in warm, human terms to which citizens can relate. Skillfully done, TV ads can be very effective in bringing home the candidate's themes. A case in point was the series of brilliant, funny—and inexpensive—television ads that helped a little-known Wisconsin state legislator, Russ Feingold, win the Democratic primary, defeat a two-term incumbent senator, and then go on to serve three terms in the U.S. Senate (1993–2011). As his opponents battered each other with negative ads, Feingold ran clever, personal spots describing himself as the "underdog candidate." One showed Elvis, alive and endorsing Feingold. Another showed Feingold walking through his modest home, opening up a closet and saying, "No skeletons."

One of the best positive ads in 2012 was run by successful Senate candidate Heidi Heitkamp, D-N.D. In this ad, Heitkamp was shown wearing a baseball pullover and helmet while hitting line drives in a batting cage. In voice-over, she narrates that her political opponents "try to hit me with all sorts of stuff." Rather than respond to those "negative ads that aren't true," she pivots to highlighting her own priorities of "Medicare" and "jobs." In the last frame, she turns to the camera, winks, smiles broadly, and says, "I'm just getting warmed up."

Negative Themes. Candidates also deploy campaign resources against their opponents. Contrast ads distinguish the candidate from the opponent on the grounds of policy and experience, and attack ads strike at the opponent's record or personal character. Republican representative Leonard Lance's 2008 winning bid for an open seat in New Jersey's Seventh District offers an example of an effective contrast ad. The ad featured a series of "man on the street"–style shots, showing male and female voters of different ages and races, each saying "Linda Stender is a spender." The ad's tone was high-spirited, with bright colors and punctuated by a cash register sound. One voter is even shown cracking up in laughter as he attempts the line. The repetition, combined with the rhyme on his opponent's name, memorably conveyed the central contrast Lance sought to draw in his campaign. Because challengers are usually less known than incumbents, they are more vulnerable to attacks and unflattering personal revelations.

Negative campaign themes are often the result of opposition research (called "oppo" by campaigners). Its purpose is "to get the skinny on the client's opponents and, if all goes well, expose them as hypocrites, liars, thieves, or just plain unsavory characters."[47] Both national parties and many campaigns invest in opposition research. A Republican National Committee self-evaluation after its 2012 electoral defeats (referred to as the "Autopsy" report) called for an "allied group dedicated solely to research to establish a private archive and public website that does nothing but post inappropriate Democratic utterances."[48]

Though not technically a campaign ad, the "push poll" is another negative campaign technique. These are not actual polls designed to elicit public attitudes, but instead are biased phone calls with questions aimed at changing voters' opinions. The caller divulges negative information—often false or misleading—in the hope of pulling the voter away from the opponent and toward the candidate paying for the call.

Negative ads are common in modern campaigning because politicians believe they work. This strategy was forcefully described by Rep. Tom Cole, R-Okla., in a memo to his House colleagues: "Define your opponent immediately and unrelentingly. Do not let up—keep the tough ads running right up to election day. Don't make the mistake of pulling your ads in favor of a positive rotation the last weekend."[49]

Recent experiments by two noted communications researchers tend to confirm the power of negative ads. Such ads, these scholars found, lift voters' information levels, even if the information conveyed is distorted or trivial. Although neither positive nor negative ads have much effect on strong partisans, negative ads can work powerfully on citizens who have little information to begin with and on those with little or no party allegiance.[50] "We should not necessarily see negative ads as a harmful part of our electoral system," argues Kenneth Goldstein, founding director of the University of Wisconsin's political advertising project. "They are much more likely [than positive ads] to be about policy, to use supporting information, and to be reliable. Few negative ads are on personal issues."[51]

Like other forms of product promotion, political ads often stretch or distort the truth. Sometimes the disinformation is so blatant that the term *dirty tricks* applies. This tactic includes not only spreading falsehoods but also using doctored photographs or faking news reports or news headlines.

One of the most controversial attack ads in the 2010 campaign was aired by Democratic candidate Jack Conway in his unsuccessful attempt to defeat Republican Rand Paul for the open Senate seat in Kentucky. The ad asserted that when Paul was a student at Baylor University he was "a member of a secret society that called the Holy Bible 'a hoax,'" and the society "was banned for mocking Christianity and Christ."[52] The subject matter of the ad was obviously inflammatory, particularly in Kentucky, one of the most religious states in the country.[53]

Victims of such tactics have some means of defense, even when attacks are leveled close to election day. The campaign can promptly air response ads or accuse the offender of mudslinging. During a candidate debate, for example, Paul repeatedly called on Conway to apologize. In the end, many analysts felt that Conway's ad backfired, undermining his support among independents and even among Democrats. "Backlash [over the ad] may have sunk Conway's campaign for good," reported one Democratic-leaning polling firm.[54]

Formal complaints can sometimes persuade opponents to disavow attack ads or local broadcasters to pull them off the air. Media outlets sometimes find themselves in the unwanted role of arbiter, when candidates demand that opponents' ads be discontinued.[55] As one deterrent to smear tactics, the BCRA of 2002 requires that candidates personally appear and vouch for their advertisements.

Evolving Mass Media. The old-fashioned media—newspapers, radio, and television networks—are on the decline. The newspaper business in the United States, in particular, appears to be in crisis. Even before the 2007–2009 recession, newspapers around the country had cut staff and closed bureaus in an effort to remain economically viable. The proportion of people who read newspapers continues to fall. According to a 2012 poll, just 23 percent reported that they read a print newspaper the day before, a decline of about half since 2000.[56] Changing media pose a threat even to television, in that young people rely far less on television news than they did in earlier years. By contrast, the Internet is an increasingly important news source. A study by the Pew Research Center reported a 300 percent increase in Internet usage for campaign news between 2000 and 2012, with the shift most pronounced among young people.[57]

Web outlets are unregulated by the government. In 2006 the Federal Elections Commission (FEC) decided to treat the Internet "as a unique and evolving mode of mass communication and political speech that warrants a restrained regulatory approach."[58] Critics of the hands-off approach point out that Web political messages can be costly to produce and are sometimes far edgier than would be permitted in traditional media outlets. At the least, the public has an interest in learning who instigates these messages, who prepares them, and who pays for them.[59]

Still, the variety and seeming spontaneity of the Web intrigue many political analysts. One observer of the Web scene calls it "word of mouth on steroids." Although campaign organizations use the medium, the knowledge and skill to make compelling videos—like those unleashed on YouTube and other outlets—have "moved out of campaign headquarters" and into the hands of private citizens.

The Ground War: Pressing the Flesh and Other Forms of Close Contact

Direct appeals to voters through personal appearances by candidates or their surrogates—at shopping centers, factory gates, or even door to door—are part of every campaign. In his successful 1948 Senate campaign, Lyndon B. Johnson swooped out of the sky in a helicopter to visit small Texas towns, grandly pitching his Stetson from the chopper for a bold entrance; an aide was assigned to retrieve the hat for use at the next stop.[60] Other candidates, preferring to stay closer to the ground, stage walking tours or other events to attract attention. Few elected officials get by without doing a great deal of what is inelegantly called "pressing the flesh."

Recent social science research has demonstrated the importance of retail, as opposed to wholesale, campaigning. TV ads, direct mail, and phone banks are less effective than old-fashioned ways of getting out the vote. An array of experiments has shown that personalized messages delivered face to face or in conversational manner over the phone are far superior to impersonal methods of reaching potential voters.[61] According to Yale political scientists Donald P. Green and Alan S. Gerber, face-to-face canvassing raises turnout by 7 to 12 percentage points.[62]

One-on-one campaigning is physically and emotionally challenging. But an obvious advantage of so-called shoe-leather campaigning is cost, at least when compared with mass media appeals. "Door-to-door canvassing is the tactic of choice among candidates and campaigns that are short on cash," explain Green and Gerber. "Precinct walking is often described as the weapon of underdogs."[63] Former representative Dan Glickman, D-Kan. (1977–1995), describes his first House campaign as a thirty-one-year-old challenger facing a long-term incumbent:

I walked door-to-door to 35,000 homes over an eight-month period. I walked from 10:30 a.m. to 2 p.m. and again from 5:30 to 8 p.m. I lost 35 pounds and learned to be very realistic about dogs. I met a woman my father had lent $100 or $150 to 30 years before. She embraced me and said, "You saved us." I won by three percentage points.[64]

Face-to-face campaigning is obligatory in smaller communities, where people expect politicians to show up at festivals, parades, or annual county fairs. "If you ain't seen at the county fair, you're preached about on Sunday," remarked a politician as he led his party's Senate candidate around the hog and sheep barns in Ada, Oklahoma.[65] In small states, first-name relationships are often valued. "They want to know you," political scientist Garrison Nelson remarked about Vermont voters. The state's Independent senator, Bernard Sanders, distributes bumper stickers that simply say, "Bernie."[66] In Bristol, on Rhode Island's coast, the Fourth of July parade—the oldest in the country—is "the first and perhaps biggest event of the campaign season."[67]

Getting Out the Vote. GOTV drives are focused on registering constituents to vote and then getting voters to the polls. Recognizing the importance of personalized voter contact, both parties have developed sophisticated GOTV operations. Each now relies on "micro-targeting" to reach sympathetic voters. This approach employs computer models to exploit a wide array of data, such as the groups to which people belong or the magazines they read, to identify potential voters and the issues that are important to them. "Micro-targeting has become so widespread that it is now used by all House and Senate candidates, on both sides, in state legislative races, and in some cases, all the way down the ballot to local school board elections," concludes one journalist.[68]

In addition, many groups finance their own field operations in support of favored candidates. In this sense, the parties' GOTV efforts are just part of a broader campaign waged by their allied groups. For example, the Service Employees International Union (SEIU) sought to knock on three million potential voters' doors before the 2014 election.[69] For their part, Republicans depend on a wide array of pro-life, evangelical, and socially conservative organizations to undertake GOTV drives for their candidates.

The Parallel Campaigns

The scene is a hospital operating room; the patient is surrounded by surgeons and nurses. One surgeon in a voice of astonished concern exclaims, "Oh my." A nurse asks, "Colitis?" Another nurse asks, "Hepatitis?" A third, "Diverticulitis?" The surgeon replies, "No, I'm afraid it's Dina Titus. Taxes up the yingyang. Her tax policy is killing us." The target of this television ad was 2008 Democratic House challenger Dina Titus, a former political science professor at University of Nevada–Las Vegas and current representative for Nevada's First Congressional District. The ad was paid for by Freedom's Watch, a lobbying group bankrolled by wealthy conservatives, notably billionaire casino developer Sheldon Adelson.

The huge increase in spending by outside groups discussed above means that campaigns no longer resemble boxing matches between two combatants. They have become free-for-alls in which multiple combatants throw punches and land roundhouse kicks. Candidates compete not only against their opponents and their parties but also against scores of groups that join the fray.

Hundreds of such organizations engage in congressional campaigning, most of them favoring one or the other major political party. As allies of a national party, these organizations contribute to the "nationalization" of congressional elections. The ads these organizations run tend to reinforce existing stereotypes about the parties. "To watch the advertisements blanketing the airwaves, every Democrat is an Obamacare-loving big spender," observes journalist Reid Wilson. "Every Republican is a Medicare-slashing tea partier."[70] Such ads undercut the candidates' ability to control their own political image. As outside-group spending becomes a paramount element of campaign finance, it becomes harder for candidates to differentiate themselves from their national parties. Candidates in swing states or districts attempting to carve out distinctive profiles run up against their opponents' Super PAC–funded ads painting with a broad brush, lumping them in with the rest of their party's team.

WHO VOTES?

Although Congress is supposed to be the people's branch of government, only around half of voting-age citizens normally take part in House elections. In the 2014 House elections just 35.9 percent of the voting-eligible population, or VEP (all eligible residents age eighteen and over), participated.[71] In 2012 turnout was 58.0 percent—slightly below the 61.6 percent turnout of 2008.[72]

As Figure 4-3 indicates, turnout varies according to whether the election is held in a presidential or a midterm year. Midterm races lack the intense publicity and stimulus to vote provided by presidential contests. Since the 1930s, turnout in midterm congressional elections has averaged about 12 percent below that of the preceding presidential election. Midterm electorates include a greater share of people who are interested in politics, and—not unrelated—who are also more affluent and better educated.[73]

Reasons for Not Voting

Political analysts disagree over the reasons for the anemic voting levels in the United States, which are near the bottom among established democratic countries. Several explanations—not all of them compatible—have been suggested.[74]

One explanation for nonvoting is simply demographic. Groups with low voting rates, such as young people, African Americans, and Latinos, have been growing as a share of the U.S. population. Young people (ages eighteen through twenty-nine) are traditional no-shows, perhaps because they have fewer of the life experiences (mortgages, taxes, school-age children, community ties) that propel older people toward activism. Four out of ten young people have not

FIGURE 4-3   **Turnout in Presidential and Congressional Elections, 1946–2014**

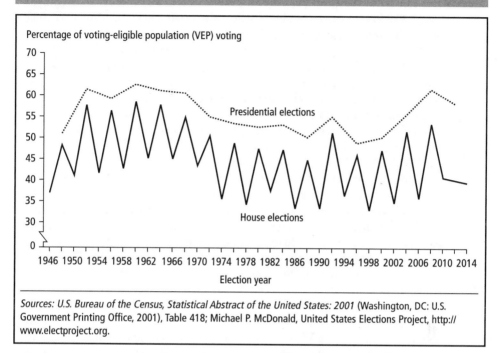

Sources: *U.S. Bureau of the Census, Statistical Abstract of the United States: 2001* (Washington, DC: U.S. Government Printing Office, 2001), Table 418; Michael P. McDonald, United States Elections Project, http://www.electproject.org.

registered to vote (three times greater than those aged fifty and older).[75] Turnout among young Americans in the 2014 midterms was estimated at 22.2 percent.[76]

A second explanation stresses legal barriers to voting. Only about 70 percent of the voting age population are registered to vote. Many democracies automatically register all adults; some even require that people vote. By contrast, U.S. citizens must take the initiative to register and vote. The National Voter Registration Act of 1993 (the so-called Motor Voter law) aimed to increase citizens' access to voter registration by, among other things, requiring states to offer voter registration as an option when citizens apply for a driver's license. Registration of eligible voters soon rose about 3.8 percent nationwide, but voting levels failed to climb—especially among the young and the poor, the targets of the measure.[77]

Other disincentives can be blamed on electoral arrangements. U.S. citizens are asked to vote far more often than are voters in parliamentary regimes; and elections are held on weekdays, not on weekends or national holidays. A number of states and localities have modernized their election procedures, making it easier to register and vote. Absentee balloting and vote by mail have become more common. Some states permit ballots to be submitted over a period of time. Oregon citizens may even vote by telephone. In recent years, however, lawmakers in many states have raised new barriers through voter ID requirements—such as photo IDs or proof-of-citizenship papers.[78] Although passed under the pretext of combating "voter fraud," these are widely understood as partisan measures intended "to depress voter turnout in minority and poor communities."[79] In 2008 the Supreme Court upheld the strictest such law, Indiana's 2005 statute that requires all voters to present a valid government ID.[80] The Supreme Court's *Shelby County v. Holder* (2013) decision overturning the Voting Rights Act of 1965's requirement for preclearance of changes in voting rules in states with a history of discrimination, opened the door to more states adopting tight voter ID laws. Hours after the Supreme Court's ruling, the state of Texas began enforcing a strict photo identification requirement for voting.[81]

Biased or careless election administration can also turn away voters or lead to a miscount of their ballots, as uncovered in voting scandals in Florida (2000) and Ohio (2004). Local election practices often weigh most heavily on minority or socioeconomically disadvantaged citizens, who are more likely to encounter insufficient numbers of poll workers, antiquated or badly designed voting machines, and longer lines. Limited voting hours and inadequate polling facilities, for example, led to extremely long lines in a number of urban Florida communities in 2012. An Ohio State University researcher estimated that the long lines that year turned away as many as 49,000 voters across Central Florida.[82]

A final explanation for low voter turnout is citizen disaffection. Noncompetitive elections, poor candidates, and contentious or negative campaigning are thought to keep people away from the polling booths. To be sure, apathy and cynicism are part of the picture. Surveys sponsored by Harvard University's "Vanishing Voters" project found that four out of ten nonvoters in 2000 claimed to care little about politics and public affairs. A quarter were dismayed or confused by the barrage of campaign messages. And another quarter were simply angry or cynical about politics.[83]

Biases of Voting

Although voting is the simplest and most accessible form of political involvement, it is still biased in favor of people at the higher rungs of the social and generational ladders—those who are older, more affluent, better educated, and more in touch with political events. Eight in ten people whose annual incomes exceed $50,000 vote in a typical election. This is twice the voting rate of the poor, defined as people with annual incomes of less than $15,000.

Alternative forms of political participation are even more sharply biased. For example, giving money is mainly an elite activity. According to a study by Sidney Verba and his colleagues, 35 percent of all political money flowed from the 4 percent of people making more than $125,000 a year. Poor people, who were 19 percent of the sample, made only 2 percent of political donations.[84]

HOW VOTERS DECIDE

What induces voters to cast their ballots for one candidate and not another? As a general rule, voters reach their decisions on the basis of party loyalty. But candidate assessments and salient issues also figure into voters' decisions. The relative strength of these elements varies over time and among specific races.

Although American voters are often uninformed or indifferent about political issues and candidates, they employ what is called low-information rationality, or gut reasoning, to make voting booth decisions. As Samuel L. Popkin explains, people "triangulate and validate their opinions in conversations with people they trust and according to the opinions of national figures whose judgments and positions they have come to know."[85] Thus voters work through imperfect information to make choices that will often roughly approximate the choices they would have made with more perfect information.

Party Loyalties

Party identification is the single most powerful factor in determining voters' choices. And it remains the strongest single correlate of voting in congressional elections. In recent elections, at least nine in every ten Democrats and Republicans voted for their parties' nominees. Independents tend to split their votes more evenly between the parties. In 2006 they veered toward Democratic candidates by a three-to-two margin.[86] But in 2014 independents preferred Republican to Democratic candidates by 12 percentage points.[87]

According to surveys, most people who claim to be independents are in fact closet partisans who lean toward one party or the other. These independent leaners—about a quarter of the total electorate—hold attitudes similar to those of partisans. Not only do they favor one party over the other, but they also share many (though not necessarily all) of the party's values and will vote for the party's candidates—if they vote at all.

Only a small percentage of citizens (6–12 percent) are true independents; they are unpredictable, however, and have dismal turnout rates. "I would encourage candidates not to play to them," advises David Magleby of Brigham Young University, "because they tend to jump on bandwagons, to follow tides. You're better off [working] on getting your weak partisans and your leaners."[88]

Partisan Resurgence. Today's voters are as loyal to their professed party identification as they have ever been.[89] Few voters who identify as either Republican or Democrat defect from their party when they cast votes in particular congressional races.

This represents a major shift from recent decades. Between 1950 and 1980, partisan loyalty declined among the American electorate, with voters identifying with one party and often supporting candidates from the other party. These weakened party ties led to an epidemic of split-ticket voting—that is, voters supporting one party's presidential candidate and the opposition party's congressional candidate. Between 1952 and 1988, the number of voters who reported in surveys that they split their ticket between presidential and House candidates rose from 12 percent to 25 percent. Those who split their ballots between different parties' House and Senate candidates grew from 9 percent to 27 percent.[90]

Most of these ticket-splitters, it turned out, were in the throes of moving from one party to another. White southern conservatives made up a large share of ticket-splitters during this era. Targeted by the GOP's so-called southern strategy, these voters were attracted to presidential candidates such as Barry Goldwater, Richard Nixon, and Ronald Reagan. At the same time, southern conservatives continued to back Democrats in congressional and state races as strong Republican candidates often failed to challenge entrenched incumbents—because the Democratic Party put up conservative candidates, and because long-serving Democrats won the "personal vote" of constituents by delivering more benefits back home through their party's control of legislative chambers. The same phenomenon occurred to a lesser degree in the Northeast, where voters were drawn to the Democrats' national policies and candidates but continued to support moderate to liberal Republican representatives or senators.[91]

Recent party realignment has brought party affiliation into sync with policy and ideological preferences. Although the process extended over many years, the long Republican courtship of southern conservatives was consummated in 1994. Merle Black of Emory University estimates that more than 80 percent of white conservatives in the South are Republicans; only 10 percent are Democrats.[92] A parallel trend, no less dramatic, has been the Democratic Party's absorption of GOP moderates and liberals. Finding acceptable candidates up and down the ballot, these voters have less need to pick and choose—hence revived partisanship and dwindling split tickets.

In short, the bulge in split-ticket voting was a by-product of gradual partisan realignment. Over the last six presidential elections, ticket-splitting has plummeted to less than 10 percent—exactly the same level it was fifty years ago. The number of congressional districts voting for one party's presidential candidate and the other party's House candidate fell as well. In 2012 only around 11 percent of districts voted for one party for the House and the other party for president. Just fifteen House Republicans won in districts that were carried by President Obama.

Midterm and Presidential Election Years. Politicians have long talked about "coattails": how House and Senate candidates could be pulled into office by the strength of a popular presidential candidate. The idea is that successful presidential candidates will entice new voters not just for themselves but for their whole party.

In presidential election years, the party that wins the presidency typically does increase its numbers in Congress. As shown in Table 4-1, the winning presidential candidate's party gains on average 15.1 seats in the House and 2.1 seats in the Senate. Boosts for the president's congressional party were considerably more modest in recent election years than they were in the 1930s and 1940s. George H. W. Bush, Bill Clinton, and George W. Bush all began their presidencies with some congressional seat losses for their party. Nevertheless, political scientists who have analyzed the influence of presidential candidates on the outcome of congressional elections have found that "nontrivial coattail effects have been discernible in recent elections."[93] President Ronald Reagan boosted his party's congressional votes by 2–3 percent in 1980 and 5 percent in 1984. In 1996 President Clinton's reelection added about 2.6 percentage points to Democrats' House and Senate totals.[94] President Obama began his presidency with the largest increases in his party's numbers in Congress for any president since Reagan in 1980.

The president's party normally suffers significant reversals in the midterm congressional elections. In fact, the president's party has lost seats in thirty-three of the thirty-six midterm elections since 1860. "This is not quite the certainty of 'death and taxes,' but it is about as dependable as things get in politics," observes political scientist James E. Campbell.[95] As evident in Table 4-2, since 1934 the presidential party has lost an average of 27 House seats and 3.9 Senate seats in midterm elections.

The "midterm law" was broken on only three occasions. Democrats gained four seats in the House and held their own in the Senate in 1998, in the midst of President Clinton's impeachment proceedings. Although voters deplored Clinton's personal behavior, his job ratings remained robust; Republicans were rebuked for insisting on impeaching him. Four years later, President George W. Bush's GOP gained eight House seats and one Senate seat, no doubt because of the post-9/11 rally effect. The only other anomaly occurred in 1934, when President Franklin D. Roosevelt's popularity strengthened the Democrats' grip on both chambers. Even set in historical context, the midterm losses faced by Democrats during the Obama administration stand out: Republicans' gain of sixty-three House seats in 2010 was the largest midterm swing since 1938, while the GOP's gain of nine Senate seats in 2014 was the most dramatic Senate midterm shift since 1958.

One theory that endeavors to explain the pattern of midterm loss is known as "surge and decline." This theory posits that the visibility and excitement of a winning presidential campaign attracts intermittent voters who tend to support the president's party in down-ticket races. When these presidential candidates are not on the ballot, the shrunken electorate of midterm years contains fewer supporters of the president's party—that is, a presidential surge, swollen by less motivated voters attracted by presidential campaigns, is followed two years later by a decline as intermittent voters drop out of the electorate. But other studies suggest that midterm voters are no more or less partisan than those in presidential years and share most of their demographic characteristics.[96] Another problem with the theory is that, no matter the circumstances, the president's party typically loses more seats at the midterm than it gains during a presidential year.

A second theory argues that midterm elections serve in part as a referendum on the president's popularity and performance in office during the previous two years.[97] Voters may hold the president's party responsible for economic reverses, unpopular policies, or military ventures. The 2010 and 2014 midterm elections were seen as referenda on President Obama's time in office: although Obama wasn't on the ballot, his Democratic legislators were, and they bore the brunt of voter dissatisfaction.

A third theory emphasizes voters' preferences for "balance." By favoring the out-party at midterm, voters can pull policy back toward the ideological center.[98] Voter behavior may not be driven so much by dissatisfaction with the president as by the desire to check potential presidential excesses. This may seem like an overly sophisticated calculation for the average voter, but even if only a relatively small portion of the electorate follows this logic it can have a sizable impact on electoral outcomes. Balance theory helps explain why the shift against the president's party in midterm elections is typically larger than one would expect based on presidents' approval ratings or based on the "surge and decline" thesis.[99]

All three schools of thought—"surge and decline," referendum theory, and balance theory—can shed light on such dramatic midterm outcomes as the Democrats' 1974 post-Watergate bonus of forty-eight representatives and five senators, the Democrats' retaking of House and Senate majorities in 2006, and the Republicans' gain of sixty-three representatives and six senators in 2010.

TABLE 4-1 Seats in Congress Gained or Lost by the President's Party in Presidential Election Years, 1932–2012

		Seats gained or lost	
Year	President	House	Senate
1932	Franklin D. Roosevelt (D)	+90	+9
1936	Roosevelt (D)	+12	+7
1940	Roosevelt (D)	+7	−3
1944	Roosevelt (D)	+24	−2
1948	Harry S. Truman (D)	+75	+9
1952	Dwight D. Eisenhower (R)	+22	+1
1956	Eisenhower (R)	−2	−1
1960	John F. Kennedy (D)	−22	+2
1964	Lyndon B. Johnson (D)	+37	+1
1968	Richard M. Nixon (R)	+5	+6
1972	Nixon (R)	+12	−2
1976	Jimmy Carter (D)	+1	0
1980	Ronald Reagan (R)	+34	+12
1984	Reagan (R)	+14	−2
1988	George H. W. Bush (R)	−2	0
1992	Bill Clinton (D)	−10	0
1996	Clinton (D)	−9	−2
2000	George W. Bush (R)	−3	−4
2004	Bush (R)	+3	+4
2008	Barack Obama (D)	+21	+8
2012	Obama (D)	+8	+2
Average seats gained (21 elections)		+15.1	+2.1

Source: Compiled by the authors.

The Appeal of Candidates

"My theory on politics is ultimately that people vote for the person they like most," declared former senator David Pryor, D-Ark. (1979–1997).[100] Apart from partisan loyalties, the appeal of given candidates is the strongest force in congressional voting. Not surprisingly, candidate appeal normally tilts toward

TABLE 4-2	**Midterm Fortunes of Presidential Parties, 1934–2014**		
		Seats gained or lost	
Year	President	House	Senate
1934	Franklin D. Roosevelt (D)	+9	+10
1938	Roosevelt (D)	−71	−6
1942	Roosevelt (D)	−45	−9
1946	Roosevelt and Harry S. Truman (D)	−55	−12
1950	Truman (D)	−29	−6
1954	Dwight D. Eisenhower (R)	−18	−1
1958	Eisenhower (R)	−47	−13
1962	John F. Kennedy (D)	−5	+3
1966	Lyndon B. Johnson (D)	−47	−4
1970	Richard M. Nixon (R)	−12	+3
1974	Nixon and Gerald R. Ford (R)	−48	−5
1978	Jimmy Carter (D)	−15	−3
1982	Ronald Reagan (R)	−26	+1
1986	Reagan (R)	−5	−8
1990	George H. W. Bush (R)	−7	−1
1994	Bill Clinton (D)	−54	−10
1998	Clinton (D)	+4	0
2002	George W. Bush (R)	+8	+1
2006	Bush (R)	−31	−6
2010	Obama (D)	−63	−6
2014	Obama (D)	−13	−9
Average seats lost (21 elections)		−27.1	−3.9

Sources: CQ Press Electronic Library, *Vital Statistics on American Politics Online Edition*, Table 1-17. Originally published in Harold W. Stanley and Richard G. Niemi, eds., *Vital Statistics on American Politics, 2009–2010* (Washington, DC: CQ Press, 2009). Each entry is the difference between the number of seats held by the president's party at the start of Congress after the midterm election and the number of seats held by that party at the start of Congress after the preceding general election. Special elections that shifted partisan seat totals between elections are not noted.

incumbents. When voters abandon their party to vote for House or Senate candidates, they usually vote for incumbents.

Incumbency Advantage. Incumbents rarely lose their bids for reelection, as is evident in Table 4-3. Incumbent reelection rates have always been robust. Even in the 2010 watershed election, incumbent winners still included 85 percent of all representatives and 83 percent of all senators who ran for reelection. House incumbents fared even better in 2014, with 96 percent of those running for reelection winning, alongside 82 percent of senators. Changes in party control of seats are attributable as much to winning seats opened up by retirements as to defeating incumbents.

Defeating a House incumbent is an uphill struggle, absent a scandal or misstep. Senate challengers—more often than not, well known and generously financed—have a stronger chance of unseating incumbents than do those seeking House seats. Nevertheless, more than four out of five Senate incumbents win the contests they enter.

Why are incumbents so formidable? Incumbents' success rates go beyond what one should expect based on the partisan character of their constituencies. In other words, incumbents often win by solid margins in constituencies that are closely divided between Republicans and Democrats. This phenomenon has led scholars to ask whether the sheer fact of incumbency itself offers advantages: Do candidates fare better running as incumbents than they would running as nonincumbents?[101]

To measure this advantage, scholars often look to the "sophomore surge" and the "retirement slump." The sophomore surge refers to the average gain in vote share by candidates running for reelection for the first time, compared with their performance in their first election. The retirement slump is the average drop in a party's vote share when an incumbent retires and the seat opens up. Scholars then average these two calculations into a single index, known as the "slurge," which is often used to measure the overall incumbency advantage. According to this measure, incumbents enjoyed about a 6 to 8 percent boost in their share of the vote simply by virtue of being incumbents from the mid-1960s through the 1990s. The incumbency advantage has fallen in the past decade, as rising levels of partisan voting and conflict in Washington make it harder for individual politicians to separate themselves from their parties. The estimated slurge hit a low of 3 points in 2014.[102] Even this relatively small edge, however, provides a significant buffer for those incumbents who do not face a district that is tilted decisively in favor of the out-party.

Political scientists have launched a veritable cottage industry to explain incumbency advantage. Certainly, one key factor is incumbents' campaign fund-raising advantages, which were described earlier (see "Incumbents versus Challengers"). It is also no secret that incumbents have many methods of gathering support—through speeches, press coverage, newsletters, staff assistance, and constituent service. Incumbents' popularity depends in large part on their success in shaping information that constituents receive about them and their performance—through advertising, credit claiming, and position taking.[103]

The unequal visibility of candidates is thus an important source of incumbency advantage. In National Election Study (NES) surveys spanning almost thirty years, nearly all respondents were able to recognize the names of, and offer opinions about, their Senate and House incumbents running for reelection (means of 97 percent and 92 percent, respectively). Senate challengers were recognized and rated by 77 percent of the respondents, House challengers by only 53 percent.[104]

Voters also report having high levels of contact with House and Senate incumbents. The more contact voters have with their legislators, the more positive their evaluations are likely to be. According to NES surveys, at least nine out of ten voters said they had some form of contact with their representative. A fifth of them reported having met the lawmaker in person. Many constituents receive mail from their representatives or read about them in newspapers or online. Virtually all voters reported some contact with their senators, mostly through mailings, TV appearances, or other media coverage.

Incumbents achieve these high levels of visibility and constituency contact in part because of their perquisites of office. The typical House member receives staff, office, and travel allocations valued at between $2 and $3 million over a two-year term; senators, with six-year terms, command between $17 and $27 million in resources. Everyone concedes the value of incumbents' perquisites, but scholars differ on how much they affect electoral success. One view is that incumbents exploit their resources to ensure reelection, seizing on their ability to assist constituents in dealing with the bureaucracy to build electoral credit. Others counter that legislators are simply responding to constituents' demands, aided by advances in communication technology. Still others question whether incumbents' resources are directly translatable into votes.[105]

Senate and House. The factors contributing to incumbency advantage help explain why senators are more vulnerable at the polls than are their House counterparts. First, Senate challengers are far more conspicuous than House challengers. Senate contests are more widely reported by the media, and challengers can gain almost as much exposure as incumbents. Media coverage of House races is more fragmentary than that of Senate races, throwing more weight to incumbents' techniques of contacting voters.

Second, senators cannot manipulate voter contacts as much as representatives do. Voters get their information about Senate races largely through the organized media, which senators do not control. Representatives gain exposure through focused means—personal appearances, mailings, and newsletters—which they fashion to their own advantage. "Somewhat ironically," observes Michael J. Robinson, "powerful senators are less able to control their images than 'invisible' House members."[106]

Among senators, constituency size is also a crucial variable in elections. Small-state senators in many respects resemble representatives. Compared with their large-state colleagues, they are more visible, more accessible, and more able to raise the campaign money they need. But they are not electorally safer, as their challengers, too, have an easier time mounting their campaigns and gaining visibility.[107]

TABLE 4-3 **Reelection Rates in the House and Senate, by Decade, 1950s–2000s, plus 2012–2014**

Decade	House					Senate				
	Sought reelection	Faced no opponent	Lost primary	General election	Percent reelected	Sought reelection	Faced no opponent	Lost primary	General election	Percent reelected
1950s	402	85	6	25	93.2%	30	4	1	6	77.3%
1960s	404	52	8	26	91.5	32	1	2	4	80.8
1970s	389	57	2	23	92.3	27	1	2	6	67.7
1980s	403	67	13	15	95.7	29	1	0	3	88.0
1990s	385	36	8	18	93.6	26	0	0	3	87.4
2000s	395	40	3	24	93.2	28	1	1	4	87.9
2012–2014	394	20	8.5	20	92.8	26	.5	.5	3.5	84.6

Sources: CQ Weekly Report, April 5, 1980, 908; November 8, 1980, 3302, 3320–3321; July 31, 1982, 1870; November 6, 1982, 2781; November 10, 1984, 2897, 2901; November 12, 1988, 3264, 3270; November 10, 1990, 3796–3805; November 7, 1992, 3557–3564, 3570–3576; November 12, 1994, 329ff; February 15, 1997, 447–455; November 7, 1998, 3027–3035; November 11, 2000, 2694–2706; December 14, 2002, 3289–3297; November 6, 2004, 2653–2660; November 13, 2006, 3068–3075; November 10, 2008, 3043–3052; November 8, 2010, 2618–1627; November 12, 2012, 2284–2293; November 6, 2014, 60–61.

Note: Statistics for each decade are election-year averages for the five elections conducted under that decade's apportionment of House districts. For example, the 1950s include the five elections 1952 through 1960. "Percent reelected" takes into account both primary and general election defeats. "Faced no opponent" means no major-party opponent.

Strategic Politicians. A very important and frequently underrated factor contributing to incumbent reelection success is simply the quality of candidates who typically run against incumbents. Jacobson surely captures the normal state of affairs when he observes that "most incumbents face obscure, politically inexperienced opponents whose resources fall far short of what is necessary to mount a formidable campaign."[108] As discussed in Chapter 3, it is often difficult to recruit strong candidates to run against incumbents. Incumbents are reelected at high rates not just because of the advantages they have over challengers in terms of funding and visibility, but simply because they are often far more skilled and more experienced politicians than their opponents.

Incumbency advantage has a self-fulfilling aspect, because good potential challengers will typically perceive the long odds of defeating an incumbent and therefore choose not to enter the race. Incumbents prevail because the system of candidate recruitment throughout the United States often fails to offer voters viable alternatives.

Issue Voting

Issue preferences and even ideological beliefs figure prominently in voters' decisions. Even if most Americans devote only modest attention to political affairs, a significant number of voters are attuned to issues and base their choices on a specific issue or cluster of issues. Not a few elections turn on those margins.

Congressional Party Platforms. Partisans care deeply about the issues with which their parties are linked. In studying the 1998 House elections, Owen G. Abbe and his colleagues found that "voters are more likely to support candidates whom they deem competent on their issues." They concluded that "party leaders and individual candidates must campaign on a well-defined agenda for party-owned issues to have an impact."[109]

At least since the mid-1970s, congressional parties have forged campaign platforms. The most notable example was the GOP's "Contract with America," the brainchild of then-representative Newt Gingrich of Georgia.[110] The contract was a set of ten proposals that candidates promised to bring to the House floor if Republicans won a majority in the 1994 midterm elections. Similarly, more than a year before the 2006 balloting, House Democrats, led by the minority leader, Nancy Pelosi of California, came up with another list of initiatives known as the "Six for '06" platform. It embraced such popular goals as national security, energy independence, and economic strength. In the lead-up to the 2010 elections, congressional Republicans embraced a platform called the "Pledge to America." It included such proposals as a $100 billion cut in federal spending, an end to tax hikes, and curbs on new federal regulations.[111]

Issues and Partisanship. Voters' responses to political issues show up in the different patterns of choice displayed by demographic groups (see Figure 4-4). Americans sort themselves out politically according to their age, sex, income, education, race or ethnicity, region, and even by frequency of attendance at religious services.

A demographic snapshot of the two parties' voters would start at the much-discussed gender gap, the difference in voting between men and women. Women lean toward Democratic candidates, men toward Republicans. The gender gap appears in virtually all recent contests. As pollster Celinda Lake remarked, "You'll get [a gender gap] in a race for dogcatcher in Montana, if it's a Republican against a Democrat."[112] The gender gap was 8 points in 2012 and 10 points in 2014. The explanation for the gender gap probably lies in differing responses to political and social issues. Men are more apt to favor military expenditures, tough anti-crime laws, and restrictions on welfare recipients and immigrants. Women are more supportive of social programs such as government-sponsored health benefits, job training, child care, and assistance to needy families.[113]

A host of similar patterns is found among congressional voters. "There's a family gap, a generation gap, a gender gap," said GOP pollster Neil Newhouse of the fissures among the voting population.[114] Many of the patterns are familiar. The Republicans attract upper-income and conservative voters; the Democrats engage lower-income and liberal voters. The Republicans draw upon married people, whites, regular churchgoers, gun owners, small-business owners, and older people; the Democrats attract singles and young people, African Americans, Hispanics, Jews, the secular, and occasional churchgoers. Such loyalties are built on issues and themes adopted by parties and candidates over the years.

Issues and Campaigns. Legislators and their advisers try to anticipate voters' reactions to their stands on issues. They devote much energy to framing positions, communicating them (sometimes in deliberately vague language), and assessing their effect. Moreover, every professional politician can relate cases in which issues tipped an election one way or another. Frequently cited is the electoral influence of single-interest groups. Some citizens vote according to a single issue they regard as paramount—for example, gun control, abortion, or gay marriage. Even if few in number, such voters can decide close contests. For that reason, legislators often shrink from taking positions on such hot-button issues.

Public policy issues also have powerful indirect effects on election outcomes. Issues motivate "opinion leaders," voters who can influence support far beyond their single vote. Organized interests also carefully monitor lawmakers' behavior and then channel or withhold funds, publicity, and other campaign assistance accordingly. Legislators devote time and attention to promoting and explaining issues to attentive publics because it pays for them to do so.

ELECTION OUTCOMES

The two Congresses are apparent throughout congressional elections. House and Senate contests are waged one by one on local turf, but always against a backdrop of national events, issues, and partisan alignments. The involvement of national party entities and their allied interest groups has imposed a greater degree of national coordination on congressional campaigns, especially those in marginal states and districts. The resulting fusion of local and national forces shapes the content and results of congressional elections.

FIGURE 4-4   **Who Were the Voters in 2014?**

Percentage of voters		For Democrat		For Republican
	Total vote	46		52
49	Men	41		57
51	Women	51		47
75	White	38		60
12	Black	89		10
8	Hispanic/Latino	62		36
3	Asian	49		50
2	Other	49		47
13	Under 30 years	54		43
22	30–44 years	50		48
43	45–64 years	45		53
22	65 years and older	41		57
2	Not a high school graduate	54		44
18	High school graduate	45		33
29	College incomplete	44		50
51	College graduate and/or postgraduate study	49		54
20	East	55		43
25	Midwest	45		53
33	South	38		59
22	West	50		48
53	Protestant	37		61
25	White evangelical or born-again Christian	20		78
24	Catholic	45		54
3	Jewish	66		33
36	Family income < $50,000	54		43
34	$50,000–$99,999	44		55
30	$100,000 or more	41		57
35	Democratic	92		7
28	Independent	42		54
36	Republican	5		94
23	Liberal	87		11
40	Moderate	53		45
37	Conservative	13		85

Source: Data from *Washington Post*, "Exit Polls," http://www.washingtonpost.com/wp-srv/special/politics/2014-midterms/exit-polls/.

Notes: Percentages based on Democratic, Republican, and other (not shown) votes. Data based on questionnaires completed by voters leaving polling places around the nation on election day, 2014.

Party Balance

Despite the oft-claimed independence of candidates and voters, almost all races are run under either the Democratic or Republican Party label, fought on playing fields tilted toward one party or the other, and aimed mainly at loyalists who are likely to turn out for their party's candidates.

Shifting Majorities. In some respects, the overall partisan outcome of the 2014 contests was fixed months and even years before the actual balloting. With voters still anxious about the economy and President Obama's approval ratings hovering around 42 percent, it was clear that the elections would be difficult for Democrats. Senate Democrats were heavily "exposed" going into 2014 in that the party had to defend more than twice as many seats as did Republicans. Conventional wisdom early in the cycle held that Democrats had a good chance of losing control of the Senate. Meanwhile, benefiting from both incumbency advantage and the favorable outcome of the 2010 redistricting process, Republicans were well positioned to maintain their House majority. In the end, the Republicans gained more than enough seats to take over the Senate, while also adding to their House majority.

Taking a longer view, the outcome was predictable in that either the Democrats or the Republicans have controlled Congress since 1855 (see Appendix A for a list of the partisan majorities in the House and Senate since 1901). Between 1896 and 1920, the two parties had approximately equal numbers of partisans in the electorate, but lower participation rates in Democratic areas favored the Republicans. The GOP's relative position improved further after 1920, when women received the vote.

The New Deal realignment of the 1930s shifted the balance to the Democrats. For many years after that, the Democrats were a perennial majority and the Republicans a permanent minority on Capitol Hill. Between 1932 and 1994, the Republicans controlled both chambers simultaneously for only four years (1947–1949, 1953–1955). Democratic sweeps in 1958, 1964, and 1974 padded their majorities. Republicans found the Democratic dominance in Congress hard to overcome, even in years when voters strongly backed Republican presidential candidates. Democrats were able to maintain their majorities, as long-serving incumbents effectively exploited their positions of influence and their ability to steer government benefits back home.

In recent decades, however, no party has been able to take control of Congress for granted. Since Republicans won control of the Senate in 1980, neither party has been secure in its control of that chamber. Similarly, control of the House has been a far more open question since the Republican victory of 1994 than during the long years of Democratic dominance. Even while Republicans clung to their post-1994 majority in the House for the next decade, Democrats steadily gained seats throughout the 1990s, and Republicans' control of the chamber progressively narrowed. In 2006 Democrats returned to majority status in both the House and the Senate. They then expanded these margins of control in the 2008 elections.

In 2010, however, all the House Democratic gains of 2006 and 2008 were wiped out. Republicans retook House control (242–193), gaining their largest majority in that chamber in sixty-four years. Republicans retained their House majority in 2012, with only a loss of eight seats, and gained another 13 seats in 2014. Even so, no analyst believes that the era of intense two-party competition for control of Congress has yet come to an end.

Regional Patterns. Recent elections have cemented long-term shifts in the two parties' power bases. Historically, the Grand Old Party was dominant in the populous states of the Northeast and Midwest. "The Democracy," by contrast, owned the solid South from the Civil War era through the 1970s, as well as the large urban political machines. Today, many of the old patterns are precisely reversed, with the Republican Party dominant in the South and the Democratic Party ascendant in the Northeast.[115] The tectonic plates of political alliances move slowly, but they sometimes produce changes of earthquake proportions.

The 1994 earthquake signaled the Republicans' conquest of the South. For the first time in history, the GOP claimed a majority of the South's seats. The party's grip on the region continued to tighten in subsequent election cycles. By 2015 Republicans held 73 percent of House seats and 86 percent of Senate seats belonging to the eleven states of the Confederacy. The modern-day GOP is currently the party of choice for conservative white southerners.

Regionally, the South, the Great Plains, and the Mountain West form the backbone of the congressional GOP. Fully 40 percent of the Republican Conference in both chambers is now from the South, even though that region accounts for only a quarter of the Senate and a third of the House districts. In its other regional bastions, the Great Plains and the Mountain West, Republicans claim 77 percent of senators and 76 percent of House districts. Taken together, these regions account for approximately 55 percent of the GOP's House majority and 72 percent of its Senate contingent. The Great Lakes states constitute a competitive region, with Republicans controlling 60 percent of its House seats but only one-third of its Senate seats.

Democrats are strongest on the coastal edges of the national map—the Northeast, the Mid-Atlantic, and the West Coast. The eleven states of New England and the Mid-Atlantic are overwhelmingly Democratic (though some have lost population and thus House seats). In these states—all of which were in the Democratic Party's column in the last three presidential elections—the party claims 65 percent of House seats and 77 percent of Senate seats. In New England, the GOP holds only two House seats and two out of twelve Senate seats. Similarly, Democrats dominate the country's western coast. All four Pacific Rim states (excluding Alaska) were won by Democratic candidates in the last four presidential elections. Democrats control fifty-one of the region's seventy House seats and all eight of its Senate seats.

Looking beyond such regional patterns, the two parties tend to represent different kinds of districts. Democratic strength lies in cities, inner suburbs, and majority-minority districts, including those in the South and Midwest.

Republicans dominate rural, small-town, and exurban areas. Meanwhile, Democratic voters are more packed together in the districts held by Democrats than are Republican voters in the districts held by their party, which means that Democratic candidates tend to win by larger majorities than Republican winners normally do. Put another way, more Democratic votes are wasted (that is, inefficiently distributed across congressional districts), giving the GOP a structural advantage.[116]

Polarized Parties, Polarized Voters? Underlying this geographic distribution is what might be called a cultural divide between the two parties. Democrats tend to represent urban areas, where most voters favor social welfare spending and environmental and other business regulations. Urban voters also tend to take a more tolerant view of the diversity of racial, ethnic, and sexual identities. Republicans tend to be traditionalists—economic and cultural conservatives who promote businesses large and small, advocate certain religious causes, and generously support military expenditures. Such long-standing issue commitments flatly contradict anyone who claims that there is scant difference between the two parties.

How pervasive are these partisan differences within the electorate? Political elites—candidates, officeholders, activists, and strong party identifiers—have long been found at the extremes of the ideological spectrum: Democrats to the left, Republicans to the right.[117] Such activists do not represent the majority of citizens, average voters, or even average party identifiers. Most voters either identify as "moderate" or reject any ideological term to describe themselves.[118] Rank-and-file party identifiers have, however, become more ideologically polarized than in the past.[119] Many, after all, respond to the rising amount of ideological rhetoric in the contemporary political arena, including that dispensed by congressional representatives and biased cable, Internet, and other partisan communications. Moreover, these loyal voters are ardently wooed by parties and candidates, both of whom seek reliable supporters (rather than waverers) to turn out at the polls.

Party Alignment and Realignment

Historically, political upheavals have shifted party control in the House or Senate with decisive results. Political scientists and journalists often talk of "critical elections" or "critical periods" in which one party yields preeminence to another, or major voting groups alter the shape of the parties' coalitions, or both. Such watershed eras include the Civil War, the turbulent 1890s, the New Deal of the 1930s, and the Republican revolution of 1994. Each of these upheavals brought to Capitol Hill new lawmakers, new voting patterns, and new legislative priorities.[120]

Between the civil rights upheavals of the 1960s and the mid-1990s, the congressional party system went through a gradual transformation that realigned the parties on ideological lines and brought them into competitive balance. The Republican Party achieved ideological consistency by attracting southern and rural conservatives and by shedding most of its moderate wing, especially members from the Northeastern, Mid-Atlantic, and Pacific Rim states. In losing most of the South to Republicans, the Democrats also became more ideologically coherent. Long split by divisions between conservative southerners and northern liberals, by the 1990s the Democratic Party was smaller than in the past, but considerably more unified.

Realignments of the party system are only apparent in hindsight. It now seems clear that the Democratic majorities of the 110th and 111th Congresses (2007–2011) were not grounded in any long-term shifts of voter alliances. Political scientist James Campbell views the post-2010 Republican House majority as a "return to the normal party balance of recent decades," reflecting the temperament of the United States as a center-right country.[121] Indeed, Republicans may enjoy an enduring congressional majority post-2010, especially in view of the hurdles to defeating incumbents and the structural advantages they hold in congressional districts. Still, the Republican margin of control is relatively narrow and vulnerable to a partisan wave election. Today's party system remains in the same tight competitive balance characteristic of the 1990s.

Turnover and Representation

Reelection rates should not be confused with turnover rates. Even in years when few members are turned out of office by the voters, many leave Capitol Hill voluntarily—to retire, to run for another office, or to follow other pursuits. In other words, the natural process of membership change is continuous. Although the vast majority of incumbents seeking reelection won in 2014, the new Congress that convened in January 2015 included thirteen new senators and sixty-one new House members. More than 25 percent of each chamber had served less than two years.[122]

For Congress to be a responsive institution, constant turnover of members is essential—whether by steady increments or by watershed elections. Even when few lawmakers are turned out of office, all of them are keenly aware of the threat of defeat. Most take steps to prevent that eventuality by continually monitoring constituents' needs and opinions through personal visits and polls. But are voters' views accurately reflected by the representatives they elect to Congress? This question is not easily answered. Popular control of policy makers is not the same thing as popular control of policies. Constituents' views are not precisely mirrored by legislators' voting behavior or by the laws passed by the legislature.

CONCLUSION

What links voters' attitudes and members' voting on issues? In the 1960s, Warren E. Miller and Donald E. Stokes found that constituency attitudes correlated differently depending on the kind of policy.[123] In foreign affairs, constituents' attitudes and legislators' votes exhibited a negative correlation; in social and economic welfare issues the correlation was moderate; in civil rights issues the correlation was very high. In other words, in at least one and possibly two major policy areas the linkage was weak enough to cast some doubt on constituency control.

Political scientists explain the absence of strong linkages by noting how difficult it is to meet all the conditions needed for popular control of policies. Voters would have to identify the candidates' positions on issues, and they would have to vote by referring to those positions. Differences among candidates would have to be transparent, and winners would have to vote in accord with their preelection attitudes. These conditions are not routinely met. Candidates' stands are not always clear, and candidates do not invariably differentiate themselves on issues.

Nevertheless, winning candidates learn from their campaign experiences, even from issues raised by their opponents. *Issue uptake* is the term coined by political scientist Tracy Sulkin to describe this effect. From her study of the issue agendas of 473 House and Senate campaigns and the winners' subsequent legislative activity, she demonstrates that the victors embrace many of their opponents' campaign themes when they return to Capitol Hill. "Congressional campaigns have a clear legacy in the content of legislators' agendas," she writes, "influencing the areas in which they choose to be active and the intensity with which they pursue these activities."[124] Legislative responsiveness is best thought of as a process:

> It begins in campaigns as candidates learn about the salience of issues and their strengths and weaknesses on them; continues throughout winning legislators' terms in office, influencing not just how they vote but also the content of legislation they introduce, cosponsor, and speak about on the floor; goes on to inform their career decisions and future electoral prospects; and leaves a tangible trace on public policy outputs.[125]

If ideological or attitudinal links between voters and their representatives are rough and variable, actual contacts between constituents and individual legislators are numerous and palpable. Much of lawmakers' time and effort while in office is devoted to responding to the folks back home. Constituency politics are ever present in the daily lives of senators and representatives. The two Congresses are distinct but inextricably linked.

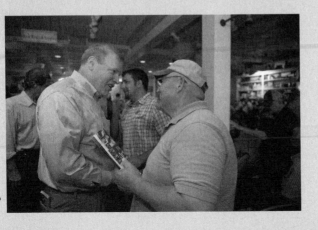

Lawmakers on the Hill and at Home. Rep. Tammy Duckworth, D-Ill., after taking her oath of office in January 2013. An Asian American, she is the first disabled woman to serve in the House, having lost both her legs in the Iraq war. Sen. Susan Collins (R-Maine) addresses the *Fortune* Most Powerful Women Summit in Washington, D.C. Collins's reputation as a pragmatic deal-maker on Capitol Hill has helped her cultivate strong support in her Democratic-leaning state. And two lawmakers reach out to their constituents: Rep. Lynn Jenkins, R-Kan., talks with district voters in Valley Falls, and Rep. Morgan Griffith, R-Va., greets constituents at the Floyd Country Store in Floyd, Virginia.

Being There:
Hill Styles and Home Styles

Touring an Alzheimer's care unit in Yarmouth, Maine, Sen. Susan Collins, R-Maine, touted a recent spending bill that she had helped steer through Congress, which provided an extra $120 million for Alzheimer's research. Collins declared that the additional funding was a "good start" but that much more was needed to find effective treatments for the devastating disease.[1] A moderate Republican from a Democratic-leaning state, Collins has used her seat on the powerful Senate Appropriations Committee to deliver programs that appeal to home-state voters across party lines. A provision in a spending bill approved in December 2014 helped an important state industry by requiring that fresh white potatoes be included in the federal Women's, Infants, and Children supplemental food assistance program. Collins hailed the change, arguing that "Potatoes are an affordable and nutrient-dense food that all WIC participants should be able to purchase."[2]

But Collins's local appeal does not rest simply on delivering for her state. She has cultivated a reputation as a deal-maker in Washington who can get things done on national issues. A Maine Democratic strategist noted admiringly that "You frequently see her right in the middle of the legislative mix in Washington. . . . I think the senator's team has done a considerable job continually pushing out that message and basically reinforcing that persona here at home."[3] One of Collins's signature legislative accomplishments was guiding a complex, bipartisan intelligence reform bill through fierce turf battles while chairing the Senate Homeland Security and Governmental Affairs Committee in 2004.[4] Collins has also at times been a key player in intense partisan fights over taxation and spending, generally trying to position herself as a voice of moderation pursuing common ground.[5] Soon after Barack Obama took office, Collins was one of just three Republicans to provide the votes necessary to push his $800 billion stimulus to enactment.[6] Facing a moderate, independent-leaning electorate, Collins also became one of the first Republican senators to endorse same-sex marriage.[7] A GOP strategist noted that "Mainers respect people who sort of break the mold a little bit, demonstrate their independence and demonstrate their willingness to chart their own course and do what they think is right instead of what the party believes and the president believes."

After initially securing election to the Senate by a fairly narrow, 49 percent to 44 percent margin in 1996, Collins has won handily in each of her reelection bids. In November 2014, she defeated her Democratic challenger, Shenna Bellows, by a 68 percent to 32 percent margin. Explaining the Maine Republican's ability to cruise to reelection in a state that voted twice for Obama, Collins's spokesperson highlighted voters' appreciation for "personal and approachable politicians who really make an effort to meet their constituents." But Collins's electoral success also reflects an approach to her Washington work that complements her reputation at home as a pragmatic problem-solver rather than a partisan warrior.

A local champion and a national leader, Susan Collins personifies the two Congresses. All members live and work in these two worlds: one on Capitol Hill and the other back home in their states and districts.

HILL STYLES

Congress is a body of transplanted locals who naturally speak up for their constituents. However, the ability of Congress to reflect the nation's large and varied population is affected by the diversity of its membership. There is no substitute for having a member of one's own group in a position of influence, and many groups do not receive representation commensurate with their presence in the population.

Who Are the Legislators?

Elections, as Aristotle first observed, are essentially oligarchic affairs that involve few active participants. The active participants are self-starters and risk-takers willing to seek an electoral "contract" for two or six years with no guarantee of renewal. In addition, by almost any measure senators and representatives constitute an economic and social elite. They are well educated. They come from prestigious occupations. The pay of senators and representatives ($174,000 since 2009) alone puts them in the top 5 percent of the nation's wage earners, but many members also have earned or inherited considerable wealth.[8] In 2014 around half of House members were millionaires, along with about two-thirds of senators.[9]

The elite character of the congressional membership raises questions of representation. One central purpose of a representative body is to bring together diverse individuals to deliberate on public policy. When the diversity of viewpoints is systematically limited, important interests and concerns are likely to be overlooked or undervalued. As John Stuart Mill argued a century and a half ago, "In the absence of its natural defenders, the interest of the omitted is always in danger of being overlooked."[10]

To meet Mill's standards for representation, must Congress closely mirror the demographics of the populace? Hannah Pitkin distinguishes between two types of representation: *descriptive* and *substantive*.[11] "Descriptive representation" refers to whether a legislature's membership reflects the diversity of backgrounds and interests in society. "Substantive representation" occurs when legislators consciously act as agents for constituents and their interests—an activity legislators can perform regardless of their personal background or group memberships. For example, legislators can voice farmers' concerns even if they have never plowed a field. Whites can champion equal opportunities for minorities.

Although descriptive representation and substantive representation are conceptually distinct, a wide range of empirical research has found that they are intertwined in the real world. The social identity of legislators affects representation in myriad ways. Representatives' racial, ethnic, and gender identities shape their priorities, positions, and legislative styles.[12] Whether constituents and representatives share a common identity has also been shown to affect trust and patterns of contact between them.[13]

Education and Occupation. By every measure, Congress is a highly educated body.[14] When the 114th Congress convened in January 2015, 94 percent of House members and 100 percent of senators held university degrees. Nearly two-thirds had graduate degrees. Twenty-two had medical degrees.

Historically, law and politics have been closely linked in the United States. A humorist once quipped that the U.S. government "of laws and not men" is really "of lawyers and not men." And indeed, at the beginning of the 114th Congress, 159 representatives and 54 senators were law school graduates.

That so many members have law degrees does not necessarily mean that they possess extensive experience in the practice of law. "They are not, by and large, successful lawyers who left thriving partnerships to run for public office," observes Alan Ehrenhalt. "Rather, they are political activists with law degrees."[15] Legal training develops skills that are useful in gaining and holding public office, such as verbalization, advocacy, and negotiation. A law degree also serves as a stepping-stone into public service at many levels. Lawyers monopolize elected law enforcement and judicial posts, two main pathways to Congress. Hill staffers are often expected to have law degrees, and many members of Congress start out on Capitol Hill as staff aides. The 114th Congress is home to at least one hundred former congressional staffers.

The historical dominance of lawyers on Capitol Hill has nevertheless declined in recent decades. Lawyers are now outnumbered by members from other careers. Today's Congress is filled with professional public servants or, in common parlance, "career politicians." The 114th Congress includes thirty-nine former mayors, ten former governors, eight former lieutenant governors, fifteen former judges, one former cabinet secretary, and three ambassadors. Just over half of senators (fifty-three) are former House members.

A significant contingent of Congress members have served in the military, though the veterans' ranks have thinned over time. After World War II, returning veterans surged into Congress. Among them were Reps. John F. Kennedy, D-Mass.; Richard M. Nixon, R-Calif.; Gerald R. Ford, R-Mich.; and Bob Dole, R-Kan. By the 1970s, more than seven of ten members were veterans. As the World War II era receded and draftees were replaced by a volunteer force, fewer veterans were elected. Just 19 percent of the members of the 114th

Congress have served in the military.[16] A small group of members currently serve in the Reserves and the National Guard.

Today's media-centered campaigns have spawned a few celebrity legislators. Several astronauts, including Sen. Bill Nelson, D-Fla., have served. Name recognition from his career as a writer and performer on *Saturday Night Live* helped launch the political career of Sen. Al Franken, D-Minn.

Many occupations are, and always have been, drastically underrepresented in Congress. Low-status occupations—including farm labor, service trades, manual and skilled labor, and domestic service—are extremely rare on Capitol Hill.[17] A recent study finds that the underrepresentation of these lower-status occupations undermines their substantive representation when Congress considers economic issues.[18] Not a few members, however, held menial jobs at some point in their lives. For example, at a hearing on Social Security taxes for household help, Rep. Carrie P. Meek, D-Fla. (1993–2003), a granddaughter of slaves, brought her own vivid experiences to the proceedings. "I was once a domestic worker," she told her colleagues. "My mother was a domestic worker. All my sisters were domestic workers."[19] Such perspectives are valuable for congressional representation and deliberation.

Race. African Americans, who make up 13.2 percent of the nation's population, account for 10.1 percent of the membership of the House of Representatives and 2 percent of the Senate. In 2015, forty-four African Americans served in the House: forty-two Democrats and two Republicans. One of the two African American senators (Sen. Tim Scott, S.C.) is a Republican. Although African American representation in Congress still does not reflect their proportion of the nation's population, black legislators have gained seniority and congressional influence over time.[20]

Other minorities are more severely underrepresented. Latinos make up 17.1 percent of the U.S. population but only 7.4 percent of the House membership and 3 percent of the Senate. Of the thirty-two Latino representatives, most are Mexican Americans. All three Latino senators, however, are Cuban Americans. Of the Latino members of the 114th Congress, twenty-three are Democrats and twelve are Republicans. Asians and Pacific Islanders claim eleven representatives and one senator—all but one are Democrats. There are two Native Americans, both House Republicans.

The growing presence of racial minorities in Congress has had beneficial effects on representational bonds with minority communities. African Americans represented by black lawmakers, for example, tend to know more about their representatives and hold them in higher esteem.[21] "Even controlling for party affiliation," Katherine Tate's survey of black constituents found, "black legislators received significantly higher ratings on average than their white counterparts."[22] Another study showed that constituents of the same race as the incumbent were 27 percent more likely than constituents of other races to recognize the name of their representative.[23]

A growing scholarly literature also suggests that descriptive representation on Capitol Hill yields substantive benefits for minority communities.

Black legislators are more active on issues of importance to their constituents of color—that is, they are more likely than their white colleagues to introduce bills on subjects of special concern to black Americans, and to attend committee meetings, offer amendments, and participate in deliberations on these issues.[24]

Gender. Neither chamber accurately reflects the nation in terms of gender. Congress historically has been a male bastion. In international comparisons, it still is: the United States ranks eightieth worldwide in the proportion of women serving in the national legislature.[25] Diversity has developed slowly. Unable to vote nationally until 1920, women have always been underrepresented in Congress. Beginning in 1917 with Rep. Jeannette Rankin, R-Mont., the presence of women in Congress has grown slowly. A record number of women serve in the 114th Congress—eighty-four representatives (nineteen of them in the California delegation) and twenty senators (two each from California, New Hampshire, and Washington).[26] More than 70 percent are Democrats. Among them, Nancy Pelosi, D-Calif., serves as House Democratic leader and was the first woman to serve as Speaker of the House (2007–2011).

The advent of a critical mass of women has changed Congress. Policy concerns once labeled "women's issues"—which, in truth, affect everyone— now receive a respectful hearing. Gender discrimination, women's health, sexual assault in the military, and issues involving the balance between family and workplace are more seriously addressed. Rep. Nita M. Lowey, D-N.Y., whose mother died of breast cancer, pressed for increased funding for research on the disease. During a debate over family leave policy, Sen. Patty Murray, D-Wash., recalled having to quit a secretarial job sixteen years earlier when she was pregnant with her first child. "When a person in this body gets up and speaks from personal experience, it changes the whole nature of the debate," observed Sen. Chris Dodd, D-Conn.[27] Referring to the women serving in the Senate, Senator Murray declared, "We've made it okay for men to talk about these [women's] issues, too."[28] Political science research offers systematic confirmation that the presence of women has had notable effects on Congress. Women legislators are more likely than men to introduce, sponsor, and press for bills of special concern to women and children.[29] Early in the 114th Congress, female Republicans took the lead in sidetracking a leadership-sponsored bill to ban abortions after twenty weeks; most of the female lawmakers favored the general principle behind the bill, but they argued that the bill did not do enough to accommodate rape victims.[30]

Only a handful of women members are mothers of school-age children. They undoubtedly face special challenges. Asked about the hardest thing about being a mother of young children while serving in Congress, Rep. Kristi Noem, R-S.D., said: "It isn't easy being away from my kids during the weeks I spend in D.C."[31] Nevertheless, the presence of moms on the Hill undoubtedly enriches representation. "Having kids is very relevant for a member of Congress," says former representative Pat Schroeder, D-Colo. (1973–1997), whose children were young when she arrived on Capitol Hill.[32]

One challenge that women lawmakers face is that voters tend to view them as less competent on military and security issues.[33] To counter voters' stereotypes of female politicians in the post-9/11 environment, scholar Michele Swers finds that women legislators have expanded their activity and visibility on defense issues, particularly on homeland security matters.[34] As noted above, Sen. Susan Collins played a key role in securing passage of a major intelligence reform bill in 2004.[35] Female senators have continued to play a crucial role in debates over security in the Obama years. As Senate Intelligence Committee chair in the 113th Congress, Dianne Feinstein, D-Calif., became a leading voice in the national conversation on the CIA's post-9/11 interrogation program, releasing a major report that rekindled an intense public debate on torture.[36] In sum, women legislators today are active far beyond the so-called women's issues.

Sexual Orientation. Gays and lesbians passed a milestone in 1998 when Tammy Baldwin, D-Wis., became the first lesbian representative whose sexual orientation was known before her initial election. (Other congressional gays and lesbians revealed their sexuality or were outed after they had served for some time; some remain in the closet.) Baldwin did not shy away from the issue. Her campaign slogan was "A different kind of candidate." In 2013 Baldwin became the nation's first openly gay senator.

As with other types of social identity, electing gay and lesbian representatives matters for the group's representation. Indeed, one recent study found that the presence of lesbian and gay elected officials was the single most important factor affecting local adoption of domestic partner benefits.[37] Still, as Rep. Barney Frank, D-Mass., has pointed out, the hardest part of running as a gay man is "convincing voters that you will not disproportionately focus on that minority's issues."[38]

Religion. Ninety-eight percent of all members of Congress cite a specific religious affiliation. By comparison, about 20 percent of Americans do not identify with any particular faith; indeed, the fastest-growing category in recent surveys of American religion is "unaffiliated."[39] Protestants collectively make up a majority of the 114th Congress, but about 30 percent of House and Senate members are Roman Catholics, the largest single religious denomination. Jews account for 5 percent. The 114th Congress also includes sixteen Mormons, two Buddhists, two Muslims, and one Hindu.[40]

Age and Tenure. When the 114th Congress convened in 2015, the average age of members was among the highest in history: fifty-seven for representatives, sixty-one for senators.[41] Tenure as well as age has risen since the early days. "Few die, and none retire," it was said as the twentieth century began. Today, the average member of Congress has served for approximately a decade.[42]

Age and tenure levels fluctuate over time. Periods of relatively low turnover (the 1980s, for example) are punctuated by dramatic changings of the guard. The 2010 election was one such moment. Fully 21 percent of the House and 15 percent of the Senate were freshmen in the ensuing 112th Congress. The GOP wave in 2014 helped bring in another relatively large freshman class, with fifty-eight new House members and thirteen new senators. Similar turn-overs occurred in the 1970s and the 1990s, involving both senior and junior members of Congress.[43] Electoral defeats play some role, but the majority of members leave voluntarily. Of course, many departing members retire just because they anticipate electoral difficulty.[44]

A certain balance between new blood and stable membership is undoubtedly optimal for legislative bodies. Rapid turnover—the early 1990s and 2006–2014, for example—can sharpen generational conflict. Many newly elected members indulge in Congress-bashing in their campaigns and want to shake up the institution, and not a few of them shun the idea of making a career of public service. The anti-establishment attitudes of members of the Tea Party caucuses on Capitol Hill are not unusual among large classes of relative newcomers. Reflecting on these troublesome freshmen, former Senate majority leader Trent Lott, R-Miss., said, "As soon as they get here, we need to co-opt them."[45] If past is prologue, many will eventually settle into the established power structure on Capitol Hill.

Equal Representation of States. The equal voice that all states have in the Senate is a central feature of congressional representation. The Senate's divergence from a population-based representation affects the welfare of many social and economic groups. It enlarges the voice of farmers, ranchers, mining interests, and users of federal lands—all groups that have far more presence in the less populous states than in the nation as a whole. At the same time, racial and ethnic minorities—already underrepresented in Congress relative to their share of the nation's population—are further disadvantaged by the Senate's makeup.[46] The nation's populous states are more racially and ethnically diverse than its less populous ones, and so one effect of Senate representation is to boost the voting power of the predominantly white residents of lightly populated states and to confer less voting power on the more racially diverse residents of populous states.[47]

Equal state representation in the Senate has other meaningful effects as well. Bonds between senators and their constituents are closer and more person-alized in less populous states than in more populous ones.[48] And when Congress makes decisions about distributing federal dollars, less populous states receive more benefits than they pay in taxes, whereas populous states provide more revenue but receive fewer returns. Small-population states are advantaged across most federal spending programs, with the effect most pronounced on the types of programs over which Congress maintains tightest control.[49]

Collective Representation. Representation does not always follow state or district boundaries. It occurs when citizens feel they are served by any member of Congress, not just their local member. Congressional represen-tation is, as Robert Weissberg put it, "collective," not just "dyadic."[50] In other words, representation involves more than the interactions between individual members and the residents of their geographic constituencies. Citizens can feel a sense of connection to Congress when the body as a whole includes members who speak for them. When someone from an ethnic or racial minority background goes to Congress, it is often a matter of pride for an entire identity group. Such legislators speak for people like themselves throughout the nation.[51]

Many constituencies are represented in the same way. One member who suffers from epilepsy defends job rights for other sufferers of the condition; another whose grandson was born prematurely champions funds for medical research into birth defects; members who are openly gay speak out for the rights of homosexuals everywhere. Such causes are close to members' hearts, even though they may pay scant political dividends. Legislators' backgrounds, religious beliefs, social identities, and experiences all shape their views and priorities. Political scientist Barry C. Burden refers to such influences as "the personal roots of representation," and he argues that analysts must take them into account to understand legislators' policy activism in Congress.[52]

Congressional Roles

Members of Congress, as Richard F. Fenno Jr. explains, spend their lives "moving between two contexts, Washington and home, and between two activities, governing and campaigning."[53] The two contexts and the two activities are continuously interwoven. How members govern is deeply affected by their constituency roots and their campaign experiences. In turn, their Capitol Hill activities affect all their subsequent contacts with people back home. As members carry out their representational functions, it is possible to distinguish three roles undertaken to some degree by most members of Congress: legislator, constituency servant, and partisan.

Legislator. The rules, procedures, and traditions of the House and Senate impose many constraints on members' behavior. To be effective, new members must learn their way through the institutional maze. Legislators therefore stress the formal aspects of Capitol Hill duties and routines: legislative work, investigation, and committee specialization. Sen. Charles E. Schumer, D-N.Y., an elected official for most of his life (he was elected to the state assembly at age twenty-three and served nine terms in the U.S. House), explained his commitment as a professional legislator during his successful 1998 Senate campaign:

> I love to legislate. Taking an idea—often not original with me—shaping it, molding it. Building a coalition of people who might not completely agree with it. Passing it and making the country a little bit of a better place. I love doing that.[54]

Legislators pursue information and expertise on issues, not only because of their personal interest in public policy but also because it sways others in the chamber. To influence other members, a legislator must be perceived as credible and knowledgeable—in other words, someone worth listening to.

The legislator's role often dovetails with that of representing constituents. Most members seek committee assignments that will serve the needs of their states or districts. One House member related why he sought a seat on the committee handling flood control and water resource development. "The interests of my district dictated my field of specialization," he explained, "but the decision to specialize in some legislative field is automatic for the member who wants to exercise any influence."[55]

Members soon learn the norms, or folkways, that expedite legislative productivity. Examining the post–World War II Senate, Donald R. Matthews identified folkways that restrained and channeled members' legislative activity. Senators were encouraged to serve an apprenticeship, deferring to elders in their early years; to concentrate on Senate work instead of on gaining publicity; to specialize in issues within their committees or affecting their home states; and to extend reciprocity to colleagues—that is, provide willing assistance with the expectation that it would be repaid in kind one day.[56]

These folkways have faded in importance in the contemporary Senate. Barbara Sinclair's major reassessment of senators' Hill styles concluded that the restrained activism of the 1950s Senate had given way to unrestrained activism in the contemporary era.[57] New senators now actively take part in most aspects of the chamber's work, ignoring the apprenticeship norm. Many senators, especially those with an eye on the White House, work tirelessly to attract national publicity and personal attention. Committee specialization, although still common, is less rigid than it once was. Senators now have many overlapping committee assignments and are expected to express views on a wide range of issues.

The House relies more on formal channels of power than on informal norms. From interviews, however, Herbert B. Asher uncovered some key House norms.[58] Among them are the beliefs that the important work of the House should be done in committees, and that members should specialize in the issues before their committees. Members should be prepared to bargain and trade votes. Members should learn the procedural rules of the chamber. They should not personally criticize a colleague on the House floor.

As in the Senate, House norms of earlier eras have eroded. New members, impatient to make their mark, assert themselves more quickly, aided by party leaders who worry about getting the freshmen reelected. Leadership comes earlier to members than it used to. Specialization remains more compelling in the House than in the Senate, but many members branch out into unrelated issues. No longer are committees the sole forums for influencing legislation. Many of today's members, more partisan and ideologically driven than their predecessors, shun norms such as reciprocity and compromise. One of the most striking violations of civility norms occurred during the highly contentious spring of 2010. While staunchly pro-life representative Bart Stupak, D-Mich., was announcing his support for health care reform legislation on the House floor, another House member interrupted him by shouting, "Baby killer!"[59]

Constituency Servant. As constituency servants, members of Congress attempt to give voice to local citizens' concerns, solve problems constituents encounter with federal programs, and ensure that their states and districts receive a fair share of federal dollars. Often the task is performed by legislators and their staffs as casework—individual cases triggered by constituent letters or visits. Even though mostly delegated to staff aides, this is a chore that weighs heavily on members. A House member expressed the philosophy of most legislators this way:

> Constituent work: that's something I feel very strongly about. The American people, with the growth of the bureaucracy, feel nobody cares. The only conduit a taxpayer has with the government is a congressional office.[60]

One recent field experiment analyzing members' response time to letters dealing with policy and letters requesting constituent services found that members prioritize service over policy.[61] Sometimes, members stress constituency service to gain breathing room for legislative stands that stray from district norms.

Research has shown that developing a reputation as working hard on behalf of constituents in these ways makes a positive difference for legislators' careers. A recent study found that "a constituent-service reputation generates the most positive notice among citizens . . . [while] policy expertise appears to be less valuable to, or less noticed by, constituents."[62]

Procuring pork-barrel projects for local constituencies tends to improve representatives' name recognition back home,[63] reduce their likelihood of facing a strong challenger,[64] and enhance vulnerable members' reelection chances.[65] Even while Congress has adopted bans against earmarking special projects for members' constituencies and creating tax breaks for ten or fewer beneficiaries, they recognize that their constituents still expect them to bring home the bacon. An Arkansas lobbyist tells the story of going to visit one of his state's Republican members known for his anti-pork speeches. "I know you're anti-pork," the lobbyist began, "but I have to tell you about our needs and how to position yourself." "What do you mean?" the representative retorted. "As far as I can tell, it's not pork if it's for Arkansas."[66] Members have especially strong incentives to perform the constituency servant role whenever Congress considers government programs with highly visible local benefits, such as highway or mass transit grants, water projects, and homeland security contracts.

Partisan. Members of Congress are elected not just as individual representatives, but as members of a political party. Nearly every member of Congress formally affiliates with one of the two major parties, and even the few members elected as independents organize with one of the two parties to receive their committee assignments. Party affiliation is more than a mere label for most members. Members work with and for their parties, and their partisan ties and activities have a pervasive effect on congressional elections, representation, and legislation.

Members have a personal stake in the collective fate of their parties. Whether their party commands a majority of seats in the House or Senate affects their power in the chamber and their ability to achieve personal legislative goals. The majority party elects leaders with agenda-setting responsibilities and controls the chairmanships of all committees and subcommittees in the two chambers. In addition, members know that voters' feelings about the parties will affect their own electoral chances. Former Republican senator Lincoln Chafee of Rhode Island lost his seat in 2006, despite high personal approval ratings, in large part because of his party's unpopularity in Rhode Island. "I give the voters credit," he said. "They made the connection between electing even popular Republicans at the cost of leaving the Senate in the hands of a leadership they had learned to mistrust."[67]

Many members hold posts within their congressional parties. Legislative party organizations are extensive, with whips, deputy whips, regional whips, and a variety of task forces. Elections for party positions are often hotly contested. As discussed in more detail in Chapter 6, members who hold or seek party positions dedicate significant effort to party causes. They do favors for fellow partisans and exhort them to vote the party position. They seek to impress leaders and other party members with their prodigious fund-raising and campaigning on behalf of their party's candidates.[68]

Even those members who do not serve as party officers will typically attend and participate in the party caucus. In the contemporary Congress, the House and Senate caucuses of both parties meet at least weekly. Members engage in internal party communications and party message development. They stage press conferences, reach out to sympathetic groups and opinion leaders, and coordinate floor speeches as they seek to shape media coverage to partisan advantage.[69] In short, partisan activities today place significant demands on legislators' time and energy. Not only do members seek to enact good policy as legislators and advance local concerns as constituency servants, but they also are partisans, heavily invested in the collective fortunes of their parties.

How Do Legislators Spend Their Time?

For senators and representatives, time is their most precious commodity, and lack of it is their most frequent complaint about their jobs.[70] Allocating time requires exceedingly tough personal and political choices. Members are barraged with requests for meetings with groups and constituents. They are expected to spend considerable amounts of time in their home states and districts.

Scheduling is complicated by the large number of formal work groups— mainly committees and subcommittees, but also joint, party, and ad hoc panels. The average senator sits on three full committees and seven subcommittees; representatives average two committees and four subcommittees. With so many assignments, lawmakers are hard-pressed to control their crowded schedules. Committee quorums are difficult to achieve, and members' attention is often focused elsewhere. All too often, working sessions are composed of the chair, the ranking minority member, perhaps one or two interested colleagues, and staff aides.[71]

Repeated floor votes, which lawmakers fear missing, are another time-consuming duty. In a typical Congress, more than a thousand recorded votes may be taken in the House and perhaps six hundred in the Senate. "We're like automatons," one senator complained. "We spend our time walking in tunnels to go to the floor to vote."[72] Rep. Debbie Wasserman-Schultz, D-Fla., shuns the House gym, explaining, "I get my exercise running around the Capitol."[73]

Members are under relentless pressure to raise campaign funds. As mentioned in Chapter 4, the Democratic Congressional Campaign Committee recommends that new members spend between 40 and 50 percent of their time in Washington on fund-raising. "Call time" takes a large bite out of members' daily schedule. In addition, members must set aside time for fund-raising events and other personal meetings.

Taken together, lawmakers' daily schedules in Washington are "long, fragmented, and unpredictable," according to a study based on time logs kept by senators' appointment secretaries.[74] "In Congress you are a total juggler," recalls former representative Pat Schroeder. "You have always got seventeen things pulling on your sleeve."[75] Often members have scant notice that their presence is required at a meeting or a hearing. Carefully developed schedules are frequently disrupted.

Political scientists may claim that Congress runs in harmony with members' needs, but the members know otherwise. In a survey of 114 House and Senate members, "inefficiency" was the thing that most surprised them about Congress (45 percent gave this response).[76] "[Congress] is a good job for someone with no family, no life of their own, no desire to do anything but get up, go to work, and live and die by their own press releases," quipped former representative Fred Grandy, an Iowa Republican who left Congress in 1995. "It is a great job for deviant human beings."[77]

The dilemma legislators face in allocating their time is far more than a matter of scheduling; it is a case of conflicting role expectations. Many members want to devote extra time to legislative duties than their schedules allow. There are always pressing demands to spend more time on constituency and political chores.[78] The two Congresses pull members in different directions. As a retiring House committee chair remarked:

> One problem is that you're damned if you do and damned if you don't. If you do your work here, you're accused of neglecting your district. And if you spend too much time in your district, you're accused of neglecting your work here.[79]

The Shape of the Washington Career

Once a short-term activity, congressional service has become a career. Accompanying this careerism, or longevity, is a distinctive pattern of Washington activity: the longer members remain in office, the more they sponsor bills, deliver floor speeches, and offer amendments. Despite the democratizing trends of the reform era (1960s and 1970s), senior lawmakers continue to take the lead in legislative activities.[80]

Long tenure also tends to pull members toward legislative specialization. Settling into their committee slots, members gain expertise in a distinct policy field and spend their time managing legislation and conducting oversight in that field. Seniority tends to boost legislative achievement. Veterans usually enjoy significantly more success than do freshmen in getting their bills passed.[81]

The link between members' service and their effectiveness reflects the indispensable role careerists play in the legislative process. As John R. Hibbing observed:

> Senior members are the heart and soul of the legislative side of congressional service. Relatively junior members can be given a sub-committee chairmanship, but it is not nearly so easy to give them an active, focused legislative agenda and the political savvy to enact it. Some things take time and experience, and successful participation in the legislative process appears to be one of those things.[82]

The wisdom of this statement is repeatedly borne out. One recent study drawing on the uniquely detailed data available for the North Carolina General Assembly reports that legislators' "effectiveness rises sharply with tenure," and "there is no evidence that effectiveness eventually declines with tenure, even out to nine terms."[83] The study concludes that "the increased effectiveness [of senior legislators] is due to the acquisition of specific human capital, most likely through learning-by-doing."[84] A comprehensive study of U.S. House members' abilities to get their bills past significant stages in the legislative process reports that "as members become more senior they become more efficient at arranging deals with key office-holders."[85] Newcomers bring with them zeal, energy, and fresh approaches. And yet many of them lack patience, bargaining skills, institutional memory, and respect for the lawmaking process.

LOOKING HOMEWARD

Not all of a representative's or a senator's duties lie in Washington, D.C. Legislators not only fashion policy for the nation's welfare, but they also act as emissaries from their home states or districts.

Independent Judgment or Constituency Opinion?

Although found in virtually every political system, representation is the hallmark of democratic regimes dedicated to sharing power among citizens. In small communities, decisions can be reached by face-to-face discussions, but in populous societies such personalized consultation is impossible. Thus, according to democratic theory, citizens can exert control by choosing "fiduciary agents" who will then deliberate on legislation just as their principals, the voters, would do if they could be on hand themselves.[86] But in attempting to serve as a faithful agent for constituents, legislators are faced with a central dilemma of representation: whether to take actions that are popular with constituents or to do what the legislator believes is in their best interest. As Pitkin explains,

> The representative must act in such a way that, although he is independent, and his constituents are capable of action and judgment, no conflict arises between them. He must act in their interest, and this means he must not normally come into conflict with their wishes.[87]

Recent opinion surveys seem to echo Pitkin's formulation. As one analyst puts it, "The public seems to want elected officials to internalize the majority's values and then try to assess how those values come to bear on an issue." No less than 85 percent agreed with the following statement: "The goal of Congress should be to make the decisions that a majority of Americans would make if they had the information and time to think things over that Congress has."[88]

Nonetheless, legislators must do more than register prevailing constituency opinion in order to represent their constituents. Public opinion often changes when controversy arises and constituents become more informed about issues. Legislators have to anticipate constituents' future views if an issue becomes more salient and more broadly understood.

Some representatives reject the idea that they ought to represent public opinion and instead see themselves as Burkean trustees charged with doing what is in constituents' interests. Speaking to a group of newly elected House members, Rep. Henry J. Hyde, R-Ill. (1974–2007), voiced the Burkean ideal:

> If you are here simply as a tote board registering the current state of opinion in your district, you are not going to serve either your constituents or the Congress well. You must take, at times, a national view, even if you risk the displeasure of your neighbors and friends back home. If you don't know the principle, or the policy, for which you are willing to lose your office, then you are going to do damage here.[89]

In short, legislators must instead use their superior information about policy, their broader perspective, and their personal judgment in making decisions. Nearly every member can point to conscience votes cast on deeply felt issues. A few, such as Rep. Mike Synar, D-Okla. (1979–1995), compile a contrarian record, challenging voters to admire their independence if not their policies. Synar was an unabashed liberal Democrat from a state that now elects mostly conservative Republicans. "I want to be a U.S. congressman from Oklahoma, not an Oklahoman congressman," Synar declared when he arrived in the capital.[90] If turned out of office by hostile sentiment (as Synar later was), the Burkean can at least hope for history's vindication.

In practice, legislators assume different representational styles according to the occasion. They ponder factors such as the nation's welfare, their personal convictions, and constituency opinions. "The weight assigned to each factor," writes Thomas E. Cavanagh, "varies according to the nature of the issue at hand, the availability of the information necessary for a decision, and the intensity of preference of the people concerned about the issue."[91]

Members of Congress are challenged to explain their choices to constituents—no matter how many or how few people truly care about the matter.[92] The anticipated need to explain oneself shapes a member's decisions and is part of the dilemma of choice. A cynical saying among lawmakers asserts that "a vote on anything [is] a wrong vote if you cannot explain it in a 30-second TV ad."[93]

What Are Constituencies?

Senators and representatives cannot respond equally to all the people within a given state or district. A subset of their constituents elected them, and so they interact more with supporters than with opponents. The constituencies that legislators see as they campaign or vote are quite different from the boundaries found on maps. Fenno describes a "nest" of constituencies, ranging from the widest (geographic constituency) to the narrowest (personal constituency), which is made up of supporters, loyalists, and intimates.[94]

Geographic and Demographic Constituencies. The average House district today numbers more than 713,000 people. As for senators, fourteen represent states with only one House district; the rest represent multidistrict states with as many as thirty-eight million people.[95] Such constituencies differ sharply from one another. More than half of the people in Manhattan's Upper East Side (New York's Twelfth District) have college degrees, compared with only 6 percent in California's central valley (Twenty-first District). Median family income ranges from $79,000 (New Jersey's Eleventh District, Morris County) to less than $21,000 in New York's Sixteenth District in the South Bronx, where 40 percent of the families live in poverty. Such disparities among districts shape their representatives' outlooks.

Demographically, constituencies may be homogeneous or heterogeneous.[96] Some constituencies, even a few whole states, remain uniform and one-dimensional—mostly wheat farmers or inner-city dwellers or small-town citizens. Because of rising population, economic complexity, and educational levels, however, virtually all constituencies, House as well as Senate, have become more heterogeneous than they used to be. The more diverse a constituency, the more challenging is the representative's task.

Another attribute of constituencies is electoral balance, especially as manifested in the incumbent's reelection chances. Heterogeneous districts tend to be more competitive than uniform ones. Incumbents predictably prefer safe districts—that is, those with a high proportion of groups leaning toward their party. Not only do safe districts favor reelection, but they also imply that voters will be easier to please.[97]

Truly competitive districts are not the norm, especially in the House of Representatives. In the last month leading up to the 2014 elections, analysts at the *Cook Political Report* estimated that just thirty-eight House seats were either toss-ups or merely leaning toward one political party. Indeed, the majority of successful candidates won handily: 74 percent of House victors won by 20 percentage points or more, and 16 percent faced no opposition at all. A mere 11 percent of House districts were decided by narrow margins.

As Table 5-1 shows, competitiveness varies over time. Senate seats are more likely to be closely contested than House races, but most incumbents still win in a walk.

Whatever the numbers might show, few incumbents regard themselves as truly safe. The threat of losing an election is very real. Even with incumbent reelection rates at above 90 percent, incumbent officeholders understandably fear even a 10 percent chance of losing a job they have worked so hard to win. Most lawmakers have a close call at some time in their congressional careers, and many of them eventually suffer defeat.[98] In addition to the incumbents who went down to defeat in 2014, a number of others—including four senators and some twenty-seven House members—survived while receiving what might be called warning signs from the home folks.[99] Incumbents thus worry not only about winning or losing but also about their margins of safety. Downturns in normal electoral support narrow the member's comfort zone in the job, may invite challengers in future years, and could block chances for further advancement.[100]

Political and Personal Constituencies. As candidates or incumbents analyze their electoral base, three narrower constituencies can be discerned: supporters (the reelection constituency), loyalists (the primary constituency), and intimates (the personal constituency).[101] Supporters are those who generally are expected to back the candidate in the November general election. Candidates and their advisers constantly monitor these voters, reassessing precinct-level political demography—registration figures, survey data, and recent electoral trends. The more elections incumbents have survived, the more precisely they can identify supporters. Areas and groups with the biggest payoffs are usually targeted.

Loyalists are the politician's staunchest supporters. They may share ties with the member from preelectoral ventures—civil rights, environmental, or Tea Party activists, for example. They may hail from the same religious or ethnic groups, or political or civic clubs as the candidate. They may be friends and neighbors. Whatever their source, they are willing volunteers who can be counted on to lend a hand in reelection campaigns.

Candidates dare not ignore these loyalists. A favorite story of House Speaker Thomas P. "Tip" O'Neill Jr., D-Mass. (1953–1987), emerged from his first campaign for city council (at which he failed). A neighbor told him, "Tom, I'm going to vote for you even though you didn't ask me." "Mrs. O'Brien," replied a surprised O'Neill, "I've lived across the street from you for 18 years. I shovel your walk in the winter. I cut your grass in the summer. I didn't think

TABLE 5-1   House and Senate Margins of Victory, 1974–2014

Chamber and election year	Percentage of vote				Number of seats
	Under 55	55–59.9	60 plus	Unopposed	
House					
1974	24	16	46	14	435
1976	17	14	56	12	435
1978	17	14	53	16	435
1980	18	14	60	8	435
1982	16	16	63	6	435
1984	12	13	61	14	435
1986	9	10	64	17	435
1988	6	9	67	18	435
1990	11	16	58	15	435
1992	20	18	58	3	435
1994	22	17	52	9	435
1996	22	18	57	3	435
1998	10	17	63	10	435
2000	18	12	56	14	435
2002	10	10	70	10	435
2004	7	14	64	15	435
2006	15	14	62	9	435
2008	14	16	57	12	435
2010	24	16	54	6	435
2012	17	21	59	2	435
2014	11	15	58	16	435
Senate					
1974	41	18	35	6	34
1976	30	33	30	6	33
1978	24	33	36	6	33
1980	58	18	21	3	34
1982	30	27	43	—	33
1984	18	21	58	3	33
1986	38	15	47	—	34
1988	33	15	52	—	33
1990	26	11	49	14	34
1992	34	34	32	—	35
1994	32	34	34	—	35
1996	59	18	24	—	34
1998	29	9	62	—	34
2000	29	15	55	—	34
2002	32	18	46	4	34
2004	32	15	50	3	34
2006	24	21	55	—	33
2008	26	20	51	3	35
2010	32	27	38	3	37
2012	39	27	33	0	33
2014	33	22	39	3	36

Sources: CQ Weekly and authors' calculations.

Notes: Percentages may not add to 100 because of rounding. "Unopposed" includes districts or states where only one major-party candidate was on the ballot.

I had to ask you for your vote." To this the lady replied, "Tom, I want you to know something: people like to be asked."[102] Expressions of gratitude are equally important. The elder George Bush reportedly "always carried a box of note cards with him on the campaign trail and penned a personal note immediately following each event to the volunteers and hosts."[103]

Even entrenched officeholders worry about keeping their core supporters energized. Loyalists are a politician's defenders in times of adversity. "There's a big difference between the people who are for you and the people who are excitedly for you," an Iowa politician told Fenno, "between those who will vote if they feel like it and those for whom the only election is [your] election. You need as many of that group as you can get."[104]

Intimates are close friends who supply political advice and emotional support. They may be members of the candidate's family, trusted staff members, political mentors, or individuals who shared decisive experiences early in the candidate's career. The setting and the players differ from state to state and from district to district. Tip O'Neill's inner circle was made up of the "boys" of Barry's Corner, a local clubhouse in Cambridge, Massachusetts, whose families O'Neill had known intimately over more than fifty years of political life. When Rep. David E. Price, D-N.C., first decided to run for Congress, he relied on what he called the "Wednesday night group," which he described as "an inner circle without whom the effort would never have gotten off the ground."[105] Such intimates play an indispensable role. Beyond their enthusiastic support, they provide unvarnished advice on political matters and serve as sounding boards for ideas and strategies.

Home Styles

Legislators evolve distinctive ways of presenting themselves and their records to their constituents—what Fenno calls their home styles. These styles are exhibited in members' personal appearances, mailings, newsletters, press releases, radio and television spots, and websites. Little is known about how home styles coalesce, but they are linked to members' personalities, backgrounds, constituency features, and resources. The ways members interact with constituents have a powerful effect on their electoral success. As Fenno notes, "It is the style, not the issue content, that counts most in the reelection constituency."[106]

Presentation of Self. A successful home style will elicit trust—constituents' faith that legislators are who they claim to be and will do what they promise.[107] Winning voters' trust does not happen overnight; it takes time, persistence, and consistency. Members must establish their qualification for office—that is, the belief that they are capable of handling the job. Members also strive to convey identification—the impression that legislators resemble their constituents, and empathy—the sense that legislators understand constituents' problems and care about them.

Because of the variations among legislators and constituencies, the use of many different home styles can effectively build the trust relationship. The legendary Speaker "Mr. Sam" Rayburn represented his East Texas district for nearly fifty years (1913–1961) as a plain dirt farmer. Once he was back in his hometown of Bonham, his drawl thickened; his tailored suits were exchanged for khakis, an old shirt, and a slouch hat; and he traveled not in the Speaker's limousine, but in a well-dented pickup truck. His biographer relates:

> If Rayburn ever chewed tobacco in Washington, a long-time aide could not recall it, but in Bonham he always seemed to have a plug in his cheek. He made certain always to spit in the fireplace at his home when constituents were visiting, so that if nothing else, they would take away the idea that Mr. Sam was just a plain fellow.[108]

The aim of a member's home style is to become "one of us" in constituents' estimation. Accomplishing this is a "difficult feat—far more difficult than establishing a reputation as a fine constituency servant or policy expert."[109]

Today's legislators are no less inventive in fashioning home styles. Some embrace what Fenno calls a "person-to-person" style that relies upon knowing constituents by name and meeting with them in small, face-to-face groups. Such an approach can forge a sense of deep connection between the member and his home community. Others adopt an "issue-oriented" approach, which typically involves holding many town hall events where the member articulates and defends her stances across a range of hot-button topics. The issue-oriented member conveys the impression that she is an activist, engaged in issues that her constituents view as important. Still other members rely upon their personal background to help forge a connection with constituents, such as the military veteran, who uses national defense issues to symbolize his oneness with a district supportive of the military. The repertoire of home styles is virtually limitless.

Although members retain some choice as they devise their home style, the most effective style will depend, in part, on how well the member's ideology and party fit with district dynamics. A recent study drawing upon thousands of member press releases to categorize types of home styles found that members from districts filled with out-partisans tend to emphasize credit-claiming for spending in the district, rather than articulating policy positions. By contrast, members from districts that are dominated by their copartisans adopt home styles that emphasize taking positions on a range of policies. This difference in strategies means that policy debates in Washington tend to be shaped by the more extreme voices of members from one-party districts.[110]

Voters are likely to remember style long after they forget issue statements or voting records. Even so, legislators know full well that they must explain their decisions to others.[111]

Explaining Washington Activity. Explaining is an integral part of decision making. In home district forums, constituents expect members to be able to describe, interpret, and justify their actions. If they do not agree with the member's conclusions, they may at least respect the decision-making style.

Although few incumbents fear that a single vote can defeat them, all realize that voters' disenchantment with their record can be fatal—more so in these days of Internet communications, when lobby groups publicize voting records. Although local news media coverage of Congress is often uncritical, it can promote political accountability. Local media devote more time and resources to monitoring representatives who are "out of step" with their district's presidential vote than those who are perceived to be in step. Such members face additional media scrutiny and must therefore account for their Washington decisions more frequently.[112]

Members stockpile reasons for virtually every position they take, often more than are needed. Facing especially thorny choices (for example, on aid to Wall Street firms, health care reform, or the appropriate reach of surveillance policy), they might seek a middle-of-the-road route. More often, they huddle under the umbrella of their party's line. Whatever course they choose, they will find that inconsistency is mentally and politically costly. Contrary to the popular stereotype of politicians speaking out of both sides of their mouths, members give much the same account of themselves regardless of the group they are talking to.

Constituency Careers. Constituency bonds evolve over the course of a lawmaker's career. Constituency careers have at least two recognizable stages: expansionism and protectionism. In the first stage, the member builds a reelection constituency by solidifying the help of hard-core supporters and reaching out to attract additional blocs of support. Aggressive efforts to reach out to new voters—exploiting the perquisites of incumbency, such as fundraising and an election-year avalanche of messages to constituents—account for the "sophomore surge," in which newcomers typically boost their margin in their first reelection bid. In the second stage, the member stops expanding the base, content with protecting support already won. Once established, a successful home style is rarely altered.

Certain developments, however, can lead to a change in a member's home style. One is demographic change in the constituency, as population movement or redistricting force a member to confront unfamiliar voters or territory. A second cause is a strategic reaction, such as when a fresh challenger or a novel issue threatens established voting patterns. Because coalitions may shift over time, members and their advisers pore over the results of the most recent election (and available survey results).

Finally, home styles may change with new personal goals and ambitions. Achieving positions of power in Washington can divert a member's attention from home state business. Family responsibilities or the need to improve one's financial situation may also lead to a shift in priorities. Faced with new aspirations or shifting constituency demands, some members decide to retire. Others struggle ineffectively and are defeated. Still others survive by rejuvenating their constituency base.

OFFICE OF THE MEMBER INC.

Home style includes the way a member answers day-to-day questions: How much attention should I devote to state or district needs? How much time should I spend in the state or district? How should I keep in touch with my constituents? How should I deploy staff aides to handle constituents' concerns?

Road Tripping

During the nineteenth century, legislators spent most of their time at home, traveling to Washington only when Congress was in session. However, after World War II (and the advent of both air travel from home and air-conditioning on Capitol Hill), congressional sessions lengthened until they spanned most of the year.

By the 1970s, both houses had adopted parallel schedules of sessions punctuated with district work periods (House) or nonlegislative periods (Senate). At the same time, members were permitted more paid trips to states or districts. Today, senators and representatives are allowed as many trips home as they want, subject to the limits of their official expense allowances. Many members (even those from the West Coast) go home every weekend. Today's home styles thus entail frequent commutes.

Seniority is also a factor. Senior members tend to make fewer trips to their districts than do junior members, perhaps reflecting junior members' greater attentiveness to their districts or senior members' greater Washington responsibilities. Finally, members' decisions to retire voluntarily are usually accompanied by large drops in trips home.

Constituency Casework

"All God's chillun got problems," exclaimed Rep. Billy Matthews, D-Fla. (1953–1967), as he pondered mail from his constituents.[113] In the early days, lawmakers lacked staff aides and wrote personally to executive agencies for help in matters such as pension or land claims and appointments to military academies. The Legislative Reorganization Act of 1946 provided de facto authority for hiring caseworkers, first in Senate offices and later in the House.

What are these cases all about? As respondents in a nationwide survey reported, the most frequent reason for contacting a member's office (16 percent of all cases) is to express views or obtain information on legislative issues. Requests for help in finding government jobs form the next largest category, followed by cases dealing with government services such as Social Security, veterans' benefits, or unemployment compensation. Military cases (for example, transfers, discharges, or personal hardships) are numerous, as are tax, legal, and immigration problems. Constituents often ask for government publications. And there are requests for flags that have flown over the U.S. Capitol.

Many citizen appeals, moreover, betray a hazy understanding of the officeholder's duties. Rep. Luis V. Gutierrez, D-Ill. (1993–2009), reported being barraged with all manner of complaints and requests when he shopped in his North Side Chicago neighborhood. Examples of what he has heard are: "They haven't picked up my trash!" (the city's job). "Can you get my son a scholarship to the state university?" (a state matter). Or "I can't pay my child support" (personal). Rep. Gutierrez's personal favorite was: "I own property in Puerto Rico and someone is blocking my driveway."[114]

Cases arrive in legislators' offices by letter, phone, e-mail, fax, or in person at district or mobile offices. All representatives and senators now have e-mail addresses and websites with contact information. Occasionally, members themselves pick up cases from talking to constituents. Indeed, many hold office hours in their districts for this purpose. When a constituent's request is received, it is usually acknowledged promptly by a letter that either fulfills the request or promises that an answer will be forthcoming.

Keeping up with incoming communications is a priority for all congressional offices. If the constituent's request requires contacting a federal agency, the contact in the executive agency is usually a liaison officer. Once the problem has been conveyed, it is a matter of time before a decision is reached and a reply forwarded to the congressional office. The reply is then sent along to the constituent, perhaps with a cover letter signed by the member. If the agency's reply is deemed faulty, the caseworker may ask for reconsideration; in some cases the member may personally intervene to lend weight to the appeal.

The volume of casework varies from state to state and from district to district. Demographic variation affects casework volume because some types of citizens simply are more likely to have contact with government agencies. Senators representing the smallest states often have casework loads that exceed those of House members, because their greater institutional clout makes them even more attractive to small-state residents than their state's House members. By contrast, large-state senators are perceived as being more distant, so constituents in those states are more likely to turn to their House members for casework requests.[115]

From all accounts, casework pays off in citizen support for individual legislators. In one National Election Study (NES) survey, 17 percent of all adults reported that they or members of their families had requested help from their own representatives. Eighty-five percent said they were satisfied with the response they received.[116] "Casework is all profit," contends Morris P. Fiorina. Unlike the positions members take on issues, casework wins friends without alienating anyone.

Some criticize constituency casework as unfair or biased in practice. Citizens may not enjoy equal access to senators' or representatives' offices. Political supporters or cronies may receive favored treatment at others' expense. But in the great bulk of cases, help is universally dispensed.

Personal Staff

Legislators head sizable office enterprises that reflect their responsibilities within the institution and toward their constituents. Staff members assist with legislative and constituency duties. Constituent representation is deemed so essential that when a member dies, resigns, or is incapacitated, the staff normally remains on the job (supervised by the secretary of the Senate or the clerk of the House, as the case may be).

Each House member is entitled to a member representational account (MRA) that ranges from $1.2 to $1.4 million annually. From this account, members pay the salaries of no more than eighteen full-time and four part-time employees. The average House member's full-time staff actually numbers about fifteen. Representatives also are entitled to an annual office allowance, which is used for travel, telecommunications, district office rental, office equipment, stationery, computer services, and mail.[117]

Senators' personal staffs range in size from thirteen to seventy-one; the average is from thirty to thirty-five full-time employees. Unlike the House, the Senate places no limits on the number of staff a senator may employ. A senator's office expense account depends on factors such as the state's population and its distance from Washington, D.C.

Members' offices always seem crowded and overburdened, but freezes on staff size have been partially offset by computerization, shifting work to state and district offices, and use of volunteers. Congressional offices depend heavily on unpaid help, mainly college-age interns. On average, each House and Senate office uses about nine interns every year (see Appendix B for information on internships).

Staff Organization. No two congressional offices are exactly alike. Each is shaped by the personality, interests, constituency, and politics of the individual legislator. State and district needs also influence staff composition. A senator from a farm state likely will employ at least one specialist in agricultural problems; an urban representative might hire a consumer affairs or housing expert. Traditions are important. If a legislator's predecessor had an enviable reputation for a certain kind of service, the new incumbent will dare not let it lapse.

The member's institutional position also affects staff organization. Committee and subcommittee chairs have committee staff at their disposal. Members without such aides rely heavily on personal staff for their committee work.

Staff Functions. Most personal aides in the House and Senate are young, well educated, and transient. Senate and House aides have served on average less than four years in their posts. Their salaries, although somewhat above the average for full-time workers in the United States, fall well below those for comparably educated workers.[118]

The mix of personal staff functions is decided by each member. Most hire chiefs of staff, legislative assistants (LAs), caseworkers, and press aides, as well as a few people from the home state or district. Chiefs of staff supervise the office and impart political and legislative advice. Often they function as the legislator's alter ego, negotiating with colleagues, constituents, and lobbyists. LAs work with members in committees, draft bills, write speeches, suggest policy initiatives, analyze legislation, and prepare position papers. They also monitor committee sessions that the member is unable to attend.

To emphasize personal contacts, many members have moved casework staff to their home districts or states. Virtually all House and Senate members have home district offices. Some members have as many as five or six such offices. Field offices have lower staff salaries, cheaper rents, and less overhead. They also are more accessible to constituents, local and state officials, and regional federal officers. Members' district staffs fill the role once performed by local party workers and simultaneously enhance members' reelection prospects.

This organizational division reflects the fundamental duality of legislative roles. Legislative functions are centered on Capitol Hill, whereas constituency functions are based in field offices. In other words, "Office of the Member Inc." is increasingly split into headquarters and branch divisions—with the Capitol Hill office handling legislative duties and the state or district office dealing with constituents.

Because members' resources—offices, staffs, and allowances—are funded by the taxpayers, they are restricted to the conduct of official business. "Any campaign work by staff members must be done outside the congressional office, and without using any congressional office resources," states a 2006 House ethics memorandum.[119] This distinction may seem cloudy; after all, members' offices are suffused with electoral concerns, and what constitutes "campaign activity" is unclear. During the campaign season, certain aides go on leave and transfer to the campaign organization's payroll.

MEMBERS AND THE MEDIA

Office allowances in both chambers amply support lawmakers' unceasing struggle for media attention. A member's office bears some resemblance to the communications division of a medium-size business. Nearly every day, messages are released for wide distribution. In addition to turning out press releases, newsletters, and individual and mass mailings, members communicate through telephone, interviews, radio and TV programs, e-mail and text messages, official and personal websites, and through Internet social networking services. Most of the time, these publicity barrages are aimed not at the national media but at individuals and media outlets back in the home state or district.

Mail

The traditional cornerstone of congressional publicity is the franking privilege—the right of members to send out mail at no cost with their signature (the frank) instead of a stamp. This practice, which dates from the First Continental Congress in 1775, is intended to facilitate official communication between elected officials and the people they represent (a rationale accepted by federal courts in upholding the practice).

Critics point out that franked mail is largely unsolicited and often politically motivated. The fact that outgoing mail costs are much higher in election years than in nonelection years seems to bear that criticism out. Most items are mass mailings, such as general-purpose newsletters blanketing home states or districts, or special messages targeted to certain categories of voters. Recipients are urged to share their views or contact local offices for help. Sometimes, the newsletter may feature an opinion poll asking for citizens' views on selected issues. Whatever the results, the underlying message is that the legislator cares what folks back home think.

Current law forbids franked mail that is "unrelated to the official business, activities, and duties of members." It also bars the frank for a "matter which specifically solicits political support for the sender or any other person or any political party." In addition, Congress has placed caps on newsletters and on total outgoing mail. Chamber rules forbid mass mailings (five hundred or more pieces) sixty days (Senate) or ninety days (House) before a primary, runoff, or general election. In the lead-up to the beginning of each cut-off period, streams of U.S. Postal Service trucks are seen pulling away from the loading docks of the congressional office buildings.

The advent of e-mail poses the problem of whether, or how, the much-debated franking restrictions should apply. The Senate has generally applied the franking rules to electronic mail. The House, however, has declined to adopt such strict rules.

Americans increasingly rely on the Internet for news. It is no wonder, then, that lawmakers have set active websites and even blogs.[120] Most sites feature the member's biography, committee assignments, and votes on major issues. Capitol Hill websites exhibit variety in their content, usability, and inter-activity.[121] Some members' websites include streaming audio or video of members' speeches or appearances on news programs. Few of them include such potentially sensitive information as the member's financial disclosure reports, travel spending, and meetings with lobbyists.

Members are quick to embrace new communications technologies. Many members now make use of social networking services such as Facebook, Vine, and Twitter.[122] Reporting on lawmakers using their BlackBerries throughout President Obama's first address to a joint session of Congress, *Washington Post* journalist Dana Milbank joked, "It's bad enough that Americans are paralyzed by economic jitters. Now the president has to deal with lawmakers paralyzed by Twitter."[123]

Feeding the Local Press

News outlets are decentralized and dispersed across America. These include daily and weekly newspapers, radio and TV stations, and cable systems. Virtually all these media outlets are locally based, centered on local issues, and funded by local advertising.

Most local media outlets have inadequate resources for covering their congressional delegations. In fact, very few have their own Washington reporters. Most rely on syndicated or chain services that rarely follow individual members consistently. "If they report national news it is usually because it involves local personalities, affects local outcomes, or relates directly to local concerns," stated a Senate report.[124]

The inadequate resources enjoyed by local press outlets create opportunities for members of Congress to ensure that they receive mostly positive attention.

Most legislators have at least one staffer who serves as a press aide; some have two or three. Their job is to generate coverage highlighting the member's work. Executive agencies often help by letting incumbents announce federal grants or contracts awarded in the state or district. Even if the member had nothing to do with procuring the funds, the press statement proclaims, "Senator So-and-So announced today that a federal contract has been awarded to XYZ Company in Jonesville." Many offices also prepare weekly or biweekly columns that small-town newspapers can reprint under the lawmaker's byline. More generally, a substantial share of local newspaper coverage is based on press releases issued by members of Congress.[125] Given these tendencies, it should be no surprise that most stories about incumbents are uncritically positive: only 6 percent of the news stories compiled by R. Douglas Arnold in his study of local congressional press coverage cited anyone who criticized the incumbent's performance.[126]

The House, the Senate, and the four Capitol Hill parties (House and Senate Republicans and Democrats) have fully equipped studios and satellite links where audio or video programs or excerpted statements (called actualities) can be produced for a fraction of the commercial cost.[127] Some incumbents produce regular programs that are picked up by local radio or television outlets. More often, these local outlets insert brief audio or TV clips on current issues into regular news broadcasts—to give the impression that their reporters have gone out and obtained the story. Members also create their own news reports and beam them directly to hometown stations, often without ever talking to a reporter. With direct satellite feeds to local stations, members regularly go "live at five" before local audiences.

Like printed communications, radio and TV broadcasts pose ethical questions. House and Senate recording studios are supposed to be used only for communicating about legislation and other policy issues, but the distinction between legitimate constituent outreach and political advertising remains blurred. (The studios run by the parties have no such limits.) Some radio and television news editors have qualms about using members' programs. "It's just this side of self-serving," said one television editor of the biweekly *Alaska Delegation Report*.[128] Others claim to see little difference between these electronic communications and old-fashioned press releases. Local editors and producers still have to decide whether to use the material, edit it, or toss it.

Local radio and television's weakness for congressionally initiated communications magnifies the advantages incumbents enjoy. ABC News commentator Cokie Roberts observed, "The emergence of local TV has made some members media stars in the home towns and, I would argue, done more to protect incumbency than any franking privilege or newsletter ever could, simply because television is a more pervasive medium than print."[129] A recent study reports a strong link between the expansion of local television stations across the country and the rise of incumbency advantage in the post-1960s era.[130]

Reports on Congress from the national press corps are far more critical than those from local news organizations. Following the canons of investigative journalism, many national reporters are on the lookout for scandals or evidence of wrongdoing. The national press reports primarily on the institution of Congress, whereas the local press focuses mostly on local senators and representatives. The content and quality of press coverage in local and national media underscore the differences between the two Congresses. Congress as collective policy maker, covered mainly by the national press, appears in a different light from the politicians who make up Congress, covered mainly by local news outlets.

CONCLUSION

How members of Congress manage the two Congresses dilemma is reflected in their daily tasks on Capitol Hill and in their home states or districts. Election is a prerequisite to congressional service. Legislators allocate much of their time and energy, and even more of their staff and office resources, to the care and cultivation of voters. Their Hill styles and home styles are adopted with this end in mind.

Yet senators and representatives do not live by reelection alone. Many bemoan the need for constant campaigning. "What drives me nuts about this place is that, when I came here, it used to be that you had at least a year after you were elected where you could get the people's business done before the next election intruded," complained former representative David Obey, D-Wis. (1969–2011). "Now the way politics has been nationalized, the election intrudes every day."[131] For those who remain in office, reelection is not usually viewed as an end in itself, but as a lever for pursuing other goals—policy making or career advancement. Fenno once remarked to a member that "sometimes it must be hard to connect what you do here with what you do in Washington." "Oh no," the lawmaker replied, "I do what I do here so I can do what I want to do there."[132]

Party Leaders. President Barack Obama meets with congressional leaders in the Old Family Dining Room of the White House on Friday, November 7, 2014. From left to right: House Minority Leader Nancy Pelosi, D-Calif.; Speaker John Boehner, R-Ohio; President Obama; Senate Democratic leader Harry Reid, D-Nev.; Senate Republican leader Mitch McConnell, R-Ky.; and Sen. Charles Schumer, D-N.Y. Senate Majority Leader Mitch McConnell, R-Ky., waits for the start of the State of the Union address in the House Chamber on January 20, 2015. House Minority Leader Nancy Pelosi hands the gavel to Speaker John Boehner after he is reelected for a third term to lead the 114th Congress.

Leaders and Parties in Congress

"The first thing I need to do is get the Senate back to normal," said the incoming Senate majority leader, Mitch McConnell, R-Ky.[1] After decades of slowly climbing the ranks, McConnell finally became the Senate's top leader when Republicans picked up nine seats and reclaimed the Senate majority in 2014. In assuming the post, he said he hoped to move the Senate past gridlock and to run the institution in a more open and inclusive fashion.

McConnell has his work cut out for him. Every political leader finds it more difficult to govern than to oppose. Furthermore, the political environment of the 114th Congress presents special challenges, including both divided government and hard questions on the political agenda, such as fiscal retrenchment, immigration, and energy policy. To legislate in this environment, McConnell will need to identify policies that can garner bipartisan support in the Senate, command a majority in a fractious Republican-led House, and win a Democratic president's signature. This is no easy task. After the defeat of so many moderate Senate Democrats in 2014, bipartisanship in the Senate may well be even more elusive. Meanwhile, the calendar will move quickly. Before the first session of the 114th Congress expires, Washington will be preoccupied with the 2016 presidential election. McConnell's path of least resistance may well be to focus on confrontation with the president, so as to clarify choices for voters in the next elections, rather than on legislative achievements.

Building electoral majorities, managing internal party politics, and passing legislation are among congressional leaders' wide-ranging duties. These responsibilities must be carried out with careful attention to the two Congresses. Leaders must facilitate lawmaking, while at the same time attending both to party members' representational ties with their constituents and to the party's public image. Of his fellow Republicans, House Speaker John Boehner, R-Ohio, says, "You've got to give them room to be rebellious from time to time. If you tighten down the pressure cooker too much, it's going to explode."[2] On the other hand, a leader must also be able to instill enough discipline to bring coherence to a party. "The leadership is going to have to find a way to deal sternly with some of these members," said former Senate Republican leader Trent Lott, R-Miss., in advice to McConnell. "I wouldn't put up with some of the stuff that they're doing."[3]

Making national policy means finding ways of persuading members who represent different constituencies, regions, ideologies, values, and interests to support legislation that addresses national concerns. "The only thing that counts is 218 votes, and nothing else is real," a House leader declared. "You have to be able [to attract a majority of the House] to pass a bill."[4] Implicit in this party leader's statement is a recognition that mobilizing winning coalitions is not easy.

Party leaders encounter what scholars call a "collective action" dilemma.[5] How can leaders mobilize majorities to legislate for the public good when it is in the self-interest of rank-and-file lawmakers to focus solely on their own individual electoral needs? Such members often prefer to free ride on the efforts of their colleagues. In many cases, they want to avoid the difficult trade-offs that are frequently required for successful legislation. Legislative deal-making can be especially painful during conditions of divided government, in which neither party is able to achieve many of its partisan aims. Of course, if there are too many free riders, little lawmaking will get done at all.

Taking account of the two Congresses requires party leaders to assume roles both inside and outside the institution. In their inside role, party leaders formulate policy agendas and use their procedural and organizational authority to advance them. In their outside role, party leaders articulate and publicize issue positions designed to galvanize partisan support and swing voters. In today's era of ideological polarization and intense electoral competition, leaders try to generate public momentum either to force legislative action on party priorities or to create issues to take to the voters in the next election. Leaders' inside and outside roles are inextricably intertwined. They serve as their party's link to the president, the press, the public, and the party faithful.

Congressional leadership is fundamentally partisan. Indeed, Congress itself is a partisan institution—that is, parties organize the legislature. The majority party in the House and Senate controls not only the top leadership posts but also the chairmanships and majorities on committees and subcommittees. With these tools, the majority party is generally able to control the legislative agenda.

THE SPEAKER OF THE HOUSE

No other congressional leader possesses the visibility and authority of the Speaker. "Because the Speakership is the only leadership position in Congress whose existence and method of selection is mandated by the Constitution," writes political scientist Matthew N. Green, "the office possesses considerable prestige."[6] Although the Constitution does not require the Speaker to be a House member, all of them have been. Under the Presidential Succession Act of 1947, the Speaker is next in line behind the vice president to succeed to the presidency.

The office of Speaker combines procedural and political prerogatives with policy and partisan leadership. Speakers preside over the House, meaning that they rule on points of order, announce the results of votes, refer legislation to committees, and maintain order and decorum in the House chamber. In addition to these procedural prerogatives, they exercise important political powers. They set the House's agenda of activities, control the Rules Committee, chair or influence the decisions of their party's committee assignment panel, bestow or withhold various rewards, coordinate policy making with Senate counterparts, and, in this age of television and Internet communications, expound party and House positions to the public at large. In practice, Speakers today seldom actually preside over the House because they focus so much attention on external activities, such as campaigning for party members, fund-raising, and message development.

Speakers are formally elected by the members of the House, but in practice the key step is to be selected by a majority of the majority party when it caucuses to select leaders. Today's Speakers have served long careers in the House, over which they have built relationships with fellow members and risen through the ranks of their party. Speakers elected since 1899 served, on average, more than twenty years before their election to the post. Both Boehner and Pelosi served twenty years before becoming Speaker.

Once in office, Speakers traditionally have been reelected as long as their party has controlled the House. Members typically vote for the speakership along straight party lines. Not since 1923 has there been a genuine floor battle over the speakership, because since that time one party has always enjoyed a clear majority in the House, and that party has been able to work out internally disagreements over control of the speakership.[7] In 2015, however, Boehner suffered twenty-five Republican defections in his election as Speaker, the most for any sitting Speaker in more than a century. This challenge to Boehner was poorly organized, in that his disaffected conservative opponents were unable to coalesce around a single candidate as an alternative.

As chief parliamentary officer and leader of the majority party (see Figure 6-1), the Speaker enjoys unique powers in scheduling floor business and in recognizing members during sessions. Occasionally, Speakers will relinquish the gavel to join in the floor debate. Recent Speakers, including Dennis Hastert and Pelosi, often voted on issues before the House.[8] The Speaker is also in charge of administrative matters. The current administrative structure was established after Speaker Newt Gingrich took office in 1994. Gingrich's reforms streamlined and modernized management, undertook an independent audit of the accounting systems, and assigned responsibility to a new chief administrative officer—elected by the House at the start of each Congress—for running the House's administrative operations in a professional manner.[9]

The Changing Role of the Speaker

The Speaker's power derives in great part from the House's majoritarian rules. A determined House majority can achieve its policy objectives via majority rule. But it was not always so. Before 1890, intense battles were fought over the minority's right to delay—and even stop—legislative action. Throughout most

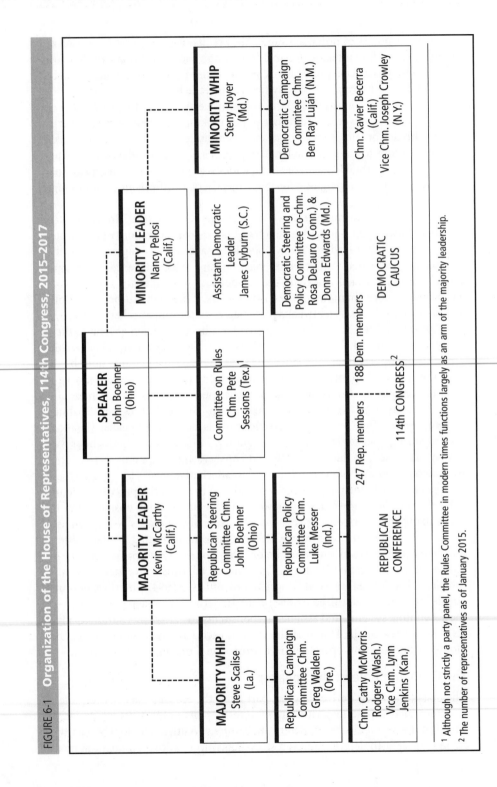

FIGURE 6-1 Organization of the House of Representatives, 114th Congress, 2015–2017

SPEAKER
John Boehner
(Ohio)

MAJORITY LEADER
Kevin McCarthy
(Calif.)

MAJORITY WHIP
Steve Scalise
(La.)

MINORITY LEADER
Nancy Pelosi
(Calif.)

MINORITY WHIP
Steny Hoyer
(Md.)

Committee on Rules
Chm. Pete
Sessions (Tex.)[1]

Republican Steering
Committee Chm.
John Boehner
(Ohio)

Republican Policy
Committee Chm.
Luke Messer
(Ind.)

Republican Campaign
Committee Chm.
Greg Walden
(Ore.)

Assistant Democratic
Leader
James Clyburn (S.C.)

Democratic Steering and
Policy Committee co-chm.
Rosa DeLauro (Conn.) &
Donna Edwards (Md.)

Democratic Campaign
Committee Chm.
Ben Ray Luján (N.M.)

Chm. Cathy McMorris
Rodgers (Wash.)
Vice Chm. Lynn
Jenkins (Kan.)

Chm. Xavier Becerra
(Calif.)
Vice Chm. Joseph Crowley
(N.Y.)

REPUBLICAN
CONFERENCE

DEMOCRATIC
CAUCUS

247 Rep. members   188 Dem. members

114th CONGRESS[2]

[1] Although not strictly a party panel, the Rules Committee in modern times functions largely as an arm of the majority leadership.

[2] The number of representatives as of January 2015.

of the nineteenth century, the House minority possessed a variety of stalling tactics that often frustrated House decision making.[10] In the 1890s, however, Republican Speaker Thomas "Czar" Reed of Maine finally curtailed the minority's capacity for obstruction. The House adopted procedures (the famous Reed Rules) to facilitate action on the basis of majority rule, including an 1890 House rule, still in effect: "No dilatory motion shall be entertained by the Speaker."

By 1910 Speaker Joseph G. Cannon, R-Ill., dominated the House: assigning members to committees, appointing and removing committee chairs, referring bills to committee, regulating the flow of bills to the House floor as chair of the Rules Committee, and controlling floor debate. Taken individually, Cannon's powers were little different from those of his immediate predecessors, but taken together and exercised to their limits, they bordered on dictatorial. The result was a revolt. Progressive Republicans joined with discontented minority Democrats to reduce the Speaker's authority.

The House forced Cannon to step down from the Rules Committee in 1910 and required the House to elect the committee's members. The next year, when Democrats took control of the House, the new Speaker, James B. "Champ" Clark of Missouri, was denied the authority to make committee assignments, and his power of recognition was curtailed. The speakership then went into long-term eclipse as power flowed briefly to party caucuses and then to committee chairs.

Over time after the 1910 revolt, committees became more powerful relative to party leaders. Power in Congress was diffused among a relatively small number of committee chairs, who were often called the "barons" of Capitol Hill. These chairs rose to power by means of a nearly inviolable seniority system, in which each committee's longest-serving majority party member served as chair until death, resignation, or retirement. This system tended to elevate to top committee posts the long-serving conservative southern Democrats from safe seats, a process that eventually yielded committee chairs who were out of step with the preferences of party leaders. But Speakers of this era had little ability to discipline the powerful, independent committee chairs whom they did not appoint and could not remove.

Working from this more constricted office, Speakers after Cannon exhibited various leadership styles. The longest-serving Speaker in history, Democrat Sam Rayburn of Texas (1940–1947, 1949–1953, 1955–1961), functioned largely as a broker or mediator, who negotiated with committee chairs to report out legislation supported by the Democratic majority. Rayburn used his personal prestige as well as his long political experience and immense parliamentary skills to lend coherence to a decentralized chamber. As he explained, "The old day of pounding on the desk and giving people hell is gone. A man's got to lead by persuasion and kindness and the best reason—that's the only way he can lead people."[11]

The distribution of power in the House of Representatives changed fundamentally during the 1970s. Frustrated by the conservative tilt of the committee barons, activist, liberal lawmakers elected during the Vietnam War and the

Watergate era joined forces with other longtime members disgruntled with the status quo to curb the power of committee chairs. These reformist Democrats took a two-pronged approach toward transforming the distribution of power in the House.

First, the reformers limited the ability of committee chairs to act independently. Rather than allowing chairs to hold their positions regardless of their adherence to the party's agenda, new party rules adopted in 1973 required that committee chairs be elected by secret ballot of the Democratic Caucus. Committee chairs were also obligated to share power with subcommittee chairs.

Second, the reformers strengthened the hand of the party leadership. The Speaker, for example, gained the right to name all the majority party members of the Rules Committee, including the chair. The Speaker was also permitted to refer measures to more than one committee.

Although the reforms enhanced party leaders' powers, Speakers did not exploit them to the fullest degree immediately. Instead, power was gradually centralized in the majority party leadership over many subsequent Congresses. Longtime Speaker Thomas P. "Tip" O'Neill Jr. (D-Mass., 1977–1987) strengthened the office by drawing Democratic rank-and-file members into the leadership orbit, expanding the whip structure, and creating leadership task forces to allow them input on party priorities.[12] O'Neill's successor, Speaker Jim Wright (D-Tex., 1987–1989), pushed the prerogatives of the office further. His unyielding personal style and knack for making "minority status more painful," as one House GOP leader put it, embittered Republicans (and even some of his own party).[13] Wright's tenure in office ended in the wake of ethics charges successfully initiated against him by an energetic up-and-coming Republican, Newt Gingrich. Although Wright's successor, Speaker Thomas S. Foley, D-Wash. (1989–1995), had a reputation for being a judicious, low-key, and consensus-oriented leader, he began to make far more extensive use of the Rules Committee to shape the floor agenda and restrict amending opportunities.[14]

The Contemporary Speaker. Speaker Newt Gingrich, R-Ga., took the office of Speaker to new heights. In the lead-up to the 1994 elections, Gingrich had spearheaded a ten-point party platform called "The Contract with America." Almost all House Republican candidates pledged to act on every item in the platform within the first hundred days of the 104th Congress if their party won a majority. Gingrich was widely credited with the GOP's sweeping victory in the 1994 elections: "[Gingrich is] the one responsible for leading the Republican Party out of the wilderness of the minority to the promised land of the majority," said one GOP House member.[15]

In the immediate aftermath of the Republicans' taking control of the House, GOP lawmakers observed a parliamentary model of governance marching in lockstep with their "prime minister." Everything in the ten-point contract except term limits for lawmakers passed the House within a hundred days. Gingrich also adopted a wide array of institutional changes that centralized power in his office. He curbed the independence of committees by personally selecting committee members and chairs who would strongly support his agenda—and, when necessary, ignored seniority in the process. In addition, he required the GOP members of the Appropriations Committee to sign a written pledge that they would heed the leadership's directives for spending reductions. Most significant, he changed the House rules to impose a six-year term limit on all committee and subcommittee chairs, so no chair could accumulate enough influence to challenge the central party leaders. In short, party power came to dominate committee power.

But Gingrich did not remain Speaker for long. Two extended face-offs with President Bill Clinton in late 1995 and early 1996 resulted in highly unpopular shutdowns of ongoing government operations, for which the public blamed the Republicans, not President Clinton.[16] In 1996 the House voted overwhelmingly to reprimand and fine Gingrich in response to ethics charges related to inaccurate financial information he had given to the House Ethics Committee. When the 1998 midterm results came in, many Republicans blamed Gingrich for their poor showing. He then left the speakership and resigned from the House.

Gingrich's successor as Speaker, Rep. Dennis Hastert, R-Ill. (1999–2007), played a less visible role outside the House, but inside the institution he was no less powerful than Gingrich. The longest-serving GOP Speaker, Hastert exercised "top-down" command of the House and followed a partisan governing strategy on party-preferred measures. "The job of the Speaker," he said, "is not to expedite legislation that runs counter to the wishes of the majority of his majority."[17] Hastert and his leadership team were not reluctant to direct rank-and-file members or committee chairs to toe the line on issues important to the party. For example, during a GOP conference meeting, Veterans' Affairs chair Christopher H. Smith of New Jersey criticized the Republicans' budget resolution and the spending proposals for veterans. Speaker Hastert "got up and shut him down," said a witness to the tongue-lashing. "I've never seen anything like that. It was scathing."[18] When Smith refused to curb his advocacy of more spending for veterans, GOP leaders removed him as Veterans' Affairs chair and even from the committee itself.

The trend toward centralization of power in the Speaker's office was not reversed under Hastert's successor, Nancy Pelosi (D-Calif., 2007–2011). Her elevation to the speakership was ground-breaking in that she was the first woman to rise so high in American politics, but Speaker Pelosi's leadership style tracked the same "top-down," centralized model of her immediate predecessors. Of her leadership style, a Brookings Institution report concluded that "a pattern of tighter, more centralized control . . . continues unabated."[19]

Although the current Speaker, John Boehner, indicated an intention to lead the House in a more inclusive manner, there is no indication that the balance of House power has shifted back in the direction of committee chairs. By selecting loyal Republicans as committee chairs, Boehner ensures that committees serve the leadership's broader interests.[20] Boehner has also informed rank-and-file members that the leadership monitors their voting behavior and makes committee assignments accordingly.[21] In 2012 Boehner's Steering Committee stripped four members of their committee assignments as punishment for their intransigence and willingness to criticize fellow Republicans.[22]

Although Boehner has asserted discipline over committees, he has taken a more tolerant stance toward the Republican rank and file. "The House works best when it is allowed to work its will," he says.[23] Boehner has repeatedly been unable to hold his party's ranks together on high-stakes issues. With conservatives refusing to go along with bipartisan deals, he has had to rely on Democratic votes to pass important legislation, such as to raise the debt ceiling or to keep the government operating. Recalcitrant conservatives also forced Boehner to scuttle plans for bipartisan immigration reform.[24]

The Speaker's Influence: Style and Context

Congressional analysts disagree about the extent to which congressional leaders can influence policy outcomes. Compared with legislative party leaders in many other democracies, party leaders in Congress unquestionably have fewer tools to induce party loyalty among lawmakers. Nevertheless, congressional leaders enjoy more institutional authority at some times than at others. In general, political scientists stress context over personal style as the main factor affecting the Speaker's institutional clout. Political scientists have developed a theory—conditional party government—to explain why congressional leaders appear to be stronger during some eras than others.[25]

Conditional party government theory posits that if partisans share common policy views and confront an opposition party with sharply different policy preferences, then these dual conditions favor strong, centralized leadership. Rank-and-file partisans (the principals) will empower their party leaders (agents) to advance an agenda that nearly all of them support. According to the two leading proponents of this theory:

> These two considerations—preference homogeneity [or policy agreement within parties] and preference conflict [or policy disagreement between parties]—together form the "condition" in the theory of conditional party government. As these increase, the theory predicts that party members will be progressively more willing to create strong powers for leaders and to support the exercise of those powers in specific instances. But when diversity grows within parties, or the differences between parties are reduced, members will be reluctant to grant greater powers to leaders. This is the central prediction of [conditional party government].[26]

Conditional party government theory provides an explanation for the changing role of the Speaker. Speaker Sam Rayburn's role as cautious broker and negotiator, for example, makes sense in light of fractures within the Democratic Party during the 1950s. During Rayburn's era—and for many years afterward—congressional Democrats were deeply divided between their northern and southern wings. Southern Democrats tended to be more conservative than their northern colleagues on significant political issues, particularly civil rights and labor regulations (such as minimum wage laws, union organizing, and business–labor relations). On such matters, southern Democrats often allied with Republicans in a voting pattern known as the "conservative coalition." Recognizing these divisions, Rayburn had to lead cautiously. Just bringing the Democratic Caucus together could be politically explosive, so Rayburn rarely convened the caucus.[27] Instead, he dealt with members on a personalized, individual basis.

According to the theory of conditional party government, Rayburn's style of leadership was not merely a personal stylistic choice; it was also a way of coping with intractable conflict within the party. Under such conditions, rank-and-file Democrats simply would not trust their Speaker with expansive procedural and political powers.

By the same token, the conditional party government perspective attributes the forceful leadership of recent Speakers to changes in the political context. Since the 1960s, regional realignments have created (1) far more ideological consensus *within* each of the two congressional parties, and (2) considerably less ideological agreement *between* the two parties than existed during the 1950s and 1960s. Partisan realignment is an important part of the story. After the enfranchisement of southern African Americans in the 1960s, the Democratic Party in the South began to elect Democrats (such as John Lewis of Georgia) who were more responsive to African American constituents and more ideologically compatible with their party colleagues from the rest of the country. Meanwhile, conservative southern whites gradually moved into the Republican Party. Because the South is now largely in the GOP camp, today's Democratic Party lacks the deep regional divisions that characterized the earlier era. The conservative coalition is no longer an important voting bloc in Congress. Constituency change in the North reinforced this ideological homogenization of the parties. Moderate "Rockefeller Republicans" have largely disappeared in the Northeast. As a result of these constituency changes, the two parties are more internally coherent in their policy preferences.

This new context helps explain the assertive styles of contemporary Speakers. The rank-and-file members of both parties are more willing to trust their leaders with institutional authority. Contemporary Speakers of both parties have been given more influence over committee assignments, allowing them to appoint like-minded members to coveted committees. By stacking important committees with loyal partisans, a Speaker raises the likelihood that they will report legislation that the Speaker favors. Individual members also recognize that they owe their committee assignments in part to the Speaker. Given the greater willingness of members to tolerate hierarchical leadership, recent Speakers have been able to direct committee chairs, advance party agendas, and take procedural actions to hamstring the minority party. In short, leaders' personal talents have been augmented by formal and informal procedural changes that have enhanced their influence.

Not all scholars accept the conditional party government account. An alternative theory—the pivotal voter theory—eschews a focus on parties and leaders as a way to understand Congress. Instead, this perspective emphasizes the power of rank-and-file members, particularly the critical members whose votes are necessary to form a majority or to clear other thresholds, such as the two-thirds supermajority needed to override a presidential veto. Proponents of this theory argue that policy outcomes on the floor rarely diverge from what is acceptable to the pivotal voter—in the House, the member who casts the 218th vote.[28] Why would members vote to support a policy with which they disagree? After all, leaders have only limited tools with which to discipline members, and are ultimately accountable to the chamber for their actions. When a majority party is internally unified, there will be no difference between what it prefers and what the chamber majority will agree. But when the majority party is divided, it is unable to enforce its agenda unless it can command a majority. In pursuit of their desired outcomes, members will coalesce across party lines to form a winning coalition, just as conservative southern Democrats once did with conservative Republicans—the so-called "conservative coalition" that shaped legislative policy making for a good part of the twentieth century. From this vantage point, the important question for understanding Congress is simply the distribution of policy preferences in the chamber as a whole, not the activities and powers of party leaders and party organizations.

Other critics of conditional party government emphasize that leadership is by no means entirely determined by the political context. "Leadership in Congress occurs within an institutional context that imposes limits," writes Randall Strahan, "but some leaders take advantage of those opportunities and others do not. Leadership involves not only the conditions that make leadership possible but also the choice of the leader to act."[29] Adroit and forceful Speakers can lead by molding circumstances and seizing opportunities favoring their own objectives.[30] In short, Speakers' personal capacities allow them to exercise that elusive quality called leadership—that is, an ability to persuade others to follow even when they disagree with their leaders' views.

House Floor Leaders

The Speaker's principal deputy—the majority leader—is the party's floor leader. As former majority leader Tom DeLay, R-Tex. (1997–2003), said of his relationship with Speaker Hastert, "I see it that Hastert is the chairman of the board and I am the chief executive officer."[31] Elected every two years by secret ballot of the party caucus, the floor leader is not to be confused with a floor manager. Floor managers—usually two for each bill and frequently the chair and ranking minority member of the committee that reported the bill—are appointed to steer particular bills to a final vote.

The House majority leader is usually an experienced legislator. However, the current majority leader, Rep. Kevin McCarthy, R-Calif., rose to leadership quickly. After entering the House as a freshman in 2007, McCarthy was elected the party's majority whip in 2011. In a short time frame, he had distinguished himself as a party activist. He was lead author of the House Republican "Pledge to America," a party platform document for the pivotal 2010 elections. In addition, he was one of the authors of *Young Guns,* a small-government manifesto designed to raise the authors' profiles as young, reform-minded Republican leaders.[32] McCarthy's effectiveness as a leader is enhanced by his ability to avoid being too closely associated with any one faction in his party. "Moderates think he's a moderate. Conservatives think he's a conservative," says Tony Strickland, a former Republican colleague of McCarthy's in the California Assembly.[33]

House and party rules are largely silent about the majority leader's duties. By tradition, the primary duties are to serve as principal strategist and spokesperson for the party and to monitor the House floor. By modern custom, neither the Speaker nor the Democratic or Republican leaders chair committees,[34] but they may serve on formal or informal task forces or panels.

To plan the daily, weekly, and annual legislative agendas, McCarthy must consult widely. He meets regularly with committee chairs to discuss their schedule of activities, review pertinent legislative issues, and coordinate chamber action with the party's floor managers. He also gauges sentiment on legislation among rank-and-file members and urges them to support or reject measures. As one majority leader said, "The Majority Leader has prime responsibility for the day-to-day working of the House, the schedule, working with the committees to keep an eye out for what bills are coming, getting them scheduled, getting the work of the House done." He added that the majority leader must also "articulate to the outside world" what his or her party stands for and is trying to do.[35]

The minority leader is the floor leader of the opposition party. Like the majority leader, the minority leader promotes unity among party colleagues, monitors the progress of bills through committees and subcommittees, and forges coalitions in support of proposals. However, the minority leader is more often in a reactive position, criticizing the majority party's initiatives and developing alternatives to them. Bertrand Snell, R-N.Y., minority leader from 1931 to 1939, described the duties:

> He is spokesman for his party and enunciates its policies. He is required to be alert and vigilant in defense of the minority's rights. It is his function and duty to criticize constructively the policies and program of the majority, and to this end employ parliamentary tactics and give close attention to all proposed legislation.[36]

Former Speaker Nancy Pelosi is minority leader in the 114th Congress. After the 2010 elections, she was "the first sitting speaker to move across the hall to the minority leader's office since 1955."[37] Even though a sizable contingent of House Democrats had questioned the wisdom of retaining Pelosi—with her low approval ratings—as the public face of the party, a large majority opted to stick with a seasoned leader rather than go with a newcomer. Her prodigious fund-raising—more than $400 million for Democratic candidates since joining the elected party leadership as whip in 2002—established a track record that many members were reluctant to question.[38] There was also no question about her effectiveness in holding the party together to achieve remarkable legislative victories.[39] In 2014 she was unchallenged in her reelection to the minority leadership.

The minority leader must forge party unity by managing internal conflicts and resolving intraparty disagreements. Perhaps the most important job of the minority leader is to craft a strategy to win back majority control of the House. In this respect, the minority leader must decide whether to cooperate with or to confront the majority party. By working with the majority, the minority party can often influence legislation more to its followers' liking. However, cooperation entails supporting the majority party's legislation on the floor—an often unpleasant task.

A minority party can instead pursue a strategy of confrontation. By consistently offering an alternative vision on issues of the day, the minority party can build the case for its return to power. In the 111th Congress (2009–2010), then–minority leader Boehner signaled that House Republicans would focus more on confrontation than on cooperation. "I have been trying to get my Republican colleagues to understand that we are not in the legislative business," Boehner remarked at a lunch with reporters.[40] There is no set formula for how to win back majority control of the House, because many of the electoral and political forces and events that influence majority status are beyond party leaders' control.[41] But in an era of slim majorities, where control of the chamber appears up for grabs, minority leaders may be more likely to spurn compromises that might end up making the majority party look capable of effective governance, and instead to pursue a strategy of confrontation that would persuade the public it is time for a change.[42]

House Whips

Another top elective party post is that of chief whip. As the term implies, the whip and the whip's team of deputies and regional whips encourage party discipline, count votes, and, in general, mobilize winning coalitions on behalf of partisan priorities. To do so, the chief whip serves as liaison between the party's rank-and-file membership and its leaders. The whip assembles and communicates political and policy intelligence, assigns deputy whips to take the "temperature" of the various factional groups within the party, and provides the party's members with scheduling information.

Accurate vote counting is a whip's most important skill. A set of veteran former whips advised one newly elected whip, "You need to know your count, and you don't share your count."[43] Members' voting predilections on important procedural and substantive issues are typically classified as "yea," "leaning yea," "undecided," "leaning no," and "no." Former majority whip James Clyburn, D-S.C., used a fishing metaphor to explain his procedure for forging winning coalitions:

When it comes to working with the Democratic Caucus I have to fish in a lot of ponds. I go fishing with the Blue Dogs [fiscally conservative Democrats]. I go fishing with the New Dems [moderate Democrats]. I go fishing with the Hispanics and I go fishing with the Asian Pacific Islanders, trying to cobble together the 218 votes I need.[44]

The current Republican majority whip is Steve Scalise, R-La., newly elected to the position after the surprise 2014 primary defeat of then–majority leader Eric Cantor, R-Va., opened a vacancy in the top House Republican Party leadership. According to Scalise, a whip's most important skill is knowing how to "pick your fights": "You've got to thread the needle between conservative areas that unite us, as opposed to things that divide us . . . and we have a lot of infighting and circular firing squads and nothing is accomplished."[45]

The parties' whip teams meet regularly to discuss issues and strategy. These large whip teams involve many members in leadership decision making and give them incentives to back their top leaders. With a sixty-person GOP whip organization, observed a former GOP majority whip, it is feasible "to reach everybody in the [Republican] Conference and deliver their votes when it counts."[46] A large whip team also ensures leadership representation for important party groups and broadens the party's appeal to outside constituencies, while allowing for a division of labor. "Grunt work is subcontracted out to whip team members: Each is typically assigned two or three House colleagues. . . . [W]hip team members take cards from the GOP cloakroom, approach their assigned colleagues and check the appropriate box on the card reflecting the lawmaker's intentions."[47]

LEADERS OF THE SENATE

Unlike the House, today's Senate is an institution that tolerates and even promotes individualism. Candidate-centered elections, the proliferation of policy and ideological interest groups, the outsized role of money in campaigns, generous staff resources, and senators' efforts to win news media coverage are among the factors that gave rise to today's individualistic Senate. Senators cherish and assert their independence, which intensifies the challenges faced by those elected to lead them. Unlike their House counterparts, Senate leaders must lead an institution largely devoid of institutional prerogatives and procedures designed to facilitate majority rule.

Presiding Officers

The House majority's highest elected leader, the Speaker, has the authority to preside over the House. By contrast, the Senate's majority leader, the majority party's highest leader, almost never presides in the Senate chamber.

The Senate has three kinds of presiding officers. First, the constitutional president of the Senate is the vice president of the United States (see Figure 6-2). Except for ceremonial occasions, the vice president seldom presides over Senate sessions and can vote only to break—not make—a tie. When votes on major issues are expected to be close, party leaders make sure that the vice president is presiding so he can break the tie.

Second, the Constitution provides for a president pro tempore to preside in the vice president's absence. In modern practice, this is the majority party senator with the longest continuous service. Sen. Orrin Hatch, R-Utah, is president pro tempore of the Senate of the 114th Congress (2015–2017). By passing a simple resolution, the Senate sometimes appoints a deputy president pro tempore. This majority party official presides over the Senate in the absence of the vice president and president pro tempore.

Third, a dozen or so senators of the majority party, typically junior members, serve approximately one-hour stints each day as the presiding officer. The opportunity to preside helps newcomers become familiar with Senate rules and procedures.

Floor Leaders

The majority leader is the head of the majority party in the Senate, its leader on the floor, and the leader of the Senate. Similarly, the minority leader heads the Senate's minority party. (Today, minority leaders prefer to be called "Republican leader" or "Democratic leader," as the case may be). The majority and minority leaders are elected biennially by secret ballot of their party colleagues. Neither position is mentioned in the Constitution; they are relatively recent creations that date from the early 1900s. Although serving as a party leader in the House is typically a full-time position, every party leader in the Senate sits on one or more committees. The smaller size of the Senate allows leaders to participate in committee work while discharging their leadership duties.

Emergence of the Floor Leader. Historically, the Senate has always had leaders, but no single senator exercised central management of the legislative process in the fashion of today's floor leader. During the Senate's first century or so—especially in the 1790s and early 1800s, when there was no system of permanent standing committees or organized senatorial parties—leadership flowed from the personal talents and abilities of individual legislators. The small size of the early Senate promoted an informal and personal style of leadership. Throughout the nineteenth century, scores of prominent senators were called "leaders" by scholars and other observers. Some were sectional or factional leaders; others headed important committees (by the mid-to-late 1840s committees and their chairs were centers of power); and still others (such as Henry Clay, John C. Calhoun, and Daniel Webster) exercised wide influence because of their special political, oratorical, or intellectual gifts. Even as late as 1885, however, Woodrow Wilson could write: "No one is the Senator. No one exercises the special trust of acknowledged leadership."[48]

FIGURE 6-2 Organization of the Senate, 114th Congress, 2015–2017

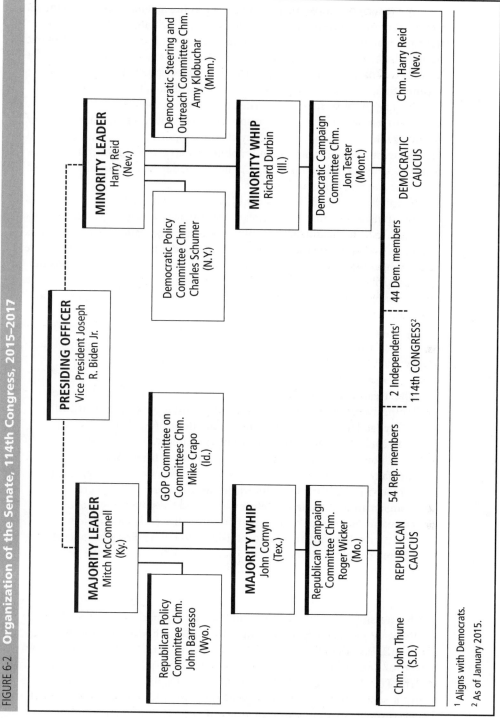

[1] Aligns with Democrats.
[2] As of January 2015.

By the turn of the twentieth century, the political landscape had changed. Party structures and leaders emerged as clearly identifiable forces for organizing and managing the Senate's proceedings. This important development occurred, according to a historian of the Senate, because of the influx of a "new breed" of senators who valued party unity and "the machinery of [party] organization," especially the party caucus.[49] In addition, fierce interparty competition may have spurred the parties to formalize their leadership.[50] Soon, those senators who chaired their respective party caucuses acquired levers of authority over senatorial affairs. They chaired important party panels, shaped the Senate's agenda of business, and mobilized party majorities behind important issues. By 1913 the position of majority leader had informally emerged out of the caucus chairmanship.[51]

Not until Lyndon B. Johnson (LBJ) became majority leader in 1955 was the post transformed into one of great authority and prestige.[52] Considered by many analysts to be the most influential majority leader ever, the Texas Democrat had an extensive network of trusted aides and colleagues who gave him better information about more issues than any other senator. Opposition party control of the White House under President Dwight D. Eisenhower gave the aggressive Johnson the luxury of choosing which policies to support and which strategies to employ to get them enacted. Armed with a pragmatic outlook, domineering style, and legendary arm-twisting abilities, Johnson became the premier vote-gatherer in the Senate. The majority leader's display of face-to-face persuasion was called the "Johnson Treatment":

> The Treatment could last ten minutes or four hours. It came, enveloping its target, at the LBJ Ranch swimming pool, in one of LBJ's offices, in the Senate cloakroom, on the floor of the Senate itself. Its tone could be supplication, accusation, cajolery, exuberance, scorn, tears, complaint, the hint of threat. It was all of these together. It ran the gamut of human emotions. Its velocity was breathtaking, and it was all in one direction. Interjections from the target were rare. Johnson anticipated them before they could be spoken. He moved in close, his face a scant millimeter from his target, his eyes widening and narrowing, and his eyebrows rising and falling. From his pockets poured clippings, memos, statistics. Mimicry, humor, and the genius of analogy made The Treatment an almost hypnotic experience and rendered the target stunned and helpless.[53]

Buttressing Johnson was an inner club, a bipartisan group of senior senators. A particularly important ally within this inner club was Sen. Richard B. Russell of Georgia. The leader of southern Democrats and a lawmaker of immense influence, Russell endorsed Johnson as Democratic leader. (The Russell Senate Office Building on Capitol Hill is named for the Georgia senator.) The club, observers said, wielded the real power in the Senate through its dominance of most of the Senate's key committees and leadership positions.[54] Furthermore, unwritten rules of behavior (for example, junior members should be seen and not heard) encouraged new senators to defer to the establishment.

Today's majority leaders encounter a Senate that is much different from the one led by Johnson. Gone is the seniority-ruled, club-like, relatively closed Senate of old. It was ended largely by three key developments: the influx of independent-minded and activist senators who wanted and expected to be major policy participants; internal senatorial changes that promoted egalitarianism, such as the provision of staff resources to all members; and external developments in the broader political environment (such as the twenty-four-hour news cycle).

Together, these developments led to an individualistic Senate where leaders were expected to serve members' personal needs and advance their individual agendas. As former majority leader Robert C. Byrd, D-W.Va. (1977–1981, 1987–1989), once remarked about the egalitarian, individualistic, and C-SPAN–covered Senate: "Circumstances don't permit the Lyndon Johnson style. What I am saying is that times and things have changed. Younger Senators come into the Senate. They are more independent. The 'establishment' is a bad word. Each wants to do his 'own thing.'"[55] Similarly, the current Democratic leader, Harry Reid, D-Nev., said:

> I don't dictate how people vote. If it's an important vote, I try to tell them how important it is to the Senate, the country, the president. . . . But I'm not very good at twisting arms. I try to be more verbal and non-threatening. So there are going to be . . . a number of opportunities for people who have different opinions not to vote the way that I think they should. But that's the way it is. I hold no grudges.[56]

Limits on Today's Leadership: Individualism and Partisanship. If individualism characterizes the post-Johnson Senate, another development has added to leaders' difficulties in managing and processing the Senate's business: escalating partisanship. Unlike in the House, having a strong and cohesive party does not necessarily enable a Senate majority leader to govern. As discussed in more detail in Chapter 8, the Senate's rules do not permit the majority party leadership to set the agenda without input from the minority party. The majority leader must negotiate with the minority leader in scheduling legislation for floor consideration. To lead the Senate successfully, then, Senate leaders must achieve considerably more cross-party consensus than is necessary in the House.

As in the House, the two Senate parties have become more cohesive internally and more ideologically distinct from one another. Differences between the parties are also grounded in the two parties' electoral interests, as each party strategizes to communicate clear reasons for voters to prefer it to the opposition.[57] Groups allied with the parties also contribute to the widening divide. The two Congresses are very much in evidence as Democratic senators champion policies favored by their core national constituencies (such as environmentalists, gays, minorities, and unions), and Republican lawmakers do the same for their constituency base (such as religious conservatives, the Tea Party, business owners, gun owners, and antiabortion advocates).

Majority Leader. Party polarization makes it extraordinarily difficult for the Senate majority leader to achieve the consensus needed to make the Senate function. Any senator has significant parliamentary powers to stymie action, which puts a premium on the leader's skill in negotiating and deal-making. In order to move legislation, Senate leaders rely heavily on patience, perseverance, personal ties, and procedural hardball. If one or more senators object to moving forward on a matter, the majority leader faces an even higher hurdle: acquiring the sixty votes needed to end debate (that is, invoking a procedure called "cloture") so the Senate can vote on the measure or matter. As a former majority leader reminisced:

> It's a tough job [being majority leader], and it has gotten tougher and tougher. Part of it is that now you don't need 50 votes—you've got to have 60 votes. The filibuster and cloture used to be used occasionally for big issues. [In more recent years] it has become an instrument used on almost every bill. You can have 51 votes, you can have 55 votes, but if you don't get 60 votes, [the bill] can die. And it is very hard to dredge up 60 votes.[58]

"The biggest challenge I have is results," said another former majority leader. "If you have more than half [in the Senate], that doesn't mean you are going to win."[59] The Senate majority leader frequently finds it impossible to push legislation past the procedural hurdles erected by the Senate minority.

Minority Leader. The Democratic leader in the 114th Congress, Harry Reid, a former Golden Gloves boxer, is by all accounts a blunt, tough, and savvy leader. "He's very shrewd and effective," said former senator John Ensign, R-Nev. "Behind the scenes he is tenacious."[60]

The job of the minority leader is to build party consensus, craft policy alternatives, and devise tactics to block or modify the majority's initiatives. The minority leader also acts as his or her party's representative in any dealings with the president. When the minority leader is a member of the president's party, he or she has the traditional duties of pushing the administration's program and responding to partisan criticisms of the president. When in opposition, the minority leader has to calculate when to cooperate with and when to confront the president.

The minority leader is always striving to win back control of the Senate. In pursuit of that goal, it is often useful for a minority leader to shun compromise. Bipartisan deals tend to blur the differences between the parties, and a minority party seeking to win more seats needs a clear argument against the majority in its campaign for change. While in the minority during President Obama's first two years in office (2009–2011), Republican leader McConnell made much use of this approach. Reflecting on the party's strategy of uniform opposition, McConnell observed, "It was absolutely critical that everybody be together because if the proponents of the bill were able to say it was bipartisan, it tended to convey to the public that this is O.K., they must have figured it out. It's either bipartisan or it isn't."[61] The approach achieved many of its desired effects: it excited the Republican base, intensified media controversy, defined party lines, and weakened public confidence in President Obama and the Democratic congressional leadership.

Party Whips. The Senate's whip system carries out functions similar to those of the House, such as counting noses before crucial votes, monitoring floor activity, and fostering party consensus.

Sen. John Cornyn, R-Tex., is the Senate's majority whip in the 114th Congress, the Republicans' second in command. Cornyn had served as chair of the National Republican Senatorial Committee from 2009 to 2012, and he might have been seen as partly responsible for the party's disappointing failure to pick up seats in the 2012 election. But his elevation to the whip position in November 2012 reflects the esteem in which he is held by his party colleagues.

Sen. Richard J. Durbin, D-Ill., is the minority whip of the 114th Congress. Durbin, quite knowledgeable about procedure, has a reputation for being "very good at taking issues and making them resonate with the public."[62] As Sen. Patty Murray, D-Wash., said, "He puts issues we're dealing with in real American language. I think he's really a good face for our party."[63]

SELECTION OF LEADERS

Before the opening of each new Congress, senators and representatives elect their top leaders by secret ballot in their party caucuses. Although the whole House votes for the Speaker, the election is pro forma. With straight-party voting—the modern unspoken rule on this and other organizational matters— the majority party elects the Speaker.

Candidates for party leadership positions usually wage elaborate campaigns to win support from their partisan colleagues. Occasionally, last-minute entrants successfully bid for leadership positions. But whether brief or lengthy, campaigns for party leadership positions are intense. Members understand that a party leadership post can be a "career launching pad either within the [Congress] or outside it."[64]

Both House and Senate leaders are generally chosen from the mainstream of their respective parties. As political scientist David Truman observed as long ago as 1959, party leaders tend to be "middlemen" in their parties—in ideological terms, from neither the far left nor the far right fringes.[65] A recent study examining all open leadership contests over the past hundred years determined that leaders tend to be closer to their party's ideological median than would happen by chance, but also that Democratic leaders tend to come from the left of the party median and Republican leaders from the right of the party median.[66] It also appears that these patterns are evident early in the selection process, suggesting that candidates with these profiles are more likely to seek leadership positions in the first place.

Seniority in Congress is one of many criteria that influence the election of party leaders. Another consideration is geographical balance within the leadership. In the 2014 contest for House Republican whip, Rep. Steve Scalise, R-La., made his successful case for the position partly on the basis of the dearth of other southerners in top Republican leadership positions.[67] Other factors influencing the choice of leaders include: parliamentary expertise; competency in organizational matters; skill in forging winning coalitions; fund-raising prowess; communication skills; sensitivity to the mood of the membership; and personal attributes such as intelligence, fairness, persuasiveness, political shrewdness, and media savvy. Gender balance may be becoming a more important consideration, as the number of women lawmakers rises. For example, female representation was a prominent consideration in the most hotly contested leadership battle of 2012, as Republicans selected Rep. Cathy McMorris Rodgers, R-Wash., for the number four leadership slot over Rep. Tom Price, R-Ga.[68]

LEADERSHIP ACTIVITIES

Leadership duties can be broadly described as institutional maintenance (ensuring that Congress and its members perform their lawmaking and oversight duties and preserving Congress's reputation and integrity) and party maintenance (crafting winning coalitions among partisan colleagues and providing assistance to their members).[69] These two tasks are often blended, as leaders perform their institutional tasks in ways that simultaneously serve their party. Nevertheless, congressional leaders have responsibilities for the basic functioning of Congress that transcend party politics.

Institutional Tasks

From an institutional perspective, party leaders have various obligations. To help them carry out these diverse responsibilities, their chamber gives them extra staff resources.

Organizing the Chamber. Party leaders select the top administrative officers of both houses of Congress, such as the clerk of the House and the secretary of the Senate. These officers are important for the day-to-day functioning of the chambers even if they are invisible to the public. Party leaders also oversee committee jurisdictional revisions and revise congressional rules. Speaker Gingrich backed the abolition of three standing committees in 1995, and Speaker Hastert supported a major recodification of House rules in 1999, the first since 1880.

Scheduling Floor Business. "The power of the Speaker of the House is the power of scheduling," Speaker O'Neill once declared.[70] Or, as Gingrich put it, "When you are Speaker you get to set the agenda. . . . [Y]ou get to decide what legislation is up."[71] After broad consultation, House and Senate party leaders decide what, when, how, and in which order measures should come up for debate. Setting the chamber's agenda and schedule—determining what each chamber will debate—is perhaps the single most important prerogative of the Speaker and Senate majority leader. Scheduling legislation is a basic task that must be managed for the institution to function at all, but leaders also act strategically in their party's interests as they make these decisions.

Once a bill is scheduled for action, the job of the leaders is to see that members vote—a task more difficult than merely herding bodies into the chamber. Party leaders may seek out certain members to speak on an issue because their endorsement can persuade other legislators to support it. Or they may delay action until the bill's sponsors are present. "The leadership must have the right members at the right place at the right time," said Robert Byrd (D-W.Va.) when he was the Senate majority whip.[72] Although leaders generally seek to influence members of their own party and chamber, they also try to win cooperation from the other chamber and from the opposition party.

Leaders' scheduling prerogatives mold policy outcomes. The point at which a bill reaches the floor can seal its fate. A week's delay in scheduling a controversial White House initiative, for example, may give the president, lobbying groups, and others additional time to muster votes for the proposal. Depending on the circumstances, delay may also afford the opposition an opportunity to mobilize its forces.

Legislative business is also scheduled with forthcoming elections in mind. Measures are postponed to avoid an electorally embarrassing defeat, or they may be brought to the floor to satisfy groups allied with the party. What better time to take up legislation revamping the Internal Revenue Service than on or around April 15, the filing deadline for federal income taxes? Reflecting the two Congresses, both parties use the floor as an election platform to raise issues that appeal to external audiences. After passing measures advocated by its electoral base, a party can say, "Look what we did for you." Conversely, a party that fails to pass a measure can say to its bedrock supporters, "Look what we tried to do."

Consulting the President. A traditional duty of party leaders is to meet with the president to discuss the administration's goals and to convey legislative sentiment about what the executive branch is doing or not doing. Although presidents spend more time dealing with leaders of their own party in Congress, they also consult with opposition leaders.

Party Tasks

From a party perspective, congressional party leaders have a number of formal and informal responsibilities. Each party's rules formally specify certain functions and responsibilities for their leaders. Parliamentary precedents and chamber rules assign additional duties to party leaders. Party leaders have also assumed a wide range of duties on an informal basis.

Organizing the Party. Congressional leaders help to organize their party by selecting partisan colleagues for standing committees, revising party rules, choosing other party leaders, and appointing party committees. A couple of examples illustrate the point. Senate Republicans' rules authorize their leader, Senator McConnell, to appoint party colleagues to certain committees. In the House, Speaker Boehner ensured that many freshmen elected in 2010 received plum committee assignments.[73] As a reward for his help in regaining majority control of the Senate in the 2006 midterms, Democratic leader Reid brought Sen. Charles Schumer, D-N.Y., into party leadership, most recently as chair of the Democratic Policy and Communications Center (DPCC). Schumer is also expected to rise to Democratic leader after Reid's retirement at the end of 2016.[74] In 2014 Reid also tapped Sen. Elizabeth Warren, D-Mass., as a "strategic policy advisor" to the DPCC in order to strengthen outreach to progressive groups nationwide.[75] Similarly, in 2015 McConnell recruited as "counselors" four senators from across the ideological spectrum: Sens. Mike Lee, R-Utah; Rob Portman, R-Ohio; Deb Fischer, R-Neb.; and Shelley Moore Capito, W.Va.[76]

Promoting Party Unity. Another leadership responsibility is to encourage party unity in Congress on priority legislation. Sen. Everett Dirksen, R-Ill. (minority leader, 1959–1969), used social gatherings to accomplish this goal:

> Dirksen brought party members together in a series of social affairs. He held cocktail parties at a Washington country club, inviting all Republican senators and sometimes their wives too. These were calculated by Dirksen to improve party harmony and to build a friendly feeling for himself with the Republican senators.[77]

Party leaders' efforts to foster party cohesion go far beyond extending social invitations. Leaders perform many services for their party rank and file that build goodwill and a sense of common purpose. They schedule members' bills, provide them with timely political information, advise them on electoral issues, visit with their constituents, help them obtain good committee assignments, and work with them to forge policy agendas. "You really have to make people feel part of the process," remarked a Senate Democratic leader.[78] Periodically, leaders organize partisan retreats where members discuss party and policy goals, consider specific legislative initiatives, air differences, and resolve disputes.

Party leaders do not have to rely solely on their powers of persuasion. Informal political networks and access to strategic information give them an edge in influencing colleagues:

> Because members will respond more candidly to leadership polls than to lobbyist or White House polls, [leaders] have perhaps the most important information in a legislative struggle—information on where the votes are and (sometimes) what it will take to win certain people over.[79]

Top leaders also can bestow or withhold a variety of tangible and intangible rewards, such as naming legislators to special or select committees, influencing assignments to standing committees, aiding reelection campaigns, and smoothing access to the White House or executive agencies.

Publicizing Party Views. Leaders are expected to publicize their party's policies and achievements. They give speeches in various forums, appear on radio and television talk shows, write newspaper and journal articles, hold press conferences, organize town meetings around the country, and maintain active websites that highlight party issues and images. Leaders are also expected to develop public relations strategies to neutralize the opposition's arguments and proposals.[80] The advocacy role has increased in importance in recent years, in part because of the twenty-four-hour news cycle. "We've created a situation," noted a scholar, "where the real way you drive the legislative process is by influencing public opinion, rather than by trading for votes."[81]

Party leaders also provide members with talking points for meetings with journalists or constituents. Parties often create communications teams that meet regularly to discuss message development and delivery, and to recommend their more telegenic members to present party positions. "We're focused on making sure we deliver the [party] message both here in Washington and out in the hinterlands," said a chair of the Senate Republican Conference.[82]

Providing Campaign Assistance. Leaders must be energetic campaigners and fund-raisers on behalf of their partisan colleagues. They help party candidates raise campaign funds. They establish their own leadership political action committees (PACs) to solicit contributions and donate to candidates of their party. Speaker Boehner, for example, raised nearly $100 million for the 2014 election cycle, a record-breaking sum.[83] Leaders direct campaign dollars to groups running issue ads in the months leading up to the November elections. They travel widely to campaign for incumbents and challengers from their party. They encourage outside groups to contribute to the party's electoral efforts. They also help vulnerable colleagues gain a higher profile by giving them a lead role on a major issue.[84]

In both the House and the Senate, the ability to raise funds for colleagues is an increasingly important criterion for judging prospective party leaders.[85] Members anticipating a run for a leadership post distribute campaign funds as standard operating practice. According to one account, "It seems that the job of fundraiser is becoming more important to senators' expectations of what a majority leader should do. . . . [They] are not trying to buy votes so much as to demonstrate how well they can fulfill that role."[86] Leaders stand at the intersection of the two Congresses—the representative assembly, where money is needed to win elections, and the lawmaking body, where power calls the shots.

PARTY CAUCUSES, COMMITTEES, AND INFORMAL GROUPS

House and Senate leaders operate in diverse institutional settings. In the larger, more impersonal House, majority party leaders sometimes ignore the wishes of the minority party. But this seldom happens in the Senate, where leaders must cope with the extensive rights of individual senators and the minority party. Despite these differences between the House and the Senate, parties in the two chambers are organized into the same three components: caucuses, committees, and informal party groups.

Party Caucuses

The organization of all partisans in a chamber is called the caucus or (in the case of Republicans) the conference. Party caucuses or conferences elect leaders, approve committee assignments, provide members with services, debate party and legislative rules and policies, appoint task forces or issue teams, develop themes to keep members on message, enable members to vent their frustrations, and discuss outreach programs that appeal to voters. In an explanation that applies equally well to both parties and chambers, a senior House Democrat said:

> The caucus is the place where a great deal of freewheeling debate over an issue takes place and where sometimes a consensus develops. Most of the discussions, although they have taken place at leadership meetings and at chairmen's meetings and in whips' meetings, have ended up in the broader forum of the caucus where every member of the Democratic party participates. You don't take a vote, but you try to develop a consensus and make concessions where they're necessary and develop the strongest possible position that can be supported by the maximum number of Democrats.[87]

In brief, party caucuses are useful forums where party members and leaders can assess sentiment on substantive or procedural issues and forge party unity. On rare occasions, party caucuses consider whether to strip particular members of their committee seniority or to oust committee leaders. Sometimes presidents attend their party's House or Senate caucus to rally the troops, as President Obama did just before the House of Representatives voted on health care reform in 2010.[88]

Party Committees

Each of the four congressional party groups—Senate and House Democrats, Senate and House Republicans—establishes committees to serve partisan needs and objectives (see Table 6-1). Three of the four party groups on Capitol Hill have policy committees, for example.[89]

Party committees do not make policy, but they do provide advice on scheduling, study substantive and political issues, distribute policy papers, track votes on issues, and discuss and implement party policy. Their influence has varied over the years, assuming greater importance when the party does not control the White House and thus needs policy and oversight assistance. The policy committees also maintain websites that party members and staff can access for information. Other important party panels are the campaign committees (discussed in Chapter 3) and the committee assignment committees (discussed in Chapter 7).

TABLE 6-1	**Party Committees in the Senate and House**

Committee	Function
Senate Democratic	
Policy and Communications Center	Considers party positions on specific measures and assists the party leader in scheduling bills; facilitates communication between Senate Democrats and to external audiences
Steering and Outreach	Assigns Democrats to committees and coordinates policy, legislative, and message issues for the Democratic Conference
Campaign	Works to elect Democrats to the Senate
Senate Republican	
Policy	Provides summaries of GOP positions on specific issues; researches procedural and substantive issues; drafts policy alternatives
Committee on Committees	Assigns Republicans to committees
Campaign	Works to elect Republicans to the Senate
House Democratic	
Steering and Policy	Assists the leadership and Democratic Caucus in establishing, implementing, researching, and communicating party priorities; assigns Democrats to committees
Campaign	Works to elect Democrats to the House
House Republican	
Policy	Considers majority party proposals and works for consensus among Republican members
Steering	Assigns Republicans to standing committees
Campaign	Works to elect Republicans to the House

Note: The official names of the parties' campaign committees are as follows: Democratic Senatorial Campaign Committee, National Republican Senatorial Committee, Democratic Congressional Campaign Committee, and National Republican Congressional Committee.

Informal Party Groups

In addition to party committees, a variety of informal partisan groups operate on Capitol Hill. Among party groups in the House are the conservative Republican Study Committee, the liberal Progressive Caucus, the centrist New Democrat Coalition, and the fiscally conservative Blue Dog Democrats. The conservative Republican Study Committee regularly reserves time at the end of the legislative day to spotlight its priorities and successes and to criticize the Democrats. Most of the hundreds of informal groups on Capitol Hill are not explicitly partisan. Instead, they typically have a policy focus—such as boating, steel, mining, soybeans, rural health, electricity, automobiles, children, bicycles, or the Internet—and promote public awareness of related issues, sometimes favoring specific policies.

PARTY CONTINUITY AND CHANGE

Several features of the contemporary party system on Capitol Hill stand out: the intensity of party conflict, the persistence of the two-party system, and the advent of new coalition-building practices.

Intense Party Conflict

By any test one can use, the four Capitol Hill party groups are flourishing. The organizational elements are healthy and active, their leaders are increasingly prominent, and party voting is at very high levels. The congressional parties are well assisted by professional staff.

The strength of today's parties has definite virtues. For one, it enables voters to better comprehend the divergent views, values, and principles of the two parties, and it may even encourage voter turnout. "Confrontation fits our strategy," said Richard B. "Dick" Cheney when he was in the House (1979–1989). "Polarization often has very beneficial results. If everything is handled through compromise and conciliation, if there are no real issues dividing us from Democrats, why should the country change and make us the majority?"[90] The public's awareness and understanding of differences between the parties has increased as a result of party polarization.[91]

Nevertheless, the intensity and extent of partisan conflict raises questions about the body's ability to engage in meaningful bipartisan deliberation and mutual accommodation. Compromise is a traditional hallmark of legislative decision making. Observers and members alike decry the dearth of legislative give and take in the contemporary Congress. The two parties are not "just opponents or rivals now. [They] are enemies, with every fight being zero-sum," exclaimed a senior GOP lawmaker. "Compromise is seen as weakness by many of your constituents, and by all your potential opponents in the next primary."[92] The goal of bipartisanship is an oft-heard refrain on Capitol Hill—but it is an elusive one. President Obama campaigned in 2008 on a promise to "turn the page" on the bitter party politics that had characterized the George W. Bush presidency. But his first major initiative, an economic stimulus package, won almost no Republican support at all.[93] As former senator Olympia J. Snowe, R-Maine, observed, "The whole Congress has become far more polarized and partisan so it makes it difficult to reach bipartisan agreements. The more significant the issue, the more partisan it becomes."[94]

The Two-Party System

The Democratic and Republican Parties have dominated American politics and Congress since the mid–nineteenth century. Scholars have advanced various theories for the dualistic party politics of a country as diverse as the United States. Plurality elections in single-member congressional districts encouraged the creation and maintenance of two major parties. Under the winner-takes-all principle, the person who wins the most votes in a state or district is elected to the Senate or House. This principle tends to discourage the formation of third parties. However, other countries using this system of representation, such as Canada and the United Kingdom, have nonetheless had a tradition of successful third parties. Some scholars also trace the origins of the national two-party system to early conflicts between Federalists (advocates of a strong national government) and Antifederalists (advocates of limited national government).[95] In addition, many states have laws that make it difficult to create new parties. Constitutional, political, and legal arrangements all contribute to the existence and maintenance of the two-party system.

Whatever mix of causes produced the two-party system, one thing is clear: few third-party or independent legislators have been elected to Congress during the last century. The high-water mark was the Sixty-third Congress (1913–1915), which had one Progressive senator and nineteen representatives elected as Progressives, Progressive-Republicans, or independents. Since World War II, only a handful of lawmakers have been elected from minor parties or as independents.[96] Most of these legislators have converted to one of the major parties or have voted with them on procedural and substantive matters. The 114th Congress has two independent lawmakers, each of whom affiliates with the Democratic Party: socialist senator Bernie Sanders of Vermont and Sen. Angus King of Maine. Third-party or independent members participate in Democratic or Republican affairs by invitation only.

Advances in Coalition Building

In Capitol Hill's highly competitive environment, party leaders are constantly searching for new ways to get the legislative results they want. Fierce competition has prompted continual innovation in media, public relations, and legislative strategies.

Media and Public Relations. Party leaders understand that media strategies—that is, the use of the press, television, radio, polls, the Internet, speeches, and so on—are essential to advance or block legislation, as well as to shape the party's public image. Leaders form issue teams, message groups, "war rooms," or theme teams to orchestrate, organize, and coordinate political events and communications strategies that promote the party's message to the general public. No longer is the inside game—working behind the scenes to line up votes—sufficient to pass major legislation.

Also necessary is the outside game—influencing public opinion, coordinating with advocacy groups, and creating grassroots support for policy initiatives. Today, both parties use the media to complement their parliamentary strategies in order to raise issues, define and frame priorities, and respond to partisan criticisms. Both congressional parties understand the importance of words as political weapons. GOP consultants found, for example, that characterizing the tax on inheritances as the "death tax"—and having GOP officeholders repeat it again and again over several years—aroused public ire against the tax. This sentiment was instrumental in the dramatic reductions of the estate tax as part of President George W. Bush's successful 2001 tax cut plan.

President Obama can use his bully pulpit to advance Democratic initiatives, but congressional Republicans have no messenger who can focus the nation's attention as effectively as a president. As a result, Republicans have embraced a wide array of communications techniques to shape national debate. Meanwhile, they have augmented the number of leadership staff handling new media, communications, and grassroots outreach. "Our effort will work to help build dynamic, multilayered, outside-the-Beltway coalitions that will help the Republican Conference explain the value of our policies and the impact they will have on the American people," predicted a House Republican coalitions director.[97] Republican leaders hold press conferences, appear on diverse media outlets, organize town meetings, prepare talking points for the press (and their own members), develop party themes, participate in Web forums and blogs, write newspaper editorials, circulate data and statistics, organize policy forums, and engage in a variety of other activities to promote their legislative agenda to the public and to criticize Democratic proposals.

Omnibus Bills. A phenomenon of modern lawmaking is the rise of megabills—legislation that is hundreds or thousands of pages in length, encompassing disparate policy topics. Many of Congress's most significant recent policy departures have been enacted through omnibus bills.

Joining several bills in a single package can help leaders garner support. In such megabills, sweeteners can be added to woo supporters, and provisions that could not win majority support in stand-alone bills can be tucked out of sight. Bundling popular programs with painful spending cuts limits the number of difficult votes lawmakers must cast and provides them with political cover. Members can explain to angry constituents or groups that they had to support the indivisible whole because its discrete parts were not open to separate votes. Leaders, however, must be wary of the reverse concern that a megabill can attract a coalition of opponents with the votes needed to reject the measure.

Megabills can also strengthen Congress's leverage with the executive branch. Measures that a president might veto if presented separately can be folded into megabills and signed in that fashion. "I assure you that in the spending bill, we will be pushing back against this bureaucracy by doing what's called placing riders," said Republican majority leader McConnell of his strategy for negotiating with President Obama over appropriations. "We're going to go after them on health care, on financial services, on the Environmental Protection Agency, across the board."[98]

Party leaders command the resources and authority to influence the packaging process. "Omnibus bills place a huge amount of power in the hands of a few key leaders and their staffs," pointed out one House member.[99] Rank-and-file members look to party leaders to formulate a package acceptable to a majority, if not all, of its members. Nevertheless, these megabills often arouse lawmakers' suspicions and complaints. "These omnibus bills . . . are abominations," one member complained. "No one member of Congress has a chance to read much of them, let alone understand them, before they are voted on."[100]

CONCLUSION

Congressional parties have elaborate organizations, and their leaders fulfill a multiplicity of roles and duties. As Sen. Robert Byrd explained when he held that post, the Senate majority leader performs many duties: "He facilitates, he constructs, he programs, he schedules, he takes an active part in the development of legislation, he steps in at crucial moments on the floor, offers amendments, speaks on behalf of legislation and helps to shape the outcome of the legislation."[101] And yet, typically party leaders cannot command their colleagues. The House party leader, according to Representative Pelosi, is a "weaver of a loom, just pulling together all the threads of different opinion in our caucus."[102] Speaker Boehner joked of his recalcitrant backbenchers: "You might notice I have a few knuckleheads in my conference." [103] But leaders' success rests chiefly on their skill in giving others reasons to follow them. "A leader without followers is simply a man taking a walk," also remarked Boehner.[104]

The party system organizes Congress. The committee system shapes the measures on which Congress acts. These two systems are often in conflict. The first emphasizes aggregation; the second, fragmentation. Party leaders have historically struggled to manage an institution that distributes policy-making authority so widely. In short, leaders provide the centripetal force to offset the centrifugal pull of committees.

A panel including Michael P. Millikin, executive vice president and general counsel of General Motors Company (far left) and Mary T. Barra, GM's chief executive officer (second from left), testifies before the Senate Commerce Committee's Subcommittee on Consumer Protection, Product Safety, and Insurance in the wake of the GM recalls. (Top right) Sen. Chuck Grassley, R-Iowa, and Sen. Mazie Hirono, D-Hawaii, attend a 2013 Senate Judiciary Committee hearing on immigration reform. Sen. John Cornyn, R-Tex. (center), consults with staff aides during the Judiciary Committee markup of the ill-fated bill to ban assault weapons. (Bottom) Committee aides sort through amendments during a break in the House Energy and Commerce Committee's markup of a 2009 bill designed to reduce greenhouse gases.

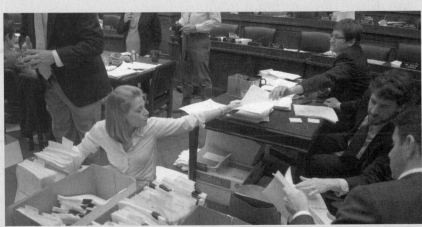

chapter 7

Committees:
Workshops of Congress

C ongress's committees serve two broad purposes: individual and institutional. Individually, lawmakers are able to use their committee assignments to benefit their constituents. "As far as I can see, there is really only one basic reason to be on a public works committee," admitted a House member. "Intellectual stimulation" is not it. "Most of all, I want to be able to bring home projects to my district."[1] At the start of the 112th Congress (2011–2013), no less than twenty House GOP freshman lawmakers won assignment to the Transportation and Infrastructure Committee, in part because the panel's agenda (highways, mass transit, and water projects) addresses investments that can bring jobs and economic growth to their districts. Nine more GOP "frosh" were added to the panel in the 113th Congress and ten more in the 114th. Legislators fully understand the connection between their committee assignments and their influence over the funding of federal projects that can help their reelection.

Committees also enable legislators to utilize or develop expertise in areas that interest them. A former teacher, for example, may seek assignment to the committee overseeing education policy. And some panels, such as the tax and appropriations committees, enable members to wield personal influence among their colleagues. For much of congressional history, members sought out the House Appropriations Committee, explained a GOP leader, because "instantaneously . . . they have a host of new friends, and we all know why": that panel controls the distribution of discretionary federal money (over $1 trillion in 2015).[2]

Institutionally, committees are the centers of policy making, oversight of federal agencies, and public education (largely through the hearings they hold). By dividing their membership into a number of "little legislatures," the House and Senate are able to consider dozens of proposed laws simultaneously.[3] Without committees, a legislative body of 100 senators and 441 House members[4] could not handle biennially the roughly 10,000 bills and nearly 100,000 nominations, a national budget in 2015 of nearly $4 trillion, and a limitless array of controversial issues. Although floor actions often refine legislation, committees are the means by which Congress sifts through an otherwise impossible jumble of bills, proposals, and issues.

Congressional committees serve another important institutional function in the political system: they act as safety valves—that is, they are outlets for national debates and controversies. Military and economic challenges, demographic shifts, trade agreements, global environmental concerns, the drug war, social dislocations caused by technological advances, and the cost of health care place enormous strains on the political system. As forums for public debates, congressional committees help to vent, absorb, and perhaps resolve these strains. The safety valve function also gives citizens a greater sense of participation in national decision making and helps educate members about public problems.

At times, the individual and institutional purposes of the committee system come into conflict. Because members tend to gravitate to committees for constituency or career reasons, they are not the most impartial judges of the policies they authorize. "It's one of the weaknesses of the system that those attracted to a committee like Agriculture are those whose constituents benefit from farm programs," acknowledged Sen. Charles E. Schumer, D-N.Y. "And so they're going to support those programs and they're not going to want to cut them, even the ones that are wasteful."[5]

THE PURPOSES OF COMMITTEES

Senator Schumer's comment highlights an ongoing debate about the development and fundamental purposes of the committee system. To explain the organizational logic of legislatures and the behavior of their committees, scholars have advanced theories emphasizing distributional, informational, and partisan motives.

Distributive theory suggests that legislatures create committees to give lawmakers policy influence in areas critical to their reelection. Members seek committee assignments to "bring home the bacon" (public goods and services) to their constituents. Because lawmakers self-select onto these kinds of committees, the committees become filled with what scholars call "preference outliers"—members whose homogeneous preferences for benefits to their constituents put them out of step with the heterogeneous views of the membership as a whole. Chamber majorities may need to restrain overreaching committees by rejecting or amending their recommended actions.[6]

Informational theory proposes that legislative bodies establish committees to provide lawmakers with the specialized expertise required to make informed judgments in a complex world. Furthermore, the division of labor under the committee system augments Congress's role in relation to the executive branch. Instead of being composed primarily of preference outliers, committees under this model have a diverse membership with wide-ranging perspectives. The basic goal of committees, then, is to formulate policies that resolve national problems.[7]

Partisan theory views committees as agents of their party caucuses. According to this perspective, committee members are expected to support their party's programs or, at minimum, not advance policies opposed by a majority of their own party.

Each of these perspectives captures an aspect of the committee system. Lawmakers are concerned with local issues of immediate concern to constituents, but every district and state is also affected by broad national concerns—the condition of the economy and the environment, for example. Certain issues may lend themselves on occasion more to the distributional than to the informational or party theory of policy making.

Because good public policy may be impeded by the parochial orientations of individual members, Congress has a small number of control, or centralizing, committees that promote institutional and policy integration over committee and programmatic particularism. For example, each house has a Budget Committee, which proposes limits on how much Congress can spend on designated functional areas.[8] However committees are characterized, they concentrate on the policy and oversight activities of individual lawmakers.

EVOLUTION OF THE COMMITTEE SYSTEM

Committees in the early Congresses were generally temporary panels created for specific tasks. Proposals were considered on the House or Senate floor and then were referred to specially created panels that worked out the details—the reverse order of today's system. The Senate, for example, would "debate a subject at length on the floor and, after the majority's desires had been crystallized, might appoint a committee to put those desires into bill form."[9] About 350 ad hoc committees were formed during the Third Congress (1793–1795) alone.[10] The parent chamber closely controlled these temporary committees. It assigned them clear-cut tasks, required them to report back favorably or unfavorably, and dissolved them when they had completed their work.

By about 1816, the Senate—and the House a bit later—had developed a system of permanent, or standing, committees, some of which are still in existence. Standing committees, as historian DeAlva Stanwood Alexander explained, were better suited than ad hoc groups to cope with the larger membership and wider scope of congressional business. Another scholar, George H. Haynes, pointed out that the "needless inconvenience of the frequent choice of select committees" taxed congressional patience. Lawmakers recognized that debating bills one at a time before the whole chamber was an inefficient way of processing Congress's legislative business. Perhaps, too, legislators turned to standing committees as counterweights to presidential influence in setting the legislative agenda.[11] Permanent committees changed the way Congress made policy and allocated authority. The House and Senate now reviewed and voted on recommendations made by specialized, experienced committees. Permanent committees also encouraged oversight of the executive branch. Members have called them "the eye, the ear, the hand, and very often the brain" of Congress.[12]

As committees acquired expertise and authority, they became increasingly self-reliant and resistant to chamber and party control. After the House revolt against domineering Speaker Joseph G. Cannon, R-Ill., in 1910, power flowed to the committee chairs. Along with a few strong party leaders, committee chairs held sway over House and Senate policy making during much of the twentieth century. In rare instances, committee members rebelled and diminished the chair's authority. But most members heeded the advice that Speaker John W. McCormack, D-Mass. (1962–1971), gave freshmen: "Whenever you pass a committee chairman in the House, you bow from the waist. I do."[13]

The chairs' authority was buttressed by the custom of seniority that flourished with the rise of congressional careerism. The majority party member with the most years of continuous service on a committee virtually always became its chair. As a result, committee chairs owed little or nothing to party leaders, much less to presidents. This automatic selection process produced experienced, independent chairs but concentrated authority in a few hands. The have-nots wanted a piece of the action and objected that seniority promoted the competent and incompetent alike. They objected, too, that the system promoted members from safe one-party areas—especially conservative southern Democrats and midwestern Republicans—who could ignore party policies or national sentiments.

The late 1960s and the 1970s saw a rapid influx of new members, many from the cities and suburbs, who opposed the conservative status quo. (In the House, this surge was abetted by U.S. Supreme Court–mandated reapportionments, as discussed in Chapter 3.) Allying themselves with more senior members seeking a stronger voice in Congress, these reformers sponsored changes that diffused power and shattered seniority as an absolute criterion for leadership posts. Today, House and Senate committee chairs (and ranking minority members) are elected by their party colleagues. No longer free to wield arbitrary authority, they must abide by committee and party rules and be sensitive to majority sentiment within their party's caucus or conference.

In fact, there has been a dramatic shift in the power of committee chairs, especially since the mid-1990s. Committee chairs are far less independent today than they were in the 1950s and 1960s. Once the dominant central players in the House and Senate, contemporary chairs are often hand-picked by party leaders, expected to raise money for the party, toe the line on top party issues, and use the media to advance party goals. Committee chairs are still important actors, but they are a shadow of what they once were.

TYPES OF COMMITTEES

Today, Congress boasts a shopper's bazaar of committees—standing, select, joint, and conference—and within each of these general types are variations. Standing committees, for example, can be classed as either authorizing or appropriating panels. Authorizing committees (such as Agriculture, Armed Services, and Judiciary) are the policy-making centers on Capitol Hill. As substantive committees, they propose solutions to public problems and advocate what they believe to be the necessary levels of spending for the programs under their jurisdictions. The House and Senate Appropriations Committees recommend how much money agencies and programs will receive. Not surprisingly, the two types of panels, authorizing and appropriating, tend to come into conflict. Typically, authorizers press for full funding of their recommendations, whereas appropriators usually recommend lower spending levels, especially in an era of spending austerity.

Standing Committees

A standing committee is a permanent entity created by public law or House or Senate rules. Standing committees continue from Congress to Congress, except in rare instances when they are eliminated or new ones are created. Table 7-1 identifies the standing committees in the 114th Congress.

TABLE 7-1 **Standing Committees of the House and Senate, 114th Congress, 2015–2017**

House	Senate
Agriculture	Agriculture, Nutrition, and Forestry
Appropriations	Appropriations
Armed Services	Armed Services
Budget	Banking, Housing, and Urban Affairs
Education and the Workforce	Budget
Energy and Commerce	Commerce, Science, and Transportation
Ethics	Energy and Natural Resources
Financial Services	Environment and Public Works
Foreign Affairs	Finance
Homeland Security	Foreign Relations
House Administration	Health, Education, Labor, and Pensions
Judiciary	Homeland Security and Governmental Affairs
Natural Resources	Judiciary
Oversight and Government Reform	Rules and Administration
Rules	Small Business and Entrepreneurship
Science, Space, and Technology	Veterans' Affairs
Small Business	
Transportation and Infrastructure	
Veterans' Affairs	
Ways and Means	

Sources: House and Senate committee web pages.

Standing committees process the bulk of Congress's daily and annual agenda. Typically, measures are considered on the House or Senate floor after first being referred to, and approved by, the appropriate committees. At the same time, committees are the burial ground for most legislation—that is, committees select from the thousands of measures introduced in each Congress those that merit floor debate. Of the hundreds of bills that clear committees, fewer still are enacted into law.

Sizes and Ratios. The biennial congressional election results frame the party negotiations over setting committee sizes and ratios (the number of majority and minority members on a panel). At the beginning of each new Congress, each chamber adopts separate resolutions, offered by Democrats and Republicans, electing party members to the committees and thus setting their sizes and ratios. In practice, committee sizes and ratios are established in the House by the majority leadership. Because the majority party has the votes, it is the final arbiter if the minority protests its allotment of seats.

At the opening of the 114th Congress, the House ratio of Republicans to Democrats was 57 percent to 43 percent. In the main, this was the approximate ratio on most House committees. As a result, there was no public protest from minority members about being underrepresented on most committees, a common complaint in years past. To be sure, some committees, such as Rules (69 percent to 31 percent in the 114th) and Ways and Means (64 percent to 36 percent in the 114th), traditionally have disproportionate ratios to ensure firm majority party control. The Ethics Committee has an equal number of majority and minority members, and the Speaker names the committee chair.

In the Senate, sizes and ratios are negotiated by the majority and minority leaders. (Senate rules, unlike those of the House, establish the sizes of the standing committees, but these can be adjusted up or down with the agreement of the majority and minority leaders.) Once it became clear after the 2014 elections by what margin the Republicans had won Senate control (54R, 46D), the two party leaders—Democrat Harry Reid, Nev., and Republican Mitch McConnell, Ky.—met and negotiated committee sizes and ratios. "We'll be negotiating committee ratios, the two of us, like we always do," remarked Senator McConnell.[14] Given the Republican gain of nine seats in the 114th Senate, Senator McConnell proposed that the Republicans be granted a two-seat advantage on most committees. On four panels—Foreign Relations, Rules and Administration, Small Business, and Veterans' Affairs—the GOP had a one-seat advantage. These committee ratio changes gave the GOP a margin similar to what Democrats had enjoyed in the preceding Congress, underscoring the adage that elections have consequences. In general, Senate leaders usually change party ratios on committees "by shifting seats between the parties, rather than by adding seats to panels."[15] The Senate's Select Committee on Ethics—which is chaired by a majority party member—always has an equal number of majority and minority members.

Party leaders sometimes enlarge panels to accommodate lawmakers competing for membership on the same committees. They recognize that intraparty harmony can be maintained by boosting the number of committee seats. When

John Boehner, R-Ohio, first became Speaker in 2011, he downsized most House committees to boost productivity and to cut costs. For example, the Appropriations Committee went from sixty seats to fifty, Transportation and Infrastructure from seventy-five seats to fifty-nine, and Ways and Means from forty-one seats to thirty-seven. Four years later, two of those committees have seen an increase. Appropriations now has fifty-one members, Ways and Means has thirty-nine, while Transportation remains at fifty-nine members. The Armed Services Committee is the largest House panel, with sixty-four members, an increase of one member since 2011. Because of the large GOP gains in the November 2014 elections, Republicans expanded their majorities on the committees by a few seats. For example, the GOP's majority on Armed Services was thirty-four to twenty-seven Democrats in the 113th Congress and thirty-six to twenty-seven in the 114th.

Minority Leader Nancy Pelosi, D-Calif., faced some discontent from her Democratic flock once the sizes and ratios of committees became known following the November 2014 elections. Several Democrats lost their seats on major committees with the GOP's reset of sizes and ratios. For example, Democrats lost a seat on the Ways and Means Committee (24R to 15D in the 114th Congress).[16]

Subcommittees. Subcommittees perform much of the day-to-day lawmaking and oversight work of Congress. Like standing committees, they vary widely in rules and procedures, staff arrangements, modes of operation, and relationships with the full committee as well as its other subcommittees. They are created for various reasons, such as lawmakers' need to subdivide a committee's wide-ranging policy domain into manageable pieces, their wish to chair these panels and to have a platform to shape the legislative agenda, and their desire to respond to the policy claims of specialized constituencies.

Under House rules, most standing committees are limited to no more than five subcommittees, though there are exceptions, most notably Appropriations (with twelve subcommittees).[17] Committees bound by the limit of five may create a sixth subcommittee if it is devoted to oversight.

Another House rule limits members to serving on no more than four subcommittees. Such limits—on the number of subcommittees for each standing committee and subcommittee assignment restrictions for each member—are designed to make Congress "more deliberative, participatory, and manageable by reducing scheduling conflicts and jurisdictional overlap."[18] Republicans are in control of the House of the 114th Congress, and their party conference rules state that the "method for the selection of Chairmen of the Committee's Subcommittees [and GOP subcommittee assignments] shall be at the discretion of the full Committee Chairman, unless a majority of the Republican Members of the full Committee disapprove the action of the Chairman."[19] In the case of the Appropriations Committee, the chair submits nominees for subcommittee chairs to the Republican Steering Committee for approval. "If any nomination is rejected by the Steering Committee, the Chair shall submit the new nomination(s) in a timely manner."

The two Congresses are also evident in the composition of subcommittees. A good example occurred in the 112th House when Lamar Smith, R-Tex., chaired the Judiciary Committee. He passed over Steve King, R-Iowa, for chairmanship of the Immigration Subcommittee. King had been the ranking GOP member on the panel in the previous Congress. But, worried that King's inflammatory statements about immigrants would alienate Latino voters in the 2012 elections, Smith selected Elton Gallegly of California, "who has a lower profile and a less strident tone than King," to head the subcommittee.[20] Although King remained a member of the panel, he did not chair the Immigration Subcommittee in either the 113th or 114th Congresses.

In dealing with House subcommittees, the minority Democrats follow the detailed procedures outlined in their party rules. Committee Democrats bid for a subcommittee ranking slot (or assignment) in order of their seniority on the full committee (or seniority on the Appropriations subcommittee), with the most senior Democrat choosing first. The choices are then subject to approval by secret ballot of the Democratic committee members. The ranking positions on four of the most influential committees—Appropriations, Energy and Commerce, Financial Services, and Ways and Means—also require approval by the Democratic Steering and Policy Committee and then the Democratic Caucus. If the Steering and Policy Committee rejects a member to serve as the ranking committee minority leader, the relevant committee is obliged to submit a new nominee to the party panel. In reviewing the nominations for ranking committee leader of each of the four committees, the Steering and Policy Committee "shall consider all relevant factors, including merit, length of service on the committee and degree of commitment to the Democratic agenda, and the diversity of the Caucus."

Assignment to the most important committees is generally "exclusive." Democrats who serve on exclusive committees may serve on no other standing committees unless they are granted an exemption, or waiver, from this requirement. (Waivers of the rule are quite common.) Waivers are granted to permit members to sit on an extra major committee that they deem important to their reelection prospects. This is another example of the two Congresses— the institution bending to suit the preferences and constituency needs of individual members. House Republicans refer to their generally exclusive panels as the "A" committees (Appropriations, Energy and Commerce, Rules, and Ways and Means).

Although silent on the number of subcommittees that standing committees may establish, Senate and party rules set subcommittee assignment limits for senators and prohibit them from chairing more than one subcommittee on any given committee. The number of subcommittees, not surprisingly, often equals the number of majority party members on a committee eligible to chair a subcommittee. Subcommittee chairs and assignments are determined in one of two ways: by the committee chair in consultation with the ranking member, or by senators' order of seniority on the full committee. It is traditional in both chambers for committee members to defer to the chair on organizational matters, such as the number of subcommittees and their respective jurisdictions.

Unlike in the House, where every standing committee except Budget, Ethics, and House Administration has subcommittees, in the Senate four standing committees customarily function without subcommittees—Budget, Rules and Administration, Small Business, and Veterans' Affairs—as do four other permanent panels—Indian Affairs, Ethics, Intelligence, and Aging. These panels are able to process their legislative business without subcommittees because of their relatively small workloads compared with those of other Senate committees.

Select, or Special, Committees

Select, or special, committees are temporary panels that typically go out of business after the two-year life of the Congress in which they are created. But some select committees take on the attributes of permanent committees. The House, for example, has a Permanent Select Intelligence Committee. Select committees usually do not have legislative authority (the right to receive and report out measures) unless it is granted by their authorizing measure; they can only study, investigate, and make recommendations. The membership of select committees is the prerogative of the Speaker. In practice, he names the majority members, including the chair, and the minority leader appoints lawmakers from her side of the aisle.

Select panels are created for several reasons. First, they can accommodate the concerns of individual members. Indeed, the chairs of these panels may attract publicity that enhances their political careers. For example, Democrat Harry S. Truman of Missouri came to the public's (and President Franklin D. Roosevelt's) attention as head of a special Senate committee investigating World War II military procurement practices. Second, special panels can be an access point for interest groups (e.g., the Senate Special Committee on Aging reflects the concerns of the elderly). Third, select committees supplement the standing committee system by overseeing and investigating issues for which the permanent panels may lack adequate time or prefer to ignore. At other times, majority party leaders may spur the creation of a select committee to draw attention to an issue or problem.

For example, on the opening day of the 114th Congress (January 6, 2015), the House reestablished a select panel entitled the Select Committee on the Events Surrounding the 2012 Terrorist Attack in Benghazi [Libya]. The panel's mandate was to conduct a comprehensive investigation of the terrorist attack on September 11, 2012, against the U.S. Consulate in Benghazi in which four Americans were killed, including the U.S. ambassador. Despite seven previous investigations, House "Republicans say a number of unanswered policy and factual questions about the deadly assault have not been fully answered by the Obama White House, the Pentagon and the CIA."[21] House Democrats viewed the investigation as a "witch hunt" aimed at "damaging [the] White House run by Hillary Rodham Clinton, who was secretary of state at the time of the attacks in Libya."[22] Democrats even discussed boycotting the select panel's proceedings.

Finally, select committees can be set up to coordinate consideration of issues that overlap the jurisdictions of several standing committees. A good example occurred following the establishment in 2003 of the Department of Homeland Security (DHS). The department was formed by merging twenty-two federal agencies with a workforce at the time of 180,000 employees. Because numerous House committees exercised jurisdiction over parts of DHS, Speaker Dennis Hastert, R-Ill., created a select homeland security panel to determine whether a new, single-focused standing committee should be created to oversee DHS. Interesting to note is that the select panel was dominated by committee chairs keen on protecting their jurisdiction rather than transferring any significant portion to a new standing committee on homeland security. As a result of the select panel's review, Speaker Hastert backed the creation of a new standing Committee on Homeland Security, which did not receive as much jurisdiction as advocates wanted. The formation of this panel is discussed in more detail later in this chapter.

Joint Committees

Joint committees, which include members from both chambers, have been used since the First Congress for study, investigation, oversight, and routine activities. Unless the composition of a joint committee is prescribed in statute, House members of these committees are appointed by the Speaker; senators are appointed by that chamber's presiding officer. The chairmanship of joint committees rotates each Congress between House and Senate members. There are now four joint committees: Economic, Library, Printing, and Taxation. The Joint Library Committee and the Joint Printing Committee oversee, respectively, the Library of Congress and the Government Printing Office. The Joint Taxation Committee is essentially a holding company for staff who work closely with the tax-writing committees of each house. The Joint Economic Committee conducts studies and hearings on a wide range of domestic and international economic issues.

Conference Committees

Before legislation can be sent to the president to be signed, it must pass both the House and the Senate in identical form. One way this result is obtained is to create a conference committee (see Chapter 8 for more on conferences). Sometimes called the third house of Congress, these bicameral panels reconcile differences between similar measures passed by both chambers. They are composed of members from each house.

Some scholars argue that congressional conference committees are powerful because they have unilateral authority to veto or negotiate alterations in legislation at a late stage in the process. Others dispute this contention and claim that the "ex post veto is not a significant institutional foundation of congressional committee power."[23] Another model suggests that conferees serve as agents of their respective chamber majorities, advocating their policy positions instead of conference committee viewpoints.[24] Whatever the claims, increasingly the top party leaders in each chamber are taking a direct and active role in determining those who should (or should not) be conferees. On occasion, the top leaders, such as the Senate majority leader or House majority leader, serve as conferees on priority measures to increase their leverage in the bicameral bargaining process.

Several recent Congresses have witnessed a decline in the convening of conference committees (see Chapter 8). The Senate, compared to the House, has difficulty at times in convening conferences for interconnected political and procedural reasons. Politically, the majority party has sometimes excluded minority party conferees from the negotiating sessions. Procedurally, it is more difficult to get to conference if senators want to filibuster a motion to do so. As a form of payback, minority party senators who are conferees in name only can stymie the creation of conference committees by extended debate.

During recent Congresses when the House and Senate were controlled by different parties—each acting in a highly polarized legislative environment—neither party nor chamber evinced much interest in considering many bills passed by the other house. Why create conference committees on politically inspired measures that have little or no chance of becoming public law, such as the GOP House voting over fifty times to repeal or change the president's signature health care law? Absent the creation of many conference committees, the House and Senate typically use the amendment exchange method: sending amendments back and forth between the chambers until the matters in bicameral disagreement are resolved. A common feature of this method is that the interchamber bargaining takes place in secret, and party leaders often exert large influence in negotiating the final legislative product, especially on "must pass" measures.

THE ASSIGNMENT PROCESS

Every congressional election sets off a scramble for committee seats. Legislators understand the linkage between winning desirable assignments and winning elections. Newly elected representatives and senators quickly make their preferences known to party leaders, to members of the panels that make committee assignments, and to others—such as friendly lobbyists or generous contributors. They may be able to help the newcomers obtain their preferred committee seats. At the same time, incumbents may try to move to more prestigious panels.

The Pecking Order

The most powerful, and thus most desirable, standing committees are House Ways and Means and Senate Finance, which pass on tax, trade, Social Security, and Medicare measures. The House and Senate Appropriations Committees, which hold the federal purse strings, are also influential panels and usually much sought after. However, their attractiveness has waned somewhat, given "the recent political focus on cutting spending, the now-routine inability of lawmakers to fund the government by the statutory deadline of Oct. 1 each year and the moratorium on earmarks that Republicans have successfully imposed on Congress."[25] Still, appropriators distribute over $1 trillion to numerous federal agencies and programs. Many lawmakers, mindful of the two Congresses, strive to ensure that some of those funds are funneled to their districts or states. Unsurprisingly, in today's contentious partisan environment, where fiscal clashes occur constantly between Democrats and Republicans over taxes, expenditures, and the size of government, party leaders have taken a much larger role in shaping appropriations measures and in mobilizing the votes to win their enactment.

The consequence of these developments is to make *some* lawmakers wary of either chairing or serving on the appropriating panels. When Republicans took control of the 112th House (2011–2013), several GOP lawmakers declined to serve on the Appropriations Committee. "We sent a sheet around, people gave us their preferences, and there weren't that many members that chose to serve on the Appropriations Committee," said Speaker John Boehner, R-Ohio.[26] These lawmakers recognized the potential perils of the two Congresses: they could be challenged electorally either by Tea Party supporters for not cutting enough, or by constituents angry at spending cuts to favorite programs. As a result, budget-cutting fiscal hawks have been recruited to the panel. Their mission is to practice the "politics of subtraction," by cutting or terminating agencies and programs. The Appropriations Committee has been "a favor factory for years; now it is going to be [an antispending] slaughterhouse," declared a House critic of the favor factory.[27] As a right-leaning GOP Appropriations member said, the mission of many conservative Republicans is to recast the panel as the "disappropriations" committee.[28]

The Senate has also seen evidence of the panel's diminished allure. When the longtime chair of the Appropriations Committee, Democrat Daniel Inouye of Hawaii, died, the two most senior Senate Democrats on that panel—Patrick Leahy, Vt., and Tom Harkin, Iowa—each chose not to head it. Although Appropriations was considered for decades to be the most powerful Senate committee, Senators Leahy and Harkin decided to remain as chairs of other committees. Their decisions would have confounded many senatorial colleagues from a different era. The result: the third-ranking Democrat on the panel, Barbara Mikulski, Md., became in the 113th Congress the first woman to chair the Appropriations Committee. She serves as the ranking Democrat on Appropriations in the 114th Congress.

Two other indicators suggest that Senate Appropriations may have lost some of its luster. Just weeks after being sworn in during her first year as a senator, GOP freshman Shelley Moore Capito of West Virginia became a "cardinal"—a term reserved for the chairs of each chamber's appropriating subcommittees. Senator Capito heads the Legislative Branch Appropriations Subcommittee. Traditionally, lawmakers who served on Appropriations waited years before they might become a subcommittee chair. Second, Sen. Dan Coats, R-Ind., who was slated to become a subcommittee cardinal in 2015, left Appropriations and won assignment to the Finance Committee. The point:

Senator Coats "saw more value being a junior member on Finance than a cardinal on Appropriations."[29] It is common for committees to change over time in their attractiveness to members. The Budget Committees, established in 1974, are sought-after assignments because of their important role in economic and fiscal matters and their guardianship of the congressional budgeting process. The House and Senate Commerce Committees, along with each chamber's banking and financial services committees, are also coveted panels: not only do they command broad jurisdictional mandates, but the many interest groups they affect can supply cash donations for the committee members' future election campaigns. For example, it is usual for GOP leaders to boost the reelection chances of their freshmen lawmakers by naming them to committees where it is relatively easy to raise campaign funds, such as Financial Services, Energy and Commerce, Appropriations, and Ways and Means. "The amount of money you can raise is almost entirely determined by committee membership," said a GOP insider.[30] For example, four of eight openings on the House Financial Services Committee went to GOP members who face competitive and expensive races in November 2016.[31]

Among those panels that seldom have waiting lists are the House and Senate Ethics Committees. These committees are not popular because legislators are reluctant to sit in judgment of their colleagues. "Members have never competed for the privilege of serving on the ethics committee, and I am no exception," remarked a House Democrat after his party's leader prevailed on him to join the Ethics panel. Or as one GOP member grumbled after serving as Ethics chair, "I've paid my debt to society. It's time for me to be paroled."[32]

Preferences and Politicking

In his analysis of six House committees, Richard F. Fenno Jr. found that three basic goals of lawmakers—reelection, influence within the House, and good public policy—affected the committee assignments that members sought. Reelection-oriented members were attracted to committees such as Natural Resources (then called the Interior Committee). Appropriations and Ways and Means attracted influence-oriented members. Policy-oriented members sought membership on the Education and Labor Committee (now Education and the Workforce) and the Foreign Affairs Committee. Members with similar goals found themselves on the same committees, Fenno concluded. Such homogeneity of perspectives may result in harmonious but biased committees (see Table 7-2).[33]

Since Fenno's study, scholars have elaborated on the link between members' goals and committee assignments. They have divided House committees into reelection (or constituency), policy, and power panels, and they concur that some mix of the three goals motivates most of the committees' activities. They agree, too, that members' goals "are less easily characterized in the Senate than in the House."[34] After all, most every senator has the opportunity to serve on one of the top committees, such as Appropriations, Armed Services, Commerce, and Finance. Thus the power associated with a particular committee assignment is less important for senators than for representatives.

Members campaign vigorously for the committees they prefer. In *Hit the Ground Running,* his guidebook for GOP newcomers to Congress, then–House majority leader Eric Cantor, R-Va., outlined the key steps for securing committee assignments (see Box 7-1).

Although both parties try to accommodate assignment preferences, some members still receive unwelcome assignments. A classic case was that of Democratic representative Shirley Chisholm of Brooklyn (1969–1983), the first African American woman elected to Congress. Initially, she was assigned to the House Agriculture Committee. "I think it would be hard to imagine an

TABLE 7-2 House and Senate Committee Comparison

Category	House	Senate
Number of standing committees	20	16
Committee/subcommittee assignments per member	About 6	About 11
Power or prestige committees	Appropriations, Budget, Commerce, Financial Services, Rules, Ways and Means	Appropriations, Armed Services, Commerce, Finance, Foreign Relations[1]
Treaties and nominations submitted by the president	No authority	Committees review
Floor debate	Representatives' activity is somewhat confined to the bills reported from the panels on which they serve	Senators can choose to influence any policy area regardless of their committee assignments
Committee consideration of legislation	More difficult to bypass	Easier to bypass[2]
Committee chairs	Subject to party and speakership influence that can limit the chair's discretionary authority over committee operations	Freer rein to manage committees
Committee staff	Often assertive in advocating ideas and proposals	More influential in shaping the legislative agenda
Subcommittee chairmanships	Representatives of the majority party usually must wait at least one term	Majority party senators, regardless of their seniority, usually chair subcommittees

[1] Almost every senator is assigned to one of these committees.

[2] For example, by allowing riders—unrelated policy proposals—to measures pending on the floor.

BOX 7-1   **How to Get the Committee Assignment You Want**

The first step is to decide which committee assignments are right for you and your district. Soon after the organizational conference, you will receive a Dear Colleague letter from your leadership requesting that you submit your committee preferences. Expect this form by early December at the latest. Your personal policy interests, the needs of your district and state, and your future goals are important factors in deciding which committees to request.

Obtaining a seat on your preferred committee may be a multi-year process depending on vacancies and which committees you select. This applies especially to the "A" committees.

Second, be prepared to make your case as to why you should be selected to your committee of choice. The competition for committees such as Financial Services, Transportation and Infrastructure, and Armed Services can be intense.

Successful arguments may include highlighting your professional experience or policy expertise within the committee's jurisdiction, the critical needs of your district or state, the fact that your region of the country may be under-represented on the committee, or the fact that you may be a vulnerable freshman. Bottom Line: This is about marketing yourself, your experience, your abilities, and your district.

Finally, you should engage the Steering Committee (the GOP's committee assignment panel). First, reach out to your class representative. They will be your primary voice on the Steering Committee and it is important that they be an advocate for your request. Keep in mind that your class representative must prioritize and balance the needs of your entire class.

You should also discuss your committee choices with the elected leaders. They hold a substantial bloc of votes on the Steering Committee. In addition, you may want to reach out to other members of the Steering Committee. Ideally, you want to have someone other than your class and regional representative speak in support of your request when the Steering Committee convenes.

---

assignment that is less relevant to my background or to the needs of the predominantly black and Puerto Rican people who elected me," she said. Chisholm's protests won her a seat on the Veterans' Affairs Committee. "There are a lot more veterans in my district than there are trees," she later observed.[35] Yet some urban lawmakers welcome service on the Agriculture Committee, where they can fuse metropolitan issues with rural issues through food stamp, consumer, and other legislation.

How Assignments Are Made

Each party in each house has its own panel to review members' committee requests and dispense assignments to standing committees: the House Republican and Democratic Steering Committees, the Senate Republican Committee on Committees, and the Senate Democratic Steering and Outreach Committee. The decisions of these panels are the first and most important step in a three-step procedure. The second step involves approval of the assignment lists by each party's caucus. Finally, there is a pro forma election by the full House or Senate.

Formal Criteria. Both formal and informal criteria guide the assignment panels in choosing committee members. One formal rule of the House Democratic Caucus is that recommendations for "committee posts need not necessarily follow seniority." Similarly, House GOP rules stipulate that lawmakers designated to serve as the chair of committees "need not be the Member with the longest consecutive service on the Committee." Senate GOP conference rules state that two Republicans from the same state should not serve on the same committee. House Democratic rules state that any member who served on either the Appropriations or Ways and Means Committees in the preceding Congress must be reported to the caucus in the new Congress for appropriate action (approval or rejection).

Since 1953, when Senate Democratic leader Lyndon B. Johnson of Texas announced his "Johnson rule," all Senate Democrats have been assigned one major committee before any party member receives a second major assignment. In 1965 Senate Republicans followed suit. Senate rules also classify committees into different categories, popularly called "A," "B," and "C". There is even a separate category of prestigious "Super A" committees. Senators may sit on only one of the four Super A panels: Appropriations, Armed Services, Finance, and Foreign Relations (unless they are granted a waiver of the rule). Senate Rule XXV states that members must serve on no more than two committees in the A category, which includes the four Super A panels; one in the B grouping (such as Budget, Rules and Administration, and Small Business); and any number of C committees (Ethics, Indian Affairs, Joint Library, Joint Printing, and Joint Taxation).

Informal Criteria. Many informal criteria affect committee assignments—including party loyalty, geography, substantive expertise, gender, and electoral vulnerability. House Democratic rules, as noted earlier, instruct the Steering Committee to consider "merit, length of service, degree of commitment to the Democratic agenda, and Caucus diversity" in granting committee assignments. When House Republicans completed their selection of committee chairs for the 113th Congress, there were no women committee leaders. As a result, female party members made it known to Speaker Boehner that he must rectify this situation by naming women to head committees (Ethics and House Administration) with leadership vacancies for which he had appointment authority. The Speaker complied with this request. Noteworthy is that the Speaker confronted the same issue in the 114th Congress: of the House committee chairs, only one was a female, Candice Miller of Michigan. She was selected by Speaker Boehner to lead the House Administration Committee, which she headed in the previous Congress. The only nonwhite GOP chair was Rep. Devin Nunes—who is of Portuguese descent. Speaker Boehner appointed Nunes to chair the Permanent Select Intelligence Committee.[36]

Members' own wishes are another criterion. Lawmakers who represent districts or states with large military installations may seek assignment to the

Armed Services Committee. Or lawmakers with a specific policy interest (education, health, and so on) may strive to win appointment to panels that deal with those topics. Finally, the committee assignment panels of each congressional party typically respect what is referred to as a "property norm." Returning lawmakers of each party are generally permitted to retain their committee seats (unless they are bumped because of committee ratio changes) before new members bid for vacant committee positions. Lawmakers who do lose their committee positions because of ratio changes may be returned to those panels in the next or subsequent Congresses.

The two Congresses are always intertwined in committee assignment decisions. Each party seeks to boost the electoral resources of its members. House Democratic and GOP leaders, for example, sometimes grant electorally vulnerable freshmen an extra committee assignment to broaden their appeal as they head toward their reelection contests. "All of these committees have constituents," said Democratic leader Steny Hoyer of Maryland. "And all of these [freshmen Democratic appointees] have people in their districts who are members of these constituencies."[37] More seasoned members who could face tough electoral competition may seek plum assignments as well, in order to boost their influence and capacity for fund-raising.

Party leaders also promise committee assignments to candidates to help them win election. When Senate GOP leader Mitch McConnell, R-Ky., was campaigning in Arkansas for John Boozman—who successfully challenged incumbent senator Blanche Lincoln, D-Ark., in 2010—McConnell vowed he would appoint Boozman to the Agriculture Committee. "John will be on the Agriculture Committee on Day One when we make the committee assignments," declared Senator McConnell. "I have the ability to put him on the Agriculture Committee, and I'm going to do that."[38] Senator Lincoln was the chair of the Agriculture Committee, and McConnell's promise helped to blunt Lincoln's claim that as the chair she could deliver for the farmers and consumers of Arkansas.

Seniority. Normally, the assignment panels observe seniority when preparing committee membership lists. The member of the majority party with the longest continuous committee service is usually listed first. Senate Republicans—unlike House Republicans and House and Senate Democrats—apply seniority rigidly when two or more GOP senators compete for either a committee vacancy or chairmanship. As a senator noted, "When I first came to the Senate, I was skeptical [of the seniority tradition]. But as I've become more senior, I've grown more fond of it."[39] (The Senate GOP leader fills half of all vacancies on the A committees; seniority determines the other half.)

By contrast, the two House party groups do not observe seniority as strictly as Senate Republicans typically do. Recall that House Democratic rules even state that members of their assignment panel are not bound by seniority in nominating members for committee posts (see Box 7-2 on party assignment committees). The issue of seniority came into play when Henry Waxman, D-Calif., the former chair and ranking member of the Energy and Commerce Committee, chose not to run for reelection to the 114th Congress.

Two Democrats on the panel wanted to assume Waxman's spot: Anna Eshoo, Calif., who was fifth in seniority, and Frank Pallone, N.J., first in seniority. Leader Pelosi, a close friend of Eshoo, strongly endorsed her candidacy in a "Dear Colleague" letter to all Democrats. On the other hand, Steny Hoyer of Maryland, the Democratic whip, backed Pallone. The battle lines were drawn and the contest for Energy's top spot was intense. Pelosi's firm control of the Steering and Policy Committee ensured that Eshoo would prevail over Pallone, but the Democratic Caucus reversed that decision and voted to make Pallone the ranking member on the Energy panel.

A number of factors contributed to Pallone's victory, including the issue of seniority. On the one hand, Pelosi contended that "seniority makes you a contender, but it does not make you a chairman. It is a consideration, not a determination." Hoyer disagreed with Pelosi's view: "I have historically been for the ranking member, the senior member, if that member is capable and able, and if that member has contributed significantly to the legislative product. I think Frank Pallone has done all those."[40] The Eshoo-Pallone contest triggered an internal party debate about the value of seniority in determining the top Democratic posts on committees.

In January 2015, a number of younger House Democrats, concerned that their advancement in the party was blocked by too many senior lawmakers, wanted to impose a six-year limit on how long a member could serve as a committee chair or ranking committee member. As one reformer said, "I think it's important that newer members, especially, see a path for career advancement." In response, a Hispanic Caucus member said: "I don't think you force the people who have given the time to the committee to [leave]."[41] To date, the six-year term limit proposal has not been adopted by House Democrats.

Speaker Boehner regularly confronts chairmanship decisions because of the term limits on committee and subcommittee chairs. Typically, the Speaker upholds the term-limit rule for chairs who have reached their six-year limit. His position has been upheld by the Steering Committee. An example makes the point.

At the start of the 113th Congress, there were term-limited chairs, such as Transportation Committee head John Mica, Fla., who wanted waivers to continue as panel leaders. Speaker Boehner rejected all such requests except in the special case of Paul Ryan, Wis., who was term-limited as head of the Budget Committee. Representative Ryan's case was special for several reasons. He had been selected as Mitt Romney's vice presidential candidate; he was the GOP's most prominent and authoritative spokesperson on fiscal and budgetary matters; and he was a rising star in the national Republican Party. Moreover, there was broad consensus among party leaders and rank-and-file Republicans that Ryan should be granted a waiver to continue as Budget Committee chair, especially during a period of continuing fiscal challenges among the two parties, chambers, and branches of government.

In the 114th Congress, Representative Ryan became chair of the Ways and Means Committee. Mindful that Ryan might compete for the presidency,

> BOX 7-2   **Party Assignment Committees**
>
> **House Republicans.** Before the official convening of the 104th Congress in January 1995, incoming Speaker Newt Gingrich, R-Ga., revamped his party's Committee on Committees, which he would chair. Gingrich renamed it the Steering Committee, transformed it into a leadership-dominated panel, and eliminated a weighted voting system wherein a GOP member of the assignment panel cast as many votes as there were Republicans in his or her state delegation. Instead, Gingrich granted the GOP leader (himself in this case) the right to cast the most votes (five); every other Steering Committee member could cast only one vote, except the majority leader, who got two votes. These changes have continued in subsequent Congresses. The Republican leader also appoints all GOP members of the Rules, House Administration, Ethics, and Permanent Select Intelligence Committees.
>
> **House Democrats.** Democrats on the House Ways and Means Committee functioned as their party's committee on committees from 1911 until 1974, when the Democratic Caucus voted to transfer this duty to the Steering and Policy Committee. The Steering Committee, cochaired by Rosa DeLauro of Connecticut and Donna Edwards of Maryland in the 114th Congress, recommends Democratic assignments to the caucus, one committee at a time. Leader Pelosi also names members of her party to the Ethics, House Administration, Rules, and Permanent Select Intelligence Committees. In a first, Pelosi named Muslim André Carson of Indiana to be a member of the House's Intelligence panel.
>
> **Senate Republicans.** The chair of the Republican Conference appoints the assignment panel of about three to five members. The floor leader is an ex officio member. Pennsylvania senator Patrick Toomey chairs the panel during the 114th Congress.
>
> **Senate Democrats.** The Steering and Outreach Committee makes assignments for Democrats. Its size (about twenty-five members) is set by the party conference and may fluctuate from Congress to Congress. The party's floor leader appoints the members of this panel and its chair. In the 114th Senate, the chair is Sen. Amy Klobuchar of Minnesota.

Republicans in mid-November 2014 adopted a new party rule that states in part: a chair who publicly announces his or her intent to seek an elected federal office must resign his or her chairmanship. In early January 2015 Ryan announced that he would not be a candidate for the White House in 2016, stating that "my job as [Ways and Means] chairman deserves undivided attention."[42] Speaker Boehner granted a waiver to a close ally, Rep. John Kline of Minnesota, to serve a fourth term in the 114th Congress as chair of the Education and Workforce Committee.

In addition to upholding the term-limit rule with only infrequent exceptions, Speaker Boehner removed from influential committees four conservative lawmakers who opposed the party on numerous issues in 2013.[43] In 2015 he removed two members from the Rules Committee as punishment for challenging his speakership.[44] In the view of a House GOP aide, Speaker Boehner's purpose in stripping these members of their committee assignments was to send a message to his GOP colleagues: "You want good things in Congress and to have a good career? Better play nicely."[45]

On the Senate side, Republicans adopted in 1997 a party rule restricting committee chairs (or ranking members) to six years of service. "The whole thrust behind this," said the Senate author of the term-limit change, "is to try to get greater participation, so new members of the Senate don't have to wait until they've been here 18 years to play a role."[46] This goal is not easy to achieve because long-serving Republicans are often senior on more than one committee. Thus when they hit the six-year limit, party rules permit them to seek the chairmanship (or ranking minority position) of another committee and leap-frog over a party member with less committee seniority.

Senate Republicans witnessed an unexpected case of leap-frog in the 114th Congress. Sen. Jeff Sessions of Alabama had served four years (2011–2014) as ranking member on the Budget Committee and fully expected to become the panel's chair in the 114th Congress. Instead, Sen. Mike Enzi of Wyoming decided to challenge Sessions for the Budget chairmanship, making it the only contested committee post. Tellingly, both senators were elected on the same day in 1996 and sworn into office on the same day. Absent any relevant background experience (service in the House, for example) that is used to determine seniority rankings among newly elected Senate Republicans, their seniority rank was determined by picking names out of a hat. Senator Enzi's name came out ahead of Session's, which meant that forever more, Enzi had more seniority than Sessions. After several weeks of negotiations between the two friends, an agreement was reached that allowed Senator Enzi to take the chairmanship of the Budget Committee. Senator Sessions remained on the Budget Committee.[47]

Senate Democrats have no term-limit rule for their committee leaders. Their long-standing tradition is to allow seniority on a panel to determine who will be either the chair or ranking minority member of a standing committee. But Senate rules also limit members to one full committee chairmanship. Recall the reference earlier in this chapter to how Senator Mikulski became chair of the Appropriations Committee. Or consider Sen. Bernie Sanders, D-Vt., who serves as ranking member on the Budget Committee in the 114th Congress because other, more senior Democrats on the Budget Committee prefer to remain as ranking on other committees.

Biases. The decisions made by the assignment panels inevitably determine the geographical and ideological composition of the standing committees. Committees can easily become biased toward one position or another. Farm areas are overrepresented on the Agriculture Committees and small-business interests on the Small Business Committees. It is no wonder, then, that committees are policy advocates. They propose laws that serve the interests of their members and the outside groups and agencies that gravitate toward them.

Both who gets on a panel and who does not affect committee policy making. Committees that are carefully balanced between liberal and conservative interests can be tilted one way or the other by new members. Meanwhile, the number of women on a committee can sometimes change committee dynamics and outcomes. And new committee leaders can shift a panel's policy agenda and outlook. The views of Sen. Barbara Boxer, D-Calif., on environmental policy when she chaired the Environment and Public Works Committee diverge sharply from those of the chair in the 114th Congress, Sen. James Inhofe, R-Okla.: "Inhofe calls global warming a hoax; Boxer ranks curbing global warming as one of her two top priorities."[48] A committee's political philosophy influences its success on the House or Senate floor. Committees ideologically out of step with the House or Senate majority are more likely than others to have legislation defeated or significantly revised by floor amendments.

Approval by Party Caucuses and the Chamber

For most of the last century, each chamber's party caucuses either simply ratified the assignment decisions of their committees on committees or took no action on them at all. Beginning in the 1970s, however, party caucuses became major participants in the assignment process. Chairs and ranking minority members were subjected to election by secret ballot of their party colleagues. Clearly, committee leadership is no longer an automatic right.

Although seniority still encourages continuity on committees, the seniority system has now become more flexible and is under party control. House Democratic rules for the 114th Congress state that upon "a demand supported by 10 or more Members, a separate vote, by secret ballot, shall be had on any member of a committee. . . . If the noes prevail on any such vote, the committee list . . . in question shall be returned to the [Steering Committee] for the sole purpose of implementing the direction of the Caucus." The term-limit rule for House Republicans prevents their members from becoming independent committee barons, as occurred in earlier eras. In the Senate, the parties can exercise control over committees but nearly always defer to the seniority rankings of lawmakers in determining who becomes ranking member on or heads a committee or subcommittee.

Each chamber's rules require that all members of standing committees, including chairs, be elected by the entire House or Senate. The practice is for each party's leaders to offer the caucus-approved assignment lists to the full chamber. Normally, these are approved quickly by voice vote.

COMMITTEE LEADERSHIP

Committee chairs call meetings and establish agendas, hire and fire committee staff, arrange hearings, recommend conferees, act as floor managers, allocate committee funds and rooms, develop legislative strategies, chair hearings and markups, function as the committee's spokesperson, and regulate the internal affairs and organization of their committees. For example, as the Senate Judiciary chair told a journalist, "I've always set the agenda in Judiciary."[49]

BOX 7-3 Committee Decision Making: A Formal Model

Political scientists use a variety of sophisticated techniques to understand legislative decision making. Employing concepts from economics such as rational choice—the notion that individuals (or lawmakers) have preferences or desires and that they will act in their self-interest to achieve their goals—these scholars utilize a number of analytical tools to consider how lawmakers devise strategies to accomplish their policy objectives. One such analytical approach is called spatial theory. The term *spatial* refers to a mathematical idea that theorists rely on called a policy space. An easy-to-understand example is that certain policy preferences can all be arrayed along a straight line, an unidimensional continuum. For example, one end of the line might be labeled "more spending" and the other "less spending." Different spending preferences could be placed at different points, or spaces, along the line.

In employing spatial theory to model legislative decision making, scholars make a number of assumptions. Two are especially important: (1) lawmakers hold consistent preferences, and (2) members have an ideal policy outcome that they prefer. Put differently, lawmakers will vote for policy alternatives that bring them closer to their policy ideal and oppose those that do the reverse. The work of these scholars highlights the importance of institutional rules and procedures in determining which of several policy alternatives will prevail. Analysts have also found that the median voter—the midpoint lawmaker with an equal number of other members to his or her left or right—is the ultimate determiner of outcomes in unidimensional cases. Another way to view the median voter is the 218th vote in the House, the Supreme Court justice who casts the fifth vote in a 5–4 decision, or the member who casts the sixth vote in a committee of eleven members.

To depict this graphically, assume that a House Appropriations subcommittee has sent to the floor a spending bill that reflects its committee median (CM). The subcommittee also must take into account a floor median (FM) if it wants its majority position to carry the day on the floor. The current policy status quo (Q) means that, if the bill does not pass, last year's funding level remains in force. If the subcommittee's bill is brought to the floor under a no-amendment rule, then the House membership can either accept or reject the panel's position. If the House rejects the subcommittee's policy recommendation, it has agreed to retain the status quo. Whether the subcommittee's position prevails on the floor can be depicted using these two examples.

If the subcommittee's position is to win on the House floor, it must devise a strategy that takes account of the majority preferences of the membership. Furthermore, the subcommittee

A chair's procedural advantages are hard for even the most forceful minority members to overcome. The chair may be able to kill a bill simply by refusing to schedule it for a hearing. Or a chair may convene meetings when proponents or opponents of the legislation are unavoidably absent. The chair's authority derives from the support of a committee majority and a variety of formal and informal resources, such as substantive and parliamentary experience and control over the agenda, communications, and financial resources of the committee. When told by a committee colleague that he lacked the votes on an issue, then–House Energy and Commerce chair John Dingell, Mich., reminded him, "Yeah, but I've got the gavel."[50] Dingell banged his gavel, must have some way to acquire information about the policy options likely to be accepted by at least a majority of the House. These types of considerations are commonplace in the real world of Capitol Hill policy making.

Example 1

More spending   Less spending
         FM   CM   Q

In Example 1, the preferences of a majority of the House clearly are closer to the committee's position than the status quo. Thus the committee's position prevails.

Example 2

More spending   Less spending
         FM   Q   CM

In Example 2, a majority of the House clearly favors the policy status quo instead of the committee's position, which loses in an up-or-down floor vote.

Most bills concern not a single dimension, such as more or less spending, but a multitude of dimensions. For example, a bill might be close to a member's ideal point on the spending dimension but be far away on another dimension, such as which governmental level (federal or state) should handle the issue. The introduction of additional dimensions (multidimensionality) produces greater difficulty in analyzing legislative decision making. By employing spatial theory and other analytical approaches, political scientists strive to better understand and explain congressional politics and decision making.[1]

---

[1] See, for example, Kenneth Shepsle and Mark Boncheck, *Analyzing Politics* (New York: Norton, 1977); Charles Stewart, *Analyzing Congress* (New York: Norton, 2001); and Gerald Strom, *The Logic of Lawmaking: A Spatial Theory Approach* (Baltimore: Johns Hopkins University Press, 1990).

---

adjourned the meeting, and the majority had no chance to work its will before the legislative session ended.

The Dingell example highlights the formidable ability of chairs to stymie action on legislation they oppose. However, committee chairs also are among the most substantively and strategically knowledgeable members of their panel and of the chamber. They are advantageously positioned to form ideas into law. When Bill Thomas, R-Calif., headed the Ways and Means Committee (2001–2007), he was acknowledged as hard-working, assertive, and shrewd. On many controversial issues (tax, trade, and health), he skillfully mobilized winning coalitions in committee, in the chamber, and in conference with the Senate.

Thomas even sought out senatorial advice on how to move legislation in the House in a way that would maximize its chances in the Senate.[51] With both chambers in the 114th Congress controlled by Republicans, efforts at bicameral coordination, cooperation, and communication are likely to increase.[52]

The ranking minority party members on committees are also influential figures, but they are often reacting to the plans of the majority. Among their powers on various committees are nominating minority conferees, hiring and firing minority staff, sitting ex officio on all subcommittees, assisting in setting the committee's agenda, managing legislation on the floor, and acting as committee spokespersons for their party. Ranking members, as appropriate, present minority alternatives to majority proposals, challenge the chair on procedural and policy matters, develop tactics and strategies to foil the majority's plans, and highlight party goals and views to the attentive public. For example, Elijah Cummings, D-Md., won the ranking position on the Oversight and Government Reform Committee over other competitors in the 113th Congress because he was viewed as better able than the others to counterattack the aggressive and media-savvy chair of the panel, Darrel Issa of California.[53] Cummings remains on the panel as ranking member now that Rep. Jason Chaffetz of Utah has replaced the term-limited Issa as chair in 2015. Both Cummings and Chaffetz have worked to develop a productive relationship. Each lawmaker, for instance, visited the congressional district of the other.[54]

POLICY MAKING IN COMMITTEE

Committee decision making tends to be deliberate and collegial, but fragmented. Committees encourage bargaining and accommodation among members. To move bills through Congress's multiple decision points from subcommittee to committee, authors of bills and resolutions typically make compromises in response to important committee members, among others. These gatekeepers may exact numerous alterations in a bill's substance. The proliferation of committees also multiplies the points of access for outside interests.

Overlapping Jurisdictions

The formal responsibilities of standing committees are defined by the rules of each house, various public laws, and precedents. Committees do not have watertight jurisdictional compartments. Any broad subject overlaps numerous committees. The Senate has an Environment and Public Works Committee, but other panels also consider environmental legislation. The same is true in the House. These House bodies, along with a brief sketch of some of their environmental responsibilities, are as follows:

Agriculture: pesticides; soil conservation; some water programs

Appropriations: funding for environmental programs and agencies

Energy and Commerce: health effects of the environment; environmental regulations; solid waste disposal; clean air; safe drinking water

Financial Services: open space acquisition in urban areas

Foreign Affairs: international environmental cooperation

Natural Resources: water resources; power resources; land management; wildlife conservation; national parks; nuclear waste; fisheries; endangered species

Oversight and Government Reform: federal executive branch agencies for the environment

Science, Space, and Technology: environmental research and development

Small Business: effects of environmental regulations on business

Transportation and Infrastructure: water pollution; sludge management

Ways and Means: environmental tax expenditures

Jurisdictional overlaps can have positive results. They enable members to develop expertise in several policy fields, prevent any one group from dominating a topic, and promote healthy competition among committees. Committees with overlapping jurisdictions sometimes formulate a written memorandum of understanding that outlines how policy topics are to be referred among them.[55] But healthy competition can quickly turn into intercommittee warfare. Various House and Senate committees periodically clash over issues that do not fit neatly into any single panel's area of responsibility (energy and environmental issues or cybersecurity, for example). Committees' formal jurisdictional mandates have not kept pace with change—nor can they, given the constant emergence of new issues (such as climate change). Another trigger of turf battles is forum shopping by outside interests, who want their carefully drafted bills referred to sympathetic committees.

The expansionist tendency of some committees also can create intercommittee tussles. The "bold jurisdictional power grab" by the House Energy and Commerce Committee for an intellectual copyright bill will not stand, declared the bipartisan leaders of the Judiciary Committee. "Rest assured, we will wholeheartedly oppose this move in a bipartisan fashion, as we would expect Energy and Commerce leaders to do if we attempted to write energy legislation."[56] The GOP chair of the Natural Resources Committee urged his party's leaders to transfer energy jurisdiction from the Energy and Commerce Committee to his panel. "In terms of legislative power, it is a Goliath," the chair declared. "[Energy and Commerce] is the committee that spawned Obamacare and the Democrats' cap-and-trade national energy tax."[57] Energy and Commerce chair Fred Upton, R-Mich., quickly defended his panel's jurisdiction. "To diminish the authority of the Energy and Commerce Committee," he wrote, "is to weaken the power of the House—the people's body—and give an upper hand to the Democrat[ic] White House."[58] In the end, the GOP Steering Committee rejected the Resources chair's effort to capture part of the Energy and Commerce panel's jurisdiction.[59]

Multiple Referrals

When a bill is introduced in the House, it usually is referred to a single committee. House rules traditionally made no provision for multiple referrals, although informally at times more than one panel reviewed the same bill. In 1975, however, the rules were changed to permit several types of multiple referrals. This change augmented the Speaker's authority and granted him or her additional flexibility in referring measures to various committees.

When Republicans assumed control of the House in 1995, they streamlined multiple referrals and placed them firmly under the Speaker's control. The Speaker must "designate a committee of primary jurisdiction upon the initial referral of a measure to a committee." The primary committee concept increases accountability for legislation while retaining for the Speaker flexibility in determining whether, when, and for how long other panels can receive the measure.

At the time of initial referral, the Speaker identifies the primary committee. It has predominant responsibility for shepherding the legislation to final passage. The Speaker may also send the measure to secondary panels. The House parliamentarian calls this practice an additional initial referral. In the following example of referral language, the Energy and Commerce Committee is the primary committee and Judiciary is the additional initial panel:

> H.R. 650. A bill to establish reasonable legal reforms that will facilitate the manufacture of vital, life-saving vaccines, and for other purposes; to the Committee on Energy and Commerce, and in addition to the Committee on the Judiciary, for a period to be subsequently determined by the Speaker, in each case for consideration of such provisions as fall within the jurisdiction of the committee concerned.

Multiple referrals may promote integrated policy making, broader public discussion of issues, wider access to the legislative process, and consideration of alternative approaches. They also enhance the Speaker's scheduling prerogatives. The Speaker can use the referral power to intervene more directly in committee activities and even to set deadlines for committees to report multiply referred legislation. The reverse is also possible: the Speaker can delay action on measures by referring them to other committees. Thus multiple referrals can be employed to slow down legislative decision making. (About 20 percent of measures introduced in the House are multiply referred.)

The Senate usually sends measures to a single committee—the committee with jurisdiction over the subject matter that predominates in the legislation. Although multiple referrals have long been permitted by unanimous consent, they are used infrequently, mainly because senators have many opportunities to influence policy making on the floor. Senate procedures provide lawmakers with relatively easy ways either to bypass the referral of legislation to committees or to raise issues for chamber consideration (see Chapter 8).

Where Bills Go

Many bills referred to committee are sent by the chair to a subcommittee. Others are retained for review by the full committee. In the end, committees and subcommittees select the measures they want to consider and ignore the rest. Committee consideration usually consists of three standard steps: public hearings, markups, and reports.

Hearings. When committees or subcommittees conduct hearings on a bill, they listen to a wide variety of witnesses. Hearings are an important way for lawmakers to learn and to keep abreast of the policy and oversight issues that come before the committees on which they serve. Witnesses who testify include the bill's sponsors, federal officials, pressure group and think tank representatives, business leaders, academics, state and local officials, and private citizens—sometimes even celebrities. Celebrity witnesses can help give a bill national visibility. As a senator put it, "Quite candidly, when Hollywood speaks, the world listens. Sometimes when Washington speaks, the world snoozes."[60]

Equally important are witnesses who add drama to hearings because of their first-hand experience with an issue or problem. The Senate Finance Committee, for example, attracted national headlines with its hearings on alleged wrongdoings by the Internal Revenue Service (IRS). Taxpayers recounted their horrendous experiences, and IRS agents donned black hoods to tell about the organization's mistreatment of taxpayers.[61] Testimony by employees who lost their jobs and retirement savings because of corporate scandals and mismanagement helped to galvanize congressional enactment of corporate accounting and accountability laws, such as the Dodd-Frank Wall Street Reform and Consumer Protection Act (P.L. 111–203).[62] Hearings, then, are often orchestrated as political theater in which witnesses put a human face on a public problem and tell stories that may generate public momentum for or against legislation.[63]

Hearings also provide opportunities for committee members to be heard on issues. Frequently, lawmakers present their views on legislation in their opening statements and in the guise of questioning witnesses. By revealing the patterns and intensity of support or opposition and by airing substantive problems, hearings indicate to members whether a bill is worth taking to the full chamber. Most hearings follow a traditional format. Each witness reads a prepared statement. Then each committee member has a limited time (often five minutes) to ask questions before the next witness is called. To save time and promote give and take, committees occasionally use a panel format in which witnesses sit together and briefly summarize their statements.

Committees will sometimes convene joint hearings with other relevant House or Senate panels. They also may organize field hearings in cities around the country to generate and solicit public support for an issue, or, in a two Congresses theme, schedule hearings in the chair's state or district to win him or her favorable publicity and visibility prior to the November elections. Party committees, ad hoc legislative groups, or individual lawmakers also may conduct informal hearings of their own. Committees may even hold pre-hearings so committee members can be better informed about the issues likely to be raised during a scheduled hearing.

Committees are harnessing contemporary technology to conduct Capitol Hill hearings. Committees utilize technology to provide live broadcasts of their hearings online ("Webcasts") in order to make the legislative process "fully accessible and transparent" to the public.[64] For example, immediately after a House Transportation hearing on transportation legislation with Transportation Secretary Anthony Foxx as the key witness, the committee chair, Bill Shuster, R-Pa., and Foxx held a Twitter "town meeting."[65] House and Senate panels have also employed interactive video, teleconferencing, e-hearings, and other technology to collect testimony from witnesses who may be located in other parts of the nation or the world. The Internet has been used to transmit testimony, and cable television viewers have e-mailed or faxed questions to witnesses.[66] And, in a first, an astronaut became the only person ever to deliver testimony from outer space to a committee hearing on Capitol Hill.[67]

Some of the overlapping purposes served by hearings are the following:

- To explore the need for legislation
- To build a public record in support of legislation
- To publicize the role of committee chairs
- To stake out committee jurisdictions
- To review executive implementation of public laws
- To provide a forum for citizens' grievances and frustrations
- To educate lawmakers and the attentive public on complex issues
- To raise the visibility of an issue

Hearings are shaped mainly by the chairs and their top staff, with varying degrees of input from party leaders, the ranking minority member, and others. Chairs who favor bills can expedite the hearings process; conversely, they can kill with kindness legislation they oppose by holding endless hearings. When a bill is not sent to the full chamber, the printed hearings are the end product of the committee's work. Committee chairs, mindful of the two Congresses, can also use hearings to try and win reelection by addressing issues that appeal to various voting groups in their state or district.

Markups. After hearings are held, committee members decide the bill's actual language—that is, they mark up or amend the bill (see Box 7-3 on committee decision making). Chairs may circulate their "mark" (the measure open for amendment) to committee colleagues and solicit their comments and suggestions.

To promote greater transparency and accountability, House Republicans adopted chamber rules that require committees to make their markup vehicle available online to the public at least twenty-four hours prior to markup meetings. In addition, committees are obligated to make amendments adopted during markup publicly available online within twenty-four hours, and record votes during markups are to be publicly available in electronic form within forty-eight hours.

Some panels adhere closely to parliamentary rules during the committee amending phase; others operate by consensus with few or no votes taken on the issues; and still others have "conceptual markups." A senator explained that Finance Committee markups "are not about legislative language. They are concept documents that are then put into legislative language and brought to the floor."[68] Concepts may include, for example, whether going to school counts as work for welfare recipients, or what kind of tax plan best fosters economic growth. Proponents try to craft a bill that will muster the backing of their colleagues, the other chamber, lobbyists, and the White House.

The markup process can be arduous because members often face the two Congresses dilemma: whether to support a bill that might be good for the nation or oppose it because of the opposition of their constituents. Not surprisingly, the bill that emerges from markup is usually one that can attract the support of most members. As a former chair of the House Ways and Means Committee stated, "We have not written perfect law; perhaps a faculty of scholars could do a better job. A group of ideologues could have produced greater consistency. But politics is an imperfect process."[69] Or as Sen. Pat Roberts, R-Kan., said about a bill revamping the intelligence community: "While this is not the best possible bill, it is the best bill possible."[70]

Outside pressures often intensify during markup deliberations. Under House and Senate sunshine rules, markups must be conducted in public, except on national security or related issues. Compromises can be difficult to achieve in markup rooms filled with lobbyists watching how each member will vote. Thus committees sometimes conduct pre-markups in private to work out their positions on various issues.

After conducting hearings and markups, a subcommittee sends its recommendations to the full committee. The full committee may conduct hearings and markups on its own, ratify the subcommittee's decision, take no action, or return the matter to the subcommittee for further study.

Reports. If the full committee votes to send the bill to the House or Senate, the staff prepares a report, subject to committee approval, describing the purposes and provisions of the legislation. Reports emphasize arguments favorable to the bill, summarizing selectively the results of staff research and hearings. Reports are noteworthy documents. The bill itself may be long, highly technical, and confusing to most readers. "A good report, therefore, does more than explain—it also persuades," commented a congressional staff aide.[71] Furthermore, reports may guide executive agencies and federal courts in interpreting ambiguous or complex legislative language.

The Policy Environment

Executive agencies, pressure groups, party leaders and caucuses, and the entire House or Senate form the backdrop against which a committee makes policy. (To be sure, outside groups, the 24/7 media, and the broad issue context of a particular period all influence committees' policy environment.) These environments may be consensual or conflictual. Some policy questions are settled fairly easily; others are bitterly controversial. Environments also may be monolithic or pluralistic. Some committees have a single dominant source of outside influence; others face numerous competing groups or agencies.

Environmental factors influence committees in at least four ways. First, they shape the content of public policies and thus the likelihood that these policies will be accepted by the full House or Senate. The Judiciary Committees are buffeted by diverse and competing pressure groups who feel passionately about volatile issues such as abortion, immigration, and gun control. The committees' chances for achieving agreement among their members or on the floor depend to a large extent on their abilities to deflect such issues altogether—or to accommodate diverse groups through artful legislative drafting and political accommodation.

Second, policy environments foster mutual alliances among committees, federal departments, and pressure groups—the "iron triangles." The House and Senate Veterans' Affairs Committees, for example, regularly advocate legislation to benefit veterans' groups, the second point in the triangle. This effort is backed by the Department of Veterans Affairs, the third point in the triangle. At the very least, issue networks emerge. These are fluid and amorphous groups of policy experts who try to influence any committee that deals with their subject area.[72]

Third, policy environments establish decision-making objectives and guidelines for committees. Clientele-oriented committees, such as the House and Senate Small Business Committees, try to promote the policy views of their clientele groups, small-business enterprises. Alliances between committees and federal departments also shape decisions, such as the traditional support given the military by the House and Senate Armed Services Committees.

Finally, environmental factors influence the level of partisanship on committees. Some committees are relatively free of party infighting, but other committees consider contentious social issues that often divide the two parties. The House and Senate Judiciary Committees are filled with conservative Republicans and liberal Democrats; ideological clashes are not uncommon. To try to reduce the intense partisanship on various committees, their chairs have organized informal gatherings or bipartisan retreats as a way for committee members "to find common ground despite the strong feelings on a lot of issues."[73] At least one committee chair employed a novel seating arrangement to promote interparty comity. Rather than use the traditional format—lawmakers of one party sitting on one side of the dais and the opposition on the other side—the innovative seating arrangement had Democrats and Republicans sitting next to each other all along the dais: Democrat, Republican, Democrat, Republican, and so on.

COMMITTEE STAFF

Staff aides play a big role in the three principal stages of committee policy making—hearings, markup, and report. Representatives and senators (the latter to a greater degree because there are fewer of them) cannot handle their large workloads on their own, so they must rely heavily on their unelected employees. Indeed, Congress needs qualified professional staff to counter the expertise lodged in the executive branch and in the lobbying community. In the House, committee resources are roughly divided between the majority and minority parties on a two-thirds to one-third basis; in the Senate, it is a 60 to 40 percent ratio. Informally, both parties rely on a network of outside experts to help them evaluate proposals from the executive branch, forge policy proposals, or provide strategic advice. For example, think tanks provide lawmakers and their staff with numerous domestic, defense, and foreign policy options and proposals.

The discretionary agenda of Congress and its committees is powerfully shaped by the congressional staff. Their influence can be direct or indirect, substantive or procedural, visible or invisible. In the judgment of one former senator, "Most of the work and most of the ideas come from the staffers. They are predominantly young men and women, fresh out of college and professional schools. They are ambitious, idealistic, and abounding with ideas."[74] However, staff tenure is relatively short. According to a 2010 survey conducted by the House's Chief Administrative Office, the tenure of personal staff ranges from 6.7 years for chiefs of staff to 1.8 years for staff assistants. The average tenure for Senate aides is about 5.3 years. Many committee, personal, and leadership aides use their experience as a stepping-stone to other jobs, such as lobbying.

Policy proposals emanate from many sources—the White House, administrative agencies, interest groups, state and local officials, scholars, and citizens—but staff aides are strategically positioned to advance or hinder these proposals. As one Senate committee staff director recounted, "Usually, you draw up proposals for the year's agenda, lay out the alternatives. You can put in some stuff you like and leave out some you don't. I recommend ideas that the [chair is] interested in and also that I'm interested in."[75] Many committee staff members are active in outside communications and issue networks (health or the environment, for example) that enhance lawmakers' abilities to make informed decisions.[76]

Staff aides negotiate with legislators, lobbyists, and executive officials on issues, legislative language, and political strategy. Staff members do the essential spadework that can lead to changes in policy or new laws. For example, a "team totaling 20 [Senate Governmental Affairs] aides, including detailees from the FBI and CIA" drafted the 2004 bill that reorganized the nation's intelligence community.[77] Staff aides sometimes make policy decisions. Consider their crucial role on a defense appropriations bill:

> The dollar figures in the huge piece of legislation [were] so immense that House–Senate conferees, negotiating their differences, . . . relegated almost every item less than $100 million to staff aides on grounds that the members themselves did not have time to deal with such items, which [a senator] called "small potatoes."[78]

In preparation for hearings, aides recruit witnesses, on their own or at the specific direction of the chair, and plan when and in what order they appear. In addition, staff aides commonly accompany committee members to the floor to give advice, draft amendments, and negotiate compromises. The number of aides who can be present on the floor is limited, however, by House and Senate regulations.

For information, analyses, policy options, and research projects, committee staff can turn to the three legislative support agencies: the Congressional Research Service, established in 1914; the Government Accountability Office, established in 1921 (as the General Accounting Office and renamed in 2004); and the Congressional Budget Office, established in 1974. Unlike committee or personal aides, these units operate under strict rules of nonpartisanship and objectivity. Staffed with experts, they provide Congress with analytical talent matching that in executive agencies, universities, and specialized groups.

Staffing reflects members' dual roles in the two Congresses: national policy maker and constituency representative. It can sometimes be a controversial process. A New Jersey senator, for example, was criticized by African American clergy in his state for "failing to appoint blacks to important positions on his personal staff" as he had promised he would when he was running for office. The senator responded that he had hired professional black staffers and "defended his efforts to hire members of racial minorities."[79] During the electoral season, staffers frequently take unpaid leave to work as campaign volunteers for their boss or "to boost their party's prospects in pivotal races."[80]

COMMITTEE REFORM AND CHANGE

Since passage of the Legislative Reorganization Act of 1946, Congress has made numerous attempts to reform the committee system but has succeeded mainly with limited rather than comprehensive approaches to change. In brief, because of strong opposition from members who stood to surrender subcommittee chairmanships or favored jurisdictions, Congress has had only mixed success in reorganization efforts. One change to the committee system—the creation of homeland security standing committees in each chamber—illustrates some of the difficulties associated with revamping the committee structure.

Homeland Security Committees

The National Commission on Terrorist Attacks upon the United States (also called the 9/11 Commission) urged the House and Senate to each create a single authorizing committee for homeland security. Its report stated that at least eighty-eight committees and subcommittees in Congress had some jurisdiction over the recently created Department of Homeland Security. Arguably, the formation of House and Senate homeland security panels would minimize turf conflicts, reduce the number of panels before which top DHS officials would have to appear as witnesses, and strengthen congressional oversight of the new department. Eventually, both chambers responded to the commission's suggestion, but in different ways.

In the Senate, the GOP and Democratic leaders created in August 2004 a twenty-two-person working group (headed by Sens. Mitch McConnell and Harry Reid) to review the commission's recommendations for improving oversight of intelligence and homeland security. Two months later, the Senate debated the McConnell-Reid plan (S. Res. 445), which called for renaming the Governmental Affairs Committee the Homeland Security and Governmental Affairs Committee and assigning it broad authority for overseeing domestic security and DHS. Achieving that objective, however, would require ten standing committees to give up some of their jurisdiction to the renamed Governmental Affairs panel.

During floor action on S. Res. 445, several amendments were successfully offered by committee chairs and ranking members reclaiming the jurisdiction that would have been lost to the renamed Governmental Affairs Committee if the resolution was adopted unchanged. "We're creating a shell," lamented Joseph I. Lieberman of Connecticut, the ranking Democrat on the Governmental Affairs Committee. "We're calling a committee a homeland security committee. But if you pick up the shell, there's not much homeland security under it."[81] The chair of the Governmental Affairs Committee, Susan Collins, R-Maine, said the changes made to S. Res. 445 left her newly renamed panel with "less than 38 percent of the Department of Homeland Security's budget and 8 percent of its personnel."[82] Dismayed by these events, both Collins and Lieberman voted against S. Res. 445, which was approved on October 9, 2004, by a 79–6 vote. S. Res. 445 also called for the creation of a Senate Appropriations Subcommittee on Intelligence, but that proposal was not acted upon.

At the opening of the 109th Congress in 2005, the House replaced its temporary select panel on homeland security with a standing committee. The permanent panel was given, among other responsibilities, jurisdiction over general homeland security policy and the organization and administration of the Department of Homeland Security. The new committee also was assigned broad oversight authority over all government "activities relating to homeland security, including the interaction of all departments and agencies with the Department of Homeland Security." Even with the creation of the new panel, however, oversight of homeland security is still spread among nine other authorizing committees.

The turf-conscious committee chairs negotiated with their party leaders to preserve some portion of their panels' jurisdiction that had been given to the new standing committee. A detailed analysis of how homeland security legislation was to be referred among all the committees with homeland security jurisdiction was included in the *Congressional Record*.[83] To illustrate, the Homeland Security Committee was to receive bills dealing with "transportation security," but the Transportation and Infrastructure Committee retained its jurisdiction over measures dealing with "transportation safety." Plainly, this jurisdictional distinction is somewhat akin to the adage, "two sides of the same coin."

At the start of the 112th Congress in 2011, House GOP leaders considered—and rejected—giving the Homeland Security Committee the predominance of jurisdiction over the Department of Homeland Security. The chair of the Homeland Security panel urged party leaders to consolidate significant policy and oversight responsibility in his committee rather than maintain the status quo of having DHS subject to the marching orders of numerous committees and subcommittees. But the head of the Transportation Committee, along with other committee chairs, argued that "their committees should get more homeland security turf, not less."[84] GOP leaders did not want to open the new Congress with a bitter and divisive jurisdictional battle over committee turf and quietly quashed the matter. And that has been the response of the majority leadership to this day. Even so, at the start of the 114th Congress, several Homeland Security members once again unsuccessfully urged their GOP leaders to consolidate more homeland jurisdiction in their committee.

Committees are remarkably durable, resilient, and stable institutions, despite the periodic forces for change that buffet them (such as public criticism of Congress and reformist sentiment among institutionally minded lawmakers). Major committee restructuring plans fail or produce only marginal adjustments in committees' jurisdictional mandates, policy-making influence, or method of operation. Scholars and lawmakers posit various theories to explain why it is difficult to accomplish major jurisdictional realignment. For example, because the control of jurisdictional turf is viewed as power, Speaker Thomas P. "Tip" O'Neill Jr., D-Mass., explained the House's rejection of a major 1973–1974 committee realignment plan in this succinct manner: "The name of the game is power, and the boys don't want to give it up."[85] A political scientist offered an electoral explanation for the demise of committee reshuffling plans that embodies the two Congresses concept:

> [A] primary and constant force hindering committee restructuring movements has been the electoral objectives of members of Congress. Under pressure to bolster their reelection prospects in order to achieve long-term legislative and personal goals, rational politicians with the ability to shape legislative structures utilize the arrangement of rules and procedures to secure targeted government benefits for needy constituents and voting blocs. Any widespread change in the established order of policy deliberation—particularly its centerpiece—the committee system—would create far too much uncertainty in members' electoral strategies and therefore would be broadly opposed from the start.[86]

Whatever other factors (such as interest group, party leadership, or committee member and staff opposition) impede major committee overhaul, these workshops of Congress evolve in response to new events and circumstances. Several recent developments highlight the dynamic quality of the committee system. These include ebbs and flows in the authority of committee chairs, the use of task forces, and the circumvention of the committee process.

Constricting the Authority of Committee Chairs

When Republicans took control of both houses of Congress in the mid-1990s, many GOP committee chairs had to take more direction from their top leaders, especially in the House. Committee chairs "have been at the mercy of top House and Senate Republican leaders," wrote two congressional analysts, who "resorted to dictating legislation from the top down in order to maintain some semblance of control."[87] Centralized control over committees was plainly evident during the speakership of Newt Gingrich (1995–1999), who sometimes circumvented committee consideration of legislation; dictated legislative changes to committees; used the Rules Committee to redraft committee-reported measures; and engaged in other actions that undermined the committee system, such as creating partisan task forces. Two changes made during the Gingrich era require emphasis because they strengthened party control of the committee chairs. First, Gingrich riveted into the House rulebook term limits for committee and subcommittee leaders, which has prevented the return of powerful committee barons. Furthermore, he took control of the committee assignment process and set aside seniority as the principal criterion in choosing committee leaders. Party loyalty, fund-raising, and legislative skills often take precedence today over seniority in naming committee chairs.

Speaker Hastert, too, was not reluctant to rein in committee chairs. He decided to use an interview process to determine replacements for full committee chairs who had completed their six years. In a letter to GOP members, Speaker Hastert explained several features of the interview process: "The candidates [for each open chairmanship] will be given an opportunity to discuss their legislative agenda, oversight agenda, how they intend to organize the committees, and their communications strategy."[88] Party loyalty and fund-raising prowess were also important factors. Even with term limits, there is no guarantee that chairs will be permitted to serve their full six-year term if they arouse the ire of party leaders. In an unprecedented event, GOP leaders ousted a colleague in 2004 (Christopher Smith of New Jersey) as chair of the Veterans' Affairs Committee, removed him from the panel, and named another member as chair. Smith's offense: outspoken advocacy of more spending on veterans' benefits, which angered Speaker Hastert. The message of Smith's removal was plain to every Republican: toe the party line and be a team player or you will be benched.

Speaker Hastert also exercised tight control over the Appropriations Committee. After Hastert won adoption in 2003 of a party rules change requiring the Appropriations subcommittee chairs to be approved by the Steering Committee, one of the subcommittee leaders said, "Now the leadership gets to have the [subcommittee chairs] come in and grovel before them."[89] Two years later, the Steering Committee warned a subcommittee chair that he could lose the chairmanship of his Appropriations subcommittee if he "does not raise or donate more money to Republicans."[90]

Speaker Pelosi worked to keep the committee chairs under control and to shape the party message and agenda at the top leadership level. After all, a major focus of Pelosi was to retain Democratic control of the House in the November 2008 and 2010 elections. She could not permit independent-minded committee chairs to do their own thing and jeopardize this fundamental party goal. At the same time, Speaker Pelosi recognized the need to have a productive relationship with her chairs, because much of the House's work is carried out by these "little legislatures." Achieving the right balance between "top-down" command and committee autonomy is no easy task. Henry Waxman, D-Calif., a committee chair and a Pelosi ally, put it this way: "I think there has to be a lot more direction from the leadership to the committees of jurisdiction. We don't want to return to the days of committee chairs that felt they didn't have to be accountable. There has to be a balance."[91]

As a former committee chair, Speaker Boehner wanted to follow the "regular order" and allow committees to produce legislative products by observing the usual deliberative process of hearings, markups, and reports. He promised that "no more bills [would be] written behind closed doors in the speaker's office. Bills should be written by legislators in committee in plain public view."[92] The reality was somewhat different, however. Significant measures were the product of private negotiations among the top House party leaders, particularly the Speaker, Senate leaders (with Senate GOP leader Mitch McConnell often playing a key role), Vice President Joe Biden, and President Barack Obama. Key staff aides to these party and executive branch leaders were also instrumental negotiators on the critical bills.

In the view of Rep. David Price, D-N.C., a former political scientist, "Partly what is going on here is the decline of the committees. The place is much more centralized. There are less active less autonomous committees."[93] Diminished autonomy filters down to subcommittees, as well. In 2015 Republican leaders reportedly issued a warning through their full committee chairs: if subcommittee leaders vote against GOP-initiated procedural motions on the House floor, they "should give up their posts" because party leaders "will not tolerate members stepping out of line."[94]

Senate committee chairs also are subject to direction from their party leadership. For example, when Harry Reid, D-Nev., was Senate majority leader, he told the Finance chair to "stop chasing Republican votes on [President Obama's] massive health care reform bill."[95] When political momentum began to build for enactment of an earlier health measure, another majority leader took the issue away from the chair of the Health, Education, Labor, and Pensions Committee and "created a [party] task force . . . to write the . . . bill."[96] The point is that on measures of utmost party importance, congressional leaders will often override the prerogatives of committee chairs to take control of crucial agenda items.

When Mitch McConnell became Senate majority leader at the start of the 114th Congress, one of his goals was "to return to the regular order. We need to get committees working again."[97] On an earlier occasion, he stated: "The committee process is a shadow of what it's been. Major legislation is now routinely drafted not in committee but in the majority leader's conference room and then dropped on the floor with little or no opportunity for members to participate in the amendment process, virtually guaranteeing a fight."[98] It is too soon to determine whether and to what extent Senator McConnell will be able to empower committees in the 114th Congress. Early on, there is some evidence that Senator McConnell is relying on committees to influence the Senate's agenda. For example, he deferred to Armed Services Committee chair John McCain, R-Ariz., on the timing of floor action on the confirmation of Defense Secretary nominee Ashton Carter; he let Senator Bob Corker, R-Tenn., chair of the Foreign Relations Committee, "take the lead on an Iran sanctions bill"; and, to spare "himself from refereeing a thorny debate" on filibuster reform, McConnell relied on Rules chair Roy Blunt, Mo., to help determine whether the Senate would adopt any filibuster rule change.[99]

To sum up, the ability of today's party leaders, particularly in the House, to exercise significant control over committee leaders represents a major change in how Congress works. The chairs are subject to centralized leadership direction on the party's top priorities and might face sanctions if their performance does not comport with party expectations. On the one hand, this development ensures that the chairs (and ranking minority members) are ultimately accountable for their actions to the Democratic Caucus or Republican Conference. On the other hand, tight leadership control, combined with term limits for House and Senate Republicans, could gradually diminish the traditional role of committees as the policy specialization system for the legislative branch. Why bother to devote years of effort to becoming substantive experts, some committee members might ask, if policy on major issues is decided at the top and committee leaders are forced to relinquish their posts after six years (if not sooner)?

Party Task Forces

Speaker Gingrich was noted for creating numerous party task forces, in part because he could determine their mandate and timetable, appoint the chair and members, and assign a deadline for drafting a product. Many of these task forces did little, but some wrote legislation. Indeed, task forces can forge consensus, draft legislation, coordinate strategy, promote intraparty communication, and involve noncommittee members and junior members in issue areas.

Speaker Hastert deemphasized the use of party task forces, but he still occasionally employed them to address issues of importance to the party. For example, Hastert created task forces to deal with health and terrorism issues. Speaker Pelosi established a bipartisan task force to consider whether the House should create an outside body to investigate ethical misconduct by lawmakers.[100] Her initiative led the House in March 2008 to create an independent Office of Congressional Ethics (OCE) with authority to initiate investigations of alleged misconduct by lawmakers.[101] Speaker Boehner, who retained the OCE, relied on a GOP high-tech working group "to propose measures that would spur growth in the high-tech industry."[102]

Senate leaders also form party task forces, sometimes to showcase senators up for reelection and to promote party priorities. For example, a senator up for reelection was named by GOP leader McConnell to head the GOP's high-tech task force. The aims of the task force are "to advise the Republican Conference on technology issues and act as an advocate for the industry."[103] Party task forces are also created to develop legislative plans or ameliorate internal party conflict. For example, Senate GOP leader Bob Dole of Kansas established a task force to cool the passions of junior Republicans who wanted to oust the Appropriations chair (Mark Hatfield of Oregon) because he did not vote for a top GOP priority, a constitutional balanced budget amendment. The task force came up with term limits for committee chairs, which, as noted earlier, are still observed by Senate Republicans.

A variation on task forces in both chambers is what commentators call "gangs." They are lawmakers of both parties in each house who come together to advance major issues that the relevant committees of jurisdiction are hard-pressed to resolve because of ideological, partisan, or other divisions. In the view of an insightful commentator, "With polarization increasingly clogging the conventional paths to agreement (either at the committee level or through leadership), [lawmakers] convene a coalition of the willing to chart a bypass." Another analyst noted that committees "have been bypassed so many times by the leadership that they are not [always] the venue [for deal-making] anymore."[104]

The "gang of eight" in the 113th Senate—composed of four Democrats and four Republicans—is a good example of this phenomenon. This gang played a major role in securing Senate passage in 2013 of a comprehensive immigration reform measure. One gang member, Sen. Lindsey Graham, R-S.C., used a two Congresses theme to remind GOP opponents of immigration reform that 70 percent of the Hispanic electorate voted for President Obama in the 2012 election. Politically, he said, "if the bill fails and Republicans are blamed . . . I think it makes it virtually impossible for us to win the White House in 2016."[105]

At the same time, the House also created a bipartisan gang of members, led by Rep. Mario Diaz-Balart, R-Fla., who met in secret to craft an immigration reform bill that might pass the House. By early 2014, they began to share the contents of their proposed bill with lawmakers they trusted. To ease the concerns of colleagues worried about supporting such a plan, they employed polls, PowerPoint presentations, and intelligence from outside supporters. The two Congresses soon ended hopes for House enactment of immigration reform. In a stunning upset, Majority Leader Eric Cantor, R-Va., was defeated in a party primary by a little-known challenger who castigated Cantor as a secret advocate of "amnesty" for illegal aliens. The outcome: support faded quickly among Republicans for immigration reform.[106]

Bypassing Committees

It has not been unusual in recent years, as noted above, for House and Senate party leaders to bypass some or all of the stages of committee consideration of legislation. In general, the circumvention of committees reflects the dominance of party power over committee power. It also represents Congress's focus on partisan gain over cooperative policy making. Specific reasons for bypassing committees are noteworthy. For example, heightened partisanship in certain committees encourages party leaders to take charge of priority measures to avoid negative media coverage of committee markups. Or factional disputes within committees may prevent them from reaching agreement on measures deemed important to party leaders. Time is a factor as well. Party leaders may believe there is not enough time for committees to hold hearings and markups on major bills they want to consider within a certain time period. Along these lines, Senator Mikulski lamented that "legislative malpractice" occurred during the Senate debate on a medical liability bill: "First of all, the procedure for considering this bill is seriously flawed. The bill was brought to the full Senate without hearings, without consideration by the Judiciary Committee."[107] While some analysts contend that "there are few consequences if [committees are bypassed] because nobody outside Congress cares whether a bill went through committee or not,"[108] many committee chairs and rank-and-file lawmakers are frustrated as the careful legislating made possible by committees takes a back seat to political messaging.[109]

CONCLUSION

Several generalizations can be made about congressional committees today. First, they shape the House and Senate agendas. Not only do they have negative power—pigeonholing legislation referred to them—but they have positive power as well. The bills they report largely determine what each chamber will debate and in what form. As one House chair stated in his testimony before the Joint Committee on the Organization of Congress, committees

> provide Congress with the expertise, skill, and organizational structure necessary to cope with the increasingly complex and technical questions in both the domestic and international arenas. They also ensure a forum for the broadest possible participation of diverse interests and constituencies in the formative stages of the legislative process. They are, in short, the window through which much of the democratic participation in lawmaking is made possible.[110]

Second, committees differ in their policy-making environments, mix of members, decision-making objectives, and ability to fulfill individual members' goals. Recruitment methods reinforce committees' autonomy; they frequently are imbalanced ideologically or geographically. And they are likely to advocate policies espoused by agencies and outside groups interested in their work.

Third, some committees still have an *esprit de corps* that flows across party lines, in part because these panels have developed a culture of bipartisanship. The military panels are a good example. Despite intermittent partisan clashes, for the past fifty-three years the House and Senate Armed Services Committees have never failed to win enactment into law of the annual National Defense Authorization Act. Committee members usually will defend their panels against criticisms or jurisdictional trespassing and criticize attempts to bypass them.

Fourth, committees typically operate independently of one another. This longtime custom fosters an attitude of mutual noninterference in the work of other committees. However, multiple referrals of bills spawn broader interrelationships among committees.

Fifth, the committee system contributes fundamentally to policy fragmentation, although a few committees—such as the House's Rules and Budget Committees—act as policy coordinators for Congress. "This is one of the anomalies here," remarked a House member. "In order to attain legislative efficiency, we say that we have to break down into committees with specialized jurisdictions. When you do that, you lose your ability to grapple with the big problems."[111] As a result, party leaders are more involved than ever in coordinating policy making and forging winning coalitions in committees and on the floor.

Finally, committee autonomy is far weaker today than it was before the 1970s, as assertive party leaders strive to move the party's agenda forward and enforce party discipline—with or without the committee leaders' cooperation. Gone are the days when committee chairs were known as the "dukes" and "barons" of Capitol Hill. In brief, the balance of power in Congress has shifted to party leaders.

House and Senate Chambers. Senators sit at assigned desks in the elegant Senate chamber (top). The House Speaker's chair is in front of the flag and to the left of the Mace—a symbol of the authority of the Sergeant at Arms that on rare occasions may be hoisted and displayed to quell disturbances in the chamber. The seats below are for clerks, and the box in the foreground is the "hopper," where members may place amendments for House consideration (center). The House chamber, seen from the rear, shows the Speaker's rostrum but also the galleries and lawmakers' seats. Members do not have assigned seats, but the majority and minority committee leaders' tables are seen to the right (bottom).

Congressional Rules and Procedures

C ongress needs written rules to do its work. Compiling the Senate's first parliamentary manual, Thomas Jefferson stressed the importance of a known system of rules:

> It is much more material that there should be a rule to go by, than what the rule is; that there may be uniformity of proceeding in business not subject to the caprice of the Speaker or captiousness of the members. It is very material that order, decency, and regularity be preserved in a dignified public body.[1]

Jefferson understood that how Congress operates affects what it does. Thus Congress's rules protect majority and minority rights, divide the workload, help contain conflict, ensure fair play, and distribute power among members. Because formal rules cannot cover every contingency, precedents—accumulated decisions of House Speakers and Senate presiding officers—fill in the gaps. These precedents are codified by House and Senate parliamentarians, printed, and distributed. There are also informal, unwritten codes of conduct, such as courtesy to other members.[2] These folkways are commonly transmitted from incumbent members to newcomers, though institutional civility is under strain in what Sen. Barbara Mikulski terms "today's era of shutdown, slowdown, slamdown politics."[3]

Before bills become laws, they typically pass successfully through several stages in each house (see Figure 8-1 for a simplified view of lawmaking). Bills that fail to attract majority (sometimes supermajority) support at any critical juncture may never be passed. Congress, in short, is a procedural obstacle course that favors opponents of legislation and hinders proponents. This defensive advantage promotes bargaining and compromise at each decision point.

Congressional rules are not independent of the policy and power struggles that lie behind them. There is very little the House and Senate cannot do under the rules so long as the action is backed by votes and inclination. And yet votes and inclination are not easily obtained, and the rules persistently challenge the proponents of legislation to demonstrate that they have both resources at their command. Little prevents obstruction at every turn except the tacit understanding that the business of the House and Senate must go on. Members recognize that the rules can be redefined and prerogatives taken away or modified. Rules also can be employed against those who use them abusively. In short, rules can be used to block or advance actions in either chamber, and proponents or opponents of measures or matters do not look on them as neutral devices.

INTRODUCTION OF BILLS

Only members of Congress can introduce legislation. Often embedded in these measures are a number of assumptions—for example, that a problem exists; that it can best be resolved through enactment of a federal law instead of allowing administrative agencies or state and local governments to handle it; and that the proposed solution contained in the bill ameliorates rather than exacerbates the problem. The GOP-controlled House recently adopted a rule requiring all sponsors of legislative proposals to provide a statement specifying the power or powers granted to Congress in the Constitution that give it the authority to enact the bill or joint resolution. The purpose of the rules change, according to Rep. Greg Walden, R-Ore., is to ensure that "Congress respects the limits imposed on it by the founding document."[4]

Lawmakers introduce legislation for many reasons: personal, political, and policy. When gasoline prices rise, members respond in two Congresses fashion by introducing numerous energy-related bills. Another motivation can be just as potent: a personal brush with adversity. Congress is an intensely human place, where personal experience sometimes has powerful repercussions.[5] As a senator stated, "Each of us, as United States senators, comes to . . . this public place with the sum of our beliefs, our personal experience and our values, and none of us checks them at the door."[6] For example, former senator Pete V. Domenici, R-N.M., whose daughter suffers from mental illness, was Congress's acknowledged champion for the mentally ill. "In the field of mental health," said a Democratic House member, "I think it's possible that nothing at all would have been done by Congress if it weren't for legislators like Domenici who were galvanized by personal experience."[7] Former representative Carolyn McCarthy, D-N.Y., was a forceful advocate for gun control. Why? A deranged gunman on a commuter train killed her husband and seriously wounded her adult son. As a journalist concluded: "Much is made of the so-called intersection of policy and politics. Hardly noticed, but perhaps more important to lawmakers themselves, is the intersection of policy and personal affairs, the bills that directly play a role in the lives of lawmakers and their loved ones."[8] Beyond personal experience, members get ideas for bills from numerous sources, such as the executive branch, interest groups, scholars, state and local officials, constituents, the media, and their own staff.

A member who introduces a bill becomes its sponsor. He or she may seek cosponsors to demonstrate wide support for the legislation. Outside groups also may urge members to cosponsor measures. "We were not assured of a

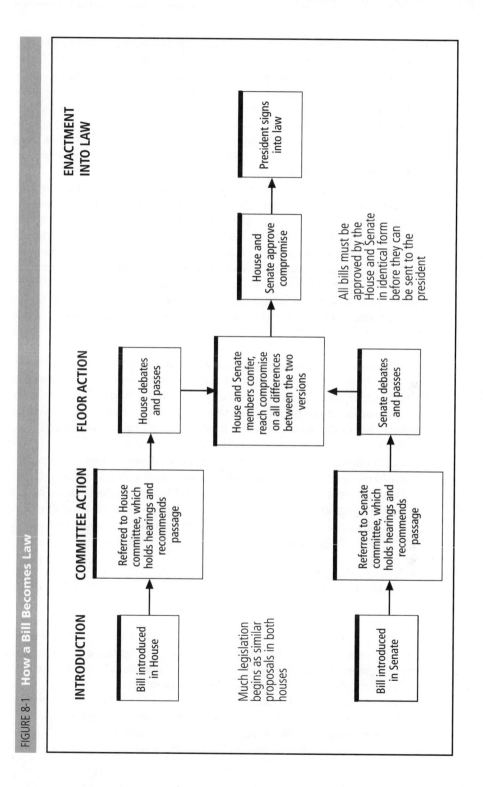

FIGURE 8-1 How a Bill Becomes Law

INTRODUCTION

COMMITTEE ACTION

FLOOR ACTION

ENACTMENT INTO LAW

Bill introduced in House

Referred to House committee, which holds hearings and recommends passage

House debates and passes

House and Senate members confer, reach compromise on all differences between the two versions

House and Senate approve compromise

President signs into law

Much legislation begins as similar proposals in both houses

All bills must be approved by the House and Senate in identical form before they can be sent to the president

Bill introduced in Senate

Referred to Senate committee, which holds hearings and recommends passage

Senate debates and passes

hearing," said a lobbyist of a bill that his group was pushing. "So it was very important to line up a lot of cosponsors to show the over-all concern."[9] A two Congresses dimension is also evident in signing (or not signing) on to legislation. For example, a lawmaker may cosponsor a labor bill to win the support of union workers back home. Conversely, the lawmaker may decide against cosponsoring the labor bill because it would mobilize business groups to oppose his or her reelection. Vulnerable lawmakers up for reelection may cosponsor measures offered by opposition members to broaden their appeal to voters in both major parties.

Equally important as the number of cosponsors is their identity, especially their leadership status and ideological stance. Members often seek out cosponsors from the opposing party to signal that the bill transcends partisan politics. In an unusual cosponsorship pairing, the former House chairs of their respective party campaign committees, Chris Van Hollen, D-Md., and Pete Sessions, R-Tex., joined to introduce bipartisan legislation.[10] When Sen. Ted Kennedy, D-Mass., an outspoken liberal, served in the Senate with Sen. Strom Thurmond, R-S.C., a southern conservative, he exclaimed, "Whenever Strom and I introduce a bill together, it is either an idea whose time has come, or one of us has not read the bill."[11]

Although identifying a bill's sponsors is easy, pinpointing its real initiators may be difficult. Legislation is "an aggregate, not a simple production," wrote Woodrow Wilson. "It is impossible to tell how many persons, opinions, and influences have entered into its composition."[12] President John F. Kennedy, for example, usually is given credit for initiating the Peace Corps. But Theodore Sorensen, Kennedy's special counsel, recalled that the Peace Corps was

> based on the Mormon and other voluntary religious service efforts, on an editorial Kennedy had read years earlier, on a speech by General [James] Gavin, on a luncheon I had with Philadelphia businessmen, on the suggestions of [Kennedy's] academic advisers, on legislation previously introduced and on the written response to a spontaneous late-night challenge he issued to Michigan students.[13]

In short, many bills have complex origins.

Required legislation, particularly funding measures, make up much of Congress's annual agenda. Bills that authorize programs and specify how much money can be spent on them (authorization bills) and bills that provide the money (appropriations bills) appear on Congress's schedule at about the same time each year. Other matters recur at less frequent intervals, every five years perhaps. Emergency issues require Congress's immediate attention. Activist legislators also push proposals onto Congress's program.

Bills not acted on die automatically at the end of each two-year Congress. "Anybody can drop a bill into the hopper [a mahogany box near the Speaker's podium where members place their proposed bills]," said a House GOP leader. "The question is, Can you make something happen with it?"[14]

BOX 8-1   **Types of Legislation**

Bill

- Most legislative proposals before Congress are in a bill form.
- Bills are designated H.R. (House of Representatives) or S. (Senate) according to where they originate, followed by a number assigned in the order in which they were introduced, from the beginning of each two-year congressional term.
- *Public bills* deal with general questions and become public laws if approved by Congress and signed by the president.
- *Private bills* deal with individual matters, such as claims against the government, immigration and naturalization cases, and land titles. They become private laws if approved and signed by the president.

Joint Resolution

- A joint resolution, designated H. J. Res. or S. J. Res., requires the approval of both houses and the president's signature, just as a bill does, and has the force of law.
- No significant difference exists between a bill and a joint resolution. The latter generally deals with limited matters, such as a single appropriation for a specific purpose.
- Joint resolutions are used to propose constitutional amendments, which do not require presidential signatures but become a part of the Constitution when three-fourths of the states have ratified them.

Concurrent Resolution

- A concurrent resolution, designated H. Con. Res. or S. Con. Res., must be passed by both houses but does not require the president's signature and does not have the force of law.
- Concurrent resolutions generally are used to make or amend rules applicable to both houses or to express their joint sentiment. A concurrent resolution, for example, is used to fix the time for adjournment of a Congress and to express Congress's annual budgeting plan. It might also be used to convey the congratulations of Congress to another country on the anniversary of its independence.

Resolution

- A simple resolution, designated H. Res. or S. Res., deals with matters entirely within the prerogatives of one house.
- It requires neither passage by the other chamber nor approval by the president and does not have the force of law.
- Most resolutions deal with the rules of one house. They also are used to express the sentiments of a single house, to extend condolences to the family of a deceased member, or to give advice on foreign policy or other executive business.

In many cases, the ideas in bills that are never passed can still become law in other ways. For example, a twenty-three-year veteran of the House who was criticized for introducing 640 unsuccessful measures during his service refuted the contention that he was "the nation's least successful lawmaker of the past two decades" by pointing out that many of his ideas "were a seed planted . . . in a larger bill." In fact, the member estimated that 110 of his ideas became law "after being stuck in somebody else's bill."[15]

Drafting

"As a sculptor works in stone or clay, the legislator works in words," observed one member.[16] Words are the building blocks of policy, and legislators frequently battle over adding, deleting, or modifying terms and phrases.

Members increasingly give their bills eye-catching titles to attract media attention and for partisan message purposes. For example, GOP lawmakers have introduced bills with titles such as "The Reducing Barack Obama's Unsustainable Deficit Act."[17] Titles, such as the Violence Against Women Act, also have a two Congresses dimension. "Obviously, you want to be for [that] title," remarked Sen. Roy Blunt, R-Mo. "If Republicans can't be for it, we need to have a very convincing alternative."[18] Creative acronyms are also increasingly popular on Capitol Hill because they attract public attention. Consider the USA PATRIOT Act (Uniting and Strengthening America by Providing Appropriate Tools Required to Intercept and Obstruct Terrorism), the DREAM Act (Development, Relief, and Education for Alien Minors), or the JOBS bill (Jumpstart Our Business Startups).

Although bills are introduced only by members, anyone can draft them.[19] Expert drafters in the House and Senate offices of the legislative counsel assist members and committees in writing legislation. Executive agencies and lobbying groups also often prepare measures for introduction by friendly legislators. Many home-state industries, for example, draft narrowly tailored tariff or regulatory measures that enhance their business prospects. These proposals are then introduced by local lawmakers—another instance of the two Congresses linkage. As a senatorial aide explained, the senator sometimes "just introduces [bills] as a courtesy to his constituents."[20] (See Box 8-1 outlining the four basic types of legislation: bills, joint resolutions, concurrent resolutions, and simple resolutions.)

Nowadays, Congress frequently acts on comprehensive (omnibus) bills or resolutions (sometimes called packages or megabills by the press). For example, during the lame duck session following the November 2014 midterm elections, Congress enacted a $1.1 trillion omnibus appropriations bill over 1,600 pages. Packages contain an array of issues that were once handled as separate pieces of legislation. Their increasing use stems in part from members' reluctance to make hard political decisions without a package arrangement. A House Budget Committee chair once explained their attractiveness. As he stated:

Large bills can be used to hide legislation that otherwise might be more controversial. By packaging difficult issues in measures that command broad support, they enable members to avoid hard votes that they would have to account for at election time and allow members to avoid angering special-interest groups that use votes [to decide] contributions to campaigns. Leaders can also use them to slam-dunk issues that otherwise might be torn apart or to pressure the President to accept provisions that he objects to.[21]

Sometimes, Congress has little choice but to use the omnibus approach. Difficulties in enacting the twelve annual appropriations bills often mean that all or many are rolled into one comprehensive package. In this way, procedural action on the outstanding measures is expedited by majority party leaders, who, in doing so, minimize the opportunities for further delay.[22]

Timing

"Everything in politics is timing," Speaker Thomas P. "Tip" O'Neill Jr., D-Mass. (1977–1987), used to say. A bill's success or failure often hinges on when it is introduced or brought to the floor. A bill that might have succeeded early in a session could fail as adjournment nears. However, controversial legislation can sometimes be rushed through during the last hectic days of a Congress. "You do learn that everything has its time," noted Sen. Bob Corker, R-Tenn. You "just wait for the moment which is going to be the best environment."[23]

Elections greatly influence the timing of legislation. Policy issues can be taken off or kept on Congress's agenda because of electoral circumstances—a good illustration of how the two Congresses are inextricably connected. For example, coming off major electoral successes, parties will usually try to capitalize on their momentum with quick action early in the new Congress. Noteworthy examples are the House's action in 1995 on the ten-point, hundred-day Contract with America agenda heralded by Speaker Newt Gingrich, R-Ga., and the hundred-hour legislative agenda pushed in 2007 by Speaker Nancy Pelosi, D-Calif. As one of its first orders of business under Speaker Boehner, the House on January 26, 2011, passed a bill to repeal Obamacare.

REFERRAL OF BILLS

After bills are introduced, they are referred formally to the appropriate standing committees by the Senate presiding officer or the House Speaker. (In practice, however, measures are referred by the Senate or House parliamentarian, who is the official procedural adviser to each chamber's presiding officer.)

A bill's phraseology can affect its referral and therefore its chances of passage. This political fact of life means that members use words artfully when drafting legislation. The objective is to encourage the referral of their measures to sympathetic, not hostile, committees. If a bill mentions taxes, for example, it invariably is referred to the tax panels. In a classic case of circumventing the Finance Committee, Senator Domenici avoided the word *tax* in a bill proposing a charge on waterborne freight:

> If the waterway fee were considered a tax—which it was, basically, because it would raise revenues for the federal treasury—the rules would place it under the dominion of the Senate's tax-writing arm, the Finance Committee. But Finance was chaired by Russell B. Long, of Louisiana, whose state included two of the world's biggest barge ports and who was, accordingly, an implacable foe of waterway charges in any form. Domenici knew that Long could find several years' worth of bills to consider before he would voluntarily schedule a hearing on S. 790 [the Domenici bill]. For this reason, [Domenici staff aides] had been careful to avoid the word *tax* in writing the bill, employing such terms as *charge* and *fee* instead.[24]

Domenici's drafting strategy worked. His bill was jointly referred to the Commerce Committee and the Environment Committee, on which he served. Because committees' jurisdictional mandates are ambiguous and overlap, it is not unusual for legislation to be referred to two or more committees—the concept of "one bill, many committees." So-called "multiple referrals" are common in the House, less so in the Senate. In the Senate, they require unanimous consent to implement. Furthermore, all senators have many opportunities to influence committee-reported measures or matters, regardless of whether they serve on the panel of jurisdiction (see Box 8-2, which describes how parliamentary convention affects the reference of legislation).

Of the thousands of bills introduced each year, Congress takes up relatively few. During the 113th Congress (2013–2015), 8,913 public bills and joint resolutions were introduced, but only 296 (3 percent) became public laws, many naming post offices and federal buildings. Many more public laws were enacted in earlier Congresses: for example, 640 in the 90th (1967–1969) and 590 in the 99th (1985–1987). Part of the general decline in the number of laws enacted can be explained by the use of omnibus or megabills. The decline may also stem from the widespread congressional sentiment that more laws may not be the answer to the nation's problems. But the decline also reflects political stalemates resulting from the complexity of issues, the intensity of partisanship, legislative-executive and bicameral conflicts, and the narrow party divisions in Congress. It is worth emphasizing that lawmakers understand that most of the bills they introduce are unlikely, as stand-alone measures, to become law. Members know that the ideas encapsulated in their legislation can be "added as amendments to a larger bill or negotiated into a markup or conference report."[25]

Lawmaking is an arduous and intricate process. As a Senate GOP leader noted, "That's the way Congress works. You work for two years and finally you get to the end and either it all collapses in a puddle or you get a breakthrough."[26] Or as former representative John Dingell, D-Mich., the longest-serving lawmaker in U.S. history in either chamber, phrased it: "Legislation is hard, pick-and-shovel work," and it often "takes a long time to do it."[27] Recall the decades-long efforts by numerous lawmakers and presidents—from Teddy Roosevelt to, finally, Barack Obama—to comprehensively overhaul the nation's health care system.

Once committees complete action on the bills referred to them, the House and Senate rules require a majority of the full committee to be physically present to report (vote) out any measure. If this rule is violated and not waived, a point of order can be made against the proposal on the floor. (A point of order is a parliamentary objection that halts the proceedings until the chamber's presiding officer decides whether the contention is valid.)

Bills reported from committee have passed a critical stage in the lawmaking process. The next major step is to reach the House or Senate floor for debate and amendment. The discussion that follows begins with the House because tax and appropriations bills originate there—the former under the Constitution, the latter by custom.

BOX 8-2   **Rules and Referral Strategy**

S ometimes, the Senate's rules can be so arcane that it takes major strategy sessions to get even the most routine bills through the legislature.

That was the case when Sen. Bob Graham, D-Fla. (1987–2005), drafted a bill (targeted only at Florida) to permit the Forest Service to sell eighteen tracts of land and use the proceeds to buy up patches of private lands within the Apalachicola National Forest. To ensure that such a low-profile bill moved, Graham wanted it to go through the Energy and Natural Resources Committee, on which he sat.

Instead, Parliamentarian Alan S. Frumin told Graham's aides that the bill, which was soon to be introduced, would be referred to the Agriculture, Nutrition, and Forestry Committee. Because Graham was not a member, such a move could have guaranteed the bill a quiet death.

Why the Agriculture Committee? For at least four decades, the jurisdiction over land bills has been split between the two committees. Bills affecting land east of the 100th Meridian—which runs through North Dakota and South Dakota and the middle of Texas—are assigned to Agriculture, while bills that affect lands west of it go to Energy.

Graham's bill dealt with the wrong side of the country. To change Frumin's mind, Graham's aides needed to turn the rules to their advantage.

They found their opportunity by uncovering the roots behind the 100th Meridian rule. The idea was to divide jurisdiction between public lands and privately owned lands. Because most land on the East Coast is privately owned, that side of the country went to Agriculture, which had jurisdiction over private lands. Everything in the West fell to Energy, which had jurisdiction over public lands.

Graham's aides, however, found out that a majority of tracts in Florida were always public lands. That persuaded Frumin that the bill belonged to the Energy panel.

Source: Adapted from David Nather, "Graham Turns Rules to His Advantage," *CQ Weekly*, June 8, 2002, 1494.

SCHEDULING IN THE HOUSE

All bills reported from committee in the House are listed in chronological order on one of several calendars. Bills that raise or spend money directly or indirectly are assigned to the Union Calendar. The House Calendar contains non-money-related public measures, such as proposed constitutional amendments. Private bills, such as immigration requests or claims against the government, are assigned to the Private Calendar.

There is no guarantee that the House will debate legislation placed on any of these calendars. The Speaker, in consultation with party and committee leaders, the president, and others, largely determines whether, when, how, and in what order bills come up. In recent years, the majority leader has assumed the role of managing the day-to-day schedule of the House. The Speaker, however, remains the ultimate decider.

The Speaker's agenda-setting authority is bolstered by rules and precedents upholding the principle of *majority rule*, a fundamental House characteristic. Majority rule means that in the House a united and determined voting majority—whether partisan or bipartisan—will prevail over resolute opposition. In the polarized environment of the contemporary House, majority rule typically means large control of decision making by the majority party. Bipartisan majorities are common because most issues voted upon do not divide the two parties, such as preventing child sex trafficking.

Shortcuts for Minor Bills

Whether a bill is major or minor, controversial or noncontroversial, influences the procedure employed to bring it before the House. Most bills are relatively minor and are taken up and passed through various shortcut procedures.

One especially important routine and time-saving procedure for considering minor or relatively noncontroversial measures is suspension of the rules. The procedure is in order Monday, Tuesday, and Wednesday of each week, but controlled by the Speaker through the power of recognizing who may speak ("Mr. Speaker, I move to suspend the rules and pass H.R. 1234"). The vote on this motion simultaneously suspends House rules and enacts (or rejects) the measure. Most public laws enacted by the House are accomplished through this procedure. An analysis of the 113th Congress (2013–2015) found that 75 percent of lawmaking vehicles (bills and joint resolutions) reached the floor via suspension of the rules procedure.[28]

Legislation considered under suspension of the rules does not have to be reported from committee before the full House takes it up. Importantly, the suspension procedure permits only forty minutes of debate, allows no amendments, and requires a two-thirds vote for passage. The procedure is often favored by bill managers who want to avoid unfriendly amendments and points of order against their legislation. Bills that fail under suspension can return again to the floor by a rule issued by the Rules Committee (discussed later in this chapter). The majority leadership "does not ordinarily schedule bills for suspension unless confident of a two-thirds vote."[29]

The heightened partisanship in the closely divided House raises the question of why the suspension procedure, which requires bipartisanship to attract the two-thirds vote, is being employed more and more in such a polarized institution. The answer seems to involve a trade-off. "As members are increasingly being denied opportunities in special rules to offer amendments to more substantive bills on the floor," explained Donald R. Wolfensberger, former staff director of the House Rules Committee, "the leadership is providing alternative mechanisms to satisfy members' policy influence and reelection needs through the relatively non-controversial and bipartisan suspension process."[30] Thus, greater use of suspensions serves two prime purposes: it provides an outlet for members to achieve their policy and political goals, and keeps the lid on members' frustration with limited or closed amendment procedures.

The current rules of the House Republican Conference establish specific guidelines for using the suspension procedure. Under Conference Rule 28, bills and resolutions are not to be scheduled using the suspension procedure if, for example, they fail to include a cost estimate; create new programs, unless they also eliminate or reduce a program of equal or greater size; or authorize appropriations without including a sunset provision. Moreover, the GOP's majority leader lists on his website a number of informal "legislative protocols," or expectations involving the suspension procedure. One of those recommends that suspension bills be available for three days prior to their consideration. Members are kept informed about the measures being considered under the suspension procedure through daily and weekly whip notices and leadership announcements. Lawmakers often refer to measures on the "suspension calendar" even though there is no formal calendar for this purpose.

To accommodate lawmakers' constituency and legislative activities (the two Congresses concept), the House instituted a cluster voting rule. The Speaker announces that record votes on a group of bills debated under the suspension procedure will be postponed and clustered until later that day or within the next two days. The bills are then brought up in sequence and disposed of without further debate. Cluster voting accommodates lawmakers returning from weekends in their district. It also minimizes interruptions of committee or constituency meetings when the House is in session throughout the week. Absent cluster voting, members would be required to run back and forth to the chamber scores of times throughout the day to vote on issues.

At times, the minority party gets upset with the majority leadership for not scheduling enough of their bills via the suspension procedure. To protest, minority party members may vote against suspension bills until more of their routine measures are taken up on the floor. They also may castigate the majority leadership for using the suspension of the rules procedure on bills that in their estimation merit more debate than forty minutes and require the offering of amendments.

Another expedited procedure is unanimous consent. The Speaker will recognize a lawmaker to call up bills or resolutions by unanimous consent "only when assured that the majority and minority floor leadership and the relevant committee chairs and ranking minority members have no objection."[31]

Without these clearances, unanimous consent is not a viable avenue to the floor. Only 5 percent of lawmaking legislation passed the 113th House by unanimous consent.[32]

Major measures reach the floor by different procedures. Budget, appropriation, and a limited number of other measures are considered "privileged"[33]—meaning that the House rulebook grants them a "ticket," or privileged access, to the floor. Privileged measures may be called up from the appropriate calendar for debate at almost any time. (Remember, the Speaker sets the agenda, even for privileged business.)

Most major bills, however, do not have an automatic green light to the floor. Before they reach the floor they need to be granted a rule (a procedural resolution) by the Rules Committee. These procedural resolutions, known as "rules" or "special rules," are how virtually all major bills reach the House floor. Special rules also establish the terms for debating and amending legislation.

The Strategic Role of the Rules Committee

The House Rules Committee has existed since the First Congress. During its early years, the committee prepared or ratified a biennial set of House rules and then dissolved. As House procedures became more complex because of the growing membership and workload, the committee became more important. In 1858 the Speaker became a member of the committee and the next year its chair. In 1880 Rules became a permanent standing committee. Three years later, the committee launched a procedural revolution. It began to issue rules, privileged resolutions granting measures priority for floor consideration.

Arm of the Majority Leadership. The Speaker and the majority party leadership have not always had firm control over the House Rules Committee. After the House rebelled against the arbitrary decisions of Speaker Joseph G. Cannon, R-Ill., and removed him from the Rules Committee in 1910, the committee became independently powerful. As such, it extracted substantive concessions in bills in exchange for rules, blocked measures it opposed, and advanced those it favored, often reflecting the wishes of the House's conservative coalition of Republicans and southern Democrats.

For example, the chair of the Rules Committee from 1955 to 1967, Howard W. "Judge" Smith, D-Va., was a diehard conservative who regularly resisted pressure from Democratic leaders and constituencies to act on liberal agenda items, especially civil rights. Smith was a master at devising delaying tactics. He might abruptly adjourn meetings for lack of a quorum, allow requests for rules to languish, or refuse to schedule meetings. House consideration of the 1957 civil rights bill was temporarily delayed because Smith absented himself from the Capitol, and his committee could not meet without him. Smith claimed he was seeing about a barn that had burned on his Virginia farm. Retorted Speaker Sam Rayburn, D-Tex., "I knew Howard Smith would do most anything to block a civil rights bill, but I never knew he would resort to arson."[34]

Liberals' frustration with the bipartisan coalition of conservatives who dominated the committee finally boiled over. After John F. Kennedy's election as president in 1960, Speaker Rayburn recognized that he needed greater control over the Rules Committee if the House was to advance the president's activist New Frontier program. Rayburn proposed enlarging the committee from twelve members to fifteen. This proposal led to a titanic struggle between Rayburn and the archconservative Rules chair:

> Superficially, the Representatives seemed to be quarreling about next to nothing: the membership of the committee. In reality, however, the question raised had grave import for the House and for the United States. The House's answer to it affected the tenuous balance of power between the great conservative and liberal blocs within the House. And, doing so, the House's answer seriously affected the response of Congress to the sweeping legislative proposals of the newly elected President, John Kennedy.[35]

In a dramatic vote, the House agreed to expand the Rules Committee. Two new Democrats and one Republican were added, loosening the conservative coalition's grip on the panel.

During the 1970s, the Rules Committee came under even greater majority party control. In 1975 the Democratic Caucus authorized the Speaker to appoint, subject to party ratification, all Democratic members of the committee, including the chair. (Thirteen years later, Republicans authorized their leader to name the GOP leader and members of the Rules Committee.) The majority party maintains a disproportionate ratio on the panel (currently nine Republicans and four Democrats in the 114th Congress). The Rules Committee, in short, has once again become the Speaker's committee. As a GOP Rules member said about the panel's relationship with the Speaker, "How much is the Rules Committee the handmaiden of the Speaker? The answer is, totally."[36] GOP representative Pete Sessions of Texas heads the panel in the 114th Congress.

Rarely are rules rejected by the House. As Speaker Thomas "Tip" O'Neill once said: "Defeat of the rule on the House floor is considered an affront both to the [Rules] Committee and to the Speaker."[37] The Speaker's influence over the Rules Committee thus ensures that the Speaker can both bring measures to the floor and shape their procedural consideration.

The Rules Committee is effectively a "traffic cop" for the House floor. In the absence of a special rule, bills in the House would have to be taken up in the chronological order listed on the calendars, and many substantial bills would never reach the floor before Congress adjourned. The Rules Committee can put major bills first in line. Equally important, a rule from the committee sets the conditions for debate and amendment. Special rules are as or more important to a bill's fate as a favorable committee vote. A request for a rule is usually made by the chair of the committee reporting the bill. The Rules Committee conducts hearings on the request in the same way that other committees consider legislation, except that only members testify. The House parliamentarian usually drafts the rule after consulting with majority Rules

Committee leaders and staff. The rule is considered on the House floor and is voted on in the same manner as regular bills (see Box 8-3 for an example of a structured rule from the Rules Committee).

Types of Rules. Traditionally, the Rules Committee has granted open, closed, modified, or structured rules as well as waivers. An open rule means that any lawmaker may propose germane amendments that are in compliance with House rules and the 1974 Budget Act. A closed rule prohibits the offering of amendments by rank-and-file members. A modified rule comes in two forms: modified open and modified closed (today commonly called a "structured" rule). The distinction hinges in part on the number of amendments made in order by the Rules Committee—few or only one under modified closed, more under modified open. Structured rules limit and specify the

---

BOX 8-3　**Example of a Rule from the Rules Committee**

*T*his is a structured rule (H. Res. 27) that sets the terms for debating and amending the Regulatory Accountability Act of 2015 (H.R. 185). This often-used rule limits the number of amendments, even naming the members in the Rules Committee report on H. Res. 27 who may offer the relatively few amendments made in order. The House adopted H. Res. 27 on January 13, 2015, by a vote of 242 to 180.

Resolved, That at any time after the adoption of this resolution the Speaker may, pursuant to clause 2(b) of rule XVIII, declare the House resolved into the Committee of the Whole House on the state of the Union for consideration of the bill (H.R. 185) to reform the process by which Federal agencies analyze and formulate new regulations and guidance documents. The first reading of the bill shall be shall be dispensed with. All points of order against consideration of the bill are waived. General debate shall be confined to the bill and shall not exceed one hour equally divided and controlled by the chair and ranking minority member of the Committee on the Judiciary. After general debate the bill shall be considered for amendment under the five-minute rule. The bill shall be considered as read. All points of order against provisions in the bill are waived. No amendment to the bill shall be in order except those printed in part A of the report of the Committee on Rules accompanying this resolution. Each such amendment may be offered only in the order printed in the report, may be offered only by a Member designated in the report, shall be considered as read, shall be debatable for the time specified in the report equally divided and controlled by a proponent and an opponent, shall not be subject to amendment, and shall not be subject to a demand for division of the question in the House or in the Committee of the Whole. All points of order against such amendments are waived. At the conclusion of consideration of the bill for amendment the Committee of the Whole shall rise and report the bill to the House with such amendments as may have been adopted. The previous question shall be considered as ordered on the bill and amendments thereto to final passage without intervening motion except one motion to recommit with or without instructions

---

Source: Congressional Record, 114th Cong., 1st sess., January 13, 2015, H237–H248.

amendments that lawmakers may offer to the pending bill. Waivers of points of order are commonly included in the different types of rules. Waivers set aside technical violations of House rules to allow bills or other matters to reach the floor.

Whether Democrats or Republicans control the House, their majority on the Rules Committee displays procedural creativity and imagination. It is common today for the Rules Committee to announce in advance that it will provide a structured (i.e., "restricted") rule and require lawmakers to submit their proposed amendments to the committee. The committee will then review the amendments and determine which to make in order for chamber consideration. The requirement that all amendments be either pre-printed in the *Congressional Record* or submitted in advance to Rules aids the majority party in preparing its floor strategy.

The trend toward creative use of complex rules reflects several developments. Among the most important are the wider use of multiple referrals, which requires Rules to play a larger coordinating role in arranging floor action on legislation; the rise of megabills hundreds of pages in length that contain priorities the Speaker does not want picked apart on the floor; the desire of majority party leaders to exert greater control over floor procedures; members' impatience with dilatory floor challenges to committee-reported bills; members' demand for greater certainty and predictability in floor decision making; and efforts by committee leaders either to limit the number of amendments or to keep unfriendly amendments off the floor. The sharp rise in partisanship has also triggered an increase in creative rules (see Box 8-4 on examples of creative rules).

Minority party lawmakers typically object strongly to the use of restrictive rules that block them from offering and getting votes on their policy alternatives. "We don't expect to win," said a minority member, "but we do expect to be able to at least offer amendments so the two parties can define their differences."[38]

When Republicans took control of the House in 1995 after four consecutive decades in the minority, they remembered their bitter experience with rules that restricted their right to offer amendments. Speaker Gingrich promised more openness and greater opportunities for all lawmakers to offer floor amendments to pending legislation. Republicans did work to provide more open amendment procedures when they first took control of the House. However, as Republican majorities declined in subsequent Congresses, the number of open rules dropped markedly (see Table 8-1), the result of heightened partisan acrimony and the GOP's determination to enact its agenda priorities with few or no changes.

Like the Republicans in 1995, Speaker Pelosi pledged to manage the chamber in an open, fair, and deliberative manner when Democrats reclaimed the House majority in the 110th Congress (2007–2009). But it was not long before the Democrats brought their legislative priorities to the floor under closed or structured rules. The Republicans regularly took the floor to criticize the

Democratic majority for reneging on its promises. The majority is "failing to live up to its commitment to run the House in an open and fair manner," exclaimed a Rules Republican.[39] In response, Democrats said the GOP's floor strategy was to offer "gotcha" amendments designed for campaign attack ads or to undermine the majority's policy priorities.

Speaker Boehner also promised to run an open, fair, and deliberative law-making process with ample opportunities for the minority Democrats to offer amendments. "To my friends in the minority," Boehner said, "I offer a commitment: Openness . . . will be the new standard."[40] But Democrats nonetheless find much to criticize in GOP-crafted rules. As the ranking Rules Democrat, Louise Slaughter, N.Y., said on one occasion: while "this rule may have the word 'open' in the title, I assure [my colleagues] that this is not an open process. [T]he Republican majority has provided an extremely convoluted and restrictive process."[41] She added that the 113th House was the most closed in history, as the Rules Committee approved eighty-three closed rules, surpassing the previous record of sixty-one.[42]

Open rules generally clash with a fundamental objective of any majority party: enactment of priority legislation. As Table 8-1 reveals, only 18 percent of rules in the 112th Congress were either open or modified open, a better percentage than under Speaker Pelosi but not compared to Boehner's two GOP predecessors (Gingrich and Hastert). However, unlike previous Speakers, Boehner has brought many appropriations bills to the floor under open rules, returning to the traditional practice of the House.

In summary, rules establish the conditions under which most major bills are debated and amended. They determine the length of general debate, permit or prohibit amendments, and often waive points of order. Writing the rules is the majority party's way of ensuring that measures reach the floor under terms favorable to the party's preferred outcomes. Put differently, the majority party limits and structures the votes to get the legislative and political results it intends, keeping the two Congresses in mind. In this era of message politics and partisan polarization, innovative rules can both protect majority party members from casting electorally perilous votes or, alternatively, make amendments in order that appeal to diverse party constituencies.

Dislodging a Bill from Committee

Committees do not necessarily reflect the point of view of the full chamber. What happens when a standing committee refuses to report a bill or when the Rules Committee does not grant a rule? To circumvent committees, members have three options: the discharge petition, the Calendar Wednesday rule, and the ability of the Rules Committee to extract a bill from committee. However, these tactics are rarely employed and seldom successful.

The discharge petition permits the House to relieve a committee of jurisdiction over a stalled measure. This procedure also provides a way for the rank and file to force a bill to the floor, even if the majority leadership, the committee

BOX 8-4   **Examples of Creative Rules**

Queen-of-the-Hill Rule

- Under this special rule, a number of major alternative amendments—each the functional equivalent of a bill—are made to the underlying legislation, with the proviso that the substitute that receives the most votes is the winner.
- If two or more alternatives receive an identical number of votes, the last one voted upon is considered as finally adopted by the membership.

Self-Executing Rule

- This special rule provides that when the House adopts a rule it has also agreed simultaneously to amend the underlying bill made in order by the special rule.
- This rule is used for various reasons such as reconciling the policies recommended by multiple committees; correcting procedural or Budget Act violations; or making changes in the base bill to pick up votes to enact the measure.
- Whether this rule is controversial or not usually depends on the nature of the policy being agreed to in the "two or more-for-one" vote.

Structured Rule

- The essential feature of the structured rule is that it limits the freedom of members to offer germane amendments to the bills made in order by those rules. The only amendments permitted are those designated in the special rule or in the Rules Committee report to accompany the procedural rule (see Box 8-3 for an example of a structured rule). The number of structured rules has increased since the 1980s. The majority party uses these rules to minimize debate, prevent unwanted amendments, and maximize its ability to mobilize winning majorities.
- Rank-and-file members often rail against these rules because they restrict their opportunities to amend committee-reported measures or majority party initiatives.

Multiple-Step Rule

- This type of rule facilitates an orderly amendment process.
- One variation is for the Rules Committee to first report a rule that regulates general debate on a bill and then report another follow-on rule to govern the amending process to the measure.
- Another variation is for the Rules Committee to state publicly that if a measure encounters difficulties on the floor, the panel will report a subsequent rule that limits time for further debate or further amendments.

Suspension Day Rule

- This type of rule authorizes the Speaker to entertain motions to suspend the rules on days other than Monday, Tuesday, or Wednesday.

TABLE 8-1 **Open and Structured Rules, 103d–113th Congresses (1993–2014)**

Congress	Open/ Modified Open		Structured		Closed		Totals	
	Number	Percent	Number	Percent	Number	Percent	Number	Percent
103d (1993–1995)	46	44%	49	47%	9	9%	104	100%
104th (1995–1997)	83	58	40	28	19	14	142	100
105th (1997–1998)	74	53	42	30	24	17	140	100
106th (1999–2000)	91	51	49	27	39	22	179	100
107th (2001–2002)	40	37	44	41	23	22	107	100
108th (2003–2004)	34	26	62	47	37	28	133	100
109th (2005–2006)	24	19	61	49	40	32	125	100
110th (2007–2008)	23	14	81	50	59	36	111	100
111th (2009–2010)	0	0	73	65	38	34	111	100
112th (2011–2012)	25	18	65	46	50	36	140	100
113th (2013–2014)	12	8	65	43	72	48	149	100

Source: Don Wolfensberger, resident scholar, Bipartisan Policy Center, Washington, D.C. Wolfensberger is a former decades-long professional staff aide and staff director of the House Rules Committee.

Note: The table applies only to special rules providing for the initial consideration for amendment of bills, joint resolutions, and significant concurrent resolutions (e.g., budget, war-related). It does not apply to privileged resolutions considered in the House, to subsequent rules for the same measure, to conference reports, or to special rules that only waive points of order against appropriations bills but do not provide for consideration in the Committee of the Whole. Rules making in order more than one bill are counted as a separate rule for each measure made in order, e.g., a rule providing for the consideration of four bills under closed rules is counted as four closed rules. An open rule is one that permits any member to offer an amendment otherwise germane in the Committee of the Whole under the five-minute rule. A modified open rule is one that either requires the pre-printing of amendments in the *Congressional Record*, sets an overall time cap on the amendment process, or both. A structured rule is one that limits the amendments that can be offered to those specified in the special rule and/or report on the rule. A closed rule is one that prohibits the offering of amendments (except those recommended by the reporting committees).

chair, and the Rules Committee oppose it. If a committee does not report a bill within thirty legislative days after the bill was referred to it, any member may file a discharge motion (petition) requiring the signature of 218 members, a majority of the House. Once the signatures are obtained, the discharge motion is placed on the Discharge Calendar for seven days. It can then be called up on the second and fourth Mondays of the month by any member who signed the petition. If the discharge motion is agreed to, the bill is taken up right away. Since 1910, when the discharge rule was adopted, only three discharged measures have ever become law. Its threatened or actual use, particularly as the number of signatures closes in on 218, may stimulate a committee to act on a bill and the majority leadership to schedule it for floor action.

The discharge procedure is rarely successful as a lawmaking device largely because members are reluctant to second-guess committees; to write legislation on the floor without the guidance of committee hearings and reports; and to use a procedure that may one day be used against committees on which they serve. Moreover, 218 signatures are not easy to obtain. The Speaker, too, is not reluctant to pressure majority party members who sign discharge petitions to remove their names, because their actions could jeopardize the majority's control of the floor schedule. If majority lawmakers add or refuse to remove their names, the message being sent, according to Rep. Tom Cole, R-Okla., is that "you're thumbing your nose at your own leadership."[43] Unwanted consequences, as noted below, might result to majority members who refuse to heed their leader's advice.

The minority party may employ discharge petitions to spotlight issues for electioneering purposes. For example, minority members may promote and publicize their high-priority issues and then circulate discharge petitions "in an attempt to force House votes—and provide a contrast with [the majority party] in an election year."[44] In brief, vulnerable House members can be subject to attack ads for failing to sign a discharge petition supported by many voters in their respective districts.

The discharge rule also applies to the Rules Committee. A motion to discharge a rule is in order after seven legislative days, instead of thirty days, as long as the bill made in order by the rule has been in committee for thirty days. Any member may enter a discharge motion, but majority members rarely break ranks with their party leaders to sign the petition. When Rep. Christopher Shays, R-Conn., signed a successful discharge petition to force House action on a landmark campaign finance reform bill (the Bipartisan Campaign Reform Act of 2002) opposed by the GOP leadership, there were charges of treason against Shays and rumblings that he might face a GOP challenger in the Republican primary.[45] Shays was subsequently passed over as chair of the Oversight and Government Reform Committee, even though he had more seniority than the two other Republicans in contention.

Adopted in 1909, the Calendar Wednesday rule provides that on Wednesdays committees may bring up from the House Calendar or Union Calendar their measures that have not received a rule from the Rules Committee. However, the clerk will not call committees on Wednesdays unless the committee chair gives notice on Tuesday that he or she will seek recognition to call up a measure under the rule. Calendar Wednesday is cumbersome to employ, seldom used, and generally dispensed with by unanimous consent. Since 1943, fewer than fifteen measures have been enacted into law under this procedure.[46]

Finally, the Rules Committee has the power of extraction. The committee can propose rules that make bills in order for House debate even if the bills have been neither introduced nor reported by standing committees. Based on an 1895 precedent, this procedure is akin to discharging committees without the required 218 signatures. It stirs bitter controversy among members who think it usurps the rights of the other committees, and therefore it is seldom used.

HOUSE FLOOR PROCEDURES

The House meets Monday through Friday, often convening at noon. In practice, it conducts the bulk of its committee and floor business during the middle of the week (to accommodate the so-called Tuesday to Thursday Club of members who go home to their constituencies every weekend). At the beginning of each day's session, bells ring throughout the Capitol and the House office buildings, summoning representatives to the floor. The bells also notify members of votes, quorum calls, recesses, and adjournments. Typically, the opening activities include a daily prayer; approval of the *Journal* (a constitutionally required record of the previous day's formal proceedings); recitation of the Pledge of Allegiance; receipt of messages from the president (such as a veto message) or the Senate; announcements, if any, by the Speaker; and one-minute speeches by members on any topic. On Mondays through Thursdays, a period of morning-hour debate takes place after the opening preliminaries but before the start of formal legislative business.

After these preliminaries, the House generally begins considering legislation. For a major bill, a set pattern is observed: adopting the rule, convening in the Committee of the Whole, allotting time for general debate, amending, voting, and moving the bill to final passage.

Adoption of the Rule

The Speaker, after consulting other majority party leaders and affected committee chairs, generally decides when the House will debate a bill and under what kind of rule. Speakers rely on their majority leader to help draft and manage the floor agenda. When the scheduled day arrives, the Speaker recognizes a majority member of the Rules Committee for one hour to explain the rule's contents. By custom, the majority member yields half the time for debate only to a minority member of the Rules Committee. At the end of the debate, which may take less time than the allotted hour, the House votes on the previous question motion. Its approval brings the House to an immediate vote on the rule. Rejection of the previous question (a rare occurrence) allows the minority party an opportunity to amend the rule.

Opponents of a bill can try to defeat the rule and avert House action on the bill itself. But rules are rarely defeated because majority party members generally vote with their leaders on procedural votes and the Rules Committee is sensitive to the wishes of the House. During the speakership of Dennis Hastert, R-Ill. (1999–2007), the House rejected only two rules offered by the Rules Committee. Splits within the majority party account for the defeats. Nancy Pelosi never lost a rule during her four years as Speaker (2007–2011); nor has Speaker Boehner (2011–) had any rules turned down by the House. Procedural votes are usually party-line votes. Once the rule is adopted, the

House is governed by its provisions. Most rules state that "at any time after the adoption of [the rule] the Speaker may declare the House resolved into the Committee of the Whole."

Committee of the Whole

The Committee of the Whole House on the state of the Union is a parliamentary artifice that the House borrowed long ago from the British House of Commons. Its function in the contemporary House is to expedite consideration of legislation and to promote member involvement in general debate and the amendment process, if amendments are permitted by the special rule. It is simply the House in another form with different rules. For example, a quorum in the Committee of the Whole is only 100 members, compared with 218 for the full House. Debate on amendments is governed by the five-minute rule rather than the one-hour rule that applies in the House. By custom, Speakers never preside over the committee; they always appoint a majority party colleague to act as chair of the committee, which then begins general debate of a bill.

General Debate

A rule from the Rules Committee specifies the amount of time, usually one to two hours, for a general discussion of the bill under consideration. Controversial bills require more time, perhaps four or more hours. Control of the time is divided equally between the majority and minority floor managers—usually the chair and ranking minority member of the committee that reported the legislation. (When bills are referred to more than one committee, a more complex division of debate time is allotted among the committees that had jurisdiction over the legislation.) The majority floor manager's job is to guide the bill to final passage; the minority floor manager may seek to amend or kill the bill.

After the floor managers have made their opening statements, they parcel out several minutes to colleagues on their side of the aisle who wish to speak. General debate rarely lives up to its name. Most legislators read prepared speeches. Give-and-take exchange occurs infrequently at this stage of the proceedings.

The Amending Phase

The amending process is the heart of decision making on the floor of the House. Amendments determine the final shape of bills and often dominate public discussion. Former representative Henry J. Hyde, R-Ill., for example, repeatedly and successfully proposed amendments barring the use of federal funds for abortions. Hyde's 1977 anti-abortion amendment remains today a regular provision of many public laws.

An amendment in the Committee of the Whole is considered under the five-minute rule, which gives the sponsor five minutes to defend it and an opponent five minutes to speak against it. The amendment then may be brought to a vote. Amendments are routinely debated for more than ten minutes, however. Legislators gain the floor by saying, "I move to strike the last word," or "I move to strike the requisite number of words." These pro forma amendments, which make no alteration in the pending matter, simply serve to give members five minutes of debate time.

If there is an open rule, opponents may try to load a bill with so many objectionable amendments that it will sink under its own weight. The reverse strategy is to propose sweetener amendments that attract support from other members. Offering many amendments is an effective dilatory tactic because each amendment must be read in full, debated for at least five to ten minutes, and then voted on.

In this amending phase, the interconnection of the two Congresses is evident: amendments can have electoral as well as legislative consequences. Floor amendments enable lawmakers to take positions that enhance their reputations with the folks back home, put opponents on record, and shape national policy. For example, "put-them-on-the-spot amendments," as one representative dubbed them, can be artfully fashioned by minority lawmakers to force the majority to vote on issues such as gun control, immigration reform, or climate change that can be used against them in the next campaign.[47] The majority party's control of the Rules Committee minimizes the use of this tactic because the panel often "scripts" the amendment process. Only the amendments made in order by Rules can be offered, often in a set order, and only by a specific member. Structured rules of this sort block spontaneous amendments and debates on issues that might stymie passage of the majority party's priorities.

The minority guards the floor to demand explanations or votes on amendments brought up by the majority. As a minority floor guardian wrote, "So long as a floor watchdog exists all members of the House are afforded some additional protection from precipitous actions."[48] In the 114th Congress, various minority members assume this role for Democrats in the House.

Voting

Before passage of the 1970 Legislative Reorganization Act, the Committee of the Whole adopted or rejected amendments by voice votes or other votes with no public record of who voted and how. Today, any legislator supported by twenty-five colleagues can obtain a recorded vote. (The member who requested a recorded vote is counted as one of the twenty-five who rise to be counted by the chair.)

Since the installation of an electronic voting system in 1973, members can insert their personalized cards (about the size of a credit card) into one of more than forty voting stations on the floor and press the "Yea," "Nay," or "Present" button. A large electronic display board behind the press gallery provides a running tally of the total votes for or against a motion. The voting tally, said a representative, is watched carefully by many members:

> I find that a lot of times, people walk in, and the first thing they do
> is look at the board, and they have key people they check out, and
> if those people have voted "aye," they go to the machine and vote
> "aye" and walk off the floor.

But I will look at the board and see how [members of the state delega-
tion] vote, because they are in districts right next to me, and they have
constituencies just like mine. I will vote the way I am going to vote
except that if they are both different, I will go up and say "Why did
you vote that way? Let me know if there is something I am missing."[49]

After all pending amendments have been voted on, the Committee of
the Whole rises. The chair hands the gavel back to the Speaker, and a quorum
once again becomes 218 members.

Recommit and Final Passage

As specified in the rule, the full House must review the actions of its agent,
the Committee of the Whole. The Speaker announces that under the rule the
previous question has been ordered, which means in this context that no further
debate is permitted on the bill or its amendments. The Speaker then asks
whether any representative wants a separate vote on any amendment adopted
in the Committee of the Whole. If not, all the amendments agreed to in the
committee will be approved.

The next important step is the motion to recommit, which provides a way
for the House to return, or recommit, the bill to the committee that reported
it. The motion to recommit has two forms: (1) the rarely used "straight" motion
to return the measure to committee (which effectively kills it), and (2) a motion
to recommit with instructions that the committee report "forthwith," which
means the bill never really leaves the House. If this form of the motion is
adopted, the bill, as modified by the instructions, is automatically before the
House again. By precedent, either form of the motion is always made by a
minority party member who opposes the legislation. Each form of the motion
is also subject to ten minutes of debate, five per side. Recommittal motions are
usually not successful because they are so heavily identified as an opposition
party prerogative, but they do serve to protect the rights of the minority.

Recent Congresses have seen a change in the major purposes of the
motion to recommit. Although still employed by the minority party to force
the House to vote on its alternative policy proposal (the "instructions" in this
motion), the motion to recommit is now frequently employed to achieve two
political purposes: to defeat, delay, or eviscerate majority party policies, and
to force vulnerable majority lawmakers to vote on "gotcha amendments"
certain to cause them electoral grief if they do not vote for the minority proposal. As Democratic leader Steny Hoyer, Md., exclaimed, "The unfortunate
fact is that the motion to recommit with instructions has for more than a
decade become a hollow vehicle and farce."[50] For example, whether a
Democratic or Republican minority, the instructions in motions to recommit
are artfully drafted to require members to vote on "hot-button" issues—
preventing child molestation, for example—while also undermining the
majority party's policy objectives. Clearly, many lawmakers would be reluctant to vote against a motion to recommit with this kind of instruction

because they would likely face a barrage of campaign attack ads suggesting that they support child molestation.

If the motion to recommit with instructions is adopted, the minority proposal is incorporated into the bill. If it is rejected, as commonly occurs, the Speaker will declare, "The question is on passage of the bill." Passage of the measure, by the House in this case, marks about the halfway point in the lawmaking process. The Senate must also approve the bill, and its procedures are strikingly different from those of the House. It is an institution noted for protecting the rights of the minority—hence its reliance on the unanimous consent of all senators to accomplish much of the chamber's business.

SCHEDULING IN THE SENATE

Compared with the larger and more clamorous House, which needs and follows well-defined rules and precedents, the Senate operates more informally. And, unlike the House, where the rules permit a determined majority to make decisions, the Senate's rules emphasize individual prerogatives (freedom to debate and to offer amendments, including nonrelevant amendments) and minority rights (those of the minority party, a faction, or even a single senator). "The Senate," said one member, "is run for the convenience of one Senator to the inconvenience of 99."[51] No wonder some commentators say the Senate has only two rules (unanimous consent and exhaustion) and three speeds (slow, slower, and slowest). As former senator Byron Dorgan, D-N.D., said, "The only thing it's easy to do in the Senate is slow things down. The Senate is 100 human brake pads."[52] In brief, the Senate's rules, practices, and traditions make it a *supermajority rule* institution compared to the majority rule House. Stated differently, "minority rule" (by one senator, a small group, or the minority party) is the Senate's core feature.

The scheduling system for the Senate appears relatively simple. There is a Calendar of Business on which are listed public and private bills reported by the committees and a separate Executive Calendar for treaties and nominations. The Senate has nothing comparable to the scheduling duties of the House Rules Committee, and the majority and minority leadership actively consult about scheduling. The Senate majority leader is responsible for setting the agenda and is aided in controlling scheduling by the priority given him when he seeks recognition on the floor. What this means is that if several senators are seeking recognition from the presiding officer and the majority leader is among them, the chair will always give preference to the majority leader.

Despite the Senate's smaller size, establishing a firm agenda of business is harder in the Senate than in the House. As a majority leader once said:

> The ability of any Senator to speak without limitations makes it impossible to establish total certainty with respect to scheduling. When there is added to that the difficulty and very demanding schedules of 100 Senators, it is very hard to organize business in a way that meets the convenience of everybody.[53]

Legislation typically reaches the Senate floor in two ways: by unanimous consent or by motion. But senators, too, can also force Senate consideration of their proposals by offering them as nonrelevant amendments to pending business. Unanimous consent agreements are of utmost importance to the smooth functioning of the Senate.

Unanimous Consent Agreements

The Senate frequently dispenses with its formal rules and instead follows negotiated agreements submitted to the Senate for its unanimous approval (see Box 8-5 on unanimous consent agreements). The objectives are to expedite work in an institution known for extended debate, to impose some measure of predictability on floor action, and to minimize dilatory activities. As a party floor leader observed:

> We aren't bringing [measures] to the floor unless we have [a unani-
> mous consent] agreement. We could bring child-care legislation to
> the floor right now, but that would mean two months of fighting. We
> want to maximize productive time by trying to work out as much as
> we can in advance [of floor action].[54]

It is not uncommon for party leaders to negotiate piecemeal unanimous consent agreements—limiting debate on a specific amendment, for example—and to hammer them out in public on the Senate floor.

Unanimous consent agreements (also called time-limitation agreements) limit debate on the bill, any amendments, and various motions. Occasionally, they specify the time for the vote on final passage and typically impose constraints on the amendment process. For example, to facilitate enactment of an omnibus crime package that contained provisions with widespread Senate support, senators agreed to a unanimous consent request barring floor amendments on controversial issues such as gun control or the death penalty.[55]

The Senate's unanimous consent agreements are functional equivalents of special rules from the House Rules Committee. Both waive the rules of their respective chambers and must be approved by the members—in one case by majority vote and in the other by unanimous consent. These accords are binding contracts and can be terminated or modified only by another unanimous consent agreement. Senators and aides often negotiate, draft, and circulate unanimous consent agreements privately, whereas the Rules Committee hears requests for procedural rules in public sessions.

Ways to Extract Bills from Committee

If a bill is blocked in committee, the Senate has several ways to obtain floor action. A senator with the Senate's approval can add the bill as a nonrelevant floor amendment to another bill, bypass the committee stage by placing the bill directly on the calendar, suspend the rules, or discharge the bill from committee. Only the first two procedures are effective; the other two are somewhat

> BOX 8-5 **Example of a Unanimous Consent Agreement**

*O*rdered, That on Wednesday, January 28, 2015 at 2:30 p.m., the Senate resume consideration of S. 1, a bill to approve the Keystone Pipeline, and proceed to vote in relation to the following amendments in the order listed:

- —Cardin Amdt. No. 75;
- —Peters Amdt. No. 70;
- —Sanders Amdt. No. 23;
- —Cruz Amdt. No. 15;
- —Merkley Amdt. No. 125;
- —Moran Amdt. No. 73;
- —Whitehouse Amdt. No. 148;
- —Daines Amdt. No. 132;
- —Coons Amdt. No. 115;
- —Collins Amdt. No. 35;
- —Carper Amdt. No. 120;
- —Murkowski Amdt. No. 166;
- —Heitkamp Amdt. No. 133;
- —Gillibrand Amdt. No. 48;
- —Barrasso Amdt. No. 245;
- —Cardin Amdt. No. 124;
- —Daines Amdt. No. 246;
- —Burr Amdt. No. 92, as modified.

Ordered further, That all amendments listed above be subject to a 60 vote affirmative threshold for adoption and that no second degree amendments be in order to the amendments; provided, that there be 2 minutes of debate equally divided between each vote; provided further, that all votes after the first in the series be 10 minute votes.

Ordered further, That with respect to S. 1, the filing deadline for first degree amendments be 3 p.m. on Monday, January 26, 2015, and the filing deadline for second degree amendments be 5 p.m. on Monday, January 26, 2015.

Ordered further, That with respect to the motions to invoke cloture on Amendment No. 2, offered by the Senator from Alaska (Ms. Murkowski), to S. 1 . . . the mandatory quorum required under Rule XXII be waived. (Jan. 23, 26, 27, 2015.)

Source: U.S. Senate, *Calendar of Business,* January 28, 2015, p. 2.

difficult to employ and seldom succeed.[56] Motions to suspend the rules require one day's notice in writing (published in the *Congressional Record*) specifying the precise rule to be suspended. The motion is debatable and requires a two-thirds vote for adoption. The discharge procedure has not been used in over forty years, in part because of its cumbersome requirements.

A fundamental and widely used prerogative of senators is offering non-germane amendments to legislation under floor consideration. Because the Senate has no general germaneness (or relevancy) rule, senators can take an agriculture bill that is stuck in committee, draft it as a nonrelevant floor amendment, and offer it to a pending health bill. "Amendments may be made," Thomas Jefferson noted long ago, "so as to totally alter the nature of the proposition." Unanimous consent agreements can limit or prohibit nonrelevant amendments. There are other circumstances under which senators may not offer nongermane amendments, such as during consideration of reconciliation legislation as prescribed by the Budget Act of 1974. But the ability to offer nongermane amendments has long afforded individual senators far greater ability to bypass committees than their House counterparts enjoy.

Senators can also bypass the referral of measures to committee by invoking one of the chamber's formal rules (Rule XIV). Typically, when senators

---

BOX 8-6   Senate Rule XIV: Bypassing Committee Referral

MEASURES READ THE FIRST TIME—S. 338 AND S. 339

Mr. CORNYN. Mr. President, I understand that there are two bills at the desk, and I ask for their first reading en bloc.

The PRESIDING OFFICER. The clerk will report the bills by title for the first time.

The assistant legislative clerk read as follows:

A bill (S. 338) to permanently reauthorize the Land and Water Conservation Fund.

A bill (S. 339) to repeal the Patient Protection and Affordable Care Act and the Health Care and Education Reconciliation Act of 2010 entirely.

Mr. CORNYN. Mr. President, I now ask for a second reading, and I object to my own request en bloc.

The PRESIDING OFFICER. Objection having been heard, the bills will be read for the second time on the next legislative day.

Source: Congressional Record, February 2, 2015, S702.

MEASURES PLACED ON THE CALENDAR—S. 338 AND S. 339

Mr. MCCONNELL. I understand there are two bills at the desk due for a second reading.

The PRESIDING OFFICER. The clerk will read the bills by title for the second time.

The legislative clerk read as follows:

A bill (S. 338) to permanently reauthorize the Land and Water Conservation Fund.

A bill (S. 339) to repeal the Patient Protection and Affordable Care Act and the Health Care and Education Reconciliation Act of 2010 entirely.

Mr. MCCONNELL. Mr. President, in order to place the bills on the calendar under the provisions of rule XIV, I object to further proceedings en bloc.

The PRESIDING OFFICER. Objection is heard. The bills will be placed on the calendar.

Source: Congressional Record, February 3, 2015, S707.

introduce bills or joint resolutions (or when bills or joint resolutions are passed by the House and sent to the Senate), they are referred to the appropriate committee of jurisdiction. Rule XIV specifies that those measures are to be read twice by title on different legislative days before they are referred. If a senator interposes an objection after the first reading and again the next day after the second reading, the bill or joint resolution is automatically placed on the Senate's Calendar of Business (see Box 8-6 for how Rule XIV works). Although not used for the vast majority of measures, Rule XIV is increasingly invoked on party issues of high priority. The majority leader, for example, may employ it to circumvent committees because no time is available for a lengthy committee review, or because he wants an issue ready to be called up at his discretion. As Sen. Lamar Alexander, R-Tenn., noted, "From the 103rd to the 109th Congress, Rule XIV to bypass [committees] was used on average 24 times per Congress. This was shattered in the 110th Congress when it was used 57 times."[57]

SENATE FLOOR PROCEDURES

The Senate, like the House, often convenes at noon, sometimes earlier, to keep pace with the workload. Typically, it opens with a prayer, followed by the Pledge of Allegiance and then leaders' time (usually ten minutes each to the majority leader and the minority leader to discuss various issues). If neither leader wants any time, the Senate typically either permits members who have requested time to make their statements, or it resumes consideration of old or new business under the terms of a unanimous consent agreement. The Senate, too, must keep and approve the *Journal* of the previous day's activities. Commonly, the *Journal* is "deemed approved to date" by unanimous consent when the Senate adjourns or recesses at the end of each day.

Normal Routine

For most bills, the Senate follows four steps:

1. The majority leader secures the unanimous consent of the Senate to an arrangement that specifies when a bill will be brought to the floor and the conditions for debating it.

2. The presiding officer recognizes the majority and minority floor managers for opening statements.

3. Amendments are then in order, with debate on each amendment regulated by the terms of the unanimous consent agreement.

4. A roll call vote takes place on final passage.

As in the House, amendments in the Senate serve various purposes. For example, floor managers might accept "as many amendments as they can without undermining the purposes of the bill, in order to build the broadest possible consensus behind it."[58] Some amendments are drafted with the two

Congresses in mind. Such amendments are often designed to embarrass members who must vote against them. "My amendment can be characterized as a 'November amendment,'" remarked a Republican senator, "because the vote . . . will provide an opportunity for Senators to go home and say, 'I voted to reduce Federal taxes' and 'I voted to cut Federal spending.'"[59] Senate Democrats make "vigorous use of amendments to strike a contrast with Republican policies."[60] Unless constrained by some previous unanimous consent agreement, senators generally have the right to offer an unlimited number of floor amendments.

Significantly, recent majority leaders have increasingly used their right of first recognition on the floor to "fill the amendment tree." The amendment tree refers to a chart that imposes a limitation on the number of amendments to a measure that may be offered and pending at the same time. Using the right of first recognition, the majority leader can offer amendment after amendment until the so-called "amendment tree" is filled. Once the amendment tree is filled, no other senator may offer amendments—that is, the amending process is frozen "until action is taken to dispose of one or more of those already pending."[61]

This practice is controversial and angers many lawmakers, especially those in the minority. When he was majority leader, Harry Reid, D-Nev., employed tree-filling far more than his Democratic or Republican predecessors. The surge in tree-filling largely reflects two general and overlapping developments: heightened partisan conflict in the chamber and wider use of amendments by the minority party for political message-sending. Understandably, members of the minority party blast the majority leader for undermining the unique deliberative character of the Senate by preventing the minority from offering their amendments. From the majority leader's perspective, tree-filling is done for several specific purposes, such as blocking unwanted, nonrelevant amendments; protecting vulnerable party colleagues from voting on amendments crafted to cause them electoral grief; or promoting negotiations with the opposition so an accord might be reached on the number of amendments each side is willing to vote on. If an accord is reached, the majority leader would drop some or all of his amendments, opening places on the tree for others to offer their amendments.

Sen. Mitch McConnell, R-Ky., is the new majority leader of the 114th Senate. He has promised to restore the "regular order" in the Senate. Traditionally, the term means that introduced bills will be referred to committee where hearings and markups would be held. Such measures might then be reported (sent) to the Senate floor for consideration by all senators. The bill would then undergo extensive debating and amending activity.

A basic objective of the regular order is to permit lawmakers to consider legislation under conditions that allow for fair, robust, and thoughtful deliberation. The regular order ideally involves various lawmakers working across the aisle and forging compromises to enact measures. Today, this general goal is hard to achieve, as members instead pursue a more parliamentary style of governance where debating and voting usually follow rigid party lines.

Needless to say, it is too soon to know whether and to what extent the traditional regular order will be observed on a consistent basis by Majority Leader McConnell. The first bill taken up in the 114th Senate, as Senator McConnell promised, was construction of the Keystone Pipeline. Consideration of that legislation might provide early clues as to McConnell's floor management style and his view of the regular order, as these four points suggest.

First, Senator McConnell employed Rule XIV on January 7, 2015, to place S.1 on the legislative calendar. The measure was never referred to the committee of jurisdiction (Energy and Natural Resources) for hearings or markup, probably because the issue has been discussed and debated for over six years with no resolution. The Energy Committee did meet to craft a committee-reported substitute amendment to S. 1.

Second, Senator McConnell provided both parties with several weeks of floor debate and amendment opportunities. There was no tree-filling, and nonrelevant amendments were in order, such as one declaring that climate change is not a hoax.

Third, after two weeks on S. 1, McConnell wanted to move forward faster in processing amendments. For example, he wanted the Senate to vote on six pending Democratic amendments and six pending GOP amendments, but Democrats objected. As Senator McConnell explained:

What we have here are at least six Democratic amendments that presumably they understand because they offered them. I assume they know what is in them because they wrote them and offered them. Yet they do not want to vote on them.[62]

Fourth, Senator McConnell called up each pending Democratic amendment and successfully moved to table each one. (Tabling motions are nondebatable.) When Democrats sought to discuss the amendments more before the tabling vote, McConnell objected to each such request. In brief, Senator McConnell used procedural hard-ball tactics to bring Senate action on S. 1 to a successful end. The legislation passed the Senate on January 29, 2015, by a 62–36 vote.

S. 1 was adopted by the GOP House without any changes. S. 1 was sent to the White House for President Obama's consideration. He vetoed the Keystone Pipeline measure, as he said he would for weeks before Congress enacted S. 1. To sum up, consideration of S. 1 suggests that a bipartisan regular order can be followed on the floor until the majority leader determines that the minority party's goal is to inhibit lawmaking progress rather than to advance it. As a congressional scholar observed, examples of budding bipartisan cooperation in the Senate "must always be tempered by a generous dose of caution."[63]

Regular order in the Senate also means that a bill is brought to a final vote whenever senators stop talking. (The Senate has no motion to end debate and vote on a measure or matter.) This can be a long process, particularly in the absence of a unanimous consent agreement. On some bills, unanimous consent agreements are foreclosed because of deliberate obstructive tactics, particularly the threat or use of the filibuster (extended debate). In these instances, bills cannot be voted upon until the filibuster has ended.

Holds, Filibusters, and Cloture

The old-style filibuster has long been associated with the 1939 movie *Mr. Smith Goes to Washington*, which featured a haggard Jimmy Stewart conducting a dramatic solo talkathon on the floor of the Senate to inform the public about political wrongdoing. In its new incarnation, the filibuster is usually threatened more than executed. Filibuster threats gain a senator bargaining power and negotiating leverage.

Today, the mere threat to filibuster is sufficient to block action on many bills or nominations, in large measure because it is so hard to mobilize sixty votes to invoke cloture (closure of debate). Moreover, cloture is a time-consuming procedure (three to five days) that impedes the Senate's ability to process its extensive workload.

Filibusters involve many blocking tactics besides extended debate in which senators might hold the floor for hours of endless speeches. In today's polarized Senate, contemporary filibusters are commonly waged by those who skillfully exploit Senate rules. For example, senators might offer scores of amendments, raise many points of order, or demand numerous and consecutive roll call votes. Holds also function as a form of silent filibuster.

Holds. Long an informal custom, a hold permits one or more senators to block floor action on measures or matters by asking their party leaders not to schedule them. A hold, explained Sen. Charles E. Grassley, R-Iowa, is "a notice by a Senator to his or her party leader of an intention to object to bringing a bill or nomination to the floor for consideration."[64] The majority leader decides whether, or for how long, to honor a colleague's hold. The power of holds is grounded in the implicit threat of senators to conduct filibusters or to object to unanimous consent agreements.

Holds have come under criticism because they often lead to delays or even the death of measures or nominations. Originally intended as a way for senators to get information about when the majority leader planned action on a measure, holds have become devices for senators to kill measures or take hostages so as to extract concessions on unrelated matters.

For years, Sens. Grassley and Ron Wyden, D-Ore., joined by Sen. Claire McCaskill, D-Mo., have tried to reform—not eliminate—the holds process. Specifically, they want to end secret holds where one anonymous senator can block bills or nominations. Some success for the trio came in 2007, when the Senate established a procedure for ending secret holds (formally called a "notice of intent to object"). However, there was no enforcement mechanism. When the 112th Congress opened in 2011, the Senate adopted a "standing order"—the functional equivalent of a formal rule—that requires every senator to make his or her hold public. If a senator does not come forward to be the claimant, then whoever objected on his or her behalf, including the two party leaders, would be identified in the *Congressional Record* as the "holder." Still, anonymous pre-floor objections to calling up measures or matters have not disappeared in the Senate. In short, there are still secret holds in the Senate.

Filibusters and Cloture. The right of extended debate is unique to the Senate. Any senator or group of senators can talk continuously in the hope of delaying, modifying, or defeating legislation. In 1957 South Carolina senator Strom Thurmond, then a Democrat, set the record for the Senate's longest solo performance—twenty-four hours and eighteen minutes; he was trying to kill a civil rights bill.

Most measures can be subject to at least two primary filibusters: the first on the motion to take up the legislation and the second on the consideration of the bill itself. "Double filibusters" underscore the expansive scope of minority rights that characterizes Senate procedure. Importantly, however, a number of laws, including trade and budget reconciliation measures, restrict a senator's right to extended debate. As a former Senate parliamentarian explained, "We have on the books probably a couple hundred laws that set up specific legislative vehicles that cannot be filibustered or only amended in a very restricted way."[65]

The success of a filibuster depends not only on how long it takes but also on when it is waged. A filibuster can be most effective late in a session because there is insufficient time to break it.[66] Even the threat of a filibuster can encourage accommodations or compromises between proponents and opponents of legislation.

During most of its history, the Senate had no way to terminate debate except by unanimous consent, exhaustion, or compromise. In 1917 the Senate adopted Rule XXII, its first cloture (debate-ending) rule. After several revisions, Rule XXII now permits three-fifths of the Senate (sixty members) to shut off debate on substantive issues or procedural motions. (A two-thirds vote is required to invoke cloture on a proposal to change the rules of the Senate.)

Once cloture is invoked, thirty hours of debate time remain before the final vote occurs on the matter identified in the cloture motion. There might also be multiple cloture votes on a measure: on the motion to proceed, on the bill itself, and on amendments. If the Senate is in a procedural "hard ball" situation, opponents of the legislation will consume the entire thirty hours of postcloture debate on each clotured item. These actions "can grind legislative business to a halt and leave the Senate in an interminable purgatory."[67]

Senators complain about the frequent use of filibuster threats and cloture attempts. In the past, filibusters generally occurred on issues of great national importance. Today, they occur on a wide range of less momentous topics. As one majority leader pointed out,

> Not long ago the filibuster or threat of a filibuster was rarely undertaken in the Senate, being reserved for matters of grave national importance. That is no longer the case. . . . The threat of a filibuster is now a regular event in the Senate, weekly at least, sometimes daily. It is invoked by minorities of as few as one or two Senators and for reasons as trivial as a Senator's travel schedule.[68]

Unsurprisingly, many commentators call it the "sixty-vote Senate." Or, as a senator observed, "It isn't good enough to have the majority. You've got to have 60 votes."[69] Today, it is not uncommon for unanimous consent agreements to require bills or amendments to attract sixty votes for passage rather than a simple majority. The interests of both sides are served by this development. Majority advocates get a vote, and the supermajority threshold protects minority opponents. Moreover, this accord saves the Senate's time by avoiding use of the cloture procedure.

Attempts to invoke cloture also have increased, particularly in recent Congresses. For example, in the decade from 1961 to 1971 there were 5.2 cloture votes per Congress, but during the 109th Congress (2005–2007) there were fifty-two cloture votes.[70] From the 110th Congress through the 113th Congress (2013–2015), there were 494 cloture votes.[71]

Importantly, a cloture vote does not mean a filibuster is underway. Cloture is sometimes employed for purposes unrelated to ending a filibuster. For example, if the sixty votes are obtained under Senate Rule XXII, there is the requirement that all amendments must be germane to the clotured measure. Or the majority leader may schedule repeated cloture votes, knowing that they will fail, in order to tar the other party as "obstructionists" in the next election.

There is little question that contemporary senators wield their procedural prerogatives for partisan advantage. It is not surprising, then, that majority and minority partisans typically provide different interpretations of the circumstances that provoke their dismay and frustration with Senate proceedings. When Democrats held the Senate majority in 2010, Sen. Dorgan declared that there was "less cooperation and more determination to block almost anything than at any time I have seen in the 30 years I have served here." He added:

> We have a noncontroversial issue, a motion to proceed [to the consideration of] something on which there is no controversy, and it is subject to a filibuster, and then a cloture motion has to be filed. Then 2 days have to pass before it ripens. We have a cloture vote, and then following the cloture vote, the minority says: Well, we insist that the 30 hours postcloture be used. So 30 hours has to be burned off. Only then can you get a vote on a noncontroversial issue. Then you have a vote, and it is 98 to 1. That has happened throughout this [Congress]— continual efforts to block everything; deciding that the best strategy politically, apparently, for the minority here in the U.S. Senate is to block everything.[72]

During his time in the minority, GOP senator Alexander insisted that the "real obstructionists have been the Democratic majority which, for an unprecedented number of times, have used their majority advantage to limit debate, not allow amendments and bypass the normal committee consideration of legislation." He continued:

So the real "party of no" is the majority party that has been saying "no" to debate and "no" to voting on amendments that minority members believe improve legislation and express the voices of the people they represent. In fact, the reason the majority leader can claim there have been so many filibusters is because he actually is counting as filibusters the number of times he filed cloture—or moved to cut off debate.[73]

In the midst of this clash of viewpoints, a number of mainly junior senators have proposed to change Senate rules. Normally, change to Senate rules requires a supermajority in support, because the chamber's Rule XXII specifies that obtaining cloture on any proposed alterations to Senate rules requires a majority of two-thirds. One reform group argued that a newly elected Senate should not be bound by this or any preexisting rule. Like the House does every two years, reform-minded members argued that the Senate has the constitutional right "to determine the rules of its proceedings" by majority vote at the start of a new Congress, notwithstanding any inherited (or continuing) rules from the previous Congress.

Another approach to changing Senate rules is what became known as the "nuclear option." Rather than amending the text of Rule XXII at the start of a new Congress, the nuclear option—which can be invoked at any time—involves establishing a new precedent of the Senate by overturning correct rulings of the presiding officer. Because overturning (or upholding) rulings of the presiding officer requires, with few exceptions, only a simple majority vote, the majority party can take such an action without any support from senators of the minority party. (This reality underscores use of the word *nuclear* because of the parliamentary fallout expected from the minority party.) The effect is the same as a formal rules change, because precedents trump Senate rules until they are modified or repealed at some later date.

On November 21, 2013, the nuclear option was triggered and produced a major procedural change in the Senate. A congressional scholar called the development "among the three or four most important events in the procedural history of the Senate."[74] Majority Leader Reid, long frustrated by his party's inability to attract sixty votes to overcome Republican obstruction and approve President Obama's executive and judicial nominees, successfully invoked the nuclear option to establish majority cloture on executive and judicial nominees, excepting only nominees to the Supreme Court.

The procedural maneuver went as follows: When the Senate voted (57 yeas to 43 nays) against cloture on a judicial nominee, Senator Reid raised a point of order (a parliamentary objection) that "the vote on cloture under Rule XXII for all nominations other than the Supreme Court of the United States is by majority vote." The presiding officer rejected Reid's point of order, mindful of Rule XXII's sixty-vote requirement to invoke cloture. Reid appealed the chair's ruling, which the Senate reversed on a 52–48 partisan vote. The Senate's authoritative new precedent "reinterpreted the provisions of Rule XXII to require only a simple majority to invoke cloture on most nominations."[75] To be sure, any majority party could use the nuclear option to change by majority vote the interpretation of Senate rules that impede favorable action on party-preferred priorities.

To say that the minority Republicans were angry is an understatement. For example, GOP senator Charles Grassley of Iowa called it a "naked power grab and nothing more than a power grab."[76] For the remainder of the 113th Congress, Republicans continued to delay action on presidential nominees by, ironically, using a Rule XXII procedure left unchanged by the new precedent: they consistently exploited all the time allowed for postcloture debate before permitting votes on the nominees. Despite these delays, the nuclear option increased substantially Senate approval of the president's nominees.[77]

With Republicans in charge of the 114th Senate, there has been ongoing debate within the party about whether they should repeal the nuclear precedent or retain it. Supporters of keeping majority cloture suggest that it will allow the Republican Senate to confirm the nominees of a future Republican president, filling the federal bench with conservative justices. Conversely, some Republicans want to repeal the precedent, mindful that they might lose the Senate in the 2016 elections and that a President Hillary Clinton would load the bench with liberal justices and the executive branch with associates of both Clintons.

The fight over the nuclear option puts the procedural quandary facing the Senate in stark terms. Most senators value the benefits provided by unlimited debate to them as individuals. Many senators also believe that it would be a grave mistake for the Senate to "become just like the House" with its majority party dominance. But in an atmosphere of bitter partisan warfare in which the minority regularly uses all the tactics available to it to obstruct the majority, the Senate may not be able to continue to function with a set of rules and precedents that assume a degree of restraint and comity.

RESOLVING HOUSE–SENATE DIFFERENCES

Before bills can be sent to the president, they must be passed by the House and the Senate in identical form. Conference committees are the best known method used to resolve bicameral differences when the two chambers pass dissimilar versions of the same bill. Another approach is to "ping-pong" House and Senate amendments between the chambers until each house is satisfied with the product.[78] There are occasions, too, when ping-ponging is used in combination with conference committees. For example, the chambers may start out using the exchange of amendments and then convene a conference to resolve the outstanding matters in bicameral disagreement.

The ping-pong procedure has increased in importance and prominence in recent Congresses. A major reason was the Senate's difficulty in convening a conference with the other chamber because of its own internal partisan disagreements. Going to conference requires a motion that can be filibustered.

Opponents of a measure can thus use extended debate to block the convening of a conference with the House, unless proponents can muster sixty votes to overcome the obstruction.

Most public laws are approved without conferences. Either they pass each chamber without any changes (roughly 70 percent of the time), or the House and Senate amend a bill in turn until both chambers agree on the wording (about 20 percent of laws follow this shuttle route). Only about 10 percent of the measures passed by Congress—usually the most important and controversial—are subject to bicameral reconciliation by conference committees. More specifically, during the 113th Congress, of the 296 laws that were enacted, 76 percent became law by one house simply adopting the other's bill; 38 percent observed the ping-pong approach; and only 2 percent (three measures) involved the conference process.

Under each chamber's rules and precedents, conference committees meet only to resolve the matters in bicameral dispute; they are not to reconsider provisions already agreed to, and they are not to write new law by inserting matter that neither house may have considered. However, parliamentary rules are not self-enforcing, and either chamber can waive or ignore them.

Selection of Conferees

Conferees usually are named from the committee or committees that reported the legislation. Congressional rules state that the Speaker and the Senate presiding officer select conferees. In fact, that decision typically is made by the relevant committee chairs and the ranking minority members. House and Senate party leaders commonly get involved in naming conferees on major legislation to ensure that the conferees will back leadership positions on the legislation.

House and Senate party leaders are sometimes named as conferees—a sign that they want to direct conference negotiations on high-stakes issues important to their party. The House majority leader, for example, often serves on important tax conferences. When the top majority party leaders of either chamber are named as conferees, this signals, as one senator declared, a "majority-party driven" conference.[79]

Each chamber may name as many conferees as it wants, and some conference delegations are very large. The 1981 omnibus reconciliation conference set the record, with more than 250 House and Senate conferees working in fifty-eight subconferences to resolve more than three hundred matters in bicameral disagreement. The ratio of Republicans to Democrats on a conference committee generally reflects the proportion of the two parties in the House and Senate.

Today's conference committees represent a sharp departure in size and composition from the pre-1980 era, when conference delegations generally ranged from five to twelve conferees from each house. And before the mid-1970s, conferees nearly always were the most senior lawmakers from the committees that reported the legislation. Although seniority frequently determines who the conferees will be, it is not unusual for junior and even first-term members to be conferees. Furthermore, conferees today commonly are chosen from several standing committees and reflect intricate selection arrangements. For example, House conferees may be named to negotiate only certain items in disagreement instead of the entire bill. Multiple referrals and megabills are the driving forces behind these two developments.

In conference each chamber has a single vote determined by a majority of its conferees, who are generally expected to support the legislation as it passes their body. But, a senator confessed, as conference committees drag on, the "individual attitudes of the various members begin to show."[80] A standard objective of conferees is to fashion a compromise product—the conference report—that will be acceptable to a majority of the membership of both chambers and that the president will sign into law.

Openness and Bargaining

Secret conference meetings were the norm for most of Congress's history. In 1975 both houses adopted rules requiring open meetings unless the conferees from each chamber voted in public to close the sessions. Two years later, the House went further, requiring open conference meetings unless the full House agreed to secret sessions. Sometimes, the Cable-Satellite Public Affairs Network (C-SPAN) televises conference proceedings.

The open conference is yet another instance of individual–institutional cleavage. Under the watchful eye of lobbyists, conferees fight harder for provisions they might have dropped quietly in the interest of bicameral agreement. And yet private bargaining sessions still permeate conference negotiations.

Senators and representatives expect certain bills to go to conference and plan their bargaining strategy accordingly. For example, whether to have a recorded vote on amendments can influence conference bargaining. In the absence of a recorded vote, amendments may be easier to drop in conference. Bargaining techniques in conference cover a range of approaches: from logrolling ("you accept my chamber's position on this provision and I'll accept yours on another provision") to threats to walk out of the negotiations unless the other side compromises. One side may fight hard for a position on which it plans to yield, so the conferees can tell their parent chamber that they put up a good battle but the other side would not relent. Conference committees are where the final version of the law is often written, sometimes making changes or additions to legislation that neither chamber ever reviewed or considered in committee or on the floor.

The Conference Report

A conference ends when its report (the compromise bill) is signed by a majority of the conferees from each chamber. House and Senate staff then prepare the conference report and the accompanying joint explanatory statement, which summarizes the conferees' recommendations. The House and Senate then vote on the conference report without further amendment. If either chamber rejects the conference report—an infrequent occurrence—a new conference may be called or another bill introduced. Once passed, the compromise bill is sent to the president for approval or disapproval.

CONCLUSION

The philosophical bias of House and Senate rules reflects the character of each institution. Individual rights are stressed in the Senate, majority rule in the House. In both chambers, however, members who know the rules and precedents have an advantage over procedural novices in affecting policy outcomes. The late senator Robert Byrd, D-W.Va.—the longest-serving Senate member in history—was the acknowledged procedural expert in the Senate. Byrd understood that passing measures often involved unorthodox processes and procedures (for example, forgoing committee hearings or markups or even floor debate).[81]

In addition to congressional rules, persistence, strategy, timing, compromise, and pure chance are important elements in the lawmaking process. To make public policy requires building winning coalitions at successive stages where pressure groups and other parties can advance their claims. Political, procedural, personal, and policy considerations shape the final outcome. Passing laws, as one former representative said, is like the "weaving of a web, bringing a lot of strands together in a pattern of support which won't have the kind of weak spots which could cause the whole fabric to fall apart."[82]

Showdown over Government Funding. Threats to shut down the federal government have become a staple of recent congressional politics. In December 2014, Republican conservatives led by Sen. Ted Cruz, R-Tex., sought to block a massive bipartisan government spending bill because it failed to roll back President Barack Obama's executive order limiting deportations of undocumented immigrants. Senate Democrats poked fun at Senate Republicans for their inability to control their Tea Party members, at one point singing "I'll Be Home for Christmas" outside the Senate floor. The bill eventually passed just hours before the government was set to close down.

Decision Making in Congress

"**I**'m upset with certain things in the bill. It's not perfect. But a longer-term funding [bill] is much better for our economy than a short-term one," tweeted outgoing Senate majority leader Harry Reid in defense of a 1,603-page bill enacted as the 113th Congress came to a close in December 2014.[1]

The carefully crafted compromise had been negotiated by Reid, Senate Republican leader Mitch McConnell, top House Republicans, and the White House in a bid to avoid another government shutdown. Dubbed the "Cromnibus," the measure combined an "omnibus" appropriations bill funding most government agencies through the end of the fiscal year in September 2015, with a more limited continuing resolution funding the Department of Homeland Security through the end of February 2015. The shorter timeline for Homeland Security was a response to Republican anger over President Obama's November 2014 executive order allowing up to five million undocumented immigrants to remain in the country. With Republicans slated to take over the Senate majority in the 114th Congress, conservatives hoped that they would be able to use their leverage over funding the Homeland Security Department—which has jurisdiction over immigration enforcement—to reverse Obama's executive order. Conservative foes of Obama's immigration move were not alone in viewing the massive spending bill as an opportunity to pursue their priorities. The urgent need to pass a bill to keep the government running became a vehicle for numerous interests to attach priorities that otherwise might face tough opposition. Most controversially, Wall Street financial interests won approval of language loosening restrictions on big banks' ability to engage in certain risky trading strategies. The provision—approved without any hearings—was largely written by Citigroup.[2] But Wall Street banks were not the only winners. McConnell added a provision dramatically increasing the amount of money that individuals could contribute to the national parties. The bill also restricted the District of Columbia's power to pursue legalization of marijuana in the district, and relaxed a regulation limiting how long truck drivers could drive without taking a rest break. Democratic leader Nancy Pelosi rallied her troops against the bill, lambasting the rules changes for Wall Street and big donors as a "taint that was placed on this valuable appropriations bill from on high. . . . This is blackmail. You don't get a bill unless Wall Street gets its taxpayer coverage."[3] This

Democratic opposition would not normally threaten passage of legislation in the Republican-controlled House. But Speaker John Boehner desperately needed some Democratic votes for the Cromnibus because a faction of ardent conservatives rejected the bill for doing too little to counter Obama's immigration executive order. These conservatives—led by Sen. Ted Cruz, R-Tex.—argued that the massive spending bill should block all funding for enforcement of the Obama order. Boehner and other top GOP leaders understood that such a provision would prompt a presidential veto, resulting in a government shutdown that they feared would damage Republicans' standing with voters. So Boehner instead found himself working with the White House to find Democratic votes to secure a floor majority for the Cromnibus. Obama, Vice President Joe Biden, National Economic Council chair Jeffrey Zients, and White House budget director Shaun Donovan phoned undecided Democrats, urging them to support the bill. In the end, a group of fifty-seven mostly moderate Democrats, led by Minority Whip Steny Hoyer, D-Md., provided Boehner with the votes necessary to pass the bill on a 219–206 roll call, despite sixty-seven Republican votes against it.[4] Striding toward the House chamber minutes before the final vote, a relieved Boehner declared that "I'm a happy warrior."[5]

But the bill faced still another hurdle in the Senate. Cruz and fellow Tea Party conservative Mike Lee, R-Utah, objected to a unanimous consent agreement that Reid and McConnell had negotiated to govern consideration of the Cromnibus. Cruz insisted that the Senate vote on his point of order that the bill violated the Constitution because it funded Obama's allegedly unconstitutional executive order. The maneuver forced the Senate to stay in session over the weekend, even as twenty Republicans joined a unified Democratic caucus in voting down the point of order. "I don't see what we're achieving here," complained Republican Jeff Flake, R-Ariz., of Cruz's strategy.[6] Indeed, Democrats used the extra time in session as an opportunity to force consideration of numerous judicial appointees that Republicans had been holding up. On the final passage vote, eighteen Republicans voted against the Cromnibus. They were joined by twenty-one Democrats and one Independent—most of whom objected to the Wall Street and campaign finance riders—but the bill nonetheless passed, with a majority of each party's senators recorded in favor.[7]

This large-scale spending measure (and hundreds more that have a lower profile) required lawmakers to make tough policy choices collectively—after discussion, debate, bargaining, and problem-solving. The end product is almost always an imperfect compromise. Indeed, before the bill arrived at his desk, Obama issued a statement expressing his "disappointment" with several provisions of the Cromnibus but nonetheless endorsing the compromise measure.[8] Legislative assemblies are deliberative bodies, and in the United States this deliberation takes place in the context of the two Congresses. Individual members confront thousands of choices: how and when to participate, how to decide, how to find allies, and how to explain their actions to constituents back home.

THE POWER TO CHOOSE

All members of Congress have the ability to shape public policy, although some members are far more influential than others. At a minimum, every legislator has the right, indeed the obligation, to vote. Legislators must cast their own votes; no colleague or staff aide may do it for them. To exchange their votes or other official acts for money or for any other thing of value is a federal crime. But aside from bribery or corruption there are no legal grounds for challenging legislators' deliberations or decisions. As discussed in Chapter 2, the U.S. Constitution specifies that "for any Speech or Debate in either House, [members of Congress] shall not be questioned in any other place."

Policy making in Congress involves far more than casting roll call votes. Matters that come before Congress for a vote have already been shaped by the participation of members at prior stages. Some of this work, like members' votes, is a matter of public record: formal meetings, markups, debates, and amending activities. Of equal importance are the less-visible informal negotiations that surround nearly every enactment—away from the eyes and ears of reporters and lobbyists. Separating formal and informal modes of participation in a study of members' committee activity, Richard L. Hall found that members' formal and informal activities do not always coincide.[9] Sometimes, members use formal actions to signal concern to constituents and other groups, but then do not follow through with the hard informal work needed to shape the legislation.

A full accounting of lawmakers' performance, then, would embrace not only how members participate in floor and committee deliberations but also how much effort they expend overall. How much attention do they pay to issues? How do they gain expertise? Whom do they consult for information on legislative decisions? How much do they rely upon party leaders for advice? How do they hire, deploy, and supervise their staffs? Countless such decisions define what it means to be a member of Congress.

TYPES OF DECISIONS

One basic decision facing legislators is how to spend their time and energy while in the nation's capital. Some try to digest the mountains of studies and reports that cross their desks. They "do their homework," in Capitol Hill parlance. Others seem to know or care little about legislative matters. They pursue other duties—communication, outreach, visits with constituents or lobby groups, partisan politics, and fund-raising. Such members may rarely contribute to committee or floor deliberations. Their votes usually follow cues from party colleagues, staff aides, the White House, or interest groups. Some are found in the ranks of the "Obscure Caucus," a list of unnoticed members compiled periodically by *Roll Call,* a Capitol Hill newspaper. These members "spend time on parochial concerns or constituent service" rather than "staff a PR portfolio with press releases, television appearances and photo ops."[10] One recent study found considerable variation in the legislative effectiveness of members of

Congress, with the most effective representatives tending to be majority party members who hold senior committee or party leadership posts.[11]

Specializing

Within the legislative realm, members may dig deeply in a particular area or range widely across issues and policies. Senators are more apt to be generalists, while representatives tend to cultivate a few specialties. Former senator Jim DeMint, R-S.C., once explained why members should specialize:

> If you've got twenty things you want to do, see where everything is. You'll find that maybe ten of those are already being worked on by people, and that while you may be supportive in that role, you don't need to carry the ball. But you can find those two or three things that are important to you that no one seems to be taking the lead on. But if you try to play the lead on everything, you'll be wasting your time.[12]

In both houses, key policy-making roles are played by those whom Rep. David E. Price, D-N.C., a political scientist, calls *policy entrepreneurs*—that is, those recognized for "stimulating more than . . . responding" to outside political forces on a given issue.[13] Often nearly invisible to the mass of citizens, these legislators are known to specialized publics for their contributions to specific policies—for example, Sen. Jeff Flake, R-Ariz., on immigration; Rep. Earl Blumenauer, D-Ore., on bike trails; and Rep. Mac Thornberry, R-Tex., on cybersecurity.

Members' policy reaches can go beyond their committee assignments— through speeches, floor amendments, caucuses, and task forces, to name a few. When only in his second term, Rep. Dick Armey, R-Tex. (1985–2003), who was not a member of the Armed Services Committee, devised an ingenious scheme to employ an outside commission—the Base Realignment and Closure Commission (BRAC)—to decide which unneeded military bases should be closed. His proposal smoothed political sensitivities regarding base closures in members' constituencies and won bipartisan support for its enactment into law (P.L. 100–526). Such feats are not everyday occurrences, but the fluidity of today's procedures makes even the most junior member a potential policy entrepreneur.

A member's knowledge and perceived expertise on issues is a vital source of legislative influence. As Sen. Edmund S. Muskie, D-Maine (1959–1980), put it:

> People have all sorts of conspiratorial theories on what constitutes power in the Senate. It has little to do with the size of the state you come from. Or the source of your money. Or committee chairmanships, although that certainly gives you a kind of power. But real power up there comes from doing your work and knowing what you're talking about. Power is the ability to change someone's mind. . . . The most important thing in the Senate is credibility. Credibility! That is power.[14]

This sort of credibility generally comes from immersion in a particular set of issues, rather than aiming to speak authoritatively across the sweep of congressional business.

Timing of Decisions

Lawmakers do more than specialize in a particular policy field. They are constantly forced to make decisions on issues, many far from their areas of specialization. Timing is key. *When* members make decisions has important consequences for the deliberative process, a point that Richard F. Fenno Jr. discussed in his work on the "politics of timing."[15]

From a study of a vote on selling AWACS (airborne warning and control system) reconnaissance planes to Saudi Arabia, Fenno identified three types of decision makers: early deciders, active players, and late deciders.

Early deciders are fervent supporters who want to get out front in the debate. "I'd rather come out early and be part of the fight," said Rep. Peter T. King, R-N.Y., of his ready support for fast-track trade authority.[16] These members are buoyed by friendly lobbyists but ignored by others because their commitments are known at the outset from declarations, bill sponsorship, or prior voting records.

Active players, by contrast, delay their commitments, inviting bids from various sides of the issue at hand and often gaining leverage over the final language of legislation.

Late deciders delay their decision (or reconsider an earlier commitment) until the very last moment. They forfeit influence over the basic framework of the measure. But late deciders are eagerly courted by all sides and may gain specific concessions. With every vote critical to Senate passage of President Obama's health care overhaul plan and pressure mounting to conclude action, Sen. Byron Dorgan, D-N.D., informed Majority Leader Reid that he would not vote for the Patient Protection and Affordable Care Act unless it included Native American health care. "That's not a threat, just a statement of fact," he said.[17] (Dorgan, now retired, was chair of the Committee on Indian Affairs.) Native American health care was included as part of the larger bill.

Taking the Lead

Senators and representatives differ widely in the rate at which they introduce and sponsor bills. Some lawmakers are inveterate initiators of bills and resolutions. Others shy away from sponsoring measures. Still others commonly take the lead in sponsoring legislation because of the position they occupy, such as the chair of the relevant committee of jurisdiction. A study by Wendy Schiller found that bills in the Senate are most likely to be introduced by senior senators, those who are chairs or ranking members of high-volume committees (such as Commerce), and those who represent large, diverse states.[18]

Senate and House rules do not limit the number of members who can cosponsor bills or resolutions. Thus cosponsorship has become common. Most bills are cosponsored; in a recent Congress, the average Senate bill had 4.1

cosponsors and the average House bill had 15.5 cosponsors.[19] Authors of measures often circulate a "Dear Colleague" letter detailing the virtues of the bill and soliciting cosponsors to demonstrate broad support and urge committee action. A researcher found that more than twelve thousand such letters were sent electronically by House members in 2007, an average of more than twenty-five letters per member.[20]

Occasionally, however, some members shun cosponsors. Introducing his waterway users' fee bill, Sen. Pete V. Domenici, R-N.M. (1973–2009), decided against seeking cosponsors for several reasons.[21] First, as ranking Republican on the subcommittee, he could arrange for hearings without the support of cosponsors. In addition, single sponsorship is easier. ("If you've got cosponsors you have to clear every little change with them.") And, finally, if the bill became law, he would get more credit on his own.

Do legislators favor the bills and resolutions they introduce? Normally they do, but as Sportin' Life, the *Porgy and Bess* character, said, "It ain't necessarily so." Members may introduce a measure to stake out jurisdiction for their committee or to pave the way for hearings and deliberations that will air a public problem. Or they may introduce measures they do not personally favor to oblige an executive agency or to placate an important interest group.

Taking Part

As members in any organization, some lawmakers take a passionate interest in what goes on; others pay selective attention to issues; a few seem just to be going through the motions. In a detailed study of three House committees, Richard L. Hall uncovered great variation in members' levels of participation. Although members' attendance at committee and subcommittee sessions was respectable (about three-quarters of the members showed up for at least part of each session), active participation—taking part in markup debate, offering amendments, and the like—was far less common. Perhaps half a subcommittee's members could be considered players, by a generous counting. The rest were nonplayers. As a subcommittee staffer remarked, "On a good day half of [the members] know what's going on. Most of the time it's only five or six who actually mark a bill up."[22]

Constituency interests strongly propel members to participate in committee business. In formal subcommittee markup sessions, "the public forum has the benefit of allowing members at once to promote—through their votes, arguments, amendments, obstructionism—constituency interests and be seen doing so."[23] But even when negotiations are not visible to the public, legislators will have an incentive to advocate for constituent interests.

Constituency-driven activity was especially common in the House Agriculture Committee, a panel historically buffeted by regional and commodity pressures. Because of the committee's composition, its membership is more favorable to agriculture programs than the House as a whole. Furthermore, only a subset of the committee's members participates in most matters, and those who choose to take part tend to be more predisposed to favor the programs under consideration than even the rest of the Agriculture Committee. Hall found in his late 1990s study that members representing constituencies with large numbers of dairy farmers and peanut growers, for example, were the most active in influencing policy affecting dairy and peanut interests. Neither the full committee nor floor deliberations counterbalanced the enthusiastic advocacy of the dozen or so lawmakers from districts that produced those commodities. Participation on Agriculture was the most biased toward members with a constituency stake in the legislation being considered; in debates over job training legislation in another committee, participating members tended to represent areas with higher unemployment rates than those of nonparticipants, but the gap was less stark than on Agriculture. No participatory biases were found when concentrated district benefits were not at stake.

Members in formal leadership positions are also more likely to take an active part in committee deliberations. Members often forgo participation because there are so many demands on their time that they must prioritize issues that are important to their constituents. Committee and subcommittee leaders, however, face fewer obstacles to participation because their seniority and authority "[place] them at the epicenter of the communications network in which most important legislative interactions take place."[24] In other words, holding leadership posts puts members "in the know" and enables them to be major players on legislation even when they do not personally have a significant constituency stake in the outcome.

Participation in House or Senate floor debates is equally varied: members who do not serve on the relevant committees, or who have only peripheral interests in the matter, are tempted to speak simply "for the record." Floor speeches vary greatly in the quality of their informational content. A study of three major congressional debates determined that it is "typically no better than moderately informed." Gary Mucchiaroni and Paul J. Quirk concluded: "Legislators frequently assert claims that are inaccurate or misleading, and reassert them after they have been effectively refuted."[25] The good news about floor debates is that opposing members often—though not always—counter erroneous or distorted arguments.

Offering Amendments

Another important way of participating is to offer amendments to bills or resolutions. Amendments propose specific changes in legislative language: they delete or add words or substitute one provision for another. They are a chief means of shaping legislation during committee and floor deliberations. However, amendments are not always intended to enact policy changes. They can instead be used as a tool of obstruction or to derail legislation. They also can serve political purposes by putting members on the record on specific issues. For example, Sen. Claire McCaskill, D-Mo., who won reelection in a tight 2012 contest, exclaimed that in the lead-up to the election, Senate GOP leader Mitch McConnell, R-Ky., had been "trying to figure out what amendments he could put on the floor to make my life miserable." McConnell's goal, she said, was "to figure out some way to put something on the floor that would get me to vote against my own mother."[26]

House majority leaders, who control the floor agenda, regularly employ special rules to limit the amendments that members can offer to particular bills. By so doing, the leaders often can engineer favored policy outcomes, expedite floor action, and prevent politically difficult issues from being raised on the floor. In 2012, for example, the House considered a GOP tax reform bill under a structured rule that granted a specific minority Democrat the opportunity to offer one free-standing amendment to the bill (H.R. 6169) that the majority Republicans knew they could defeat. The measure was entitled "Pathway to Job Creation through a Simpler, Fairer Tax Code Act." A senior minority member of the Rules Committee blasted the rule, stating that other than one minority amendment, "every single amendment the Democrats had to try to influence this bill was defeated [in the Rules Committee] on a strictly partisan vote—every single one of them." This bill, he added, is "a press release masquerading as a meaningful piece of legislation."[27] The measure passed the House on a party-line vote.

Compared to the House, in the Senate—because of individual senators' prerogatives—amendments are more freely offered and form a central part of floor debate. Sometimes, amendments are offered simply to test the strength of support for a proposal rather than to immediately alter policy outcomes. During a debate on reauthorizing the National Aeronautics and Space Administration, a House member introduced an amendment to cancel the costly space station program. Instead of losing by a wide margin (as in previous years), the amendment failed by only a single vote. That narrow margin signaled plunging support for the space station and other "big science" projects.[28]

Some amendments are designed to force members to declare themselves on issues that command public attention. Sen. David Vitter's, R-La., amendment to an omnibus appropriations bill to end automatic cost-of-living increases in congressional salaries is an example. Lawmakers who vote for salary increases, especially during hard economic times, risk having the voters turn them out of office.

Other amendments are poison pills. So-called killer amendments are intended to make a bill so unpalatable that if adopted, they will kill the underlying measure. Although killer amendments upset the sponsors and managers of bills, they rarely alter a measure's ultimate fate. Examining seventy-six killer amendments considered in the mid-1990s, a scholar concluded that they "rarely, if ever, cause bills to fail. . . . Most were easily defeated."[29]

Casting Votes

Lawmakers' most visible choices are embodied in the votes they cast. Voting is a central ritual of any legislative body. Members know that their voting records communicate a great deal of information about their policy and political commitments to their constituents. Reflecting on his vote on a financial institutions bailout package, a House member said, "This is a legacy vote; these are the votes you have to live with for the rest of your life."[30] Several months after the 112th Congress convened, many Tea Party–supported congressional Republicans found themselves facing a legacy vote. These lawmakers, having promised in the 2010 elections to cut and curb government spending, now faced an unavoidable vote: the electorally painful decision to raise the national debt ceiling. A failure to raise the debt ceiling when needed would risk global financial instability, but voting to increase it is never popular with constituents, particularly those most concerned about government debt. Raising the "must-pass" debt ceiling is "beautiful politics—the brutal kind," declared former senator Alan Simpson, R-Wyo. (1979–1997), cochair of President Obama's deficit reduction commission.[31]

Members anticipate that constituents will review their votes at reelection time. Outside groups closely follow members' votes on specific measures and publicize them during election campaigns. Special interests want to know whether members' promises on the campaign trail tracked their voting decisions in Congress. Groups may grade lawmakers as "heroes" or "zeros" based on their votes for environmental or business measures. Nevertheless, members' own personal judgments sometimes outweigh political expedience. Members may be willing to risk their reelection chances by casting a vote contrary to the strong preferences of many of their constituents (for example, voting for gun control in a state or district with a pro-gun culture), especially if they have explained to voters in advance the reasons for their decision.

Senators and representatives strive to be recorded on as many floor and committee votes as possible. On 640 roll call votes on the House floor in 2013, members voted 96 percent of the time. Senators recorded a participation rate of 97 percent on the 291 votes taken in 2013.[32] Members seek to compile a record of diligence to forestall charges of absenteeism by potential opponents. They also want to compile a good voting record to demonstrate their commitment to the voters back home. Just before casting her 5,000th consecutive vote, Sen. Susan Collins, R-Maine, said, "While I recognize that not every vote is a critical vote, at this time when the public's confidence is so low, casting every single vote sends a strong signal to one's constituents of dedication to the job and to respect for the high privilege that we have been given."[33]

House and Senate leaders make it easier for members by trying to schedule votes at predictable times; stacking votes back to back in midweek; or holding fewer votes on Mondays, when lawmakers are returning to Capitol Hill from their states or districts, and Fridays, when many members are anxious to depart for their constituencies.

If members cannot vote in person, they can still be recorded on an issue by announcing their views in floor statements or in press releases. A member who wishes to be recorded on an issue but cannot be present for the roll call vote may also ask another member who plans to vote on the other side for a "pair" arrangement in which both announce their positions in the *Congressional Record* but neither casts a vote (they cancel each other out). Members often grant such requests as a courtesy to their colleagues. Members might also vote "present" for various reasons. For example, Sen. Charles Schumer, D-N.Y., cast a rare "present" vote on a judicial nominee because the nominee was married to his sister.[34]

What Do Votes Mean?

Like other elements of the legislative process, votes are open to multiple interpretations. House and Senate floor votes do not perfectly register members' views. Members sometimes vote against a bill that they prefer to the status quo because they hope that a better bill on the matter might emerge later. Members know that a weak reform can deplete political will for bolder action. Killing a modest measure may lead to action on a more wide-ranging proposal later. Politicians may also refuse to accept a compromise when they can force a confrontation that will sharpen the differences between the parties. At times, members prefer to keep the issue alive rather than to pass a bill. As a scholar wrote, "Advocates often anticipate that having the party differences clearly displayed will help them win in the next election, after which they will be able to enact an unadulterated form of the bill."[35]

Members also may vote for a bill that they do not favor because they fear that if they fail to support it the end result will be something even worse. For example, some conservative Republicans voted for a federal program providing prescription drug coverage for elderly Americans because they believed it was the best bill they could get. "I don't think we'll write a better bill if we defeat this," explained a conservative senator.[36] Members may also go along with legislation because on the whole they deem the bill a step forward, even though they dislike specific provisions.

In some cases, recorded votes are wholly misleading. Given the multiplicity of votes—procedural as well as substantive—on many measures, lawmakers can come out on more than one side of an issue, or at least appear to do so. For example, members may vote to authorize a program and later vote against funding it. Or they may vote against final passage of a bill but for a substitute version. This tactic, which may open a lawmaker to the charge of being a "flip-flopper," assures the bill's backers that the lawmaker favors the concept, while pleasing voters who oppose the bill. Such voting patterns may reflect either a deliberate attempt to obscure one's position or a thoughtful response to complex questions. As in so many aspects of human behavior, lawmakers' motivations are often difficult to discern.

Members can also take advantage of "free votes" when their own individual vote will not affect the final outcome. Some members delay voting until the outcome of the vote is already assured. For example, during the debate on a constitutional amendment to prohibit flag burning, there was "strategic waiting" on the part of members.[37] Democratic members were cross-pressured on the issue—Democratic leaders opposed the anti–flag burning amendment, but it was very popular with constituents. Before it was clear that the amendment was going to fail, only 28 percent of the voting Democrats supported the amendment. Once enough votes had been cast to defeat the amendment,

73 percent of the remaining Democrats voted in favor of it. After the amendment had failed, members could take the popular position without any legislative consequences. Opportunities for insincere votes proliferate in the U.S. system of the separation of powers. Members can deliberately vote for measures that they believe will fail in the other chamber of Congress or be vetoed by the president. And they can support popular measures that they expect the courts will strike down as unconstitutional.

Lawmakers' voting rationales are sometimes hard to explain to outsiders. In some cases, members face a dilemma: either vote their convictions and deal with the consequences, or swallow their misgivings and vote for appearance's sake. A GOP House member chose the former course when he joined fourteen other Republicans in voting against a popular bill authorizing U.S. sanctions against nations that persecute religious minorities—an appealing idea but fraught with problems. "This was an awfully awkward vote, and I know I'll hear from the folks back home," he explained. "But the devil was in the details."[38]

More often, lawmakers decide to go with the crowd. Regarding a highly appealing constitutional amendment requiring a balanced budget, a senator admitted that he planned to vote for it because he got "tired of explaining" its deficiencies. It was easier "just to say put it in."[39] It no doubt eased the member's conscience to know that the chances were slim that the amendment would ultimately be ratified.

Scholars and journalists often mistakenly treat votes as if they were unambiguous indicators of legislators' views. Lobbyists, too, are prone to assess lawmakers on the basis of floor votes. Many groups construct voting indexes that label legislators as "friendly" or "unfriendly." Citizens should be cautioned to examine such indexes closely. How many votes does the index include? Are they a fair sample of the group's concerns? Does the index embody a partisan or ideological agenda, hidden or otherwise? The bottom line is: beware of an interest group's voting scorecards, even if you agree with its policy leanings.

DETERMINANTS OF VOTING

Votes, particularly on single issues, should be examined, interpreted, and categorized with care. Party affiliation, ideological leanings, constituents' views, presidential leadership, and cues from trusted fellow members are among the factors that shape congressional voting.

Party and Voting

Party affiliation is the strongest single correlate of members' voting decisions. In a typical year, from half to two-thirds of all floor votes could be called party unity votes, defined as votes in which a majority of voting Republicans oppose a majority of voting Democrats. Figure 9-1 depicts House and Senate party unity votes from 1953 to 2013. Party voting is far more prevalent today than it was in the 1970s or early 1980s. Indeed, contemporary levels of party voting recall the militant parties of the late nineteenth century.

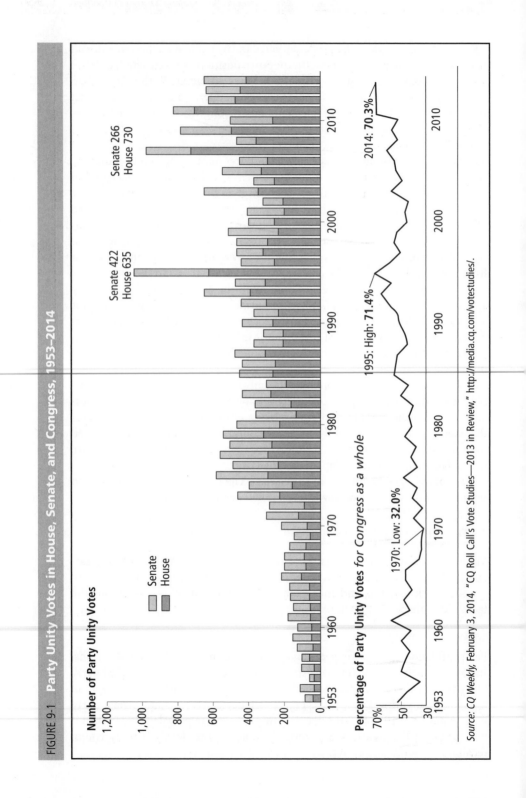

FIGURE 9-1 Party Unity Votes in House, Senate, and Congress, 1953–2014

Number of Party Unity Votes

Senate 266
House 730

Senate 422
House 635

Senate
House

Percentage of Party Unity Votes for Congress as a whole

2014: **70.3%**

1995: High: **71.4%**

1970: Low: **32.0%**

Source: CQ Weekly, February 3, 2014, "CQ Roll Call's Vote Studies—2013 in Review," http://media.cq.com/votestudies/.

In the GOP-controlled 113th House, party unity was near record-setting levels.[40] In 2013, 70.5 percent of the 1,202 House roll call votes divided the parties. House party unity scores were high in large measure because Republican leaders "persistently brought up proposals to unify their conference, including bills attacking President Barack Obama's health care law."[41] In 2013 in the Senate, 68 percent of 657 votes split along party lines, again close to a record for the chamber.[42]

Figure 9-2 depicts unity scores for the two parties in each chamber from 1956 to 2013. Both House Republicans and Democrats achieved extremely high cohesion in 2013: 91.5 percent of Republicans and 89 percent of Democrats voted with their own party when the two parties disagreed. The Republicans' unity level was at an all-time high. Senate Democrats achieved even greater unity, also setting a record for their party with a 93.5 percent unity rate in the 113th Congress. Senate Republicans enjoyed slightly lower success in holding their troops together, recording an 85 percent unity rate. The GOP's score was driven down by the frequent defections of two members—Susan Collins of Maine and Lisa Murkowski of Alaska, each of whom had a unity score below 70 percent. But leaving aside these two frequent defectors, Senate GOP leaders kept the vast majority of their troops in line.[43]

Party cohesion stems from a number of roots. Members of a political party vote similarly because they are elected by many of the same sorts of constituencies and organized interests throughout the country. As one study noted, on a wide range of unrelated issues—"gun control, the economy, war, same-sex marriage, abortion, the environment, the financial bailout—the views of Republicans and Democrats have become increasingly monolithic."[44]

Party members also vote together because of their shared ideological commitments. Changes in the ideological composition and the constituency base of the two congressional parties have contributed to the increased levels of partisanship in the contemporary Congress. Each of these sources of party unity—constituency and ideology—is discussed here. However, it is important to note that congressional party unity also has a source in explicitly *partisan* motives, meaning party members' shared political interests in helping their party win elections and control Congress.[45] These interests bring fellow partisans together despite the diversity of their policy preferences. Indeed, even when interparty conflict in Congress was at a low ebb in the late 1960s and early 1970s, the parties still successfully organized the committees and leadership of Congress, and party affiliation remained the strongest single predictor of members' voting behavior.

Members of Congress cooperate with their fellow partisans in part because their personal fate as politicians is bound up with their party's public image and collective reputation. Members know that they do not win or lose elections solely as individual legislators. Voters' attitudes about the national parties affect their choices in particular congressional elections.[46] As a result, members have reason to take into account how their individual actions will affect public perceptions of their party as a whole.

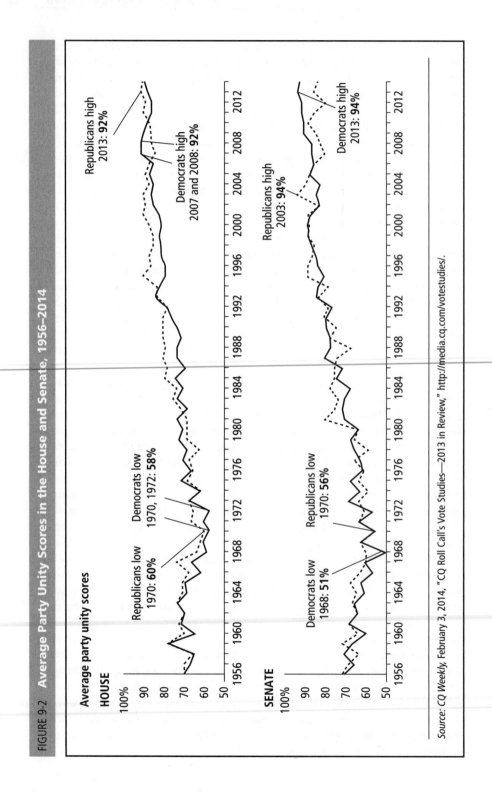

FIGURE 9-2   Average Party Unity Scores in the House and Senate, 1956–2014

Average party unity scores

HOUSE

Republicans high
2013: **92%**

Democrats high
2007 and 2008: **92%**

Republicans low
1970: **60%**

Democrats low
1970, 1972: **58%**

SENATE

Republicans high
2003: **94%**

Democrats high
2013: **94%**

Democrats low
1968: **51%**

Republicans low
1970: **56%**

Source: CQ Weekly, February 3, 2014, "CQ Roll Call's Vote Studies—2013 in Review," http://media.cq.com/votestudies/.

Members also care about the collective image of their party because they want their party to command a congressional majority. Members gain power personally when their party is in the majority. Members of the majority party chair all committees and subcommittees, and majority leaders set the floor agenda. It is easier for members to advance their personal policy initiatives when they are in the majority.

Members concerned with winning elections and wielding influence will therefore pay attention to their party's collective reputation. To foster positive public impressions of their party, fellow partisans work to find common ground. They collaborate in efforts to construct an appealing policy agenda and then cooperate in promoting it. They also exploit opportunities to call into question the other party's competence and integrity.

Common political interests nurture bonds of trust and communication among fellow partisans. To deepen these bonds, the congressional parties now hold regular lunches, conferences, and retreats for members. In addition, the socialization of new members largely takes place in partisan settings. Thus fewer friendships cross party lines these days. As one senator explained, "If the only knowledge you have of 'the other side of the aisle' is what you have read in an attack press release written by the party operatives, you wouldn't want to talk to them, and you certainly wouldn't want to be friends."[47]

Majority and minority party leaders regularly appeal to their members' common partisan interests in order to rally their troops behind the party agenda. The leaders of both parties strive to give the electorate a favorable view of the party's "brand." They hire consultants to devise messages and strategies crafted to generate broad public support for their policy goals and objectives. Contrasting his party's image with the clearer Republican brand, a Democratic senator said, "I can tell you what the Republicans stand for in eight words: family values, strong defense, lower taxes and less government."[48] Reflecting on these partisan motives, political scientists Gary Cox and Mathew McCubbins wrote, "Modern political parties facing mass electorates, similar to corporations facing mass markets, have a strong incentive to fashion and maintain a brand name."[49]

The common political interests of Democrats and Republicans mean they are predisposed to support their party. Political scientists who have studied members' voting decisions have found that members decide mainly by consulting the views of their partisan colleagues.[50] The typical member of Congress feels "duty bound to ascertain the views of the party leaders and [to] go along in the absence of contrary inclinations."[51] In other words, members cooperate with their parties unless they have a reason to defect. Wavering members who have reservations about the party's position may be subject to heavy pressure from party leaders. A classic example involved House Speaker Newt Gingrich, R-Ga. (1995–1999), and his lieutenants. During the GOP's first year in power after forty consecutive years of Democratic control, a junior Republican described the leadership's approach at persuasion:

> They pull us into a room before almost every vote and yell at us. . . . They say, "This is a test of our ability to govern," or "This is a gut check," or "I got you here and you hired me as your coach to get you through, but if you want to change coaches, go ahead."[52]

Party leaders in both chambers can usually rely on a high level of reflexive support from fellow partisans, especially on procedural matters. Political scientists have repeatedly shown that members are more likely to vote with their parties on procedural motions than directly on the substance of legislation.[53] Indeed, members often support their party leaders on procedural matters related to a bill, even when they do not intend to support the bill on final passage. Procedural votes, in brief, are usually partisan votes. As a senator once observed, "This is a procedural vote, and in the Senate we traditionally stick with the leadership on such votes."[54]

House leaders have broad authority to exploit procedures to strengthen party unity. Through their control of key committees, scheduling powers, and use of special rules, majority party leaders arrange for votes they are likely to win and avoid those they are apt to lose. For example, the majority leadership can use their agenda-setting prerogative in positive and negative ways. They can bring legislation to the floor under procedures that advantage the majority party, or the leaders can block unwanted measures (or amendments) from even being brought up for chamber consideration.

Senate leaders have fewer procedural tools than do House leaders, but majority leaders can use their right to be recognized first on the floor to regulate the timing, order, and content of debates to partisan advantage. For example, then–Senate majority leader Reid deliberately scheduled a series of votes he knew he would lose in fall 2010. Why? He wanted to portray Republicans as "obstructionists," to indicate to the bill's supporters that he tried, to demonstrate that Senate rules need revision (the measures were blocked by filibuster threats), and to direct the public's attention to these issues. Minority Leader McConnell viewed the entire exercise as political theater: "Are we here to perform, or are we here to legislate?"[55] At the same time, minority party members also have strong incentives to stick together on procedural and other matters, forcing vulnerable majority party members to cast difficult votes and making it increasingly difficult for the majority party to pursue its program.

Ideology and Voting

Most lawmakers today hold strong ideological views on such topics as the proper role and purpose of government.[56] Indeed, many members of Congress entered politics through various ideological causes. Opposition to the Iraq war and the huge income disparity between the rich 1 percent and the other 99 percent spurred political activism for members on the left of the political spectrum. Many members on the right entered politics because of their small-government views or traditionalist social values. Long before they take their first oath of office, members bring ideological loyalties that inspire voting decisions throughout their political careers.

Both political parties encompass ideological diversity, which reflects their demographic and behavioral differences. The Republican Party, for example, embraces both economically conservative voters—educated, higher-income cohorts who are often associated with business—along with less-educated, lower- or middle-income people who are drawn to the party's traditional social values and its emphasis on limited government, national and border security, and a hard line on crime. Balancing the party's ideological wings is not an easy assignment for GOP congressional leaders. They work to accommodate both the party's social and religious conservatives, as well as its economically conservative business wing, not to mention the Tea Partiers.

Thus the journey to an acceptable compromise among House Republicans since their 2010 election victory has often been difficult, sometimes impossible. Many junior Republicans have been in no mood to contain their zeal to cut spending, repeal health care, and overturn unwanted federal regulations. During a House GOP Conference meeting, freshman representative Steve Southerland, Fla., said he understood the party leadership's plea for party unity: "I want you to know there is a limit to how far I will follow. I may lose in 2012 [he won reelection] but I will not lose me."[57] The 114th Republican House is also likely to confront continued disunity within party ranks. Indeed, the twenty-five conservative Republicans who refused to vote for John Boehner's reelection as Speaker as the new Congress opened used the vote to signal their opposition to any compromises in the name of finding common ground with the Democratic White House.[58]

The Democratic Party also embraces ideological variety. In brief, Democrats include across-the-board liberals who are committed to a vigorous government redressing economic grievances, to tolerant stances on social and lifestyle issues, and to international treaties and institutions guiding foreign policy. But the party also includes factions advocating for a more conservative position on economic issues or on social issues, such as abortion. For example, a group of centrist House Democrats who belong to the informal New Democratic Coalition tacks left on social issues but veers "toward the center on business- and economic-oriented policies that could appeal to independent and moderate voters."[59] The party's diversity reflects its voters, who range from union members—who are concerned with economic issues but less liberal on social causes—to the "creative class" of professionals in university towns and urban enclaves who are far more libertarian on social issues but often less concerned with "bread and butter" issues like jobs, housing, and minimum wage.[60] Free-trade pacts also tend to split these groups: union members fear losing jobs to low-wage foreign labor, while educated professionals tend to be more open toward globalization. Democratic leaders have to navigate these ideological divisions, often by avoiding issues that fracture the party.

When political scientists began seriously to analyze congressional roll call voting in the 1950s, ideological diversity within each of the two parties was far greater than it is today. Conservatives and liberals had a meaningful presence in both legislative parties. Although members often voted along party lines, at other times they would unite across parties in recognizable ideological coalitions.

Frequently, Republicans and southern Democrats would cooperate in a voting pattern known as the conservative coalition.[61] The coalition's success rate was impressive in both chambers during the 1939–1965 period—no matter which party controlled the White House or Capitol Hill.

Since the 1960s, the two legislative parties have sorted themselves out along ideological lines, with conservatives largely in the Republican Party and liberals exclusively in the Democratic Party. Scholars have found that "the most conservative Democrat is more liberal than is the most liberal Republican," with Republicans moving further to the right than Democrats to the left (called "asymmetric polarization").[62] As a consequence, the cross-party conservative coalition surfaces so rarely these days that the respected *CQ Weekly* stopped scoring it.[63] Bipartisan conservatism fell victim to the increasing ideological consistency of both political parties. In short, "Democrats are perched on the left, Republicans on the right, in both the House and the Senate as the ideological centers of the two parties have moved markedly apart."[64]

The polarization of the contemporary Congress—in which partisanship and ideology are closely intertwined—can be shown spatially on a left–right (liberal–conservative) continuum. Using the congressional roll call voting record, political scientists Keith T. Poole and Howard Rosenthal have devised a scaling methodology to generate ideological scores for all members of Congress.[65] Their data show marked divergence between the parties in recent years.

Figure 9-3 displays the distribution of ideological preferences for Republicans and Democrats among activists and the general public and within Congress. When voters are asked to locate themselves on the ideological spectrum, the result roughly follows a normal bell-shaped curve. As shown in panel A, citizens are bunched together around the middle of the ideological spectrum, with relatively few respondents identifying themselves as very liberal or very conservative.[66] The same centrist pattern appears when voters are asked to position themselves on specific policy issues, even on hot-button topics such as taxes and abortion. By contrast, political activists are more likely to identify as either liberal or conservative. The survey results displayed in panel A of Figure 9-3 reveal Republican and Democratic activists clustering to the left or right of the median, with far less overlap between the two parties at the elite level than exists in the mass public.

In 1968 the ideological divisions in the House of Representatives (displayed in panel B in Figure 9-3) looked similar to those of the party elites. Democrats appeared in almost every ideological niche, from far left to far right. Although Republicans were more tightly clustered on the right, a number spilled over to the liberal side of the scale.[67] Political moderates—members at or near the midpoint between the parties—constituted a substantial bloc.

The contemporary Congress (represented by panel C) is almost completely polarized along party lines. Only a handful of members fall at the midpoint— not a single Republican falls on the liberal side of the scale, and only a few Democrats stray into the conservative category.

In today's Congress, members' party affiliation and ideological views overlap almost perfectly. (These figures are for the House; patterns in the Senate are

FIGURE 9-3   **Ideological Divisions in Congress and the Public**

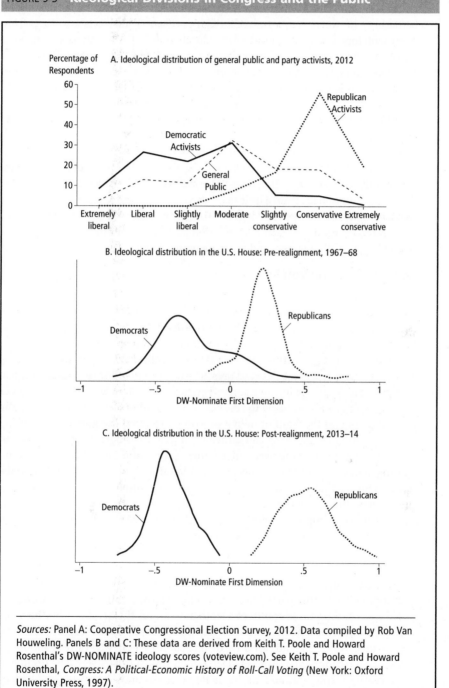

A. Ideological distribution of general public and party activists, 2012

Percentage of Respondents

Republican Activists

Democratic Activists

General Public

Extremely liberal   Liberal   Slightly liberal   Moderate   Slightly conservative   Conservative   Extremely conservative

B. Ideological distribution in the U.S. House: Pre-realignment, 1967–68

Democrats

Republicans

DW-Nominate First Dimension

C. Ideological distribution in the U.S. House: Post-realignment, 2013–14

Democrats

Republicans

DW-Nominate First Dimension

Sources: Panel A: Cooperative Congressional Election Survey, 2012. Data compiled by Rob Van Houweling. Panels B and C: These data are derived from Keith T. Poole and Howard Rosenthal's DW-NOMINATE ideology scores (voteview.com). See Keith T. Poole and Howard Rosenthal, *Congress: A Political-Economic History of Roll-Call Voting* (New York: Oxford University Press, 1997).

similar, though somewhat less dramatic.) This polarization and the resulting collapse of the middle (the "shrinking center") have produced clear ideological battle lines between the parties. Although partisan rigidity gets a bad rap from commentators, one must consider how closely political convictions are linked to partisanship in the minds of lawmakers and their activist supporters. "If you can't find common ground, that doesn't mean you're partisan," explained Nancy Pelosi when she was Speaker (2007–2011). "It just means you believe different things."[68]

The proportion of political moderates—conservative Democrats or liberal Republicans—hovered at about 30 percent in the 1960s and 1970s. Today, however, fewer than one in ten lawmakers fall into this centrist category.[69] Conservative Democrats, the larger of the two centrist groupings, once represented a third of their party's members; today they could caucus in a small room. The fiscally conservative "Blue Dog" Democrats, as they called themselves, saw their ranks cut in half (from a little over fifty to twenty-six) in the November 2010 elections. The Blue Dogs are down to fourteen members in the 114th Congress. Even rarer are moderate Republicans, who account for no more than 2 percent of all House GOP members and no more than 3 to 6 percent of senators.[70]

Constituency and Voting

Constituency context is another powerful influence on members' vote choices. Constituencies control lawmakers' choices in two ways. First, people usually elect representatives whose views mirror their own. In this sense, representatives vote their constituency because they are transplanted locals. Second, members listen to constituents because it is politically imperative to do so. Representatives feel great electoral pressure to respond to the dominant political interests and opinions in their constituencies. For example, pleas for stronger gun control laws are unlikely to resonate with members from Idaho, where the culture embraces the right of men and women to purchase guns.

Constituency concerns can either reinforce or undermine party unity in Congress. For much of the twentieth century, it was not unusual for conservative-leaning states to elect Democrats and for liberal-leaning states to elect Republicans. During that period, constituency influence often led members to buck their party. But since the 1960s, constituencies have gradually sorted themselves out according to ideological and policy preferences. In the current era, constituency pressure tends to bolster party unity.

Relatively few Democrats in the 114th Congress represent conservative districts or states. In 1960 all senators from the South were Democrats, and they constituted a large conservative bloc that often resisted Democratic Party leaders and cooperated across party lines with Republicans. But in the 114th Congress (2015–2016), only three southern Democrats are in the Senate.[71] By the same token, many areas once represented by GOP liberals have been captured by Democrats. New England, an area of the country that was once a moderate Republican stronghold, now elects Democrats almost exclusively. The decline of conservative Democrats and moderate Republicans underlies much of the ideological cohesion within, and the chasm between, today's Capitol Hill parties.[72]

Partisans in the contemporary Congress vote together in great part because they reflect the same kinds of states and districts. Republicans tend to represent rural areas and outer suburbs. Democrats tend to represent urban areas, inner-ring suburbs, and majority-minority districts.[73] Two interrelated demographic trends are worth noting briefly. First, today the GOP is strongest among white voters and older citizens, while Democrats fare much better among minority groups and young voters. Democrats also hold an advantage among women, while Republicans attract a greater share of men.

Second, diversity characterizes Democrats more than Republicans and House Democrats more than Senate Democrats. Starting with the 113th Congress, white males have been—for the first time in American history—a minority in the House Democratic caucus.[74] The consequences of having a white-male-dominated, largely "southernized" House Republican Party and a minority and female-dominated House Democratic Party are not self-evident. However, it is reasonable to suggest that compromises on significant issues may be harder to obtain, disagreements over the role of government are likely to be more contentious, and conflicts over social issues could increase. In the judgment of a political scientist, "When you have parties so divergent in views, regions, and genders, the culture wars could escalate from conventional to nuclear weapons."[75]

The few remaining party mavericks in today's Congress tend to come from parts of the country where their party generally does not do well electorally. This is especially the case among Democrats; the least loyal Democratic senators in the 114th Congress all came from states that voted Republican for president, such as Joe Manchin of West Virginia.[76] Several of the most independent Republicans likewise represent Democratic-leaning constituencies, such as Susan Collins of Maine and Mark Kirk of Illinois. But Republican mavericks also include some hardline conservatives who at times differentiate themselves from the party mainstream by defecting. Tea Party conservatives Mike Lee of Utah and Justin Amash of Michigan were thus among the Republicans with the lowest unity scores in the 114th Congress.[77] Constituency affects congressional decision making as politicians take both attentive and inattentive publics into account. Political scientist R. Douglas Arnold has tracked how both groups can influence members' electoral calculations.[78] Attentive publics are those citizens who are aware of issues facing Congress and hold decided opinions about what Congress should do. It is thus relatively easy for politicians to consider their views. A politician's natural instinct is to yield to the strongly voiced preferences of an attentive public, unless the issue in question mobilizes two equally vociferous but opposing interests. Especially feared are single-interest groups that threaten to withhold electoral support if their preferences—for example, on abortion or gun control—are ignored.

Inattentive publics are those who lack extensive knowledge or firm preferences about a specific issue. Frankly, this definition describes most people most of the time. People pay attention to only a small fraction of the issues before Congress, yet a reelection-minded legislator dare not ignore those who seem indifferent to an issue. "Latent or unfocused opinions," Arnold cautions, "can quickly be transformed into intense and very real opinions with enormous political repercussions. Inattentiveness and lack of information today should not be confused with indifference tomorrow."[79] Legislators are well advised to approach even the most minor choices with this question in mind: Will my decision be defensible if it were to appear on the front pages of major newspapers in my state or district?

Calculating the electoral consequences of a lawmaker's multitude of daily decisions is no easy task. Arnold summarizes the components of such calculations:

> To reach a decision, then, a legislator needs to (1) identify all the attentive and inattentive publics who might care about a policy issue, (2) estimate the direction and intensity of their preferences and potential preferences, (3) estimate the probability that the potential preferences will be transformed into real preferences, (4) weigh all these preferences according to the size of the various attentive and inattentive publics, and (5) give special weight to the preferences of the legislator's consistent supporters.[80]

Fortunately, lawmakers need not repeat these calculations every time they face a choice. Most issues have been around for some time. The preferences of attentive and even inattentive publics are fairly well known. Moreover, Congress is well structured to amass information about individual and group preferences. And prominent officials—party leaders and acknowledged policy experts, for example—can often legitimize members' choices and give them cover in explaining those choices to voters.

The Presidency and Voting

Although Congress often pursues an independent course and members differ in their feelings toward the occupant of the White House, presidents can persuade members to support their agendas. Figure 9-4 depicts the percentage of the time presidents—from Dwight D. Eisenhower to Barack Obama—have prevailed in congressional roll call votes on which they announced a position. Presidents take positions on a wide range of issues, from the momentous (health care and financial reforms, in Obama's case) to large numbers of routine and noncontroversial matters (most Senate confirmations of executive nominations, for example).[81]

During President Obama's first two years in office, he enjoyed large success in winning congressional support on those issues where he took a clearly stated position. In fact, in 2009 he had a 96.7 percent success rate. A year later, his success rate dropped to 85.8 percent, "the tenth highest on record and the fourth highest for a president in his second year." Moreover, his 2010 score "does not capture the sheer size of the legislation enacted during his second year: the tax deal [extending President George W. Bush's 2001 and 2003 tax cuts to 2012], in addition to overhauls of [the] health care system and financial regulations, not to mention student loans, food safety, a strategic weapons treaty with Russia and a repeal of the ban on gays serving openly in the military."[82]

President Obama's legislative success rate declined significantly in the aftermath of the November 2010 elections. Republicans reclaimed control of the House and gained seats in the Senate. For the next four years, Obama enjoyed an overall success rate that hovered in the 50 to 60 percent range. But this masked a huge gap between the Republican House and Democratic Senate. In 2014, for example, the president won on just 15 percent of the roll call votes in the House where he took a position; by contrast, he succeeded on 93 percent of the Senate roll calls where he took a stand. Since legislation must pass both chambers, the battles between the president and House Republicans meant that "Obama signed fewer new laws than any president this century, or in the half-century before that."[83]

Indeed, party control of Congress dramatically affects presidential success rates. As long as their party controls Congress, presidents win at least three of every four votes on which they take a position; when the government is divided, presidents fall well below that level. Another important pattern evident in Figure 9-4 is that presidents tend to lose congressional support as their administrations age. Presidents' best years in dealing with Congress are usually their first. This could be due to a "honeymoon" effect in which legislators are more likely to side with a popular president, though it also may result from presidents tackling issues where the opportunity for success is strongest early in their terms and being left with harder problems as their term continues.

Cue-Givers and Roll Call Votes

It is impossible for a single member to make an informed decision on the hundreds of roll call votes confronted in each Congress. As a result, members rely heavily upon their colleagues and other informants as a source of cues as they make up their minds. A good cue-giver will tend to be a member with expertise on the issue under consideration who shares the partisan, ideological, and perhaps regional affiliations of the member seeking out help in making a decision. Exchanges of voting cues are endemic in both chambers. The exchange not only saves the recipient the time and trouble of mastering the subject matter, but it also can provide credible cover in defending the vote. Cue-giving is a key element in John W. Kingdon's model of representatives' decisions, derived from interviews with members immediately after their votes on specific issues.[84]

Legislators have little difficulty making up their minds when they receive no conflicting cues from party leaders, respected fellow members, constituents, or key interest groups. If all the cue-givers in their field of vision concur, members operate in a consensus mode of decision making. If the actors are in conflict, the lawmaker will have to weigh the alternatives.

Fellow members emerge in Kingdon's study as the most influential cue-givers, with constituencies ranking second. As one lawmaker observed:

> I think that the other members are very influential, and we recognize it. And why are they influential? I think because they have exercised good judgment, have expertise in the area, and know what they are talking about.[85]

FIGURE 9-4   Presidential Success History, 1953–2014

■ Fifth year of presidency

Source: CQ Weekly, February 3, 2014, "2013 Vote Studies: Presidential Support," 170.

Note: Presidential success is defined as the percentage of the time the president won his way on roll call votes on which he had taken a clear position.

When members deviate from a consensus stance among their cue-givers, it is usually to follow their own conscience or their constituencies.

LEGISLATIVE BARGAINING

Whatever their sources of influence, in the end individual legislators have only a single vote on any given bill or, more typically, on an amendment. At that moment, the vote is reduced to a "yea" or "nay" question, with no hedging or nuance allowed. Legislators have to decide how to cast these binary votes on a bewildering array of issues. They rarely have adequate—or even much—information on any particular bill or amendment. Legislators must weigh their goals—which often may conflict—and process their limited information in a relatively short period of time to arrive at a decision.[86]

Such a state of affairs—disparate goals and widely scattered influence—is hazardous. Stalemate is a constant threat. The "collective action problem" is the way political scientists refer to the challenge of merging individual goals into group achievements. To overcome this predicament, members have to resort to politicking—that is, they must trade off goals and resources to get results. It is no wonder, then, that Congress is "an influence system in which bargain and exchange predominate."[87]

Implicit and Explicit Bargaining

Bargaining is a general term that refers to several related types of behavior. It describes in an overall sense the process by which two or more parties arrive at a mutually beneficial exchange. Such processes may be implicit or explicit.

Implicit Bargaining. Implicit bargaining occurs when legislators take actions designed to elicit certain reactions from others, even though no negotiation has taken place. For example, legislators often introduce bills or sponsor hearings not because they expect the measure to pass but to prod someone else—an executive branch official, or a committee chair with broader jurisdiction on the question—to take action. Or a bill's managers may accept a controversial amendment knowing full well that the objectionable provision will be dropped in the other chamber or in conference. At other times, a committee's judgment about the merits of a bill may receive deference from noncommittee members, with the expectation that the committee members will reciprocate when it comes to other committees' proposals. These are examples of the so-called law of anticipated reactions.[88]

Explicit Bargaining. Explicit bargains also take several forms. In making compromises, legislators may agree to split their differences. Compromises are straightforward on issues dealing with quantitative elements that can easily be adjusted upward or downward—for example, funding levels or eligibility criteria. Compromise on substance is also possible. For example, members who favor a major new program and members who oppose any program at all may agree to a two-year pilot project to test the idea.

"You cannot legislate without the ability to compromise," declared former senator Alan Simpson, R-Wyo., who often found fault with militant junior members of his own party. He recounted the following tale:

> On a recent bill, I went to [conservative House members] and said: "Here's what I'm doing. I've got six senators who will vote this far, and then the next time if you go any further, they will not be there." So [my GOP colleague] and I delivered on this singular bill, and they said, "We want you to get more." And we said, "There is no more to get." Next vote on this bill, we lost six votes. Then they came in and said, "We are going to probably kill the whole thing. . . . " [A]nd they got nothing.[89]

The lesson is that compromise is inevitable in crafting laws; those who are unwilling to give ground are bound to be disappointed. On occasion, both parties avoid compromise and engage in brinksmanship, with each expecting the other to "blink" first before the interparty deadlock produces bad political and policy repercussions. Winning concessions from the opposing side is a key aim of this form of strategic bargaining.[90]

The classic compromise—a "win win" for the contending sides—has been hard to achieve in recent Congresses. A significant number of lawmakers have instead preferred a "no compromise" stance. There was simply an unwillingness on their part to engage in the traditional "give and take" negotiating process: members give up legislative provisions or positions but take others they find acceptable enough to move legislation forward. A view expressed by a House Republican reflected one shared by many others on Capitol Hill: "When it comes to compromise, half of a bad deal is still a bad deal."[91] Effective governance is challenged when issues provoke high-stakes brinksmanship and compromise implies political weakness, a sellout, or a betrayal of principle.

Logrolling

Logrolling is bargaining in which members exchange support so that all parties to the deal can attain their individual goals. The term originated in the nineteenth century when neighbors helped each other roll logs into a pile for burning. Its most visible form is a something-for-everyone enactment, sometimes called a "Christmas tree" bill. Such bills are prevalent in legislative areas such as public works, omnibus taxation, or tariffs and trade. Describing a classic logroll, former representative Edward J. Derwinski, R-Ill. (1959–1983), explained how the country's two million farmers put together a majority coalition every five years to pass the omnibus farm bill's basket of price supports, acreage allowances, and marketing agreements:

> What [the farmers] do is very interesting. The agriculture people from North Carolina, where agriculture means tobacco, discuss their problems with the man representing the rice growers in Arkansas or California. The sugar beet growers in Minnesota and sugar cane

interests in Louisiana and Hawaii and the wheat and corn and soybean and other producers just gather together in one great big happy family to be sure there is a subsidy for every commodity. They put those numbers together again so that they have at least 218 supporters in the House and 51 in the Senate. A supporter of the tobacco subsidy automatically becomes a supporter of the wheat subsidy, or the sugar quota, or the soybean subsidy, or whatever else follows.[92]

Logrolling draws lawmakers into the finished legislative product by embracing their special interests, proposals, or amendments. Henry M. "Scoop" Jackson, D-Wash. (House, 1941–1953; Senate, 1953–1983), when asked how he had assembled a majority for a new proposal, responded this way: "Maggie [Sen. Warren Magnuson of Washington] talked to Russell, and Tom promised this if I would back him on Ed's amendment, and Mike owes me one for last year's help on Pete's bill."[93] Such reciprocity especially pervades the Senate, dominated as it is by individuals. Sponsors of a Senate bill often must placate most or all interested legislators to gain clearance to bring a bill to the floor.

Lawmakers who enter into, and stand to profit from, a logroll are expected to support the final package, regardless of what that package looks like. A broad-based logroll is thus hard to stop. "It's not a system of punishment. It's a system of rewards," explained a House member.[94]

Logrolling can turn narrowly targeted programs into broad-scale ones, as many lawmakers want a piece of the policy pie. This development can dilute a program's impact by spreading funds throughout the nation rather than in targeted areas. Similarly, if resources are spread too thinly among too many sites, the program may not make a noticeable difference in any single area.

When faced with an austere fiscal environment, logrolling is often aimed at equalizing sacrifices instead of distributing rewards. Broad-spectrum bills—authorizations, omnibus tax measures, continuing resolutions, and budget resolutions—may include numerous less-than-optimal provisions, many of which would fail if voted on separately. Such a negative logroll enables lawmakers to support the measure as "the best deal we can get."

In a time logroll, members agree to support one measure in exchange for later support for another measure. A time logroll was crucial to the initial House passage in 2003 of a major new prescription drug benefit for seniors. Rep. Jo Ann Emerson, R-Mo., had been fighting for years to allow U.S. consumers to purchase generic drugs from Canada and other countries where prices were lower, but she could not convince her Republican leadership to permit a vote. "I felt like a darned broken record," Emerson said.[95] When Emerson realized that Republican leaders would need her vote to pass the new prescription drug benefit, she took advantage of the opportunity. She demanded that they promise to bring her reimportation bill up for a vote, and eventually she was able to get a good-faith pledge from the leadership to greenlight her bill. "I'm extremely pleased with the outcome," she said.[96] Republican leaders fulfilled their promise to Emerson the following month by permitting the House to take a vote on the matter.[97]

Sometimes, logrolls can be constructed on the basis of side payments to members. A lawmaker's support is exchanged for benefits on an unrelated issue—for example, a federal project for the state or district, a better committee assignment, inclusion in an important conference, help with fund-raising, or access to the White House. Although such side payoffs may seem trivial or parochial, they can enable members to achieve valued goals.

Bargaining Strategy

For bargaining to take place, participants in the House and Senate must be able to rely on one another's future actions. Rep. John P. Murtha, D-Pa. (1974–2010), a master deal-maker, cited two elements of power on Capitol Hill: "Develop expertise on an issue that makes you vital to colleagues, and keep your word."[98] Relying on his expertise and contacts within the defense community, he often cut deals quietly in the back corner of the Democratic side of the House. On the Senate side of the Capitol, the same kind of deal-making occurs. Democratic leader Reid, for example, was not reluctant to provide Sens. Ben Nelson, D-Neb., and Mary Landrieu, D-La., with what each wanted in order to win their votes for the president's controversial health overhaul plan. The press soon called the special health benefits each received for their states, respectively, the "Cornhusker Kickback" and the "Louisiana Purchase."[99]

For bargaining to succeed, the participants must agree on the need for a legislative product—that is, the benefits of reaching a decision must exceed the costs of failing to do so. In many cases, politicians may prefer a course of strategic disagreement, the "efforts of politicians to avoid reaching an agreement when compromise might alienate supporters, damage their prospects in an upcoming election, or preclude getting a better deal in the future."[100]

According to bargaining theory, a measure's sponsors will yield only what they absolutely must to gain a majority of supporters. "Parties wish to use their votes efficiently, winning victories at the cheapest possible price."[101] By this logic, if bargainers act rationally and have perfect information about one another, minimum winning coalitions should predominate.[102] Recounting Senate majority leader Lyndon B. Johnson's meticulous vote-counting before a floor fight, a top Senate aide concluded: "And once a sufficient majority had been counted, Johnson would seldom attempt to enlarge it: Why expend limited bargaining resources which might be needed to win future battles?"[103]

Most legislative strategists, however, lack Johnson's extraordinary skills. Uncertainty about outcomes leads them to line up more than a simple majority of supporters. Moreover, at many points in the legislative process supermajorities are required—for example, in voting under suspension of the rules, in overriding vetoes, or in ending Senate filibusters. Not surprisingly, therefore, minimum winning coalitions are not typical of Congress, even in the majoritarian House of Representatives.[104]

Yet coalition size is the crux of legislative strategy. Bargainers repeatedly face the dilemma of how broadly or how narrowly to frame their issues and how many concessions to yield in an effort to secure passage.

CONCLUSION

Congressional deliberation is at risk today. With both parties unified and seemingly uninterested in debate or compromise, life on Capitol Hill has become, in Thomas Hobbes's words, "nasty" and "brutish" (though hardly "short"). Take-no-prisoners strategies are encouraged by today's highly competitive, polarized party system. As a senator observed,

> The pressure on congressional leaders both from interests in the party and from outside groups is severe. Many would rather fight and lose, rather than reach out and find common ground. Congress should not be like the Super Bowl, in which one team always has to win and the other team inevitably loses. There's nothing wrong with reaching legitimate compromise and getting something done for the American people.[105]

Political scientist Sarah Binder's findings echo this sentiment. "The decline of the political center," she writes, "has produced a political environment that more often than not gives legislators every incentive not to reach agreement."[106] The result is often legislative inaction, which may be criticized as stalemate or gridlock.

Yet the enterprise of lawmaking rests on the premise that at least where urgent matters are concerned, bargainers will normally prefer some sort of agreement to none at all. As Everett M. Dirksen, R-Ill., the legendary Senate Republican leader (1959–1969), once remarked, "I am a man of fixed and unbending principle, and one of my principles is flexibility."[107] Flexibility is especially crucial with "must-pass" legislation that, if not approved, can imperil government functions. When dealing with some reauthorizations and appropriations, the alternative to lapses in the timely enactment of appropriations bills—called "funding gaps"—can be the total or partial shutdown of federal activities and programs and the furlough of governmental employees.[108] Indeed, budget impasses have resulted in seventeen funding gaps since 1977. The two most controversial funding gaps occurred when the GOP-controlled 104th Congress (1995–1997) and President Bill Clinton clashed over spending policy. Two partial government shutdowns occurred (November 15–16, 1995, and December 16–January 6, 1996) that led to the furlough of about 800,000 federal employees. More recently, thousands of federal furloughs occurred in October 2013 due to the controversy over Republican efforts to use an omnibus spending bill to defund the Affordable Care Act. Bargaining is a necessary part of legislative life. It shapes the character of bills, resolutions, and other forms of congressional policy making. It also underlies many attributes of the legislative process—delay, obfuscation, compromise, and norms such as specialization and reciprocity.

Deliberation is the hallmark of legislative decision making. Coalitions are constructed as diverse views are voiced and a variety of members, executive officials, and interest groups participate. It is yet another point of contact and conflict between the two Congresses—the Congress of individual wills and the Congress of collective decisions.

Multiple **Presidential Roles.** President Barack Obama meets with congressional leaders in the Oval Office in September 2014 to discuss options for combating the Islamic State. Standing before Vice President Joe Biden and Speaker John Boehner, the president waves to the crowd before delivering his 2015 State of the Union address. The president meets with female Congress members in the Roosevelt Room of the White House in March 2014.

10

Congress and the President

The November 2014 midterm elections produced another major defeat for congressional Democrats, in part because many voters viewed the election as a way to express their opposition to the policies and priorities of President Barack Obama. With 254 House members in the 114th Congress (2015–2017), the GOP enjoyed its largest majority since the 71st Congress (1929–1931), when Herbert Hoover was president. Republicans also took control of the Senate with a 54 to 46 advantage.

However, to the consternation of many Republicans, President Obama did not act like the "lame-duck" chief executive they expected, one whose job approval ratings at the time were in the low forties and whose party had suffered an electoral debacle.[1] Instead, according to one account, the president acted "as though his party won the midterms."[2] Immediately after the midterms, Obama took a series of decisive executive actions, such as forging a major climate change agreement with China, a major emitter of greenhouse gas; suspending the deportation of about five million undocumented immigrants; and ending the fifty-four-year U.S. policy of sanctions against Cuba with the goal of normalizing relations with the island nation.

Sen. Ted Cruz, R-Tex., called President Obama's executive actions "unprecedented," and he explained why. "Previous Presidents, particularly second-term Presidents, have been repudiated by the voters, and there is a way Presidents typically responded: They react with humility. They react acknowledging the American people, trying to course correct. Sadly, President Obama did not do that."[3] Perhaps because he would no longer be on the ballot seeking reelection, the president acted not like a lame duck whose administration was essentially over, but as a forceful chief executive on the policy offensive. As President Obama said: "I'm going to try to squeeze every last ounce of possibility and the ability to do good out of this job in these last two years."[4] Added David Axelrod, a longtime political strategist for the president: "He sees problems he wants to solve, and he's going to use the tools that are available to him to solve them. I certainly do not expect him to curl up in a fetal position."[5]

The tools available to President Obama in his dealings with the GOP Congress involved a mixture of confrontational and cooperative approaches. For example, on the confrontational front, President Obama issued two veto threats during the first two days of the GOP-controlled 114th Congress. One involved legislation (S.1) to construct the long-delayed and controversial Keystone pipeline project bringing oil from Canada to the Gulf Coast. Upset with President Obama's veto threat, GOP senator John Hoeven of North Dakota declaimed: "Here we have legislation that has bipartisan support in this body. . . . [Yet] the President issues a veto message right out of the gates. Why? For whom? Whom is he working for?"[6]

The other veto threat issued by Obama concerned a bill (H.R. 30) to delete part of the Affordable Care Act, the president's signature domestic achievement. Since its enactment in 2010, House Republicans have tried nearly sixty times to "repeal and replace" the statute. As a House Democrat said of the GOP's latest attempt to eviscerate the health care reform law, Republicans continue to use the chamber as a "campaign studio," bringing "legislation to the floor [to accommodate their conservative base] that the President will veto" with little chance of it being overridden by a two-thirds vote of either chamber.[7] GOP senator Richard Burr, N.C., expressed dismay at the surge of veto threats by the president, several more made during his 2015 State of the Union address: "When you start out with multiple veto threats and you show no willingness to even meet somewhere in the middle on issues that have been percolating for some time, it gives you very little hope that there's going to be a breakthrough."[8]

Despite the president's sometimes combative rhetoric directed at the new GOP Congress, the interests and incentives of the nation's top legislative and executive leaders converge today in certain respects, creating opportunities for progress on various issues. Republicans excelled in previous Congresses at frustrating many of the administration's legislative priorities. The president called Republicans the "Party of No." Now in the majority in both chambers, Republican leaders want to prove that they can actually govern by finding common ground with the president and minority Democrats on specific issues. A two Congresses incentive contributes to the GOP's urge to govern: twenty-four GOP senators are up for reelection in 2016, several representing states carried by President Obama. Their defeat could return the Senate to Democratic control. In the House, an analyst noted that there are fifty-one "Obama Republicans" who represent "congressional districts that the president won in 2012 or that Mitt Romney won by fewer than five percentage points."[9]

GOP leaders in both chambers have identified a number of potential bipartisan initiatives (cybersecurity, for example) that the president might sign into law. Success at congressional governance also could bolster the GOP's presidential candidate in 2016 by boosting public support for the party's agenda and brand. On the other hand, there are GOP lawmakers who dislike the president personally and disagree with almost anything he proposes. Some of them suggest that compromises with Obama are unnecessary since "we may win the White House and control all levers of power after the 2016 election."[10]

As for President Obama's incentives for cooperation with the GOP Congress, they are at least twofold: First, during his final two years of office, he wants to burnish his eight-year legacy with additional legislative accomplishments.

Second, certain issues might be easier to enact working with the majority Republicans rather than the minority Democrats. Trade is a prime example. Many Democrats in Congress and their outside supporters (labor unions, for example) oppose trade agreements with other nations because of their perceived negative impact on U.S. jobs. The president, however, is lobbying Democratic lawmakers to join with Republicans to pass legislation granting him trade promotion authority: allowing trade agreements negotiated by the administration with other nations to be subject in Congress to a so-called "fast track" procedural process in each chamber: limits on debate, no amendments, and an up-or-down vote. Senate Finance chair Orrin Hatch, R-Utah, has said he would move "carefully but quickly" to produce trade legislation.[11] On May 22, 2015, the Senate passed the trade bill by a 62–37 vote.

Other potential areas for interbranch cooperation during the 114th Congress might include corporate tax reform, a new authorization of the use of force resolution to combat terrorist groups, and more funds for infrastructure projects (highways, bridges, ports, and so on). At issue is "whether the two sides can get past [the rancor] of the past several years by agreeing to disagree on certain issues where their philosophies diverge, and engaging on issues where there is room for compromise."[12]

Compared to the 2011–2014 period of often acrimonious interchamber and interbranch battles, there was considerable legislative–executive cooperation during Obama's first two years in office (2009–2010), when Democrats controlled both legislative chambers. Although the president inherited huge problems (two wars, a financial meltdown, and high unemployment, among others), Obama in his first two years won passage of truly consequential legislation. Some analysts called the achievements transformative, comparable to President Lyndon B. Johnson's "Great Society" accomplishments such as Medicare in 1965. With a Democratic-controlled Congress, the president won enactment of a massive overhaul of the health care system, something many of his predecessors from Theodore Roosevelt on had wanted but had failed to do. He revamped the financial regulatory system; championed a $787 billion stimulus package to revive the economy and prevent another Great Depression; and, during one of the most productive "lame-duck" sessions in decades, succeeded in winning Senate approval of a major nuclear arms treaty with Russia and terminated the "don't ask, don't tell" law that prevented gays and lesbians from serving openly in the military. To be sure, not all Obama proposals were enacted even under unified government; immigration reform and climate change legislation both failed to make it through the legislative process, and even successful initiatives—such as health care reform—required many compromises and concessions. But the 111th Congress nonetheless stands out as being highly productive.

Legislative successes were much harder to come by in the next two Congresses after Republicans won control of the House. GOP ranks were filled with many conservative Tea Party–endorsed lawmakers who opposed the very idea of compromising with the opposition party. They were determined to cut spending, reduce the deficit, abolish federal programs, and repeal unwanted regulations. Moreover, many were willing to provoke government shutdowns or risk allowing the government to default on its debt obligations unless the Obama administration agreed to their demands. Over in the Senate, GOP minority leader Mitch McConnell of Kentucky proclaimed that "the single most important thing we want to achieve is for President Obama to be a one-term president."[13] Instead, President Obama won a second term handily in 2012, with Republicans losing eight seats in the House (but still in control) and Democrats unexpectedly picking up two Senate seats. Republicans were devastated by their losses. Many had been convinced that they would win the White House, retain the House, and take control of the Senate.

Given the president's resounding 2012 electoral victory, Obama anticipated that he could advance an expansive agenda, including immigration reform and climate change legislation. His belief was that past policy impasses would be replaced in the main by bipartisan compromises and that the GOP's "fever" of blanket opposition to the president's initiatives would be broken. The president's expectations were not realized. An array of factors foiled Obama's hopes, such as unexpected crises that refocused the White House's time and attention away from his preferred priorities; the inability of the two parties to reach across the aisle to resolve their differences; and presidential miscues. Examples of unforeseen developments that provoked legislative–executive disputes included:

> The botched rollout of HealthCare.gov; long waits at veterans hospitals; Edward Snowden's disclosures of the National Security Agency's secrets; a pileup of foreign children along the southern border; Islamist terrorists marauding across Syria and Iraq and beheading foreigners, including Americans; and the arrival of the Ebola virus in the United States.[14]

Clearly, tensions between the executive and legislative branches are inevitable. The two policy-making branches have divergent responsibilities and different constituencies and terms of office, and typically they are jealous of each other's prerogatives. Executive officials see the decentralized Congress as inefficient and meddlesome. Legislators perceive the hierarchical and highly centralized executive branch as arrogant and arbitrary. At times, these differences lead to conflicts that the news media dramatize as the "battles on the Potomac." Many times during recent legislative sessions, the elective branches engaged in the "politics of brinksmanship"—which branch would blink first and capitulate to the demands of the other—before legislation was enacted to resolve bitter interbranch clashes. A dramatic instance occurred during summer 2011 over legislation to raise the debt ceiling (see Chapter 14).[15]

Divided government often complicates relationships between Congress and the executive branch, as was evident in the highly polarized 2011–2014 period when Republicans held the House but Democrats controlled the Senate.

Gridlock was often the order of the day on major legislation. The GOP House passed many measures on largely party-line votes that simply died in the Democratic Senate, with the reverse the case as well. The truncated 112th Congress enacted "fewer bills into law than any Congress in decades"—the same refrain heard for the 113th Congress, whose chambers were also controlled by different parties. In response, GOP representative Jason Chaffetz of Utah exclaimed, "Numbers of bills passed should not be a litmus test for a Congress."[16] Even with the often hostile relationship between the branches, a defender of Congress's performance could note that appropriations measures were eventually enacted and the government kept afloat. A key issue, however, is how much more than that can be accomplished under current conditions of divided government and fierce partisan warfare?

THE PRESIDENT AS LEGISLATOR

The president is sometimes called the chief legislator because of his close involvement in congressional decision making. Article II, section 3, of the Constitution directs the president from time to time to "give to the Congress Information of the State of the Union and recommend to their Consideration such Measures as he shall judge necessary and expedient." (Today, this means annually and during television's prime time.) Soon after delivering the annual State of the Union address, the president sends to Congress draft administration bills for introduction on his behalf. By enlarging the list of messages required from the president—the annual budget and economic reports, for example—Congress has further involved the chief executive in designing legislation. Indeed, Congress often delegates authority to the president because it appreciates the strengths of the White House—such as its capacity for coordination—and recognizes its own shortcomings, such as its decentralized committee structure, which inhibit swift and comprehensive policy making. Crises, partisan considerations, and public expectations all make the president an important participant in congressional decision making. And the president's constitutional veto power ensures that White House views will be listened to, if not always heeded, on Capitol Hill.

The legislative presidency emerged after World War II. By then, it was conceded that this new presidential role was institutionalized, performed not because of some unique combination of personality and circumstance but because everyone expected it—including Congress, the press, and the public.[17] This deeply entrenched expectation will not change anytime soon.

Understanding the chief executive's relations with Congress is no easy task. The founders did not clearly define the legislative–executive relationship, and so it has always been a work in progress. Presidents bring their own style to the relationship, which political scientist Charles O. Jones characterizes as either the "partnership model" or the "independent model." The partnership model means that presidents consult regularly with lawmakers and involve them directly in the policy and political affairs of the White House. The independent model holds that presidents should minimize their involvement with Congress and strive on their own to accomplish their top priorities.[18]

Scholars have long analyzed America's complex system of separate institutions sharing, and competing for, power. Different theories, such as Jones's, have been formulated to define effective presidential leadership. Some studies focus on the person in the White House; others examine the bureaucracy and the institutional functions and structures of the presidency; and still others analyze discrete aspects of the relationship between Congress and the president, such as presidential spending power versus the legislative branch's power of the purse.[19] Here we discuss four prominent presidential theories—persuasion, rhetoric, administrative, and the "two presidencies"—as a way to illuminate important aspects of the chief executive's relations with Congress. To varying degrees, these analytical perspectives overlap and capture the activities of all presidents.

The Power to Persuade

"Presidential power is the power to persuade," wrote Richard E. Neustadt, a former staff aide in the Truman White House and adviser to President-elect John F. Kennedy.[20] Power, Neustadt asserted, meant more than the executive's ability to persuade Congress to enact a bill. "Strategically, the question is not how he masters Congress in a peculiar instance, but what he does to boost his chances for mastery in any instance."[21] Presidents striving to be successful are urged to employ all their powers—constitutional, political, bureaucratic, personal, and more—to persuade Congress and others to follow their lead. Setting Congress's agenda—that is, determining the policies that the legislature heeds by taking them up in committee and on the floor—epitomizes the president's power to persuade.

Presidents have shaped Congress's agenda since the earliest days of the Republic. The First Congress of "its own volition immediately turned to the executive branch for guidance and discovered in [Treasury Secretary Alexander] Hamilton a personality to whom such leadership was congenial."[22] Two decades later (by 1825), the "initiative in public affairs remained with [Speaker Henry] Clay and his associates in the House of Representatives" and not with the president.[23] Thus dominance in national policy making may pass from one branch to the other. Strong presidents sometimes provoked efforts by Congress to reassert its own authority and to restrict that of the executive. Periods of presidential ascendancy are often followed by eras of congressional assertiveness. Still, Congress has usually expected the White House to outline its legislative program in the annual State of the Union message and in other formal and informal presidential messages.

Presidents follow different patterns in setting agendas. They also study the decisions of their predecessors to learn from their mistakes and successes. For example, President Ronald Reagan (1981–1989) and his staff studied the clumsiness of his predecessor, Jimmy Carter (1977–1981), in dealing with his two Congresses (with large Democratic majorities). Reagan found that Carter quickly overloaded Congress's agenda and never made clear what his priorities were. There were three major consequences:

> First . . . there was little clarity in the communication of priorities to the American public. Instead of galvanizing support for two or three major national needs, the Carter administration proceeded on a number of fronts. . . . Second, and perhaps more important, the lack of priorities meant unnecessary waste of the President's own time and energy. . . . Third, the lack of priorities needlessly compounded Carter's congressional problems. . . . Carter's limited political capital was squandered on a variety of agenda requests when it might have been concentrated on the top of the list.[24]

By contrast, agenda control was the hallmark of Reagan's leadership during his first year in office. By limiting his legislative priorities, Reagan focused Congress's and the public's attention on one priority issue at a time. Most were encapsulated as "Reaganomics"—tax and spending cuts. He exploited the usual honeymoon period for new presidents by moving his agenda quickly, during a moment of widespread anticipation of a new era of GOP national political dominance.

Reagan also dealt skillfully with Congress, meeting, negotiating, and socializing with lawmakers, including a private dinner with Democratic Speaker Thomas P. "Tip" O'Neill Jr. of Massachusetts and his wife. Enjoying a Republican majority in the Senate, the Reagan White House focused primarily on lobbying the Democratic House to pass the president's economic program— the "greatest selling job I've ever seen," said Speaker O'Neill. Reagan personally called or telegraphed all of the "Boll Weevils," the forty-seven southern Democrats in the Conservative Democratic Forum.[25] And he persuaded several governors to meet with members from their states who were opposing the program. Top executive officials were dispatched to targeted Democratic districts to drum up public support. On the key House vote, all 191 GOP members and 63 Democrats backed the president's budget plan.

Overall, after only eight months in office Reagan scored some of the biggest victories of his eight years in office. Later, when his control over the agenda slackened, Congress was still confined to a playing field he had largely set out. Lawmakers were forced to respond to, though not always accept, the positions the president had staked out on taxes, spending, defense, and social issues.

President Obama is in his final two years in the White House, but the character of his relationship with the GOP Congress remains unsettled. Obama must decide when to compromise with the GOP lawmakers, when to challenge their legislative decisions, and when to bypass Congress and use his executive authority to try to accomplish his domestic and international objectives. As the president stated, "My job over the next couple of years is to do some practical, concrete things as much as possible with Congress. If it's not possible with

Congress, on my own."[26] The president may focus on the international arena, where presidents traditionally enjoy greater independence—shifting U.S. policy toward Cuba, opening negotiations with Iran, and addressing global climate change are examples. At the same time, the president is reaching out to congressional Democrats to ensure that they will vote to protect his accomplishments, such as the Affordable Care Act, from GOP attempts to repeal or eviscerate them. In short, as House minority whip Steny Hoyer of Maryland put it, President Obama "needs to rely on [Democrats] in both houses to sustain a veto."[27]

Persuading Congress is not easy. Presidents recognize the importance of maintaining informal contacts with Congress as a means for facilitating trust and open lines of communication. As Lyndon Johnson—who had served as Senate minority leader (1953–1955) and majority leader (1955–1960)—once declared, "Merely placing a program before Congress is not enough. Without constant attention from the administration, most legislation moves through the congressional process at the speed of a glacier."[28] Johnson regularly (and sometimes crudely) admonished his aides and departmental officers to work closely with Congress. "[Get off] your ass and see how fast you can respond to a congressional request," he told his staff. "Challenge yourself to see how quickly you can get back to him or her with an answer, any kind of an answer, but goddamn it, an answer."[29]

Critics of President Obama charge that he has not made effective use of informal contacts to persuade members of Congress to support his programs. Obama has shown less interest in socializing with members of Congress than some of his predecessors, and his office of legislative liaison has not enjoyed especially close ties to legislative leaders and rank-and-file members. Defenders of the president note that no amount of socializing or informal persuasive efforts will bridge the deep divisions separating GOP and Democratic leaders. Still, even key Democrats have expressed exasperation that the president has not been as attentive to members of Congress as they would like.[30]

To persuade members to support their programs, presidents often grant or withhold their patronage resources. Broadly conceived, patronage involves not only federal and judicial positions but also federal construction projects, location of government installations, campaign support, access to strategic information, plane rides on *Air Force One*, White House entry for important constituents, and countless other favors, large and small. Some presidents even keep records of the political favors they grant to lawmakers, IOUs that they can cash in later for needed support in Congress. There are limits, however, to the persuasive power of patronage. As one White House congressional relations chief said, "The problem with congressional relations is that with every good intention, at the end of the day you can't accommodate all the requests that you get."[31] More important, many factors influence how members vote on issues important to the White House. Although a president's persuasive skills can sometimes tip the balance, other considerations—lawmakers' constituency interests, policy preferences, and ideological dispositions, as well as public opinion and the number of partisan seats in each chamber—usually are more important in shaping congressional outcomes.

Going Public: The Rhetorical President

"With public sentiment, nothing can fail; without it nothing can succeed," Abraham Lincoln once observed.[32] Lincoln's idea is the essence of the rhetorical presidency: how and when a chief executive strategically employs contemporary campaign techniques and the technology of the mass media to promote "himself and his policies in Washington by appealing to the American public."[33] The rhetorical president's ultimate objective is to produce an outpouring of public support that encourages lawmakers to push his ideas through the congressional obstacle course. However, "if he had the votes he would pass the measure first and go to the public only for the bill-signing ceremonies."[34]

Going public on an issue is not without its risks. The strategy may alienate legislators who feel that the president is going over their heads, cutting them out of the process, and disregarding their constitutional role. The president can also raise expectations that cannot be met, make inept appeals, or stiffen the opposition. Furthermore, many legislators are more popular than the president in their districts or states. Political scientists, such as George Edwards, argue that presidents rarely succeed in moving public opinion.[35] Presidents do better when they champion issues that the public already favors. Contextual factors, such as the mood of the country, the state of the economy, the president's popularity, and the president's partisan strength in Congress, largely account for their legislative success.

President Reagan was an acknowledged master at using the electronic media to orchestrate public support. The Hollywood actor-turned-president was at home in front of cameras and microphones, and he had a keen sense of public ritual and symbolism as means of rallying support. After the March 30, 1981, assassination attempt, Reagan returned a month later and made a dramatic appeal for his economic program. "The White House shrewdly tied Reagan's return to action to the budget and tax debate, scheduling an April 28 comeback speech before a joint meeting of Congress. It was a triumph, and people began to call him the 'Great Communicator.'"[36] Reagan's adroitness with the media is a legacy that looms large for subsequent presidents and Congresses. He showed that "one man using the White House's immense powers of communication can lift the mood of the nation and alter the way it does business."[37]

President Bill Clinton used various media technologies to reach voters and employed campaign-style practices to generate public support for his programs. His empathetic response to the April 1995 bombing of a federal office building in Oklahoma City reminded people of the human face of the federal government, the very entity House Republican "revolutionaries" were warring against. When Republicans added provisions that Clinton opposed to a flood relief bill, the president used the bully pulpit to paint the GOP position as "extreme" and generated a flurry of favorable publicity for his position. One reporter noted:

> News accounts portrayed Republicans as, well, crazy extremists bent on playing games with flood victims. Rank-and-file Republicans writhed in political agony. Michigan Republican Fred Upton's mother watched the news accounts with alarm and warned her son, "You're getting killed." "When your mom tells you that, you know you're in trouble," said Upton.[38]

The White House also used "nightly tracking polls and weekly focus groups to help determine its daily message and the approach President Clinton should take to important national issues."[39]

George W. Bush was initially dubbed "the reticent president" by some analysts on several grounds: his preference for not seizing the public spotlight by addressing every major event or issue that might arise; his determination to stay "on message" by sticking to prepared talking points; his predilection for carefully staged and scripted appearances; and his propensity for committing verbal gaffes. Nevertheless, Bush worked diligently to win public and political support for his policy and political objectives.[40] Bush also became the first president to deliver his weekly radio address in Spanish—political recognition of the electoral potential of the growing Hispanic population.

Bush came into his own as both communicator in chief and commander in chief in the aftermath of the terrorist attacks on the World Trade Center in New York City and the Pentagon. He gave powerful and eloquent speeches in a variety of forums, such as before Congress and at the United Nations (UN), on the need to go after terrorists who threatened the United States and to disarm Saddam Hussein's regime in Iraq. His direct and confident manner resonated with most Americans and boosted domestic and congressional support for his antiterrorism and war plans.

In addition, the Bush White House went to great lengths to use television to promote the president, employing former network television aides with expertise in lighting, camera angles, and backdrops. The most elaborately staged event was Bush's flight to and speech on the aircraft carrier *Abraham Lincoln* during which he prematurely announced the end of major military combat in Iraq. White House aides "choreographed every aspect of the event, even down to the members of the *Lincoln* crew arrayed in coordinated shirt colors over Mr. Bush's right shoulder and the 'Mission Accomplished' banner placed to perfectly capture the president and the celebratory two words in a single shot."[41] As the war continued for years without producing stability and security in Iraq, those same images were used to ironic effect by war critics, Democratic candidates, and late-night comedians.

President Obama, like Reagan, is an exceptionally skilled and eloquent speaker who enjoys addressing citizens in a variety of locales and settings. Winston Churchill once said that of "all the gifts bestowed upon [modern leaders], none is so precious as the gift of oratory."[42] Obama has that gift.[43] In a modern version of Franklin Roosevelt's "fireside" chats, Obama became the first president to appear on *The Tonight Show,* a late-night television program that draws about five million viewers. The president's purpose was "to broaden his audience beyond cable news junkies and political elites, appealing to those who don't already know the intricacies" of his policy proposals.[44]

President Obama recognized that "in a fragmented media universe, presidents must communicate nearly constantly across an array of platforms, both traditional and new."[45] One of those new platforms was a live Internet "town hall" meeting in which Obama fielded questions in the White House from citizens across the nation as well as from a live audience in the East Room. That video chat was the first of its kind for any modern presidency.[46] Another first for the president was to hold a Twitter town hall meeting, as well as participating in town hall events conducted on YouTube and Facebook.[47] The president also created a Web page called "We the People" where citizens were "able to create and sign petitions seeking the government's action on a range of issues."[48] A petition that attracts at least 100,000 signatures within thirty days, such as making the opening day of major league baseball a national holiday, is usually guaranteed a response from the White House.[49]

In the Internet age with its 24/7 media cycle, "presidents must exploit an array of traditional and nontraditional communication methods if they are to influence and shape the public conversation. The pace at which news travels" in the social media age also means that it is difficult at times for presidents to stay on message, because issues or stories can quickly go viral and require a response from the administration.[50] Little surprise that the Internet strategy of President Obama is both sophisticated and unconventional in reaching Americans. A few examples make the point. Prior to his 2015 State of the Union address, "the White House hyped nearly every recent major policy announcement—on LinkedIn and other websites."[51] When critics attack the White House, an array of friendly opinion-makers on various websites and on Twitter launch counterattacks on a day-by-day, minute-by-minute basis, "giving the president cover while savaging the opposition."[52] Celebrities of various types—movie stars, professional athletes, and others—are integral to the White House's messaging operations. "After several YouTube stars met with the president in late February [2014] to discuss the Affordable Care Act, they created 25 videos touting the law—garnering more than 32 million viewings."[53]

Despite his communication innovations and gifts as a speaker, which helped him twice win the presidency, Obama—by many accounts, including his own—has not employed the "bully pulpit" in an effective manner as chief executive. He has delivered many important, thoughtful speeches, but they appear to have done little in moving public opinion toward supporting his ambitious agenda. As a Democratic governor put it, "Ironically, the best communicator I ever saw in a campaign has turned out to be not so good at getting out the message as president."[54] Two years after the president first took office, he agreed with some of this criticism. As Obama said during a 2010 interview:

"What I have not done as well as I would have liked to is to consistently communicate to the general public why we're making some of these decisions."[55] Four years later, the president admitted that he still encountered problems selling his policies to American voters. As he said:

> One of the things that I do need to constantly remind myself and my team of is, it's not enough to build the better mouse trap. People don't automatically come beating to your door. We've got to sell it. We've got to reach out to the other side, and where possible, persuade.
>
> And I think there are times—there's no doubt about it—where I think we have not been successful in going out there and letting people know what it is that we're trying to do and why this is the right direction. So there is a failure of politics there that we've got to improve on.[56]

President Obama also held fewer press conferences than his predecessors, such as George W. Bush and Bill Clinton.[57]

By not employing the huge megaphone of the White House as effectively as he might have, the president enabled congressional Republicans, hostile media outlets, and others who opposed his agenda to dominate the public relations battle at important moments. Health care is a prime example. Republicans constantly and successfully framed the national debate on health care reform as a "government takeover," "socialized medicine," or a bill with "death panels." President Richard Nixon made a keen observation on how administrations can win favorable congressional action on their policies: "In the final analysis, [legislative successes] are not won or lost by programs. They are won or lost on how these programs are presented to the country, and how all the political and public relations considerations are handled."[58]

Advancing administration priorities requires skill at both the inside game of mobilizing winning coalitions on Capitol Hill and the outside game of stirring popular support for the president's agenda. Indeed, some suggest that the traditional "inside game" of presidents wooing legislators to enact laws might be in decline. Forging congressional consensus in today's hyperpartisan era is much harder to achieve for a number of reasons, including the fragmentation of media outlets, the power of social media, public mistrust of government, fiscal constraints, and strong political divisions in the country. The point is that the growing importance of the "outside game" is changing the inside game and transforming presidential power:

> [T]he old pattern of exercising presidential power by proposing programs, cajoling Congress into passing them and then setting up a government apparatus to implement them may be giving way to a new pattern in which a president uses the White House as a platform to focus national attention on an issue and to mobilize forces outside

Washington to devote time and resources to address it. . . . Consider it the 21st century version of what Teddy Roosevelt called the bully pulpit.[59]

For example, the president can use his "convening power" to persuade Congress, states, nongovernmental entities, and others to resolve various issues. The convening power concerns "the ability to use the clout and magnetism of the Oval Office to bring together people and organizations to take on problems, contributing time, focus and money."[60]

The Administrative President

Presidents understand that getting Congress to pass legislation is an arduous process, and that even when laws are enacted bureaucratic indifference may hamper implementation of presidential initiatives. Thus a president's core administrative strategy is to win policy goals by statute whenever feasible but, when such an effort falls short, to accomplish those aims through organizational or managerial techniques. Administrative presidents employ a variety of methods, such as naming loyal political appointees to supervise and monitor agency activities, reorganizing executive departments to advance presidential goals, using the budget process to reduce unwanted programs or increase favorite activities, and employing executive orders and rule-making authority to achieve outcomes blocked by Congress.[61] Presidents have an array of methods to bypass Congress and act unilaterally to advance their objectives. Important to note is that acting unilaterally often means that the president has failed to win congressional support for his policies.

Nonetheless, using executive orders and reorganization plans, presidents can act on their own to create entirely new administrative entities. In doing so, presidents are, at times, able to institutionalize policies that Congress would never have created. Based on a study of all the administrative agencies established between the end of World War II and 1995, William G. Howell and David E. Lewis report that "presidents have unilaterally created over half of all administrative agencies in the United States."[62] Among them are such important agencies as the Peace Corps. Facing significant opposition in Congress to the Peace Corps idea, President Kennedy opted to create the agency by executive order. By the time Congress got around to reviewing the president's actions the Peace Corps already had 362 employees and 600 volunteers at work in eight countries.[63] By establishing this "fact on the ground," the president pressured Congress into accepting the new organization. Another example stems from the September 11, 2001, terrorist attacks. In the immediate aftermath of the attacks, President George W. Bush unilaterally created an Office for Homeland Security in the White House; constructed a prison for suspected terrorist noncitizens at Guantánamo Bay, Cuba; and established a new court system for handling cases involving "unlawful enemy combatants."[64] Despite candidate Obama's 2008 campaign promise to close the Guantánamo Bay military prison, the facility to date remains open. Faced with continuing congressional opposition to closing the facility, President Obama is reportedly using prisoner transfers from Guantánamo "to shrink the size of the Gitmo population [in early 2015] from the current 127 to as low as 60, so he can more easily make the case that keeping the facility is not worth the cost."[65]

Presidents have long employed executive orders—a form of administrative lawmaking using (or expanding) authority that the legislative branch has delegated—to achieve objectives not explicitly authorized by Congress.[66] President Harry S. Truman, for example, issued an executive order racially integrating the armed services. Stymied by the GOP-controlled Congress on issues such as antismoking legislation, a patients' bill of rights, and subsidies for school construction, President Clinton made extensive use of executive orders. "His formula include[d] pressing the limits of his regulatory authority, signing executive orders and using other unilateral means to obtain his policy priorities when Congress fail[ed] to embrace them."[67] Congressional Republicans railed against Clinton's "go-it-alone" governing.

George W. Bush similarly exploited administrative tools to advance his policy goals. For example, Bush quickly exercised executive authority to roll back, suspend, or challenge many Clinton-era regulations. He also was not reluctant to implement by executive fiat administration programs stalled in Congress. When the Senate blocked action on Bush's faith-based initiative (assisting religious groups in winning government grants for charitable and social service work), the president ordered his administration to implement the program through executive orders and changes in agency regulations.[68] Moreover, like presidents before him, Bush encouraged his departments and agencies to move rapidly to enact a wide array of so-called "midnight regulations." By rushing them through in the administration's waning months, executive officials could burnish the president's legacy and—as a senior think tank analyst observed—"extend its influence into the future."[69]

Upon entering office in 2009, the Obama administration moved quickly to block or reverse many of Bush's rules and regulations. Even before Obama was sworn into office, his transition team "compiled a list of about 200 Bush administration actions and executive orders that could be swiftly undone to reverse White House policies on climate change, stem cell research, reproductive rights and other issues."[70] True to form, in his first seven days in office President Obama blocked action on Bush's last-minute rules. And like many other presidents, Obama has not shied away from using executive power to achieve his goals. "If Congress refuses to act [on my priorities]," declared the president, "I've said that I'll continue to do everything in my power to act without them."[71] He informed lawmakers in his 2014 State of the Union address that he planned to bypass Congress and use the "pen and phone" to advance his policy agenda. And the president has done just that, such as raising the minimum wage for federal contractors; banning federal contractors from discriminating against gay workers; and expanding a federal program to assist students in repaying their federal loans.[72] Once legislation addressing climate change stalled in Congress, President Obama used executive power to promulgate greenhouse gas emission regulations issued by the Environmental Protection Agency. When Congress failed to reauthorize the No Child Left Behind law, the president waived many of its requirements for more than half the states— so long as they followed guidelines issued by the administration, such as promoting charter schools.[73]

One executive action of President Obama's, which he announced in a nationwide address on November 20, 2014, triggered a loud negative outcry from GOP lawmakers on Capitol Hill, their supporters in the country, and many others who believed Obama's actions were unconstitutional. By executive action President Obama granted about five million undocumented immigrants protection from deportation. GOP lawmakers were infuriated and called Obama's action "mass amnesty by executive fiat." Many called the president a monarch, emperor, or king. There was talk of impeachment. Others called it a lawless act because the president was rewriting law, the responsibility of Congress.[74] President Obama justified his decision by noting that other chief executives (Kennedy, Reagan, and both Bushes) had used executive authority "to defer immigration enforcement against a class of non-citizens"; that immigration laws passed by Congress granted the president broad prosecutorial discretion in enforcing those statutes; and that after months of analysis the White House concluded that the president had the authority to "alter the way immigration laws are enforced."[75] The president also delivered a stark message to lawmakers who challenged his unilateral action on immigration: "Pass a bill."[76]

The "Two Presidencies"

"The United States has one president, but it has two presidencies; one presidency is for domestic affairs, and the other is concerned with defense and foreign policy."[77] According to this formulation by political scientist Aaron Wildavsky, presidential proposals are likely to achieve more success in the international arena than in the domestic arena, in part because Congress asserts itself more in domestic policy making than in foreign policy. Since its emergence, Wildavsky's thesis has sparked considerable controversy on, for example, how to measure success rates in the two arenas and whether the concept is relevant today in a world in which the international and domestic constantly overlap.[78] Scores of issues are transnational in character, such as climate change, global economic crises, or the ongoing struggle against terrorism. Even voter rejection of President Obama's party in the November 2014 midterm elections was noticed by foreign friends and adversaries alike. A Beijing newspaper wrote that "U.S. public opinion has downgraded Obama," raising concerns that China, Russia, and others might be emboldened to take actions that threaten American interests at home and abroad.[79]

Whatever the strengths or weaknesses of the two-presidencies idea as Wildavsky laid it out, the concept seems especially relevant to the presidency of George W. Bush before and after the September 11, 2001, terrorist attacks. The pre-9/11 period constituted George W. Bush's first presidency, with its focus on domestic issues; then the post-9/11 era constituted his second presidency, with its strong focus on defense and national security issues.

The Pre-9/11 Phase. Despite Vice President Al Gore's plurality in the 2000 popular vote tally, President Bush quickly advanced an ambitious agenda as though he had won a huge victory. This approach surprised the many pundits who had predicted that Bush would move slowly to implement his "compassionate conservative" campaign promises. "This is the farthest thing from a caretaker administration you could get," declared a Brookings Institution analyst.[80]

Bush scored major policy successes early in his first term, largely by staking out an assertive policy-making approach that combined bipartisan and partisan governing strategies. Three days after being sworn into office, for example, Bush proposed the No Child Left Behind Act. A bipartisan and bicameral group of lawmakers worked cooperatively with the administration to win passage of the legislation. Bush took a more partisan approach in pushing Congress to enact the largest across-the-board tax cut ($1.35 trillion) since Ronald Reagan's presidency. Although there were partisan complaints that the tax cut was too large, lawmakers on both sides of the aisle were reluctant to vote against tax reductions for their constituents.

A different legislative dynamic emerged after May 2001, when Vermont GOP senator Jim Jeffords switched parties and Senate Democrats suddenly found themselves the majority party. Democratic control of the Senate produced significant problems for the Bush administration. Now the Democrats could initiate and force votes on their priorities, hold hearings to spotlight their agenda and critique Bush's, modify or block administration bills coming from the GOP House, reject the president's nominations, and require the White House to develop "a defensive strategy for responding to Democratic ideas."[81] Bush's position was further weakened by polls showing that the public preferred the Democrats' positions over GOP ones. By June 2001, Bush's public standing had fallen "to a tepid 50 percent approval rating, the lowest presidential approval rating in more than five years."[82] As a result, congressional Democrats became increasingly optimistic that they could reclaim control of Congress in the midterm elections of November 2002. It was not to be, however.

The Post-9/11 Phase. The George W. Bush presidency was transformed by the terrorist attacks. After an uncertain response during the first days, Bush became a resolute, decisive, and strong commander in chief. Images of the president consoling firefighters and others at the site of the World Trade Center, his calm and confident demeanor, and his eloquent statements to the public—including the September 20, 2001, national address before a joint meeting of Congress—rallied the nation to fight a global war against terrorists and the states that provided them safe haven. He called this global struggle "the first war of the twenty-first century," an open-ended fight that continues to this day.

Meanwhile, Bush's public approval ratings soared to a record-level 91 percent, breaking his father's record of 89 percent during the 1991 Persian Gulf

War.[83] The levels of bipartisanship on Capitol Hill were also remarkable in the first weeks after the terrorist attacks. Congress moved quickly to enact significant measures, including passage of legislation authorizing the president to employ "all necessary and appropriate force" against those groups or nations involved in the terrorist attacks. Subsequently, as directed by the president, the military ousted the Taliban regime in Afghanistan, which had provided safe haven for Osama bin Laden, the al Qaeda leader behind the September 11 attacks. (On May 2, 2011, bin Laden was killed at his compound in Pakistan in a daring U.S. Navy commando operation authorized by President Obama.)

President Bush's focus then turned to Iraq, a nation he declared to be part of the "axis of evil" that threatened the world. In October 2002, the administration persuaded Congress to enact a joint resolution granting the president unilateral authority to launch a preemptive military strike against Iraq. On March 19, 2003, President Bush went on national television and informed the nation of the start of the war in Iraq. Three weeks later, on April 9, U.S. forces entered Baghdad, ending the regime of longtime dictator Saddam Hussein.

President Bush justified the invasion of Iraq on several grounds: al Qaeda operated in Iraq, and Saddam Hussein was somehow involved in the 9/11 attacks; Saddam had weapons of mass destruction and posed a threat to American and world safety; and Saddam was obtaining uranium from Niger for his nuclear weapons program. However, the rationales for invading Iraq proved to be false. A few weeks before he left office, in a valedictory interview with ABC News, Bush came close to admitting that the Iraq war had been a mistake. "The biggest regret of all the presidency has to have been the intelligence failure in Iraq," he said.[84]

THE VETO POWER

Article I, section 7, of the Constitution requires the president to approve or disapprove bills passed by Congress. When the president disapproves (vetoes) a measure, it dies unless it "shall be repassed by two thirds of the Senate and House of Representatives." Because vetoes are so difficult to override, the veto power transforms the president into, in Woodrow Wilson's words, a "third branch of the legislature."[85] Presidents can usually attract enough of their supporters in Congress to sustain a veto. From 1789 through the end of Barack Obama's first six years in office, thirty-six of forty-four presidents exercised their veto authority on 2,566 occasions. Congress overrode these vetoes on 110 occasions (4.3 percent).[86] President Obama vetoed just two bills during his first six years in office (see the section "Pocket Vetoes" for more discussion of Obama's two vetoes during this period). Not since 1881 has a president issued fewer vetoes than Obama.[87]

When contemplating a veto, presidents seek advice from numerous administration sources, such as agency officials, the Office of Management and Budget, and White House aides, as well as allied lawmakers and interest groups. Presidents commonly give various reasons for vetoing a bill: the bill is unconstitutional, it encroaches on the president's independence, it is unwise public policy, it cannot be administered, or it costs too much. Political calculations may underlie any or all of these reasons. The veto is more than a negative power, however. Presidents use the threat of a veto to advance their policy objectives by, for example, inducing legislators to accommodate executive preferences and objections. "We try to use the veto threat wisely, to change votes or to change the language of the underlying document," explained a top White House legislative aide. "And we succeed."[88]

Presidents also practice the politics of differentiation through the veto: a veto fight with Congress may suit presidents who want to underscore how their views differ from the other party's. For its part, Congress can discourage vetoes by adding items to must-pass legislation or to measures the president strongly favors. Congress may also deliberately send the president of the opposite party a measure that lawmakers want him to veto, so they can use the issue on the campaign trail—a "winning by losing" strategy.[89] Bills may also be signed in a public ceremony closer to the November elections as a way to energize the electoral base of the president's party—another example of the two Congresses.

Veto Options

Once the president receives a bill from Congress, he has ten days (excluding Sundays) in which to exercise one of four options:

1. He can sign the bill. Most public and private bills presented to the president are signed into law. The president also may issue a signing statement that expresses his interpretation of the provisions of the new law.

2. He can return the bill with his veto message to the originating house of Congress.

3. He can take no action, and the bill will become law without his signature. This option, which is seldom employed, is reserved for bills the president dislikes but not enough to veto.

4. He can pocket veto the bill. Under the Constitution, if a congressional adjournment prevents the return of a bill, the bill cannot become law without the president's signature.

Veto Strategies

George H. W. Bush (1989–1993) was among the most successful chief executives in employing the veto against an opposition Congress. He used it to block unwanted legislation and as a potent bargaining weapon to wring concessions from the Democratic-controlled Congress. Not until his term was nearly over, and after thirty-five consecutive veto victories, did Congress manage to override a Bush veto—on a 1992 measure to reregulate the cable television industry. Part of the explanation for Bush's veto successes was that he announced his intentions early and stuck by them unless the compromises he wanted were agreed to. Furthermore, he convinced congressional Republicans that their strength depended on sustaining his vetoes.

By contrast, President Clinton did not veto a single measure during his first two years in office—something that had not happened since the days of Millard Fillmore in the 1850s. Part of the explanation is that Clinton was dealing with a Democratic Congress. Not until 1995 did Clinton use his veto pen, rejecting an appropriations bill sent to him by the Republican Congress. Subsequently, the president either exercised or threatened to exercise the veto against numerous GOP-sponsored bills. (Presidents often use Statements of Administration Policy to express their concerns about measures moving through Congress, even threatening to veto them.)

President George W. Bush claimed that he would not hesitate to use his veto power to enforce his budgetary goals if Congress passed legislation he considered excessive or objectionable. But he did not veto a single bill, spending or otherwise, during his entire first term, although he did issue 145 veto threats during that time. One has to reach back all the way to James Garfield (1881) to find a veto-less president, and Garfield did not even serve a full year before being assassinated. Partial-term presidents William Henry Harrison, Zachary Taylor, and Millard Fillmore never issued a veto; nor did one-termers John Adams and John Quincy Adams. Only Jefferson survived two terms without one.[90]

Several factors account for Bush's no-veto first term: unified Republican control of the House and Senate during much of the period and the resulting consensus on many issues; the refusal of top party leaders, such as Speaker Dennis J. Hastert, R-Ill., to send to the White House bills that Bush might veto; the desire of Republicans to demonstrate their capacity to govern with narrow majorities; the ability of the White House and GOP congressional leaders to work out their disagreements; and the president's pragmatism in redefining his positions "to accommodate the direction in which lawmakers were leaning."[91]

Like other presidents, Barack Obama has threatened to veto measures because of objections to provisions in the legislation. During President Obama's 2011 State of the Union address, he declared, "If a bill comes to my desk with earmarks in it, I will veto it" (as discussed in Chapter 14, earmarks are special-interest provisions in measures that benefit members' districts or states). The president's threat had a direct effect on the lawmakers. As Senate Democratic whip Richard Durbin of Illinois exclaimed, "We're out of the earmark business."[92] President Obama seldom followed through on veto threats in his first six years in large measure because the Democratic Senate could block anti-administration bills coming out of the GOP House.[93]

With Republicans in control of both chambers of the 114th Congress, President Obama is likely to make greater use of the veto during his final two years in office. "Now, I suspect," remarked Obama, "there are going to be some times where I've got to pull that [veto] pen out."[94] Recall that the president, acting swiftly, issued two veto threats (on the Keystone pipeline and a bill modifying the Affordable Care Act) just before the new GOP Congress convened.

In response, Speaker John Boehner said: "At a minimum, he could have waited a few hours."[95] Worth noting is that "two vetoes" are available to the president: his own veto prerogative and that of his party in the Senate given its sixty-vote requirement to end filibusters. If forty-one Senate Democrats stay united, they can block legislation unwanted by the president or win policy concessions acceptable to the White House on veto-threatened legislation.

Veto threats are used for many reasons, such as protecting administration priorities, defining party differences and positions, or encouraging negotiations. Research by political scientist Samuel Kernell suggests that veto threats encourage legislative–executive bargaining and "are a big part of divided government." Interestingly, his research "shows that measures that prompt them are 'highly likely' to become law."[96]

Post-Veto Action

Just as the president may feel strong pressure to veto or to sign a bill, Congress may feel intense political heat after it receives a veto message. A week after President Nixon's televised veto of a 1970 bill funding welfare programs, House members received more than fifty-five thousand telegrams, most of them urging support for the veto. And Congress did uphold the veto, in part because of Nixon's televised appeal. However, despite a massive telephone campaign to congressional offices (as many as eighty thousand calls an hour) urging members to sustain President Reagan's veto of a 1988 civil rights bill, the House and Senate easily overrode the veto.[97]

Actually, Congress need not act at all on a vetoed bill. If party leaders lack the votes to override, the chamber that receives a vetoed measure may refer it to committee or table it. Even if one house musters the votes to override, the other body may do nothing. A vetoed bill cannot be amended—it is all or nothing at this stage—and the Constitution requires that votes on overriding a veto be recorded.

Signing Statements

At times, presidents issue proclamations called "signing statements" to accompany bills they have signed into law. Even though they are not mentioned in the Constitution, signing statements have been used since James Monroe's presidency (1817–1825). Ronald Reagan was the first president to use signing statements as a way to challenge congressional enactments on constitutional grounds. George W. Bush, however, employed them more often than any other president to reassert and strengthen the so-called unitary theory of executive power.[98] As interpreted by Bush, this theory allowed the president to override laws that he claimed would impinge upon his constitutional prerogatives as commander in chief. When Congress banned torture of war prisoners, for example, the president held that the law trespassed on his powers as commander in chief. (See Box 10-1 for three examples of Bush's signing statements.)

Even though the Constitution requires the president to "take care that the laws be faithfully executed," Bush's signing statements asserted that he had "the power to set aside the laws when they conflict with his legal interpretation."[99] Signing statements have raised concerns in Congress because they seem to provide the president with an unofficial line-item veto, allowing him to decide which parts of bills to implement or ignore. Some observers believe that signing statements have little effect on the administration of laws. Studies have shown that "federal agencies seem to have generally complied with thousands of legislative provisions that [Bush] had questioned."[100] Still, one legal scholar noted that a president who has no intention of enforcing the law as Congress intended should "face the political music by issuing a veto and subjecting that veto to the possibility of an override in Congress."[101]

Running for president in 2008, Obama criticized President Bush's use of signing statements. As president, Obama vowed he would use such statements with restraint and "only when it is appropriate to do so as a means of discharging my constitutional responsibilities."[102] On March 11, 2009, President Obama issued his first signing statement, "reserving a right to bypass dozens of provisions in a $410 billion government spending bill even as he signed it into law."[103] The most contentious of these provisions enhanced protections for government whistleblowers. Sen. Charles E. Grassley, R-Iowa, attacked the signing statement for going back on Obama's campaign promises to protect whistleblowers and to avoid Bush's sentiment that some parts of laws are optional.[104] In a White House memorandum to all departments and agencies, President Obama made clear that signing statements are appropriate in limited circumstances, and that "they promote a healthy dialogue between the executive branch and Congress."[105]

Healthy dialogue or not, Obama's signing statements aroused the ire of lawmakers and influential outside organizations. The American Bar Association, for example, sent a letter to President Obama "urging him instead to veto bills if he thinks sections [of a measure] are unconstitutional."[106] Nonetheless, President Obama continues to use signing statements. Moreover, the objections that Obama raises in his signing statements are often similar to President Bush's: that the legislation contained provisions that infringed on the constitutional prerogatives of the president.[107]

Pocket Vetoes

The pocket veto has been a source of some controversy and confusion over the years. Article I, section 7, of the Constitution states:

> If any bill shall not be returned by the President within ten days (Sundays excepted) after it shall have been presented to him, the same shall be a law, in like manner as if he had signed it, unless Congress by the adjournment prevents its return, in which case it shall not be a law.

BOX 10-1 **Examples of Signing Statements**

	Congressional directive	Signing statement
Intelligence Reform and Terrorism Prevention Act of 2004 (P.L. 108-458) Signed December 17, 2004	Created a position for a national intelligence director, in response to past intelligence failures, and required the president to consult with Congress on the person's responsibilities.	"To the extent that provisions of the Act . . . purport to require consultation with the Congress as a condition to execution of the law, the executive branch shall construe such provisions as calling for, but not mandating, such consultation."
Fiscal 2006 Defense Appropriations (P.L. 109-148) Signed December 30, 2005	Outlawed "cruel, inhumane or degrading treatment" of suspected terrorists in U.S. custody.	"The executive branch shall construe Title X in Division A of the Act, relating to detainees, in a manner consistent with the constitutional authority of the President to supervise the unitary executive branch and as Commander in Chief."
Department of Defense Appropriations Act, 2007 (P.L. 109-289) Signed September 29, 2006	Blocked money from being spent to process foreign intelligence if it was gathered unlawfully. Stipulated that information gathered on U.S. citizens must comply with constitutional limits on searches and seizures.	"The executive branch shall construe [the provision] in a manner consistent with the President's constitutional authority as Commander in Chief, including for the conduct of intelligence operations, and to supervise the unitary executive branch."

Source: Adapted from Chris Wilson, "Memo to Congress: Bush Asserts Final Say," *CQ Weekly*, October 30, 2006, 2863.

The framers wanted to ensure that presidents would not be forced into signing last-minute legislation and that Congress would have time to consider, and perhaps override, the president's objections. The issue, however, is exactly when a congressional adjournment prevents the return of the president's veto. Several court decisions, such as *Kennedy v. Sampson* (1974), established the principle that pocket vetoes are not to be used during congressional sessions but only after Congress's final adjournment at the end of its second session.

The Ford and Carter administrations adhered to this understanding, but not other administrations. For example, President Reagan twice used intersession (between the first and second sessions) pocket vetoes, and President Clinton employed intrasession (in the middle of a session) pocket vetoes. In December 2007, President Bush invoked the pocket veto and returned it to the

House (which originated the measure) "to leave no doubt the bill is being vetoed." The House majority voiced strong objection, with Speaker Pelosi declaring, "Your successful return of H.R. 1585 establishes that you were not prevented from returning it."[108]

President Obama's two vetoes were what some refer to as "hybrid vetoes" or "protective return" pocket vetoes (see Box 10-2). Obama returned the two unsigned bills to the originating chamber as if he were exercising a regular (or traditional) veto. In both cases, Congress objected to his pocket veto approach, treated it as a regular veto, and sustained the veto.

Thus it appears that neither an intra- nor an intersession pocket veto prevents its return to Congress. Until the Supreme Court makes a definitive ruling involving the use of the pocket veto both during and between legislative sessions, it is likely that legislative–executive conflicts over the pocket veto will occur periodically. In summary, the scope of the pocket veto power, as public law scholar Louis Fisher has written, "has been left largely to practice and to political understandings developed by the executive and legislative branches."[109]

The Line-Item Veto

Congress's habit of combining numerous items into a single measure obliges the president to accept or reject the entire package. Presidents and supporters of executive power have long advocated allowing the president to veto items selectively. They argue that it would give the president an effective way to eliminate wasteful spending and reduce the federal deficit. Opponents counter that the item veto is about interbranch power and not fiscal restraint. Granting the item veto to the president, they argue, would undermine Congress's power of the purse and give chief executives added bargaining leverage over lawmakers. "The president could say, 'I'm going to zap your dam, but I've got another piece of legislation coming around, and I won't be so inclined to do that [if you support me],'" said Rep. Jack Kingston, R-Ga.[110] Critics also say that presidents already have the only tool they need to control spending: the veto.

After much debate, Congress eventually passed a line-item veto, as part of the "Contract with America." After a president signed a bill into law, he could exercise the line-item veto prerogative to cancel dollar amounts specified in any appropriations law, or even in the accompanying House or Senate committee reports; strike new entitlement programs or expansions of existing programs; and delete tax breaks limited to one hundred or fewer beneficiaries. The measure required the president, after using the line-item veto, to send a special message to Congress identifying what he had rescinded. To overturn his decisions, Congress would have to pass another bill that the president could then veto, requiring Congress to override it by a two-thirds vote of each chamber. On June 25, 1998, in the case of *Clinton v. New York*, the Supreme Court by a 6–3 vote held the Line-Item Veto Act to be unconstitutional because it gave the president "unilateral authority to change the text of duly enacted statutes," as Justice John Paul Stevens wrote for the majority.[111] The Clinton administration soon announced that it would release funds for the projects that had been subjected to line-item vetoes.

Since the Court's decision, and in view of today's high deficits, there has been renewed interest among some lawmakers in enacting a constitutionally valid line-item veto. President Obama also supports enactment of enhanced rescission legislation that would guarantee within a specified number of days an up or down vote on a package of spending cuts. Many lawmakers oppose rescission bills, because they believe it would cede too much power to the president.

BOX 10-2 Deep Presidential Pockets

When he quietly vetoed his first piece of legislation last week—a stopgap military appropriation that turned out not to have been needed—Barack Obama renewed a rather obscure constitutional debate about the way recent administrations have employed the "pocket veto," in which a president fails to either sign or veto a bill after Congress has already adjourned.

In his Dec. 30 "memorandum of disapproval," the term usually applied when announcing a pocket veto, Obama indicated that he was withholding his signature from the short-term continuing resolution that Congress sent him to ensure military spending until the fiscal 2010 Defense spending bill could be signed into law—which Obama had done Dec. 19. But the president also returned the short-term bill to the House.

There is no question that, as Obama asserts in his memorandum, his signing the Defense bill made the short-term continuing resolution unnecessary. But constitutional law experts question whether Obama and other recent presidents who have done the same thing actually have the authority to issue hybrid veto messages that combine both a traditional and pocket veto.

"This never made any sense," says Louis Fisher, a specialist on constitutional law at the Library of Congress. "It seems you have either a returned veto or a pocket veto, but not both."

President Gerald R. Ford was the first to use one of these "protective return" vetoes. . . .

Nevertheless, presidents of both parties subsequently issued several hybrid vetoes.

Although it may seem like just "constitutional trivia," [political science professor Robert] Spitzer says he views it as a way that presidents of both parties have quietly tried to expand executive power.

Presidents view the pocket veto, originally envisioned as protection against Congress passing laws and then skipping town before a president had a chance to veto them, as particularly attractive because there's no way legislators can override them.

"This whole protective return pocket veto is a back-door way to expand the pocket veto so that the president can use it any time Congress is literally not in session," Spitzer says.

Source: Reprinted from Seth Stern, "Deep Presidential Pockets," *CQ Weekly,* January 4, 2010, 10.

SOURCES OF LEGISLATIVE–EXECUTIVE COOPERATION

Unlike the legislative assemblies of many nations where executive authority is lodged in the leader of parliament—called the prime minister or premier—Congress truly is separate from the executive branch. And yet the executive and legislative branches are mutually dependent in policy making. The 124 volumes (as of 2011) of the *United States Statutes at Large* underscore the cooperative impulses of the two branches. Each volume contains the joint product of Congresses and presidents over the years, from the 108 public laws enacted by the First Congress (1789–1791) to the 296 enacted by the 113th Congress (2013–2014). These accomplishments are the result of party loyalties and public expectations, bargaining and compromise, and informal links between the president and lawmakers.

Party Loyalties and Public Expectations

Presidents and congressional leaders have met informally to discuss issues ever since the First Congress, when George Washington frequently sought the advice of Virginia representative James Madison. But meetings between the chief executive and House and Senate leaders were not common until Theodore Roosevelt's administration (1901–1909). Today, congressional party leaders are two-way conduits who communicate legislative views to the president and inform other members of executive preferences and intentions. A president and the members of his party are linked psychologically and ideologically. This means that "bargaining 'within the family' has a rather different quality than bargaining with members of the rival clan."[112] Congressional Democrats want President Obama to succeed in moving his agenda, even though they do not always share his priorities. As Rep. Chris Van Hollen, D-Md., once said, "Our political fortunes are tied to Barack Obama's."[113] This statement certainly was evident when congressional Democrats suffered disastrous midterm election results in 2010 (Republicans captured the House) and 2014 (the Senate went Republican as well). In both cases, President Obama's low popular standing contributed to the Democratic congressional losses. With President Obama's approval rating on the increase, from 40 percent to 48 percent in early 2015, many Democrats are now anxious to have Obama use his bully pulpit in all its media manifestations to mobilize Democrats and independents across the country to support the party and its agenda in 2016.

To be sure, there will be intense competition between the two parties to shape the political narrative leading to November 2016. As president, Obama's capacity to attract media coverage, love of campaigning, and desire to keep a Democrat in the White House will drive him to try to shape, focus, and amplify the party's agenda to the general electorate.

Bargaining and Compromise

The interdependence of the two branches provides each with the incentive to bargain. Legislators and presidents have in common at least three interests: shaping public policy, winning elections, and attaining influence within the legislature. Executive officials can help or hinder members of Congress to achieve their goals. Agency personnel, can heed legislators' advice in formulating policies, help them gain favorable publicity back home, and give them advance notice of executive actions. By the same token, executive officials rely on legislators for help in pushing administrative proposals through the legislative process.

Bargains and compromises are essential to public policy making in a diverse nation of over 320 million people. Most recently, compromise-making has proven to be exceptionally difficult among the parties, chambers, and branches. Many factors account for this development, including the ideological divide between the two political parties and intense party competition for control of national institutions.[114] Bipartisan compromises may be good or bad, but they cannot be achieved if the two parties emulate parliamentary systems: one party governs (or tries to), and the other is united in opposition.

Deal-making between the branches is hard because, as a GOP House member said, "Compromise has a very small constituency—very small."[115] This view, combined with the country's political and ideological polarization, has created what might be called a new normal on Capitol Hill: policy making by brinksmanship. Each side waits until the final hours before accepting a compromise in the belief that it heightens its bargaining leverage. A scholar summed up the pitfalls of the high-risk, "no compromise" brinksmanship tactic: it "aims at claiming a large portion of the pie: 'Give me everything or I walk.' That's a very aggressive approach, and doesn't foster creative deal-making at all." In brief, contemporary leaders face the challenge of how they can come together to address the nation's problems when many in both parties disdain the idea of compromise.

Informal Links

Some presidents deal with Congress more adeptly than others. Lyndon Johnson assiduously courted members. He summoned legislators to the White House for private meetings, danced with their wives at parties, telephoned greetings on their birthdays, and hosted them at his Texas ranch. He also knew how to twist arms to win support for his programs. Johnson's understanding of what moved members and energized Congress was awe-inspiring. "There is only one way for a President to deal with the Congress," he said, "and that is continuously, incessantly, and without interruption."[116]

President Obama meets periodically with the bicameral leadership—the Speaker, House minority leader, Senate majority leader, and Senate minority leader—to discuss issues of common concern. His top legislative aides are often present at every key stage of a major bill's development, suggesting ways to resolve contentious issues. As a former senator, the president also has informal and friendly relationships with several lawmakers, including Sen. Tom Coburn, R-Okla., until his retirement in 2014. According to Senator Coburn, however, the president is not especially adept at schmoozing or developing social relationships with lawmakers:

My friend the president isn't a great people person in terms of reaching out ... how many times do you just invite four or five Republicans over, just sit down just to get to know them? Or how many times do you call people? What you have to do is invest in relationships. And I think that's probably one of his biggest failings, is not investing enough in the relationships in the Congress.[117]

President Obama is mindful of the need for social and personal engagement and, according to aides, is reaching out to more and more lawmakers. For example, the president has set aside "45 minutes in his schedule to call a handful of Republican and Democratic lawmakers ... to discuss issues."[118]

To a large extent, Obama has outsourced the congressional liaison role to Vice President Joe Biden—given his more than three decades of Senate service. Biden's close ties to many House and Senate members, especially Senate GOP leader McConnell, have enabled him to craft bipartisan compromises on major measures that have passed both chambers. When Senator McConnell found he could not reach a compromise on a major issue with Senate Democrats, he opened negotiations with Vice President Biden to produce a successful result in what many commentators called a dysfunctional Congress. "The vice president and I have worked together on solutions before," remarked Senator McConnell, because of the trust they developed after decades of serving together in the Senate.[119]

Informal and personal relationships between the president and the top House and Senate party leaders, as well as rank-and-file members, can promote, but not guarantee, productive problem-solving. "These kinds of relationships just don't pop up out of the air or out of necessity," observed a former aide to Speaker Boehner. "They require trust, and they take time. You just don't grow that necessary trust and relationship overnight."[120]

SOURCES OF LEGISLATIVE–EXECUTIVE CONFLICT

Legislative–executive conflicts were evident in 1789, they are present today, and they can be expected in the future for at least three reasons. First, the Constitution specifies neither the precise policy-making roles of Congress and the president nor the manner in which they are to deal with one another. Second, presidents and Congresses serve different constituencies. Third, important variations exist in the timetables under which the two branches operate.

Constitutional Ambiguities

Article I invests Congress with "all legislative powers," but it also authorizes the president to recommend and to veto legislation. In several specific areas, the Constitution splits authority between the president and Congress. The Senate, for example, is the president's partner in treaty making and nominations under the "advice and consent" clauses. And before treaties can take effect, they require the concurrence of two-thirds of the Senate. The Constitution is silent, however, on how or when the Senate is to render its advice to the president.[121]

In 1919 and 1920, a historic confrontation occurred when the Senate vehemently opposed the Treaty of Versailles negotiated by President Woodrow Wilson. The treaty contained an agreement binding the United States to the proposed League of Nations. Many senators had warned the president against including the League provision in the treaty, and during floor deliberations the Senate added several reservations that the president strongly opposed. Spurning compromise, Wilson launched a nationwide speaking tour to mobilize popular support for the treaty. Not to be outdone, senators opposed to the pact organized a "truth squad" that trailed the president and rebutted his arguments. During his tour, Wilson suffered a stroke from which he never fully recovered. And in the end, the treaty was rejected. This example illustrates that under the Constitution's separation of powers, presidents' abilities to achieve even their most urgent foreign policy goals are limited by Congress's institutional prerogatives.

Different Constituencies

Presidents and their vice presidents are the only public officials elected nationally. To win, they must create vastly broader electoral coalitions than are necessary for legislators, who represent either states or districts. Only presidents, then, can claim to speak for the nation at large. It is important to note, however, that

> there is no structural or institutional or theoretical reason why the representation of a "single" broader constituency by the President is necessarily better or worse than the representation of many "separate" constituencies by several hundred legislators. Some distortion is inevitable in either arrangement, and the question of the good or evil of either form of distortion simply leads one back to varying value judgments.[122]

Presidents and legislators tend to view policies and problems from different perspectives. Members of Congress often subscribe to the view that "what's good for Portland is good for the nation." Presidents are apt to say that "what's good for the nation is good for Portland."

In other words, public officials may view common issues differently when they represent diverging interests. For example, a president might wish to reduce international trade barriers. A representative from a district where a manufacturer is threatened by imported products is likely to oppose the president's policy, whereas retailers of imported products are likely to support the president. The challenge to national policy making is to forge consensus within an electorate that simultaneously holds membership in two or more competing constituencies.

Disparities in constituencies are underscored by differences in the ways voters judge presidents and members of Congress. Studies of presidential popularity ratings suggest that presidents are judged on the basis of general factors—economic boom or bust, the presence or absence of wars or other crises, the impact of policies on given groups.[123] The news media, too, can affect the assessment of presidents. Legislators, by contrast, tend to be assessed on the basis of their personalities, their communication with constituents, and their service in material ways to the state or district. Not only do presidents and legislators serve different constituencies, but they also labor under divergent incentives.

Party ties can at times bridge the differences in constituency interests that separate presidents from Congress. Both the president and his party in Congress tend to be judged together by voters, creating a common interest in cooperation. But these same party ties will pull in the opposite direction when different parties control the White House and Congress.

Different Time Perspectives

Finally, Congress and the president operate on different timetables. Presidents have four years, at most eight, to win adoption of their programs. They are usually in a hurry to achieve all they can before they leave office. In practice, they have even less time because of the typical falloff in presidential support after the initial "honeymoon." Indeed, presidents and their advisers actually often have a year, perhaps less, to sell their basic programs to Congress and the public. "A president's most effective year is his first," explained Sen. Richard Durbin, D-Ill., President Obama's close friend and confidant. "He is brand new to the office, has a national mandate of varying degrees, and Congress is usually more open to working with him. After the first year, an election year is under way and people look at him differently."[124] Presidents think in terms of four years; most lawmakers think in terms of two.

On major, long-standing issues, however, Congress typically moves slowly. Seldom does it pass presidential initiatives quickly unless an emergency or crisis of some sort is looming. Moreover, many legislators are careerists. Once elected, House members are likely to be reelected, and senators serve six-year terms. Most members hold office a good deal longer than the presidents they deal with. Skeptical legislators, reluctant to follow the president, realize that if they resist long enough someone else will occupy the White House.

THE BALANCE OF POWER

"The relationship between the Congress and the presidency," wrote Arthur M. Schlesinger Jr., "has been one of the abiding mysteries of the American system of government."[125] Part of the mystery inheres in the Constitution, which enumerates many powers for Congress as well as those "necessary and proper" to carry them out, while leaving the president's powers largely unstated. Where does the balance of power lie? There is no easy answer, but at certain times the scale has tipped toward Congress and at other times toward the president. Scholars have even identified periods of "congressional government" or "presidential government."[126]

Four points need to be remembered about the ups and downs of Congress and the presidency. First, even during periods in which one branch appears to dominate, the actual balance of power in specific policy areas is complex. The stature of either branch is influenced by issues, events, partisan circumstances, personalities, or public opinion.

The mid-1960s and early 1970s, for example, are cited as a time of "imperial presidents" and compliant Congresses.[127] Nonetheless, although Congress enacted much of President Johnson's Great Society program, it also initiated scores of laws, including consumer, environmental, health, and civil rights legislation. Nor did executive actions go unchallenged. Nationally televised hearings conducted in 1966 by the Senate Foreign Relations Committee helped to mobilize congressional and public opposition to the Vietnam War. The refrain "imperial presidents" and "compliant Congresses" was heard again when Republicans were in charge of Congress from 2001 to 2007 and George W. Bush was in the White House. More recently, a former House majority leader called President Obama an "imperial president" for using his regulatory and executive authority to govern without Congress.[128]

Second, power also shifts within each branch. In Congress, aggressive leaders may be followed by less assertive leaders. In the executive branch, the forces for White House leadership regularly battle the forces for agency decentralization. These internal power fluctuations clearly affect policy making. During the Eisenhower presidency in the 1950s, powerful committee and party leaders could normally deliver blocs of votes to pass legislation. Today, even with the resurgence of partisanship on Capitol Hill, the president can never be sure which of the 535 members will form a winning coalition.

Third, legislative–executive relationships are not zero-sum games. If one branch gains power, the other does not necessarily lose it. If one branch is up, the other need not be down. The expansion of the federal government since World War II has augmented the authority of both branches. Their growth rates were different, but each expanded its ability to address complex issues, initiate legislation, and frustrate the proposals of the other. According to the conventional wisdom, wars, crises, nuclear weapons, military expansion, and public demands fostered the imperial presidency. Such factors certainly enlarge the likelihood of executive dominance, but in the wars of 1812 and 1898, for example, military action was encouraged in part by aggressive Congresses. Economic panics and depressions under Presidents James Monroe, James Buchanan, and Ulysses S. Grant did not lead to losses of congressional power.

Political scientist David Mayhew has asserted that with respect to productivity of laws and investigations, it "does not seem to make all that much difference whether party control of the American government happens to be unified or divided."[129] Mayhew examined the period from 1946 to 1990, when the mobilization of cross-party majorities on Capitol Hill was commonplace. President Ronald Reagan, for example, enjoyed large successes on his policy priorities (tax cuts, defense hikes, and program reductions) in 1981 when he won the support of conservative "Reagan Democrats" in the Democratic-controlled House. Today, in an era of strong, largely cohesive, and ideologically distinct congressional parties—reflecting the conditional party government model discussed in Chapter 6—it may be that unified government is more important for legislative productivity, though the sixty-vote requirement to end Senate filibusters makes impasses quite possible even under unified control.

Conflict between Congress and the president is embedded in the system of separation of powers and checks and balances. But the founders also expected their governmental arrangement to promote accommodation between the branches. Historical patterns have veered between these two extremes. The two branches worked together in the early days of Woodrow Wilson's progressive New Freedom (1913–1916); during the New Deal (1933–1937) and World War II (1941–1945); during the brief Great Society years (1964–1966) following John F. Kennedy's assassination in 1963; for the even briefer "Reaganomics" juggernaut during Ronald Reagan's first year in office (1981); during most of George W. Bush's first six years in office (2001–2007); and during Barack Obama's first two years (2009–2011). At other times, the two branches fought fiercely—during Wilson's second term (1919–1921); after 1937 during the Franklin Roosevelt administration; after 1966 during the Lyndon Johnson administration; and for much of the Nixon, Reagan, George H. W. Bush, and Clinton administrations, the final two years of George W. Bush's presidency, and Obama's presidency after 2010.

Finally, a wide gap often separates what presidents want from what they can achieve. Congress can influence what, when, how, or even whether executive recommendations are sent to Capitol Hill. Expectations of what will pass Congress frequently shape White House agendas. This indirect priority-setting power of the House and Senate can affect whether the president even transmits certain proposals to Congress. It also works in the other direction. Recommendations may be forwarded or endorsed because the White House knows they have broad legislative support. "The president proposes, Congress disposes" is an oversimplified adage.

Congress and the president are institutions shaped by diverging imperatives. Executive officials want flexibility, discretion, and long-range commitments from Congress. They prefer few controls and consultations with a limited number of legislators. The executive tends to be hierarchical, or vertical, in decision making, whereas Congress tends to be collegial and horizontal—with power spread among 535 independent-minded lawmakers. One of the legislative branch's strengths is that it is able to give voice and visibility to diverse viewpoints that the executive branch may have overlooked or ignored. The dispersion of power can slow down decision making, but it also can promote public acceptance of the nation's policies. Thus what are often viewed as Congress's vices are also genuine virtues.

CONCLUSION

Conflict would seem to be the inevitable result of a system that intentionally divides lawmaking and other powers between the executive and legislative branches. Much of the relationship between Congress and the executive, however, is better characterized as accommodation than as conflict. Neither branch is monolithic. Presidents find supporters in both chambers even when presidents are opposed by congressional majorities. Both branches seek support for their policy preferences from each other and from outside allies. Congress and the president must find ways to work together to achieve common goals.

Nevertheless, confrontation is a recurring element in dealings between Capitol Hill and the White House. The framers of the Constitution consciously distributed and mixed power among the three branches. They left it unclear how Congress or the president would assert control over the bureaucracy and over policy making. Even when both houses of Congress are controlled by the same party as the White House, the two branches have different constituencies and often become adversaries.

Finally, legislative–executive relations are constantly evolving. Either branch may be active on an issue at one time and passive at another time. So many circumstances affect how, when, what, or why shifts occur in the relationship that it is impossible to predict the outcome.

AP Photo/Pablo Martinez Monsivais

AP Photo/Carolyn Kaster

Bureaucracy: The Fourth Branch. Sen. Marco Rubio, R-Fla., speaks at a news conference on Capitol Hill to discuss Veterans' Affairs' accountability legislation. A "Closed" sign hangs on a barricade before the Lincoln Memorial in Washington, D.C. Congress's inability to pass a funding bill due to a long-running dispute over President Obama's health care law caused a partial government shutdown in 2013, which forced 800,000 federal workers off the job and suspended most non-essential federal programs. Health and Human Services Secretary Kathleen Sebelius is sworn in on Capitol Hill, prior to testifying before the House Energy and Commerce Committee hearing on the problems plaguing the implementation of the Affordable Care Act.

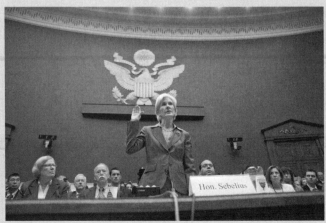

AP Photo/ J. Scott Applewhite

Congress and the Bureaucracy

In his 2015 State of the Union address, President Barack Obama articulated a sweeping role for the national government. He urged the GOP Congress to enact legislation that would provide, for example, free community college for everyone (paid for by tax hikes on the wealthy); seven days of paid sick leave for every worker; high-quality child care for American families; and the resources to build a twenty-first-century infrastructure—"modern ports, and stronger bridges, faster trains and the fastest Internet." Clearly, the president's view of the proper role of government diverged significantly from that of the GOP Congress. A fundamental goal of many Republican lawmakers is to shrink the government's domestic role, which makes it unlikely that Congress will enact many of Obama's recommendations. As advocates of greater reliance on the business sector, states, localities, and individuals, GOP opponents castigated the president for suggesting a larger federal role in policy making, particularly during a time of large fiscal deficits (nearly $500 billion), huge debt (over $18 trillion), and low public trust and confidence in government.

Public confidence and trust in government ebb and flow over time. In 1964 nearly 80 percent of Americans said they trusted the government "to do the right thing most of the time."[1] Confidence fell, however, during the Vietnam War and the Watergate scandal. Different eras, in brief, can provoke different views of government. Suffice it to say, as a noted scholar put it, "The role of government in a free society must be a matter of continuous negotiation among members of its public."[2]

The national government has grown under presidents of both parties throughout the modern era despite pronouncements such as that of President Bill Clinton in 1996, "The era of big government is over." The administration of Republican president George W. Bush (2001–2009) oversaw substantial governmental growth, only in part triggered by increased domestic security and military expenditures after the terrorist attacks of September 11, 2001. As respected journalist David S. Broder wrote, President Bush presided over one of the largest expansions of government in history: He "created a mammoth Cabinet department [Department of Homeland Security], increased federal spending, imposed new federal rules on local and state governments, and injected federal requirements into every public school in America."[3]

When Democratic president Obama began his first term, the country was in the midst of the most serious national economic crisis since the Great Depression. The federal government spent hundreds of billions of taxpayer dollars to revive the ailing economy. The effort undoubtedly helped halt the recession's downward spiral, perhaps preventing another depression. "Not since Lyndon B. Johnson and Franklin D. Roosevelt," wrote a congressional journalist, has a president "moved to expand the role of government so much on so many fronts—and with such a demanding sense of urgency."[4] Many Americans railed against the major, even transformative, laws enacted during the first two years of the Obama administration, particularly the economic stimulus of 2009, the Affordable Care Act, and financial regulatory reform.

With the public deeply split over Obama's agenda, subsequent elections in 2010, 2012, and 2014 yielded six years (2011–2017) of divided government. The three elections reignited the age-old national conversation between those who view government as a constructive force for collective action and those who emphasize private-sector and nongovernmental problem-solving.

President Obama provided his own perspective on the government's size and scope. "It's not an issue of big government versus small government. It's an issue of smart government," where "we can probably do more and do it smarter with less money, if we are actually making some tough choices."[5] A key challenge for the president's concept of smart government is an unsettled political and policy reality: today's big government is supported with revenue for a small government. In the judgment of a former representative, Democrat Lee Hamilton of Indiana: "The nation's current fiscal difficulties will surely force government to do less than many people want, and the public sector will have to become smarter, more effective, and more efficient."[6]

Yet history demonstrates that it is often difficult for presidents or Congress to shrink the size, role, or reach of the federal government. Setting aside war and other national crises, one basic reason is the ambivalence of the public. Although they profess to want to get the government off their backs, Americans of virtually all ideological persuasions often turn to the government to help fulfill their goals and to provide assistance during times of need. As William S. Cohen, former GOP senator from Maine (1979–1997), put it: "The government is the enemy until one needs a friend."[7]

The paradox, then, is that citizens and various groups oppose the general idea of big government, but they support many of the government's specific roles in ensuring clean air and water, a strong national defense, access to quality health care, the safety of food products and prescription drugs, and protection from terrorist attacks. Understandably, lawmakers typically defend government programs supported by their constituents. In brief, many people may dislike or resent government, but they usually support federal programs that benefit themselves.

To implement any government program, an organized bureaucracy is required—often federal *and* state bureaucracies. Importantly, Washington relies on the states to administer many national programs. By the same token, states rely on federal resources to fund many of their health care, transportation, and education priorities. Each level of government needs the other. Although the federal–state relationship is rife with tensions and turf battles, today's federal–state relationship is usually more symbiotic than confrontational.

The two Congresses contribute to an expanding bureaucracy. In today's complex and interdependent world, constituents typically look to the national government rather than the private sector to secure collective goods such as security, justice, and protection. Similarly, nationwide corporations often lobby for federal regulation so they do not have to contend with the different rules of the fifty states. Members of Congress respond to such demands.

CONGRESS ORGANIZES THE EXECUTIVE BRANCH

Just as the president and Congress share influence over lawmaking, they share responsibility for the executive branch of government—the bureaucracy. The Constitution requires the president to implement the laws, and by implication it empowers him to manage the executive branch. But Congress "has at least as much to do with executive administration as does an incumbent of the White House."[8] Congress is constitutionally authorized to organize and fund the executive branch.

The framers, of course, did not foresee the huge federal bureaucracy that has arisen from their sparse references to "executive departments." George Washington supervised only three departments (State, War, and Treasury); Barack Obama heads fifteen. Beyond the cabinet departments, the federal bureaucracy also includes independent agencies (such as the Central Intelligence Agency), independent regulatory commissions, and government corporations (see Figure 11-1).

Congress has extensive influence over the structure and composition of the federal bureaucracy.[9] Among other things, it can enact statutes that establish or abolish executive agencies and departments (see Table 11-1). The newest cabinet creation is the Department of Homeland Security (DHS). Other ways Congress can influence the structure of the executive branch include: instructing departments and agencies to reorganize themselves, establishing an outside commission to make recommendations, or authorizing the president to reorganize on his own or to develop reorganization plans that will then be subject to some form of congressional review. Congress extends its long arm into the bureaucracy in many different ways. The Senate confirms (or not, as the case may be) presidential appointments of high-level officials. Congress authorizes the basic personnel systems of federal entities. It also grants rulemaking authority to administrative agencies.

Senate Confirmation of Presidential Appointees

High-level federal appointments—executive, diplomatic, and judicial—are subject to the Senate's "advice and consent" under Article II, section 2, of the Constitution. After the president has decided whom to nominate, the Senate decides whether to confirm (see Figure 11-2).

FIGURE 11-1   **The Government of the United States**

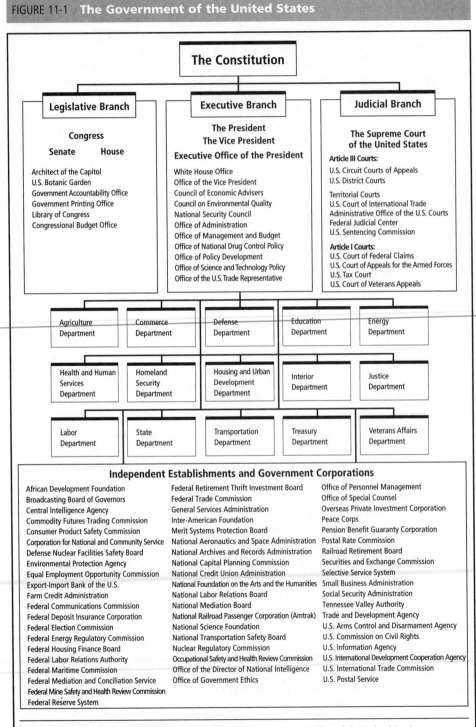

The Constitution

Legislative Branch

Congress

Senate   **House**

Architect of the Capitol
U.S. Botanic Garden
Government Accountability Office
Government Printing Office
Library of Congress
Congressional Budget Office

Executive Branch

**The President
The Vice President**

Executive Office of the President

White House Office
Office of the Vice President
Council of Economic Advisers
Council on Environmental Quality
National Security Council
Office of Administration
Office of Management and Budget
Office of National Drug Control Policy
Office of Policy Development
Office of Science and Technology Policy
Office of the U.S. Trade Representative

Judicial Branch

**The Supreme Court
of the United States**

Article III Courts:
U.S. Circuit Courts of Appeals
U.S. District Courts

Territorial Courts
U.S. Court of International Trade
Administrative Office of the U.S. Courts
Federal Judicial Center
U.S. Sentencing Commission

Article I Courts:
U.S. Court of Federal Claims
U.S. Court of Appeals for the Armed Forces
U.S. Tax Court
U.S. Court of Veterans Appeals

Agriculture Department	Commerce Department	Defense Department	Education Department	Energy Department

Health and Human Services Department	Homeland Security Department	Housing and Urban Development Department	Interior Department	Justice Department

Labor Department	State Department	Transportation Department	Treasury Department	Veterans Affairs Department

Independent Establishments and Government Corporations

African Development Foundation
Broadcasting Board of Governors
Central Intelligence Agency
Commodity Futures Trading Commission
Consumer Product Safety Commission
Corporation for National and Community Service
Defense Nuclear Facilities Safety Board
Environmental Protection Agency
Equal Employment Opportunity Commission
Export-Import Bank of the U.S.
Farm Credit Administration
Federal Communications Commission
Federal Deposit Insurance Corporation
Federal Election Commission
Federal Energy Regulatory Commission
Federal Housing Finance Board
Federal Labor Relations Authority
Federal Maritime Commission
Federal Mediation and Conciliation Service
Federal Mine Safety and Health Review Commission
Federal Reserve System

Federal Retirement Thrift Investment Board
Federal Trade Commission
General Services Administration
Inter-American Foundation
Merit Systems Protection Board
National Aeronautics and Space Administration
National Archives and Records Administration
National Capital Planning Commission
National Credit Union Administration
National Foundation on the Arts and the Humanities
National Labor Relations Board
National Mediation Board
National Railroad Passenger Corporation (Amtrak)
National Science Foundation
National Transportation Safety Board
Nuclear Regulatory Commission
Occupational Safety and Health Review Commission
Office of the Director of National Intelligence
Office of Government Ethics

Office of Personnel Management
Office of Special Counsel
Overseas Private Investment Corporation
Peace Corps
Pension Benefit Guaranty Corporation
Postal Rate Commission
Railroad Retirement Board
Securities and Exchange Commission
Selective Service System
Small Business Administration
Social Security Administration
Tennessee Valley Authority
Trade and Development Agency
U.S. Arms Control and Disarmament Agency
U.S. Commission on Civil Rights
U.S. Information Agency
U.S. International Development Cooperation Agency
U.S. International Trade Commission
U.S. Postal Service

Source: The United States Government Manual, 2014 (Washington, DC: Office of the Federal Register, Government Printing Office), 22.

TABLE 11-1 **Growth of the Cabinet**	
Department	Year created
State	1789
Treasury	1789
War (reorganized and renamed Defense in 1947)	1789
Interior	1849
Justice (position of attorney general created in 1789)	1870
Agriculture	1889
Commerce (created as Commerce and Labor)	1903
Labor (split from Commerce and Labor)	1913
Health, Education, and Welfare (reorganized and renamed Health and Human Services in 1979)	1953
Housing and Urban Development	1965
Transportation	1966
Energy	1977
Education	1980
Veterans Affairs	1989
Homeland Security	2002

Source: CQ Daily Monitor, January 10, 2003, 3.

Senators use their confirmation power to wield influence over executive branch priorities. Senate committees usually elicit the following promise from departmental and agency nominees they have confirmed: "The above nomination [a cabinet secretary, for example] was approved subject to the nominee's commitment to respond to requests to appear and testify before any duly constituted committee of the Senate."[10] Or, as Sen. Charles Grassley, R-Iowa, declared, "I'm going to hit every [Obama] nominee with the question, 'Are you open to congressional oversight?'"[11] The confirmation process also reflects the two Congresses principle. As a top Senate official once remarked, "It looks very, very good in California or some place to put out a press release that says, 'Today, I questioned the new Secretary of Transportation about the problems of our area.'"[12]

Presidents can bypass the Senate's advice and consent role in three broad ways. First, the Constitution (Article II, section 2) provides that "[t]he President shall have Power to fill up all Vacancies that may happen during a Recess of the Senate, by granting Commissions which shall expire at the End of their next Session." For example, a recess appointee named in 2012 could serve until late 2013. Presidential recess appointments are not unusual, and they have occurred during intersession—the interval between the first and second sessions of a Congress—and intrasession breaks. For example, a study by the Congressional Research Service found that since the inauguration of President Ronald Reagan

FIGURE 11-2　**The Appointments Process**

THE WHITE HOUSE

The selection process

1. Vacancy occurs or future vacancy identified.
2. Determination of appropriate position requirements (job description).
3. Search and recruitment of candidates.
4. Initial selection and clearances.
5. Final selection; announcement of nomination.

Nomination sent to the Senate

THE SENATE

The confirmation process

1. Nomination referred to committee.
2. Committee staff investigation.
3. Committee hearings and committee vote.
4. Floor debate and final action in full Senate.

Presidential appointee assumes office.

in 1981, "presidents have made 329 intrasession recess appointments and 323 intersession appointments."[13] Over time, presidents came to rely more on recess appointments in response to the wider use of Senate filibusters and holds to block the confirmation of presidential appointments.

Senators have long resented presidential use of the recess appointment option, especially if the chief executive is not of their party, because it undermines their constitutional advice and consent role. In response, the Senate would sometimes adopt a simple formula to block recess appointments: no Senate recesses, no presidential recess appointments. The Senate would meet in *pro forma* session, convening for only a few seconds and seldom conducting any official business. Use of these sessions prevented President Obama from employing recess appointments for people opposed by Senate Republicans. By precedent, presidents respected the fiction that the Senate was in session during *pro forma* meetings and did not make recess appointments.

However, in 2012 President Obama broke precedent, ignored the Senate's *pro forma* sessions, and recess-appointed Richard Cordray as chair of the new Consumer Financial Protection Bureau. His approval had been blocked by

Senate Republicans for months because they wanted a law enacted to have a commission-led agency rather than one person in charge of the bureau. In addition, because the National Labor Relations Board (NLRB) lacked a quorum to function, the president recess-appointed three individuals during the Senate's *pro forma* meetings. The president contended that the Senate was not actually in session because nearly every senator, except for a few Republicans, had departed for the winter holidays. Senate Republicans countered that official business was conducted during the *pro forma* sessions, and that the president had no authority to determine what constitutes sessions of the Senate. Obama's action set off a storm of protest in the Senate and prompted review by the Supreme Court.

In 2014 the Supreme Court for the first time considered the president's recess appointment authority in the case of *NLRB v. Noel Canning*. It unanimously invalidated President Obama's 2012 recess appointments to the National Labor Relations Board. The Court also concluded that a vacancy must be of "substantial length"—meaning in historical practice more than ten days—before a recess appointment by the president could be made. Finally, the Court held that whether the Senate is in session for a few seconds or minutes, *pro forma* sessions mean that the president cannot make recess appointments: "When the Senate declares that it is in session and possesses the capacity, under its own rules, to conduct business, it is in session for the purposes of the [Recess Appointments] Clause."[14]

The president has other ways to bypass the Senate's advice and consent role. The president can name individuals, on a temporary acting basis, to fill vacant positions that require confirmation by the Senate. In some cases, however, Congress has enacted laws that set up an automatic mechanism to fill temporary vacancies. For example, if the director of the Office and Management and Budget (OMB) is absent or unable to serve, the deputy director then acts as the OMB director.[15]

Furthermore, many prominent officials, such as White House advisers, are not subject to the advice and consent of the Senate. President Obama may be a record-breaker in naming so many individuals, informally called "czars," to head up important policy initiatives—the "environmental czar," the "economic czar," the "Ebola czar."[16] Czars oversee and coordinate the forming of policies that cut across the jurisdictions of several departments and agencies. For example, Harvard professor (now U.S. senator) Elizabeth Warren was asked to set up the new Bureau of Consumer Financial Protection in the Treasury Department. The bureau was created as part of the landmark financial regulatory reform bill (P.L. 111-203), and she was largely the intellectual force behind its creation. Because of significant Senate opposition to Warren, President Obama bypassed the nominations process and named Warren an assistant to the president and special adviser to the Treasury secretary. GOP senator Bob Corker of Tennessee dubbed Warren "the czar of all czars."[17]

The appointment of numerous czars reflects the amassing of further power in the White House. Yale law professor Bruce Ackerman contends, "We need to seriously consider requiring Senate approval of senior White House staff positions."[18] And yet the slow pace of confirmations no doubt provides incentives for presidents to name policy czars as a way to avoid lengthy Senate approval.

Nominations to high-level executive posts are subject to standards of judgment and evaluation that go far beyond reasonable questions of competence or conflict of interest. As one commentator explained:

> These days, if you want to . . . accept a position of public trust, everything is relevant. Your moral, medical, legal and financial background, even your college records, become the subject of public scrutiny. In the old days, the scrutiny was done in private, and certain transgressions could be considered irrelevant.[19]

This shift in standards stems in part from changed attitudes on the part of the press and the public. The contemporary press is far more aggressive in reporting on the private activities of public officials.[20] This trend is also driven in large measure by a hyperpartisan environment in which the president's opponents seek to embarrass or obstruct the administration at every turn.

These developments have produced a rigorous vetting process for nominees. Each nominee must fill out several lengthy questionnaires and undergo security checks. According to political scientist Norman Ornstein, "Each security check is a massive operation, involving up to 40 face-to-face interviews, and is basically the same for the assistant secretary of Education for public affairs as it is for the secretary of State."[21] Investigators from the White House, Federal Bureau of Investigation (FBI), IRS, and Senate ask nominees difficult and uncomfortable questions about their personal and professional lives. "I have never been subjected to such personally insulting and expensive scrutiny in my life," said one Obama nominee, who was asked for receipts for furniture he donated to charity more than a decade ago. Another nominee was questioned about "his wife's sexual activity when she was at university."[22] The importance of a thorough vetting process was emphasized by an Obama adviser: "The real purpose of vetting is to understand the person's ability to perform the job and be confirmed for the position. We also want to avoid surprises."[23]

The intense scrutiny and loss of privacy deter talented people from accepting the call to presidential service. Presidential recruiters report that it takes more calls to find candidates willing to subject themselves to the process and more work to keep the candidates from bolting once the process begins.[24]

Today, there is substantial frustration with the confirmation process. "The nomination system is a national disgrace," wrote a scholar of the presidential appointment process.[25] The problems are many, afflicting the administrations of both parties—even when the same party controls the White House and the Senate. Although the Senate eventually confirms most nominees, three concerns with the process merit mention.

First, it takes longer and longer to fill the full-time cabinet and agency positions requiring Senate confirmation. Public administration expert Paul C.

Light studied five hundred of Obama's nominees for full-time jobs in his administration "and found they've waited an average of more than nine months to be confirmed, longer than at any time since the 1960s."[26] Additional delays are caused by the administration's slowness in nominating people to serve in high federal positions.[27]

Individual senators regularly threaten filibusters or place holds on nominations—that is, senators notify party leaders that they oppose floor consideration of certain nominees (see Box 11-1). The Senate may also refuse to consider a nominee if members invoke senatorial courtesy. This tradition, dating from the nation's earliest years, means that the Senate will usually delay or not act on nominees for offices in a state if opposed by a senator of the president's party from that state.

Second, an expanding bureaucracy raises concerns about public accountability. Over time, Congress and the president have created more and more job titles in the top echelons of government. The result is additional layers of bureaucracy—in some federal agencies there are as many as fifty layers between the president and frontline executive employees—"a bureaucratic fog in which Congress and the president are hopelessly isolated from the people they most need to guide."[28] Among the numerous new titles are deputy associate deputy secretary, principal assistant deputy undersecretary, principal senior deputy assistant secretary, deputy associate assistant secretary, and deputy executive associate administrator.[29] The Pentagon is a glaring example. In 1960 there were 78 deputy assistant secretaries of defense, and today there are 530.[30]

BOX 11-1 **Lifting of Objection**

Mr. GRASSLEY. Madam President, on June 27, I provided notice of my intent to object to proceeding to the nominations of Mark J. Mazur, to be an Assistant Secretary of the Treasury, and Matthew J. Rutherford, to be an Assistant Secretary to the Treasury. My support for the final confirmation of these nominees depended on receiving information from both the Treasury Department and the Internal Revenue Service regarding their implementation of the tax whistleblower program. Since I have received the responses, I no longer object to proceeding to these nominations. [. . .]

I began asking questions about the program's implementation in 2010. I wrote again in 2011 and then again on April 30 of this year. Unfortunately, I did not get complete answers until I objected to proceeding to the nominations of Mr. Mazur and Mr. Rutherford. [. . .]

It is unfortunate that objecting to these nominees, both of whom were approved by the Finance Committee by unanimous, bipartisan votes, was the only way I could get information about the whistleblower program. At least there is now more information than ever before about the IRS whistleblower program.

Source: An excerpt from the *Congressional Record*, July 30, 2012, S5655–S5656.

According to Light, this "thickening of government" makes it difficult to know whom to hold accountable for what goes wrong in the executive branch, and "impossible for the bottom to hear the top when messages go through dozens of interpretations on their journey down."[31]

Third, the Senate's confirmation process can be difficult, especially in this period of polarized politics. Many nominees are subjected to rough treatment. For example, former GOP senator Chuck Hagel, Neb., Obama's defense secretary (2013–2014) and a decorated Vietnam War combat officer, confronted harsh criticism and interrogation from many Republicans on the Senate Armed Services Committee, some of whom were his former colleagues. In the end, the Senate confirmed Hagel as defense secretary despite an outside media campaign funded by secret donors "unmatched in the annals of modern presidential cabinet appointments."[32] Sometimes, the purpose of Senate confirmation hearings "seems less to ensure that nominees are fit than to cripple the chief executive's political leadership."[33]

To address some of the problems with delays in confirmations, the bipartisan Senate leadership created a "working group," headed by Sens. Charles Schumer, D-N.Y., and Lamar Alexander, R-Tenn., to suggest reforms to the confirmation process. Two modest measures emerged, and both were agreed to by the Senate in 2011. First, the president signed into law (P.L. 112-166) the Presidential Appointment Efficiency and Streamlining Act. This law reduced by 163 the number of non-policy-making executive positions subject to the advice and consent of the Senate, such as nominations to various federal boards and commissions. Second, the Senate adopted a resolution (S. Res. 116) that expedited chamber consideration of 272 nominations—different from the 163 noted above—to various federal entities (departmental posts, independent agencies, federal advisory boards, etc.).

Even with passage of these measures, the Obama administration and its allies grew increasingly frustrated with the delays facing both executive branch and judicial nominees. The Democratic Senate voted in November 2013 to require only a simple majority to end debate on all executive branch appointments and all judicial nominees other than to the Supreme Court (see Chapter 8 for a detailed discussion). Although Republicans objected vociferously to the change, Senate GOP leaders made no move to eliminate the provision when they gained control of the Senate in the 114th Congress. As a result, executive branch nominees will no longer need to overcome filibuster threats.

The Personnel System

Congress wields constitutional, legal, and informal authority over the federal personnel system. The civil service itself was created after a disgruntled job seeker assassinated President James A. Garfield in 1881. That event prompted Congress to curb the abuses of the spoils system, the practice of handing out federal jobs to supporters of the party that had won the presidency. In 1883 Congress passed the first civil service law that substituted merit for patronage. But those patronage practices have a modern equivalent: the political appointee system. The latest figures show that the fifteen cabinet departments are home to more than 2,500 political appointees (see Table 11-2).[34] The number of political appointees, however, is small compared with the number of federal employees: as of 2014, there are 2 million civil servants and 1.3 million active uniformed personnel.

Not all political appointees have the requisite experience to meet the challenges of their office. A classic example involved Hurricane Katrina, which devastated the Gulf Coast in late August 2005. At the time, the chief of the Federal Emergency Management Agency (FEMA) was Michael Brown. A former commissioner of the International Arabian Horse Association, Brown had little experience in emergency management. Despite President George W. Bush's praise—"Brownie, you're doing a heck of a job!"—FEMA's response to this crisis was widely viewed as inept and inadequate. One response by Congress was to pass the Post-Katrina Emergency Management Reform Act of 2006 (P.L. 109-295), which requires that any nominee named to head FEMA must meet certain qualifications.[35]

Periodically, various lawmakers recommend a reduction in the number of political appointees. They contend that there are simply far more appointees than the president can manage effectively. Far from enhancing responsiveness, said one senator, the large number of political appointees undermines "presidential control of the executive branch."[36] Not everyone agrees. Amid rising partisanship, one scholar argued, "presidents need to stock departments with people who understand politics and the importance of interaction with Congress, lobbyists and the media."[37]

Pay and Other Legal Standards. By law, Congress has wide control over federal employees. It can establish retirement programs; special requirements for holding office; personnel ceilings; employee performance standards; wages, benefits, and cost-of-living adjustments (COLAs); and protections from reprisals for whistleblowers (employees who expose waste and corruption).

Importantly, the 1939 Hatch Act, named for Sen. Carl Hatch, D-N.M. (1933–1949), restricts federal employees' partisan activity. The act was passed during the New Deal after reports that civil servants were being bullied to back President Franklin D. Roosevelt in his reelection efforts. The purposes of the Hatch Act are "to ensure that federal programs are administered in a nonpartisan fashion, to protect federal employees from political coercion in the workplace, and to ensure that federal employees are advanced on merit and not based on political affiliation."[38] Today, civil servants can engage in political activity in accord with regulations prescribed by the U.S. Office of Special Counsel. For example, most career civil servants can run for nonpartisan office, contribute money to political organizations, or attend political rallies. They may not run for partisan office, use their authority to exert influence over an election, or wear political buttons while on duty.[39] As a sign of the times, the special counsel's office has also issued guidelines for federal employees on the use of social media such as Facebook and Twitter in election campaigns.[40]

TABLE 11-2 **Political Appointees by Department and Appointment Type, 2012**

Department	Presidential appointment requiring Senate approval	Presidential appointment not requiring Senate approval	Noncareer Senior Executive Service	Schedule C	Total
Agriculture	14	3	39	164	220
Commerce	24	0	36	84	144
Defense	53	0	74	101	228
Education	17	1	14	115	147
Energy	23	0	21	69	113
Health and Human Services	20	1	72	68	161
Homeland Security	21	2	55	83	161
Housing and Urban Development	14	0	19	47	80
Interior	18	0	39	46	103
Justice	225	0	49	65	339
Labor	18	0	24	80	122
State	254	5	38	104	401
Transportation	23	0	27	38	88
Treasury	36	0	30	44	110
Veterans Affairs	15	0	10	10	35
Total	775	12	547	1,118	2,542

Sources: Policy and Supporting Positions (Washington, D.C.: U.S. Government Printing Office, 2012). This volume is called "The Plum Book" because of the color of its cover. The authors acknowledge the assistance of Maeve P. Carey, regulatory expert at the Congressional Research Service.

Other limits are placed on bureaucrats as well. After leaving public office, many executive officers, top legislative staffers, and legislators themselves pass through the "revolving door" to jobs with private firms that deal with the government. However, various laws impose a "cooling-off" period before these officials and employees may lobby their former agencies, departments, or branches of government. For example, under the Honest Leadership and Open Government Act of 2007, high government officials and senators are subject to a two-year cooling-off period after leaving office; House members must

comply with a one-year cooling-off period.[41] Nevertheless, government officials regularly move to the private sector and vice versa. Enactment of the
landmark Dodd-Frank Wall Street Reform and Consumer Protection Act (P.L.
111-203) in 2010 saw many government regulators walk through the revolving
door to join various Wall Street firms.[42] Similarly, top White House officials
have also left the administration to take high-paying jobs in business, law, and
public relations firms, despite signing Obama-required pledges barring them
for two years from trying to influence executive officials on behalf of their
clients. However, the pledge does not prevent "outgoing Obama aides from
lobbying Congress or from helping employers or clients influence the administration by charting strategy or even supervising lobbyists."[43]

Size of Government. Americans have debated the size and reach of the
federal government since the nation's founding. Recall that Thomas Jefferson
advocated limited government: "That government governs best that governs
least." Alexander Hamilton, Jefferson's rival, favored a strong national government and an energetic chief executive. In the view of Abraham Lincoln,
"Government is people coming together collectively to do that which they
could not do as well, or at all, individually."[44]

The national government's role has expanded dramatically since the turn
of the twentieth century—from the Progressive Era to World War I, from the
New Deal to the Great Society, to today's governmental interventions in the
private sector. Growth has been driven by overlapping factors. Wars and crises,
of course, expand federal obligations and centralize authority in the national
government. The intelligence community mushroomed during the Cold War
as the United States faced a major threat from the other nuclear-armed super-
power, the Soviet Union, and expanded dramatically after the September 11,
2001, terrorist attacks. As a result, some 854,000 people with top secret clearances are now in place at ten thousand sites across the United States.[45]

Complexity is another factor triggering governmental growth. New problems and issues repeatedly demand national action. Today, the federal government must address issues with global dimensions, from trade to currency
exchange rates to climate change. As the nation's population grew to over 320
million and government expanded its responsibilities and capacities, it was
only natural that individuals and groups would look to their national officeholders to solve problems in health care, transportation, law enforcement,
energy, and so on.

People often complain about the overly large federal establishment, but
what does "too big" really mean? There is considerable disagreement about
how the federal government's size should be measured: the share of the gross
domestic product (GDP) devoted to federal expenditures, the magnitude of
the federal budget, or the number of federal employees. As to the first standard, federal spending relative to the size of the U.S. economy is a mixed picture, from 21.8 percent of GDP in 1990 to 18.4 percent in 2000, 20.2 percent
in 2008, 23.8 percent in 2010, and 20.8 percent in 2013. Moreover, since 2011
and despite Congress's penchant for legislating by crisis, the federal deficit is

projected to shrink by nearly $4 trillion over a decade because of large cuts in discretionary spending, some tax increases, and savings on interest payments. However, this is a short-term outlook. The Congressional Budget Office noted that "total government spending is falling compared with the size of the economy but will rise again in the next decade" because of more baby boomer retirements and rising medical costs.[46]

Another measure of the government's size is the federal budget, which is large (nearly $3.8 trillion in the president's budget submitted in 2015 to Congress). It is President Obama's view that "the economy has recovered enough that it's time to begin spending again," especially after years of cost-cutting and escalating national obligations.[47] Given a stronger economy, the president ignored the statutory sequestration budget cap of $1.017 trillion—set for his budget plan in a 2011 law—and increased discretionary spending to $1.091 trillion to provide extra funding for his domestic and defense priorities.[48] New taxes would largely pay for the increased spending. Congressional "deficit hawks" called the president's budget "dead on arrival," citing its nearly $500 billion estimated annual deficit—the mismatch between revenue and expenditures—and a national debt of over $18 trillion. The large federal budget represents to a significant degree the disconnect between what citizens want and what they are willing to pay for. It is this decades-long trade-off that dominates contemporary American politics.

Contrary to what many people believe, the federal workforce has remained relatively constant in size. How can the government continue to perform services while generally keeping its size down? One answer is that much of what the federal government does is transfer money to eligible recipients, such as the elderly who receive Social Security. This function does not require large numbers of federal workers. Another answer is that federal work has been outsourced to contract firms, or privatized. The Pentagon, for example, reached a milestone in 2001 when the number of its private-sector employees (734,000) exceeded its civilian workforce (700,000). Nine years later, the Defense Department said it employed 766,000 contractors compared with 745,000 civilian employees; however, another study calculated that Pentagon-employed contractors numbered 1.2 million.[49] These contract employees "perform service jobs from mowing lawns to testing weapons systems."[50] As one analyst explained, "Everybody wants the federal government to look smaller than it really is. By contracting out jobs rather than having civilian workers in those jobs, you can say, 'Look, the government's smaller.'"[51] Another scholar has put the true personnel size of the government at about 15 million employees: the 4.1 million civilian, military, and postal workers plus the 10.5 million "shadow" employees who work "under federal contracts and grants or mandates imposed on state and local governments."[52]

Whatever the outcome of this debate about government size, privatizing (or outsourcing) the federal government's work has certain benefits and costs. Outsourcing has distinct advantages in many instances: contractors can be faster, more flexible, and cheaper than the career bureaucracy. They can provide

security services, technological skills, intelligence capabilities, and other benefits that government agencies are unable to fulfill. However, many analysts
believe that certain functions are inherently governmental, which means they
are "so intimately related to the public interest as to require performance by a
federal government employee."[53] Because contractors are not directly responsible to Congress, the so-called third-party (or shadow) government raises serious questions of accountability, resulting in fraud, waste, and cost overruns.

The Rulemaking Process

Congress creates and funds executive agencies and defines their legal mandates, but rarely can it specify the details needed to implement policies and
programs. By statute, Congress delegates to federal entities the task of implementing rules and regulations (the terms are interchangeable) for carrying out
the mandates contained in laws. As Senator Grassley explained, "All regulations are based ultimately on the authority granted by this Congress. When an
agency promulgates a rule, it is engaging in a legislative task—in effect, filling
in the gaps on the implementation that we in Congress have established
through statute."[54] Executive agencies through their rule-writing authority
(their final regulations have the full force and effect of statutes) enact more
"laws" annually than the legislative branch. In other words, executive branch
officials who write regulations are lawmakers operating in a bureaucratic context. Congress delegates such authority to federal agencies largely because
lawmakers lack the time and technical expertise to devise the detailed language
required to implement the goals of complex statutes. Moreover, Congress
retains broad legislative power to amend, modify, or repeal regulations.

For example, lawmakers can employ procedures specified in the
Congressional Review Act (CRA) to try to nullify, one at a time, unwanted
regulations promulgated by executive agencies. The CRA is a section of the
1996 small-business regulatory fairness law requiring regulators to submit all
proposed major rules and regulations—those with an economic impact over
$100 million in any one year—to the House and Senate. Lawmakers then have
sixty legislative days from the time a regulation is published in the *Federal
Register*—the government's daily publication of regulatory activities—to reject
it via a joint resolution of disapproval, considered under expedited procedures
(meaning, for example, restrictions on the length of debate).[55]

Important to note is that the president can veto joint resolutions of disapproval, and mustering the two-thirds vote needed to override the chief executive
is a high hurdle. Since CRA's enactment in 1996, there have been forty-three
attempts to disapprove a rule with only one success (in 2001 on an ergonomics
rule to curb workplace injuries).[56] Nevertheless, as an aide to a former Senate
GOP majority leader noted, the CRA "provides an important public relations tool
to highlight real concerns and perhaps force the administration to make some
changes [to the challenged regulation] that they would otherwise not be willing
to make."[57] Wider GOP use of the CRA can also "put Democrats on record as to
whether they stand with the President" in supporting bad regulations.[58]

BOX 11-2   **The Rulemaking Process**

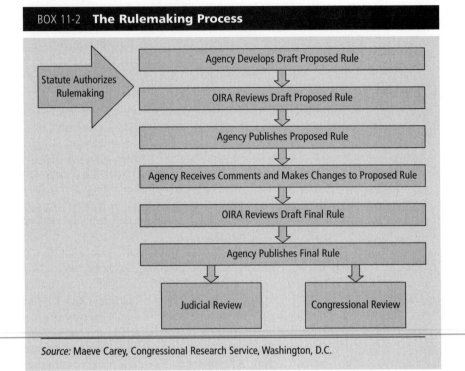

Source: Maeve Carey, Congressional Research Service, Washington, D.C.

Disapproval resolutions also signal regulatory agencies that Congress is keeping a close eye on their work.

Statutory Standards for Rulemaking. In the Administrative Procedure Act (APA) of 1946 and later amendments to it, Congress established standards for rulemaking by government agencies. Under the APA, regulatory agencies are required to publish a notice in the *Federal Register* of their proposed rulemaking. The notice includes such information as where and when "interested parties" can comment on the proposed rule. Typically, the public comment period runs for at least thirty days. Interested parties can take part in the process by testifying in public about the merits or demerits of proposed regulations. Citizens can comment on federal rulemaking through the government's official websites—www.federalregister.gov or www.reginfo.gov—as well as through comparable sites. Record numbers of public comments on proposed regulations are being received by government agencies, both because comments can be made easily on federal websites and the issues provoke controversy among businesses, outside groups, and other stakeholders:

> The State Department received more than 2.5 million comments on whether to permit construction of the Keystone XL oil pipeline. More than 1.26 million have weighed in this summer [2014] on Federal

Communications Commission rules on how broadband providers treat traffic on their networks. At the Environmental Protection Agency, officials are sorting through hundreds of thousands of comments on new emission rules for power plants.[59]

The federal courts also ensure that executive officials do not repeal rules by fiat. A federal appeals court has held that once a rule is published in the *Federal Register,* "it cannot be reversed without a lengthy administrative process, even if [the rule] has not yet taken effect."[60] Although presidents can overturn executive orders with the stroke of a pen, they cannot treat regulations the same way. "It is not easy for a president to stop a final rule that has been published in the *Federal Register* short of putting the whole process [as prescribed in the Administrative Procedures Act of 1946] in reverse and beginning the process of rulemaking anew—with public notices, comment periods and agency reviews that could take years."[61]

Legislative–Executive Clashes. Congress and the White House frequently skirmish over rulemaking. GOP administrations tend to have a pro-business regulatory perspective, favoring voluntary compliance and giving key regulatory jobs to corporate and industry officials who are keen on easing or reducing regulation. Democratic presidents appoint individuals to head agencies that support worker safety and consumer and environmental protections. Inevitably, these disparate party views of federal regulation produce sharp disagreements. Congressional Republicans blame President Obama for creating job-killing regulations that stifle economic growth by imposing expensive costs and red tape on businesses. For his part, President Obama contends that Republicans want the end of regulations "that protect Americans from risky financial deals and other reckless behavior that crashed our economy."[62] Nonetheless, the Obama administration has directed federal agencies to be "sensitive to the costs and cumulative effects of regulations on businesses." The president also issued an executive order (13563) requiring "executive agencies to reduce regulations that place unnecessary burdens on U.S. businesses and the public."

An ongoing controversy between Congress and the executive agencies has centered on the authority of the Environmental Protection Agency (EPA) to regulate carbon emissions. The EPA used its authority under the Clean Air Act (P.L. 101-549) to require power plants, electric utilities, and oil refineries to employ the best available technologies to reduce their carbon emissions. (On April 2, 2007, the U.S. Supreme Court, in *Massachusetts v. EPA,* agreed that greenhouse gases were air pollutants and subject to regulations imposed by the EPA.) In response to the EPA's actions, House and Senate members from energy-producing states immediately went on the offensive to limit or strip the EPA's climate change authority. "We are not going to let this administration regulate what they've been unable to legislate," declared House Energy and Commerce chair Fred Upton, R-Mich.[63] Upton also promised that the EPA administrator would be testifying so frequently before his committee "that he'll guarantee her a permanent parking space on Capitol Hill."[64] Jason Chaffetz,

R-Utah, the chair of the House Oversight and Government Reform Committee, referred to EPA officials as "the 'poster children' of waste, fraud, and abuse."[65]

However, after several years of committee hearings and passing bills in their chamber repealing EPA regulations, House Republicans started to recognize that their chances of curbing environmental regulations were not good. As Joe Barton, R-Tex., chair *emeritus* of the House Energy and Commerce Committee, explained: "Congress can do something [about EPA regulations], but you need a majority in the House and 60 percent in the Senate, plus the president to avoid a veto. In this environment, we don't have that." Instead, mindful of the two Congresses, Barton said Republicans should push messaging bills. "Message bills are different. I'm open to that," he said.[66] "Over-regulation is always a good message for us," added a spokesperson for the Republican National Committee.[67] Cutting federal red tape was a theme employed regularly by GOP candidates in the midterm elections of November 2014.

Hundreds of rules and regulations issued each year by executive agencies must be reviewed by the White House regulatory "czar" before agencies may publish them in the *Federal Register*. (For a summary of the rulemaking process, see Box 11-2.) This czar is the chief of the Office of Information and Regulatory Affairs (OIRA) within the Office of Management and Budget. OIRA devotes considerable time to analyzing economically significant regulations, those that would impose more than $100 million in costs on affected industries. OIRA can reject these major rules, require their revision, or approve them in line with the president's priorities. (For a list of the number of final federal rules published for selected years, see Table 11-3.)

Proposed rules and regulations are typically subject to cost-benefit review. Measuring costs and benefits is at best a tricky undertaking. Risk analysis experts hold that this traditional tool should be used "to sort through a complex world of threats to human and environmental health so we can identify the choices that will do the most people the most good at the least cost."[68] Critics of this approach, however, point out that measuring costs is usually easier than estimating benefits; costs are more easily quantified, whereas benefits are often intangible and long-term. How valuable are regulations? Lawmakers, like their constituents, are of two minds. Some, such as Sen. Barbara Boxer, D-Calif., emphasize their positive aspects:

> The purpose of the Federal regulatory process is to improve and protect the high quality of life that we enjoy in our country. Every day, the people of our Nation enjoy the benefits of almost a century of progress in Federal laws and regulations that reduce the threat of illness, injury, and death from consumer products, workplace hazards, and environmental toxins.[69]

Other lawmakers call for regulators to issue "smarter, more cost-effective regulations."[70] Meanwhile, corporations complain that federal rules and regulations require them to spend billions in compliance costs. A difficult challenge is to distinguish between inflexible, pointless, or overly burdensome regulations and the beneficial regulations that are necessary to promote and protect the public's health and safety.

Whatever their view of the regulatory process, legislators must act as intermediaries between their constituents and federal agencies. Constituents' problems are handled within members' offices by personal staff aides called caseworkers. In addition to courting the electoral payoff of effective casework—evidence of the two Congresses once again—some members appreciate its value as oversight. "The very knowledge by executive officials that some Congressman is sure to look into a matter affecting his constituents acts as a healthy check against bureaucratic indifference or arrogance," wrote a former senator.[71]

CONGRESSIONAL CONTROL OF THE BUREAUCRACY

"Congressional power, like chastity," explained a scholar, "is never lost, rarely taken by force, and almost always given away."[72] Because no law can be sufficiently detailed to cover every conceivable circumstance, Congress allows executive officials wide discretion in implementing the laws it passes. This delegation of authority occurs because legislators lack the time, knowledge, or expertise to address the complexities of contemporary administration.

Congress is often sharply criticized for drafting vague or sloppy legislation that gives executive officials and judges too much leeway in interpretation and administration. "Administration of a statute is, properly speaking, an extension of the legislative process," pointed out political scientist David B. Truman; therefore, Congress must watch over its programs lest they undergo unintended change.[73] Because of the size and reach of the executive establishment, Congress's oversight role is even more important today than when Woodrow Wilson wrote in 1885, "Quite as important as lawmaking is vigilant oversight of administration."[74]

The Constitution does not refer explicitly to the oversight role, but it implicitly flows from Congress's right, among other things, to make laws, raise and appropriate money, give advice and consent to executive nominations, and impeach federal officials. The Supreme Court has explicitly recognized Congress's oversight authority. For instance, the Supreme Court held in *Watkins v. United States* (1957) that Congress's investigatory power "is inherent in the legislative process. That power is broad. It encompasses inquiries concerning the administration of existing laws as well as proposed or possibly needed statutes." Two years later, in *Barenblatt v. United States*, the Supreme Court stated: "The scope of [Congress's] power of inquiry . . . is as penetrating and far-reaching as the potential power to enact and appropriate under the Constitution."

Congress has formalized its oversight duties in laws and House and Senate rules. The Legislative Reorganization Act of 1946 directed all House and Senate committees to exercise "continuous watchfulness" over the programs and agencies under their jurisdiction. Subsequent statutes and House and Senate rules

TABLE 11-3 **Number of Documents (Final Rules) Published in the *Federal Register*, 2000–2013**

Year	Number of final rules
2000	4,313
2001	4,132
2002	4,167
2003	4,148
2004	4,101
2005	3,943
2006	3,718
2007	3,595
2008	3,830
2009	3,503
2010	3,573
2011	3,807
2012	3,708
2013	3,659

Source: Maeve Carey, "Counting Regulations: An Overview of Rulemaking, Types of Federal Regulations, and Pages in the *Federal Register*," Congressional Research Service Report R43056, November 26, 2014.

Note: The data are provided by the Government Accountability Office (GAO) in its Federal Rules Database, available on GAO's website.

have extended Congress's authority and resources for oversight. The Government Accountability Office (GAO), the chief investigative arm of the legislative branch, provides the House and Senate at the start of each new Congress with "high risk" reports on the management and accounting practices of federal agencies and departments. The high risk reports also identify "areas in need of broad-based transformation."[75] Overall, GAO issues annually more than a thousand audits and reports on administrative management.

Members understand their review responsibilities. "Congress's duty didn't end in passing this law," remarked a senator. "We have to make sure the law works." Another senator said, "I have always felt that one-third of the role of Congress should be in oversight."[76] Or as Speaker John Boehner emphasized, "I think the biggest part of Congress's job is to provide proper oversight of the executive branch of government."[77]

The purposes of oversight are many, but three are especially important: (1) to check the power of the executive branch; (2) to determine how laws are being implemented and whether they need adjustments and refinements; and (3) to shine the spotlight of public attention on significant executive actions and activities. As Woodrow Wilson wrote in 1885, "The informing function of Congress should be preferred even to its legislative [lawmaking] function." He went on to say:

> Unless Congress [has] and use[s] every means of acquainting itself with the acts and dispositions of the administrative agencies of government, the country must be helpless to learn how it is being served; and unless Congress both scrutinize[s] these things and sift[s] them by every form of discussion, the country must remain in embarrassing, crippling ignorance of the very affairs which it is most important it should understand and direct.[78]

Political purposes are served by oversight as well, such as generating favorable publicity for programs; urging the elimination or reduction of agencies; responding to requests from special interests to influence agency decisions; or winning electoral support from constituents or groups. Oversight thus occurs in a political context, within which Congress's relationship with administrative agencies can range from cooperation to conflict.

To ensure that laws are working, Congress relies on a varied array of formal and informal processes and techniques. Each has its strengths and weaknesses, and it is often necessary to use several in combination if the House and Senate are to challenge or assess executive branch performance. Many oversight activities are indirect, ad hoc, and not subject to easy measurement or even recognition. "Oversight isn't necessarily a hearing," said John D. Dingell, D-Mich., a noted and feared House overseer when he chaired the Energy and Commerce Committee. "Sometimes it's a letter. We find our letters have a special effect on a lot of people."[79]

Hearings and Investigations

Many of Congress's most dramatic historical moments have occurred during legislative probes into administrative or business misconduct or manmade and natural disasters. Examples are the Teapot Dome inquiry (1923); the Senate's Watergate hearings (1973–1974); the Iran-Contra investigation (1987); the joint hearings into the disintegration of the space shuttle *Columbia* (2003); the hearings on the Iraq war (2007); or the hearings into taxpayer-funded bonuses for Wall Street executives (2009). The mere threat of a congressional hearing is often enough to keep agencies in line. But Congress's investigative authority is not without limits. Earl Warren, when he was chief justice of the U.S. Supreme Court, wrote in the aforementioned *Watkins v. United States* (1957):

> There is no general authority to expose private affairs of individuals without justification in terms of the functions of Congress. . . . Nor is the Congress a law enforcement or trial agency. These are functions of the executive and judicial departments of government. No inquiry is an end in itself; it must be related to, and in furtherance of, a legitimate task of the Congress.[80]

By collecting and analyzing information, House and Senate inquiries can clarify whether new laws are needed to address public problems. They also sharpen Congress's ability to scrutinize executive branch activities, such as the expenditure of funds, the implementation of laws, and the discharge of duties by administrative officials. Investigations inform the public by providing "a forum for disclosing the hidden aspects of governmental conduct," wrote two senators. It allows a "free people to drag realities out into the sunlight and demand a full accounting."[81] Hearings and investigations are, in short, valuable devices for making government accountable to the people. They can spawn new laws or their functional equivalent: change in bureaucratic operations.

Congressional Vetoes

Congress has little choice but to delegate sweeping authority to administrative agencies. The question, then, is how can Congress control those agencies? One answer historically has been the legislative veto (or congressional veto), a statutory enactment that permits presidents or agencies to take certain actions subject to later approval or disapproval by one or both houses of Congress (or in some cases by committees of one or both houses). Legislative vetoes are arrangements of convenience for both branches. Executives gain decision-making authority they otherwise might not have, and Congress retains a second chance to examine decisions.

In 1983 many forms of the legislative veto were declared unconstitutional by the Supreme Court (*Immigration and Naturalization Service v. Chadha*). The Court's majority held that the device violated the separation of powers, the principle of bicameralism, and the presentation clause of the Constitution (legislation passed by both chambers must be presented to the president for his signature or veto). The decision, wrote Justice Byron R. White in a vigorous dissent, "strikes down in one fell swoop provisions in more laws enacted by Congress than the court has cumulatively invalidated in its entire history."[82]

Congress has repealed some veto provisions since *Chadha* and amended others, while continuing to employ a wide range of oversight techniques to monitor executive actions. Yet despite the *Chadha* ruling, legislative vetoes of the committee variety continue to be enacted into law. Public law scholar Louis Fisher has summed up the status of legislative vetoes:

> Are they constitutional? Not by the Court's definition. Will that fact change the behavior between committees and agencies? Probably not. An agency might advise the committee: "As you know, the requirement in this statute for committee prior-approval is unconstitutional under the Court's test." Perhaps agency and committee staff will nod their heads in agreement. After which the agency will seek prior approval of the committee.[83]

Self-interest impels agencies to pay close attention to the wishes of members of Congress, especially those who sit on their authorizing or appropriating panels.

Mandatory Reports

Congress can require the president, federal agencies, or departments to assess programs and report their findings.[84] Reports can act "as a mechanism to check that laws are having the intended effect." Moreover, they can "drive a reluctant bureaucracy to comply with laws it would otherwise ignore."[85] Each year, executive agencies prepare several thousand reports for submission to Congress. Because of the massive size and important role of the Defense Department, it is not surprising that the Pentagon is tasked with preparing numerous reports for Congress. At a 2010 departmental briefing, Defense Secretary Robert Gates noted, "In 1970, the Pentagon produced a total of 37 reports for the Congress, a number that topped off at more than 700 reports in last year's cycle."[86] Trying to reduce the number of outdated or duplicative reports—which Congress does periodically—often comes with the requirement that agencies be more responsive to committees' requests for information. A spokesperson for the former chair of the House Armed Services Committee said his boss would be happy to work with the secretary of defense to eliminate various reporting requirements if the Pentagon would do "a better job of providing specific programmatic and policy information in a timely manner" to the committee.[87]

Nonstatutory Controls

Congressional committees also use informal means to review and influence administrative decisions. These range from telephone calls, letters, personal contacts, and informal understandings to statements in conference reports, hearings, and floor debates.[88] Committee reports frequently contain phrases such as "the committee clearly intends that the matter be reconsidered" or "the committee clearly intends for the Secretary to promote" or "the committee clearly expects."

On occasion, OMB directors tell federal agencies to ignore report language because it is not legally binding. Lawmakers of both parties and chambers (and even executive officials), however, may seek to thwart such directives. Sometimes, members threaten to make all report language legally binding on agencies, thereby limiting the agencies' flexibility and discretion in resolving issues.[89] Although their usage is not measured, nonstatutory controls may be the most common form of congressional oversight.

Inspectors General

In 1978 Congress created a dozen independent offices for inspectors general (IGs). Since then, Congress has established inspectors general offices in nearly every federal department and agency. IGs conduct audits and investigations of agency programs and operations; prevent and detect fraud and abuse in such programs and operations; and keep Congress and agency heads fully informed on a timely basis about problems and the need for corrective actions. Granted wide latitude and independence, IGs are "the government's first line of defense against fraud."[90]

Inspectors general testify frequently before congressional committees and submit directly to Congress reports on their efforts to root out waste, fraud, and abuse. For example, the Labor Department IG determined that a departmental initiative to improve worker safety in hazardous industries "rarely fulfilled its promise" because of uneven inspections and enforcement. The result was fifty-eight fatalities that might have been prevented.[91] The Pentagon's IG detailed billions of dollars in waste and fraud by military contractors.[92]

The Appropriations Process

Congress probably exercises its most potent oversight of agencies and programs through the appropriations process. By cutting off or reducing funds (or threatening to do so), Congress can abolish agencies, curtail programs, or obtain requested information. Upset that the secretary of the Department of Housing and Urban Development (HUD) was flying off to various conferences rather than dealing with the housing foreclosure crisis, appropriators eliminated the secretary's travel budget. "Frankly, I want to cause [HUD] officials a little personal pain," declared one legislator. He said he wanted them to "just plant their butts at their desks and do the job that they were appointed to do."[93] In another case, a House Appropriations subcommittee chair, angry because the Homeland Security Department had not provided reports on its spending priorities, declared, "They've just been ignoring us. They'll pay for that."[94] The chair of the House Appropriations Committee, Hal Rogers, R-Ky., bluntly stated that there will be consequences if agencies are not responsive to information requested by Congress. "When you request information from an agency it's not a friendly, nice, convenient thing," he declaimed. "It's a demand for information that's required to do your work in allocating federal dollars."[95] By the same token, Congress can build up program areas by increasing its appropriations—sometimes beyond the levels that the administration has requested.

The appropriations power is exercised mainly through the House and Senate Appropriations Committees, especially through each panel's twelve standing subcommittees. These panels annually recommend funding levels for federal agencies and departments so that they can carry out their program responsibilities. The budgetary recommendations of the Appropriations subcommittees are generally accepted by their parent committee and by the House or Senate.

The Appropriations Committees and their subcommittees, or members from the House or Senate floor, may offer amendments that limit the purposes for which money may be spent ("limitation riders") or that impose other spending limits on federal agencies. Funding bills also may contain various policy directives to federal agencies—for example, prohibiting agencies from using funds to promulgate or issue certain regulations. Such directives are often in the form of floor amendments. "These amendments," wrote two GOP senators, "are an important way for Congress to save taxpayers from wasteful agency spending, and they enjoy a long-standing precedent because of their use by Republican and Democratic Congresses alike to rein in the excesses of Republican and Democratic administrations."[96] Today, limitation amendments are a key component of the GOP strategy to dismantle the Affordable Care Act. Political scientist Jason A. McDonald has underscored the legislative importance of limitation amendments in influencing agency actions. They provide "Congress with much more influence than scholars have appreciated over not only everyday policy decisions within agencies . . . but also over the substance of regulations about which members of Congress, and their constituencies, care for political and policy reasons."[97]

Impeachment

Article II, section 4, of the Constitution states: "The President, Vice President, and all Civil Officers of the United States, shall be removed from office on Impeachment for, and Conviction of, Treason, Bribery, or other high Crimes and misdemeanors." This removal power is the ultimate governmental check vested in Congress.[98] The House has the authority to impeach an official by majority vote. It then tries the case before the Senate, where a two-thirds vote is required for conviction.

Only impeached federal judges have been convicted by the Senate. The most recent case occurred on December 8, 2010, when the Senate voted for only the eighth time to convict and remove a federal district judge.[99] As for presidents, the House impeached President Andrew Johnson in 1868, after Radical Republicans in the House charged that he had violated the Tenure of Office Act by dismissing the secretary of war. The Senate acquitted Johnson by a single vote. Facing probable impeachment and conviction, President Richard M. Nixon resigned in 1974 after the House Judiciary Committee voted articles of impeachment. In December 1998, President Clinton became the first elected president to be impeached by the House. (Johnson was not elected; he became president when Abraham Lincoln was assassinated.) The charges against Clinton were perjury and obstruction of justice. Two months later, the Senate voted acquittal on both articles of impeachment.[100] The lack of impeachment cases against presidential appointees likely reflects the effectiveness of political mechanisms for holding them accountable. Numerous lower-level federal officials have been pressured to resign amid scandals—or have been directly fired by the president.

Oversight: An Evaluation

Congress's willingness to conduct regular and meaningful oversight stems from several factors: public dissatisfaction with government; revelations of executive agency abuses; the influx of new legislators skeptical of government's ability to perform effectively; concern about the growth of a regulatory state; the availability of seasoned congressional staff; and recognition by Congress that it must make every dollar count.[101]

Two factors stand out as especially important motivators of oversight since Republicans won control of the 112th House in the November 2010 elections and the Senate four years later. First, top GOP leaders have made cutting agencies and programs a major priority. For example, House Majority Leader Kevin McCarthy, Calif., stressed in a memo to House Republicans the importance of "reforming and streamlining federal agencies so government works as it should." He added that the "government's role in our lives must be measured, limited in its ambitions, constitutionally based, and focused on the big things that only governments can address."[102] The second major factor prompting oversight is simply that many in the populace want to rein in the reach of the federal government.

The perspective of the two Congresses highlights the electoral, political, and policy incentives that encourage members to oversee the bureaucracy. One of these incentives is the opportunity to claim credit for assisting constituents and to receive favorable publicity back home. Another is the prodding by interest groups and the media. Committee and subcommittee chairs "seek a high pay off—in attention from both the press and other agencies—when selecting federal programs to be their oversight targets."[103] Members on the relevant committees of jurisdiction are also motivated to induce favorable agency and departmental action on pet policies or programs.

Divided government—the president of one party, Congress (or one chamber) controlled by the other—encourages vigorous congressional oversight. Oversight simultaneously enables majority party lawmakers in Congress to monitor closely agency activities and look for ways to undermine the administration's policy goals or public reputation. Simply responding to scores of subpoenas issued by committees controlled by the opposition party can sap the time and energy of the White House and agency officials. By comparison, under unified government, the majority party in Congress tends to engage in less oversight. As one senior GOP lawmaker said of the unified period (2003–2007) when Republicans were in charge of the elective branches, "Our party controls the levers of government. We're not about to go out and look beneath a bunch of rocks to cause heartburn."[104] Party loyalty, in short, overcame institutional responsibility.

Whether there is unified or divided government, congressional oversight may not probe as deeply as some might wish. "We have not done our job in terms of oversight," declared Sen. Tom Coburn, R-Okla.[105] Friendly alliances can develop among the committees that authorize programs, the agencies that administer them, and the interest groups that benefit from governmental services. Many committees are biased toward the programs or agencies they oversee. They want to protect and nurture their progeny and make program administration look good. This kind of cooperative relationship can dissuade committees from conducting meaningful inquiries that require agencies to justify their existence and contribution to the public's well-being. Without concrete allegations of fraud or mismanagement, committees may lack the incentive to scrutinize and reevaluate their programs.

A standard rationale for oversight is that it ensures that laws are carried out according to congressional intent. But because many laws are vague and replete with multiple objectives, they are difficult to assess. Moreover, proof that programs are working as intended may not emerge for years. Congressional patience may wane as critics conclude that there are no demonstrable payoffs for the taxpayer. Alternatively, oversight may identify program flaws but not reveal what would work or even whether there is any ready solution. To address these issues requires sustained efforts by congressional committees to determine if programs are working effectively, efficiently, and economically. A key oversight objective is to link program performance to the funding decisions of the House and Senate. Thus the House and Senate employ an array of oversight techniques to evaluate federal programs.

Each oversight technique has limitations. Hearings may provide dramatic episodes, but they often result in minimal follow-up. The appropriations process is usually hemmed in by programmatic needs for financial stability. And statutes are often blunt instruments of control. Other obstacles to effective oversight include inadequate coordination among committees sharing jurisdiction over a program; sporadic review by committees of departmental activities; and frequent turnover among committee staff aides, a situation that limits their understanding of the programs created by Congress.

Critics who fault Congress's oversight may be erecting unattainable standards. Many analysts are looking for what scholars have come to call "police-patrol" oversight—active, direct, systematic, planned surveillance of executive activities. Instead, Congress often waits until the "fire alarms" sound—set off by interest groups, the press, staff aides, and others concerned about administrative violations—before it begins to review in detail agencies' activities.[106]

Congress may be benefitting from some extra police-patrol assistance offered by a combination of individual lawmakers, civic-minded individuals, and technology. A current trend is the "public as watchdog." A good example is the enactment in 2006 of the Federal Funding Accountability and Transparency Act, informally called the "Google your government" law because it required OMB "to provide a user-friendly, searchable database" of nearly $1 trillion in federal grants and contracts.[107] Government websites such as USASpending.gov allow citizens to monitor the projects that receive taxpayer dollars. The GAO has a website and hotline to enable citizens to report allegations of waste, fraud, or mismanagement of federal funds. A House chair established a whistleblower website where agency employees could alert committee staff of fraud and abuse in their agency. A House party leader's website contained a feature dubbed YouCut that allowed the public to vote on "which government programs should be cut."[108]

GOP senator Coburn of Oklahoma, who retired at the end of the 113th Congress for health reasons after a decade of Senate service, made oversight a major priority. He was a one-person fiscal watchdog. Annually, he issued a volume called "Wastebook" that listed tens of billions of dollars that he considered wasteful spending by federal agencies. As a former official in both the Clinton and Obama administrations said of Senator Coburn's investigative work: "Washington is full of politicians who love to talk about waste. Coburn sends his teams to go find it and name names, and that makes all the difference."[109]

There are even informal "citizen regulators" who test children's toys and clothing to protect them from harmful chemicals. "I'm not going to rely on an agency that changes personnel based on administrations and takes years to make any kind of change," remarked the mother of a three-year-old.[110] The promise of these actions is that they enable any interested person or watchdog group to monitor federal spending or products available in stores across the nation and make their evaluations known to congressional lawmakers. Evolving communications technologies, in short, add millions of extra eyes to congressional oversight.

Micromanagement

Because oversight often means legislative intrusion into administrative details, executive branch officials sometimes complain about congressional micromanagement. Even though the executive bureaucracy may react with dismay, Congress's focus on administrative details is as old as the institution itself. The structural fragmentation of the House and Senate encourages examination of manageable chunks of executive actions. Members realize that power inheres in details, such as prescribing personnel ceilings for agencies. "It is one of the anomalies of constitutional law and separated powers," writes Louis Fisher, "that executive involvement in legislative affairs is considered acceptable (indeed highly desirable) while legislative involvement in executive affairs screams of encroachment and usurpation."[111]

CONCLUSION

Because of continual shifts in the balance of legislative and executive prerogatives, the age-old issue of executive independence versus congressional scrutiny will not be settled. Yet the recent interest in oversight has had limited discernible effect on the size and scale of the executive branch or on the main roles and responsibilities of the legislative branch. After all, committees are not disinterested overseers; rather, they are guardians of the agencies and programs under their purview. Together with their satellite interest groups, committees and agencies form subgovernments or issue networks that dominate many policy-making areas.

Court Politics. Solicitor General Elena Kagan begins the third day of Senate Judiciary Committee hearings on her nomination to the Supreme Court. Rep. Louie Gohmert, R-Tex., speaks at a rally outside the Supreme Court in March 2015 as the justices were hearing arguments in *King v. Burwell,* an important case challenging the Obama administration's implementation of the Affordable Care Act. Supporters of the Affordable Care Act celebrate outside the Supreme Court in 2012, after a divided Court upheld the law.

Congress and the Courts

"Scarcely any political question arises in the United States that is not resolved, sooner or later, into a judicial one," wrote Alexis de Tocqueville in *Democracy in America,* his classic 1835 study of early American life.[1] No recent controversy has illustrated Tocqueville's truism so perfectly as the events following passage of the Patient Protection and Affordable Care Act of 2010 ("Obamacare"). Obamacare was quickly challenged as unconstitutional in courts across the country. The lower courts split—some upholding it, others agreeing with the opponents of the law.

The Supreme Court heard extended arguments on multiple challenges to Obamacare. Following the oral arguments in the first case to reach the high court—*National Federation of Independent Business v. Sebelius*[2]—commentators wrote innumerable analyses speculating about how the case would be resolved. On the fateful day (June 28, 2012) when the justices handed down their decision, hundreds of demonstrators gathered outside the Supreme Court building in a circus-like atmosphere that included Tea Party activists, dueling chants and signs, and even a trio of belly dancers gyrating in Obamacare's favor. In the end, the Court, in a rather convoluted fashion, upheld the most controversial aspect of Obamacare, the individual mandate to purchase health insurance. But the complexity of the Court's ruling caused CNN initially to report that Obamacare had been struck down, leading its opponents gathered outside to cheer. Those cheers quickly turned to groans and angry words as the actual nature of the Court's 5–4 decision to uphold the individual mandate became clear.

The ruling in *NFIB v. Sebelius* was not the last word on the "political questions" posed by Obamacare. A second challenge to the law—based on the statute's language rather than its constitutionality—subsequently made its way to the high court. The plaintiffs in *King v. Burwell*[3] argue that, given the plain language of Obamacare, the tax credits to assist low-income persons in buying health insurance should not be available in the states that did not set up their own health insurance exchanges. Because thirty-six states declined to set up their own exchanges, a Supreme Court holding in favor of the plaintiffs in this case would likely cripple Obamacare. The Supreme Court announced that it would hear the case in November 2014. A decision should be announced before the end of the Court's term in July 2015.

As in the first Obamacare case, the Supreme Court is typically viewed as having the final, authoritative interpretation of the Constitution—a power referred to as "judicial review." The U.S. Supreme Court first asserted the prerogative of judicial review in the landmark case of *Marbury v. Madison* (1803).[4] However, both Congress and the president interpret the Constitution, as well. As the Supreme Court stated in *United States v. Nixon* (1974), "In the performance of assigned constitutional duties each branch of the Government must initially interpret the Constitution, and the interpretation of its powers by any branch is due great respect from the others."[5]

Conflicts between Congress and the federal courts are inevitable. The most famous episode occurred during the New Deal when the Supreme Court invalidated thirteen acts of Congress in one term (1935–1936). Frustrated, President Franklin D. Roosevelt proposed legislation to increase the number of justices, and thus to provide him the opportunity to nominate judges more sympathetic to his program. Widespread legislative and public opposition, however, defeated Roosevelt's Court-packing scheme. Nevertheless, the Court, perhaps sensitive to the changes under way in the country, became more accommodating in interpreting key constitutional provisions. In 1937 the Court handed down a decision that upheld a state minimum wage law similar to one that it had previously ruled unconstitutional.[6] In that same year, the Court also upheld a federal law governing management–labor relations, recognizing a far greater congressional power to regulate commerce than the Court's precedents had permitted. This abrupt turnaround by the Court was, as a wit of the period put it, "the switch in time that saved nine."

THE FEDERAL COURTS

In contrast to the Constitution's detailed provisions specifying the structure and authority of Congress, Article III leaves the creation of the federal courts other than the Supreme Court wholly to the discretion of Congress. Thus the judicial branch owes less to constitutional mandates and more to the legislation establishing its structure and the rulings of the early justices, such as Chief Justice John Marshall (1801–1835). As a noted legal scholar explained:

> Congress was created nearly full blown by the Constitution itself. The vast possibilities of the presidency were relatively easy to perceive and soon, inevitably materialized. But the institution of the judiciary needed to be summoned up out of the constitutional vapors, shaped and maintained. And the Great Chief Justice, John Marshall—not single-handed, but first and foremost—was there to do it and did.[7]

The most important constitutional provision related to the courts is the guarantee of lifetime tenure for Article III judges. The framers of the Constitution wanted an independent judiciary—that is, a judiciary insulated from political pressure. This independence is an important part of the American system of separation of powers and a source of friction between Congress and the courts. Although Congress is not without influence, the federal courts, including the Supreme Court, have the institutional ability to frustrate congressional policy.

The federal court system today is comprised of district courts, courts of appeals, and the Supreme Court. The district courts are the federal trial courts, which deal with a range of civil matters and federal criminal cases. In addition to Article III district judges, the district courts are staffed by magistrate judges, who serve a fixed term and assist the district judges in handling the civil and criminal caseloads. The district courts also house the federal bankruptcy courts, which are staffed by specialized judges serving a fixed term.

District courts are analogous to congressional committees in the sense that most of the work of the federal courts is done at that level. District courts are organized by state, in a manner similar to congressional districts. Each state, and the District of Columbia, has at least one, with larger states (such as Texas and California) having as many as four. The primary function of the district courts is "norm enforcement"—that is, applying relatively settled law to disputes.

Above the district courts are the courts of appeals, which are organized in eleven regional circuits. There is also a circuit for the District of Columbia, and one additional circuit, the Federal Circuit, with a nationwide but specialized jurisdiction centering mainly on appeals of administrative agency rulings and patent cases. Parties unhappy with the outcome of a case at the district court level typically have an automatic right of appeal to the appellate level. These courts are staffed by judges typically called circuit judges. The courts of appeals hear oral arguments and decide cases in three-judge panels. In rare circumstances, a three-judge panel's decision will be reviewed by a larger number of circuit judges, sitting "en banc." The primary function of the courts of appeals is "error correction"—that is, reviewing the work of lower courts, and some executive branch agencies, for mistakes of law or fact.

Parties unhappy with the outcome of an appeal can seek Supreme Court review of their cases, but unlike at the court of appeals level, Supreme Court review is almost never automatic. Instead, the Court decides which cases from the courts of appeals and the state courts of last resort it will hear. Typically, the Supreme Court will hear and decide about 1 percent of the cases in which one or both parties have requested review. As a result, the Court's docket is dominated by cases raising important questions of constitutional and statutory interpretation. Unlike the lower federal courts, the Supreme Court does not engage in norm enforcement, and it rarely takes a case for the sole purpose of correcting an error committed by a lower court. Instead, its policy-making role is paramount.

The Supreme Court's policy making is carried out in two main ways. First, its interpretive decisions can broaden or restrict the legislative powers of Congress. The ruling upholding Obamacare, for example, was a significant victory for President Barack Obama and his congressional allies. In deciding that Congress's powers extended far enough to mandate that all Americans purchase health insurance, the Court established what is arguably a new "outer limit" for Congress's power over interstate commerce. Five justices agreed that Congress could not impose the individual mandate using its "commerce clause" power because those being regulated were not, in a practical sense, engaged in economic activity when not buying health insurance. However, five justices (with only Chief Justice John Roberts in both majorities) agreed that Congress could achieve the same result using its taxation power—indeed, the penalty for failing to purchase health insurance is to be administered by the Internal Revenue Service.[8] By the same token, the Supreme Court can check overreaching by Congress through its implied power of judicial review. Checking Congress was, naturally, the role that opponents of Obamacare argued the Court should play.

Second, and equally significant, the Supreme Court can act as a policy-making catalyst, especially when the House or Senate is stymied in making decisions. The landmark civil rights case of *Brown v. Board of Education* (1954) is a classic example. The decision struck down the separate-but-equal doctrine that had upheld state laws mandating racially segregated public schools. Before this decision, filibusters by southern senators had thwarted enactment of meaningful civil rights bills. The *Brown* ruling galvanized Congress to enact the Civil Rights Act of 1957, the first civil rights law since 1875. "The genius of a system of divided powers," wrote one law professor, "is that when one branch is closed to the desires of the populace or the demands of justice, another may open up."[9] Even so, the *Brown* decision alone had little impact on the actual desegregation of public schools until Congress began to pass landmark legislation such as the Civil Rights Act of 1964 and the Elementary and Secondary Education Act of 1965.

THE COURT AS REFEREE AND UMPIRE

The Supreme Court polices both the separation of powers between the two nationally elective branches and the allocation of powers between the states and the national government. Ever since the Court claimed the power of judicial review in 1803, it has considered a large number of separation-of-powers and federalism issues. In both roles, the Supreme Court is often attacked for usurping the prerogatives of the other national branches, or of the state and local governments. Members of Congress "often reserve their most vituperative criticism of federal courts for decisions that, in their view, unduly limit the prerogatives of state and local governments to regulate such matters as abortion, school prayer, prison overcrowding, school busing, local elections, and so on."[10]

A common refrain in criticism of the courts is that judges are acting as a "super legislature" in their rulings—that is, they are legislating from the bench. The charge of "judicial activism" is premised on the view that at least in some cases, judges are making decisions based on their personal values and not the dictates of law, or that they are making decisions that their critics believe should be settled by the elective branches of government.

Judicial activism, however, is frequently in the eye of the beholder. When, for example, the Supreme Court ruled 5–4 in *District of Columbia v. Heller*[11] that the Second Amendment protects an individual's right to own firearms— thereby overturning long-standing law in the District and, by implication, elsewhere—relatively few conservative commentators charged the Court with judicial activism. Many liberals, by contrast, saw the *Heller* case as a clear example of conservative judicial activism.[12] On the other hand, when the Supreme Court ruled, also 5–4, in *Kelo v. City of New London* that the power of eminent domain could be used to condemn a private residence to promote local economic development, liberals praised the Court's judicial restraint in permitting democratically accountable local governments to make such decisions free from judicial second-guessing.[13] Meanwhile, conservatives denounced the case as "liberal activism."[14] The charge of judicial activism often serves as a way of denouncing judicial decisions that politicians and opinion leaders oppose on other grounds.

In the broader context of partisan and ideological polarization, the judiciary has come in for harsh attacks from many quarters. Retired Supreme Court justice Sandra Day O'Connor commented that "the breadth and intensity of rage currently being leveled at the judiciary may be unmatched in American history. The ubiquitous 'activist judges' who 'legislate from the bench' have become central villains on today's domestic political landscape."[15]

Separation of Powers

Like the federal courts, Congress interprets the Constitution. When it makes national policy through its lawmaking processes, it is also asserting that it has the constitutional power to do so. As a result, it is not uncommon for the two branches to view issues differently. The Court sometimes frustrates congressional or executive policy, which can, in some cases, trigger a reaction.

The Lily Ledbetter case (2007) illustrates how congressional majorities may react to Supreme Court decisions with which they strongly disagree. Ledbetter received less pay than her male counterparts at Goodyear. After twenty years on the job, she learned of Goodyear's discriminatory treatment and sued on the grounds of gender-based pay and employment discrimination. The Supreme Court determined, however, that the statute of limitations in Title VII of the Civil Rights Act had expired and precluded Ledbetter's suit. The Court ruled, in a 5–4 decision, that Ledbetter's lawsuit was not timely because she did not file the suit within 180 days of the date on which the lower pay had been agreed to by the parties. The Court rejected the argument that the statute of limitations restarted with every discriminatory paycheck. A vigorous dissent by Justice Ruth Bader Ginsburg chided the Court's majority for their ignorance of workplace realities and noted that Congress could clarify the law.

Many lawmakers rejected the Court's interpretation of legislative intent in the *Ledbetter* decision. As one of its first actions, the 111th Congress (2009–2011) passed legislation, which President Obama signed into law, overturning *Ledbetter* and resetting the statute of limitations with every discriminatory paycheck, thereby making it easier for workers to challenge gender-based employment discrimination.[16]

Mindful of the courts' role in separation of powers, lawmakers have sought to employ it in their own conflicts with presidents. On a number of occasions, members of Congress have tried to enlist the courts to defend congressional prerogatives against the executive branch. Most recently, in November 2014, the House GOP filed a lawsuit in district court in Washington, D.C., challenging a number of President Obama's unilateral actions regarding the implementation of Obamacare.[17] But war-making offers the principal example. Recent presidents of both parties have committed American troops to combat on their own initiative. In response, members have gone to court to seek limits on the president's powers. As for war power suits brought by lawmakers, scholar Louis Fisher takes a cautionary view:

> In most of these cases, the courts held that the lawmakers lacked standing to bring the case. Even when legislators were granted standing, the courts refused relief on numerous grounds. Judges pointed out that the legislators represented only a fraction of the congressional membership and that often another group of legislators had filed a brief defending the president's action. Courts regularly note that Congress as a whole has failed to invoke its institutional powers to confront the president.[18]

Usually courts dismiss these suits and offer two rationales: first, the lawsuits raise political questions best left to the elective branches to resolve; and second, they represent conflicts between groups of lawmakers, not constitutional clashes between Congress and the president.

The fundamental question is how much deference the Court should show to the elected branches. Lawmakers and presidents are accountable to their constituents every time they face reelection. Although judges are not immune to the tides of public opinion, they do not face accountability through elections. On the other hand, a key virtue of an independent judiciary is that it can, in theory, protect unpopular or politically weak minority groups against unconstitutional deprivations of liberty. The tension between policy making by elected officials versus judge-made decisions is perennial.

Federalism

When there is a dispute, the Supreme Court is the ultimate arbiter of federal and state powers. This role was also front and center in the Supreme Court battle over Obamacare. One controversial aspect of the law was its expansion of the state mandates under the federal Medicaid program. Medicaid is a health insurance program for low-income Americans. The federal government provides funding to states to establish their own Medicaid programs, provided that the states comply with federal rules that create minimum standards for who and what is covered by the (state) program. States thus have a choice to participate in the Medicaid program or not, in keeping with their residual sovereignty. Medicaid funding has become an important part of many state budgets, and by the 1980s, all fifty states participated in the program. From time to time, however, state governors complain that the regulations imposed as a condition of receiving Medicaid funding are onerous on the states.

The Obamacare legislation imposed new Medicaid guidelines on the states to expand health insurance coverage to the uninsured poor not previously covered by existing Medicaid guidelines. To encourage all states to adopt these new guidelines, the legislation included a provision that states rejecting the new Medicaid coverage requirements would lose not only the expansion of Medicaid dollars, but also the support they currently received for their Medicaid programs. Several states argued this was federal coercion—that is, because Medicaid has become such an important part of state budgets, a threat to deprive states of all Medicaid revenue would leave the states with no choice at all but to accept the new expansion of the program.

As with the individual mandate, the Court decided this issue in a rather convoluted manner. Indeed, seven justices agreed that the conditions attached to the Medicaid expansion were unconstitutional, but they split in terms of the remedy. The two justices who would have upheld the conditions in their entirety joined with three justices who rejected the new mandate to hold that states declining to expand Medicaid under Obamacare could maintain their existing Medicaid funding as long as they complied with the applicable federal guidelines for that funding. In the end, the ruling permitted states to choose whether or not to expand their Medicaid rolls to cover those newly qualified under Obamacare without losing all federal support for their existing Medicaid program.[19] In this case, as in many others, the Court regulates the balance between federal and state power.

Statutory Interpretation

The distinction between statutory and constitutional interpretation is very important. In statutory interpretation, federal judges construe the meaning, or intent, of the often vague language embedded in laws. Constitutional interpretation occurs when federal or state laws are challenged as violating the U.S. Constitution.

Carr v. United States provides an example of the Court engaging in statutory interpretation. In 2006 Congress enacted the Sex Offender Registration and Notification Act (SORNA), which, among other things, made it a federal crime for sex offenders who travel "in interstate or foreign commerce" to fail to register in a new jurisdiction. The defendant in the case had moved from Alabama, where he was a registered sex offender, to Indiana prior to SORNA's enactment. The lower court, however, held that SORNA's registration requirement was retroactive. The Court, in an opinion by Justice Sonia Sotomayor, disagreed, holding that the text of the statute showed that Congress did not intend the "travels in" provision to have retroactive effect. That the provision "sets forth the travel requirement in the present tense ('travels') rather than in the past or present perfect ('traveled' or 'has traveled') reinforces the conclusion that preenactment travel falls outside the statute's compass," she wrote.[20] In short, statutory interpretation in this case and in others requires the Court to construe what is and is not covered by laws passed by Congress.

The major difference between statutory and constitutional interpretation is the relative ease with which Congress can reassert its understanding of the law against the Supreme Court. When the Court misinterprets a statute, Congress can amend or clarify the law, as it did in the *Ledbetter* case. By contrast, a constitutional decision of the Court is binding on Congress and can be undone only by a subsequent constitutional amendment—which is very rare—or by the Court itself when it overrules one of its precedents.

Judicial interpretation of federal statutes is fraught with difficulty because communications between Congress and the federal courts are highly imperfect. Neither branch understands the workings of the other very well.[21] Ambiguity, imprecision, or inconsistency can often be the price of winning enactment of legislative measures. The more legislators try to define precisely the language of a bill, the more they may divide or dissipate congressional support for it. Abner J. Mikva, a four-term House Democrat from Chicago who went on to become a federal judge and later counsel to President Bill Clinton, recounted an example from his Capitol Hill days. The issue involved a controversial strip-mining bill being managed by Arizona Democrat Morris K. Udall, then chair of the House Interior (now called Natural Resources) Committee:

> They'd put together a very delicate coalition of support. One problem was whether the states or the feds would run the program. One member got up and asked, "Isn't it a fact that under this bill the states would continue to exercise sovereignty over strip mining?" And Mo replied, "You're absolutely right." A little later someone else got up and asked, "Now is it clear that the Federal Government will have the final say on strip mining?" And Mo replied, "You're absolutely right." Later, in the cloakroom, I said, "Mo, they can't both be right." And Mo said, "You're absolutely right."[22]

Called upon to interpret statutes, judges may not appreciate the efforts required to get legislation passed on Capitol Hill or understand how to examine legislative history, as manifested in hearings, reports, and floor debate. Within the courts and among legal scholars, there is a lively debate over the proper way to approach statutory interpretation. Should judges focus only on the plain meaning of the statutory language, or should they delve into legislative history to ascertain what Congress intended when it employed certain statutory phrases? A group of federal judges, led by Supreme Court justice Antonin Scalia, argues that legislative history is unreliable as an indicator of legislative intent because it is open to manipulation by lawmakers, executive officials, and congressional staffers.

One remarkable example of the manipulation of legislative history occurred in the context of the Senate passage of the Detainee Treatment Act (DTA) in late 2005. An important issue before the federal courts at the time was whether the DTA would retroactively nullify all the pending legal challenges of the Guantánamo detainees. Two sponsors of the legislation, Sen. Lindsey O. Graham, R-S.C., and Sen. Jon Kyl, R-Ariz., sought to quash all such challenges, while another sponsor, Sen. Carl Levin, D-Mich., wanted to allow cases filed before the passage of the DTA to go forward.[23] But just before passage of the legislation, Graham and Kyl inserted into the *Congressional Record* a colloquy designed to show that the Senate intended to invalidate all pending legal challenges brought by Guantánamo detainees. Written in informal style, the colloquy contained banter suggesting that the exchange occurred live on the Senate floor. Such a colloquy would have alerted all senators that Graham and Kyl believed the legislation would foreclose all pending cases, and the absence of subsequent objections would imply that senators agreed with this interpretation. However, a C-SPAN recording showed that the discussion never actually occurred on the Senate floor. Justice Department lawyers nevertheless cited the colloquy in their legal brief arguing that Congress intended to remove all the pending cases from federal jurisdiction.[24] In response, a lawyer for one of the detainees objected: "This colloquy is critical to the government's legislative history argument, and it's entirely manufactured and misrepresented to the court as having occurred live on the Senate floor before a crucial vote."[25]

Rather than relying on legislative history, Scalia contends that justices should follow a textualist approach, examining the wording of laws or constitutional clauses and interpreting them according to what they meant at the time of enactment.[26] Justice John Paul Stevens took a contrary view, saying that a "stubborn insistence on 'clear statements' [in the law] burdens the Congress with unnecessary reenactment of provisions that were already plain enough." Former representative Barney Frank, D-Mass., once remarked that if Scalia's view on legislative history became dominant, Congress would be required to develop a new category of legislation: "the 'No, we really meant it' statute."[27] The chief counsel of the Senate Judiciary Committee observed that difficulty in textual interpretation "encourages us to write clearer legislation. But unclear bills are still written. If they were not, we would not have this fight over [the confirmation of] judges."[28]

King v. Burwell,[29] which the Court will likely decide in 2015, highlights how these differing approaches to statutory interpretation matter in terms of policy outcomes. The statutory scheme in Obamacare providing for tax credits to assist the purchase of health insurance assumed, to some extent, that states would set up their own insurance "exchanges," which are online marketplaces where people can select among a variety of health insurance plans. But the law also provided for a federal exchange in the event that states declined to set up their own. Due to political opposition to the law, a large majority of states declined to establish their own exchanges. The challenge to these subsidies focuses on the section that authorizes the Internal Revenue Service (IRS) to provide tax credits for exchanges "established by the State under 1311." The challengers argue that, given the plain meaning of this phrase, a "State" cannot be the federal government. Thus the IRS regulations providing tax credits for insurance purchased on both state and federal exchanges go beyond what the statute permits. Obamacare's defenders at first found this challenge hard to fathom. After all, the failure to provide for subsidies in states not establishing their own exchanges would frustrate Congress's intent in enacting the law, i.e., in providing all Americans with access to affordable health insurance. A major tenet of statutory interpretation is that the language of a statute should not be read in isolation from the overall purpose of the law. And there can be no doubt that a Supreme Court decision limiting the subsidies to the fourteen states that established their own exchanges would frustrate the 111th Congress's policy goals in enacting Obamacare. Whatever the outcome of the case, the ambiguous language adopted by the Obamacare Congress paved the way for this statutory interpretation challenge.

Legislative Checks on the Judiciary

Many factors are likely to generate conflict between Congress and the courts. With federal judges serving life tenure, turnover on the courts is often far slower than in Congress. Meanwhile, the ideological and partisan composition of Congress can diverge widely from that of the federal courts. In addition, some Supreme Court rulings have direct and profound effects on Congress and its members. Cases involving the redistricting of House seats and campaign finance are recent examples. Scores of interest groups also monitor court decisions, and, when they disagree with them, these groups are not reluctant to lobby Congress to seek their statutory reversal.

Congress has a variety of tools by which it can influence the Supreme Court and lower federal courts. In addition to the Senate's constitutional advice and consent role regarding judicial nominations, four legislative powers merit some mention: (1) to withdraw jurisdiction; (2) to impeach judges; (3) to influence the size, procedures, and pay scales of the courts; and (4) to pass constitutional amendments.

Withdrawal of Jurisdiction. The jurisdiction of the federal courts, including the Supreme Court, is delimited by both Article III and statute. Congress can thus alter the jurisdiction of the federal courts to achieve policy goals.

In some circumstances, Congress may seek to expand federal court jurisdiction—usually at the expense of state courts—to achieve particular policy goals. In the post–Civil War period, for example, Congress expanded federal court jurisdiction in an effort to protect the civil rights of African Americans.[30] Republican Congresses in the latter half of the nineteenth century also expanded federal court jurisdiction in order to protect commercial interests against state controls.[31] Similarly, the Class Action Fairness Act of

2005 expanded federal jurisdiction over many large class-action lawsuits, a key goal of business groups that had been frustrated by plaintiff lawyers' "forum shopping" to find the most friendly state courts.

But Congress's power over the jurisdiction of the federal courts also serves as a potential check on judicial overreach. Under its constitutional authority to determine the Supreme Court's appellate jurisdiction, for example, Congress may threaten to withdraw the Court's authority to review certain categories of cases. For example, one such controversy concerned a Ninth Circuit Court of Appeals decision that a 1954 federal law adding the phrase "one Nation under God" to the Pledge of Allegiance was unconstitutional on First Amendment grounds. In response, House majority leader Tom DeLay, R-Tex., remarked, "I think that [legislation limiting the court's jurisdiction] would be a very good idea to send a message to the judiciary [that] they ought to keep their hands off the Pledge of Allegiance."[32] Other topics—such as same-sex marriage and the public display of the Ten Commandments—evoked similar responses in Congress. Some scholars have argued that such threats of court-curbing legislation affect judicial decision making. One recent study found that the Supreme Court responds to the introduction of court-curbing legislation by striking down fewer laws in subsequent years.[33] Despite the ongoing conflicts between Congress and the courts, on only one occasion in U.S. history did Congress prevent the Supreme Court from deciding a case by removing its appellate jurisdiction:

> This extraordinary action was taken by a Congress dominated by Radical Republicans who wanted to prohibit the Supreme Court from reviewing the constitutionality of the Reconstruction Acts of 1867. The acts substituted military rule for civilian government in the ten southern states that initially refused to rejoin the Union and established procedures for those states to follow to gain readmittance and representation in the federal government.[34]

Congress simply passed legislation repealing the Supreme Court's right to hear appeals involving these matters, thereby preventing "a possibly hostile Court from using the power of judicial review to invalidate a piece of legislation."[35] Various scholars have identified a variety of reasons why court-curbing legislation is so rarely adopted: "the historically broad consensus in Congress to protect, or at least tolerate, an independent judiciary; judicial opponents' reluctance to emasculate an institution that they may someday need as an ally; . . . and resistance by the organized bar."[36]

Impeachment of Judges. Federal judges, like other national civil officers, are subject to impeachment under Article II of the Constitution. They are appointed "during good behavior," effectively for life. Only one Supreme Court justice, Samuel Chase, has ever been impeached by the House. It occurred in 1804, during bitter partisan battles between Federalists and Jeffersonian Republicans. The judiciary was the last bastion of Federalist influence after

Thomas Jefferson won the presidency in the 1800 election. Chase's intemperate and arrogant behavior—he even campaigned for John Adams's reelection in 1800—raised the ire of Jefferson and his allies in Congress. On March 12, 1804, the House voted 73–32 along party lines to impeach Chase. The Senate, however, failed to convict (and thus remove) him. The importance of Chase's acquittal by the Senate was underscored in a book by Chief Justice William Rehnquist:

> The acquittal of Samuel Chase by the Senate had a profound effect on the American judiciary. First, it assured the independence of federal judges from congressional oversight of the decisions they made in the cases that come before them. Second, by assuring that impeachment would not be used in the future as a method to remove members of the Supreme Court for their judicial opinions, it helped to safeguard the independence of that body.[37]

Other Supreme Court justices have been either threatened with impeachment or subjected to impeachment investigations. One example is William O. Douglas in 1953 and in 1970.

Fifteen federal judges have been impeached, and eight have been removed by a two-thirds vote in the Senate.[38] The 111th Congress (2009–2011) saw active impeachment proceedings against two district judges. In May 2009, Judge Samuel B. Kent of the Southern District of Texas was convicted of obstruction of justice, resulting from an investigation of claims that he had sexually abused two female court staffers, and sentenced to prison. Nevertheless, he refused to resign from the bench, meaning that he continued to collect his judicial salary. His refusal to step down drew protests from Capitol Hill, and the House soon voted unanimously to impeach him. Kent then resigned, before the Senate could try him. In 2010 Judge Thomas Porteous Jr. of the Eastern District of Louisiana was impeached and removed from the bench based on charges of corruption and making false statements on his financial disclosure reports.

These recent examples of judicial impeachments are representative of such cases throughout U.S. history. Judges have been impeached for unethical and illegal acts, but not because of the legal and policy judgments rendered during the course of their judicial duties. The "Impeach Earl Warren" billboards and bumper stickers that appeared all across the South in the 1960s in the wake of *Brown v. Board of Education* do not represent how impeachment has been used. It is outside congressional norms to employ impeachment as a mechanism to exert political influence over the judiciary.

Size, Procedure, and Pay. Historically, the size of the Supreme Court has ranged from six to ten members. "Generally, laws decreasing the number of justices have been motivated by a desire to punish the president; increases have been aimed at influencing the philosophical balance of the Court itself" (such as Roosevelt's Court-packing plan).[39] But since 1869 Congress has not changed the Court's size from its current nine justices, so this power is unlikely to be invoked in the foreseeable future.

Procedurally, lawmakers have occasionally proposed that Supreme Court decisions overturning federal laws be accomplished by a supermajority vote of the justices.[40] None of these proposals has been adopted. Instead, they serve as signals to the judiciary that lawmakers disapprove of certain court decisions. Lawmakers have also communicated complaints to the judicial branch by calling for stronger ethical guidelines for judges to ensure their impartiality, though the judicial branch claims that such oversight would violate judicial independence.[41]

Another legislative proposal that has generated interbranch controversy is opening federal courtrooms to television cameras. Several justices have opposed televising Supreme Court proceedings, in part because the cameras might alter decision making, intrude on the privacy of the justices by making them public celebrities, and threaten their personal security. During an appearance before the Senate Judiciary Committee, Justice Anthony Kennedy implored senators not to pass legislation mandating the televising of their open proceedings.[42] His concern was that televised Court sessions would eventually undermine the collegial character of the Court and encourage the justices to speak in sound bites. Attitudes toward cameras in the courtroom may be changing, however. In her confirmation hearings, the Court's newest member, Elena Kagan, said that she thought "it would be a great thing for the institution and for the American people" to be able to watch Supreme Court arguments on television.[43] Justice Sotomayor has expressed similar views. The justices' individual and collective views may not carry the day in the 114th Congress, as incoming Senate Judiciary chair Sen. Charles Grassley, R-Iowa, is a major proponent of televising Supreme Court arguments. One top journalist summarized the chair-to-be's position this way: "Grassley has made it a signature cause as part of his general push to expand government transparency."[44]

A current concern is that fewer aspirants are seeking federal judgeships. Part of the reason is pay: "Salaries are far lower [for federal judges] than what fresh-faced law-school grads can make at big corporate firms."[45] Chief Justice John Roberts devoted much of his 2008 annual year-end report on the federal judiciary to the inadequacy of judicial salaries. The judicial branch as a whole made a major, but unsuccessful push in the 110th Congress for a judicial pay increase.

Congressional opposition to increased judicial pay has stemmed, in part, from so-called "linkage." For a long time, the salaries of federal judges and members of Congress were for all practical matters linked.[46] Lawmakers' reluctance to raise their own salaries—for obvious political reasons—was a large part of the reason why federal judges' salaries had not kept pace with inflation. To raise judicial salaries substantially, members of Congress would have to agree to "de-link" their salaries from those of judges, thereby depriving members of political cover on the occasions when they did decide to raise their own salaries. In 2014, however, there were substantial increases in federal judges' pay, oddly enough, as a result of long-running litigation over the meaning of Article III's Compensation Clause.[47] The chief justice currently receives an annual salary of $255,500; associate justices, $244,400; appeals court judges, $211,200; and federal district judges, $199,100.[48] Even with the recent pay increase, judges' earnings lag behind other high-status legal professionals. Law school deans, for example, can earn over $400,000 a year, and top law firm partners $1 million or more a year.[49] Some analysts, however, question whether there are benefits to paying judges more.[50] The present state of the federal budget makes any further increases in judges' salaries (other than cost-of-living adjustments) unlikely in the near future.

Constitutional Amendments. On four occasions, Congress successfully used the arduous process of amending the Constitution to overturn decisions of the Supreme Court. In *Chisholm v. Georgia* (1793), the Court held that citizens of one state could sue another state in federal court.[51] To prevent a rash of citizen suits against the states, Congress oversaw passage of the Eleventh Amendment to reverse this decision and protect states' sovereign immunity from lawsuits brought by citizens of other states and foreign countries. The *Dred Scott v. Sandford* (1857) decision[52]—denying African Americans citizenship under the Constitution—was nullified by the Thirteenth Amendment (abolishing slavery) and Fourteenth Amendment (granting African Americans citizenship). The Sixteenth Amendment overturned *Pollock v. Farmer's Loan and Trust Co.* (1895), which struck down a federal income tax. The Twenty-sixth Amendment invalidated *Oregon v. Mitchell* (1970), which held that Congress had exceeded its authority by lowering the minimum voting age to eighteen for state elections.[53]

Generally, lawmakers are reluctant to amend the Constitution. The view of Rep. Melvin Watt, D-N.C., reflects that of many members: "I just think the Constitution has served us very well over a long, long period of time, and one needs to make a compelling case before we start amending the Constitution to do anything."[54] However, certain constitutional amendments have appeared regularly on the legislative agenda. One would ban desecration of the American flag. The proposal is a response to a 1989 Supreme Court ruling in *Texas v. Johnson* that state laws banning flag burning violate the First Amendment right of free speech. The House has passed an anti–flag desecration amendment several times, but the Senate has never approved the measure.

Eliminating life tenure for federal judges is another proposal that sometimes surfaces on Capitol Hill. Bitter judicial nomination battles have prompted some observers to suggest term limits (such as fifteen years) for federal judges. "If the Senate can't figure out how to reach a [partisan] truce in its battles over these all-important jobs," wrote one analyst, "maybe the best solution is to make the jobs not quite so important."[55] Others simply contend that Supreme Court justices serve too long. Aging justices, it is argued, may become arrogant, out of touch with contemporary values, or too impaired to serve. To avoid the difficulties of winning approval of a constitutional amendment, they propose a legislative approach that would move "justices into senior status after roughly eighteen years on the high court."[56]

ADVICE AND CONSENT FOR JUDICIAL NOMINEES

Article II, section 2, of the Constitution states that the president "shall nominate, and by and with the Advice and Consent of the Senate, shall appoint . . . Judges of the Supreme Court." The founders rejected giving the power to appoint judges solely to the executive, to Congress as a whole, or to the Senate. In the end, they compromised and required joint action by the president and the Senate. The president has the sole prerogative to nominate, but the power to confirm (or not) belongs to the Senate. Alexander Hamilton, in *Federalist* No. 66, viewed this division of responsibility in stark terms: "There will, of course, be no exertion of CHOICE on the part of the Senate. They may defeat one choice of the Executive and oblige him to make another; but they cannot themselves CHOOSE—they can only ratify or reject the choice he may have made."

Hamilton's perspective, however, requires some refinement. Giving two elective institutions a voice in the appointments process necessarily means that the Senate is able to influence the president's choice of nominees. Indeed, individual senators, House members, interest groups, the American Bar Association (which since 1952 has rated judicial candidates), the Federalist Society, the press and media, and even sitting judges can all sometimes influence both the choice of judicial nominees and Senate action, if any, on those nominees. The fact that federal district and appellate court jurisdictions are geographically based means that senators from those states (especially if they are of the president's party) commonly have a big say in recommending judicial candidates to the White House (see Table 12-1 for judgeship appointments by presidents).

Any discussion of the various norms, practices, and controversies associated with the confirmation process for federal judges must be prefaced by a description of the half-dozen principal stages in filling a vacancy on the Supreme Court.

First, the president puts together a short list of nominees. Considerable thought and research go into the list. Presidents want to nominate individuals who reflect their political and policy views and are generally perceived as being competent and knowledgeable. Many political considerations also enter the selection process. The gender, race, geographic, and religious makeup of the Court may be relevant to the choice. Presidents consider the nominee's age, seeking a qualified candidate who will be able to serve a lengthy tenure on the Court. They look to the composition of the Senate and assess the prospects of an easy or difficult confirmation battle.

The contemporary selection process also includes careful vetting of potential nominees' personal and professional lives. Typical of recent presidents, the research process conducted for the nominees on Obama's short list when Justice David Souter announced his retirement was intensive. Researchers

TABLE 12-1   **Judgeship Appointments by President, 1933–2015**

President	Supreme Court	Regional Court of Appeals	USCAFC[1]	District Courts	Total
F. Roosevelt (1933–1945)	9	52	—	136	197
Truman (1945–1953)	4	27	—	102	133
Eisenhower (1953–1961)	5	45	—	127	177
Kennedy (1961–1963)	2	20	—	102	124
L. Johnson (1963–1969)	2	41	—	125	168
Nixon (1969–1975)	4	48	—	182	231
Ford (1974–1977)	1	12	—	52	65
Carter (1977–1981)	0	56	—	206	262
Reagan (1981–1989)	3	78	5	292	378
G. H. W. Bush (1989–1993)	2	37	5	149	193
Clinton (1993–2001)	2	62	4	306	374
G. W. Bush (2001–2009)	2	61	2	261	326
Obama[2] (2009–2015)	2	47	6	250	305

Sources: Adapted from "Judgeship Appointments by President," *The Third Branch,* newsletter of the federal courts, February 2009. Data for the Obama administration are from the Federal Judicial Center, www.fjc.gov/history/home.nsf/page/research_categories.html. The work of CRS experts Steven Rutkus and Barry McMillion is gratefully acknowledged.

[1] The U.S. Court of Appeals for the Federal Circuit (USCAFC) was established in 1982.

[2] Data are through December 19, 2014.

scoured "the real estate transactions, taxes, ethics, the backgrounds of spouses and adult children, as well as a particularly close look at the early jobs held right after law school—often at the Justice Department—when early views could have been formed and when a paper trail of thousands of documents was probably created."[57] Second, once the president has made his choice, he sends a written nomination to the Senate, which is then referred to the Judiciary Committee. The nominee is escorted to various Hill offices to meet with key senators. Meanwhile, the nominee begins extensive preparation for the hearings before the Judiciary Committee. Part of the preparation commonly involves participation in mock confirmation hearings called "murder boards."

Third, the Judiciary Committee launches its own investigation of the nominee's background and qualifications. After that stage is completed, the Judiciary chair schedules public hearings on the nomination. The members of the committee have the opportunity to ask the nominee questions and also to receive testimony from other witnesses. Although it is unthinkable today that the committee would not proceed in this way, it is notable that confirmation hearings were unheard of for most of the nation's history. In 1925 Attorney General Harlan Fiske Stone was the first Supreme Court nominee to testify in public before the Judiciary Committee. Stone had made political enemies cleaning up the Justice Department in the aftermath of the Teapot Dome scandal—and by vigorously enforcing the nation's antitrust laws. Certain senators signaled that they might block Stone's appointment in light of the Justice Department's handling of a related indictment against Sen. Burton K. Wheeler, D-Mont. To answer questions about his handling of the Wheeler case, Stone offered to appear before the committee in a public hearing.[58] Still, confirmation hearings did not become customary until the mid-1950s.

Fourth, after the hearings are concluded, the Judiciary Committee meets in open session to report the nomination to the Senate either with a favorable or negative recommendation, or with no recommendation at all. Dating back to at least the 1880s, the "Judiciary Committee's traditional practice has been to report even those Supreme Court nominations that were opposed by a committee majority, thus allowing the full Senate to make the final decision on whether the nominee should be confirmed."[59] (This practice does not apply to nominees for district or appellate court judgeships.) Once reported by the committee, the nomination is assigned to the Senate's executive calendar.

Fifth, the Senate majority leader decides when to call up the nomination for chamber consideration after consultation with various lawmakers, including the minority leader. Once the nomination reaches the floor, all senators have an opportunity to discuss the nominee's credentials, philosophy, or anything else they believe is relevant for the public record. A filibuster is unusual on Supreme Court nominations. Cloture is available to curb talkathons but has been moved only four times.[60] After debate ends, in a practice begun in 1967, the Senate decides whether to confirm the Supreme Court nominee by a roll call vote. If a majority of the Senate votes to confirm, the secretary of the Senate transmits the resolution of confirmation to the president, and the president then signs the commission officially making the appointment. The nominee then takes the constitutional oath of office making him or her a justice of the U.S. Supreme Court.

Norms and Practices

Extraconstitutional norms and practices shape the confirmation process. President George Washington, for example, quickly learned the importance of the newly emerging norm of senatorial courtesy—an informal practice in which presidents consult home-state senators before submitting nominees for federal positions in their state. When he "failed to seek the advice from the Georgia senate delegation regarding a nomination for a federal position in Savannah, Washington was forced to withdraw the nomination in favor of the person recommended by the senators."[61]

Related to senatorial courtesy is the blue slip policy of the Judiciary Committee, which applies only to district and court of appeals nominees. In recent years, the practice has been for both home-state senators to be consulted through this procedure, regardless of party. Interestingly, the Obama administration worked diligently to secure the blue slip approval of GOP home-state senators and had a great deal of early success in doing so.[62] That success was undercut, however, by what one observer described as "systematic leadership-led refusal to consent" to moving ahead with nominations.[63] It seems that as in many other aspects of Senate procedures, the individual prerogatives of senators are losing ground to the leadership's partisan strategies.

An array of other Senate practices also influence whether any action occurs on judicial nominations, such as the hold, the committee chair's prerogative of determining whether hearings will be held, and the majority leader's willingness to schedule floor consideration of the nominations.

An unresolved issue is the balance between advice and consent. Presidents usually favor consent over advice. The Senate tilts in the other direction. "It's advice and consent, not nominate and rubber stamp," declared Sen. Patrick Leahy, D-Vt.[64] The qualifications appropriate for service as a federal jurist are not self-evident. The Constitution makes no reference to what presidents or senators should consider when exercising their respective roles (being a lawyer is not even a prerequisite). Setting aside the standard qualifications that everyone expects in prospective judges—legal experience, ethical behavior, recognized competence, and so on—an age-old question is whether people should be subject to litmus tests for a judicial position. Should judicial nominees disclose their views on hot-button issues likely to come before the Court? Most recent nominees have studiously refused to reveal much about their views on such issues when questioned by senators.

Nomination Battles

Over the last two centuries, the Senate has "rejected about 20 percent of all Supreme Court nominees."[65] Most of the rejections occurred in the nineteenth century, with President John Tyler holding the record: five of his six nominees were rejected by the Senate (see Table 12-2).

The bitter confirmation battles of the present originate with President Ronald Reagan's nomination of conservative Robert H. Bork to the Supreme

TABLE 12-2 Supreme Court Nominations Not Confirmed by the Senate

Nominee	President	Date of nomination	Senate action	Date of Senate action
William Paterson	George Washington	February 27, 1793	Withdrawn[1]	
John Rutledge[2]	Washington	July 1, 1795	Rejected (10–14)	December 15, 1795
Alexander Wolcott	James Madison	February 4, 1811	Rejected (9–24)	February 13, 1811
John J. Crittenden	John Quincy Adams	December 17, 1828	Postponed	February 12, 1829
Roger Brooke Taney	Andrew Jackson	January 15, 1835	Postponed (24–21)[3]	March 3, 1835
John C. Spencer	John Tyler	January 9, 1844	Rejected (21–26)	January 31, 1844
Reuben H. Walworth	Tyler	March 13, 1844	Withdrawn	
Edward King	Tyler	June 5, 1844	Postponed	June 15, 1844
Edward King	Tyler	December 4, 1844	Withdrawn	
John M. Read	Tyler	February 7, 1845	Not acted upon	
George W. Woodward	James K. Polk	December 23, 1845	Rejected (20–29)	January 22, 1846
Edward A. Bradford	Millard Fillmore	August 16, 1852	Not acted upon	
George E. Badger	Fillmore	January 10, 1853	Postponed	February 11, 1853
William C. Micou	Fillmore	February 24, 1853	Not acted upon	
Jeremiah S. Black	James Buchanan	February 5, 1861	Rejected (25–26)	February 21, 1861
Henry Stanbery	Andrew Johnson	April 16, 1866	Not acted upon	
Ebenezer R. Hoar	Ulysses S. Grant	December 15, 1869	Rejected (24–33)	February 3, 1870
George H. Williams[2]	Grant	December 1, 1873	Withdrawn	

(Continued)

TABLE 12-2 **(Continued)**

Nominee	President	Date of nomination	Senate action	Date of Senate action
Caleb Cushing[2]	Grant	January 9, 1874	Withdrawn	
Stanley Matthews	Rutherford B. Hayes	January 26, 1881	Not acted upon[1]	
William B. Hornblower	Grover Cleveland	September 19, 1893	Rejected (24–30)	January 15, 1894
Wheeler H. Peckham	Cleveland	January 22, 1894	Rejected (32–41)	February 16, 1894
John J. Parker	Herbert Hoover	March 21, 1930	Rejected (39–41)	May 7, 1930
Abe Fortas[2]	Lyndon B. Johnson	June 26, 1968	Withdrawn	
Homer Thornberry	Johnson	June 26, 1968	Not acted upon	
Clement F. Haynsworth Jr.	Richard M. Nixon	August 18, 1969	Rejected (45–55)	November 21, 1969
G. Harrold Carswell	Nixon	January 19, 1970	Rejected (45–51)	April 8, 1970
Robert H. Bork	Ronald Reagan	July 1, 1987	Rejected (42–58)	October 23, 1987
Douglas H. Ginsburg	Ronald Reagan	October 29, 1987	Withdrawn	
Harriet Miers	George W. Bush	October 3, 2005	Withdrawn	

Source: Joan Biskupic and Elder Witt, *Guide to the U.S. Supreme Court,* 3d ed., vol. 2 (Washington, DC: Congressional Quarterly, 1997), 707, authors' notes.

[1] Later nominated and confirmed.

[2] Nominated for chief justice.

[3] Later nominated for chief justice and confirmed.

Court in 1987. A Democratic-controlled Senate rejected Bork, who was perceived as too conservative, by a 58–42 margin. Conservative groups were outraged by the ways in which Bork was treated by the Democratic-controlled Senate. The political campaign mobilized against the nomination gave rise to a new verb, to *bork*.

Since the failed Bork nomination, senators have become increasingly unwilling to support Supreme Court nominees selected by presidents of the opposing party.[66] In 1986 Antonin Scalia was confirmed by the Senate 98–0, even though it was clear that he was a staunch judicial conservative. President Clinton's two nominees in the early 1990s—Ruth Bader Ginsburg in 1993 and Stephen Breyer in 1994—each garnered opposition from a handful of conservative senators. President George W. Bush's nominees—John Roberts and Samuel Alito—were met with even more widespread Democratic opposition, with only half of Senate Democrats voting in favor of Roberts and only four Democrats in favor of Alito. Senate votes on President Obama's Supreme Court nominations—Sonia Sotomayor and Elena Kagan—broke down along party lines, with only nine Republicans voting for Sotomayor and only five Republicans voting for Kagan. "We have shifted from a basic expectation that absent a reason to vote against a nominee members of the opposing party will support a president's nominee," said Benjamin Wittes, senior fellow at the Brookings Institution. "In a very short period of time, that has reversed to a presumption that members of the opposition party will oppose the president's nominee, absent a reason to support him or her. That is a very profound change."[67]

The Kagan nomination in many ways illustrates the underlying partisan logic of opposition to Supreme Court nominees in the contemporary era. One criticism raised of Kagan's nomination was her lack of judicial experience. Other than Kagan, every current justice is a former federal appeals court judge. Opponents of her nomination cast Kagan's lack of judicial experience as a "qualifications" issue.

It is, of course, an open question whether membership on the highest court should reflect a broader diversity of backgrounds. From Chief Justice John Marshall's day through Earl Warren's, for example, the Court typically included members steeped in legislative or executive experience. In the Court's recent history, only Supreme Court justice Sandra Day O'Connor ever held an elective office; she was an Arizona state senator. Some legal scholars suggest that a wider range of occupational experiences on the Court would serve an important representational function and enhance decision making "with a variety of issues in the electoral and legislative spheres."[68]

Rather than oppose a nominee based on ideology, there is every reason to think that a president's partisan opponents prefer to fight Supreme Court nominations on the qualifications issue. Sen. Charles E. Schumer, D-N.Y., has argued that senators should forthrightly take ideology into account in voting on Supreme Court nominations rather than look for other pretexts for opposing judges with whom they disagree. "For one reason or another, examining the ideologies of judicial nominees has become something of a Senate taboo," writes Schumer. "Unfortunately, the taboo has led senators who oppose a nominee for ideological reasons to justify their opposition by finding non-ideological factors, like small financial improprieties from long ago. This 'gotcha' politics has warped the confirmation process."[69]

Recent research suggests that the relationship between qualifications and the ideology of nominees has shifted since the Bork nomination fight. Political scientist Lee Epstein and her coauthors found that before Bork, senators were willing to vote for moderately qualified nominees, even if there was some ideological distance between them and the nominee. Post-Bork, however, they found that senators were less willing to vote for ideologically distant nominees, regardless of qualifications. Epstein and her coauthors summed up the situation: "the president's discretion over whom to nominate to the Supreme Court has grown far more circumscribed over the last two decades."[70] Perhaps this observation helps to explain recent presidents' preferences for nominees with court of appeals experience rather than controversial political records.

Consent and Dissent

Until recently, little controversy was associated with scrutinizing judges named to serve on the lower federal courts. Today, fierce conflict between the parties and branches overlays the confirmation process for many judicial nominees, especially for the appellate courts. "The politicization of the judiciary has recently been the most focused, and most virulent, at the appellate, or circuit level," said federal judge James Robertson.[71] Indeed, during the Obama administration even district court nominations have become more controversial. Several factors explain these developments.

First, interest groups are aware that federal judges make critical decisions across a broad spectrum of policy issues. Both parties understand that although the Supreme Court is viewed as the court of last resort, it decides only about seventy to eighty cases each year.[72] By contrast, the courts of appeals decide tens of thousands of cases annually. The courts of appeals are "playing a more important role in setting law for vast areas of the country. A decision by the Ninth Circuit, for example, is binding on nine states, where 19 percent of the nation's population lives."[73] According to one law professor, the courts of appeals are "the Supreme Courts for their region."[74] Interest groups may also be growing more sensitive to the discretion of district judges, especially in complex commercial litigation and employment discrimination cases. Many of the procedural rulings district judges make in such cases are not reviewed by appellate courts, but can seriously affect cases involving corporate defendants.

Second, some confirmation fights are clearly warm-ups for potential Supreme Court vacancies down the line. Because of the preferences of recent presidents for court of appeals judges, blocking a (potentially) controversial nominee from the appellate bench likely eliminates that person from future consideration for the high court.

Third, in presidential election years there is often a drop-off in the number of judges confirmed by the Senate. Senate majority leader Harry Reid, D-Nev., has even called this informal slowing down the "Thurmond rule," after former senator Strom Thurmond, R-S.C. In the 112th Congress, press reports indicated that Senate minority leader Mitch McConnell, R-Ky., implemented the Thurmond rule for court of appeals judges in June, but that district court confirmations would end sometime in September.[75] Although some dispute that there is a so-called Thurmond rule, and in order to share the blame with Democrats, others prefer to call it the "Leahy-Thurmond rule,"[76] the political reality is indeed a roughly 40 percent decline in the number of appellate judges confirmed during presidential election years.[77] A law professor explained why this pattern occurs: "The priority for the party not in control of the White House is not so much in stopping candidates based on their ideology, but keeping as many vacancies open as possible on the theory that the next president may be someone of your party and will be able to fill those slots."[78]

Finally, it is simply far more difficult for the Senate to provide advice and consent for lifetime judicial appointments in an environment where the ideological chasm between the two parties is so wide. Confirmation battles represent a clash between the president and the opposition party in the Senate over who will control the ideological balance of power on the courts. Unlike with legislation, once the Senate confirms a judicial nominee there is no opportunity for a subsequent Senate to reverse the decision except through the impeachment process. President George W. Bush, for example, was "more consistent and insistent than, say, [Gerald R.] Ford or Reagan" in nominating conservatives to the bench.[79] "If Democrats just rolled over on Bush's nominations," said one political analyst, "they would be guilty of oppositional malpractice."[80] There is no doubt that President Bush was successful in recasting federal courts in a more conservative direction.

In his first term, President Obama was not equally aggressive. On the ideological front, the Obama administration gravitated toward relatively centrist jurists, perhaps in an effort to avoid "culture war" issues in the confirmation process.[81] That effort was unsuccessful, as Senate Republicans, in the words of one prominent journalist, "ratchet[ed] up partisan warfare over judges . . . by delaying even uncontroversial picks who would have been quickly approved in the past."[82] Many supporters of the Obama administration were criticized the administration's slow pace in making nominations.[83] However, the Obama administration's slow pace in making judicial nominations is consistent with longer-term trends. Political scientists Sarah Binder and Forrest Maltzman found that presidents in the postwar period have been taking progressively longer in making lower-court nominations, even after taking into account other factors.[84] It is likely that much of the growing delay in making nominations results from enhanced vetting of potential nominees. Because of the increased Senate obstruction of lower-court nominations, presidents react by scouring nominees' backgrounds in search of possible grounds for Senate opposition. In other words, to avoid a stalled nomination, presidents may be stalling before making the nominations.

Following the 2012 election, however, the Obama administration became more aggressive on pressing judicial nominees.[85] The issue of judicial nominations came to a head as the Senate GOP blocked three nominees to the U.S. Court of Appeals for the District of Columbia Circuit. Unlike in past disputes over judicial nominations—as in 2005, when the so-called "Gang of Fourteen" negotiated a process for clearing several of President Bush's controversial nominees—bipartisan negotiations failed. On November 21, 2013, the Senate invoked the "nuclear option" and eliminated the filibuster for executive branch and judicial branch nominations, with an exception for Supreme Court nominations.

In the remainder of the 113th Congress, the Obama administration was able to move judicial nominations, with critics complaining that the president was "pack[ing]" the courts with "far-left" judges.[86] Fully ninety-six judges were confirmed by the Senate after going nuclear,[87] including an incredible twelve judges confirmed on the Senate's last day in session in 2014. At the end of the 113th Congress, 132 district and court of appeals judges had been confirmed,[88] and Democratic appointees made up majorities on nine of the thirteen courts of appeals.[89] Worth noting is that President Obama's federal court selections have set the record for judicial diversity. More African Americans, Hispanics, women, Asians, and gays have been confirmed as judges than ever before. Female judges "make up 42% of his confirmed nominees, more than double the average of his five predecessors combined, while African Americans make up 18% and Latinos 6%. Eleven openly gay judges now serve where there was only one."[90] Recall that President Obama named two women to the Supreme Court, one of whom is the first Hispanic to serve on the Court. All told, about 60 percent of Obama's appointments have gone to nontraditional candidates, meaning people who are not white males.[91]

The prospects for Obama's judicial picks in the 114th Congress, however, are bleak. The GOP majority, after all, will not need to filibuster nominees to block them. One thing to watch in the new Congress is the tone struck by Sen. Charles Grassley, R-Iowa, the first nonlawyer to chair the Senate Judiciary Committee. Senator Grassley said, shortly after the 2014 election, that the committee would "carefully vet" Obama's nominees.[92]

CONCLUSION

Federal courts, like Congress and the president, are central forums for resolving the political, social, and economic conflicts that characterize American society. All three branches of government interact constantly to shape the laws under which Americans live. Sometimes, as presidents say, "the buck stops here." In Congress, the buck may stop nowhere, and either elective branch may pass the buck to the courts when it is unable to resolve certain issues. "Through this process of interaction among the branches," writes scholar Louis Fisher, "all three institutions are able to expose weaknesses, hold excesses in check, and gradually forge a consensus on constitutional values."[93]

Big ISPs want the power to slow (and break!) sites like ours.
Tell lawmakers: "Protect Internet freedom. Defend net neutrality."

Read the letter | Learn More

| Name | Email | Address | Zip / Postcode |

SIGN OUR LETTER TO LAWMAKERS

✓ **Free Press Action Fund** may contact you about future campaigns.

We'll deliver this letter to your members of Congress, the FCC, and the White House. We'll
never share your email with anyone else. Privacy Policy

Cable companies are strong in Congress.

Cable giants have been lobbying Congress for years. Now they're asking for big
favors. We have to stop them. Find out if your leaders work for you, or your cable
company.

Choose your state: Key Players ▾

■ TEAM CABLE   ■ UNKNOWN   ■ TEAM INTERNET

Rubio · McConnell · Thune · Cruz · Rush · Upton · Boehner · Latta · Walden · Blackburn · Green · Moran

McCarthy · Scalise · Pelosi · Blumenthal · Nadler · Markey · Warren · King · Franken · Klobuchar · Booker · Gillibrand

Interest Group Influence. David Cohen, executive vice president of the Comcast Corporation, testifies before a House Judiciary subcommittee on the proposed merger of Comcast and Time Warner Cable in May 2014. Many interest groups circulate petitions and encourage constituents to contact their congressional representatives, such as this organization favoring net neutrality. Many interest groups also develop scorecards rating members of Congress as friendly or unfriendly to their goals. The above rating was assembled by Fight for the Future, a group that coordinates a coalition of nonprofit and tech-sector allies and organizes Internet users in support of net neutrality and privacy issues. Protesters march past the Federal Communications Commission headquarters demanding net neutrality.

Congress and Organized Interests

F ive thousand protestors picketed the Ritz Carlton Hotel in Washington, D.C., on March 9, 2010. Inside the hotel, the trade association of the health insurance industry, America's Health Insurance Plans (AHIP), was holding its annual lobbying conference. A goal of the conference was to lay out a strategy to oppose passage of health reform unless it protected the interests of the industry.

The protestors outside, a coalition of over a thousand organizations (including labor, consumer, and civil rights groups), wanted to confront the insurance industry, win media attention, and secure public and legislative backing for President Barack Obama's health care plan. "The message we have is simple," exclaimed the director of Health Care for Americans Now (HCAN), the group organizing the protest. "Congress should listen to us, not the insurance industry."[1]

Lawmakers could not help but hear the cacophony of voices advocating for and against health care reform in 2009–2010. Record numbers of lobbyists and activists swarmed Washington, seeking influence over virtually every facet of the plan. Health companies and trade associations hired "more than 4,500 lobbyists . . . about eight lobbyists for each member of Congress."[2]

Marches, rallies, demonstrations, conferences, radio and television advertising, the print media, YouTube, blogs, and more were used to influence congressional decision makers. MoveOn.org sponsored a "virtual march" on Capitol Hill, sending more than one million pro-reform e-mails to lawmakers' offices. Conservative groups such as the National Right to Life Committee purchased television ads and organized grassroots campaigns to pressure wavering congressional Democrats to vote against "Obamacare." The U.S. Chamber of Commerce commissioned an economic study designed to portray the health bill as a job killer, and sought to enlist hundreds of economists to sign a letter opposing the legislation, which would then be used in advertisements, lobbying, and grassroots mobilization.[3]

Groups on all sides of the health care issue spent huge sums to mold the final product. Medical interests (doctors, hospitals, drug companies, and various health businesses) spent $876 million over fifteen months (January 2009 to March 2010) to influence the debate. Unlike the Clinton administration's 1993–1994 health reform plan, when the health industry was united in its opposition, much of the $876 million was spent in support of President

Obama's plan, though medical interests were hardly monolithic in their preferences. Even after the Affordable Care Act was enacted on March 23, 2010, lobbying expenditures on health care continued as various interests sought to shape how the legislation was implemented.[4]

AMERICAN PLURALISM

The fifteen-month battle to enact comprehensive health care reform—an idea advocated at least since the administration of President Teddy Roosevelt—illustrates the dual nature of American pluralism. On the one hand, a vast array of organized interests, most of them headquartered in the nation's capital, seek to influence government policy. This is the "Washington system" of lobbyists and insider access that incites so much populist rhetoric and public distaste.[5] Narrow profit motives were hardly absent from the health reform debate, as lobbyists sought legislative concessions to line their clients' pockets.

On the other hand, also weighing in on the issue were membership organizations, some of them huge. By means of such organizations, Americans assemble "to petition the government for redress of grievances," in the words of the Constitution's First Amendment. Groups of Americans legitimately concerned about how health care reform might affect the quality, affordability, and accessibility of medical treatments made their concerns known.

The controversy surrounding health care reform illustrates the ambivalence that characterizes both scholarly and journalistic considerations of American pluralism. The world of interest groups prompts fears of a government corrupted by narrow special interests. And yet organized interests are not only constitutionally protected, but also a foundation of civil society and a natural by-product of democratic freedom. President Harry S. Truman, in a wry response to a reporter's question—"Mr. President, would you be against lobbyists who are working for your program?"—remarked: "Well, that's a different matter. We probably wouldn't call these people lobbyists. We would call them citizens appearing in the public interest."[6]

A Capital of Interests

Organized interests wield vast resources—money, connections, personnel, information, and organization—to win passage of legislation they favor, block legislation they oppose, and reward the politicians who help them. Capitol Hill lobbyists, emissaries of these interests, walk the halls of congressional office buildings, request personal meetings with lawmakers and aides, hold informational briefings for members and staff, and jam committee meeting rooms.

Practically every major corporation, trade association, and professional group has Washington lobbyists. There are so many lobbyists working in Washington that they have their own professional association: the American League of Lobbyists. Mindful that lobbyists have a poor public image, the league's president organized a public relations offensive to "help people understand that the 'L' word is not a bad word." He added:

Everybody has a lobbyist out there. The second you get up in the morning and you have your toast and eggs, the wheat and poultry lobbyists are involved. Then you get into your car, and you have the Toyota lobbyists. When you log on to your computer and surf the Web, don't forget about the Google lobbyists. Most people have no idea that they have so many lobbyists in their day.[7]

A look inside the Washington telephone directory under "associations" reveals as much as the Constitution about what moves Congress. Washington is home to more national associations than any other city. Numerous law, financial, technology, and public relations firms also have offices in the District of Columbia. "A financial institution . . . needs to have a Washington office," said the head of one financial trade group. "It puts you at a competitive advantage to have a Washington presence [because you] can have input into the [lawmaking] process."[8]

The lobbying community probably constitutes the third-largest industry employer in the nation's capital, behind government and tourism. "The more the government gets involved in an industry's affairs," declaimed an experienced lobbyist, "the more industry hires people to figure that out."[9] When control of one or both houses of Congress moves from one party to another, the changeover often sparks a boost in lobbying hiring and expenditures as organized interests seek out better access to new congressional leaders. "It's standard operating procedure in Washington that whenever there is a shift in power, there is a scramble by companies to make sure they have adequate representation with the new power brokers," explained the head of the Center for Responsive Politics, a D.C.-based think tank.[10]

More than $3.2 billion was spent lobbying in 2013.[11] Interestingly, lobbying expenditures have declined every year since 2010. Gridlock in Congress may have led companies, unions, and interest groups to scale back on lobbying costs. But it is not possible to track all the expenditures organizations make to influence policy making. The recent declines in outlays for direct lobbying may also mean that organized interests are spending more on other forms of influence peddling that are not subject to disclosure, such as funding nonprofit groups, think tanks, and grassroots organizations.[12] "Lobbyists are also beating a path to the agencies more than the House and Senate," noted a lobbyist, because of the extensive regulatory activity associated with the statutory enactment of financial reform legislation and the Affordable Care Act.[13]

A Nation of Joiners

Americans' zest for joining groups was noted long ago by Alexis de Tocqueville. Americans of all "conditions, minds, and ages daily acquire a general taste for association," he wrote in 1835.[14] Throughout American history, groups speaking for different subsets of "the people" have swayed public policies and politics. The nineteenth-century abolitionists fought to end slavery. The Anti-Saloon

League crusaded for the prohibition of alcohol in the 1900s. Activists in the 1960s and 1970s protested the Vietnam War, racial discrimination, and abuse of the environment. In the 1970s and 1980s, interest groups galvanized support for and against equal rights for women. In the 1990s, conservative groups pushed term limits for lawmakers, a balanced budget amendment, and tax cuts. A wide array of liberal and conservative membership organizations have been prominent in recent American politics, such as antiabortion groups, immigration reformers, gun rights and gun control advocates, Moveon.org, Tea Party groups, and Occupy Wall Street.

A free society nurtures politically active groups. "Liberty is to faction what air is to fire," wrote James Madison in *Federalist* No. 10. For decades, interest groups have grown in number and diversity. For example, the American Medical Association dominated health lobbying in the 1950s, but today hundreds of health advocacy groups woo lawmakers and orchestrate grassroots activity, up from about 90 in 1975 to at least 750 by the early 1990s. "You name a disease, there's probably a Washington lobby for it," said an official of the American Heart Association.[15] Many factors account for the proliferation of interest groups: social and economic complexity; scientific and technological developments; the government's regulatory role; the competition for federal dollars; and the diffusion of power in U.S. national government, which enhances access for outside interests (see Box 13-1 on theories of interest group formation).

Despite the tradition of vibrant associational life in the United States, there is some evidence that Americans' civic engagement has declined since the 1960s. Most famously, Harvard University professor Robert Putnam showed across a wide array of indicators that citizen participation in associations had waned. Fewer Americans were participating in organizations like Cub Scouts, Brownies, PTA, volunteer fire departments, and civic associations, such as Elks and Rotary Clubs. Putnam drew his most famous example from the nation's bowling alleys. His data showed that more people are bowling but doing so outside of traditional bowling leagues, resulting in a drop in the number of bowling leagues.[16] They are, in short, "bowling alone." People "would rather be alone in front of a television set than out with a group," Putnam wrote.[17] Rather than taking personal part in broad-based civic associations, many middle-class citizens now rely on professionally run advocacy groups to speak on their behalf.[18]

In contrast to Putnam, some other scholars have documented growth in newer civic organizations, such as environmental groups and youth soccer leagues. Although membership in older groups such as Lions Clubs or Elks or Moose Lodges has unquestionably declined, other forms of volunteering have increased.[19] Social media (such as blogs, Facebook, and Twitter) also enable the formation of new social and political communities. With so many people engaging via online and other "virtual" (rather than face-to-face) interactions, even the meaning of "civic activism" is being transformed.[20]

BOX 13-1   **Some Theories on Interest Group Formation**

Scholars have suggested a number of theories to explain the development of interest groups. Special interests have long been a source of fascination, in part because of their ability to influence policy making even though they may not reflect majority sentiment within the country. The case of vocal minorities prevailing over apathetic or disengaged majorities rivets scholarly attention. The implication is that organized interests are more powerful than unorganized interests. Among the various theories of group formation are the following.

- The proliferation hypothesis suggests that as society becomes more complex and interdependent, groups naturally form to reflect the country's intricate array of issues and entities. As new conditions, issues, or forces emerge, new groups are formed to reflect or respond to these developments. "The reasoning behind the proliferation hypothesis is straightforward: groups need a clientele from which to draw members."[1]
- The disturbance hypothesis posits an unstable equilibrium among groups. If something disturbs the equilibrium, such as war, technological innovations, the emergence of new concerns (acquired immune deficiency syndrome [AIDS], homeland security, and so on), then new groups emerge. As two scholars wrote, "Groups organize politically when the existing order is disturbed and certain interests are, in turn, helped or hurt." As an example, they note: "Mobilization of business interests since the 1960s often has resulted from threats posed by consumer advocates and environmentalists, as well as requirements imposed by the steadily growing role of the federal government."[2]
- The exchange hypothesis states that groups form because of the efforts of "entrepreneurs." The argument asserts that "group organizers invest in a set of benefits which they offer to potential members at a price—joining the group. Benefits may be material [private gains], solidarity [camaraderie], or expressive [the reward of belonging to a group with shared values and causes]."[3]

[1] Scott H. Ainsworth, *Analyzing Interest Groups* (New York: W. W. Norton and Co., 2002), 40.

[2] Alan J. Cigler and Burdett A. Loomis, eds., *Interest Group Politics,* 6th ed. (Washington, DC: CQ Press, 2002), 8. See also David B. Truman, *The Governmental Process,* 2d ed. (New York: Knopf, 1971).

[3] Robert Salisbury, "An Exchange Theory of Interest Groups," *Midwest Journal of Political Science* (February 1969): 1–32.

Biases of Interest Representation

Not all societal interests are organized and represented in the pressure group system. Organizations do not necessarily emerge just because people share a common policy goal or political interest. Economist Mancur Olson Jr. famously analyzed the difficulties of organizing to bring about policy change.[21]

Organizing requires time, energy, and money, and individuals know that the small contributions they can make usually will not be decisive or even important. If a group exists and successfully presses for policy changes, the benefits will spread beyond those who worked to bring about the results. If, for example, an environmental group successfully calls for clean air regulations, urban residents will benefit from the reduced smog, regardless of whether they personally made any contribution to the group's efforts. As a consequence, individuals will prefer to free ride on the work of others.

The issue of the free rider is especially problematic for large groups, where failure to help with the collective effort is totally anonymous. According to Olson's analysis, organizing is easier for small groups with a strong material stake in policy outcomes. In small groups, social pressure can be effectively applied to discourage free riding. In some cases, a single individual or firm will bankroll the cost of organizing because it can benefit even while bearing the costs alone.

The free rider problem is also less of an obstacle for the many groups that exist as a "by-product" of enterprises organized for other purposes. Businesses, for example, exist to make a profit. But businesses often elect to devote some share of their profits to subsidizing organizations that represent their political interests.

Under Olson's logic, the pressure group system should be tilted toward narrow economic interests that are easier to organize, and it should underrepresent broad public interests. Congress will thus receive more input from narrow groups with a financial stake in policy issues than from groups representing wider public concerns. Consistent with this theory, there are indeed biases in the composition of the interest group universe. One survey found that business interests make up 72 percent of all groups having Washington representation.[22]

The composition of the interest group world also reflects economic inequality. Put simply, it takes money to create and sustain organized interests, so groups representing the well off are more likely to emerge and survive. As political scientist E. E. Schattschneider famously put it, "the flaw in the pluralist heaven is that the heavenly chorus sings with a strong upper-class accent."[23] Frank Baumgartner, a political scientist who was part of a group that studied the lobbying community over a ten-year period, underscored how the poor and less well off are disadvantaged in having their issues advocated on Capitol Hill. "The biggest indictment of the lobbying community is that it amplifies the voice of those who already have the most resources in society and leaves the people with the greatest needs completely voiceless."[24]

The well off and the well educated in U.S. society participate more in politics than the less fortunate, and lawmakers hear disproportionately from them. In her analysis of legislator-constituent interactions in health care policy, Kristina C. Miler discovered that legislators' perceptions of their constituencies were systematically distorted by the fact that they and their offices interacted so much more frequently with resource-rich groups.[25] The rich and poor are interested in different things. The advantaged talk about taxes, government spending, and social issues, whereas the disadvantaged are primarily concerned about "basic human needs . . . [food], jobs, housing, and health."[26] Elected officials are inundated with messages from groups that represent the politically active (such as the elderly, veterans, and small-business owners). But lawmakers receive comparatively little information about the policy preferences of the needy, who are often only marginally engaged in civic life.

An example of this political reality occurred following the "sequester," a series of across-the-board spending cuts imposed as a consequence of the Budget Control Act of 2011. One immediate result of these indiscriminate fiscal reductions was nationwide flight delays as numerous air-traffic controllers were furloughed from their jobs. Powerful interests—the airlines, businesses, and an angry traveling public—lobbied Congress to get the furloughed controllers back to work. The result: a month after the sequester took effect, a law was enacted that ended the furloughs of the air-traffic personnel. As a House member noted, "When you [vote for sequester exceptions], what happens is the most politically strong groups with the most lobbyists get relief, at the expense of everybody else. Meals on Wheels, or kids on Head Start, or grants on biomedical research—all of those get left behind."[27]

PRESSURE GROUP METHODS

Pressure groups employ a variety of techniques to influence Congress's decisions. These methods have not always been ethical. Bribes and corruption have periodically fueled public outrage. During the nation's early technological and industrial expansion, railroad interests lobbied for federal funds and land grants to build their routes. Some of these early lobbyists' methods rightfully inspired public ire. In 1874 Sen. Simon Cameron, R-Pa., described an honest politician as one who "when he is bought, stays bought."[28] Samuel Ward, the "king of the lobby" for fifteen years after the Civil War, wrote to his friend Henry Wadsworth Longfellow:

> When I see you again I will tell you how a client, eager to prevent the arrival at a committee of a certain member before it should adjourn, offered me $5,000 to accomplish this purpose, which I did, by having [the member's] boots mislaid while I smoked a cigar and condoled with him until they could be found at 11:45. I had the satisfaction of a good laugh [and] a good fee in my pocket.[29]

But the legislator-lobbyist connection is a two-way street. It is a mistake to envision the relationship as only involving pressure from one direction. Reverse lobbying is pervasive. Lawmakers lobby the lobbyists to achieve their policy priorities.[30] In 2009, for example, Senate Republican leader Mitch McConnell reportedly urged the National Rifle Association to oppose the nomination of Sonia Sotomayor to the U.S. Supreme Court. McConnell knew that NRA opposition would put pressure on conservative Democrats and any Republicans leaning toward support of Sotomayor.[31] Members also try to persuade key groups that are on the fence to back their proposals or at least not publicly oppose them. The passage in 2003 of a major prescription drug benefit for Medicare enrollees was facilitated by Speaker J. Dennis Hastert's wooing of AARP—the multimillion-member seniors' lobby. Seven years later, congressional Democrats and President Obama lobbied AARP and won its backing for the Affordable Care Act.

Given this interdependence, members and leaders actively reach out to organized interests, rather than just passively waiting for group input. For example, House and Senate Democratic leaders and aides schedule regular meetings with their lobbying allies, such as labor unions.[32] The chair of the Senate Democratic Steering and Outreach Committee works "hand in hand with outside advocacy groups to raise public support for bills on the Democratic agenda."[33] Similarly, congressional GOP leaders and their top aides regularly consult with business lobbyists to formulate goals and strategy.[34] House Republican leader John Boehner of Ohio even streamed live on the Internet a Capitol Hill meeting with twenty GOP lobbyists as party leaders solicited "suggestions for a new [GOP] policy agenda" for the 112th Congress (2011–2013).[35] The lobbyists then mobilized grassroots support for these initiatives through petition drives, rallies, radio and television advertising blitzes, national door-to-door campaigns, and other techniques.[36]

Lobbying relationships have evolved in variety and sophistication. Modern-day lobbying varies according to the nature and visibility of the issue and groups' resources. Among the most important practices are direct and social lobbying, coalitions, grassroots mobilization, and electronic advocacy.

Direct Lobbying

In the traditional method of direct lobbying, lobbyists present their clients' cases directly to members and congressional staff. When a group hires a prominent lawyer or lobbyist, such as Ken Duberstein, Heather Podesta, or Steve Elmendorf, the direct approach involves personal contact with senators or representatives. An aide to Speaker Thomas P. "Tip" O'Neill Jr., D-Mass. (1977–1987), explained the importance of the personal touch:

> [Lobbyists] know members of Congress are here three nights a week, alone, without their families. So they . . . [s]chmooze with them. Make friends. And they don't lean on it all the time. Every once in a while, they call up—maybe once or twice a year [to] ask a few questions. . . . Anne Wexler [a former official in the Carter White House, and later a lobbyist] will call up and spend half an hour talking about . . . politics, and suddenly she'll pop a question, pick up something. They want that little bit of access. That's what does it. You can hear it. It clicks home. They'll call their chief executive officer, and they've delivered. That's how it works. It's not illegal. They work on a personal basis.[37]

Former members of Congress are particularly effective at direct lobbying. A retired twenty-year House member wrote to prospective clients that he could "unravel red tape, open doors, make appointments, work with the Administration or government agencies, influence legislation, and assist in any other service required."[38] Recognizing their value, lobbying firms and clients eagerly enlist the services of former lawmakers. "Each member is part of a network of reciprocity," observed scholar James A. Thurber. "You help me, and I'll help you. That's what a lobbying client is buying."[39]

Member-to-member lobbying can be uniquely effective. No outsider has the same access to lawmakers (and certain precincts of Capitol Hill) that former colleagues have. For example, former GOP senators who may be lobbyists can attend the regularly scheduled Tuesday Republican Policy Committee lunch, "where legislative tactics are plotted on issues ranging from tax cuts to foreign policy—information that gives them a decided edge over other lobbyists."[40] Although ethics rules impose restrictions on the former lawmakers (for example, they may not lobby their colleagues while in the chamber), former members still retain privileges denied to others. As former Speaker J. Dennis Hastert, R-Ill., explained, "It's hard to take away benefits from former members. We're all going to be former members one day."[41] (Hastert is now a lobbyist with a D.C.-based firm.) Turnover in Congress hampers direct lobbying. The longer former members have been out of Congress, the fewer personal contacts they have with current lawmakers.

Former top Capitol Hill staff aides are similarly sought after as lobbyists because of their personal knowledge and understanding of key members and congressional processes.[42] The ease with which members and staff rotate from congressional service into lobbying is often referred to as the "revolving door." "The Congress-to-K Street connection has been institutionalized," observed Sheila Krumholz of the nonpartisan Center for Responsive Politics. "It's Plan A for former members of Congress."[43] The revolving door also comes full circle in that many former lobbyists also return to take high-ranking staff jobs on Capitol Hill.[44]

A new type of lobbyist is also much sought after these days: the experienced fund-raiser. The talents that some fund-raisers bring to lobbying were summarized as follows:

The hiring equation for lobby firms is simple: Campaign fund-raisers spend time with lawmakers—often more than policy staffers. They also have the kinds of connections with CEOs and in-house government relations heads that could mean more business for the lobby shop. And they are comfortable making "the ask," not only to sign clients but also to try to get members of Congress and staff to take action on behalf of clients.[45]

Direct lobbying involves many activities beyond meeting with lawmakers. Lobbyists monitor committees; testify (or have their clients appear as witnesses) at hearings; interpret Hill decisions for clients; articulate clients' interests to legislators; draft legislation, speeches, and "Dear Colleague" letters for members; and give campaign assistance. The House offers more occasions for contacting members directly than does the Senate, where lobbyists are more likely to target staff aides.

Taken together, lobbyists are major players in congressional policy making. Members rely heavily on them for information. "[Lobbyists] provide continuity and institutional memory," observed former representative James P. Moran, D-Va. "Most of them have been around longer than members."[46] Or as a GOP senator put it, "I would have to say the best information I get in the legislative process comes from people directly involved in the industry that is going to be affected—and from people who represent them: the 'nefarious' lobbyists."[47] "Most members may know one or two issues well, if that," said one financial services lobbyist. "Then you have a 26-year-old kid, maybe he's even 30 and went to a good law school, who's on the staff working 10 hours a day and is supposed to tell his boss how to do derivatives regulation or credit-card reform. Are you kidding?"[48]

Social Lobbying

Lobbying also occurs in social settings outside the legislative context, such as at dinner parties, receptions, sporting and entertainment events, or on the golf course or tennis court. Successful direct lobbying is grounded in trust.[49] Lobbyists must convince lawmakers that they are credible and knowledgeable before lawmakers will accept advice from or even listen to them. Social interactions are extremely useful for fostering and developing the personal relationships that lobbyists need to be effective. Lobbyists thus seek out opportunities to interact casually with lawmakers, even when no client business will be discussed.

Travel with members of Congress has long afforded opportunities for lobbyists to engage in social lobbying, but recent ethics laws have placed restrictions on the practice. Until the 2007 ethics rules were in place, it was not unusual, for example, for legislators to accept flights on corporate jets, reimbursing their sponsors only for the cost of commercial airfare. Such settings afforded many possibilities for relationship-building and casual interaction among lobbyists, legislators, and lobbyists' clients. The 2007 ethics reforms, however, "effectively ban travel with registered lobbyists."[50] Lobbyists "may not accompany lawmakers or aides 'on any segment' of a trip."[51] And, although there are some exceptions for nonprofit organizations, lawmakers must receive prior approval for all such travel from the Committee on Ethics of their chamber. Lobbyists are not permitted to pay for meals for legislators, banning the lobbyist-funded lavish dinners that were the source of so much public distaste. There is, however, the "reception exception" or the "toothpick rule," which permits "members and aides to [eat] food [on toothpicks] at receptions, but bans them from attending sit-down meals with lobbyists."[52] As one lobbyist hosting a reception for legislators ruefully put it, "I'm sitting here as vice president of corporate affairs for the National Association of Manufacturers, and I'm making sure that there's nothing you need a fork for."[53] Members and aides may also attend lobbyist-paid events when carrying out "official duties," and when more than twenty-five people not connected with Congress are in attendance.

A large loophole in all these ethics rules involves political fund-raising. Social and direct lobbying is unrestricted at campaign events. Many fund-raising events such as golf outings, fishing trips, and sit-down dinners offer wide-open opportunities for casual interactions with lawmakers. For example, Heather Podesta hosted a dinner at her home for five Democratic female senators. The fee for attendees, who in return were given a chance to discuss issues with the senators in a private setting, was $30,400 for a "co-chair" of the event, $10,000 for a "vice chair," $5,000 for a "co-host," and $1,000 for an "individual sponsor." Checks, said Podesta, were to be made payable to the Democratic Senatorial Campaign Committee (DSCC).[54] Lawmakers can continue to invite lobbyists to attend "lavish birthday parties in a lawmaker's honor ($1,000 a lobbyist), weekend golf tournaments ($2,500 and up), a Presidents Day weekend at Disney World ($5,000), or parties in South Beach in Miami ($5,000)."[55] Lobbyists end up paying for such events because "they pay a political fund-raising committee set up by the lawmaker. In turn, the committee pays the legislator's way."[56] In short, what is illegal if done directly—such as paying for legislators' meals, travel, or gifts—is legal if done indirectly through campaign contributions.

Coalition Lobbying

To enhance their chances of success, lobbyists often construct coalitions in support of their legislative initiatives. Coalitions bring more resources, contacts, and money to lobbying efforts. When individuals and organizations "band together and support one another," noted former senator John B. Breaux, D-La. (1987–2005), now a Washington lobbyist, it makes for "a smoother and more effective [legislative] operation than if fifty or more voices [are] all arguing for the same principle without any coordination."[57]

Examples of such coalitions abound. In 2013 a coalition of university, military, public health, and science groups joined together to try to stop across-the-board budget cuts.[58] Two years earlier, environmental and public health groups worked together to stop legislative efforts to strip the Environmental Protection Agency of its authority to regulate greenhouse gas emissions. The Pharmaceutical Research and Manufacturers of America (PhRMA) worked successfully with a variety of technology and financial interests to push for more favorable tax treatment of corporate income earned overseas. A study by researchers at the University of Kansas determined that this single tax break earned companies $220 for every dollar they spent lobbying on the issue, "a 22,000 percent rate of return on their investment."[59]

"We have no permanent friends or permanent enemies—only permanent interests." That oft-repeated line helps to explain why "coalitions, like politics, make strange bed fellows."[60] A coalition between the American Petroleum Institute and the Environmental Working Group to fight subsidies to ethanol offers one recent example. As the head of the environmental group observed,

"This is not a sign of any great, broad alliance with the oil industry."[61] Not surprisingly, these marriages of convenience are often difficult to sustain.

Grassroots Lobbying

Instead of contacting members directly, many organizations mobilize citizens in districts and states across the country to pressure their senators and representatives. For example, when eBay, the online auction website, wanted to influence federal telecommunications policy so that phone and cable companies could not favor certain types of Web traffic at the expense of others, it sent an e-mail to more than a million eBay users urging them to contact their members of Congress in support of "network neutrality."[62] Similarly, Uber aggressively employs its large base of smartphone-wielding customers to pressure government officials.[63] One researcher recently estimated grassroots lobbying as a "$1-billion-a-year industry."[64]

Interest groups use tools such as e-mail, phone banks, and social media to stir up public opinion on issues and generate communications to members' offices. Although lawmakers recognize that lobbying groups orchestrate these campaigns, they also realize they may serve as a rough measure of sentiment and organizational strength behind an issue:

> The congressman has to care that somebody out there in his district has enough power to get hundreds of people to sit down and write a postcard or a letter—because if the guy can get them to do that, he might be able to influence them in other ways. So, a member has no choice but to pay attention. It's suicide if he doesn't.[65]

Lawmakers often try to distinguish between genuine grassroots and fake grassroots (often called "Astroturf") groups. Many so-called grassroots groups are nothing more than front organizations for their financial backers. One group with an environmentally friendly name, the Save Our Species Alliance, was actually pushing "a rewrite of the Endangered Species Act to ease paper and logging business's access to federal lands where those species live."[66] An attractive name can often be a way for a single interest to bankroll an initiative while masking its identity. To combat such efforts, Congress adopted reforms in 2007 that require more disclosure of the groups that fund and lead coalition efforts.

Mass mobilizations have become so common that some firms now specialize in "grass tops" lobbying. Whereas the goal of grassroots lobbying is to mobilize the masses, the goal of grass tops lobbying "is to figure out to whom a member of Congress cannot say no: his chief donor, his campaign manager, a political mentor. The lobbyist then tries to persuade that person to take his client's side" during talks with the lawmaker.[67]

Electronic Lobbying

As in most other areas of life, advances in communication technology have transformed lobbyists' work. Smartphones, tablets, and other devices allow lobbyists sitting in a congressional hearing room or office to instantly send out alerts on legislative developments to clients, coalition partners, and their home offices.

Similarly, text messaging, e-mail, and social networking sites such as Twitter, YouTube, and Facebook have all greatly increased the speed with which lobbyists can galvanize supporters. For example, a debate over how to deal with online piracy and file sharing triggered, according to one account, the "biggest online protest in history," resulting in ten million petition signatures, three million e-mails, and 100,000 telephone calls to lawmakers.[68] On a smaller scale, the conservative Family Research Council, which opposed the confirmation of Elena Kagan to the Supreme Court, hosted webcasts with legal experts during her confirmation hearings to explain why Kagan should not serve on the Supreme Court. The council also provided people visiting their website with a letter they could send to their senators objecting to Kagan's confirmation. Individuals only had to put in their ZIP code and hit "Enter."[69]

Messages can be conveyed immediately to sympathizers anywhere in the country to bring pressure to bear when and where it is most needed. A Twitter message sent to AARP members concerning President Obama's 2013 State of the Union message said: "Keep your word, Mr. President. Protect seniors. No Social Security Cuts!"[70] One of the most influential of all lobbying groups, the National Rifle Association, draws much of its political clout from its ability to generate an outpouring of communications to members' offices. According to Sen. Charles Schumer, D-N.Y., the NRA can mobilize "2, 3, 4 million people who care passionately about this issue . . . at the drop of a hat," without a similar intense and sustained grassroots activism that backs additional gun-control legislation.[71]

GROUPS AND THE ELECTORAL CONNECTION

Today it is often hard to differentiate the roles of interest groups and political parties in electoral politics. "The standard distinction between interest groups and parties used to be that parties were committed to winning elections and that pressure groups let elections happen and then tried to influence the people who got elected," remarked a political scientist. "Now interest groups through their PACs [political action committees] and a variety of other methods are very much involved in the pre-policy arena."[72] As one example, the grassroots operation of the U.S. Chamber of Commerce "has begun to rival those of the major political parties."[73] Box 13-2 provides an interesting example of a group that is blending issue advocacy and electoral politics. Union workers are being trained as lobbyists in order to make them more effective advocates, organizers, and potential candidates for elective office.

Some groups are so extensively involved in partisan electoral politics that they are effectively "party allies"—a vital part of their party's "enduring multilayered coalition," in the words of Paul S. Herrnson.[74] Increasingly, the electoral coalitions of the two parties exhibit greater ideological homogeneity. For Democrats, group allies include labor unions, environmental and women's rights organizations, and liberal membership groups such as People for the American Way and Moveon.org. For Republicans, allied groups include the U.S. Chamber of Commerce, pro-life and pro-gun organizations, oil and gas interests, and conservative ideological groups such as the Club for Growth. Between elections, congressional party leaders and their allied interest groups cooperate to promote their party's message, enhance its public image, and advance its agenda.

Interest groups help elect members to Congress in three principal ways: they raise funds and make financial contributions through political action committees; they conduct their own, independent campaigns for or against issues and candidates; and they rate the voting records of legislators.

Groups and Campaign Fund-raising

Legislators who dislike raising money—almost certainly a majority of them— turn to lobbyists or professional fund-raisers to arrange parties, luncheons, dinners, or other social events to which admission is charged. Lobbyists buy tickets or supply lists of people who should be invited. They even serve as treasurers of members' reelection campaigns or political action committees.[75]

Fund-raising events consume more and more of legislators' limited time (recall Chapter 4) and create new scheduling conflicts—another example of the competing imperatives of the two Congresses, the representative assembly versus the lawmaking institution. Members cannot chase money and do legislative work at the same time. To minimize these conflicts, "windows" are opened in the Senate's schedule:

BOX 13-2 Union Workers Trained as Lobbyists

The United Steel Workers brings a group of legislative interns to the capital several times a year. It pays them what they make in their normal jobs plus expense allowances, lodges them in hotels, and gives them desks in the Steel Workers' offices near Dupont Circle. The visitors are technically on sabbaticals authorized by the union's collective bargaining agreements.

The program combines schooling and work. Interns often are sent to Capitol Hill to track down lawmakers or congressional aides to make the union's case on legislative issues. During a typical week, they also study congressional procedures and history, attend hearings, and observe union policy meetings.

The purpose is to give rank-and-file workers a deeper knowledge of Congress and to inspire activism at the local level. The union hopes its interns will go home more politically savvy and better prepared to rally coworkers on union issues and at election time. A spokesman for the Steel Workers said the union hopes the program will "get more plumbers and steamfitters and electricians into public office."

Source: Adapted from Matthew Tully, "Union Program Fields Blue-Collar Washington Lobbyists," *CQ Daily Monitor,* March 29, 1999, 7.

A window is a period of time in which it is understood that there will be no roll-call votes. Senators are assured that they won't be embarrassed by being absent for a recorded vote. Windows usually occur between six and eight in the evening, which is the normal time for holding fund-raising cocktail parties.[76]

Sen. Robert C. Byrd, D-W.Va., the longest-serving lawmaker ever in that chamber, complained that members must spend more time raising money than legislating.[77] A former senator said he "had to become an expert [at fund-raising] to survive." He described three principles of raising money based on his experiences. First, you have to ask. "People who give once are likely to give again," but if you stop asking, they will stop giving or give to someone else. Second, "it's a compliment . . . to ask someone for a large sum." Third, "people who have given to other causes may give to yours." For this reason, "keep track of all who give what to whom."[78]

Congressional critics, and even legislators and lobbyists themselves, question the propriety of fund-raising practices. Members worry about implied obligations when they accept help or money from groups. For their part, lobbyists resent pressure from members to give repeatedly.

"Bundling" is a widely used fund-raising technique that allows lobbyists and fund-raising entities to raise more money for candidates than they can contribute individually under campaign finance laws. Political action committees (PACs), for example, are limited to giving a candidate $5,000 for use in the primary and general election. There are no limits, however, on "how much a PAC can forward to candidates from other donors."[79] To bundle, a lobbyist or another type of fund-raiser will solicit checks from various sources and then give them all at once to a candidate's campaign committee or to the House and Senate party campaign committees. The candidate knows the bundler's identity because the checks are submitted to the campaign together or, in some cases, because the checks contain identifying information. Lobbyists are not "bundling this cash for altruistic reasons," said the president of a nonpartisan election watchdog group. "They want to get the [lawmakers'] attention and interest."[80] Until the 2007 ethics reforms, the public was entirely in the dark about the identities of bundlers and the amounts they raised. Under the current rules, limited disclosure requirements are imposed. Campaign committees must identify persons "reasonably known" to be registered lobbyists if they have provided two or more "bundled" contributions totaling more than $16,000 during any semiannual reporting period.[81]

Groups and Advocacy Campaigns

Interest groups are heavily involved in elections. Incumbents must contend with opposing interests, as well as other candidates. Labor unions, for example, spent $1.1 billion from 2005 through 2011 supporting federal candidates and lobbying Washington. But they spent considerably more ($3.3 billion) during this period on getting out the vote, persuading union members to support certain candidates, and so on. Such political mobilization efforts are not required to be reported to the Federal Election Commission.[82] Numerous other groups spend considerable amounts targeting voters in selected states or districts, urging them to vote for or against certain candidates. To name a couple: the U.S. Chamber of Commerce spent $33.5 million on the 2014 midterms, and the National Rifle Association spent $27.2 million.[83]

Rating Legislators

About a hundred groups keep pressure on members of Congress by issuing "report cards" on their voting records. Groups select a number of major issues and then publicize members' scores (on a scale of zero to one hundred) based on their "right" or "wrong" votes on them. Members are often warned by colleagues that certain votes will be scored. "You'll hear this as you walk into the chamber: 'This is going to be a scored vote. The environmentalists are going to score this vote, or the AFL-CIO is going to score this vote,'" explained a House member.[84] Congressional aides sometimes check with lobbying groups to determine whether certain votes will be scored.

To be sure, advocacy groups are not reluctant to announce that they will be grading lawmakers on certain votes. Lawmakers who sign pledges, such as the Taxpayer Protection Pledge or the Social Security Protectors' Pledge, are certain to have their votes monitored closely by outside organizations for any deviations from their promises. If pledges are violated, such as voting for tax hikes, members might face a primary challenge in the next election.[85]

Interest groups use scorecards to influence members' decisions on selected issues. The liberal Americans for Democratic Action and the conservative American Conservative Union issue score-based ratings that are well known and widely used. The ratings game, however, is always simplistic. The selected votes are often inadequate to judge a member's full record because they are identified with an agenda in mind. Group strategists defend ratings as "a shorthand way for voters to tell something about their congressman."[86] After creating these scorecards, interest groups may assign attention-getting names to Congress members who score high or low, such as "heroes and zeroes" (from the Consumer Federation of America) or the "dirty dozen" (from the League of Conservation Voters).

Groups use legislative scorecards to determine which candidates will win endorsement and receive campaign contributions. Vulnerable incumbents who hold closely contested seats, mindful of the two Congresses, will cast votes carefully to avoid antagonizing powerful interest groups back home. On the other hand, members may also use negative scores in their campaigns. A liberal lawmaker, for example, might "wear bad scores from conservative groups like a badge of honor."[87] Some of the groups that rate lawmakers maintain websites that allow visitors to compare how they personally would vote on issues with the actual voting record of their senators or representatives.[88] Interest groups may also canvass door to door in certain areas, "to talk to voters about the results" of their scorecards.[89]

GROUPS, LOBBYING, AND LEGISLATIVE POLITICS

How much influence do organized interests wield over congressional legisla-tion? The American public is convinced that their sway is excessive. Overwhelming majorities of survey respondents agree with the statement, "Congress is too heavily influenced by interest groups."[90] Political science research, by contrast, offers no such clarity on this question. According to a thorough review of the literature, the subject of interest group influence has generated "more debate than progress, more confusion than advance."[91] But one conclusion is clear: the results of empirical research do not support sweep-ing populist characterizations of Congress as bought and paid for by moneyed interests. A ten-year study by a group of political scientists who examined ninety-eight issues found that the side with the most PAC donations, lobbyists, money, and members won only half of the time. They concluded, "A better predictor than money in winning or killing legislation was the support of gov-ernment agency heads, congressmen-turned-lobbyists, high-level congressio-nal and government officials—and best of all—party leaders and the president."[92] The study also pointed out that it is always difficult for lobbyists to change policy because there are "people benefiting from the status quo" and entrenched interests on both sides of the issue.[93]

The Role of Money

Journalists and campaign reform groups often posit a direct linear correlation between members' votes and the amounts they have received from various groups. Scholarly researchers reject such simple cause-and-effect inferences. Simply correlating the campaign contributions legislators receive with their voting behavior ignores the possibility that members might just as well have voted as they did without any group influence or campaign contributions. Instead, it is necessary to determine whether lawmakers vote differently than we would have expected given their party, ideology, and constituency. The more careful research designs used by scholars frequently fail to find any causal connection between PAC contributions and members' votes.[94] As the manager of a corporate PAC pointed out, money is "only one tool. We use it to defeat people who do not agree with us and elect those who do. I wish we could just 'buy' votes, but we can't. That's not the way it works in the real world."[95]

Rather than altering members' behavior, the principal finding of empirical research on interest group behavior is that lobbyists tend to donate to members who are already friendly to their objectives. Labor unions, for example, donate the bulk of their funds to Democrats.[96] Similarly, oil and gas interests contrib-ute primarily to Republicans.[97] Generally speaking, groups do not regard donating to legislative opponents a good investment of their campaign money. Citing E. E. Schattschneider, who said, "moneyed interests sing with an upper-class accent," political scientists Richard L. Hall and Frank W. Wayman write, "they also spend a good deal of effort singing to the choir."[98] Furthermore, with the proliferation of interest groups and PACs, candidates have many different groups to which they can turn for fund-raising help. No single group is likely to exert overwhelming financial leverage over any given member of Congress.

In short, the patterns in campaign contributing simply do not conform to crude vote-buying theories. The relationship between lobbyists and legislators rarely resembles a simple economic exchange of money for support. Contributions signal and reinforce a relationship more often than they create one. The influence of money must be weighed along with other considerations influencing members' votes, including constituency pressures, party ties, friendships, and personal conscience, idiosyncrasies, and prejudices. As Rep. Barney Frank, D-Mass., put it: "Votes will beat money any day. Any politician forced to choose between his campaign contributions and strong public sentiment is going to vote public sentiment. Campaign contributions are fungible, you can get new ones. You can't get new voters."[99]

This is hardly to claim that the enormous sums that interest groups spend on political campaigns have no effect on legislative politics and policy making. Contributions almost certainly buy access to legislators. "There is no question— if you give a lot of money, you will get a lot of access. All you have to do is send in the check," explained one corporate executive.[100] Furthermore, on issues that are less visible to the public and where the bulk of money is on one side, there is good reason to think that the playing field will be tilted somewhat in favor of those with financial clout. Nevertheless, the linkages between money and policy making are not simple or easy to trace. Under the right circumstances, organized interests can reframe issues, sway members, mobilize support, or demobilize opposition, but there is very little evidence that organized interests are able to convert outright opponents.[101]

Lobbying and Legislation

An open, decentralized institution, Congress presents lobbyists with numerous opportunities to shape the fate of legislation. Groups play a direct or indirect part throughout the congressional process—in individual members' work, committee activities, legislative agenda-setting, and floor decision making. Nevertheless, tracing the nature and extent of lobbyists' influence on legislation is no less difficult than untangling the relationship between campaign contributions and lawmaking.

Just as organized interests contribute primarily to their legislative allies, lobbyists also spend most of their time with friendly legislators. Lobbyists rarely target their opponents in Congress; nor do they generally devote significant effort to trying to influence fence-sitters.[102] Instead, they work with lawmakers who share their policy views—providing them with appropriate information, data, and political intelligence that they can perhaps use to persuade wavering colleagues.

Along these lines, many organized interests have ties to sympathetic informal congressional groups. For example, the steel industry maintains links with the Steel Caucus and textile manufacturers with the Textile Caucus. Interest groups can be instrumental in forming these informal legislative entities. The idea for the Mushroom Caucus (to protect mushroom producers from foreign imports) originated at a May 1977 luncheon for House members sponsored by the American Mushroom Institute.[103] The Institute of Scrap Recycling Industries lobbied for two years (successfully) to encourage formation of the Senate Recycling Caucus and the House Recycling Caucus. These two recycling groups focus "on ways Congress can help improve recycling and develop new markets for recycled products."[104] Several of the informal legislative caucuses are closely affiliated with nonprofit entities such as the Congressional Black Caucus Foundation, which can collect unlimited donations from corporations, unions, and others. The nonprofits often sponsor policy forums, meetings, conventions, and other events where lobbyists can mingle with lawmakers and discuss the issues of the day.[105]

The relationship between lobbyists and legislators is better understood as a "legislative subsidy" than as a simple exchange in which legislators trade policy for political support.[106] Legislators benefit from the help of lobbyists because successful legislating requires so much work and expertise. Lobbyists' primary role is to assist and underwrite the efforts of their legislative allies. Lobbyists provide their congressional supporters with information, legislative language, policy analysis, useful arguments, and political advice. Working with friendly legislators, lobbyists steer policy toward their clients' goals, exerting influence that in practice is hard to distinguish from legislators' own policy preferences.

The value of lobbyists to legislators thus extends far beyond campaign contributions. "Essentially, we operate as an extension of congressmen's staff," explained one lobbyist. "Occasionally we come up with the legislation, or speeches—and questions [for lawmakers to ask at hearings] all the time. We look at it as providing staff work for allies."[107]

Lobbyists' information and expertise are thus one of their most valuable assets. A survey conducted by the American League of Lobbyists revealed that lobbyists rated delivering "good information/analysis" as the most effective way to influence a lawmaker.[108] Reflecting on the changing styles of modern lobbying, a lawyer-lobbyist said, "Because of the increasing sophistication of staff, you have to be armed with facts, precedents and legal points. Sure it's a political environment, but it's much more substantive. The old-style, pat-'em-on-the-back lobbyist is gone, or at least going."[109] Lobbying is substantive because Washington is a town filled with experts and saturated with data, analyses, and reports on all sides of an issue. The result: "Facts compete in Washington, just like Democrats and Republicans."[110]

Subgovernments

Many congressional committees deal with policies of concern to specific groups such as farmers, teachers, or veterans. Lawmakers whose constituencies contain many members of these groups tend to seek seats on the relevant committees.[111] Members from farming areas seek assignment to the agriculture committees; members from states with many users of federal lands (such as ranchers and miners) seek assignment to the natural resources committees. Such committees often form alliances with the bureaucrats and lobbyists who regularly testify before them and with whom members and staff aides frequently meet. At hearings before the House or Senate veterans' affairs committees, for example, the triple alliance is on public view. In attendance are the committee members, along with witnesses from various veterans' organizations (such as the American Legion) and executive officials from the Department of Veterans Affairs. Scholars and journalists use the term *subgovernment* for the three-way policy-making alliances of committees, executive agencies, and interest groups.

These triangular relationships dominate policy making less today than in the past. Other contending forces (citizens' groups, aggressive journalists, assertive presidents) have ended their policy monopoly. Term-limited committee chairs also have less time and incentive to cultivate ties with external constituencies. Still, there is evidence that the triangular relationships remain influential in various policy domains. On January 17, 1961, President Dwight Eisenhower in his farewell address urged citizens to guard against a "military-industrial" complex to which political evolution has added Congress to the mix. This phenomenon, stated Sen. John McCain, R-Ariz., "should now rightly be called the military-industrial-congressional complex."[112] A description of the triple alliance was provided by former defense secretary Robert Gates in a 2009 speech:

> First, there is Congress, which is understandably concerned . . . about protecting jobs in certain states and congressional districts. There is the defense and aerospace industry, which has an obvious financial stake in the survival and growth of these programs. And there is the institutional military itself—within the Pentagon, and as expressed through an influential network of retired generals and admirals.[113]

Even this subgovernment is not immune to outside developments over which it has little control, as evidenced by the 2011 Budget Control Act's sequestration requiring the Pentagon to make significant spending cuts in defense programs, projects, and accounts.

REGULATION OF LOBBYING

For more than a hundred years, Congress intermittently considered ways to regulate lobbying—a right protected by the First Amendment's free speech principle and "the right of the people . . . to petition the Government for a redress of grievances." Not until 1946 did Congress enact its first comprehensive lobbying law, the Federal Regulation of Lobbying Act (Title III of the Legislative Reorganization Act). The ineffectiveness of this law finally led to passage of the Lobby Disclosure Act of 1995.[114] In 2007 Congress enacted another major lobbying reform measure, the Honest Leadership and Open

Government Act (P.L. 110-181). In general, there have been three main statutory approaches to the regulation of lobbying: defining and prohibiting abusive lobbying practices, requiring registration for lobbyists, and providing for disclosure of lobbyists' activities.[115]

The 1946 Lobbying Law

The main objective of the 1946 act was public disclosure of lobbying activities. Persons trying to influence Congress were required to register with the clerk of the House or the secretary of the Senate and to report quarterly the amounts of money they received and spent for lobbying. The law's drafters, although reluctant to propose direct control of lobbying, believed that "professionally inspired efforts to put pressure upon Congress cannot be conducive to well-considered legislation." Thus the law stressed registration and reporting:

> The availability of information regarding organized groups and full knowledge of their expenditures for influencing legislation, their membership and the source of contributions to them of large amounts of money, would prove helpful to Congress in evaluating their representations without impairing the rights of any individual or group freely to express its opinion to the Congress.[116]

The lobby law soon proved ineffective. In 1954 the Supreme Court upheld its constitutionality, but the decision (*United States v. Harriss*) significantly weakened the law.[117] First, the Court said that only lobbyists paid to represent someone else must register—exempting lobbyists who spent their own money. Second, the Court held that registration applied only to persons whose "principal purpose" was to influence legislation. As a result, many trade associations, labor unions, professional organizations, consumer groups, and law firms avoided registering because lobbying was not their principal activity. Some lobbyists claimed immunity from the law on the pretext that their job was to inform, not influence, legislators. Finally, the Court held that the act applied only to lobbyists who contacted members directly. This interpretation excluded indirect lobbying activities that, for example, generated grassroots pressure on Congress.

Lawmakers tried repeatedly to plug the 1946 law's loopholes. The attempts foundered largely because it was difficult to regulate lobbying without trespassing on citizens' rights to contact their elected representatives. After repeated efforts to "change the way Washington does business"—a campaign theme that many members advocated—the two parties finally came together to enact the first major overhaul of the 1946 act.

The Lobby Disclosure Act of 1995

The Lobby Disclosure Act of 1995 applied new rules to individuals and firms that lobby Congress and senior executive branch officials. The law broadened the definition of those who must register as lobbyists to include all those who spend at least one-fifth of their time trying to influence lawmakers, congressional aides, or high-level executive officials, and who are paid $5,000 or more over a six-month period. Registrations of lobbyists quickly soared.

A study by the Government Accountability Office determined that when the law took effect "only 6,078 individuals and organizations had registered" under the outdated 1946 act. "After the new law took effect, a total of 14,912 lobbyists registered."[118] But the number of registered lobbyists began to fall after 2006. In 2014 there were 11,509 registered lobbyists. This decline did not necessarily reflect a decline in the number of people engaged in lobbying. As with the 1946 act, organized interests have learned how to exploit loopholes in the 1995 regulations, and thus to avoid registering.[119] James Thurber's research suggests that the true number of working lobbyists is closer to 100,000.[120]

In addition to registration, the law requires lobbyists to "provide semi-annual disclosures showing who their clients are, what policies they are trying to influence, and roughly how much money they are spending for lobbying."[121] Civil fines of up to $50,000 can be imposed on those who fail to comply. Grassroots lobbying is exempt from the law, as are lobbyists paid $5,000 or less semiannually and organizations that use their own employees to lobby.

Although the 1995 lobby law was an improvement over the old one, it was minimally enforced. A 2005 report by the Center for Public Integrity said that the disclosure system was in disarray.[122] Former representative Lee H. Hamilton, D-Ind., described the situation:

> Roughly one in five of the companies registered to lobby failed to file the required forms . . . while another fifth of the required lobbying forms were filed late. The Center [for Public Integrity] found that "countless forms are filed with portions that are blank or improperly filled out. An unknown number of lobbyists neglect or refuse to file any disclosure forms whatsoever." In essence, we have a lobby disclosure system in name only.[123]

Some firms and organizations also underreport their lobbying expenditures. "Companies, trade associations, and lobby firms often misreport—intentionally or inadvertently—how much money they shell out or take in."[124]

The Honest Leadership and Open Government Act of 2007

A confluence of events beyond the perception that the 1995 law was weakly enforced compelled the 110th Congress (2007–2009) to take up another major lobbying reform bill. Public attention focused on ethics reform as a result of the Jack Abramoff bribery scandal (2005–2006), which resulted in the convictions of numerous high-ranking officials and staffers, including one member of Congress. Democrats made the "culture of corruption" on Capitol Hill a major theme of the November 2006 elections, in which they won majority control of both chambers. Following the elections, Democratic leaders realized that they had to make ethics and lobbying reform a top priority.

Some of the most notable provisions of the 2007 ethics reforms are high-lighted in Box 13-3. Allegations of ethical violations are handled by each chamber's ethics committee; lobbying violations are under the purview of the Department of Justice. In March 2008, the House created an Office of Congressional Ethics (OCE) composed of eight private citizens. The OCE may investigate any alleged rules violations by members and report their findings to the House Ethics Committee for further review. OCE reports are eventually made public even if the ethics panel chooses to dismiss the cases submitted to them.[125]

Enforcement of the registration and disclosure requirements under the 1995 and 2007 laws remains problematic. Some Washington insiders say, "I don't lobby," because they do not meet with lawmakers directly or spend more than 20 percent of their time over three months lobbying for a client. (These individuals might be called "unlobbyists."[126]) A former Senate party leader does not register as a lobbyist even though he provides clients with lawmaking and other relevant advice. "I provide my clients with analysis, not access," he said.[127] In July 2014, for the first time, the Office of Congressional Ethics accused an entity of lobbying Congress illegally; the case was referred to the Department of Justice.[128]

Foreign Lobbying

The 1995 Lobby Disclosure Act also amended the Foreign Agents Registration Act of 1938, which required those who lobby on behalf of foreign governments or political parties to register with the Justice Department and file twice-yearly reports with the department on their contacts with lawmakers and federal agencies. The 1995 law broadened the definition of foreign lobbyists to include individuals who lobby on behalf of foreign-owned commercial enterprises. Although foreigners who are lobbyists cannot make campaign contributions, one "in every $8 spent lobbying Congress and federal agencies comes from foreign governments."[129]

Numerous foreign governments sponsor cultural exchange programs for lawmakers and legislative staff, which are organized by Washington-based lobbyists who work for those governments. From 2006 to 2011, there were more than eight hundred of these cultural exchange trips paid for by foreign countries located in most parts of the world (Asia, the Middle East, and Europe, for example). Despite the detailed rules (pre-approval, the itinerary, etc.) governing congressional travel, there are loopholes. For example, registered foreign lobbyists may organize these trips and, importantly, accompany lawmakers and staff on the cultural trips. The benefits to these lobbyists can be significant. As one account noted, "Lobbyists for foreign countries use the trips to build relationships with staffers and often contact them about legislative business [involving the host countries] after the trips are over."[130]

Because of the role of the United States in the global economy and in military security, many foreign governments and lobbyists who work for foreign clients spend considerable amounts of time and money promoting their interests on Capitol Hill and with the broader citizenry. For example, to hasten

---

BOX 13-3 **The Honest Leadership and Open Government Act of 2007**

Lobby Registration

The clerk of the House and the secretary of the Senate are required to make registration and disclosure forms available, in a searchable and suitable format, on the Internet for public inspection.

Lobbying Disclosure

Lobbyists must file quarterly reports for an electronic database, with a maximum fine of $200,000 for not complying.

Gifts, Meals, and Travel

Lobbyists may not give lawmakers or staff gifts, even those less than $50 in value, and they cannot pay for lawmakers' or staffers' meals or travel expenses.

Members and staff must receive advance approval from the appropriate ethics committee before accepting any travel with any private organization.

Revolving Door

Senators and very senior executive officials are prohibited from lobbying for two years after they leave government; House members, for one.

Senior staff members who left Capitol Hill would be prohibited from lobbying for one year.

All Senate staff members are prohibited from lobbying the member or committee for whom they worked for one year after leaving.

Campaign Contributions

Registered lobbyists would have to reveal all their political contributions, including bundling of contributions from friends and colleagues.

Lobbying the Executive Branch

Lobbyists who contact executive branch officials, called "covered officials," must register with the clerk of the House and secretary of the Senate and disclose their contacts and activities. (The 1946 act did not address lobbying the executive branch.)

Source: Adapted from Jack Maskell, legislative attorney, "Lobbying Law and Ethics Rules Changes in the 110th Congress," Congressional Research Service Report RL34377, September 17, 2007.

---

passage of a trade agreement with the United States, the South Korean embassy "signed four different lobbying and public relations firms to advocate for the trade deal."[131] Several Washington firms lobbied for the Libyan rebels who led the successful revolt against dictator Muammar Gaddafi.[132] Many other nations also hire lobbyists to forge closer ties with Congress, the executive branch, and various U.S. industries, such as oil.[133]

Local lobbyists also operate globally. Many U.S.-based corporations hire lobbyists who can protect their interests in Europe or other parts of the world when disputes arise about trade, agriculture, antitrust laws, the environment, and other issues.[134] The National Rifle Association formed a transnational organization of gun groups and firearms manufacturers from eleven other countries (the World Forum) to fight international restrictions and regulations that might adversely affect the gun trade.[135] The NRA also informed the United Nations that "the effort to craft international rules for weapons sales will go nowhere in Congress if it includes civilian arms."[136]

Globalization of the world's economy also influences congressional lobbying. Toyota is the world's largest auto manufacturer, with plants located in eleven states. By locating plants around the country, the company enhances its political clout on Capitol Hill, gaining supporters in the House, Senate, and state houses. Toyota can now "call on 151 House members, 22 senators, and 11 governors from the states where it operates."[137]

CONCLUSION

Since the nation's beginning, lobbying and lawmaking have been closely intertwined. Lobbying "has been so deeply woven into the American political fabric that one could, with considerable justice, assert that the history of lobbying comes close to being the history of American legislation."[138]

Recent years have witnessed an explosion in the number and types of groups organized to pursue their ends on Capitol Hill. Compared with decades past, many more industry associations, public affairs lobbies (such as Common Cause), single-issue groups, political action committees, and foreign agents are engaging in the influence trade. Some of these groups employ new grassroots and technological lobbying techniques. Many victories today are won in Washington because of sophisticated lobbying campaigns waged in home states or districts.

No one questions that groups and lobbyists have a rightful public role, but some aspects of lobbying warrant concern. Groups often push Congress to pass laws that benefit the few and not the many. They inflate disagreements and hinder compromise. They often misrepresent the voting records of legislators in their rating schemes and pour money into the campaigns of their allies (mainly incumbents). Lawmakers who defy single-issue groups find at election time that those organizations are bent on defeating them.

Built-in checks constrain group pressures, however. The immense number of organized interests enables legislators to play one competing group off against another. Knowledgeable staff aides also provide members with information to counter lobbyists' arguments. Lawmakers' own expertise is another informal check on lobbyists. Finally, there are self-imposed constraints. Lobbyists who misrepresent issues or mislead members soon find their access permanently closed off. As Rep. Barney Frank, D-Mass, explained: "I feel better about a position when I can hear from both sides. . . . You can use [lobbyists] to inform you, as long as they know that if they lie, they lose. They will never be allowed to come back to this office."[139]

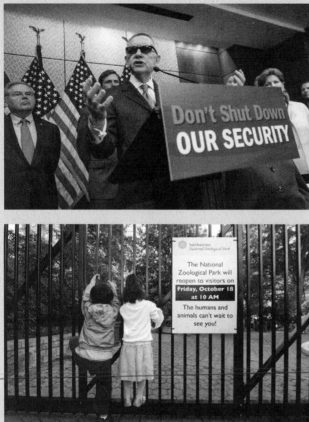

Budget and Domestic Policy Showdowns. Senate Democratic leader Harry Reid of Nevada rallies his party and the public against Republicans' insistence that a bill to fund the Department of Homeland Security include a provision repealing President Obama's executive order allowing undocumented immigrants to stay in the United States. An earlier fight over Republican efforts to defund the Patient Protection and Affordable Care Act ("Obamacare") resulted in a government shutdown that left many agencies, including the National Zoo, shuttered for weeks. Policy makers grapple with a range of domestic policy challenges beyond the recurrent budget fights. Former representative Gabrielle Giffords of Arizona (below) works the halls of Congress seeking support for a bill to expand background checks on gun purchases.

14

Congress, Budgets, and Domestic Policy Making

" There are no winners here," observed President Barack Obama on October 17, 2013, as he signed legislation to reopen the federal government after a sixteen-day shutdown. "These last few weeks have inflicted completely unnecessary damage on our economy," continued the president. Although Obama did not declare victory, the Republican chair of the House Ways and Means Committee, Dave Camp, R-Mich., counted House Republicans as among the losers: "We lost," he flatly declared.[1]

The government shutdown fight, which dominated the national news in the early fall of 2013, reflected the deep split between Democrats and Republicans on the general issue of spending priorities, and more specifically, on the future of the landmark health reform legislation passed by the Democratic Congress and President Obama in 2010. With crucial aspects of the Patient Protection and Affordable Care Act about to take effect—including the launch of insurance exchanges that would provide health insurance for millions of Americans and the implementation of the so-called individual mandate, requiring all Americans to purchase health insurance—conservative Republicans viewed the budget battle as one of their final opportunities to halt the law before it became entrenched.

Earlier in the spring, the Republican House had passed, on a party-line vote, a budget framework that called for cuts in domestic spending, major changes in Medicare, and repeal of Obama's health care law. The Democratic Senate, by contrast, narrowly approved a budget plan that kept Obamacare in place while providing for greater domestic spending and $975 billion in additional tax revenues over ten years.[2] The vast differences between the two plans made finding an agreement difficult before the start of a new fiscal year on October 1.

Meanwhile, government borrowing was set to exceed the nation's statutory debt ceiling sometime in October. When the government raises less in revenue than it spends, it must borrow money—by issuing bonds—to cover the difference. The debt limit is a statutory cap on the total amount of borrowing that the federal government can undertake. Treasury Secretary Jack Lew notified Congress in late August that the debt ceiling would be breached in mid-October unless Congress passed legislation raising the limit.[3]

House Republican leaders had entered the summer of 2013 hoping to avoid a knock-down political fight over funding the government and increasing the debt limit. But conservative members returned from their August recess having heard from conservative activists urging a final stand against Obamacare. "This is our last chance," declared a woman attending a town hall meeting held by Oklahoma representative Tom Cole. She continued that "it is more than who's gonna win the political power play if we shut down government. It's going to be, what will the future of our country look like in a decade? Because once the tentacles [of Obamacare] are there, it's too late to dial it back. Look at Social Security."[4] Rep. Tim Huelskamp, R-Kan., echoed this concern: "My more immediate thought is, what happens . . . if we don't defund it? The exchanges start up. Millions of Americans start going on there and finding out what they get for free."[5] Facing intense demands from conservative activists, House Republicans adopted a temporary measure on September 20, 2013, to keep the government running, but only on the condition that the president agree to defund the Affordable Care Act.

With the Democratic Senate and president firmly opposed to repeal of Obamacare, many political observers expected House Republicans to give up the fight before an actual government shutdown took place. Indeed, GOP leaders were keenly aware that their party had shouldered most of the blame in opinion polls and news coverage during past shutdowns.[6] But Sen. Ted Cruz, R-Tex., a leader of Tea Party Republicans, ratcheted up the pressure with a twenty-one-hour-long Senate floor speech advocating for a shutdown unless Democrats agreed to roll back Obamacare.[7] Cruz's speech sparked a barrage of e-mails from Tea Party activists urging Republicans to stand firm. Although the Texan's strategy found support from just a smattering of Senate Republicans, it carried more weight with House members from deep red districts.

After the Senate removed the provision defunding Obamacare, the House GOP sent back a bill that included a one-year delay of the individual mandate to buy insurance. This revised proposal failed in the Senate, resulting in 800,000 federal workers being furloughed on October 1. National parks closed down. Federal agencies sent home all but essential employees. The press was full of stories on the inconveniences—small and large—affecting citizens dependent on government programs, not to mention the financial pain felt by unpaid federal workers.

Democrats and Republicans vied to blame the other side for the impasse. Democrats pounced on a comment from Republican Marlin Stutzman, R-Ind., that "We're not going to be disrespected. We have to get something out of this. And I don't know what that even is." Republicans countered by highlighting a quote attributed to a senior administration official asserting that "We are winning. . . . It doesn't really matter to us" how long the shutdown lasts "because what matters is the end result."[8]

Amid the gamesmanship, however, Republican leaders quickly concluded that a deal had to happen in order to save their party's electoral brand from serious damage. Speaker John Boehner sought approval of a short-term bill to fund the government and raise the debt ceiling, while buying time for a longer-term deal on government priorities. Boehner's proposal gave in to the president on Obamacare funding, except for a provision forcing members of Congress and their staffs to pay more for their health insurance. The provision was intended to win over Tea Party conservatives, but cost the Speaker any chance of winning Democratic votes. When die-hard conservatives remained opposed to funding Obamacare, Boehner had to pull the bill, even as the Fitch Ratings put the United States AAA bond rating on a "negative watch."[9]

The action then shifted to the Senate, where Republican leader Mitch McConnell and Democratic leader Harry Reid negotiated a settlement. The deal funded the government through January 2014, raised the debt ceiling, kept Obamacare in place, and called for a conference committee of the two chambers to work out a broader spending and revenue deal by December 13, 2013. The agreement sailed through the Senate 81–18, with the only nay votes coming from Republicans. House GOP leaders brought the bill to the floor, where it passed with the votes of all 198 Democrats and 87 Republicans.[10] Most House Republicans voted against what the Tea Party group FreedomWorks labeled "a total surrender."[11] Following passage, Republican senator Kelly Ayotte, R-N.H., concluded that "if we learned nothing else from this whole exercise, I hope we've learned that we shouldn't get behind a strategy that cannot succeed."[12]

Two months later, House Budget Committee chair Paul Ryan and Senate Budget chair Patty Murray reached agreement on a longer-term funding bill intended to provide a respite from the political uncertainty. The bill included a modest increase in military spending sought by Republicans, alongside a similar hike in domestic spending.[13] Once again, it did not challenge the implementation of Obamacare, but the bill nonetheless passed with little fanfare and bipartisan support.

The two Congresses were clearly in evidence during the shutdown fight. As a lawmaking assembly, members of both parties faced the urgent need to act decisively to forestall a disaster. But passing legislation to fund the government and increase the debt limit required addressing members' electoral calculations. Many Republicans were elected by constituencies determined to see Obamacare repealed. For these members, voting for a bill that allowed the law's implementation to go forward risked provoking a difficult primary challenge from the right.

The shutdown and debt ceiling battle also illustrates other aspects of the contemporary policy-making process in Congress. In the context of deep party divisions and frequently divided government, legislators and the president find it extremely difficult to agree unless there is a deadline that makes the consequences of stalemate disastrous. The drawn-out, messy negotiating process may veer close to disaster before generating a resolution that neither side is particularly happy about and that may well once again postpone some of the difficult decisions for yet another, new deadline.

Plainly, conflicts about policies and the money to pay for them lie at the vortex of today's lawmaking process. This chapter will first provide a general overview of the policy-making process. It will then turn to a more detailed discussion of budgeting, which has increasingly come to dominate politics and policy making in Congress.

STAGES OF POLICY MAKING

Public policy is what the government says and does about perceived problems.[14] Policy making normally has four distinct stages: (1) setting the agenda, (2) formulating policy, (3) adopting policy, and (4) implementing policy.

Setting the Agenda

At the initial stage, public problems are spotted and moved onto the national agenda, which can be defined as "the list of subjects to which government officials and those around them are paying serious attention."[15] In a large, pluralistic country such as the United States, the national agenda at any given moment is extensive and vigorously debated.

How do problems move onto the agenda? Some emerge as a result of a crisis or an attention-grabbing event—an economic depression, a terrorist attack, a devastating hurricane or earthquake, or a high-visibility corruption scandal. For example, in December 2012 a devastating shooting in an elementary school in Newtown, Connecticut, led to renewed attention to gun control on the national political agenda. Other agenda items are occasioned by the gradual accumulation of knowledge—for example, rising awareness of an environmental hazard such as global warming. Still other agenda items represent the accumulation of past problems that no longer can be avoided or ignored, such as the safety of the nation's food supply and the crumbling infrastructure.

Agendas are also set in motion by political processes—election results (1964, 1994, 2006, and 2010 are good examples), turnover in Congress, or shifts in public opinion.[16] For example, Democrats took a "shellacking" in the 2010 midterm elections. The eighty-seven House GOP freshmen, backed by an assertive Tea Party movement, made cost-cutting and downsizing government their top priorities. Scores of members in both parties and both chambers shared their concerns and mobilized to address the nation's mounting deficit and debt.

Agenda items are pushed by policy entrepreneurs—that is, people who are willing to invest their time and energy in promoting a particular issue. Especially at the beginning of a new president's term, many of Washington's think tanks and interest groups issue reports that seek to influence the economic, social, or foreign policy agenda of the nation. Elected officials and their staffs or appointees are more likely to shape agendas than are career bureaucrats.[17]

Lawmakers are frequently policy entrepreneurs. Party and committee leaders are especially influential. But even rank-and-file members can play the role of entrepreneur. For example, Sen. Rand Paul, R-Ky., responded to the violent confrontations between police and protestors in Ferguson, Missouri, that took place in the summer of 2014 by pushing to demilitarize the police.[18] Paul hoped to shift attention to an issue that potentially united his libertarian constituency with groups—such as African Americans—who generally side with the Democrats. Generally speaking, politicians gravitate toward issues that are visible, salient, and solvable. Tough, arcane, or controversial problems such as entitlements may be shunned or postponed because they arouse significant public controversy.

The nation's recent experience with climate change is a good example. The vast majority of climate scientists believe that continued high levels of carbon dioxide emissions will generate severe environmental consequences over the next several decades. These consequences likely include more frequent severe weather (e.g., hurricanes, droughts, wildfires), coastal flooding as sea levels rise, and disruptions to food production. The policy solutions to address climate change are complex, and would require changes in national policy that impose real costs on energy producers (and likely consumers), along with international agreements that demand sacrifices by both developed and developing countries. Given that the immediate effects of climate change are not readily apparent to most voters today, forging a political consensus to take on the issue is difficult.[19] Indeed, this kind of creeping crisis is often difficult for members of Congress to grapple with, in part because of the two-Congresses dilemma. As conscientious lawmakers, members might want to forge long-term solutions. But as representatives of their constituents, they must respond to more immediate constituent concerns.

Formulating Policy

In the second stage of policy making, lawmakers and others discuss items on the political agenda and explore potential solutions. Members of Congress and their staffs play crucial roles by conducting hearings and writing committee reports. They are aided by the policy experts in executive agencies, interest groups, legislative support agencies, think tanks, universities, and private-sector organizations. Another term for this stage is *policy incubation,* which entails "keeping a proposal alive while it picks up support, or waits for a better climate, or while a consensus begins to form."[20] Sometimes, this process takes only a few months; more often it requires years. During Dwight D. Eisenhower's administration (1953–1961), for example, congressional Democrats explored and refined domestic policy options that, while not immediately accepted, were ripe for adoption by the time their party's nominee, John F. Kennedy, was elected president in 1960.[21]

The incubation process refines the solutions to problems and brings policies to maturity. The process may break down, however, if workable solutions are not available. The seeming intractability of many modern issues complicates problem solving. Thomas S. Foley, D-Wash. (Speaker, 1989–1995), held that in the years after he entered Congress in 1965 issues became far more perplexing. At that time "the civil rights issue facing the legislators was whether the right to vote should be federally guaranteed for blacks and Hispanics. Now members are called on to deal with more ambiguous policies like affirmative action and racial quotas."[22] Complex topics such as the escalating cost of a college education, stagnating wages, unconventional warfare, cybersecurity, and global climate change are contemporary examples of the difficult issues facing lawmakers. Solutions to problems normally involve "some fairly simple routines emphasizing the tried and true (or at least not discredited)."[23] A repertoire of proposals—for example, blue-ribbon commissions, trust funds, or pilot projects—can be applied to a variety of unsolved problems. Problem solvers also must guard against recommending solutions that will be viewed as worse than the problem.

Adopting Policy

Laws often embody ideas whose time has come. The right time for a policy is what scholar John W. Kingdon calls the "policy window": the opportunity presented by circumstances and attitudes to enact a policy into law. Policy entrepreneurs must seize the opportunity before the policy window closes and the idea's time has passed.

Once policies are ripe for adoption, they must gain popular acceptance. This is the function of legitimation, the process through which policies come to be viewed by the public as right or proper. Inasmuch as citizens are expected to comply with laws or regulations—pay taxes, observe rules, and make sacrifices of one sort or another—the policies themselves must appear to have been properly considered and enacted. One of the lingering liabilities of the landmark Patient Protection and Affordable Care Act of 2010 is the impression among some Americans that it was rammed through without bipartisan support.

Symbolic acts, such as members voting on the House or Senate floor or the president signing a bill, signal to everyone that a policy was adopted within the traditional practices. Hearings and debates serve to fine-tune policies as well as to cultivate support from affected interests. As for the pace of the overall process, responding to critics of Congress's glacial progress in adopting energy legislation, a senator posed these questions:

> Would you want an energy bill to flow through the Senate and not have anyone consider the impacts on housing or on the automotive industry or on the energy industries that provide our light and power? Should we ignore the problems of the miner or the producer or the distributor? Our legislative process must reflect all of the problems if the public is to have confidence in the government.[24]

Legitimating policies, in other words, often requires a measured pace and attention to procedural details. But a measured pace and painstaking attention to procedural niceties often provide opponents of change with an opportunity to mobilize. In many circumstances, policy makers may be forced to enact bold changes quickly in response to public outcry or demand, knowing that the details will have to be refined and adjusted later. The legislative passage in three weeks of President Obama's 2009 economic stimulus package is an example.

Implementing Policy

In the final stage, policies shaped by the legislature and at the highest executive levels are put into effect, often by a federal agency. Most policies are not self-executing; they must be promulgated and enforced. Congress and the president usually delegate most decisions about implementation to the responsible agencies under broadly worded guidelines. Implementation determines the ultimate effect of policies. Officials of the executive branch can thwart a policy by foot-dragging or sheer inefficiency. By the same token, overzealous administrators can push a policy far beyond its creators' intent.

Congress, therefore, must exercise its oversight role. It may require executive agencies to report to or consult with congressional committees or to follow other formal procedures. Members of Congress receive feedback on the operation of federal programs through a variety of channels: media coverage, interest group protests, and even casework for constituents. With such information Congress can adjust funding, introduce amendments, or recast the legislation on which the policy is based.

TYPES OF DOMESTIC POLICIES

One way to understand public policies is to analyze the nature of the policies themselves. Scholars have classified policies in many different ways.[25] Our typology identifies three types of domestic policies: distributive, regulatory, and redistributive.

Distributive Policies

Distributive policies or programs are government actions that convey tangible benefits—subsidies, tax breaks, or advantageous regulatory provisions—to private individuals, groups, or firms. These benefits are often called *pork,* a derogatory term for program benefits or spending specifically designated for members' states or districts. But pork is often difficult to define objectively. After all, "one person's pork is another person's steak." The projects come in several varieties, including "old-fashioned pork" (bridges and roads), "green pork" (wind, solar, and other alternative energy projects), "academic pork" (research grants to colleges and universities), or "high-tech pork" (cybersecurity).

Distributive policy making, which makes many interests better off and few, if any, visibly worse off—comes easily to Congress, a collegial and nonhierarchical institution that must build coalitions to function. A textbook example was the $1 billion–plus National Parks and Recreation Act of 1978. Dubbed the "Park Barrel Bill," it created so many parks, historic sites, seashores, wilderness areas, wild and scenic rivers, and national trails that it sailed through the Interior (now Resources) Committee and passed the House 341–61. "Notice how quiet we are. We all got something in there," said one House member after the Rules Committee cleared the bill in five minutes flat. Another member quipped, "If it had a blade of grass and a squirrel, it got in the bill."[26] Distributive politics of this kind throws the two Congresses into sharp relief: national policy as a mosaic of local interests.

The politics of distribution works best when tax revenues are expanding, fueled by high productivity and economic growth. When productivity declines or tax cuts squeeze revenues, it can become difficult to add new benefits or expand old ones. Yet distributive impulses remain strong even in these circumstances, as lawmakers in both parties work to ensure that money is spent for specific purposes in their districts or states. This type of particularistic spending is known by a variety of different names—"pork," "spending with a zip code," "member projects," "congressional directed spending," or, more common today, "earmarks." By whatever name, the fundamental purpose of this spending is to "bring home the bacon." Recently, earmarks have fallen into disfavor, in part because of their cost, political use ("greasing" the legislative wheels), and the circumvention of competitive procedures for funding such constituency-based projects.

The Controversy over Earmarks. During the 1990s and early 2000s, the number of earmarks in spending bills increased in number and dollar value. In 1993 there were 892 earmarks worth $2.6 billion; in 1998 there were nearly 2,000 earmarks worth $10.6 billion; and by 2005 there were "nearly 14,000 earmarks, costing $27.3 billion."[27] The cost of over 9,000 earmarks peaked at $29 billion in 2006, with a falloff to $15.9 billion (9,500 earmarks) in 2010.[28]

Various factors accounted for the explosion in earmarks and then their rapid drop-off. As for the increase, with narrow partisan divisions in the House and Senate, party and committee leaders used earmarks to attract the votes they needed to pass priority legislation and, in a two-Congresses tactic, to help electorally vulnerable lawmakers facing tough challenges at home. A longtime GOP appropriator also stated that in 1995, when Republicans took control of the House, they "democratized the earmark process" by making earmarks "available to everyone, Republican or Democrat, leader and rank-and-file alike."[29] The decline in earmarks occurred for three principal reasons. First, there was significant criticism of wasteful and unnecessary earmarks, especially in an era of rising fiscal deficits. The classic example highlighted by opponents of earmarks was "the bridge to nowhere"—a $230 million bridge connecting a small Alaskan town of eight thousand to an island with fifty residents.[30] Second, there was an unseemly and sometimes corrupt connection between earmarks and campaign contributions. One lawmaker (who ended up in jail) took $2.4 million in bribes from lobbyists to insert earmarks for defense contractors, who would then contribute to his reelection campaign. Third, aggressive watchdog groups, bloggers, and several lawmakers, such as

Rep. (now Sen.) Jeff Flake, R-Ariz., and Sen. John McCain, R-Ariz., exposed and challenged on the floor what they viewed as bad earmarks.

Earmark Reform. The 110th and 111th Congresses (2007–2010), as well as President Obama, instituted reforms intended to bring transparency and accountability to the earmark process. For example, the procedures required public disclosure of the lawmaker requesting an earmark; the name and location of the intended recipient; the purpose of the earmark; and certification that neither the requesting lawmaker nor his or her spouse had a financial interest in the earmark.

The 112th Congress (2011–2012) went even further. The GOP-controlled House imposed a complete ban on earmarks for all House members. Their party regulation stated that "no Member shall request a congressional earmark, limited tax benefit, or limited tariff benefit, as such terms have been described in the Rules of the House." Some House committees also established their own guidelines for excluding earmarks from their measures.[31] The Senate resisted for a time but then moved to ban earmarks. After President Obama declared in his 2011 State of the Union message that he would veto any legislation containing earmarks and the House indicated that it would not pass any bills that contained them, Senate Appropriations chair Daniel Inouye, D-Hawaii, said in a statement: "Given the reality before us, it makes no sense to accept earmark requests that have no chance of being enacted into law."[32] But key senators have promised to revisit the issue and to explore ways "to improve the earmarking process."[33]

The debate over earmarks did not end in either chamber for a fundamental two-Congresses reason. As one lawmaker explained, earmarking is "part of the genetic makeup of a legislator," who must try to find a way to help his or her community.[34] Earmark advocates in both chambers argued that a blanket ban impeded the lawmaking process, granted too much authority to unelected bureaucrats to make spending decisions that reside constitutionally with House and Senate members, and urged a rethinking of how to define an earmark. Writing to their Appropriations Committee's leaders, several senators stressed the need "to operationalize a clear definition" of earmarks. Authorized earmarks that benefit the entire nation, they argued, "are quite different from congressionally directed spending items, which only benefit a separate state, congressional district or region, and change year-to-year."[35]

Members also employed other, less transparent means to finance projects back home: earmarks by another name. They include "lettermarking"— lawmakers writing to administrators to urge that home-based projects be funded; "phonemarking"—calling executive officials to request money for projects in their states or districts; and "soft earmarks"—simply "suggesting" to agency officials that money should be spent on the lawmaker's project. Members also might hike the dollar amounts in certain budgetary accounts and "then forcefully request that the agency spend the money on the member's pet project."[36] Some lawmakers continue to solicit funding for earmarked local projects. They ask constituents to send in letters identifying community projects in need of federal money. As Rep. Mike Thompson, D-Calif., wrote in a letter to constituents:

> I disagree with this decision [banning earmarks] because it prevents full and open congressional consideration of many worthwhile project proposals critical to the health, safety and economic well-being of the people of our district. As your representative in Congress, I am committed to working with you to pursue alternative strategies to support critical infrastructure improvements in our communities.[37]

To sum up, many lawmakers and analysts contend that eliminating earmarks saves a trivial amount of money, and that the lengthy debates over earmarks only detract from the big-budget items that dominate spending such as entitlements and defense, which need members' attention. Earmarks are also an important way that leaders can build a coalition of support for larger national policy shifts.[38] Some observers have argued that the earmark ban has made successful negotiation more difficult in Congress.[39] Moreover, many earmarks are not wasteful and serve worthwhile national purposes, such as repairing decrepit bridges, establishing the Human Genome Project, and requiring the Pentagon to procure more body armor for troops.[40]

Regulatory Policies

Regulatory policies are designed to protect the public from the harm or abuse that might result from unbridled private activity. For example, the Food and Drug Administration monitors standards for foodstuffs and tests drugs for purity, safety, and effectiveness, and the Federal Trade Commission guards against illegal business practices such as deceptive advertising.

Federal regulation against certain abuses dates from the late nineteenth century, when the Interstate Commerce Act and the Sherman Antitrust Act were enacted to protect against abuses in transportation and monopolistic practices. As the twentieth century dawned, scandalous conditions in slaughterhouses and food-processing plants led to meatpacking, food, and drug regulations. The stock market collapse in 1929 and the Great Depression of the 1930s paved the way for the New Deal's regulation of the banking and securities industries and of labor–management relations. Consumer rights and environmental protection policies came of age in the 1960s and 1970s. The reversal of some of the protections of the 1930s enactments, plus lax oversight by federal agencies, contributed to the banking crisis of 2008–2009, which in turn fueled the Great Recession. Predictably, the fresh wave of Wall Street scandals led to a new round of regulatory fervor. Among its legacies is the Consumer Financial Protection Bureau (P.L. 111-203). Its job is to act as a watchdog for consumers in their purchase of various financial products, such as credit cards or mortgages.

Regulation inevitably arouses controversy. Much of the clean air debate, for example, involves the basic issue of costs versus benefits: Do the public health benefits of cleaner air outweigh the financial costs of obtaining it?[41] Environmentalists and health advocates argue that tougher standards for regulating air pollution save the lives of thousands who are afflicted with asthma and other lung diseases. Industries and conservative groups attack these claims, contending that the regulations are unnecessary, too expensive, and produce little health benefit.[42]

Reviewing federal agencies' regulation-writing process is a priority of today's Congress and of President Obama. Like presidents before him, Obama took steps to further centralize overall control over regulation writing in the Office of Management and Budget (OMB), specifically OMB's Office of Information and Regulatory Affairs (OIRA). For example, the president issued an executive order on January 18, 2011 (E.O. 13563), requiring agencies to produce affordable and less intrusive regulations: "We're looking at the [regulatory] system as a whole to make sure we avoid excessive, inconsistent and redundant regulation."[43] To achieve these regulatory goals, the president relies on OMB, which uses cost-benefit analysis to curb excessive and burdensome regulations. Rep. Jason Chaffetz, R-Utah, the chair of the House Oversight and Government Reform Committee, also cites regulatory reform as a priority.

Redistributive Policies

The most difficult of all political feats is redistributive policy—that is, one in which the government purposefully shifts resources from one group to another. Typically controversial, redistributive policies engage a broad spectrum of political actors, not only in the House and Senate but also in the executive branch and among interest groups and the public at large. Redistributive issues tend to be ideological, dividing liberals and conservatives on fundamental questions of equality, opportunity, and property rights. The battle over efforts to increase taxes on the wealthy is an example of a redistributive controversy. Redistribution can even be future-oriented: excessive amounts of deficit spending today mean larger financial burdens for the next generation.

Most of the divisive socioeconomic issues of the past generation—civil rights, affirmative action, welfare, immigration, tax reform—were redistributive problems. A redistributive issue for the twenty-first century is the growing share of the federal budget that goes to the elderly compared with everyone else in society. Spending on entitlement programs, principally Social Security and Medicare, absorbs an ever-increasing proportion of federal dollars, which then are unavailable for other important social, domestic, or security needs.

When redistributive issues are at stake, federal budgeting is almost always marked by conflict. In recent years, the conflicts have tended to be over the progressivity of the income tax code and how to cut entitlements. Various techniques have been employed to disguise benefit cuts and to make them more palatable. Omnibus budget packages permit legislators to approve cuts en bloc instead of one by one, and across-the-board formulas (such as freezes) give the appearance of spreading the misery equally to affected groups. In all such vehicles, provisions are added to placate the more vocal opponents of change.

CHARACTERISTICS OF CONGRESSIONAL POLICY MAKING

As a policy-making body, Congress displays the traits and biases of its membership and structure, as well as those of the larger political system. As for the first, the two houses of Congress have divergent electoral and procedural traditions. As for the second, Congress is representative, especially where geographic interests are concerned, and it is decentralized, having few mechanisms for integrating or coordinating its policy decisions. As for policy itself, Congress is often inclined toward enacting symbolic measures instead of substantive ones. Finally, Congress is rarely ahead of the curve—or the public—tending to reflect conventional perceptions of problems.

Bicameralism

Differences between the House and Senate—their relative sizes, members' terms of office, the character of their constituencies—shape the policies they make. Six-year terms, it is argued, allow senators some freedom to act as statesmen for at least part of each term before the approaching elections force them to concentrate on fence-mending.[44]

House and Senate constituencies tend to pull in divergent directions. Homogeneous House districts often promote clear, unambiguous positions on a narrower range of questions than those embraced by an entire state. A senator, then, as a representative of an entire state, must weigh the claims of many competing interests on a broad range of matters.

The sizes of the two chambers dictate procedural biases. House rules are designed to allow majorities to have their way. By contrast, Senate rules give individual senators great latitude to influence action. As a GOP senator once said, "The Senate has the strongest minority of any minority on earth, and the weakest majority of any on earth."[45] In short, the two chambers differ in outlook, constituency, and strategy. This can make forging agreement across the two chambers more challenging and therefore adds to the more general difficulty of changing or terminating existing policies, not to mention passing new legislation.

Localism

Congressional policies respond to constituents' needs, particularly those that can be mapped geographically. Sometimes, these needs are pinpointed with startling directness. For example, an aviation noise control bill required construction of a control tower "at latitude 40 degrees, 43 minutes, 45 seconds north and at longitude 73 degrees, 24 minutes, 50 seconds west"—the very location of a Farmingdale, New York, airport in the district of the Democratic representative who requested the provision.[46]

Usually, however, programs are directed toward states, municipalities, counties, or geographic regions. Funds are often transferred directly to local government agencies, which in turn deliver the aid or services to citizens. But sometimes Congress will require states and localities to fund some national priorities without federal assistance. These "unfunded mandates" strain state budgets and rouse the ire of state and local officials. For example, the No Child Left Behind (NCLB) education law (P.L. 107-110), which President Obama is urging the 114th Congress to revise and reauthorize, prescribes mandatory standardized testing in all public schools in today's cash-strapped states. School systems in many states complain that the federal government has failed to provide enough money to cover the expense of meeting the law's requirement. The law's fundamental goal is to ensure that every student in grades 3–8 is proficient in reading and math. If not, schools might close and teachers could be fired.[47]

National and local policies are necessarily intertwined. National policies can be advanced by state and local governments; in turn, states or localities can develop innovations that spur national action. The threat of terrorist attacks in the United States demands that any such calamity be confronted by first responders—police officers, firefighters, public health officials, and others—at the state and local levels. On other issues as well, the states are the testing grounds, or laboratories, for social, economic, and political experiments.

Many policy debates revolve around not only which government level can most effectively carry out a responsibility, but also which level best promotes particular values. Liberals tend to prefer that the national government lead in enforcing civil rights and environmental protection. Conservatives support an activist national government on defense and security matters. When it suits their purposes, both liberals and conservatives are capable of advocating either national mandates or local autonomy, depending on which level of government would best serve their objectives.

Piecemeal Policy Making

Policies all too often mirror Congress's scattered and decentralized structure. Typically, they are considered piecemeal, reflecting the patchwork of committee and subcommittee jurisdictions. The structure of a policy frequently depends on which committees have reported it. Working from varying jurisdictions, committees can take different approaches to the same problem. The taxing committees gravitate toward tax provisions to address problems; the appropriations committees will prefer a fiscal approach to issues; the commerce panels typically adopt a regulatory perspective; and so forth. Each approach may be well or ill suited to the policy objective. The approach adopted will depend on which committee is best positioned to promote the bill.

Symbolic Policy Making

Congressional policy making can be more about appearance than substance. Bills are often passed to give the impression that action is being taken, even when the measure adopted is unlikely to have any real impact on the problem. The general public and interest groups continually demand, "Don't just stand there, do something." Doing something is often the only politically feasible choice, even when no one knows exactly what to do or whether inaction might be just as effective.[48] For example, when rising gas prices provoked a national outcry in May 2008, Congress responded by passing a law cutting off the flow of oil to the nation's Strategic Petroleum Reserve. Though the move was touted as a way to boost supply and thus reduce gas prices, most analysts argued it would have no effect on energy prices.[49]

Still, symbolic actions are important to all politicians. This is not the same thing as saying that politicians are merely cynical manipulators of symbols. Words and concepts—*equal opportunity, income inequality, cost of living, affirmative action*—are contested earnestly in committee rooms and on the House and Senate floor. The result, however, is that policy goals are often stated in vague, optimistic language and not spelled out in terms of specific measures of success or failure.

Reactive Policy Making

It would be naive to expect a deliberative body to routinely adopt bold or radical solutions to problems. Elected officials are seldom far ahead of or far behind the collective views of their constituencies. Members know that out-of-the-mainstream views are unlikely to attract widespread public support. Indeed, Congress is essentially a reactive institution. As one House member explained,

> When decision rests on the consent of the governed, it comes slowly, only after consensus has built or crisis has focused public opinion in some unusual way, the representatives in the meantime hanging back until the signs are unmistakable. Government decision, then, is not generally the cutting edge of change but a belated reaction to change.[50]

Ending the statutory "don't ask, don't tell" policy toward gays in the military, for example, came late in 2010—only after public attitudes on the matter had shifted and the Joint Chiefs of Staff had assured lawmakers that the change would not adversely affect military performance.

The reactive character of Congress's policy making is evident in its budget process. Under pressures to reform in recent decades, Congress has embraced formal and informal changes in the way it makes budget decisions. The current budget process, dating from the mid-1970s, was intended to bring coherence to the way standing committees handle the president's budget. It has decisively shaped both Congress's internal decision making and its relations with the executive.

CONGRESSIONAL BUDGETING

Congressional budgeting is a complex process that involves two types of federal spending: discretionary and mandatory (entitlements). Discretionary spending is under the jurisdiction of the House and Senate Appropriations Committees; mandatory or entitlement spending embedded in statutes is the purview of the authorizing (or policy-recommending) committees of each chamber. Virtually all House and Senate members and committees, the president and executive branch officials, and scores of other participants actively seek to influence Congress's power of the purse. That congressional budgeting is usually contentious should come as no surprise, considering the high political and policy stakes associated with fiscal decision making (see Box 14-1 for some of the terminology used in budgeting).

Authorizations and Appropriations

Congress's budget procedures are shaped by two customary and longtime processes: authorizations and appropriations. Generally, legislative rules stipulate that before agencies or programs receive any money, Congress should first pass authorization laws that do three fundamental things: (1) establish or continue (reauthorize) federal agencies and programs; (2) define the purposes, functions, and operations of programs or agencies; and (3) recommend (that is, authorize) the appropriation of funds for programs and agencies. As Senate Democratic leader Harry Reid explained, "Authorizations allow programs to be created and funded. When we pass an authorizing bill, we hope the authorized level will be looked at in [the] appropriations committee—as I did as a longtime member. But we realize there are competing priorities, and full funding doesn't come very often."[51]

As an example, the defense authorization bill might authorize the construction of three new submarines and recommend $15 billion for this purpose. Does that mean the Pentagon has the money to build the submarines? No. Congress must enact the defense appropriations bill that would grant the Pentagon legal authority to spend a specific amount of money for the submarines. In short, an authorization can be viewed as a "hunting license" for an appropriation, a law that actually supplies programs and agencies with public funds (budget authority).

By custom, the House initiates appropriations bills. The House Appropriations Committee (usually one of its twelve subcommittees) would recommend how much money the Pentagon should receive for the submarines. The amount is called "budget authority" (BA), and it is equivalent to depositing money in a checking account. The budget outlay (BO) is the check written by the Pentagon to the contractors hired to construct the submarines. The House Appropriations Committee can provide up to the authorized $15 billion (but not more), propose less funding, or refuse to fund the submarine purchases at all. Assume that the House votes to approve $10 billion. The Senate Appropriations Committee, acting somewhat like a court of appeals, then hears navy officials asking the Senate to approve the full $15 billion. If the Senate accedes, a House–Senate compromise is worked out, either in a conference committee or by the bicameral exchange of amendments.

BOX 14-1   A Budget Glossary

Appropriations. The process by which Congress provides budget authority, usually through the enactment of twelve separate appropriations bills.

Budget authority. The authority for federal agencies to spend or otherwise obligate money, accomplished through enactment into law of appropriations bills.

Budget outlays. Money that is spent in a given fiscal year, as opposed to money that is appropriated for that year. One year's budget authority can result in outlays over several years, and the outlays in any given year result from a mix of budget authority from that year and prior years. Budget authority is similar to putting money into a checking account. Outlays occur when checks are written and cashed.

Cut-as-you-go (CUTGO) rule. This House rule requires new mandatory spending to be offset with cuts to existing entitlement programs. Tax increases cannot be used to offset new spending.

Discretionary spending. Programs that Congress can finance as it chooses through appropriations. With the exception of paying entitlement benefits to individuals (see mandatory spending below), almost everything the government does is financed by discretionary spending. Examples include all federal agencies, Congress, the White House, the courts, the military, and programs such as space exploration and child nutrition. About a third of all federal spending falls into this category.

Fiscal year. The federal government's budget year. For example, fiscal year 2016 runs from October 1, 2015, through September 30, 2016.

Mandatory spending. Made up mostly of entitlements, which are programs whose eligibility requirements are written into law. Anyone who meets those requirements is entitled to the money until Congress changes the law. Examples are Social Security, Medicare, Medicaid, unemployment benefits, food stamps, and federal pensions. Another major category of mandatory spending is the interest paid to holders of federal government bonds. Social Security and interest payments are permanently appropriated. And although budget authority for some entitlements is provided through the appropriations process, appropriators have little or no control over the money. Mandatory spending accounts for about two-thirds of all federal spending.

Pay-as-you-go (PAYGO) rule. This Senate rule requires that all tax cuts, new entitlement programs, and expansions of existing entitlement programs be budget-neutral—that is, offset either by additional taxes or by cuts in existing entitlement programs.

Reconciliation. The process by which tax laws and spending programs are changed, or reconciled, to reach outlay and revenue targets set in the congressional budget resolution. Established by the 1974 Congressional Budget Act (P.L. 93-344), it was first used in 1980.

Rescission. The cancellation of previously appropriated budget authority. This is a common way to save money that already has been appropriated. A rescissions bill must be passed by Congress and signed by the president (or enacted over his veto), just as an appropriations bill is.

> **Revenues.** Taxes, customs duties, some user fees, and most other receipts paid to the federal government.
>
> **Sequester.** The cancellation of spending authority as a disciplinary measure to cut off spending above preset limits. Appropriations that exceed annual spending caps can trigger a sequester that will cut all appropriations by the amount of the excess. Similarly, tax cuts and new or expanded entitlement spending programs that are not offset under the pay-as-you-go law could trigger a sequester of nonexempt entitlement programs.
>
> *Source:* Adapted from Andrew Taylor, "Clinton's Strength Portends a Tough Season for GOP," *CQ Weekly,* February 6, 1999, 293.

The authorization-appropriation sequence is not required by the U.S. Constitution. The dual procedure dates from the nineteenth century and stems from inordinate delays caused by adding riders—extraneous policy amendments—to appropriations bills. "By 1835," wrote a legislator, "delays caused by injecting legislation [policy] into these [appropriations] bills had become serious and [Massachusetts representative] John Quincy Adams suggested that they be stripped of everything save appropriations."[52] Two years later, the House required authorizations to precede appropriations. The Senate followed suit. Both chambers have rules and precedents designed "to segregate decisions about what the government should do [authorizations] from those about how much it can afford [appropriations]."[53] However, as discussed shortly, policy riders are often added to appropriations bills despite the dual procedure.

The Constitution provides that "No Money shall be drawn from the Treasury, but in Consequence of Appropriations made by Law" (Article I, section 9). As a result, appropriations have priority over authorizations. An appropriations measure may be approved even if the authorization bill has not been enacted. Some programs have not been authorized for years, but they still continue to operate. Why? If money is sprinkled on programs or agencies, they continue to exist and function even if their authorization has lapsed. As one House Appropriations subcommittee chair said about the "must-pass" appropriations bills, "It's not the end of the world if we postpone the Clean Air Act or a tax measure. But the entire government will shut down if . . . appropriations [are not enacted annually]."[54]

Authorizations can be annual, multiyear, or permanent. Through the end of World War II, most federal agencies and programs were permanently authorized. They were reviewed annually by the House and Senate Appropriations Committees, but not by the authorizing committees (such as Agriculture or Commerce). Since the 1970s, the trend has been toward short-term authorizations, giving the authorizing committees more chances to control agency operations.[55] Generally, authorizing committees are eager to enact their bills on a timely basis, because otherwise they cede their lawmaking power to the appropriating panels. As Sen. Dianne Feinstein, D-Calif., a senior member of the Intelligence Committee, exclaimed, "If this committee can't pass authorization bills . . . which give scope and force of law to what we do, we are in fact a paper tiger."[56] But authorizers also try from time to time to hitch a ride on an appropriations bill heading to the White House. "Ideally, it's not great to use [appropriations] bills," remarked former representative Barney Frank, D-Mass. "But they may be the only vehicles we can use [for] some [authorization measures] where we're facing a veto or we have problems in the Senate."[57]

In practice, it is hard to keep the two stages distinct. Authorization bills sometimes carry appropriations, and appropriations bills sometimes contain legislation (or policy provisions). Chamber rules that forbid these maneuvers can be waived. In the House, so-called limitation riders make policy under the guise of restricting agency use of funds. Phrased negatively ("None of the funds may be used for a specified purpose . . . "), such limitation riders bolster congressional control of the bureaucracy.[58] A well-known limitation amendment—barring the use of federal funds for abortions except under limited circumstances—was first adopted in 1976 and has been readopted ever since in appropriations bills. The Senate, too, is not reluctant to add extraneous policy proposals to appropriations bills. Policy riders can provoke bicameral, party, and legislative–executive disputes.

Committee Roles and Continuing Resolutions. Among the authorizing committees, House Ways and Means and Senate Finance have especially powerful roles in the budget process. These tax panels have access to the staff experts of the Joint Taxation Committee. Because the House under the Constitution initiates revenue measures, it usually determines whether Congress will act on legislation to raise, lower, or redistribute the tax burden. The House jealously guards its constitutional authority to originate tax measures and typically will return to the Senate any bill that violates the origination clause.[59] Occasionally, however, the Senate takes the lead. The Senate technically complies with the Constitution by appending a major tax measure to a minor House-passed revenue bill. In 1981 the Republican-controlled Senate used this tactic to act on President Ronald Reagan's sweeping tax cut plan. It used the same ploy the next year on the president's tax increase package.

Whenever Congress cannot complete action on one or more of the twelve regular appropriations bills (generally one for each subcommittee) by the beginning of the fiscal year (October 1), it provides temporary, stopgap funding for the affected federal agencies through a joint resolution known as a continuing resolution. In the past, continuing resolutions were usually employed to keep a few government agencies in operation for short periods (usually one to three months). In some years, Congress has packaged all the regular appropriations bills into one massive continuing resolution. As polarization and the increased use of the Senate filibuster have made passage of even routine spending bills difficult, it has become more common for Congress to rely on continuing resolutions to fund much or all of the government.[60] Each year, Congress also passes one or more supplemental appropriations bills to meet unforeseen contingencies. To sum up, there are three basic types of appropriations: *regular* (made annually), *supplemental* (furnishing funds for unexpected contingencies), or *continuing* (providing funds when one or more annual appropriations bills have not been enacted by the start of the fiscal year).

A Shift in Thinking. Congress has witnessed shifts in the role and culture of the two Appropriations Committees over time. Once known as guardians of the federal Treasury, the two panels gradually developed an affinity for spending as they evaluated and compared the budgetary requests of federal agencies and departments. Some lobbyists even referred to the committees as "favor factories" where taxpayer dollars could be won for their clients. Several committee members won the appellation the "King of Pork" or the "Prince of Pork" for the hundreds of millions of dollars they earmarked for projects in their states or districts.

Recently, a House appropriator called the panel "the Dis-Appropriations Committee."[61] Subtraction, not addition, now characterizes budgeting by the two panels. As Harold Rogers, R-Ky., the chair of House Appropriations, said, "The atmosphere in the country is that government has to get serious about cutting spending. . . . And the place where the spending is controlled is the Appropriations Committee."[62] To what extent and for how long the "atmosphere in the country" will support program-funding reductions is unclear. Government programs have constituencies—which is often why they were created in the first place—likely to oppose severe funding cuts or outright program terminations. As scholars and others have long known, people favor spending cuts in the abstract but not for programs they support and from which they benefit. For example, senior citizens often tell lawmakers, "Keep your hands off my Social Security!" A key question, then, is, are Americans ready and willing to shrink the size and scope of government and roll back federal spending?[63]

Backdoor Spending Techniques

To sidestep appropriators' abilities to slash their recommended funding levels, authorizing committees evolved backdoor funding provisions to bypass the front door of the two-step authorization-appropriation sequence. Backdoors are authorization laws that mandate, rather than simply recommend, the expenditure of federal funds. This type of spending legislation, which is reported solely by the authorizing committees, is called direct (or mandatory) spending, as opposed to the discretionary spending under the House and Senate Appropriations Committees. There are three types of backdoor or direct spending provisions: (1) contract authority permits agencies to enter into contracts that subsequently must be covered by appropriations; (2) borrowing authority allows agencies to spend money they have borrowed from the public or the Treasury; and (3) entitlement programs grant eligible individuals and governments the right to receive payments from the national government.

The fastest-growing of the three types is entitlements, which establish legally enforceable rights for eligible beneficiaries. Spending for entitlement programs (such as Medicare and Social Security) is determined by the number of citizens who qualify and the benefit levels established by law. No fixed dollar amount is established for these programs. Budget wonks sometimes call entitlements "uncontrollable under existing law." Statutory changes are difficult to make because entitlements benefit millions of people. Tellingly, the GOP-controlled House of the 112th Congress (2011–2012) sought to defund President Obama's health care law by changing the mandatory spending features embedded in the health law into discretionary spending. If such a law were enacted, it would be easier for House appropriators to defund the statute's implementation.[64]

The Challenge of Entitlements

Entitlements are the real force behind the escalation of federal spending (see Figure 14-1). Approximately two-thirds of federal spending consists of entitlements that avoid the annual appropriations review process. This ratio of discretionary (determined through yearly appropriations) to mandatory spending represents a dramatic reversal from that of a half-century ago. Unlike defense or domestic discretionary programs—for which the Appropriations panels recommend annual amounts and on which all lawmakers may vote—entitlement spending occurs automatically under the terms outlined in the statute.

Congress has done a reasonable job of containing discretionary spending, but reining in costly entitlements has proved to be a much more difficult task. In 1996 Congress passed legislation ending a decades-old national welfare entitlement program, Aid to Families with Dependent Children.[65] However, the recipients of the largest share of entitlement spending—senior citizens—are highly protective of these programs and also very likely to vote. A classic example of how hard it is to revamp entitlements occurred in the second term of President George W. Bush. He launched an intense lobbying drive to win public and congressional support for replacing Social Security with individual retirement accounts, but his reform effort failed to gain any traction. Even many Republicans opposed the plan's reliance on private accounts. "Social Security [is] the bedrock of support for seniors," said Sen. Olympia J. Snowe, R-Maine, "precisely because it's defined and guaranteed. What cost and what risk is it worth to erode the guaranteed benefit [through variable stock or bond investments]?"[66] President Obama also faces the challenge posed by the escalating costs of the big three entitlement programs—Medicare, Medicaid, and Social Security. But this is hardly news. Public officials and analysts have been warning for years—without too much effect—that the projected expenditures of entitlement programs are unsustainable. For example, Medicare faces a prospective funding gap of $3.6 trillion; the Medicare fund is expected to run out of money in 2030.[67] Social Security is slated to pay full benefits to the elderly until 2033, after which seniors would receive 75–80 percent of their promised benefits unless changes are made to the existing laws.[68] Medicaid covers much of the cost of nursing home care for the disabled elderly. The long-term

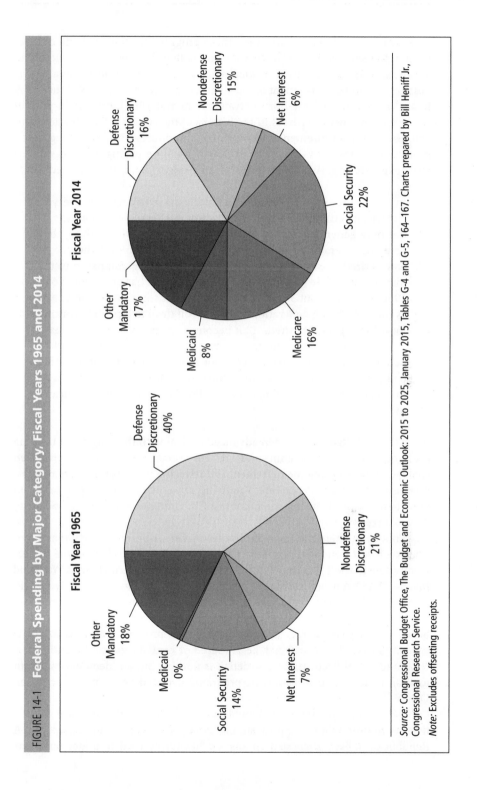

FIGURE 14-1 Federal Spending by Major Category, Fiscal Years 1965 and 2014

Fiscal Year 1965

Defense Discretionary 40%

Nondefense Discretionary 21%

Net Interest 7%

Social Security 14%

Medicaid 0%

Other Mandatory 18%

Fiscal Year 2014

Defense Discretionary 16%

Nondefense Discretionary 15%

Net Interest 6%

Social Security 22%

Medicare 16%

Medicaid 8%

Other Mandatory 17%

Source: Congressional Budget Office, The Budget and Economic Outlook: 2015 to 2025, January 2015, Tables G-4 and G-5, 164–167. Charts prepared by Bill Heniff Jr., Congressional Research Service.

Note: Excludes offsetting receipts.

demographic challenge confronting these programs is that the United States is an aging society with a population that is living longer, thanks in part to advances in often-expensive medical technology. The nation is already witnessing the gradual retirement of the seventy-six million members of the "baby boom" generation (those born between 1946 and 1964), creating a pool of the largest number of retirees in the history of the country. This development will lead to huge retirement and medical expenditures. But, according to the projections, fewer workers (a "birth dearth") will be paying taxes to support these expenditures. As a chair of the Senate Budget Committee pointed out,

> In 1950 there were about 16 Americans working for every 1 American retired. That meant programs such as Social Security . . . not only generated money to support those who were retired, they actually generated more money than needed to support the people who retired. . . . But the number of people retiring compared to the number of people working has been changing. It has gone from 16 in 1950 down to about 3 and a half today. And further into this century, as the baby boom generation retires, it will drop to 2 people working for every 1 person retired. . . . It becomes pretty obvious, if you have only two people working to pay for one person retired, those two people are going to have to pay a lot more in taxes to support that one person. . . . So this creates a huge . . . unfunded liability. We do not know how we are going to pay for [Social Security and Medicare] in the out years.[69]

Many proposals have been advanced to deal with the long-term funding challenge, but each is controversial. For Social Security, the proposed changes include raising the retirement age, reducing benefits for future retirees, increasing the payroll tax rate, requiring affluent retirees to pay taxes on their benefits, and raising the amount of income subject to Social Security payroll taxes.[70]

Politically, there are risks for any lawmaker or political party that advocates such recommendations. Rep. Paul Ryan, R-Wis., the chair of the Budget Committee in the 112th and 113th Congresses (and current chair of Ways and Means), has been one of many members of the fiscally conservative GOP-controlled House willing to take that risk. Representative Ryan has proposed overhauling Medicare and partially privatizing Social Security and cutting benefits. Many Democrats strongly oppose such proposals, arguing in Social Security's case that it will not be a source of escalating deficits until 2037. "Blaming Social Security for our deficit is nothing but an ideological attempt to slash benefits and privatize the program," declared Sen. Charles Schumer, D-N.Y.[71]

Why would congressional Republicans hand Democrats a political weapon that could erode GOP support among elderly voters in a future election? A Republican pollster suggested an answer. "It may be hard to understand why someone would try to jump off a cliff" to resolve a long-term entitlement spending issue, he said, "unless you understand that they are being chased by a tiger, and that tiger is the Tea Party."[72] Other GOP strategists disagree. They underscore that because of crushing budget realities the time is right politically for entitlement reform, provided the party does not move so fast as to "outstrip public opinion."[73] Many analysts and public officials contend that the real entitlement budget buster of the future is not Social Security but the soaring costs of Medicare and health care in general: "The long-term fiscal problem truly is fundamentally one involving the rate at which healthcare costs grow. . . . Social Security and aging are important, but it is not where the money is," explained President Obama's former budget director.[74] Representative Ryan's 2012 budget plan proposed a major overhaul of Medicare—federally subsidized vouchers for seniors so they can purchase health insurance in the private sector—and Medicaid—block grants to the states to care for low-income individuals and families. The GOP-controlled House passed the Ryan budget each year from 2012–2014, but the proposals went nowhere in the Democratic Senate. Even with the Senate in Republican hands in the 114th Congress (2015–2016), substantial changes to Medicare and Medicaid would still be a tough sell to moderate Republican senators facing reelection in competitive states—and would face a veto from President Obama unless they were paired with a substantial increase in revenues as part of a "Grand Bargain" on taxes and spending. The pressure to act aggressively on Medicare and Medicaid has also diminished slightly in the past few years as the growth in health care expenditures has slowed. President Obama claims that his landmark health care law, the Patient Protection and Affordable Care Act, is partly responsible for this slowdown in costs. Nonetheless, Medicare's actuaries warn that "notwithstanding recent favorable developments . . . Medicare still faces a substantial financial shortfall that will need to be addressed with further legislation."[75] In short, citizens want Lexus health services on a Chevrolet budget.

Setting aside the president's health care law and Representative Ryan's health proposals, the other steps "Congress could take now to restrain Medicare's growth are politically perilous. Deny end-of-life care? Restrict eligibility? Reduce treatments? Raise costs?"[76] Even more frightening from a budget perspective is the prospect of providing long-term nursing home or other care for the elderly. Long-term care, said former representative Earl Pomeroy, D-N.D., is "the elephant in the living room that no one's talking about."[77] And Medicaid, a federal entitlement program for indigent and low-income persons that is jointly funded by the national and state governments, has "now surged past Medicare to become the nation's largest health care program."[78] In short, an entitlement revolution is under way as the government today transfers more than half of federal monies to eligible families and individuals. "Call it government by ATM," remarked an analyst. "You walk up, hit the buttons, and the cash to which you're entitled pops out."[79] This transformation in the federal budget—away from discretionary to direct (or mandatory) spending—raises the question of whether this funding ratio is sustainable. Congress and the president face at least a dual fiscal challenge: the battle for scarce resources between entitlements and discretionary spending, and the struggle within the discretionary category between domestic versus defense and homeland security spending.

Two other major components of the budget merit separate mention as well: tax expenditures and interest on the national debt.

Tax Expenditures. An estimated $1 trillion is consumed by indirect spending, also called tax expenditures or tax preferences. This is the revenue that is forgone through various tax credits, subsidies, or deductions such as the home mortgage interest deduction. Rep. Jim Cooper, D-Tenn., declared that if "there is anything more out of control than entitlement spending," it is tax expenditures.[80] Compared with mandatory or discretionary spending, these expenditures receive scant public attention. One study noted that "much like entitlement programs, [tax expenditures] are on automatic pilot and do not receive sufficient scrutiny as part of the budget process."[81] Significantly, the total value of all tax preferences is virtually equal to the total value of all discretionary spending.

Negotiations between the White House and congressional leaders on deficit reduction since 2012 have focused on ways to cap or otherwise limit deductions and other tax expenditures.[82] In 2014 the House Ways and Means Committee, led by Rep. Dave Camp, R-Mich., made a serious attempt to rein in tax expenditures and simplify the tax code, but the effort never gained steam.[83] Like other government programs, tax expenditures have their own political constituencies that fight attempts to eliminate or reduce this conglomeration of tax breaks and subsidies. Of the some 250 tax expenditures, most "disproportionately benefit those at the top of the economic ladder."[84] Scholars who study tax expenditures sometimes refer to this form of federal largess as "the submerged state," or the "hidden welfare state."[85]

Interest on the Debt. "There is a cancer eating away at the budget from within," wrote a journalist, and it is the ever-increasing interest that must be paid to service the national debt.[86] In 2014 interest payments on the national debt were $231 billion, and in 2024 they are projected to reach nearly $800 billion.[87] This development further compounds the difficulty of resolving the long-term deficit. In 2014 interest payments exceeded the combined federal budget for the Education Department, Veterans Affairs, Housing and Urban Development, the Energy Department, NASA, and Transportation. By 2020, interest payments will surpass the amount projected to be spent on all discretionary programs outside of defense.[88] The options for Congress to slow the growth of interest payments on the debt appear straightforward, but they are politically controversial and substantively complex: tax more, spend less, combine those two, and foster economic growth.

To focus greater attention on issues such as tax expenditures, the debt ceiling, interest on the debt, entitlements, and much more, Congress passed more than forty years ago a landmark budgetary measure, the Congressional Budget and Impoundment Control Act of 1974. The goals of that act included bringing greater coordination and coherence to legislative budgeting and strengthening Congress's power of the purse. However, the results have been mixed because it is no easy task to control and monitor federal budgeting.

THE 1974 BUDGET ACT

Congress refocused its budgetary attention in the 1970s after its loose control of the purse strings gave rise to charges of financial irresponsibility. President Richard Nixon blamed Congress for annual deficits, consumer price hikes, high unemployment, and inflation. He also refused to spend monies duly appropriated by Congress, a practice called impoundment. Even though his administration lost every court challenge to the impoundments, Nixon held the political high ground. These diverse pressures prompted Congress to tighten its budget procedures.

The Budget and Impoundment Control Act of 1974 was landmark legislation. Among its principal features was the creation of House and Senate Budget Committees, as well as the Congressional Budget Office (CBO). The nonpartisan CBO prepares economic forecasts for Congress, estimates the costs of proposed legislation, and issues fiscal, monetary, and policy reports. The 1974 act also limited presidential use of impoundments and established a timetable for action on authorization, appropriation, and tax measures. The timetable has been changed periodically, and Congress commonly misses some of the target dates (see Box 14-2 for the timetable).

Of the many complex features of the 1974 act, two are central components of Congress's current budget process: the concurrent budget resolution and reconciliation. These two elements compel much of the time-consuming work, attract the attention of many interests and participants clamoring for fiscal resources, and influence policy decisions and outcomes.

Concurrent Budget Resolution

The core of Congress's annual budget process is adoption of a concurrent budget resolution. This measure is formulated by the House and Senate Budget Committees, which consider the views and estimates of numerous committees and witnesses.

The resolution consists of five basic parts. First, the budget resolution estimates what the federal government will spend in a fiscal year and for at least the four following fiscal years. For each fiscal year covered by the resolution, the spending is expressed in terms of both budget authority and budget outlays. Second, the total aggregate spending is then subdivided among twenty functional categories such as defense, agriculture, or energy. For each category, the target indicates what Congress expects to spend in those substantive areas. Third, the budget resolution stipulates the recommended levels of federal revenues needed to pay for the projected spending during each of the fiscal years. Fourth, the budget resolution identifies the estimated deficits (or surpluses should they occur, which is infrequent). Fifth, the total outstanding public debt

---

BOX 14-2   **The Congressional Budget Timetable**

Deadline	Action to be completed
First Monday in February	President submits budget to Congress
February 15	Congressional Budget Office submits economic and budget outlook report to Budget Committees
Six weeks after president submits budget	Committees submit views and estimates to Budget Committees
April 1	Senate Budget Committee reports budget resolution
April 15	Congress completes action on budget resolution
May 15	Annual appropriations bills may be considered in the House, even if action on budget resolution has not been completed
June 10	House Appropriations Committee reports last annual appropriations bill
June 15	House completes action on reconciliation legislation (if required by budget resolution)
June 30	House completes action on annual appropriations bills
July 15	President submits mid-session review of his budget to Congress
October 1	Fiscal year begins

Source: Bill Heniff Jr., The Congressional Budget Process Timetable, Congressional Research Service Report 98–472 GOV, March 20, 2008.

(savings bonds, Treasury securities, and other government obligations) permitted by law is also specified for at least the five-year period. In effect, the budget resolution sets the overall level of discretionary spending for each fiscal year.

The budget resolution is Congress's fiscal blueprint. It establishes the context of congressional budgeting; guides the budgetary actions of the authorizing, appropriating, and taxing committees; and reflects Congress's spending priorities. A senator described the purposes of the budget resolution: "[The budget] resolution would be analogous to an architect's set of plans for constructing a building. It gives the general direction, framework, and prioritization of Federal fiscal policy each year. Those priorities then drive the individual appropriations and tax measures which will support that architectural plan."[89] In a period of polarized politics, partisan issues dominate debate on these resolutions as Democrats and Republicans battle over spending levels for their competing priorities. Since Republicans took over the House in 2010, the Republican-controlled House Budget Committee has pushed a bold, politically risky budget blueprint that would slash nearly $6 trillion in federal spending over ten years, including, as noted earlier, the two health care entitlement programs (Medicare and Medicaid). Republicans called this budget blueprint the "path to prosperity." House Democratic leader Nancy Pelosi dubbed it a "path to poverty."[90] It is not unusual for minority party members in both chambers to vote as a bloc against the majority party's budget resolution.

The House and Senate each consider a budget resolution. In the House, budget resolutions are typically considered under special rules from the Rules Committee, which limit debate and impose restrictions on the number and types of amendments. In the Senate, the 1974 budget act sets a fifty-hour limitation for consideration of the budget resolution, unless members accept a unanimous consent agreement imposing other time restrictions. Amendments can be taken up and voted on after the fifty hours, but without debate. This circumstance often leads to "vote-a-ramas" over several days, when senators may "cast back-to-back votes on a dizzying array of dozens of amendments," often with the two Congresses in mind. As national policy makers, members of Congress may have to cast tough, but responsible, votes, which will "serve as valuable campaign fodder" for opponents in the next election.[91] When the chambers pass budget resolutions with different aggregate and functional spending levels, as is normal practice, House and Senate members usually meet in conference to resolve their disagreements. The conference report is then submitted to both chambers for final action. Because Congress's budget resolution is not submitted to the president, it has no binding legal effect. Instead, it outlines a fiscal framework that enables Congress, through its Budget Committees, CBO, and other entities, to monitor all budget-related actions taken during the course of a year. When the House and Senate are late or unable to adopt a concurrent budget resolution, each chamber usually adopts a resolution (H. Res. or S. Res.) reflecting the budget levels and enforcement procedures contained in the resolution adopted by one chamber but not the other. The failure to pass a budget has become far more common in recent years amid the fierce partisan warfare over spending and taxes. The Democratic Senate did not pass a budget from 2010–2012, prompting severe criticism from Republicans. When Congress passed a bill temporarily increasing the debt limit in January 2013, House Republicans insisted on a provision that would dock the pay of members of either chamber if it failed to pass a budget. Although some observers doubted the legality of the provision, it highlighted the breakdown in the budget resolution process.

Reconciliation

The 1974 budget act established a special procedure called reconciliation, which is an optional process authorized when Congress adopts the budget resolution. Its basic purpose is to bring revenue and direct spending (entitlement) legislation into conformity (or reconciliation) with the fiscal targets established in the concurrent budget resolution.[92] Its basic objective is to make changes in federal policies that result in budgetary savings. First used in 1980, reconciliation has been employed over twenty times since. It is a controversial process that "forces committees that might not want to reduce spending for entitlements under their jurisdiction to act and report legislation."[93]

Reconciliation is a two-step process. In the first step, Congress adopts a budget resolution containing a provision that usually instructs two or more House and Senate committees to report legislation that changes existing law. The instructions name the committees required to report legislation; they give each committee a dollar figure for mandated savings but do not specify the policies to achieve those goals; and they establish a deadline for reporting legislation to achieve the savings. In the second step, the House and Senate Budget Committees compile into an omnibus reconciliation bill the legislative changes in revenue or direct (entitlement) spending programs recommended by the named committees. If the instructions involve only one committee in each chamber, then those panels would bypass the Budget Committee and report their recommendations to the full House or Senate. On several occasions, reconciliation directives have provided for the maximum of three reconciliation bills during each fiscal year: one involving taxes, another on spending, and a third on raising the statutory debt limit.

Reconciliation in the House is considered under the terms of a rule from the Rules Committee. Procedurally, however, reconciliation is focused on the Senate, because measures governed by that optional process are treated differently from other bills or amendments. Reconciliation bills cannot be filibustered (a statutory time limit of twenty hours is placed on debate); passage requires a simple majority instead of the supermajority (sixty votes) needed to stop a talkathon; and amendments must be germane (the Senate has no general germaneness rule) and deficit-neutral (tax cuts or spending increases must be offset by equivalent revenue increases or spending reductions). There is little surprise that measures likely to arouse controversy in the Senate, such as tax bills, are attached to filibuster-proof reconciliation measures that could pass by majority votes. Democratic senator Robert Byrd lamented that reconciliation "can be used by a determined majority to circumvent the regular rules of the Senate in order to advance partisan legislation. We have seen one party, and then the other, use this process to limit debate and amendments on nonbudgetary provisions that otherwise may not have passed under the regular rules."[94] To prevent just such a usage of reconciliation bills, senators adopted the so-called Byrd Rule (named after Senator Byrd) in the mid-1980s. Under this complex rule, measures cannot be included in the Senate reconciliation package if they are viewed as extraneous provisions that are not primarily budget-related. When the parliamentarian rules that a provision violates the Byrd Rule, it is dropped from the bill unless sixty senators vote to waive the Byrd Rule.[95] Such provisions have been called "Byrd droppings."

The Byrd Rule played an important role in the 2009–2010 fight over health care reform. Some Democrats hoped to pass the massive overhaul through reconciliation, but doing so would have resulted in numerous provisions being dropped due to Byrd Rule violations. Democrats passed the overhaul through the standard sixty-vote cloture process in December 2009. However, before the bill could go to conference, Democrats lost their filibuster-proof margin in the Senate when Republican Scott Brown pulled off a dramatic upset in a January 2010 special election in Massachusetts.[96] To enact reform, Democrats had to resort to a complicated procedure in which the House adopted the previously passed Senate bill without any amendments, and the two chambers subsequently approved a set of minor changes to the legislation through reconciliation. The latter changes, however, were limited to budget-related adjustments that could pass muster with the Byrd Rule.

In summary, reconciliation offers a powerful procedure for fiscal policy. In a classic case, President Ronald Reagan and GOP congressional leaders used it for the first time on a grand scale in 1981. A reconciliation bill dictated deep, multiyear reductions (about $130 billion over three years) in domestic spending. Not long afterward, Congress also agreed to Reagan's tax legislation, the Economic Recovery Tax Act of 1981, which sharply cut tax rates for individuals and businesses. The revenue losses caused by the tax cut, combined with increased defense and entitlement expenditures and insufficient spending reductions in other areas, soon pushed annual budget deficits to levels unprecedented in peacetime, from double- to triple-digit shortfalls. Since the 1980s, Congress has been grappling with large deficits, with only a brief interlude of surpluses during the Clinton presidency.

A Revised Budget Process

The growth of budget deficits after 1981 became the prime congressional issue as lawmakers and presidents adapted to a new world: the politics of deficit reduction. Numerous proposals were put forth to deal with the problem. A prominent approach has been to set binding deficit or spending targets, which would be enforced through across-the-board cuts—known as "sequestration"—if the targets were not met. One difficulty with sequestration, however, was that it could always be forestalled by adoption of a new budget law delaying the pain. An additional strategy, embodied in the Budget Enforcement Act of 1990 (BEA), was to subject tax and entitlement programs to a new pay-as-you-go (PAYGO) procedure, which required that any tax reductions or any increases in mandatory (entitlement) spending be offset by tax hikes or reductions in other entitlement programs. As the chief counsel of the Senate Budget Committee explained, "The 'pay-as-you-go' label implies that Congress and the President may cut taxes or create [new entitlement spending] programs—that is 'go'— if they also agree to provide offsetting increased revenues or spending reductions—that is 'pay.'"[97]

Throughout much of the 1990s, the GOP-controlled Congress and President Clinton waged fierce battles over deficit reduction. As part of their political game plan, Republicans sent Clinton appropriations and reconciliation bills making deep cuts in federal programs. The president vetoed the measures, forcing two partial shutdowns of the government—the longest in congressional history. A fiscal breakthrough soon emerged, however. Indeed, much to the surprise of most observers, an era of budget surpluses arrived in the late 1990s. The robust economy and booming stock market led to much higher federal revenues, while presidential and congressional budgetary decisions during the first George Bush administration, such as passage of the Budget Enforcement Act (BEA) of 1990, as well as President Clinton's 1993 economic package, encouraged fiscal restraint and led to budgetary savings. The end of the Cold War also led to reductions in defense expenditures. "Just about everything broke right that could have broken right," said Robert Reischauer, a former CBO director.[98]

Shortly after President George W. Bush entered office, he and congressional Democrats began to argue about what to do with the huge projected surplus. Although many lawmakers and pundits recognized that the ten-year projection might never materialize—a slowing economy, international crises, or other reasons could intervene—politicians of both parties had their own ideas on how the surplus should be spent. It was a case of fiscal projections driving policy making, even though the money was not yet in the bank.

President Bush's top priority when he took office was a sizable tax cut. And on June 7, 2001, he signed into law the largest tax cut ($1.35 trillion) since Reagan's twenty years earlier. A little more than three months later, terrorists attacked the United States, and new demands and challenges confronted the country. The brief era (1998–2002) of surpluses came to a quick end.

What happened to the surplus? It disappeared because the factors that produced it reversed themselves. Instead of defense cutbacks, the nation was paying for military conflicts in Afghanistan and Iraq, reconstruction of those countries, and enhanced homeland security. A record ten years of uninterrupted economic growth ended and the stock market performed poorly, shrinking federal revenues. The large tax cuts pushed by the Bush administration also contributed to revenue shortfalls. Moreover, Congress's statutory fiscal constraints—spending caps and PAYGO—expired on September 30, 2002. Thus policy makers were now free to let the deficit increase. While PAYGO had been effective when it was in place, it clashed with Republicans' goal of cutting taxes since it required finding savings to pay for lost revenues. When Republicans took control of the House in the 112th Congress, they put in place a "cut-as-you-go" (CUTGO) rule, which focused on spending cuts to mandatory (entitlement) programs. Thus increases in entitlement spending must be offset only by spending reductions in other mandatory programs. However, tax initiatives are exempt from the CUTGO rule. House Republicans could thus cut taxes without finding offsets for the lost revenue.[99] In January 2015, House Republicans enacted another controversial rule change that could make it easier to cut taxes, this time requiring that the CBO use what is called "dynamic scoring" when it assesses the fiscal impact of major policy changes. This technique considers the macroeconomic consequences of new legislation, including potential increases in revenue that may arise if tax reductions spur greater economic growth.[100]

Budget deficits peaked at over a trillion-dollar level during the Great Recession (2009–2012) as revenues plummeted amid the shrinking economy and the Obama administration embraced stimulus spending to jumpstart growth. A deficit reduction agreement forged in 2011—following a lengthy showdown over raising the debt limit—required serious across-the-board reductions in domestic discretionary spending and defense spending if Congress failed to reach a broader agreement that would include some combination of entitlement savings and new revenues. The hope at the time was that Republicans' opposition to defense cuts and Democrats' resistance to the domestic reductions would bring both sides to the table for a "Grand Bargain." Although the Grand Bargain did not materialize, the revival in economic growth and the discretionary spending cuts have brought deficits down to the $400–$500 billion range. The CBO estimates that deficits will remain in that range over the next several years, before rising once again in the early 2020s as rising medical costs and retiree benefits increasingly stress the federal government's fiscal situation.[101] If deficits remain high in the years ahead, the federal government faces a serious dilemma: how to fund competing priorities and commitments.

The problem for Congress and the White House is determining what set of policies aimed at improving the nation's long-term fiscal prospects can attract the necessary votes. As one analyst observed, on one side are people who stress the "national neglect" theory. Being competitive globally and flourishing at home require major government investments in areas such as education and transportation. On the other side are those who emphasize the "national gluttony" model, which holds that excessive federal spending must be curbed first, based on the theory that a nation cannot spend its way to prosperity.[102] Any attempt to reconcile these competing worldviews underscores the fact that federal budgeting is about more than numbers. It reflects the divergent views of the two political parties about what policies best serve the country's short- and long-term interests.

CONCLUSION

Today, lawmakers are preoccupied with scores of important policy issues: stagnant wages, defense and homeland security, energy sources and usage, and the health of various domestic social programs. Former representative Barney Frank, D-Mass., has posed a question that crystallizes the debate over these various concerns: "What is the appropriate level of public activity in our society?"[103] Democrats and Republicans tend to answer that question differently. Governing, however, means making choices. Future decisions about budgeting and national priorities will surely reflect the values, goals, and interests that result from the confrontations and accommodations inherent in America's pluralist policy-making system.

A Ukrainian soldier rides on an armored vehicle near Artemivsk, eastern Ukraine. In 2014 Congress passed a law authorizing President Obama to supply defensive military equipment to Ukraine in its fight against Russia-backed rebels. Israeli prime minister Benjamin Netanyahu waves as he prepares to address a joint meeting of Congress on Capitol Hill in March 2015. Diplomacy is deployed as new secretary of state John Kerry (bottom left) joins South Korean foreign minister Yun Byung-se in a news conference in Seoul in April 2013 concerning North Korea's bellicose threats. Likewise, the Agriculture Department's P.L. 480 program (bottom right) distributes surplus farm products abroad.

15

Congress and National Security Policies

During President Barack Obama's second term, Congress and the White House confronted a "convergence of security crises . . . playing out around the globe."[1] Consider, for example, the rapid rise in 2014 of a barbaric and dangerous terrorist group in Iraq and Syria calling itself the Islamic State; civil wars in Iraq and Syria; or Russian president Vladimir Putin's aggression against the nation of Ukraine, including the annexation of Crimea. There are also escalating tensions and territorial disputes between China and various Asian nations, not to mention Beijing's ongoing cyber-espionage campaign against America's governmental entities and corporations. The Ebola outbreak in West Africa aroused fear that the disease might spread to many other nations, including America. Elected officials struggle to find consensus on how the United States might best respond to the wide range of security threats facing the nation, whether through diplomatic, humanitarian, economic, military, or other means.

In coping with the crises that drive national security policy making, presidential leadership typically takes center stage. In this arena, Congress is usually cast in a reactive role.

Individual presidents certainly differ in their general approaches. President George W. Bush referred to himself as "the decider," and was not reluctant to use military force. For example, after the September 11, 2001, terrorist attacks on the United States, President Bush and Congress backed the military invasion of the Taliban-led nation of Afghanistan, which had provided safe haven to Osama Bin Laden and the other plotters of the horrific 9/11 attacks. Combat operations began in October 2001 and ended in December 2001 when the Taliban fled Afghanistan. Subsequently, President Bush convinced Congress and the American people that a war of choice against the Saddam Hussein–led Iraq was in the national interest. There was no doubt that Hussein was a tyrant. However, the Bush administration claimed that Hussein had ties to al Qaeda, and it asserted mistakenly that he possessed weapons of mass destruction that could be used against the United States. In March 2003, a coalition of U.S., British, Australian, and Polish troops invaded Iraq. Iraq's capital, Baghdad, was captured two months later. Hussein's removal, according to administration officials, would lead to a new, self-governing Iraqi nation that respected democratic ideals (free speech, free association, and so on). Instead, violent disorder and sectarian strife soon supplanted democracy-promotion and nation-building.

In contrast to President Bush's quick-to-act approach, "Obama has been painstaking" in deliberating on military interventions and analyzing their potential consequences. Moreover, where "Bush was frequently accused of ignoring allies, Obama has consulted exhaustively."[2] President Obama's preference is for multilateral rather than unilateral actions to resolve global threats and to defend national interests. In the Middle East, for example, he persuaded Saudi Arabia, Jordan, Qatar, Bahrain, and the United Arab Emirates to join the United States in air strikes against the Islamic State. To avoid dispatching ground troops to every "hot spot," the president's preference is to authorize training, intelligence, communication, or other support to "moderate" rebel forces fighting to vanquish radical Islamists or to overthrow extremist regimes. As he said: "[I]t is more effective to use our unique capabilities in support of partners on the ground so they can secure their own countries' futures. And that's the only solution that will succeed over the long term."[3] Added the chair of the Joint Chiefs of Staff, Gen. Martin Dempsey: "Over the past 10 years we've done most of our heavy lifting on the direct action side [in Afghanistan and Iraq]. Increasingly, we are doing more, however, to build partners so that they can counter threats in their own regions."[4]

After more than a decade of wars in Afghanistan and Iraq, popular sentiment in the United States has largely backed the president's hesitancy in sending military troops to fight abroad. For example, Americans opposed getting involved in Syria's four-year civil war, which began in 2011, even though its president (Bashar Assad) repeatedly used chemical weapons against his own people. President Obama, who unsuccessfully demanded that Assad depart Syria, said that Assad's use of chemical weapons in the civil war would cross a "red line" triggering negative consequences. There were no military consequences, however, until the Islamic State shocked the nation by conducting in mid-August 2014 the first public beheading of an American journalist over Internet video. Other public beheadings followed the first. These grisly murders underscored for many Americans that the Islamic State aimed to send terrorists to attack Americans at home and abroad. Calls for "a severe response were growing fast."[5] Accordingly, in August 2014, the United States and its allies began air attacks against the Islamic State in Iraq. A month later the United States commenced air strikes in Syria. The goal, as President Obama stated, is "to degrade and ultimately destroy" the Islamic State. The United States has not, however, taken military action against Assad, who is opposed both by the Islamic State and by more moderate armed rebels.

Such extensive international involvement has not always marked U.S. foreign policy. Earlier generations of Americans tended to view themselves as special people set apart from the world's conflicts. Having forsaken Old World "wars and alarms," U.S. citizens—protected by two oceans—historically resolved to remain aloof from other nations' struggles. The most famous passage of President George Washington's 1796 Farewell Address counsels:

The great rule of conduct for us, in regard to foreign nations is in extending our commercial relations to have with them as little political connection as possible. . . . 'Tis our true policy to steer clear of permanent alliances, with any portion of the foreign world. . . . Taking care to keep ourselves, by suitable establishments, on a respectable defensive posture, we may safely trust to temporary alliances for extraordinary emergencies.[6]

Although Washington's Farewell Address is dutifully read in the chambers of Congress every year on the first president's birthday, Washington's vision bears little resemblance to twenty-first century conditions. As a world power today with numerous alliances spanning the globe, the United States and its foreign policies would scarcely be recognized by the nation's founders.

Formulating and implementing U.S. foreign and national security policies are not episodic activities but continual obligations. Congress and the president share in these duties—just as in domestic and budgetary matters. Congress has broad constitutional authority to take part in foreign and domestic security decisions. Even the most decisive chief executives can find themselves constrained by active, informed, and determined policy makers on Capitol Hill.

CONSTITUTIONAL POWERS

The U.S. Constitution is, in Edward S. Corwin's classic words, "an invitation to struggle for the privilege of directing American foreign policy."[7] In other words, foreign and military powers are divided between the branches. "While the president is usually in a position to *propose,* the Senate and Congress are often in a technical position at least to *dispose.*"[8] The struggle over the proper role of each branch in shaping foreign policy involves conflict over policy as well as over process.

The President Proposes

The chief executive enjoys certain innate advantages in dealing with foreign affairs. As John Jay wrote in *Federalist* No. 64, the office's unity, its superior information sources, and its capacity for secrecy and dispatch give the president daily charge of foreign intercourse.[9] In Jay's time, Congress was not in session the whole year, whereas the president was always on hand to make decisions.

The president's explicit international powers are to negotiate treaties and appoint ambassadors (powers shared with the Senate), to receive ambassadors and other emissaries, and to serve as commander in chief of the armed forces. The latter power looms large over the interbranch politics of the modern period, during which presidents have at their disposal huge military, security, and intelligence capabilities.[10] Presidents have claimed not only their explicit prerogatives but also others not spelled out in the Constitution. Whether they are called "implied," "inherent," or "emergency" powers, presidents increasingly invoke them in conducting foreign policy.

The executive branch tends to be favored by foreign policy specialists, who often denigrate legislative involvement in foreign policy. U.S. leadership in the world, declared a former secretary of state, could be sustained only "if we understand that the president has primary responsibility for the conduct of the nation's foreign policy."[11] Many lawmakers and scholars have a different view. Edward Corwin, the noted presidential and constitutional scholar, provided this balanced assessment of the legislative–executive relationship in foreign policy:

> What the Constitution does, *and all that it does,* is to confer on the President certain powers capable of affecting our foreign relations, and certain other powers of the same general kind on the Senate, and still other powers upon the Congress; but which of these organs shall have the decisive and final voice in determining the course of the American nation is left for events to resolve.[12]

Louis Fisher, an expert on legislative–executive relations, emphasized: The "Constitution does not allocate foreign policy to a single branch. It assigns portions to Congress, to the President, and to the president working jointly with the Senate." He added: "The framers deliberately dispersed political functions, including foreign affairs, to avoid concentrating too much power in a single branch."[13]

Divided control of the two policy-making branches spurs Congress to cast a more critical eye upon executive actions. Perhaps the most sensible statement of the separation of powers came from Justice Robert Jackson in *Youngstown Sheet and Tube Co. v. Sawyer* (1952). He wrote that "the president might act in external affairs without congressional authority," but he may not act "contrary to an act of Congress."[14] The president's advantages are magnified in times of warfare or crisis. It was Congress's clumsy management of affairs during the Revolutionary War that, among other things, led the founders to champion an independent, energetic executive, and to designate the president as commander in chief. Authority tends to become more centralized during wars and crises, so presidential powers reach their zenith at such times. This held true during the Cold War between the United States and the Soviet Union (1947–1989) and the hot wars in Korea (1950–1953) and Vietnam (1964–1975). The same pattern was evident in the period following the terrorist attacks of September 11, 2001. Heightened security fears and the wars in Afghanistan and Iraq brought new and sometimes unprecedented assertions of executive authority. Initially, at least, Congress's voice was muted.

Presidential powers usually contract and are subjected to sharper scrutiny from Capitol Hill when tensions ease or when the public tires of a prolonged conflict. Public opinion eventually came to oppose the Korean and Vietnam conflicts, a pattern that has repeated itself in Iraq and Afghanistan. A 2011 poll found that nearly two-thirds of Americans agreed that "the war in Afghanistan is no longer worth fighting."[15] Also in 2011 the Obama administration began a several-year transition to reduce the role and size of U.S. combat forces in

Afghanistan. In mid-June 2013, the security and defense of the country were formally handed to Afghan leaders and their country's armed forces. President Obama stated in May 2014 that America's combat missions would conclude at the end of the year with Afghans, starting in 2015, "fully responsible for security of their country."[16] Subsequently, after discussions with Pentagon leaders, President Obama revised his May order and authorized U.S. combat missions in Afghanistan against the Taliban and other terrorist groups for at least another year.

Congress Reacts

Congress has an impressive arsenal of explicit constitutional duties, such as the power to declare war, to regulate foreign commerce, to raise and support military forces, and to make rules governing military forces, including for "captures on land and water" (Article I, section 8). Paramount is the power of the purse. According to Crabb, Antizzo, and Sarieddine, "It is within the power of Congress to determine the course of American diplomacy, by virtue of its control over expenditures by the federal government."[17]

From examining the historical record, Crabb and his colleagues identify three conditions for congressional activism in foreign and defense affairs: (1) periods of weak presidential leadership in foreign policy, (2) public groundswells of concern over America's international role, and (3) pressing domestic issues that impinge on foreign affairs. Their assessment of legislative activism in foreign affairs is pessimistic. They contend that legislative activism has been associated with "the least successful and impressive chapters in the annals of American diplomacy."[18]

Our own review of the historical record, however, yields a more positive assessment of legislative influence on foreign policy. Congress asserted itself following the Revolutionary War and at the outset of the other nineteenth-century wars. At the same time, it moved to rein in excessive presidential assertions of authority both before, during, and after those wars—an impulse that extends to the more recent wars: Korea, Vietnam, Afghanistan, and Iraq, as well as the later phases of the Cold War. In brief, history demonstrates that neither branch has a monopoly on wisdom and effectiveness in shaping the nation's foreign policy.

WHO SPEAKS FOR CONGRESS?

The wide-ranging subjects of foreign policy and military affairs fall within the purviews of some twenty-three congressional committees. Other House panels and Senate panels consider matters with a tangential bearing on foreign and military policy.

The foreign affairs and national security panels are among the most visible on Capitol Hill. The Senate Foreign Relations Committee considers treaties and the nominations of key foreign policy officials. It normally regards itself as a working partner and adviser to the president. In the late 1960s and early

1970s, during the height of dispute over the Vietnam War, the committee became a forum for antiwar debate under the leadership of its chair, J. William Fulbright, D-Ark. (1959–1974). A later chair, Jesse Helms, R-N.C. (1995–2001), attacked international agencies and thwarted many of the Clinton administration's diplomatic objectives. When Sen. (now Vice President) Joseph R. Biden Jr. chaired the panel, he and his Senate committee colleagues laid out alternatives to President George W. Bush's international policies.

Sen. John Kerry, D-Mass., chaired the committee for four years (2009–2013). At the age of twenty-seven, Kerry had been the first Vietnam veteran to appear before the panel. On April 22, 1971, Kerry posed a now-famous question: "How do you ask a man to be the last man to die for a mistake?"[19] A senator steeped in international issues, Kerry was named Obama's second-term secretary of state in 2013. He was replaced as Foreign Relations chair by Sen. Robert Menendez, D-N.J. The son of Cuban immigrants, Senator Menendez took a harder line toward the Castro regime than has President Obama. GOP senator Bob Corker of Tennessee assumed the chairmanship of the foreign relations panel at the start of the 114th Congress (2015–2017). Senator Corker has called for the Obama White House "to take stronger action in Syria, stiffen sanctions against Russia, and provide lethal weapons to Ukraine."[20] He has also taken the lead in asserting Congress's right to approve or disapprove any White House–led international agreement designed to prevent Iran from building nuclear weapons.

For most of its history, the House Foreign Affairs Committee has worked in the shadow of its Senate counterpart. Even so, the House committee tends to attract members with a more global outlook than the House as a whole. It also addresses nearly as wide a range of issues as the Senate committee. For example, Rep. Ed Royce, R-Calif., the chair of Foreign Affairs in both the 113th and 114th Congresses, advocates a number of issues, such as human rights, trade with Asia, a free-market system, and the promotion of democracy in diverse regions of the world. He is also a critic of President Obama's foreign policy, advising the administration to "lay out a strategy to reverse ISIS's momentum."[21]

The Senate and House Armed Services Committees, which traditionally have a culture of bipartisanship, oversee the nation's military establishment. Annually, they authorize Pentagon spending for research, development, and procurement of weapons systems; construction of military facilities; and rules for civilian and uniformed personnel. The latter jurisdiction includes the Uniform Code of Military Conduct, which governs the lives of men and women in uniform and which has attracted congressional scrutiny of diverse matters such as sexual orientation, sexual harassment, treatment of enemy prisoners, overseas voting rights, and even the right of Jewish officers to wear yarmulkes while in uniform. Although global strategy and military readiness are important matters for the committees' members, what rivets their attention are issues closer to home such as force levels, military installations, and defense contracts. Thus constituency politics often drive military policy.

Because of their funding jurisdictions, House and Senate Appropriations subcommittees exert detailed control over foreign and defense policies. Tariffs and other trade regulations are the domains of the taxing committees (House Ways and Means, Senate Finance). Committees involved in banking handle international financial and monetary policies. And the Commerce committees have jurisdiction over foreign commerce generally.

The House and Senate Select Intelligence Committees were created in the late 1970s, following revelations of widespread abuses, illegalities, and misconduct on the part of intelligence agencies, particularly the Central Intelligence Agency (CIA) and the Federal Bureau of Investigation (FBI). After forty years, however, the two oversight panels are hampered in conducting vigorous scrutiny of the intelligence community because, according to a scholar, they have "limited expertise and weak budgetary authority."[22] However, under the leadership of Sen. Dianne Feinstein, D-Calif., the Senate Select Intelligence Committee conducted a five-year investigation into the CIA's post-9/11 detention and interrogation programs. The committee released a report in 2014 documenting a wide range of abusive practices. This so-called "torture report" sparked both calls for reform and a firestorm of controversy.

Two other panels are important to note: the House Homeland Security Committee and the Senate Homeland Security and Governmental Affairs Committee. With respect to homeland security, both panels have roughly comparable responsibilities. Both, for example, have legislative and/or oversight jurisdiction over such matters as border security, threats to the United States, cybersecurity, the protection of the nation's critical infrastructure, and the Department of Homeland Security.

Faced with a profusion of congressional power centers, executive branch policy makers complain that they do not know whom to consult when crises arise, that they have to testify before too many committees, and that leaks of sensitive information are inevitable with so many players. But executive branch officials or their emissaries are often free to consult with as few or as many lawmakers as they choose—in some cases with only the joint party leaders, in others with chairs and ranking members of the relevant committees. And when Congress tries to step in to influence administration policies, executive officers predictably complain about "micromanagement."

TYPES OF FOREIGN AND NATIONAL SECURITY POLICIES

Foreign policy is the total of decisions and actions governing a nation's relations with other nations and consists of national goals to be achieved and resources for achieving them. Statecraft is the art of selecting preferred outcomes and marshaling the appropriate resources to attain them. As former secretary of state Henry A. Kissinger, a foreign policy pragmatist, put it, "Values are essential for defining objectives; strategy is what implements them by establishing priorities and defining timing."[23]

Defining a nation's goals is no simple matter. The subject has sparked intense conflict both between Congress and the president and within Congress itself. Momentous congressional debates have displayed widely diverging views on subjects such as ties to England and France during the nation's early decades, American expansion abroad, tariff rates, involvement in foreign wars, approaches to combating terrorists, and U.S. involvement in nation-building or forcible regime change.

Lee H. Hamilton, D-Ind., a former chair of the House Foreign Affairs Committee and an acknowledged authority on international relations, summarized what he viewed as the major components of the national interest: (1) to preserve the territorial integrity of the United States and the safety and security of its people; (2) to sustain U.S. economic prosperity; (3) to promote democratic values; (4) to promote basic human rights; and (5) to protect the health and welfare of the American people.[24] Today, the national interest has been broadened to include a number of other components that affect the United States' security, such as soaring obesity rates that prevent many individuals from joining the military; the "dysfunction" in Washington that raises questions, noted a defense secretary, "about the capacity of our democracy to respond to crisis"; and global climate change.[25] Secretary of State Kerry called climate change "perhaps the world's most fearsome weapon of mass destruction."[26]

As for resources for meeting such goals, military strength and preparedness immediately come to mind. However, other assets such as wealth, productivity, creativity, political ideals, cultural values, and global credibility are even more potent in the long run. Jane Harman, a former nine-term House member and an expert in national security policy making, emphasized the importance of assessing the nation's strategic interests: "It should be obvious that both our resources and our power are less than they have been in prior decades, and that requires a new assessment of how to deploy our scarce assets against the biggest threats to the U.S. homeland."[27]

In balancing national goals and national resources, policy makers confront several different and sometimes overlapping types of foreign and national security policies. Structural policies involve procuring and deploying resources or personnel; strategic policies advance the nation's objectives militarily or diplomatically; and crisis policies protect the nation from specific foreign or domestic threats.

STRUCTURAL POLICIES

National security programs involve millions of workers and the expenditure of billions of dollars annually. Decisions about deploying such vast resources are called structural policy decisions. Examples include choices of specific weapons systems, contracts with private suppliers, the location of military installations, sales of weapons and surplus goods to foreign countries, and trade policies that affect domestic industries and workers. Structural policy making on foreign and defense issues shares important commonalities with distributive policy making in the domestic realm.

The last sixty years have seen a growing imbalance in the military versus nonmilitary elements of foreign policies. In 2015 the U.S. military budget

($577 billion) was larger than those of the next eight nations of the world combined.[28] But the singular military machine of the United States is, historically speaking, a fairly recent phenomenon. After earlier wars, the United States quickly "sent the boys home" and, under congressional pressure, shrank its armed forces—though each time to somewhat higher plateaus.[29] After World War II, however, the Cold War threat led to unprecedented levels of peacetime preparedness. By 1960, when retiring president Dwight D. Eisenhower, a career military officer, warned against the "military-industrial complex" (his speech draft said "military-industrial-congressional complex"), the new militarism was already deeply embedded in the nation's political and economic system.

After health and human services, Department of Defense (DOD) spending is the biggest discretionary portion of the federal budget. The high-water mark recently for defense spending was $691 billion in 2010. Since enactment of the Budget Control Act of 2011 (see Chapter 14), fiscal belt-tightening is required each year over ten years for defense (and domestic) discretionary spending, with sequestration (automatic spending cuts) an enforcement mechanism if defense spending exceeds the budget caps. Sequestration and its threat have aroused significant concern among Pentagon leaders, lawmakers, and defense contractors, especially at a time of rising military costs and multiple international challenges. Even so, efforts "to come up with a long-term agreement to eliminate spending caps" on defense have yet to materialize.[30]

Meanwhile, the Pentagon has used a separate war account—the Overseas Contingency Operation (OCO), which is exempt from the 2011 law—as a source of extra funds to ease budgetary pressures. OCO was "originally meant to cover the costs of the wars in Iraq and Afghanistan, but it has grown into an all-purpose funding mechanism for almost anything the Pentagon wants."[31] The House and Senate are scrutinizing the OCO budget to determine if it is the equivalent of a "slush fund" for the Pentagon. In the view of Rep. Chris Van Hollen, D-Md., the ranking minority member on the Budget Committee, "The OCO budget has been misused to get around discretionary funding caps over the years. Billions of dollars of non-war-related activities have been funded in the OCO budget."[32]

As spending reductions occur in all the military services, the Obama administration's structural plan is to have a military that will be "smaller and leaner, but it will be agile, flexible, rapidly deployable and technologically advanced."[33] Even with cutbacks, the Pentagon remains the nation's largest employer, its largest customer, and its largest procurer of equipment and services. DOD controls a huge number of structural outlays, which attract a wide swath of political interests. As a venture capitalist put it, "The military is like a Fortune No. 1 company."[34]

The State Department, by contrast, makes relatively few such decisions. For every twenty-one federal dollars spent on the military, only about one dollar goes to international affairs—including not only diplomatic representation but also military assistance, foreign development, and humanitarian aid.[35] The State Department's services and achievements are largely intangible, and in any event it spends much of its energy and money overseas. It is little surprise, then, that it has few strong domestic clients and, compared with DOD, fewer champions on Capitol Hill. Although State and Defense are typically rivals for resources and influence, former defense secretary Robert Gates (2006–2011) urged Congress to provide more money for State. He stressed the importance of strengthening national security by better integrating diplomacy and development (soft power) with military action (hard power). "We must focus our energies beyond the guns and steel of the military," said Gates. "Success will be less a matter of imposing one's will and more a function of shaping [the] behavior of friends, adversaries and, most importantly, the people in between."[36] To be sure, there are tensions between the two departments, such as the Defense Department's large role in matters usually handled by the State Department: nation-building and economic development, for example.

The Military-Industrial-Congressional Complex

Defense dollars for projects, contracts, and bases, among other things, are sought by business firms, labor unions, and local communities. As champions of local interests as highlighted by the two Congresses, lawmakers are naturally drawn into the process. The distributive impulse is wholly bipartisan. (Some observers have even suggested that a "surveillance-industrial complex" has emerged in the post-9/11 era, in which the government's interception of communications is contracted to private companies.[37])

Weapons Systems. Pentagon procurement officers anticipate congressional needs in planning and designing projects. The perfect weapons system, it is said, is one with a component manufactured in every congressional district in the nation. The Air Force's F-22 Raptor jet fighter, which has a price tag of nearly $300 million each, is assembled at Georgia and Texas factories from parts made by a thousand suppliers in forty-three states. "What it means to the company is the technology and the jobs," explained a factory manager.[38] When a defense secretary characterized the F-22 fighter as reflecting "an outdated Cold-War mind-set" and recommended significant reductions in the jet's production, it set off howls of protest from lawmakers whose states and districts would lose jobs. In the end, the Obama administration prevailed, and further procurement of F-22s was limited in number, effectively ending their production.

Another warplane the Air Force wants to retire for cost-saving reasons is the A-10 Warthog, a jet fighter that provides close (tree-top level) air support to military troops on the ground. With defense budget cuts looming, the "Air Force has no other choice," exclaimed the Air Force secretary. "Retiring the A-10 would save $4.2 billion over five years."[39] Many lawmakers with A-10s located in their states and districts—the two Congresses—quickly mobilized in both chambers to save the A-10. More than thirty lawmakers wrote to the defense secretary, stating, "It would be unconscionable to further cut an asset like the A-10 . . . increasing the risks to our service members."[40] Retired Air Force officers lobbied to save the A-10. Sen. John McCain, R-Ariz., the chair of Senate Armed Services during the 114th Congress (2015–2017), was reported to be "incensed upon hearing of the A-10's retirement."[41] Rep. Candace Miller, R-Mich., over the objections of the House Armed Services and Appropriations Committees, won adoption of an amendment that prevented any federal funds from being spent to eliminate the A-10.[42] In the end, Congress kept the A-10 flying for another year, "forbidding the Air Force from taking it out of service."[43]

An ostensible replacement for the F-22, the A-10, and other military jets is the F-35 Joint Strike Fighter, the largest and most expensive Pentagon weapons program in history. The acquisition and development costs of the weapons program have soared from $233 billion for 2,852 planes in 2011 to $397 billion for 2,443 planes in 2012. Given design flaws, delays, and growing cost overruns, some Pentagon officials have indicated that in an era of spending cutbacks "the F-35s 30-year, $1 trillion operating bill is not affordable."[44] According to a March 2014 Government Accountability Office (GAO) report, "If F-35 procurement plans remain unchanged and developmental testing continues into 2018, the cost risks . . . will likely increase as DOD expects to have invested $83.4 billion in 459 aircraft by that point in time," which amounts to around $180 million per plane.[45] However, the prospect for serious spending reductions remains murky at best. Sequestration, so far, did little to trim the program. And Lockheed Martin, the F-35s principal designer and builder, engaged in what is called "political engineering." The company "supports about 133,000 jobs [spread over 1,300 companies] in 45 states and Puerto Rico," which in turn has "generated broad bipartisan support [for the F-35] on Capitol Hill."[46] To cancel weapons systems designed and built in the districts and states of numerous lawmakers is simply not easy to accomplish.

Military Base Closures. The proliferation and geographic dispersion of military installations is another example of distributive military policy making. L. Mendel Rivers, D-S.C., chair of the House Armed Services Committee from 1965 to 1971, kept defense money flowing to bases in Charleston, South Carolina, campaigning on the slogan "Rivers delivers!" More recently, Sen. Trent Lott, R-Miss. (1989–2007), helped a Pascagoula, Mississippi, firm that builds ships for the Navy: "If I were not supportive of my hometown, that shipyard and the workers in that shipyard, I wouldn't deserve to be in Congress, now would I?"[47]

In the post–Cold War era, Congress tried to surmount the politically unpalatable problem of closing unneeded military installations. In 1988 it passed a law intended to insulate such decisions from congressional pressure by delegating them to bipartisan Base Realignment and Closing Commissions (BRACs). The BRACs were also intended to eliminate pressure on lawmakers to vote for an administration's programs in exchange for keeping open military bases in their districts. As Rep. Dick Armey, R-Tex., the champion of the BRAC legislation, stated: "The fact is, unfortunate as it is, that historically base closings have been used as a point of leverage by administrations, Democratic and Republican administrations, as political leverage over and above Members of Congress to encourage them to vote in a manner that the administration would like."[48]

Using the defense secretary's recommendations, a BRAC would draw up a list of installations targeted for closure. To make the decisions hard to overturn, the list had to be accepted or rejected as a whole by the president and Congress. The House and Senate each employ so-called expedited (or "fast track") procedures—a limit on floor consideration and a prohibition on amendments, for example—when they consider base closure legislation. Despite political hurdles, base closures are part of Congress's wider effort to balance the budget by closing unneeded military installations.

Five rounds of BRACs (1988, 1991, 1993, 1995, and 2005) reduced or eliminated hundreds of defense installations. The political pressures were intense. One commission chair was greeted at base entrances by parents holding children who, they said, would starve if the base closed.[49] Anti-BRAC lawmakers from affected areas fought the closure lists and nearly succeeded in overturning them. From the Pentagon's perspective, the closures of excess infrastructure meant that the savings could be spent on higher military priorities. Communities where bases were shuttered looked for new uses for the military facilities, such as the land and buildings, and in some cases requested federal assistance for the cleanup of environmental contamination at these installations.

The Pentagon in 2015 proposed another BRAC round to close unneeded military facilities as the armed forces are reduced because of the sequester and the post–Middle East drawdown of troops. However, many lawmakers are upset that the 2005 BRAC cost more to implement ($35 billion) than the savings ($15 billion) it produced by closing or consolidating facilities. "BRAC is a painful process with questionable cost savings," observed a senator.[50] Thus a new BRAC round is probably several years away. Lawmakers who negotiated the 2015 defense authorization measure "rejected the Pentagon's request to begin the politically painful process of shuttering domestic bases. Indeed, the final bill [denied] the Pentagon its latest request for base-closures beginning in 2017."[51]

Trade Politics

Another arena for distributive politics is foreign trade. Since the First Congress (1789–1791), the legislative branch's constitutional power to "regulate commerce with foreign nations" and to "lay and collect taxes, duties, imposts, and excises" has been used to protect and enhance the competitive position of U.S. goods and industries, whether cotton, wheat, textiles, or computer software. Until the 1930s, tariff legislation—long the primary source of federal revenue—was contested on Capitol Hill by political parties and economic regions. Northern manufacturers, for example, wanted protectionist tariffs, and southern exporting states wanted low tariffs to avoid other nations' retaliatory tariffs against their agricultural products.

Starting with the Reciprocal Trade Agreements Act of 1934 (P.L. 73-316), however, Congress began to delegate the details of tariff negotiations to the executive branch. The 1974 Trade Act is a key statute that transfers trade negotiating authority to the president, subject to Congress's ability to approve or disapprove the agreements under expedited procedures (for example, limited floor debate and no amendments in either chamber). Expedited procedures provide assurances to trading partners that Congress will act on any negotiated agreements within a certain time period. Important to note is that the 1974 trade law specifically recognized the constitutional authority of either chamber to make or change its own rules regardless of any statutory provisions addressing the procedural operations of the House or Senate.

Divergent Views on Trade. Protectionist impulses have not waned, however; myriad trade interests are represented on Capitol Hill. One trade expert suggests that three groups largely shape the trade debate in Congress.[52] To varying degrees, the perspectives of all three groups are represented in both parties. Republicans are generally "trade liberalizers," which reflects the views of many in the business community, among others. They tend to favor lowering trade barriers at home and combating them abroad in order to open world markets for U.S. goods. After all, "95 percent of the world's consumers now live somewhere other than the United States."[53] As a House GOP committee chair wrote: "Opening up new markets for U.S. producers, farmers, service providers and investors is essential for spurring growth and creating new job opportunities for both union and nonunion workers."[54]

Many Democrats are in the "fair trade" camp. They represent areas of union strength and favor barriers to curb the loss of jobs to low-wage countries. Fair traders argue that the poor labor, human rights, and environmental conditions in many countries enable them to undercut U.S. businesses through lower production costs. Fair traders want trade agreements—before they are entered into—to stipulate that nations must meet specific labor, environmental, and human rights standards.

The third group could be called "trade skeptics." They contend that trade agreements undermine U.S. sovereignty and largely benefit multinational corporations over small businesses, small farmers, and workers. Lawmakers who support labor unions and the Tea Party movement generally believe that trade has hurt the American economy by lowering wages and outsourcing jobs overseas.

The three different perspectives underscore the complexities and crosscurrents that suffuse trade policy and politics. Because both parties contain lawmakers in all three groups, it is too simple to identify one party (Republicans) as free trade and the other (Democrats) as protectionist.

A two-Congresses example illustrates the point. Republican senator Jeff Sessions of Alabama blocked a bipartisan trade bill supported by numerous business associations. His purpose was to prevent the duty-free import of sleeping bags from Bangladesh. Alabama is home to the only domestic manufacturer of inexpensive sleeping bags. As Senator Sessions explained:

> I do believe in trade. I think it's best for the world. But I would say to my colleagues we have got to have fair trade. And nations around the world . . . have taken advantage of the United States and . . . [think] that they can cheat on agreements and manipulate agreements and close down businesses . . . and somehow we're just going to pass on by.[55]

From a bicameral perspective, the Senate generally leans toward free trade because export-minded agricultural interests are overrepresented. The House, with its constituency-attentive focus, has stronger protectionist leanings.

Fast-Track Trade Negotiations. Having delegated most decisions to the executive, lawmakers who want to review specific trade deals must struggle to get back in the game. The Trade Act of 1974, as noted earlier, addressed this dilemma. The president, it said, must actively consult, notify, and involve Congress as he negotiates trade agreements. These agreements would take effect only after an implementing law is enacted, and such legislation would be handled under a fast-track procedure.

Most presidents since 1974 have been awarded fast-track (or trade promotion authority, TPA) to negotiate trade pacts subject to up-or-down votes in both houses of Congress within ninety days. However, that authority lapsed during the Clinton presidency and was not renewed by the Republican-led Congress. In 2002, after a vigorous lobbying effort, President Bush won a five-year renewal of the fast-track procedure. To gain the needed House votes, numerous concessions were made to placate textile workers and citrus growers, among others. The fast-track authority lapsed again in 2007.

With GOP control of the 114th Congress (2015–2017), President Obama might win congressional backing for fast-track authority that would facilitate adoption of major trade agreements, such as the Trans-Pacific Partnership, a free-trade accord with eleven Asian nations. The president met with the top party leaders of the House and Senate, and made "a strong case on the merits as to why [TPA] has to get done."[56] A Teamster union official opposed to fast track noted, "I'll be blunt, [GOP control of Congress] increases the chances of fast track passing" in the 114th Congress. As Senate Majority Leader Mitch McConnell, R-Ky., said to President Obama, "Send us trade agreements."[57]

Distributive politics underlie many other foreign and defense programs as well. For example, P.L. 480 (Food for Peace) dispenses food assistance to needy nations. This law, wrote two former lawmakers, "provides vital humanitarian and emergency assistance to people facing famine, natural disasters or conflict." They add that the food produced by American farmers is a "key component of the U.S. national security strategy. Nations that struggle with severe poverty and hunger are at greater risk from terrorists and instability."[58]

The United States is the world's largest seller of arms to developing nations. The value of all arms transfer agreements with developing nations in 2009 was over $45 billion. Two years later, overseas weapons sales surged to $66.3 billion.[59] The Pentagon also trains military forces in numerous nations to use its weapons. Arms sales are a profitable enterprise for the government that—for good or ill—affects civil and military affairs in every corner of the globe.[60]

STRATEGIC POLICIES

To protect the nation's interests, decision makers design strategic policies on spending levels for international and defense programs; total military force levels; the basic mix of military forces and weapons systems; arms sales to foreign powers; foreign trade inducements or restrictions; allocation of economic, military, and technical aid to developing nations; treaty obligations to other nations; U.S. responses to human rights abuses abroad; and its stance toward international bodies such as the United Nations (UN), the North Atlantic Treaty Organization (NATO), and world financial agencies.

Strategic policies overlap and embrace most important foreign policy questions. They engage executive decision makers as well as congressional committees. Such debates can express citizens' ideological, ethnic, racial, or economic interests.[61] Strategic issues typically involve broad themes and invoke policy makers' long-term attitudes and beliefs. The key agencies for strategic decision making include the State Department, the Office of the Secretary of Defense, the intelligence agencies, and the National Security Council—all advising the president.

The Power of the Purse

Congress uses its spending power to establish overall appropriations levels for foreign and defense purposes. Under those ceilings, priorities must be assigned among military services; among weapons systems; between uniformed personnel and military hardware; and to economic, cultural, or military aid—to name just a few of the choices. The president leads by presenting the annual budget, lobbying for the administration's priorities, and threatening to veto options deemed unacceptable. Yet if it chooses, Congress also can write its own budget down to the smallest detail. And the omnibus character of appropriations measures places pressure on the president to accede to the outcome of legislative bargaining on expenditures. To get the largest percent of the budget the administration wants, the president may have to swallow the smaller percent he opposes.

Post–Cold War Spending. Congress responds both to perceived levels of international tension and to shifting public views about global engagement. After the collapse of the Soviet Union, a bipartisan consensus in the Pentagon and in Congress agreed that defense funding and force levels could be cut gradually. That consensus arose either from the belief that a sizable "peace dividend" could be realized or from the hope that savings could be gained from smarter planning and trimming waste, fraud, and abuse. However, footing the bill for combat operations poses dilemmas for Congress. How much money is needed, and how much freedom should the president have in spending it? President Lyndon B. Johnson gradually deepened U.S. involvement in Vietnam, but he hesitated to ask Congress to appropriate the needed funds. Thus the first supplemental funding bill was passed in February 1966, even though Congress had signed on to the war as early as August 1964 (with the Gulf of Tonkin Resolution). Johnson's effort to hide the escalating war costs while maintaining domestic programs elevated both inflation and the federal debt.

After the September 11, 2001, attacks on the United States, Congress acted swiftly to pass a $40 billion supplemental appropriations package, one-fourth of which was under the president's near-total control. Following the U.S. invasion of Afghanistan in October 2001, Congress approved another $30 billion, again featuring flexibility. However, some lawmakers, especially on the funding committees, expressed their doubts. "All presidents want unlimited authority. In any time of conflict, there's a tendency to allow a little more leeway," said an Appropriations subcommittee chair. "We have a responsibility to maintain a balance . . . and we're struggling with that."[62]

The power of the purse is a blunt instrument in time of war. In the final analysis, no major foreign or military enterprise can be sustained unless Congress provides money and support. A president can conduct an operation for a time using existing funds and supplies, just as Johnson did at first in Vietnam, but sooner or later Congress must be asked for funding. The U.S. role in South Vietnam finally ended in 1974, when Congress simply refused to provide emergency aid funds.

Today, because of the intense focus on cutting federal spending, the size of the military budget makes it a prime target for spending reductions (after 9/11, the defense budget doubled in size). In the view of a defense specialist,

> we can't afford to keep policing a world in which many of our trading partners are growing faster and our military [missions] are contributing to national bankruptcy. The last thing America needs is a concept of its role in the world that is beyond the capacity of our economy and our political system to sustain, purchased with borrowed dollars that will make the emergence of new "peer competitors" more likely.[63]

Thus, a major challenge for defense planners is how to allocate scarce resources among competing security priorities. Should budgetary considerations determine defense strategies, or should the nature of the threats determine, within reason, the Pentagon's spending?

Spending on Foreign Aid. Unlike national defense, international affairs funding represents a relatively small expenditure. In fiscal year 2013, $43.6 billion was spent on foreign assistance, about 1% of the total federal budget.[64] The fundamental rationales for foreign aid are three: promote national security by strengthening global prosperity, democracy, and the rule of law; expand markets for U.S. exports by augmenting economic growth in developing countries; and provide humanitarian assistance to countries and peoples in need.

Historically, the nation's foreign operations required relatively small outlays. In the immediate post–World War II years of 1947–1951, however, programs to rebuild devastated Europe and Japan consumed as much as 16 percent of U.S. annual spending. Throughout the Cold War, the United States was a major provider of economic, military, and technical aid throughout the world. As a defense secretary once said, "economic development is a lot cheaper than sending soldiers."[65]

Today, of the approximately 150 countries that receive foreign aid, most of the assistance goes to a handful of states. Typically, these are "countries that are strategic allies in the Middle East, important partners in counterterrorism efforts, or global health focus countries."[66] The top five bilateral recipients are Afghanistan, Israel, Egypt, Pakistan, and Jordan. (Iraq ranks eighth.) Foreign assistance, two lawmakers point out, is "a critical tool in the diplomatic toolkit. A great power must have the tools to act—beyond simply intervening militarily. [F]oreign aid . . . help(s) avoid the enormous costs in blood and treasure that inevitably result from military intervention."[67] U.S. foreign aid ranks first in the world in dollar terms, but ranks twentieth among the world's wealthiest nations as a proportion of its gross national income.[68] (Norway ranks first by this measure.)

Treaties and Executive Agreements

The Constitution calls for Congress and the president to be partners in a key element of strategic policy: treaties with foreign powers. Under Article VI of the Constitution, all treaties "shall be the supreme Law of the Land" unless the treaty itself requires implementing legislation.

Although the president initiates them, treaties are made "by and with the advice and consent of the Senate." The Senate's consent is signified by the concurrence of two-thirds of the senators present and voting, a quorum being present. Treaty approval by the Senate entails more than a simple up-or-down vote; it is conducted in two steps. First, the Senate takes up the treaty. If it must be amended, an infrequent occurrence, it must be renegotiated with the nations that were parties to it.

Second, the Senate considers a resolution of ratification. To this document can be added reservations, declarations, or understandings; their adoption by majority vote does not require renegotiation of the treaty. According to one scholar, the "three qualifiers demarcate future U.S. behavior, intent, or policy positions as a result of the treaty. . . . They can also specify U.S. policy on unrelated issues."[69] The Senate, of course, can simply refuse to consider a treaty.

Congress may or may not be taken into the president's confidence when treaties and executive agreements are negotiated. To avoid humiliation like that experienced by President Woodrow Wilson when the Senate rejected the Treaty of Versailles after World War I, modern chief executives typically inform key senators during the negotiation process. Rarely does the Senate reject a treaty outright. In fact, it has turned down only twenty-one treaties since 1789. The most recent was the Senate's rejection of the Convention of the Rights of Persons with Disabilities in December 2012.

A major success for President Obama was winning Senate approval of a major arms control treaty with Russia. Dubbed "New START" (Strategic Arms Reduction Treaty)—the original START treaty was negotiated in the late 1980s—the president won the treaty approval battle after an intensive lobbying campaign:

> He mounted a five-week campaign that married public pressure and private suasion. He enlisted the likes of Henry Kissinger, asked

Chancellor Angela Merkel of Germany to help and sent a team of officials to set up a war room of sorts on Capitol Hill. Vice President Joseph R. Biden, Jr. had at least 50 meetings or phone calls with Senators.[70]

Because of the hurdle of obtaining a two-thirds Senate vote, since World War II presidents have relied increasingly on executive agreements—international accords that are not submitted to the Senate for its advice and consent. As explained by two legal scholars:

> As a matter of historical practice, the president may also make international agreements if authorized to do so by a law passed by Congress. (These are called "congressional–executive" agreements; the North American Free Trade Agreement is a prominent example.) And in some narrow cases, the president may create an international agreement all by himself through his own constitutional powers. [All are] legally binding on the United States and future presidents.[71]

Executive agreements may also be made pursuant to an earlier treaty. The "narrow cases" mentioned in the quotation often involve military matters. According to a legal expert, between 1939 through 2013, the United States concluded about 17,300 executive agreements compared with some 1,100 treaties.[72]

Although the conventional wisdom typically attributes the rise of executive agreements to presidential evasion of the Senate's treaty confirmation role, political scientists Glen S. Krutz and Jeffrey S. Peake argue that executive agreements constitute "a rational response by the president and Congress to the challenges faced by the United States during the daunting complexity brought on by the emergence of its international leadership in the twentieth century" and beyond.[73] Executive agreements go into force more quickly than treaties and offer a much less cumbersome process for management of international affairs—efficiency gains that can benefit Congress as well as the president.

In federal court cases challenging whether such agreements should have been treaties, the justices have invoked the political questions doctrine and declined to rule on the merits. This doctrine holds that the issue is best left "to the discretion and expertise of the legislative and executive branches."[74]

Other Policy-Making Powers of Congress

In addition to its control of the purse strings, Congress employs an array of other techniques to shape or influence strategic policies. The most common tools of congressional policy leadership are informal advice, legislative prodding through nonbinding resolutions or policy statements, policy oversight, legislative directives or restrictions, and structural or procedural changes.[75]

Advising, Prodding. Congressional leaders and key members routinely provide the president and other executive officials with informal advice. Sometimes, this advice proves decisive. In 1954 President Eisenhower dispatched Secretary of State John Foster Dulles to meet with a small bipartisan group of congressional leaders to determine whether the United States should intervene militarily in Indochina (Vietnam). The leaders unanimously declined to sponsor a resolution favoring involvement until other nations indicated their support of military action. Lacking assurances from either Congress or foreign allies, Eisenhower decided against intervening.[76]

Congress engages in legislative prodding by proposing legislation or suggesting ideas to the administration. For example, six GOP senators introduced legislation (S. 2650) to provide for congressional review of any final agreement the Obama administration negotiates with Iran relating to its nuclear program.[77] This move was widely seen as a warning to the president against making concessions to Iran as part of the negotiations. Frequently, Congress passes resolutions that are not legally binding or enforceable. Every recent Congress has approved numerous simple or concurrent resolutions. These measures may lend support to the executive branch, advance certain policies, or signal assurances or warnings to other nations. Occasionally, nonbinding resolutions put forward fresh policy ideas; at other times they are little more than posturing.

Congressional speeches are also important in framing media and public opinion. These speeches, two scholars note, can "shape media coverage of prospective uses of force, which in turn impacts public opinion about the war." They add: "All sorts of trouble, political or otherwise, await the president who loses public support for an ongoing military venture."[78]

Oversight. Congress shapes foreign policy through oversight of the executive branch's performance. Hearings and investigations often focus on foreign policy issues. Recurrent hearings on authorizing and funding State Department and Defense Department programs offer many opportunities for lawmakers to voice their concerns, large and small. Another device is to require that certain decisions or agreements be submitted to Congress before they go into effect. Congress and its committees may also require reports from the executive that "provide not only information for oversight but also a handle for action."[79] Hundreds of foreign and defense policy reporting requirements are embedded in current statutes.

Oversight in time of war or crisis is especially hazardous. The president resists intrusions, and lawmakers are reluctant to impede the action. "The trick is to rein in the White House but not seem unpatriotic," writes historian Bruce J. Schulman.[80] The boldest legislative foray into wartime oversight occurred during the Civil War. While Confederate guns were threatening Washington, D.C., the Joint Committee on the Conduct of the War (1861–1865), controlled by Radical Republicans, held hearings on Capitol Hill and published reports that questioned President Abraham Lincoln's war policies, criticized military operations, berated generals who failed to pursue the enemy, and exposed waste and fraud in military procurements.

During World War II, Missouri senator Harry S. Truman headed the Special Committee to Investigate the National Defense Program, which uncovered profiteering, contract abuses, and shoddy workmanship in wartime projects. The committee saved taxpayers billions of dollars and, not incidentally, boosted the career of its chair (it was the "Truman Committee," proclaimed its letterhead). The Senate Foreign Relations Committee hearings launched in 1966 raised doubts in the public's mind about the Vietnam War.

More recently, when Republicans won control of the House and Senate in the midterm elections of November 2014, oversight of the Obama administration became a major focus of the 114th Congress. In conditions of divided government and high partisan polarization, oversight is often employed for partisan advantage, rather than to resolve executive branch problems. Bipartisan investigations still occur, but they are harder to create and sustain given the competing incentives of the two parties. Consider these two examples, one from the House and one from the Senate, that highlight the partisan overtones that suffuse many contemporary investigations.

House. Recall from Chapter 7 that the House of Representatives in 2015 established the Select Committee on Benghazi (Libya) to investigate the September 2012 terrorist attack on the U.S. Consulate that resulted in the death of the U.S. ambassador (Christopher Stevens) and several other Americans. This tragedy had triggered seven previous congressional investigations, including the most recent investigative report (November 2014) by the House Permanent Select Intelligence Committee.[81] That panel determined that the consulate was ill-prepared to defend itself from attack, but also found no intelligence failure by the CIA, no order to block a rescue attempt, no denial of air support, and no subsequent cover-up by the administration. On the other hand, nearly all of the seven investigative reports were "critical of the State Department's pre-attack planning," given the high threat environment in Benghazi.[82] The chair of the select committee, Trey Gowdy, R-S.C., said the House Intelligence Committee's report would assist the members of his panel to produce the "final, definitive accounting of the attack" on the American consulate.[83]

Suffice it to say that many Democrats view yet another investigation as a waste of taxpayer dollars and unnecessary, given the prior inquiries. "I am not sure what the [select] committee can productively do that hasn't been done already," remarked Rep. Adam Schiff, D-Calif., a member of both the select panel and the Intelligence Committee.[84] Democrats are also concerned that the select committee's implicit goal is to castigate Hillary Clinton, the secretary of state at the time of the Benghazi attack, and in the process tarnish her reputation and undermine her chances of winning both the 2016 Democratic presidential nomination and, if nominated, the presidency itself.

Senate. On November 24, 2014, President Obama announced that Defense Secretary Chuck Hagel, who assumed the post in early 2013, would be leaving as soon as a replacement was confirmed by the GOP-controlled Senate. Some senators employed the confirmation process for Hagel's successor, Ashton Carter, a former deputy defense secretary, as a proxy to critique the president's Middle East policies, and to raise an array of other international issues. Carter, a respected defense expert, had no problems being confirmed. However, Sen. John McCain, the chair of the Armed Services Committee, said that the Ashton Carter confirmation hearings would "fully ventilate all of the issues around the administration's feckless foreign policy."[85] As Senator McCain once said, the leverage the Senate has is "to gauge our support for confirmation of a nominee on whether they are forthcoming with information or not."[86]

Legislative Mandates. Congress sometimes makes foreign policy by legislative directives—to launch new programs, to authorize certain actions, or to set guidelines. A landmark enactment of the Cold War era was the Jackson-Vanik amendment to the Trade Act of 1974 (named for Sen. Henry M. "Scoop" Jackson, D-Wash., and Rep. Charles Vanik, D-Ohio). Prompted by concern over the Soviet Union's treatment of its Jewish minority, the amendment denied government credits and most-favored-nation trade status (now called "normal trade relations") to any communist country that restricted the free emigration of its citizens.

Foreign policy statutes may include explicit legislative restrictions, which perhaps are Congress's most effective weapon. Often, they are embedded in authorization or appropriations bills that the president is unlikely to veto. Throughout the Reagan presidency, for example, Congress passed many limits on military aid to Central American countries.

Legislation also shapes the structures and procedures through which policies are carried out. "Congress changes the structure and procedures of decision making in the executive branch in order to influence the content of policy," writes James M. Lindsay.[87] When lawmakers wanted to reform military procurement, they restructured the Defense Department to clarify and streamline the process; when they wanted more say in trade negotiations, they wrote themselves into the process by enacting various trade laws.

CRISIS POLICIES: THE WAR POWERS

An international crisis endangering the nation's safety, security, or vital interests pushes aside other foreign policy goals. Examples range from Japan's attack on the U.S. naval fleet in Pearl Harbor in 1941 to the al Qaeda attacks of September 11, 2001.

Crisis policies engage decision makers at the highest levels: the president, the secretaries of state and defense, the National Security Council, and the Joint Chiefs of Staff. Congressional leaders are sometimes brought into the picture. More rarely, congressional advice is sought out and heeded—as in President Eisenhower's 1954 decision against military intervention in Indochina. Often when executive decision makers fear congressional opposition, they simply neglect to inform Capitol Hill until the planned action is under way. A failed attempt in 1980 to rescue American hostages in Iran, for example, was planned in strictest secrecy, and no legislative consultations were undertaken by the Carter administration. Strict secrecy also surrounded a major success of President Obama's in May 2011: sending special operations forces to kill Osama Bin Laden—the al Qaeda leader and architect of the 9/11 attack on the United States—at his residence in Abbottabad, Pakistan.

As long as a crisis lingers, policy makers keep a tight rein on information flowing upward from line officers. The attention of the media and the public is riveted on crisis events. Patriotism runs high. Citizens hasten to "rally 'round the flag" and support, at least initially, whatever course their leaders choose.[88]

Constitutional Powers

War powers are shared by the president and Congress. The president is the commander in chief of the military and naval forces of the United States (Article II, section 2), but Congress has the power to declare (authorize) war (Article I, section 8). The framers vested the power to declare war in Congress because they understood that monarchs and presidents often took their nations to war for personal reasons, such as ambition or military glory, rather than the national interest. As John Jay wrote in *Federalist* No. 4, "These and a variety of other motives, which affect only the mind of the sovereign, often lead him to engage in wars not sanctified by justice or the voices and interests of his people." The framers expected the commander in chief to defend the nation against sudden attacks, implying a limited military role for the president. Lawmakers and scholars have argued for decades about this division of the war powers.

Congress has declared war only five times: the War of 1812 (1812–1814), the Mexican War (1846–1848), the Spanish-American War (1898), World War I (1917–1918), and World War II (1941–1945). In four instances, Congress readily assented to the president's call for war, acknowledging in the declaration that a state of war already existed. Only once did Congress delve into the merits of waging war, and that was in 1812, when the vote was close. In two cases—the Mexican and Spanish-American conflicts—lawmakers later had reason to regret their haste.

In an age of undeclared wars, more problematic than formal declarations are the more than three hundred other instances in which U.S. military forces have been deployed abroad. (The number is uncertain because of quasi-engagements involving military or intelligence advisers.)[89] The examples range from an undeclared naval war with France (1798–1800) to the invasion of Iraq (2003). Since the last declared war—World War II in 1941—numerous military interventions have taken place abroad. Some were massive and prolonged wars: Korea (1950–1953), Vietnam (1964–1975), Afghanistan (2001–), and Iraq (1991, 2003–2011). Still others were short-lived actions (for example, military coordination of medical and disaster relief after the U.S. embassies in Kenya and Tanzania were bombed in 1998) and rescue or peacekeeping missions, some of which involved casualties (Lebanon, 1983; Somalia, 1992–1993).

Most of these interventions were authorized by the president as commander in chief on the stated grounds of protecting American lives, property, or interests abroad. Some were justified on the grounds of treaty obligations or "inherent powers" derived from a broad reading of executive prerogatives. Others were peacekeeping efforts under UN or NATO sponsorship. There were also humanitarian relief operations in nations hit by natural disasters, such as typhoons in the Philippines.

A fundamental change has occurred in the division of war powers between Congress and the president. The change occurred in 1950 when President Truman took the nation to war against North Korea, without seeking a declaration of war or any formal congressional authorization. Congress retains an arsenal of tools to challenge the president (such as the purse strings, advice and consent, lawmaking, investigations, and debate), but it often defers to the chief executive rather than asserting its formidable constitutional prerogatives.

Members of Congress, though wary of armed interventions, are reluctant to halt them: "No one actually wants to cut off funds when American troops are in harm's way," a House leadership aide explained. "The preferred stand is to let the president make the decisions and, if it goes well, praise him, and if it doesn't, criticize him," observed former representative Lee Hamilton.[90] Interventions go well if they come to a swift, successful conclusion with few American lives lost. Actions that drag on without a satisfactory resolution or that cost many lives will eventually tax both lawmakers' and citizens' patience.

Although Congress has rarely used its power of the purse to withhold funds for executive war-making, it has many other indirect mechanisms to influence military policy. Tough congressional oversight, public criticism of the president in the news media, and resolutions of disapproval can all raise the political costs to presidents of continuing a military action. In a recent study, political scientist Douglas L. Kriner finds that the level of congressional opposition that presidents encounter to their military policies depends heavily on the share of Congress held by the opposition party.[91] Based on an analysis of all major U.S. military actions between 1877 and 2004, Kriner finds that presidents who encounter significant congressional opposition are more likely to limit the scope and duration of military engagements.

The War Powers Resolution

The Johnson and Nixon administrations' conduct of the war in Vietnam left many lawmakers skeptical of presidential war-making initiatives. In 1973 Congress passed the War Powers Resolution (WPR, P.L. 93-148) over President Richard Nixon's veto. This law requires the president to consult with Congress before introducing U.S. troops into hostilities; report to Congress any commitment of forces within forty-eight hours; and terminate the use of forces within sixty days—there is an additional thirty-days to ensure a safe withdrawal—if Congress does not declare war, does not extend the period by law, or is unable to meet.

Presidents commonly issue reports to Congress within forty-eight hours after troops have been deployed abroad. Congress, however, regularly abdicates its responsibility after the sixty-day period to pass legislation supporting U.S. military actions. For example, President Obama reported on March 21, 2011, "consistent with the War Powers Resolution" that he had deployed U.S. military forces in Libya.[92] However, the president missed the sixty-day deadline for securing congressional approval for military operations and thus was evidently required to withdraw U.S. forces. Other presidents have also missed the sixty-day deadline, arguing that the WPR is unconstitutional; that the conflict or intervention is too small or limited to be called a "war"; or that the United States is not really engaged in hostilities because NATO leaders are in command of the military operation, as in Libya.[93]

The WPR has few outright defenders, but lawmakers are not ready to repeal or replace it. Although it diminishes Congress's constitutional power of declaring war, the WPR has some practical virtues. It accommodates the rapid use of armed force without the traditional step of formally declaring war. With respect to some threats, declaring war may not be a viable option, in part because it is difficult to declare war against an array of terrorist groups. Moreover, the WPR gives at least a nodding respect to the framers' belief that Congress, the branch most representative of the people, is the sole source of legal and moral authority for major military enterprises.

Even with its apparent weakness, every post-1973 president has challenged the WPR's legality. Nonetheless, few at either end of Pennsylvania Avenue are willing to risk having the Supreme Court resolve the question. Congress unquestionably has the constitutional authority to end wars by refusing funds. Whether it can make the president withdraw troops through inaction—i.e., by failing to pass a resolution authorizing the use of force—remains in dispute.

The WPR is an awkward compromise of executive and legislative authority, and presidents still intervene as they see fit. Members of Congress tend to sit on the sidelines and allow presidents to ignore the WPR. Yet the WPR stands as a reminder of the ultimate need to gain congressional approval for major military deployments. There are, of course, lawmakers who challenge presidents for unilaterally authorizing military attacks without congressional consent. GOP senator Rand Paul of Kentucky even introduced legislation (S.J.Res. 46) on December 3, 2014, that would declare the United States is at war against the Islamic State. In response, Speaker John Boehner said that it is "President Obama's job, not Congress's responsibility, to write a war authorization."[94]

Authorization of U.S. Military Action against the Islamic State

With the rapid advances of ISIS forces in Iraq and later Syria, the Iraqi government requested that the United States provide military and intelligence assistance to its beleaguered forces. Although President Obama authorized aircraft and drone strikes against ISIS positions in Iraq and Syria, he said that he had no intention of deploying combat troops to fight in the Middle East. Nevertheless, numerous lawmakers were concerned that the president's strategy amounted to "mission creep" and could embroil the United States in another long and costly war. Moreover, lawmakers disputed the president's claim that he had broad authority to order these military operations based on his constitutional role as commander in chief and two laws: the 2001 Authorization for Use of Military Force (AUMF) in Afghanistan (P.L. 107-40) and the 2002 Authorization for Use of Military Force in Iraq (P.L. 107-243).

Many lawmakers contend that neither of these laws applies to the actions against the Islamic State. Failure to authorize military action would set another bad precedent of allowing the president unilaterally to initiate combat operations without seeking legal authority from Congress. Inaction by Congress could be viewed as ratification of the president's war-making authority.[95] Congress has provided funds to train and arm moderate rebel groups seeking to combat ISIS and overthrow the Assad regime in Syria,[96] and U.S. military personnel are also assisting and advising Iraqi forces. A worry on Capitol Hill is that such limited actions may not work, and could prompt this president or the next to deploy ground troops to the region. In the view of Rep. Gerald Connolly, D-Va.:

> The President actually needs specific congressional authority, whether he wants it or not, for what he himself acknowledges will be a prolonged campaign to eradicate the cancer-like ISIL. Anything short of that is an abrogation of our sworn duty to defend and uphold the Constitution of the United States.[97]

At this juncture, neither Congress nor the White House is rushing to win approval of a new AUMF. If there is consideration of a new AUMF, debate over its provisions might include: its duration (one year, two years, or more); whether there are geographical limitations (only the Middle East and not the entire world); or a prohibition against the use of combat troops in Syria and Iraq to emphasize that the "focus is on helping people help themselves."[98] On the other hand, at a hearing of the Senate Foreign Relations Committee, Secretary of State Kerry stated that any AUMF should *not* prohibit the deployment of combat troops to Iraq and Syria because it would hamstring the ability of President Obama and the generals in the field to respond to unexpected contingencies, which might mean sending troops to other countries to battle ISIS.[99] By spring 2015, a draft AUMF (submitted by President Obama in February) has "languished, caught in the stalemate between those who want tighter restrictions and those who want the president to have as free a hand as possible." [100]

Changes in Warfare

The nature of warfare today has evolved and created new challenges for Congress and the White House. Increasingly, the future of warfare is being reshaped by at least these five developments. First, consider the reality of cyberwar. For example, U.S. intelligence agencies have determined that the Chinese military has an army unit that specializes in cyberattacks against American corporations, organizations, and governments.[101] As President Obama said in his 2013 State of the Union address, "Now our enemies are also seeking the ability to sabotage our power grid, our financial institutions and our air traffic control systems."

The U.S. military has a Cyber Command, which reportedly launched a cyberattack (a computer worm called Stuxnet) against Iranian nuclear facilities. Later, a group of Iranian hackers attacked corporate and government entities in the United States "that manage critical energy, transportation, and medical services."[102] Regularly, cyberattacks occur against the Defense Department. Nations or nonstate groups troll constantly for military secrets through cybertheft. As a chair of the Senate Armed Services Committee said, "These have got security implications, these intrusions. These are not just commercial intrusions we're trying to defend against."[103] Two prominent national leaders concluded: "We are at war in the digital world," but "the American people remain largely unaware of the danger."[104] Adm. Michael Rogers, the head of the National Security Agency and U.S. Cyber Command, predicted that in the next decade there would be a major cyberattack on critical U.S. infrastructure, such as our electrical system. It is "only a matter of when, not if, we are going to see something dramatic. This is not theoretical."[105]

Cyberwar raises a number of questions, such as: What is the role of Congress in cyberwarfare? Can presidents order cyberattacks on any nation or group without congressional knowledge or approval? According to one account, the Obama administration "has been engaged in a largely secret debate about whether cyberarms should be used like ordinary weapons, whether they should be rarely used covert tools or whether they ought to be reserved for extraordinarily rare use against the most sophisticated, hard-to-reach targets."[106] Are the enemies the president mentioned in his State of the Union message nations, terrorist groups, other nonstate actors, or a combination of all? As a member of NATO, would the United States be obligated to engage in cyberwarfare if an alliance state is the target of cyberattacks against, for instance, its electrical grid or military command system? As a noted law professor wrote, "stealth wars require rules, too." This implies a key role for Congress in defining "the scope of the new war, the authorities and limitations on presidential powers and the forms of review of the president's actions."[107]

Second, there has been a rapid increase in the use of drones: remote-controlled, pilotless vehicles that have become the counterterrorism weapon of choice for the targeted killing of insurgents. Drones are also valuable for gathering intelligence, surveillance, and reconnaissance for the military. "A platoon of soldiers wanting to look beyond the building in front of them; an intelligence agency tracking a target; a general staff trying to understand what was going on across a broad area: today there is a drone for them all."[108] The United States' military drone program is largely secret, with little analysis publicly available as to whether the benefits of targeted killings outweigh the costs, such as the killing of innocent civilians and the outrage that can provoke new terrorist recruits to attack the Unites States.[109]

There is also concern in the United States that drone technology developed for the military can be used to spy and eavesdrop on Americans, arousing privacy fears among many people. Another concern is how to hold the president accountable for his secret decisions to target and kill individuals abroad, including U.S. citizens, through drone strikes. As Sen. Angus King, I-Maine, put it: "Having the executive being the prosecutor, the judge, the jury and the executioner all in one is very contrary to the traditions and laws of this country."

A third type of modern warfare has its own special vocabulary. Some call it irregular warfare, police actions, asymmetric conflicts, hybrid wars, counter-insurgencies, proxy engagements, peacekeeping (not peacemaking) missions, interventions, or something else.[110] These are "no win" wars, often against nonstate actors, that can go on for years without the traditional end point of a treaty-signing or surrender ceremony between or among the combatants. As one commentator explained:

> The United States' problem since World War II is that it has chosen to fight limited wars that had ambiguous outcomes, at best. This was the case in Korea, Vietnam, Iraq and Afghanistan. Only in 1991's Operation Desert Storm did the United States win a decisive victory [by rolling back Iraq's invasion of Kuwait], but it had limited objectives and faced a weak adversary.[111]

Conventional warfighting between nations seems less likely today. Instead, the past several decades have witnessed the rise of insurgent groups, terrorists, and various nonstate actors who are sometimes both hard to identify and difficult to defeat. There are no formal surrenders or peace treaties signed in counterinsurgency warfare.

Fourth, today's irregular warfare requires a complex of integrated activities. The United States' domestic and international intelligence-gathering agencies, since 9/11, are working together as multi-agency networks (for example, the CIA, the FBI, and the DEA [Drug Enforcement Agency]) to gather data and intelligence on insurgent groups and their leaders on a global scale. These networks "are collecting more and better intelligence at a faster pace, and turning it around to shooters in the field more rapidly than at any time in history."[112] This fusion of intelligence activities and military specialists is being conducted in large measure through "spies, special forces, and drone strikes," as well as in other ways (satellite surveillance and reconnaissance, for example).[113]

Fifth, the scope of contemporary warfare is global. Terrorist groups, failed states, or insurgents can emerge anywhere on the planet. Understandably, the United States requires likeminded coalition partners to help ensure global security. In brief, it is simply much harder today for the United States to be the sole global police officer. As one commentator put it, "in resolving international crises, other nations have become indispensable to the United States."[114]

Together, these five changes in warfare have heightened the challenge for Congress as its members seek to have ongoing and meaningful influence over the conduct of American foreign policy.

CONCLUSION

Three key developments enhance Congress's obligations in foreign policy. First, the United States continues to exert influence in every corner of the globe: militarily, diplomatically, and culturally. Second, global interdependence blurs the line that once demarked domestic policy from foreign policy. Insofar as the resulting issues trespass upon traditional domestic matters, they are bound to encourage congressional intervention and influence. Finally, the question of whether the nation is willing or able to underwrite its costly international projects is forcing Congress and the White House to reassess the nation's global commitments, relying more on multilateral rather than unilateral actions and policies.[115]

Members of Congress cannot avoid foreign and national security policies. As the world grows ever more interdependent, those policies impinge upon every citizen and every local community. An internationally minded electorate, sensitive to famines and plagues in Africa, deforestation in the Amazon, foreign competition for jobs and trade, earthquakes and tsunamis in Japan, and anti-Americanism and terrorism in various regions, draws fewer distinctions between domestic and global matters than in the past.

Today's legislators know that global developments touch their local constituencies, and they believe (rightly or wrongly) that they will be judged to some degree on their understanding of those subjects. It especially behooves lawmakers to debate, challenge, and question presidential war-making policies that could involve the blood and treasure of the nation. As West Virginia senator Robert C. Byrd once stated, "Two constitutional power centers—set up by the framers to check and balance one another—and do battle over politics, policies, and priorities—occupy their distinct ends of Pennsylvania Avenue. What makes it all work for the good of the nation is the character of the individuals who serve."[116]

Citizens and Congress. Tourists in the 1930s gawk at the Capitol's elaborately decorated rooms (left). Today's tourists (top right) can take a Segway tour of Capitol Hill, stopping at the Capitol's east front plaza. The $621 million Capitol Visitor Center, opened in 2008, informs people about Congress's duties and achievements; guides them toward tours of the building and its chambers; offers food, souvenirs, and restrooms; and treats citizens to an unusual underground view of the Capitol dome (bottom).

The Two Congresses and the American People

"T hat meeting was one of the most astounding experiences I've had in my 34 years in politics," remarked Sen. Charles E. Schumer, D-N.Y.[1] Schumer had just emerged from a summit with Treasury Secretary Henry M. Paulson Jr. and Federal Reserve chair Ben Bernanke. House and Senate leaders, along with a group of lawmakers responsible for oversight of financial markets, had assembled at 7:00 p.m. on September 18, 2008. Seated under a portrait of Abraham Lincoln, Bernanke somberly detailed the unfolding financial crisis and warned that the entire economy "was on the brink of a heart attack."[2]

Over the preceding ten days, the government had seized Fannie Mae and Freddie Mac, the investment bank Lehman Brothers had filed for bankruptcy, Merrill Lynch had been sold at a fire-sale price, and the giant insurance firm American International Group (AIG) had been pulled back from collapse by the federal government's $85 billion emergency loan. Credit markets were frozen, denying credit access to consumers and small businesses throughout the country. "I gulped," said Schumer. "We all realized we're not in normal times."[3]

To contain the crisis, the George W. Bush administration sought immediate congressional support for a plan that would allow the Treasury Department to buy up to $700 billion of the distressed assets weighing down the balance sheets of major financial institutions. To put this request in context, $700 billion is more than the Pentagon's annual budget.[4] The three-page proposal asked for unfettered authority to spend these vast sums, with nothing more than semiannual reports to Congress.

"Do you know what you are asking me to do?" said Senate majority leader Harry Reid, D-Nev. "It takes me 48 hours to get the Republicans to agree to flush the toilets around here."[5] The administration wanted Congress to act in a matter of days. "This is the United States Senate," said Reid. "We can't do it in that time frame."[6]

The 2008 financial crisis was so urgent that "the Capital almost had the feel of wartime."[7] Still, lawmakers understandably balked at authorizing so much taxpayer money with so little deliberation. "Just because God created the world in seven days doesn't mean we have to pass this bill in seven days," quipped Rep. Joe Barton, R-Tex.[8] Not all members were willing to trust the administration's claims of impending financial disaster. "Where have I heard

454 CONGRESS AND ITS MEMBERS

this before? The Iraqis have weapons of mass destruction, and they're ready to use them," complained Rep. Gene Taylor, D-Miss. "I'm in no rush to do this."

The bailout proposal was extremely unpopular with constituents, who flooded members' offices with calls that ran as much as 30–1 against.[9] The first effort to pass the bill, on September 30, went down to defeat 228–205 in the House of Representatives.[10] The House's action caused a large-scale sell-off on Wall Street, with the Dow Jones stock index plunging 7 percent in one day.

As days unfolded without a congressional consensus, opinion leaders began to speak of "financial Armageddon" and a "credibility test for Congress."[11] Congress eventually acceded to the administration's $700 billion request, but lawmakers imposed some limits on the administration of the program. They amended the administration's proposal to restrict executive compensation, mandate program oversight, and require aid to Americans in danger of losing homes to foreclosure. The amended proposal was approved by Congress and signed into law on October 3, 2008.[12]

In the end, however, Congress's efforts to assert more control over the bailout's implementation failed. In carrying out the program, the administration used the funds not to buy toxic assets but to recapitalize banks. It quickly became clear that the banks could not be held accountable for their use of these funds. Treasury also refused to act on mortgage relief. A Brookings Institution report concluded:

> Congress designed a financial package that allowed the Treasury to spend nearly $350 billion with no accountability for how the money was used, little transparency in how institutions were selected for infusions, no metrics for determining program effectiveness, and no mechanism for forcing the Treasury to comply with the terms of the law that required action to mitigate foreclosures.[13]

Congressional handling of the financial crisis was flawed in many respects. And long afterward, the bailout remained highly unpopular with voters.[14] Nevertheless, the program proved not nearly so expensive for taxpayers as had been expected: most of the funds disbursed to financial firms were paid back,[15] and by 2015 investments under the program had actually yielded a $53.1 billion profit to the U.S. Treasury.[16] Many economists judged that the program helped to stabilize the financial system and forestall a second Great Depression.[17]

A crisis poses a severe challenge for legislative assemblies. The demand for immediate action runs counter to the deliberative processes that legislatures follow. The congressional process is inherently ponderous as different perspectives and interests are consulted and majorities are constructed. The United States is not, as some people have claimed, a "presidential nation"; it is a "separated system" marked by the ebb and flow of power among the policy-making branches of government.[18] As former Speaker Newt Gingrich, R-Ga. (1995–1999), said of the nation's complex and frustrating governing arrangements,

We have to get the country to understand that at the heart of the process of freedom is not the presidential press conference. It is the legislative process; it is the give and take of independently elected, free people coming together to try to create a better product by the friction of their passions and the friction of their ideas.[19]

The legislative "give and take" Gingrich described inevitably takes time. But fast-moving crises—all too common in an interconnected world of complex financial and security relationships—often demand that Congress act quickly, frequently without due deliberation.

The American system of government is one of deliberate interplay among institutions. Citizens' ambivalence toward the popular branch of government is yet another reminder of the dual character of Congress—the theme that has pervaded our explanations of how Congress and its members work. The two Congresses are manifest in public perceptions and assessments. Citizens evaluate Congress using standards and expectations that differ from those they use to assess their own senators and representatives.[20] This same duality appears in media coverage: the two Congresses are covered by different sets of reporters working for different kinds of media organizations.

CONGRESS-AS-POLITICIANS

Lawmakers' working conditions and schedules are far from ideal.[21] The hours are killing, the pay comparatively modest, and the toll on family life heavy. A *Washington Post Magazine* profile of Rep. Joe Courtney, D-Conn., sketched his life as follows:

> Rising, going to hearings, meeting with lobbyists, fundraising, speaking on the House floor, taking more meetings, walking to the apartment, crashing, rising. . . . The [DCCC] continues to send him reminders about his fundraising goals: *Get off the Capitol grounds; get to the phone bank; make the call.* . . . Another knock. An aide pops in with a reminder: The fundraiser back home is that weekend. . . . "It just never stops. Never."[22]

Courtney's schedule is broadly representative. According to a 2013 study, 85 percent of members' spouses live back home in their district, not in D.C. with them, and 66 percent of members said they had missed an important family event because of their job.[23] "Your schedule is not your own," remarked Sen. Fred Thompson, R-Tenn. (1994–2003), on announcing his retirement.[24] Rep. Joe Scarborough, R-Fla. (1995–2001), complained that "the conflict between being a good congressman and full-time father has grown."[25] "I'm basically single-parenting," said Courtney's wife.[26]

Members' Bonds with Constituents

The public has different expectations for individual members compared to Congress as a whole. From the institutional Congress, the public expects answers to the nation's problems developed in an open and fair policy process. By contrast, in assessing their own representatives, voters take into account far more than lawmakers' work on public policy. They weigh members' service to the state or district, their communication with constituents, and their home style. Voters consider the policy positions their members take, but they have little insight into their member's effectiveness in advancing policy proposals in the legislative process.[27] Put differently, Congress is viewed as a national policy-making institution, but individual members of Congress are only partly assessed in terms of their contributions to policy making. Local representatives are primarily evaluated in light of the personal bonds they forge with constituents and the political positions they take.

Members' high visibility in their states or districts reinforces their local ties. Constituents receive mail from their local representatives, read about them in newspapers and magazines, and see them on television. Large numbers of citizens report having contacts with their representatives. Incumbents miss few opportunities to do favors for constituents, gestures that are usually appreciated and remembered. It is no wonder, then, that constituents view their local representatives in more sympathetic, personal terms than they view the institution of Congress as a whole.

Senators and representatives present themselves to constituents largely on their own terms through advertising, self-promotion, and uncritical coverage by local or regional news media. Members devote countless hours to fundraising to ensure that they have the money to purchase all the paid media they need. Reflecting on the hundreds of fund-raising calls he makes daily, Representative Courtney said, "You could be Abraham Lincoln, but if you don't have the heart of a telemarketer, you're not going to make it to Congress."[28]

Members and their staffs devote constant attention to generating publicity and local press. "I am never too busy to talk to local TV," said a prominent House member. "Period. Exclamation point."[29] A survey of House press secretaries showed virtually unanimous agreement: "We'd rather get in [the hometown paper] than on the front page of the *New York Times* any day."[30] Individual lawmakers tend to bask in the flattering light cast by their local media. Hometown reporters, especially for broadcast media, usually work on general assignment stories and are ill prepared to question the lawmaker in detail about issues or events. Often their primary goal is simply to get the legislator on video or audio. For politicians, this is an ideal situation. They can express their views in their own words with a minimum of editing and few challenges from reporters.

The importance of personal connections and public relations does not mean that constituents are uninterested in their representatives' issue stances. Lawmakers also forge bonds with voters out of mutual agreement on important national issues. At the same time, members' personal ties with voters can help insulate them from disapproval on the occasions when their issue positions diverge from local preferences.

Questions of Ethics

Congressional ethics, however, are perennially in doubt. In a 2014 survey, a mere 7 percent of respondents rated the honesty and ethical standards of Congress members as high or very high.[31] Voters, however, do view their own representatives as more ethical than the rest of Congress. In a 2006 poll, for example, although 69 percent of respondents assessed the honesty of members of Congress generally as either "not so good" or "poor," only 30 percent took such a negative view of their own representatives.[32]

Public assessments of congressional ethics stand at odds with the views of most political scientists and close observers of the institution. The conventional wisdom among experts is that the vast majority of lawmakers are dedicated and ethical in their behavior. "Members of Congress behave better than people think," declared former representative Lee H. Hamilton, D-Ind. (1965–1999).[33]

Despite public distrust, lawmakers' behavior today is more transparent and less corrupt than in the past. Members' rising qualifications, more intense media scrutiny, and reforms in campaign finance and ethics procedures have all helped to curtail corruption. Money used to flow freely under the table. "Back in the old days, it was a common occurrence that you walked around with envelopes of cash in your pocket" to hand out to powerful lawmakers, recalled a Washington lobbyist.[34] Today, campaign contributions and direct lobbying expenses are subject to considerably more scrutiny by reporters and civic groups. Although large loopholes remain, financial abuses today are rare by pre-1970s standards.

Why, then, do citizens and commentators remain so contemptuous of lawmakers' ethics? A variety of factors, some of which are beyond members' control, drive public skepticism.

Unethical Behavior. One reason the public distrusts members' ethics is that, unfortunately, unethical behavior persists despite the network of laws and rules intended to restrain it. In 2015, for example, Staten Island representative Michael Grimm, R-N.Y., resigned from Congress after pleading guilty to felony tax fraud. Rep. Aaron Schock, R-Ill., also resigned in 2015 after questions were raised about whether he had fraudulently billed the government for excessive mileage reimbursements. House Speaker John Boehner, R-Ohio, made no secret of his low tolerance for members embroiled in scandal, telling a reporter who asked about Grimm, "I think all members should be held to the highest ethical standards."[35]

Scandals, even when they are uncovered and punished, weaken public confidence. Most notable was the mega-scandal centered on lobbyist Jack Abramoff, who advanced the interests of the gambling industry by means of donations, luxury trips, and favors for some half-dozen lawmakers. In 2006

Abramoff pleaded guilty to fraud, tax evasion, and conspiracy to bribe public officials.[36] The Abramoff scandal ended the political careers of at least six members of Congress, along with those of many congressional staffers and lobbyists. One House member was sentenced to jail for bribery.[37]

Ethics Rules and Processes. Congress's internal processes to police members' ethical violations fail to inspire public confidence. Members typically cringe at passing judgment on their peers. "The House Ethics Committee and the Senate Ethics Committee are structured in a way to protect incumbents rather than to discipline them," observed an ethics lobbyist for Public Citizen. "Members are overseeing each other, and they make sure that nothing comes back to haunt them."[38] But even energetic ethics enforcement does not improve public perceptions. The House Ethics Committee conducted eighty-nine inquiries into members' activities in the 113th Congress and empaneled subcommittees to investigate cases involving four members.[39] Despite all this enforcement activity, Americans continue to rate the ethics of Congress lower than any other profession and below that of advertisers and car salespeople.[40]

Paradoxically, the intensified regulation of public life actually fuels public distrust. So many rules govern the public activities of lawmakers that they can run afoul of them unintentionally. "High-level public officials are particularly good targets for investigation," explains law professor Cass R. Sunstein, "if only because of the complex network of statutes that regulate their behavior."[41] Elected officials are scrutinized by the Federal Election Commission, the House and Senate ethics committees, the Office of Congressional Ethics, and occasionally by the Justice Department and federal prosecutors (see Box 16-1 on congressional ethics). A number of "watchdog" groups such as Citizens for Responsibility and Ethics in Washington and Public Citizen also closely monitor ethics issues and publicize the results of their investigations.

Changing Standards of Personal Behavior. Politicians today are held to higher standards of personal habits and conduct than were politicians in the past. The contemporary news media exert great enterprise and energy investigating personal indiscretions and ethical violations, a shift from the journalistic norms of earlier eras. The effect on public perceptions is to heighten awareness of congressional shortcomings, regardless of how atypical such failings might be. The diligent work of law-abiding members attracts little attention, while an ethical lapse—or even a rumor of one—makes headlines.

In particular, sexual misconduct and substance abuse are far less tolerated today than they were a generation ago. In November 2013 freshman representative Trey Radel, R-Fla., pleaded guilty to buying 3.5 grams of cocaine and, despite initial resistance, was persuaded to resign his seat the following January.[42] Rep. Vance McAllister, R-La., came under strong pressure from Louisiana Republican leaders to step aside after the revelation of a surveillance video in which he was seen kissing a married female staffer.[43] When he refused to yield to the pressure, he was defeated for reelection in 2014. Reports of adulterous activities have ended the careers of several other members in recent years.[44]

BOX 16-1   **Congressional Ethics**

Members of Congress are bound by the U.S. Constitution, federal laws, party provisions, and House and Senate rules and conduct codes. Although many observers criticize loopholes, the panoply of regulations is extensive.

- **Constitution.** Each chamber has the power to punish its members for "disorderly behavior" and, by a two-thirds vote, to expel a member. Members are immune from arrest during attendance at congressional sessions (except for treason, felony, or breach of peace) and "for any speech or debate in either house, they shall not be questioned in any other place" (Article I, section 6). This latter provision protects lawmakers from any reprisals for expressing their legislative views.
- **Criminal Laws.** Federal laws make it a crime to solicit or accept a bribe; to solicit or receive "anything of value" for performing any official act or service, or for using influence in any proceeding involving the federal government; to enter into or benefit from any contracts with the government; or to commit any fraud against the United States.
- **Ethics Codes.** Adopted in 1968 and substantially tightened in 1977, 1989, 1995, 1997, and 2007, the House and Senate ethics codes apply to members and key staff aides. The codes require extensive financial disclosure; restrict members' outside earned income (to 15 percent of salaries); prohibit unofficial office accounts that many members used to supplement official allowances; impose stricter standards for using the frank for mailings; and ban lawmakers from accepting most meals and gifts from lobbyists. The House Committee on Standards of Official Conduct and the Senate Select Ethics Committee implement the codes, hear charges against members, issue advisory opinions, and recommend disciplinary actions.
- **Party Rules.** Congressional parties can discipline members who run afoul of ethics requirements. House Democratic and Republican rules require a committee leader who is indicted to step aside temporarily; a leader who is censured or convicted is automatically replaced.
- **Federal Election Campaign Act Amendments of 1974.** As amended again in 1976 and 1979, the Federal Election Campaign Act imposes extensive requirements on congressional incumbents as well as challengers. Additional rules and penalties were set in the Bipartisan Campaign Reform Act of 2002.
- **Office of Congressional Ethics.** Established by the House of Representatives in 2008, the Office of Congressional Ethics is an independent, nonpartisan board of eight private citizens charged with reviewing allegations of misconduct against House members and staff and, when appropriate, referring matters to the Committee on Standards of Official Conduct.

Opposition Research. Many scandals are driven by political opponents of the accused. Members of Congress, challengers, and party operatives all opportunistically seize on any ethical miscue, real or manufactured, for political advantage. For example, House Speaker Jim Wright (1987–1989),

D-Tex., was forced to step aside because of an ethics scandal that was initially brought to light via opposition research spearheaded by Rep. Newt Gingrich, R-Ga.[45] In the early weeks of the 110th Congress (2007–2009), a variety of media outlets ran stories criticizing the new Speaker, Nancy Pelosi, for apparently demanding a larger jet for trips home than the one used by her predecessor. It later surfaced that the request for a larger jet came not from the Speaker herself but from the House sergeant at arms because of security concerns and the added distance. (Pelosi lived in California, her predecessor in Illinois.)[46] That did not, however, prevent Speaker Pelosi's detractors from pushing the story to generate a media narrative that she was abusing the privileges of her office.

In his study of the impact of what he calls the "ethics culture" on federal appointments, G. Calvin Mackenzie writes:

> Instead of getting out of the way so the winners can govern, the losers begin guerrilla operations that never cease, using every weapon and every opportunity to attack, harass, embarrass, and otherwise weaken those who hold office. If you cannot beat them in an election, current practice now suggests, then do everything in your power to keep the winners from governing and implementing their policy priorities.[47]

In other words, ethics charges and countercharges are often nothing more than "politics by other means."[48] Nevertheless, the political payoffs from such accusations encourage political actors to launch them at their opponents at every opportunity, undercutting perceptions of lawmakers generally.

"A Small Class of People." Do these hazards of public life deter "the best and the brightest" from seeking elective office? It is hard to answer that question. Young people, for example, show lamentably scant interest in government careers.[49] The difficulties of balancing a parental or caregiving role with the round-the-clock demands of the lawmaker's life fall especially hard on women.[50] The poor esteem in which the public holds Congress is another deterrent for potential candidates.[51]

American democracy requires that ambitious people put themselves forward as candidates. But many of the ablest individuals decide to sit on the sidelines. Although open seats seem to have little shortage of claimants, parties frequently have great difficulty recruiting good challengers to run against officeholders. Indeed, the absence of strong challengers, especially for House seats, is a significant factor in persistently high incumbent reelection rates. Meanwhile, the outcomes of congressional elections almost always reveal at least a few underperforming incumbents who would have been vulnerable to defeat, had they only drawn a credible opponent.[52] Congressional elections would be more competitive, incumbents would be more accountable, and voters would have better choices if greater numbers of talented individuals were willing to enter the fray.

CONGRESS-AS-INSTITUTION

Americans expect Congress to be active and productive. Opinion surveys have consistently found that people want Congress to play a strong, independent policy-making role. They look to Congress to vet the president's initiatives carefully.[53]

Policy Success and Stalemate

Although most citizens believe that Congress is an important institution that should share power equally with the president, they lack awareness of the specific ways Congress affects their daily lives. Lee Hamilton tells the following story:

> [A] group of [young people] visiting my Indiana office told me that Congress was irrelevant. So I asked them a few questions. How had they gotten to my office? On the interstate highway, they said. Had any of them gone to the local university? Yes, they said, admitting they'd got some help from federal student loans. Did any of them have grandparents on Social Security and Medicare? Well sure, they replied, picking up on where I was headed. Their lives had been profoundly affected by Congress. They just hadn't focused on all of the connections before.[54]

Its poor public reputation notwithstanding, Congress has produced many innovative and effective policies. In an intriguing study, Paul C. Light of the Brookings Institution set out to identify the federal government's most influential actions over a fifty-year period.[55] A survey of historians and political scientists winnowed a preliminary roster of 588 items to a list of fifty "greatest achievements." For the record, the top three successes were judged to be rebuilding Europe after World War II (the Marshall Plan, 1947), expanding the right to vote (Voting Rights Act of 1965), and promoting equal access to public accommodations (Civil Rights Act of 1964).

In every case Light uncovered, Congress played a vital role in the policy's inception, ratification, or implementation. Although Congress was not always the initiator, many programs associated with given presidents—for example, the Marshall Plan (Harry S. Truman) and Medicare (Lyndon B. Johnson)—began as proposals on Capitol Hill. "No one party, Congress, or president can be credited with any single achievement. . . . Rather, achievement appears to be the direct product of endurance, consensus, and patience."[56]

Despite its past achievements, the contemporary Congress is frequently described as "dysfunctional" and unproductive.[57] Most observers could compile a must-do legislative agenda that would include many items left unaddressed by recent Congresses. Citizens are worried that Congress pays too little attention to long-term problems such as the cost of entitlements, the public debt, immigration, climate change, and infrastructure maintenance. Setting aside large-scale policy problems, Congress also struggles with routine matters of governance, such as budgeting, appropriations, and appointments.

Assessing the Congressional Process

Congress's institutional shortcomings are numerous and obvious. Beyond its structural and procedural complexities, the quality of its deliberations often falls short of democratic ideals. Lack of comity and bipartisanship, the growth of Senate roadblocks, and questions about appropriate transparency undercut Congress's reputation. Are reforms possible?

Deliberation. The primary function of a legislative assembly is to foster deliberation. "The assembly makes possible a deliberation in which conflicting judgments about the public good . . . can be examined, debated, and resolved," writes Richard Hall. "And through such a process the actions of government achieve legitimacy."[58] Recent developments have undermined the quality and quantity of congressional deliberation.

In order to cope with the pressures of lawmaking in a highly polarized and partisan environment, leaders of both parties tend to "short-circuit regular deliberative procedures in committee, on the floor, and in conference."[59] The legislative process has morphed into a wide variety of highly centralized improvisations—what Barbara Sinclair has termed "unorthodox lawmaking."[60] Leaders package together disparate policies into omnibus vehicles so bulky that only a small number of staff aides and members know what provisions have been inserted or left out. Outcomes are normally predetermined, especially in the House, where majority party leaders oversee the pre-floor negotiations and craft the rules for debate. Most important House measures are considered under restrictive or closed rules permitting few or no amendments.[61] Floor deliberations are just a series of desultory recitations—public speaking in this country has become something of a lost art. Under such circumstances, lawmakers are sometimes embarrassed by provisions they have voted into law.

Committee deliberation has been similarly weakened. Committee meetings are poorly attended, with the outcomes laid out by the chair and the chair's majority party colleagues. Rank-and-file committee members struggle to obtain information about pending legislation and often have little time to offer amendments.[62] Furthermore, leaders may opt to bypass committee consideration altogether, bringing unreported bills directly to the floor. "Committee budgets also remain under downward pressure."[63] Staff resources for House and Senate committees were cut by around 30 percent between 1979 and 2009.[64] Legislative branch appropriations have trended down further since 2010.[65] Staff levels at the Government Accountability Office, Congress's primary oversight and investigatory agency, were reduced by more than 14 percent after 2010.[66] According to two analysts, "Committees have been marginalized in myriad ways, from central party direction to ad hoc groups to omnibus bills."[67] As committees become less consequential policy-making arenas, members have less incentive to develop policy expertise in the matters before their committees.

Even House–Senate interactions are less deliberative in character. Today's congressional leaders frequently avoid the conference process altogether, convening "pro forma" conferences to ratify deals worked out in leadership offices or exchanging bills back and forth between the chambers. On occasion, House–Senate negotiations have excluded minority party conferees. Such tactics streamline the legislative process but forfeit the benefits of deliberation.

Another factor weakening congressional deliberation is Congress's frantic stop-and-go work schedule. Although earlier members did not live in the nation's capital, most of them stayed in town for weeks at a stretch, their days dominated by extended hearings or deliberations. By the mid–twentieth century, a minority of members—mostly from the eastern corridor—constituted a "Tuesday–Thursday club," spending long weekends at home. Nowadays, nearly all members follow such a schedule. Members arrive in Washington for votes on Tuesday evening and leave after votes conclude on Thursday afternoon. "This truncated schedule," reports a Bipartisan Policy Center commission, "leaves only one full day—Wednesday—for committee hearings, markups, and the other necessary ingredients for fruitful legislating."[68] Extended nonlegislative or "district work periods" surround all the major holidays.

Thirty-four-year House veteran Hamilton has offered a blunt assessment of the situation:

> Congress doesn't work enough at its true job. Members of Congress spend too much of their week campaigning, and not enough of it doing the hard work of governing. Building a consensus behind an approach to a national problem is tough; it takes negotiation, extended discussion, and hard study. This is impossible when you spend three days on Capitol Hill and then rush home for an extended weekend of appearances.[69]

One remedy would seem simple: longer sessions (two weeks at least), alternating with periods for constituency work or official travel. Because of the pressures of campaigning in today's highly competitive environment, reforms permitting extended deliberation are not likely.

Comity and Bipartisanship. Another institutional malady is the decline of interpersonal comity. This decline is the product of several converging factors, most notably the escalating cohesion within, and polarization between, the two parties. Nelson W. Polsby aptly termed the contemporary period an "era of ill feeling" in Congress.[70] Former representative and deputy GOP whip Mickey Edwards of Oklahoma (1977–1993) points to intense party competition for majority control as a key factor undercutting bipartisan cooperation in today's Congress:

Instead of morphing from candidates to members of Congress on the day they are sworn in, today's legislators engage in permanent campaigning. Neither party is willing to allow the other to gain credit for an achievement that might help it in the next election, so the center aisle that divides Democrats from Republicans in the House has become a wall.[71]

Critics have persuasively faulted the contemporary Congress for engaging in a "destructive form of partisanship" that prevents bipartisan give and take.[72] When the two congressional parties were more internally divided between the 1930s and 1990s, there was greater potential for cross-party coalitions and minority party input. "Oh, those were frustrating years," recalled former Republican leader Robert Michel of Illinois, who served in the minority for all of his thirty-eight years in the House (1957–1995):

> But . . . I never really felt I was out of the game or that I had no part to play. Under the rules of the House, the traditions of the House . . . there is a role to play for the minority. . . . We struck a deal, we made a bargain [and worked at] bringing dissident factions together . . . to craft good legislation for the country. That was the joy of it![73]

As leaders centralize power, minority party members are less likely to be heard.

An earlier generation of political scientists had lamented the absence of party government in the United States. They argued in favor of a democratic politics in which parties would run on coherent platforms and command the leadership and unity to enact their programs into law. Key elements of the party government model have now come to pass. The parties are far more internally cohesive; the caucuses meet regularly to decide policy; members' party-line voting presents clear alternatives to voters. But no analyst contends that these changes have lifted the quality of policy making. Instead, partisanship has been blamed for escalating the level of rancor and stalemate.

Fierce and pervasive partisan conflict undermines the public's trust in government. Congressional partisanship has a direct, negative effect on Americans' assessment of the institution.[74] According to one study:

> Citizens appear to equate partisan conflict with partisan biases and the notion that members of Congress are avoiding the facts—whatever they may be—when formulating policy. . . . [T]he public perceives partisan conflict as a waste of time and resources that could be spent trying to solve the nation's problems.[75]

Senate Roadblocks. Nowhere has the rise of partisanship created more obstacles for policy making than in the Senate. For much of the Senate's history, filibusters were rare, employed for matters of great constituency or regional importance. Today, they have become a partisan tool. The partisan filibuster—in which most or all of the Senate majority party's agenda is systematically blocked by an organized minority party filibuster—is a recent innovation. Barbara Sinclair's research dates the partisan filibuster to the first two years of the Clinton presidency (the 103d Congress, 1993–1995), in which Republican-led filibusters obstructed half of all major measures.[76] The practice has escalated since the 1990s. "As long as I've served," remarked Vice President Joe Biden in 2010, "this is the first time every single solitary decision has required 60 senators."[77]

The emergence of the partisan filibuster has made governance in the Senate exceptionally difficult. "Requiring a supermajority to pass legislation that is at all controversial makes the coalition-building process much more difficult and increases a status quo–oriented system's tendency toward gridlock," writes Sinclair. "The costs of gridlock can be severe: a government that cannot act, that cannot respond satisfactorily to its citizens' demands, loses its legitimacy."[78]

The widespread use of delaying tactics in the Senate has effects that extend far beyond the highly controversial issues. It is not merely that the Senate's majority party faces great obstacles to passing a partisan agenda. The delays also impede the Senate's ability to manage the rest of its workload. As Scott Lilly, senior fellow at the Center for American Progress, explains, "The legislative calendar is so consumed by extended debate" that there is not enough time for the Senate to reauthorize expiring programs."[79] Similarly, appropriations bills almost never pass on time, denying federal agencies the information they need to plan budgets, evaluate competing contract proposals, and maximize value for taxpayers.[80] Many uncontroversial matters that pass the House never receive Senate consideration simply because of the lack of floor time.

Transparency. Another important issue in evaluating Congress is transparency, the ability of the public to monitor and understand congressional proceedings. Questions of transparency present difficult trade-offs for legislative assemblies. On the one hand, a lack of transparency is a major source of public mistrust. People fear that a lack of public access will allow special interests to dominate the legislative process in secret. The Sunlight Foundation, a nonprofit group founded to champion congressional transparency, has pushed popular initiatives such as the online availability of members' financial statements and lobbying expenses, among other reforms. Generally speaking, the public does not trust legislators to act in the public interest in the absence of public scrutiny and accountability.

On the other hand, transparency can hamper internal legislative bargaining and compromise. It is more difficult for members to accept trade-offs that impose costs on their constituencies when those decisions are made in full public view.[81] Instead, lawmakers have a greater incentive to play to their external constituencies and refuse to engage in meaningful negotiations.[82] One of the most significant transparency reforms ever adopted was to permit C-SPAN to telecast congressional proceedings.[83] This reform gave Americans much more access to the lawmaking process. But, just as opponents of televising Congress feared, it may have hindered congressional work. Television "has probably done more to make the Senate a more partisan place," points out veteran senator Orrin G. Hatch, R-Utah. "There's a lot of posturing before the camera."[84]

The Perils of Reform. Reforming Congress is often touted as a solution to its organizational or procedural faults. The House and Senate themselves periodically engage in self-examination (the last broad-scale inquiry took place in 1993). But such efforts are often impeded by the two-Congresses dilemma— that is, structural reforms can threaten members' electoral interests. E. Scott Adler warns, for example, that "any widespread change in the established order of policy deliberation—particularly in its centerpiece, the committee system— would create far too much uncertainty in members' electoral strategies."[85]

Congress's history nevertheless includes some major planned innovations affecting deliberative processes, committee jurisdictions, and electoral arrangements. At key moments, reformers with different and often conflicting goals— enhancing legislative power and efficiency, gaining partisan or policy advantage, or augmenting individual lawmakers' perquisites—have coalesced around significant changes. Because of the variety of goals involved, however, the results achieved were often different from those anticipated.

Reformers typically find that they must build upon preexisting institutions, rather than sweep away current practices and start afresh. An example was the series of new budget procedures piled like so many building blocks on top of the existing authorization-appropriations process by the Congressional Budget Act of 1974. Little wonder that such reforms typically fall short of their sponsors' objectives. Based on a survey of forty-two major institutional innovations over the last century, one author concludes that instead of achieving stable, effective arrangements, congressional reforms result in "a set of institutions that often work at cross-purposes."[86]

Media Coverage

The most open and accessible of the three branches of government, Congress is covered by a large press corps populated by some of the nation's most skilled journalists. Long-time CBS News anchor Bob Schieffer claimed that Capitol Hill was the best news beat in Washington.[87] Paradoxically, however, few reporters are able to convey the internal subtleties or the external pressures that shape lawmaking. Moreover, the media best suited to reporting on Congress—serious daily newspapers and magazines—are suffering long-term declines in circulation.[88] In response, newspapers have curtailed their coverage of Congress and national and global politics in general. Pressrooms have been downsized; most foreign bureaus have been closed. Bottom-line pressures on the media threaten the nation's democratic processes by leaving people less informed.

The decline has been equally drastic in television (including the so-called all-news channels). "Apart from technology," says journalist Bill Moyers, "the biggest change in my thirty years in broadcasting has been the shift of content from news about government to consumer-driven information and celebrity features."[89]

Political news has changed in content as well as coverage. Fewer stories appear on policy issues and more on scandal, wrongdoing, or corruption.

Following the canons of investigative journalism, reporters play the role of suspicious adversaries on the lookout for good guys and bad guys, winners and losers. Ethical problems, congressional pay and perquisites, campaign war chests, and foreign junkets are frequent targets. Generally speaking, political radio and TV talk shows are ill-informed, combative, and contemptuous of politicians and their work.[90]

As mentioned earlier, divergent press coverage—local versus national media—widens the gap between the two Congresses' distinct images. The tone and content of news reporting is more positive for individual members than for the institution. Congress as an institution is covered by the national press with lots of skepticism and cynicism, while individual lawmakers are covered respectfully by the local media.

Citizens' Attitudes toward Congress

The institutional Congress almost always ranks well below respondents' own representatives in public esteem (see Table 16-1). Citizens' ratings of the job Congress is doing fluctuate with economic conditions, wars and crises, scandals, trust in government overall, and levels of partisan conflict (see Figure 16-1).[91] Approval of Congress surged briefly after it handled the Watergate affair in 1974, after the Republican takeover twenty years later, and after the terrorist attacks of September 11, 2001. The overall trend has been markedly downward since 2002, however, with Congress plumbing historic depths of public

TABLE 16-1   High Approval for Members, Low Approval for Congress

Individual members	Congress as an institution
Serve constituents	Resolves national issues only with difficulty or not at all
Run against Congress	Has few defenders
Emphasize personal style and outreach to constituents	Operates as collegial body that is difficult for citizens to understand
Are covered by local media in generally positive terms	Is covered by national media, often negatively (with focus on scandals and conflicts)
Respond quickly to most constituent needs and inquiries	Moves slowly with cumbersome processes that inhibit rapid responses
Are able to highlight personal goals and accomplishments	Has many voices, but none can speak clearly for Congress as a whole

Sources: Timothy E. Cook, "Legislature vs. Legislator: A Note on the Paradox of Congressional Support," *Legislative Studies Quarterly* 4 (February 1979): 43–52; Glenn R. Parker and Roger H. Davidson, "Why Do Americans Love Their Congressmen So Much More Than Their Congress?" *Legislative Studies Quarterly* 4 (February 1979): 53–61; Richard Born, "The Shared Fortunes of Congress and Congressmen: Members May Run from Congress but They Can't Hide," *Journal of Politics* 52 (November 1990): 1223–1241.

FIGURE 16-1   **Public Assessments of the Two Congresses, 1974–2014**

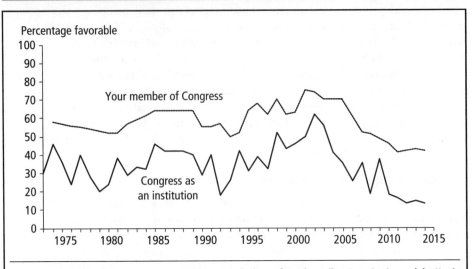

Sources: Authors' interpolations of survey results, primarily drawn from the Gallup Organization and the Harris Survey.

Notes: The Gallup Organization's questions are: "Do you approve of the way the U.S. Congress is handling its job? Do you approve or disapprove of the way the representative from your own congressional district is handling his/her job?" The Harris Survey's question is: "How would you rate the job done this past year by [Congress] [your member of Congress]—excellent, pretty good, only fair, or poor?" Responses are dichotomized as favorable ("excellent," "pretty good") or unfavorable ("only fair," "poor"). The plotted points in the figures indicate respondents having opinions who approve of or are favorable toward congressional performance. Polling data for 2010 and 2011 are from ABC News/ *Washington Post* polls.

dissatisfaction. Congressional approval (in Gallup's poll) has not reached 25 percent since December 2009 and has averaged 16 percent since January 2010. In August 2014, only 13 percent of respondents approved of the way Congress was handling its job.[92]

Congress is not well understood by the average citizen. Partly to blame are the institution's size and complexity, not to mention the arcane twists and turns of the legislative process. But many citizens simply find the whole legislative process distasteful.

Dissension is on display on Capitol Hill to a greater extent than in other branches of government. The president speaks with one voice: even though there is fierce competition for the president's ear, a statement from the president defines the administration's position. As for the judiciary, opinions are frequently divided or unclear as judges and justices disagree about law and policy, but their decisions are usually accepted as law. By contrast, no single member—not even the institution's top leaders—speaks for Congress.

The public's ambivalence toward Congress goes far deeper than unhappiness with specific policies or disgust with scandals, according to the sobering conclusions of John R. Hibbing and Elizabeth Theiss-Morse:

> People do not wish to see uncertainty, conflicting opinions, long debate, competing interests, confusion, bargaining, and compromised, imperfect solutions. They want government to do its job quietly and efficiently, sans conflict and sans fuss. In short . . . they often seek a patently unrealistic form of democracy.[93]

In other words, people seem to abhor the very attributes that are the hallmarks of robust representative assemblies. As Hibbing and Theiss-Morse observe, Congress "is structured to embody what we dislike about modern democratic government, which is almost everything."[94]

TWENTY-FIRST-CENTURY CHALLENGES

The U.S. Congress is now in its third century. Survival for more than two centuries is no mean feat. Congress has withstood repeated stress and turbulence, including a civil war, political assassinations, terrorist attacks, domestic scandals, and contentious foreign involvement. The U.S. constitutional system is far older than most of the world's existing governments.

Security

The physical setting of the U.S. Capitol now exhibits the stepped-up security arrangements prevalent elsewhere since the September 11, 2001, terrorist attacks. Just over a decade ago, visitors and Hill personnel moved freely in and out of the Capitol and surrounding office buildings. Members of the public may still visit most Capitol Hill facilities, but they now encounter uniformed officers, metal detectors, and concrete barriers. One welcome development, however, is the long-needed U.S. Capitol Visitor Center—constructed under the east front that enhances the building's safety while introducing visitors to Congress and its work.

Checks and Imbalances?

The constitutional system of divided powers and competing branches does not yield a stable equilibrium. Powers ebb and flow among the branches. Crises tend to empower the executive branch, whereas more peaceful times are friendlier to congressional power. An activist bench can drive the judiciary into political thickets; at other times the bench defers to the other branches.

Executive Hubris. Executive branch encroachments upon legislative prerogatives are neither new nor confined to crisis periods. Most modern presidents have asserted their discretion over program administration, fought for broader leeway in spending appropriated funds, and exploited their freedom to reorganize agencies and redeploy their personnel. Presidents and their appointees naturally seek to control information about what they are doing. There is no question that recent presidents have pushed the boundaries of presidential authority in ways that threaten to eclipse Congress.

Executive dominance is most apparent in military affairs. Throughout the post–World War II era, presidents have regularly embroiled the United States in military conflicts without seeking congressional support. In fact, none of the United States' military actions has been accompanied by a congressional declaration of war since President Truman single-handedly intervened in the Korean War in 1950.[95] Although Presidents George H. W. Bush and George W. Bush both asked for congressional authorizations of the use of force in Iraq, they—along with all other contemporary presidents—contended that they did not need congressional approval to act. President Bill Clinton did not ask for any kind of congressional support before launching cruise missiles against the Iraqi intelligence services in 1993; nor did he seek congressional authority before launching air strikes against the Serbs in 1994 and 1995.

The pattern continues in the Obama administration. When President Barack Obama decided at a contentious White House meeting in March 2011 to support military action against the Gaddafi regime in Libya, he did so without broadly consulting with Congress or seeking any kind of congressional authorization.[96] Obama also did not seek congressional authorization in 2014 before launching airstrikes in Iraq and Syria as part of a campaign against Islamic State rebels.

Presidents have also become more assertive in denying information to Congress. Recent presidents, including both Barack Obama and George W. Bush, have made secrecy a watchword. The Bush White House refused to share documents with Congress, permit certain executive officials to testify before congressional committees, or otherwise cooperate with investigative hearings.[97] In 2012 Congress voted to hold Obama's attorney general, Eric Holder, in contempt of Congress over his refusal to turn over documents relating to the "Fast and Furious Scandal," a failed sting operation managed by the Arizona field office of the U.S. Bureau of Alcohol, Tobacco, Firearms and Explosives.[98]

Despite such complaints, it is also clear that Congress has been complicit in its loss of power. Congress surrendered vast grants of power to the president and the executive branch immediately after the terrorist attacks of 9/11 by approving open-ended military action, the USA Patriot Act, and the 240,000-employee Homeland Security Department. More generally, Congress often prefers to avoid responsibility for difficult decisions. Indeed, a key reason why there was no authorization for the use of military force against the Islamic State in 2014 was that congressional leaders were in no hurry to weigh in on such a politically fraught issue, especially before the November elections.[99] "Congress has ceded its war power to the president," concluded former representative Hamilton.[100]

Party polarization may also have contributed to Congress's refusal to assert its prerogatives more vigorously during recent episodes of unified government. Reflecting on the relationship between the Republican Congress and President

George W. Bush, Rep. Ray LaHood, R-Ill., conceded the point: "Our party controls the levers of government. We're not about to go out and look beneath a bunch of rocks and try and cause heartburn."[101] Loyalty to a president should be no excuse for congressional timidity. Partisan loyalties did not immunize past presidents, from Franklin D. Roosevelt to Ronald Reagan to Bill Clinton, against probing oversight and sometimes fierce opposition led by their party's leaders on Capitol Hill—even in wartime. If lawmakers do not fiercely defend their prerogatives, they have only themselves to blame when executives ignore them.

Judicial Lawmaking. Congress also faces attacks upon its powers from an activist federal judiciary, which has invalidated congressional enactments in more than thirty cases since 1995. Since the 1990s, the courts have overturned federal laws in areas such as interstate commerce and civil and voting rights, in some cases raising questions that were last litigated in the 1930s. By narrow majorities, for example, the U.S. Supreme Court curbed the 1990 Americans with Disabilities Act on grounds that it had not dared to apply to earlier civil rights statutes. Recent Court rulings have all but eliminated Congress's ability to impose regulations on campaign finance. The Court came within one vote of striking down Obamacare in the summer of 2012.

The loss of congressional power extends beyond the contemporary Court's propensity to engage in judicial review. The Court also engages in statutory interpretation, sometimes in ways that many members criticize as being far at odds with Congress's intent. Even so, congressional party polarization and gridlock make it much more difficult for Congress to reassert its authority by overturning the Court's statutory interpretations.[102] If, for example, the Court declares that the Affordable Care Act does not provide health insurance subsidies in the states using the federal exchange, it is unlikely that Congress would be able to offer any kind of legislative response. A Congress that cannot act is unable to protect its authority against judicial encroachment.

Members of Congress regularly criticize the courts for "judicial activism," by which they typically mean decisions on a handful of ideological issues, principally involving abortion and religious establishment clause jurisprudence. Meanwhile, fewer members denounce judicial rulings regarding fundamental state and federal authority. The judiciary retains the capacity to constrict legislative powers in much the same way that late-nineteenth-century courts gutted the Civil War constitutional amendments. Senior federal circuit court judge John T. Noonan Jr. explains: "If five members of the Supreme Court are in agreement on an agenda, they are mightier than five hundred members of Congress with unmobilized or warring constituencies."[103]

Is Congress Permanently Damaged? The Congress of the 1970s sought to reclaim prerogatives that had slipped away during the Cold War period. It passed major reforms designed to reassert congressional power over budgets, as well as domestic and foreign policy. In his detailed account, James L. Sundquist sums up that era: "The 1970s were a period of upheaval, of change so rapid and so radical as to transform the pattern of relationships that had evolved and settled into place over the span of half a century or more."[104]

The 1970s reform fervor was short-lived. Reflecting on the subsequent period, Andrew Rudalevige revisits the question: Is there an imperial presidency? His short answer is yes: "Presidents have regained freedom of unilateral action in a variety of areas, from executive privilege to war powers to covert operations to campaign spending. . . . The default position between presidents and Congress has moved toward the presidential end of the inter-branch spectrum—and irreversibly so."[104]

Is this trend irreversible? As defenders of the constitutional system, we remain cautiously hopeful of the future. After all, partisans of all stripes have a long-term stake in an active, robust legislative branch. Executive initiatives, as popular as they may seem, demand critical review; executive programs must be overseen and evaluated.

What does the future hold? Much depends on a series of questions: Will members of Congress resolve partisan conflicts to make needed progress on pressing problems? Can Congress assert itself to protect its constitutional prerogatives against power-seeking presidents and judges? Unfortunately, no advocate of the framers' constitutional design can offer confident answers.

We conclude with a question for the twenty-first century: Are the two Congresses ultimately compatible, or are they diverging, each detrimental to the other? The burdens placed on both Congresses become increasingly heavy from an ever-growing and diverse nation in an increasingly complex world. Congress-as-institution is expected to resolve all kinds of problems. Meanwhile, members are pulled away from their legislative duties by the constant press of fund-raising, party competition, constituency expectations, and short legislative workweeks. Legislators struggle to keep abreast of conflicting demands.

Recent events are not encouraging, but the question remains whether representative democracy will in the end be a winning or losing effort. History is only mildly reassuring, and the future poses new and difficult challenges for which the margin of error may be narrower than ever before. And yet representative democracy itself is a gamble. The proposition that representation can yield wise policy making remains a daring one. As always, it is an article of faith whose proof lies inevitably in the future.

Reference Materials

APPENDIX A   Party Control: Presidency, Senate, House, 1901–2017

Congress	Years	President	Senate D	Senate R	Senate Other	House D	House R	House Other
57th	1901–1903	William McKinley/ Theodore Roosevelt	31	55	4	151	197	9
58th	1903–1905	T. Roosevelt	33	57	—	178	208	—
59th	1905–1907	T. Roosevelt	33	57	—	136	250	—
60th	1907–1909	T. Roosevelt	31	61	—	164	222	—
61st	1909–1911	William Howard Taft	32	61	—	172	219	—
62d	1911–1913	Taft	41	51	—	228	161	1
63d	1913–1915	Woodrow Wilson	51	44	1	291	127	17
64th	1915–1917	Wilson	56	40	—	230	196	9
65th	1917–1919	Wilson	53	42	—	216	210	6
66th	1919–1921	Wilson	47	49	—	190	240	3
67th	1921–1923	Warren G. Harding	37	59	—	131	301	1
68th	1923–1925	Calvin Coolidge	43	51	2	205	225	5
69th	1925–1927	Coolidge	39	56	1	183	247	4
70th	1927–1929	Coolidge	46	49	1	195	237	3
71st	1929–1931	Herbert Hoover	39	56	1	167	267	1
72d	1931–1933	Hoover	47	48	1	220	214	1
73d	1933–1935	Franklin D. Roosevelt	60	35	1	313	117	5
74th	1935–1937	F. D. Roosevelt	69	25	2	319	103	10
75th	1937–1939	F. D. Roosevelt	76	16	4	331	89	13
76th	1939–1941	F. D. Roosevelt	69	23	4	261	164	4
77th	1941–1943	F. D. Roosevelt	66	28	2	268	162	5
78th	1943–1945	F. D. Roosevelt	58	37	1	218	208	4
79th	1945–1947	Harry S. Truman	56	38	1	242	190	2
80th	1947–1949	Truman	45	51	—	188	245	1
81st	1949–1951	Truman	54	42	—	263	171	1
82d	1951–1953	Truman	49	47	—	234	199	1
83d	1953–1955	Dwight D. Eisenhower	47	48	1	211	221	1
84th	1955–1957	Eisenhower	48	47	1	232	203	—
85th	1957–1959	Eisenhower	49	47	—	233	200	—
86th[a]	1959–1961	Eisenhower	65	35	—	284	153	—
87th[a]	1961–1963	John F. Kennedy	65	35	—	263	174	—
88th	1963–1965	Kennedy/ Lyndon B. Johnson	67	33	—	258	177	—
89th	1965–1967	Johnson	68	32	—	295	140	—

Congress	Years	President	Senate			House		
			D	R	Other	D	R	Other
90th	1967–1969	Johnson	64	36	—	247	187	—
91st	1969–1971	Richard M. Nixon	57	43	—	243	192	—
92d	1971–1973	Nixon	54	44	2	254	180	—
93d	1973–1975	Nixon/Gerald R. Ford	56	42	2w	239	192	1
94th	1975–1977	Ford	60	37	2	291	144	—
95th	1977–1979	Jimmy Carter	61	38	1	292	143	—
96th	1979–1981	Carter	58	41	1	276	157	—
97th	1981–1983	Ronald Reagan	46	53	1	243	192	—
98th	1983–1985	Reagan	45	55	—	267	168	—
99th	1985–1987	Reagan	47	53	—	252	183	—
100th	1987–1989	Reagan	55	45	—	258	177	—
101st	1989–1991	George H. W. Bush	55	45	—	260	175	—
102d	1991–1993	Bush	57	43	—	268	166	1
103d	1993–1995	Bill Clinton	56	44	—	258	176	1
104th	1995–1997	Clinton	47	53	—	204	230	1
105th	1997–1999	Clinton	45	55	—	207	227	1
106th	1999–2001	Clinton	45	55	—	211	223	1
107th	2001–2003	George W. Bush	50	49	1	210	222	3
108th	2003–2005	Bush	48	51	1	205	229	1
109th	2005–2007	Bush	44	55	1	202	232	1
110th[b]	2007–2009	Bush	49	49	2	233	202	—
111th[c]	2009–2011	Barack Obama	58	40	2	257	178	—
112th	2011–2013	Obama	51	47	2	193	242	—
113th	2013–2015	Obama	53	45	2	200	233	—
114th	2015–2017	Obama	44	54	2	188	247	

☐ Republican control   ▨ Democratic control

Sources: Encyclopedia of the United States Congress, ed. Donald C. Bacon, Roger H. Davidson, and Morton Keller (New York: Simon and Schuster, 1995), 1556–1558; data compiled by authors for 103d through 114th Congresses.

Note: Figures are for the beginning of the first session of each Congress and do not include vacancies, subsequent shifts, or changes in party affiliation.

[a] The House in the 86th and 87th Congresses had 437 members because of an at-large representative given to both Alaska (January 3, 1959) and Hawaii (August 21, 1959) prior to redistricting in 1962.

[b] The two Senate independents caucused with the Democrats, giving them a 51–49 majority for the purpose of organizing the chamber.

[c] For the Senate, we have counted as Democrats Arlen Specter, who shifted parties in April 2009, and Al Franken of Minnesota, who was sworn in on July 7, 2009.

Capitol Hill is an excellent place to obtain first-hand experience with the U.S. government. With 541 lawmakers (representatives, senators, delegates, and resident commissioners); hundreds of committees and subcommittees; scores of informal caucuses; and three congressional support agencies (the Congressional Research Service, Government Accountability Office, and Congressional Budget Office), intern opportunities abound for students interested in experiencing Congress and its members up close and personal.

Undergraduates will find useful information about landing an internship on Capitol Hill in several sources. One of the best is published under the auspices of the American Political Science Association and is titled *Studying in Washington: Academic Internships in the Nation's Capital.* Political scientist Stephen E. Frantzich discusses how to get a good internship, make the most of the experience, and find a place to live in Washington, D.C.

From our own years of "soaking and poking" around Capitol Hill, we offer five observations about getting congressional experience. First, no central clearinghouse exists for internships. Every congressional office, committee, caucus, and support agency manages its own internship program. Contact information and intern applications may be found on member and committee websites (www.house.gov and www.senate.gov). For example, the House Judiciary Committee's website outlines the application process for undergraduates and law students seeking an internship with the full committee or one of its five subcommittees.

Many intern opportunities are available for minority students, such as through the Congressional Hispanic Caucus Institute (www.chci.org) or the minority access internship program (www.minorityaccess.org). You must be persistent, patient, and determined to find a position that will be a rewarding learning experience. Not only should you find out what duties and functions will be assigned to you as a volunteer intern (it is sometimes possible to secure paid internships), but you also need to remember that you have something useful to offer. Most congressional offices and committees are understaffed and subject to high staff turnover. Although the market for interns is competitive, congressional lawmakers, committees, and staffers want and need your talent.

Second, develop some notion as to where you would like to intern. Do research on the committee, lawmaker, support agency, or caucus that interests you. Remember that every office has its own personality. Senate offices, for example, are often large enterprises with many staff aides, while House offices are generally smaller. Interns thus will have more opportunities for personal, day-to-day contact with House members than with senators. The best way to determine the office environment is by interviewing people who have worked in a particular office, talking with the internship coordinators at your college or university, or visiting the office yourself.

Third, target your own representative and senators. Many congressional members prefer interns from their own state or district, who are likely to be familiar with the geography and concerns of that area. In addition, potential interns probably will have family and friends who are constituents of the lawmaker. Do not hesitate to use your contacts. You might also volunteer to work in a state or district office of the lawmaker. Before accepting an internship, consider your own views and ideals. If your views are conservative, working for a lawmaker who espouses liberal causes may be difficult. However, if you are tactful and open-minded, working for someone whose views differ from yours may be instructive.

Fourth, intern placement opportunities are plentiful. Many colleges and universities sponsor semester programs in Washington, D.C. Several schools, including American University, Boston University, Hamilton College, Georgetown University, State University of New York, University of Southern California, University of Illinois, and University of California run programs in Washington, D.C. Some accept students from other accredited colleges and universities. The Washington Center for Internships and Academic Seminars, in existence since 1975, has placed thousands of students from hundreds of colleges. To be sure, students can Google "congressional internships" and find numerous intern listings to peruse.

Finally, Congress needs and welcomes the influx of new ideas and experiences that interns bring with them. The work at times may be drudgery— answering mail and telephones, entering information into computers, and running errands—but the opportunity to learn about Congress and to pick up political smarts not easily available from textbooks is nearly without equal. You may even want to keep a private journal of your experiences: what you have done and what you have learned. In sum, an internship on Capitol Hill is likely to be rewarding intellectually and in other ways that are impossible to predict.

RESOURCES

Bailey, Christina M., and Jennifer E. Manning. "Internships, Fellowships, and Other Work Experience Opportunities in the Federal Government." CRS Report 98-654, November 18, 2014.

Best Intern Ever: Roll Call's Guide to Acing Your Internship. Washington, DC: CQ Roll Call Publishing Group, 2014.

The Congressional Intern Handbook. Washington, DC: Congressional Management Foundation, 2006.

Fleishman, Sandra. "The Annual Scramble: Washington Interns Line Up for Their First Lesson— in Housing Supply and Demand." *Washington Post,* May 29, 2004, F1.

Frantzich, Stephen E. *Studying in Washington: Academic Internships in the Nation's Capital.* 5th ed. Washington, DC: American Political Science Association, 2002.

Lee, Jennifer. "Crucial Unpaid Internships Increasingly Separate the Haves from the Have-Nots." *New York Times,* August 10, 2004, 16.

Maxwell, Bruce. *Insider's Guide to Finding a Job in Washington: Contacts and Strategies to Build Your Career in Public Policy.* Washington, DC: CQ Press, 1999.

Mershon, Erin. "Hill Internships 101: What You Need to Know," *Roll Call,* June 1, 2011 (online version).

Princeton Review. *The Internship Bible,* 10th ed. New York: Random House, 2005.

Reeher, Grant, and Mack Mariani, eds. *The Insider's Guide to Political Internships: What to Do Once You're in the Door.* Boulder, CO: Westview Press, 2002.

Strand, Mark, Michael S. Johnson, and Jerome F. Climer. *Surviving Inside Congress.* Washington, DC: Congressional Institute, 2009.

Washington Center for Internships and Academic Seminars. Address: 2301 M Street N.W., Washington, DC 20037. Telephone: (202) 336-7600 or (800) 486-8921. Website: www .twc.edu/internships/index.htm.

Washington Information Directory. Washington, DC: Congressional Quarterly. Annual publication that provides information about governmental and nongovernmental groups as well as addresses and phone numbers for congressional offices and committees.

CHAPTER 1

Bianco, William, ed. *Congress on Display, Congress at Work.* Ann Arbor: University of Michigan Press, 2000.

Hamilton, Lee H. *How Congress Works, and Why You Should Care.* Bloomington: Indiana University Press, 2004.

Hibbing, John R., and Elizabeth Theiss-Morse. *Congress as Public Enemy.* Cambridge: Cambridge University Press, 1995.

———. *Stealth Democracy: Americans' Beliefs about How Government Should Work.* Cambridge: Cambridge University Press, 2002.

Mayhew, David R. *Congress: The Electoral Connection.* 2d ed. New Haven, CT: Yale University Press, 2004.

CHAPTER 2

Binder, Sarah A. *Minority Rights, Majority Rule: Partisanship and the Development of Congress.* Cambridge: Cambridge University Press, 1997.

Jenkins, Jeffery A., and Charles Stewart III. *Fighting for the Speakership: The House and the Rise of Party Government.* Princeton, NJ: Princeton University Press, 2013.

Polsby, Nelson W. *How Congress Evolves: Social Bases of Institutional Change.* New York: Oxford University Press, 2004.

Rakove, Jack N. *Original Meanings: Politics and Ideas in the Making of the Constitution.* New York: Vintage, 1997.

Schickler, Eric. *Disjointed Pluralism: Institutional Innovation and the Development of the U.S. Congress.* Princeton, NJ: Princeton University Press, 2001.

Swift, Elaine K. *The Making of an American Senate: Reconstitutive Change in Congress, 1787–1841.* Ann Arbor: University of Michigan Press, 1996.

Wirls, Daniel, and Stephen Wirls. *The Invention of the United States Senate.* Baltimore: Johns Hopkins University Press, 2004.

CHAPTER 3

Canon, David T. *Race, Redistricting, and Representation.* Chicago: University of Chicago Press, 1999.

Ehrenhalt, Alan. *The United States of Ambition.* New York: Random House, 1991.

Fowler, Linda L., and Robert D. McClure. *Political Ambition: Who Decides to Run for Congress.* New Haven, CT: Yale University Press, 1989.

Jacobson, Gary C. *The Politics of Congressional Elections.* 8th ed. New York: Pearson Longman, 2013.

Jacobson, Gary C., and Samuel Kernell. *Strategy and Choice in Congressional Elections.* New Haven, CT: Yale University Press, 1981.

Lawless, Jennifer L. *Becoming a Candidate: Political Ambition and the Decision to Run for Office.* New York: Cambridge University Press, 2015.

Lawless, Jennifer L. and Richard L. Fox. *Running From Office: Why Young Americans are Turned Off to Politics.* New York: Oxford University Press, 2015.

CHAPTER 4

Abramowitz, Alan I. *The Disappearing Center: Engaged Citizens, Polarization, and American Democracy.* New Haven, CT: Yale University Press, 2010.

Dolan, Kathleen A. *Voting for Women: How the Public Evaluates Women Candidates.* Boulder, CO: Westview Press, 2003.

Fiorina, Morris P., Samuel J. Abrams, and Jeremy C. Pope. *Culture War? The Myth of Polarized America.* 2d ed. New York: Pearson Longman, 2005.

Herrnson, Paul S. *Congressional Elections: Campaigning at Home and in Washington.* 6th ed. Washington, DC: CQ Press, 2013.

Jacobson, Gary C. *The Politics of Congressional Elections.* 8th ed. New York: Pearson Longman, 2013.

Thurber, James A., ed. *The Battle for Congress: Consultants, Candidates, and Voters.* Washington, DC: Brookings, 2001.

Wattenburg, Martin. *Is Voting for Young People?* New York: Pearson Longman, 2007.

CHAPTER 5

Arnold, R. Douglas. *Congress, the Press, and Political Accountability.* Princeton, NJ: Princeton University Press, 2004.

Baker, Ross K. *House and Senate.* 4th ed. New York: Norton, 2008.

Burden, Barry C. *Personal Roots of Representation.* Princeton, NJ: Princeton University Press, 2007.

Davidson, Roger H. *The Role of the Congressman.* Indianapolis: Bobbs-Merrill, 1969.

Fenno, Richard F., Jr. *Home Style: House Members in Their Districts.* Boston: Little, Brown, 1978.

Fiorina, Morris P. *Congress: Keystone of the Washington Establishment.* 2d ed. New Haven, CT: Yale University Press, 1989.

Grimmer, Justin. *Representational Style in Congress: What Legislators Say and Why it Matters.* New York: Cambridge University Press, 2013.

Price, David E. *The Congressional Experience: A View from the Hill.* 3d ed. Boulder, CO: Westview Press, 2004.

Sellers, Patrick. *Cycles of Spin: Strategic Communication in the U.S. Congress.* New York: Cambridge University Press, 2010.

Swers, Michele L. *Women in the Club: Gender and Policymaking in the Senate.* Chicago: University of Chicago Press, 2013.

Volden, Craig, and Alan E. Wiseman. *Legislative Effectiveness in the United States Congress: The Lawmakers.* New York: Cambridge University Press, 2014.

CHAPTER 6

Aldrich, John H. *Why Parties? The Origins and Transformation of Party Politics in America.* Chicago: University of Chicago Press, 1995.

Baker, Richard A., and Roger H. Davidson, eds. *First among Equals: Outstanding Senate Leaders of the Twentieth Century.* Washington, DC: Congressional Quarterly, 1991.

Cox, Gary W., and Mathew D. McCubbins. *Setting the Agenda: Responsible Party Government in the U.S. House of Representatives.* New York: Cambridge University Press, 2005.

Curry, James M. *Legislating in the Dark: Information and Power in the House of Representatives.* Chicago: University of Chicago Press, 2015.

Davidson, Roger H., Susan Webb Hammond, and Raymond W. Smock, eds. *Masters of the House: Congressional Leaders over Two Centuries.* Boulder, CO: Westview Press, 1998.

Green, Matthew N. *Underdog Politics: The Minority Party in the U.S. House of Representatives.* New Haven, CT: Yale University Press, 2015.

Heberlig, Eric and Bruce A. Larson. *Congressional Parties, Institutional Ambition, and the Financing of Majority Control.* Ann Arbor, MI: University of Michigan Press, 2012.

Lee, Frances E. *Beyond Ideology: Politics, Principles, and Partisanship in the U.S. Senate.* Chicago: University of Chicago Press, 2009.

Peters, Ronald M. Jr. *The American Speakership: The Office in Historical Perspective.* 2nd edition. Baltimore, MD: The Johns Hopkins University Press, 1997.

Rohde, David W. *Parties and Leaders in the Postreform House.* Chicago: University of Chicago Press, 1991.

Sinclair, Barbara. *Legislators, Leaders, and Lawmaking: The U.S. House of Representatives in the Postreform Era.* Baltimore: Johns Hopkins University Press, 1995.

———. *The Transformation of the U.S. Senate.* Baltimore: Johns Hopkins University Press, 1989.

Strahan, Randall. *Leading Representatives: The Agency of Leaders in the Politics of the U.S. House.* Baltimore: Johns Hopkins University Press, 2007.

CHAPTER 7

Deering, Christopher J., and Steven S. Smith. *Committees in Congress.* 3d ed. Washington, DC: CQ Press, 1997.

Evans, C. Lawrence. *Leadership in Committee: A Comparative Analysis of Leadership Behavior in the U.S. Senate.* Ann Arbor: University of Michigan Press, 1991.

Fenno, Richard F., Jr. *Congressmen in Committees.* Boston: Little, Brown, 1973.

Frisch, Scott A., and Sean Q. Kelly. *Committee Assignment Politics in the U.S. House of Representatives.* Norman, OK: University of Oklahoma Press, 2006.

Hall, Richard L. *Participation in Congress.* New Haven, CT: Yale University Press, 1998.

King, David C. *Turf Wars: How Congressional Committees Claim Jurisdiction.* Chicago: University of Chicago Press, 1997.

Krehbiel, Keith. *Information and Legislative Organization.* Ann Arbor: University of Michigan Press, 1991.

Maltzman, Forrest. *Competing Principals: Committees, Parties, and the Organization of Congress.* Ann Arbor: University of Michigan Press, 1997.

Wilson, Woodrow. *Congressional Government.* Reprint of 1885 ed. Baltimore: Johns Hopkins University Press, 1981.

CHAPTER 8

Arenberg, Richard A., and Robert B. Dove. *Defending the Filibuster.* Bloomington, IN: Indiana University Press, 2012.

Binder, Sarah A. *Stalemate: Causes and Consequences of Legislative Gridlock.* Washington, DC: Brookings, 2003.

Binder, Sarah A., and Steven S. Smith. *Politics or Principle? Filibustering in the United States Senate.* Washington, DC: Brookings, 1996.

Evans, Diana. *Greasing the Wheels: Using Pork Barrel Projects to Build Majority Coalitions in Congress.* New York: Cambridge University Press, 2004.

Koger, Gregory. *Filibustering: A Political History of Obstruction in the House and Senate.* Chicago: University of Chicago Press, 2010.

Krehbiel, Keith. *Pivotal Politics: A Theory of U.S. Lawmaking.* Chicago: University of Chicago Press, 1998.

Longley, Lawrence D., and Walter J. Oleszek. *Bicameral Politics: Conference Committees in Congress.* New Haven, CT: Yale University Press, 1989.

Loomis, Burdett, ed. *Esteemed Colleagues: Civility and Deliberation in the U.S. Senate.* Washington, DC: Brookings, 2000.

Oleszek, Walter J., Mark J. Oleszek, Elizabeth Rybicki, and Bill Heniff, Jr. *Congressional Procedures and the Policy Process.* 10th ed. Washington, DC: CQ Press, 2016.

Schickler, Eric, and Frances E. Lee. *The Oxford Handbook of Congress.* New York: Oxford University Press, 2011.

Sinclair, Barbara. *Unorthodox Lawmaking: New Legislative Processes in the U.S. Congress.* 3d ed. Washington, DC: CQ Press, 2007.

Smith, Steven S. *The Senate Syndrome: The Evolution of Procedural Warfare in the Modern U.S. Senate* Norman, OK: University of Oklahoma Press, 2014.

CHAPTER 9

Arnold, R. Douglas. *The Logic of Congressional Action.* New Haven, CT: Yale University Press, 1990.

Binder, Sarah A. *Stalemate: Causes and Consequences of Legislative Gridlock.* Washington, DC: Brookings, 2003.

Edwards, George C. *At the Margins: Presidential Leadership of Congress.* New Haven, CT: Yale University Press, 1989.

Kingdon, John W. *Congressmen's Voting Decisions.* 3d ed. Ann Arbor: University of Michigan Press, 1989.

Lapinski, John S. *The Substance of Representation: Congress, American Political Development, and Lawmaking.* Princeton, NJ: Princeton University Press, 2013.

Mucchiaroni, Gary, and Paul J. Quirk. *Deliberative Choices: Debating Public Policy in Congress.* Chicago: University of Chicago Press, 2006.

Sulkin, Tracy. *The Legislative Legacy of Congressional Campaigns.* New York: Cambridge University Press, 2011.

Theriault, Sean M. *Party Polarization in Congress.* New York: Cambridge University Press, 2008.

CHAPTER 10

Binkley, Wilfred. *President and Congress.* New York: Knopf, 1947.

Bond, Jon R., and Richard Fleisher, eds. *Polarized Politics: Congress and the President in a Partisan Era.* Washington, DC: CQ Press, 2000.

Canes-Wrone, Brandice. *Who Leads Whom? Presidents, Policy, and the Public.* Chicago: University of Chicago Press, 2006.

Edwards, George C., III. *On Deaf Ears: The Limits of the Bully Pulpit.* New Haven, CT: Yale University Press, 2006.

Fisher, Louis. *Constitutional Conflicts between Congress and the President.* 4th ed. Lawrence: University Press of Kansas, 1997.

Gilmour, John B. *Strategic Disagreement: Stalemate in American Politics.* Pittsburgh: University of Pittsburgh Press, 1995.

Howell, William G. *Power without Persuasion: The Politics of Direct Presidential Action.* Princeton, NJ: Princeton University Press, 2003.

Mayhew, David R. *Divided We Govern: Party Control, Lawmaking, and Investigations, 1946–2002.* New Haven, CT: Yale University Press, 2005.

Rudalevige, Andrew. *The New Imperial Presidency.* Ann Arbor: University of Michigan Press, 2005.

Thurber, James, ed. *Rivals for Power: Presidential-Congressional Relations,* 5th ed. Lanham, MD: Rowman and Littlefield, 2013.

CHAPTER 11

Aberbach, Joel D. *Keeping a Watchful Eye: The Politics of Congressional Oversight.* Washington, DC: Brookings, 1990.

Arnold, R. Douglas. *Congress and the Bureaucracy: A Theory of Influence.* New Haven, CT: Yale University Press, 1979.

Foreman, Christopher J., Jr. *Signals from the Hill: Congressional Oversight and the Challenge of Social Regulation.* New Haven, CT: Yale University Press, 1988.

Jenkins, Jeffrey, and Eric Patashnik, eds. *Living Legislation: Durability, Change, and the Politics of American Lawmaking.* Chicago: University of Chicago Press, 2012.

Light, Paul C. *A Government Ill Executed: The Decline of the Federal Service and How to Reverse It.* Cambridge, MA: Harvard University Press, 2008.

———. *Government By Investigation: Congress, Presidents, and the Search for Answers 1945-2012.* Washington, DC: Brookings Institution Press, 2014.———. *The True Size of Government.* Washington, DC: Brookings, 1999.

Rosenbloom, David. *Building a Legislative-Centered Public Administration: Congress and the Administrative State, 1946–1999.* Tuscaloosa: University of Alabama Press, 2000.

Wilson, James Q. *Bureaucracy: What Government Agencies Do and Why They Do it.* New York: Basic Books, 2000.

CHAPTER 12

Berger, Raoul. *Congress v. The Supreme Court.* Cambridge, MA: Harvard University Press, 1969.

Binder, Sarah A., and Forrest Maltzman. *Advice and Dissent: The Struggle to Shape the Federal Judiciary.* Washington, DC: Brookings, 2009.

Fisher, Louis. *Constitutional Dialogues.* Princeton, NJ: Princeton University Press, 1988.

Geyh, Charles Gardner. *When Congress and Courts Collide.* Ann Arbor: University of Michigan Press, 2006.

Katzmann, Robert A. *Courts and Congress.* Washington, DC: Brookings, 1997.

Noonan, John T., Jr. *Narrowing the Nation's Power: The Supreme Court Sides with the States.* Berkeley: University of California Press, 2002.

Wittes, Benjamin. *Confirmation Wars: Preserving Independent Courts in Angry Times.* Lanham, MD: Rowman and Littlefield, 2006.

CHAPTER 13

Andres, Gary. *Lobbying Reconsidered.* New York: Pearson Education, Inc. 2009

Baumgartner, Frank R., Jeffrey M. Berry, Marie Hojnacki, David C. Kimball, and Beth L. Leech. *Lobbying and Policy Change: Who Wins, Who Loses and Why.* Chicago: University of Chicago Press, 2009.

Birnbaum, Jeffrey H., and Alan S. Murray. *Showdown at Gucci Gulch: Lawmakers, Lobbyists, and the Unlikely Triumph of Tax Reform.* New York: Random House, 1987.

Hall, Richard L., and Alan V. Deardorff. "Lobbying as Legislative Subsidy." *American Political Science Review* 100 (February 2006): 69–84.

Hojnacki, Marie, and David Kimball. "Organized Interests and the Decision of Whom to Lobby in Congress." *American Political Science Review* 92 (December 1998): 775–790.

Loomis, Burdett A., Peter L. Francia, and Dara Z. Strolovich, eds. *Guide to Interest Groups and Lobbying in the United States.* Washington, DC: CQ Press, 2011.

Rozell, Mark, Clyde Wilcox, and David Madland. *Interest Groups in American Campaigns: The New Face of Electioneering.* 2d ed. Washington, DC: CQ Press, 2005.

Truman, David B. *The Governmental Process, Political Interests, and Public Opinion.* 2d ed. New York: Knopf, 1971.

CHAPTER 14

Adler, E. Scott, and John D. Wilkerson. *Congress and the Politics of Problem Solving.* New York: Cambridge University Press, 2013.

Elving, Ronald D. *Conflict and Compromise: How Congress Makes the Law.* New York: Simon and Schuster, 1995.

Hilley, John L. *The Challenge of Legislation.* Washington, DC: Brookings, 2008.

Kelman, Steven. *Making Public Policy.* New York: Basic Books, 1987.

Kingdon, John W. *Agendas, Alternatives, and Public Policies.* Boston: Little, Brown, 1984.

Mettler, Suzanne. *The Submerged State: How Invisible Government Policies Undermine Democracy.* Chicago: University of Chicago Press, 2011.

Schick, Allen. *Congress and Money: Budgeting, Spending, and Taxing.* Washington, DC: Urban Institute, 1980.

———. *The Federal Budget: Politics, Policy, Process.* Rev. ed. Washington, DC: Brookings, 2007.

CHAPTER 15

Auerswald, David P., and Colton C. Campbell, eds. *Congress and National Security.* New York: Cambridge University Press, 2012.

Crabb, Cecil V., Jr., Glenn J. Antizzo, and Leila E. Sarieddine. *Congress and the Foreign Policy Process.* Baton Rouge: Louisiana State University Press, 2000.

Fisher, Louis. *Constitutional Conflicts between Congress and the President.* Lawrence: University Press of Kansas, 2007.

———. *The Constitution and 9/11.* Lawrence: University Press of Kansas, 2008.

Goldsmith, Jack. *The Terror Presidency: Law and Judgment inside the Bush Administration.* New York: Norton, 2007.

Hinckley, Barbara. *Less Than Meets the Eye: Foreign Policy Making and the Myth of the Assertive Congress.* Chicago: University of Chicago Press, 1994.

Howell, William G., and Jon C. Pevehouse. *While Dangers Gather: Congressional Checks on Presidential War Powers.* Chicago: University of Chicago Press, 2007.

Kriner, Douglas L. *After the Rubicon: Congress, Presidents, and the Politics of Waging War.* Chicago: University of Chicago Press, 2010.

Thorpe, Rebecca U. *The American Warfare State: The Domestic Politics of Military Spending.* Chicago: University of Chicago Press, 2014.

Lindsay, James M. *Congress and the Politics of U.S. Foreign Policy.* Baltimore: Johns Hopkins University Press, 1994.

CHAPTER 16

Adler, E. Scott. *Why Congressional Reforms Fail: Reelection and the House Committee System.* Chicago: University of Chicago Press, 2002.

Cook, Timothy E. *Making Laws and Making News: Media Strategies in the U.S. House of Representatives.* Washington, DC: Brookings, 1989.

Hamilton, Lee H. *How Congress Works, and Why You Should Care.* Bloomington: Indiana University Press, 2004.

Hibbing, John R., and Elizabeth Theiss-Morse. *Stealth Democracy: Americans' Beliefs about How Government Should Work.* Cambridge: Cambridge University Press, 2002.

Mackenzie, G. Calvin, with Michael Hafken. *Scandal Proof: Do Ethics Laws Make Government Ethical?* Washington, DC: Brookings, 2002.

Mann, Thomas E., and Norman J. Ornstein. *The Broken Branch: How Congress Is Failing America and How to Get It Back on Track.* New York: Oxford University Press, 2006.

———. *It's Even Worse Than It Looks: How the American Constitutional System Collided with the New Politics of Extremism.* New York: Basic Books, 2012.

Persily, Nathaniel, ed. *Solutions to Political Polarization in America.* New York: Cambridge University Press, 2015.

Taylor, Andrew J. *Congress: A Performance Appraisal.* Boulder, CO: Westview Press, 2013.

Wolfensberger, Donald. *Congress and the People: Deliberative Democracy on Trial.* Washington, DC: Woodrow Wilson Center Press, 2000.

CHAPTER 1

1. Quoted in Matea Gold and Tom Hamburger, "Loss Is Inspiration to Conservatives Hoping For More," *Washington Post,* June 12, 2014, A8.

2. Jonathan Weisman and Jennifer Steinhauer, "Cantor's Loss a Bad Omen for Moderates," *New York Times,* June 10, 2014, A1.

3. Shane Goldmacher, "Eric Cantor's Pollster Tries to Explain Why His Survey Showed Cantor Up 34 Points," *National Journal's,* June 11, 2014, http://www.nationaljournal.com/politics/eric-cantor-s-pollster-tries-to-explain-why-his-survey-showed-cantor-up-34-points-20140611.

4. Quoted in Olympia Meola and Jim Nolan, "Cantor Out," *Richmond Times-Dispatch,* June 11, 2014, A1.

5. Quoted in Jake Sherman and Anna Palmer, "The Last Days of Eric Cantor," *Politico,* July 30, 2014, 12.

6. Jeff E. Shapiro, "What Lifted Cantor to Power Ultimately Laid Him Low," *Richmond Times-Dispatch,* June 15, 2014, B1.

7. Quoted in Charlie Cook, "Untended Fences," *National Journal's,* June 14, 2014, http://www.nationaljournal.com/the-cook-report/eric-cantor-s-untended-fences-20140612.

8. Quoted in David Carr, "Eric Cantor's Defeat Exposed a Beltway Journalism Blind Spot," *New York Times,* June 15, 2014, B1.

9. Quoted in Jeff E. Schapiro, "Brat Gives Voters Way to Vent in New Kent," *Richmond Times-Dispatch,* May 25, 2014, B1.

10. Dave Brat, "A Challenger for the 7th District," *Richmond Times-Dispatch,* June 6, 2014, http://www.timesdispatch.com/opinion/their-opinion/columnists-blogs/guest-columnists/brat-a-challenger-for-the-th-district/article_20886f1d-bae2-5764-94bc-52494877c27a.html.

11. Ibid.

12. Jeremy W. Peters, "Potent Forces of Conservative Media Propelled Cantor Opponent," *New York Times,* June 11, 2014, http://www.nytimes.com/2014/06/12/us/dave-brat-was-aided-by-laura-ingraham.html.

13. Byron Tau and Tarini Parti, "How Big Money Failed to Rescue Eric Cantor," *Politico,* June 11, 2014, http://www.politico.com/story/2014/06/2014-virginia-primary-big-money-eric-cantor-107699.html.

14. Quoted in Olympia Meola, "Cantor's Campaign Costs Extend Far Beyond District," *Richmond Times-Dispatch,* July 17, 2014, A1.

15. Quoted in Jeff E. Shapiro, "What Lifted Cantor to Power Ultimately Laid Him Low," *Richmond Times-Dispatch,* June 15, 2014, B1.

16. Paul S. Herrnson, *Congressional Elections: Campaigning at Home and in Washington,* 5th ed. (Washington, DC: CQ Press, 2008), 272.

17. Sam Rayburn, *Speak, Mr. Speaker,* ed. H. G. Dulaney and Edward Hake Phillips (Bonham, TX: Sam Rayburn Foundation, 1978), 263–264. Rayburn was Speaker from 1940 to 1947, 1949 to 1953, and 1955 to 1961.

18. Quoted in Marin Cogan, "Allen West Gets Brushback from Veteran Bishop," *Politico's On Congress: Congressional News and Analysis Blog,* December 21, 2010, www.politico.com/blogs/glenthrush.

19. Frank E. Smith, *Congressman from Mississippi* (New York: Random House, 1964), 127.

20. David R. Mayhew, *Congress: The Electoral Connection* (New Haven, CT: Yale University Press, 1974), 16.

21. Alan Abramowitz, "A Comparison of Voting for U.S. Senator and Representative in 1978," *American Political Science Review* 74 (September 1980): 633–640; Richard F. Fenno Jr., *The United States Senate: A Bicameral Perspective* (Washington, DC: American Enterprise

Institute, 1982), 29ff; Frances E. Lee and Bruce I. Oppenheimer, *Sizing Up the Senate: The Unequal Consequences of Equal Representation* (Chicago: University of Chicago Press, 1999), 111–113.

22. U.S. Congress, Joint Committee on the Organization of Congress, *Organization of the Congress, Final Report,* 2 vols., H. Rep. 103–14, 103d Cong., 1st sess., December 1993, 2: 275–287. Also see Table 5-1 in this book.

23. Glenn R. Parker and Roger H. Davidson, "Why Do Americans Love Their Congressmen So Much More Than Their Congress?" *Legislative Studies Quarterly* 4 (February 1979): 53–61; Kelly D. Patterson and David B. Magleby, "Public Support for Congress," *Public Opinion Quarterly* 56 (Winter 1992): 539–540; and Randall B. Ripley, Samuel C. Patterson, Lynn M. Mauer, and Stephen V. Quinlan, "Constituents' Evaluations of U.S. House Members," *American Politics Quarterly* 20 (October 1992): 442–456.

24. For how the public's perceptions of the policy process affect Congress's institutional image, see John R. Hibbing and Elizabeth Theiss-Morse, *Congress as Public Enemy: Public Attitudes toward American Political Institutions* (New York: Cambridge University Press, 1995).

25. Alexander Hamilton, James Madison, and John Jay, *The Federalist Papers,* No. 51, ed. Clinton Rossiter (New York: Mentor, 1961), 322.

26. *Federalist Papers*, No. 52, 327.

27. Edmund Burke, "Speech to Electors at Bristol," in *Burke's Politics,* ed. Ross J. S. Hoffman and Paul Levack (New York: Knopf, 1949), 116.

28. Ibid.

29. Quoted in *Roll Call,* September 9, 1993, 16.

30. *U.S. Term Limits v. Thornton,* 115 S.Ct. 1842 (1995).

31. Quoted in Mark Carl Rom, "Why Not Assume That Public Officials Seek to Promote the Public Interest?" *Public Affairs Report* 37 (July 1996): 12.

32. For an accessible discussion of different voting systems, see Douglas J. Amy, *Behind the Ballot Box: A Citizen's Guide to Voting Systems* (Westport, CT: Praeger, 2000), 65.

33. For a classic analysis of members facing this representational difficulty, see Richard F. Fenno Jr., *Home Style: House Members in Their Districts* (Boston: Little, Brown, 1978), esp. 91–99 and 102–114. For an update, see Justin Grimmer, *Representational Style in Congress: What Legislators Say and Why It Matters* (New York: Cambridge University Press, 2013).

34. Alan I. Abramowitz, *The Disappearing Center: Engaged Citizens, Polarization, and American Democracy* (New Haven, CT: Yale University Press, 2010), 37.

35. Morris P. Fiorina, with Samuel J. Abrams, *Disconnect: The Breakdown of Representation in American Politics* (Norman: University of Oklahoma Press, 2009).

36. Fenno, *Home Style,* 168.

37. Matt Taibbi, "The Worst Congress Ever: How Our National Legislature Has Become a Stable of Thieves and Perverts—in Five Easy Steps," *Rolling Stone,* November 2, 2006, 46.

38. Woodrow Wilson, *Congressional Government* (1885; reprint, Baltimore: Johns Hopkins University Press, 1981), 210.

39. Thomas E. Mann and Norman J. Ornstein, *The Broken Branch: How Congress Is Failing America and How to Get It Back on Track* (New York: Oxford University Press, 2006), 141–191.

CHAPTER 2

1. Joseph J. Ellis, *His Excellency George Washington* (New York: Knopf, 2006), 184–186.

2. Alvin M. Josephy Jr., *On the Hill: A History of the American Congress* (New York: Simon and Schuster, 1980), 41–48.

3. Charles A. Beard and John P. Lewis, "Representative Government in Evolution," *American Political Science Review* (April 1932): 223–240.

4. Peverill Squire, *The Evolution of American Legislatures: Colonies, Territories, and States, 1619–2009* (Ann Arbor: University of Michigan Press, 2012).

5. Jack P. Green, ed., *Great Britain and the American Colonies, 1606–1763* (New York: Harper Torch Books, 1970), xxxix.

6. Edmund C. Burnett, *Continental Congress* (New York: Norton, 1964).

7. *Congressional Quarterly's Guide to Congress,* 5th ed., vol. 1 (Washington, DC: CQ Press, 2000), 9.

8. Burnett, *Continental Congress,* 171. The authors use modern capitalization when quoting the Declaration of Independence (as here) or the Constitution in this volume.

9. Jack N. Rakove, *The Beginnings of National Politics: An Interpretive History of the Continental Congress* (New York: Knopf, 1979), 43.

10. Charles C. Thach Jr., *The Creation of the Presidency, 1775–1789: A Study in Constitutional History* (Baltimore: Johns Hopkins University Press, 1969), 34.

11. James Sterling Young, "America's First Hundred Days," *Miller Center Journal's* 1 (Winter 1994): 57.

12. On the framers' general consensus on the need for a stronger national government, see Lance Banning, "The Constitutional Convention," in *The Framing and Ratification of the Constitution,* ed. Leonard W. Levy and Dennis J. Mahoney (New York: Macmillan, 1987); and John P. Roche, "The Founding Fathers: A Reform Caucus in Action," *American Political Science Review* 55 (1961): 799–816.

13. John Locke, *Two Tracts on Government,* ed. Philip Abrams (New York: Cambridge University Press, 1967), 374.

14. *National Federation of Small Business v. Sebelius,* 132 S. Ct. 2566, 2587 (2012).

15. Alexander Hamilton, James Madison, and John Jay, *The Federalist Papers,* No. 48, ed. Clinton Rossiter (New York: Mentor, 1961), 322.

16. Ibid., 308.

17. Joseph Story, *Commentaries on the Constitution of the United States,* 5th ed., vol. 1 (Boston: Little, Brown, 1905), 396. For Justice Robert Jackson's comments, see *Youngstown Sheet and Tube Co. v. Sawyer,* 343 U.S. 579, 635 (1952).

18. Mark A. Peterson, "The Three Branches of Government: Powers, Relationships and Checks," in *A Republic Divided,* ed. Annenberg Democracy Project (New York: Oxford University Press, 2007), 105. From his own survey, David R. Mayhew finds the same six out of ten success rate for presidential initiatives in *Partisan Balance: Why Political Parties Don't Kill the U.S. Constitutional System* (Princeton, NJ: Princeton University Press, 2011, 58).

19. In the 2014 case of *NLRB v. Noel Canning* (133 S. Ct. 2550), the Supreme Court restricted the president's ability to circumvent Senate approval of nominations via recess appointments to circumstances when the Senate is not able to transact Senate business. Not all executive nominees require Senate approval. According to the Constitution, "inferior officers" need not be confirmed by the Senate, and Congress can vest the power to appoint inferior officers "in the President alone."

20. William Howell and Jon Pevehouse, "When Congress Stops Wars," *Foreign Affairs* (September/October 2007).

21. In *Nixon v. United States,* 506 U.S. 224 (1993), the Supreme Court refused to review the Senate's procedures. A former federal judge, Walter L. Nixon Jr. objected that although he had been convicted by a vote of the full Senate, the evidence in his case had been taken by one of the chamber's committees.

22. *Federalist Papers,* No. 65, 396.

23. Emily Field Van Tassel and Paul Finkelman, *Impeachable Offenses: A Documentary History from 1787 to the Present* (Washington, DC: Congressional Quarterly, 1999). The only Senate impeachment trial since 1999 was that of Judge G. Thomas Porteous Jr. of the federal district

court in Louisiana. See Jennifer Steinhauer, "Senate, for Just the 8th Time, Votes to Oust a Federal Judge," *New York Times*, December 8, 2010.

24. *U.S. v. Rayburn House Office Bldg., Room 2113, Washington, DC, 20515*, 497 F.3d 654 (D.C. Cir. 2007).

25. *Marbury v. Madison*, 1 Cranch 137 (1803).

26. *The Constitution of the United States of America: Analysis and Interpretation*, S. Doc. 111-39 111th Congress, 2d sess., 199–201. Recent figures are courtesy of Kenneth Thomas, legislative attorney, American Law Division, Congressional Research Service.

27. J. Mitchell Pickerill, "Congressional Responses to Judicial Review," in *Congress and the Constitution*, ed. Neal Devins and Keith E. Whittington (Durham, NC, and London: Duke University Press, 2005), 159.

28. *Dred Scott v. Sandford*, 60 U.S. 393 (1856).

29. *Citizens United v. Federal Election Commission*, 130 S.Ct. 876 (2010).

30. *Immigration and Naturalization Service v. Chadha*, 463 U.S. 919 (1983).

31. William N. Eskridge Jr., "Overriding Supreme Court Statutory Interpretation Decisions," *Yale Law Journal's* 101 (November 1991): 331–455. Also see R. Shep Melnick, *Between the Lines: Interpreting Welfare Rights* (Washington, DC: Brookings, 1994).

32. See Richard L. Hasen, "End of the Dialogue? Political Polarization, the Supreme Court, and Congress," *Southern California Law Review* 86 (2013): 205–262.

33. Louis Fisher, *Constitutional Dialogues: Interpretation as Political Process* (Princeton, NJ: Princeton University Press, 1988), 275.

34. Quoted in Charles Warren, *The Making of the Constitution* (Boston: Little, Brown, 1928), 162.

35. Quoted in Charles Warren, *The Supreme Court in United States History* (Boston: Little, Brown, 1919), 195.

36. Wendy J. Schiller, "Building Careers and Courting Constituents: U.S. Senate Representation: 1889–1924," *Studies in American Political Development* 20 (Fall 2006): 185–197.

37. See Wendy J. Schiller and Charles Stewart III, *Electing the Senate: Indirect Democracy before the Seventeenth Amendment* (Princeton, NJ: Princeton University Press, 2014); and Gregory J. Wawro and Eric Schickler, *Filibuster: Obstruction and Lawmaking in the U.S. Senate* (Princeton, NJ: Princeton University Press, 2006).

38. Elaine K. Swift, *The Making of an American Senate* (Ann Arbor: University of Michigan Press, 1996), 5.

39. Joel H. Silbey, *The Partisan Imperative: The Dynamics of American Politics before the Civil War* (New York: Oxford University Press).

40. Sarah A. Binder, *Minority Rights, Majority Rule* (New York: Cambridge University Press, 1997), 49.

41. Norman J. Ornstein, Thomas E. Mann, and Michael J. Malbin, *Vital Statistics on Congress, 2008* (Washington, DC: Brookings, 2002), 110–111.

42. See *Jefferson's Manual, and Rules of the House of Representatives*, Section XI, H. Doc. 105–358, 105th Cong., 2d sess., 1999, 145–148.

43. Nelson W. Polsby, "The Institutionalization of the House of Representatives," *American Political Science Review* 62 (March 1968): 146–147.

44. Norman J. Ornstein, Thomas E. Mann, Michael J. Malbin, Andrew Rugg, and Raffaela Wakeman, *Vital Statistics on Congress: Data on the U.S. Congress—A Joint Effort from Brookings and the American Enterprise Institute*, July 2013, http://www.brookings.edu/research/reports/2013/07/vital-statistics-congress-mann-ornstein, Tables 6-1, 6-2, 6-3, and 6-4.

45. Ibid., Table 6-4.

46. Eric Schickler, "Institutional Development of Congress," in *The Legislative Branch*, ed. Paul J. Quirk and Sarah A. Binder (New York: Oxford University Press), 40; Ornstein, Mann, and Malbin, *Vital Statistics on Congress, 2001–2002*, 149.

47. George B. Galloway, *History of the House of Representatives* (New York: Crowell, 1961), 67.

48. Joseph Cooper and Cheryl D. Young, "Bill Introduction in the Nineteenth Century: A Study of Institutional Change," *Legislative Studies Quarterly* 14: 67–105.

49. Ronald Brownstein, "Bold Is Beautiful: The Super Committee Offers a Glimmer of Hope," *National Journal's*, August 5, 2011.

50. Barbara Sinclair, *Unorthodox Lawmaking: New Legislative Processes in the U.S. Congress* (Washington, DC: CQ Press, 2005).

51. Andrew J. Taylor, "Size, Power, and Electoral Determinants: Exogenous Determinants of Legislative Procedural Choice," *Legislative Studies Quarterly* 31 (August 2006): 338.

52. Schickler, "Institutional Development of Congress," 40.

53. Roger H. Davidson and Walter J. Oleszek, *Congress against Itself* (Bloomington: Indiana University Press, 1977), 14.

54. Quoted in Eric Schickler, *Disjointed Pluralism: Institutional Innovation and the Development of the U.S. Congress* (Princeton, NJ: Princeton University Press, 2001), 142.

55. James L. Sundquist, *The Decline and Resurgence of Congress* (Washington, DC: Brookings, 1982).

56. Julian E. Zelizer, *On Capitol Hill: The Struggle to Reform Congress and Its Consequences, 1948–2000* (New York: Cambridge University Press, 2004), 153.

57. Roy Swanstrom, *The United States Senate, 1787–1801*, S. Doc. 99–19, 99th Cong., 1st sess., 1985, 283.

58. Jeffery A. Jenkins and Charles Stewart III, *Fighting for the Speakership: The House and the Rise of Party Government* (Princeton, NJ: Princeton University Press, 2013).

59. Ibid.

60. Binder, *Minority Rights, Majority Rule*, 17.

61. Gregory Koger, *Filibustering: A Political History of Obstruction in the House and Senate* (Chicago: University of Chicago Press, 2010).

62. Ibid., 84.

63. David R. Mayhew, *Congress: The Electoral Connection* (New Haven, CT: Yale University Press, 1974), 95.

64. See David W. Rohde, *Parties and Leaders in the Postreform House* (Chicago: University of Chicago Press, 1991); and Nelson W. Polsby, *How Congress Evolves: Social Bases of Institutional Change* (New York: Oxford University Press, 2004).

65. See Sarah A. Binder and Steven S. Smith, *Politics or Principle? Filibustering in the United States Senate* (Washington, DC: Brookings, 1997); Gregory J. Wawro and Eric Schickler, *Filibuster: Obstruction and Lawmaking in the U.S. Senate* (Princeton, NJ: Princeton University Press, 2006); and Sarah A. Binder, Anthony J. Madonna, and Steven S. Smith, "Going Nuclear, Senate Style," *Perspectives on Politics* 5(4): 729–740.

66. Schickler, *Disjointed Pluralism*, 13.

67. Ibid., 141–146.

68. Ibid., 213–217.

69. Ibid., 267.

70. Ibid.

71. James Sterling Young, *The Washington Community, 1800–1828* (New York: Harcourt Brace Jovanovich, 1966), 89.

72. Noble Cunningham Jr., ed., *Circular Letters of Congressmen, 1789–1839*, 3 vols. (Chapel Hill: University of North Carolina Press, 1978), 57.

73. Swanstrom, *United States Senate*, 80.

74. Mildred Amer, "Average Years of Service for Members of the Senate and the House of Representatives, First–109th Congresses," Congressional Research Service Report RL32648, November 9, 2005. Earlier studies include Nelson W. Polsby, "The Institutionalization of the

House of Representatives," *American Political Science Review* 62 (March 1968): 146–147; and Randall B. Ripley, *Power in the Senate* (New York: St. Martin's Press, 1969), 42–43.

75. Sam Goldfarb, "Term Limits Win Out in Chairmen Picks," *CQ Weekly,* December 13, 2010, 2868.

76. Joe Martin, as told to Robert J. Donovan, *My First Fifty Years in Politics* (New York: McGraw-Hill, 1960), 49–50.

77. Robert H. Salisbury and Kenneth A. Shepsle, "U.S. Congressman as Enterprise," *Legislative Studies Quarterly* 6 (November 1981): 559–576.

78. Curtis W. Copeland, "The Federal Workforce: Characteristics and Trends," Congressional Research Service Report RL34685, April 19, 2011, Table 2.

79. Cunningham, *Circular Letters of Congressmen.*

80. Martin, *My First Fifty Years*, 101.

81. Colleen J. Shogan, "Blackberries, Tweets, and YouTube: Technology and the Future of Communicating with Congress," *P.S.* 42 (April 2010): 231. See also Matthew E. Glassman, "Tweet Your Congressman: The Rise of Electronic Communications in Congress," in *The Evolving Congress*, Senate Committee on Rules and Administration Prt. 113-30 (Washington, DC: U.S. Government Printing Office, 2014), 95–106.

CHAPTER 3

1. *U.S. Term Limits v. Thornton*, 514 U.S. 779 (1995).

2. Arend Lijphart, *Democracies: Patterns of Majoritarian and Consensus Government in Twenty-one Countries* (New Haven, CT: Yale University Press, 1984), 174.

3. Based on data on 2014 population from the U.S. Census Bureau, "National, State, and Puerto Rico Commonwealth Totals Datasets: Population, Population Change, and Estimated Components of Population Change: April 1, 2010 to July 1, 2014," https://www.census.gov/popest/data/national/totals/2014/NST-EST2014-alldata.html. See also David Samuels and Richard Snyder, "The Value of a Vote: Malapportionment in Comparative Perspective," *British Journal's of Political Science* 31, no. 4 (2001): 651–671.

4. See Daniel H. Pink, "Givers and Takers," *New York Times,* January 30, 2004, A21.

5. John D. Griffin, "Senate Apportionment as a Source of Political Inequality," *Legislative Studies Quarterly* 31 (August 2006): 425.

6. The idea is that proportional differences in the number of persons per representative for any pair of states should be kept to a minimum. The first fifty House seats are taken because the Constitution ensures that each state has at least one representative. The question then becomes, which state deserves the fifty-first seat, the fifty-second, and so forth? The mathematical formula yields a priority value for each seat, up to any desired number. The bottom line is to ensure that states are "entitled to a percentage of representatives equal to [their] portion of the national population."

7. Jeffrey W. Ladewig and Mathew P. Jasinski, "On the Causes and Consequences of and Remedies for Interstate Malapportionment of the U.S. House of Representatives," *Perspectives on Politics* 6 (2008): 90.

8. In 1960 the size of the House was temporarily increased from 435 to 437 members to accommodate the admission of Alaska and Hawaii as states. Three years later, after the 1960 reapportionment, the House reverted back to 435 members.

9. On the role of the Prohibition issue in the congressional failure to reapportion House seats in 1920, see Daniel Okrent, *Last Call: The Rise and Fall of Prohibition* (New York: Scribner, 2010), 239–241, 327–328.

10. *Congressional Quarterly's Guide to Congress,* vol. 2 (Washington, DC: CQ Press, 2000), 898.

11. Clark Bensen, "The Political Impact of Katrina: Apportionment in 2010," POLIDATA Press Release, December 22, 2006, 2.

12. Haya El Nasser, "For 2010 Census, the Counting Gets Tougher," *USA Today,* October 8, 2008, 1A.

13. Kathleen Hunter, "Minority Lawmakers to Ask Leadership to Address U.S. Census Undercounts," *CQ Today,* October 29, 2007, 6.

14. Sandy Hume, "GOP Fears 2000 Census Plan Will Overestimate Minorities," *The Hill,* May 7, 1997, 1.

15. *Department of Commerce et al. v. U.S. House of Representatives,* 525 U.S. 316 (1999).

16. Quoted in Charles Mahtesian, "Dollars and Census," *Government Executive,* December 2007, 50.

17. *Lepak v. City of Irving,* 453 Fed. Appx. 522 (5th Cir. 2011).

18. For a more detailed discussion of districting than is provided here, see Thomas S. Arrington, "Redistricting in the U.S.: A Review of Scholarship and Plan for Future Research," *The Forum* 8 (2010): art. 7.

19. Arizona, California, Hawaii, Idaho, Montana, New Jersey, and Washington have established commissions for drawing congressional district lines.

20. Juliet Eilperin, "The Gerrymander That Ate America," *Slate,* April 17, 2006. Quoted from her book *Fight Club Politics: How Partisanship Is Poisoning the House of Representatives* (Lanham, MD: Rowman and Littlefield, 2006).

21. The classic study is still Gordon E. Baker, *The Reapportionment Revolution: Representation, Political Power, and the Supreme Court* (New York: Random House, 1966).

22. Alan Ehrenhalt, "Redistricting and the Erosion of Community," *Governing* (June 1992): 10.

23. *League of United Latin American Citizens v. Perry,* 548 U.S. 399 (2006).

24. *Davis v. Bandemer,* 478 U.S. 109 (1986).

25. See also *Vieth v. Jubelirer,* 541 U.S. 267 (2004), for another example of the Court grappling with issues of partisan gerrymandering but unable to articulate a definitive judicial standard to guide mapmakers.

26. Aaron Blake, "GOP Can Draw Nearly Half of New House Districts," The Fix, *Washington Post* weblog, November 4, 2010, http://voices.washingtonpost.com/thefix/redistricting/gop-can-draw-nearly-half-of-ne.html.

27. Griff Palmer and Michael Cooper, "How Maps Helped Republicans Keep an Edge in the House," *New York Times,* December 14, 2012, A10.

28. Sundeep Iyer, "Redistricting and Congressional Control Following the 2012 Election," Analysis, Brennan Center for Justice, New York University School of Law, November 28, 2012, www.brennancenter.org/content/resource/redistricting_and_congressional_control_following_the_2012_election/.

29. *Congressional Record,* 110th Cong., 2d sess., July 29, 2008, H7285.

30. Sean M. Theriault, *Party Polarization in Congress* (New York: Cambridge University Press, 2008), 83.

31. Nolan McCarty, Keith T. Poole, and Howard Rosenthal, "Does Gerrymandering Cause Polarization?" *American Journal's of Political Science* 53 (2009): 678.

32. Rhodes Cook, "Do the Math, and the Result Is: Not Much of a Contest," *Washington Post,* October 6, 2002, B3.

33. The sole incumbent defeated in California between 2002 and 2010 was Republican Richard Pombo, who served from 1993 to 2007.

34. Charles Backstrom, Samuel Krislov, and Leonard Robins, "Desperately Seeking Standards: The Court's Frustrating Attempts to Limit Political Gerrymandering," *PS* (July 2006): 409.

35. See Andrew Gelman and Gary King, "Enhancing Democracy through Legislative Redistricting," *American Political Science Review* 88 (1994): 541–559.

36. Aaron Blake, "Breaking Down the Florida GOP's Redistricting Map," The Fix, *Washington Post* weblog, January 1, 2012, www.washingtonpost.com/blogs/the-fix/post/breaking-down-the-florida-gops-redistricting-map/2012/01/26/gIQAdCFYTQ_blog.html.

37. Steven Hill, "Schwarzenegger versus Gerrymander," *New York Times,* February 19, 2005, A29. See also Steve Lawrence, "Experts Question Redistricting Plan," *Santa Barbara News-Press,* February 20, 2005, A7.

38. Quoted in Bill Bishop, "You Can't Compete with Voters' Feet," *Washington Post,* May 15, 2005, B2. Also see James G. Gimpel and Jason E. Schucknect, *Patchwork Nation: Sectionalism and Political Change in American Politics* (Ann Arbor: University of Michigan Press, 2003); and Bill Bishop, *The Big Sort: Why the Clustering of Like-Minded America Is Tearing Us Apart* (Boston: Houghton Mifflin, 2008).

39. Jowei Chen and Jonathan Rodden, "Unintentional Gerrymandering: Political Geography and Electoral Bias in Legislatures," *Quarterly Journal's of Political Science* 8, no. 3 (2013): 239–269.

40. Quoted in Tricia Miller, "Redistricting Reform Is Tough Task Every Time," *Roll Call,* December 14, 2010.

41. Definition is from *Shaw v. Reno,* 509 U.S. 630 (1993), quoting *Davis v. Bandemer,* 478 U.S. 109 (1986).

42. Eric Foner, *Reconstruction: America's Unfinished Revolution, 1863–1877* (New York: Harper and Row, 1988), 590.

43. The "retrogression" standard was established in *Beer v. U.S.,* 425 U.S. 130 (1976).

44. The ruling in *Shelby County* v. *Holder,* 570 U.S. ___ (2013), invalidated Section 4b of the VRA.

45. Ibid., 21.

46. National Conference of State Legislatures, *Redistricting Law 2010* (Washington, DC: National Conference of State Legislatures, 2009), 3.

47. *Shaw v. Reno,* 509 U.S. 630 (1993).

48. *Miller v. Johnson,* 515 U.S. 900 (1995).

49. Ibid.

50. The Court's interpretation of Section 2 of the VRA was laid out most clearly in *Thornburg v. Gingles,* 478 U.S. 30 (1986).

51. *Shaw v. Hunt,* 517 U.S. 899 (1996).

52. *Beer v. U.S.,* 425 U.S. 130 (1976). In *Shaw v. Reno* (509 U.S. 630, 655 [1993]), the Court stated, "A reapportionment plan would not be narrowly tailored to the goal of avoiding retrogression if the State went beyond what was reasonably necessary to avoid retrogression."

53. *Shaw v. Reno,* 509 U.S. 630 (1993); *Miller v. Johnson,* 515 U.S. 900 (1995); *Bush v. Vera,* 517 U.S. 952 (1996); *Shaw v. Hunt,* 517 U.S. 899 (1996).

54. *Miller v. Johnson,* 515 U.S. 900 (1995).

55. *Easley v. Cromartie,* 532 U.S. 234 (2001).

56. *Hunt v. Cromartie,* 526 U.S. 541 (1999).

57. *Alabama Legislative Black Caucus v. Alabama,* 575 U.S. ___ (2015); and *Dixon v. Rucho,* 575 U.S. ___ (April 20, 2015) (summary disposition).

58. Robert Barnes, "Supreme Court Hands Win to Opponents of Alabama Redistricting Plan," *Washington Post,* March 25, 2015.

59. Lani Guinier, "What Color Is Your Gerrymander?" *Washington Post,* March 27, 1994, C3.

60. David Lublin, Thomas L. Brunell, Bernard Grofman, and Lisa Handley, "Has the Voting Rights Act Outlived Its Usefulness? In a Word, 'No,'" *Legislative Studies Quarterly* 34 (2009): 547.

61. Scott Bland, "More Minorities, Less Clout?" *National Journal's,* April 19, 2012.

62. Ehrenhalt, "Redistricting and the Erosion of Community," 10.

63. Kevin A. Hill, "Does the Creation of Majority Black Districts Aid Republicans? An Analysis of the 1992 Congressional Elections in Eight Southern States," *Journal's of Politics* 57 (1995): 384–401. See also Seth C. McKee, *Republican Ascendancy in Southern U.S. House Elections* (Boulder, CO: Westview Press, 2010).

64. Carol M. Swain, *Black Faces, Black Interests: The Representation of African Americans in Congress* (Cambridge, MA: Harvard University Press, 1995), 205. But see Desmond S. King and Rogers S. Smith, "Strange Bedfellows? Polarized Politics? The Quest for Racial Equity in Contemporary America," *Political Research Quarterly* 64 (2008): 686–703. King and Smith argue, "Republicans benefited from the new districts but not via an unholy alliance" (p. 698).

65. David Lublin, *The Paradox of Representation: Racial Gerrymandering and Minority Interests in Congress* (Princeton, NJ: Princeton University Press, 1997).

66. Carol M. Swain, "The Voting Rights Act: Some Unintended Consequences," *Brookings Review* 10 (Winter 1992): 51. See also Lublin, *Paradox of Representation*.

67. Alexander Bolton, "Dems Seek to 'Unpack' Minority Districts," *The Hill*, May 9, 2001, 4.

68. Louis Sandy Maisel, *From Obscurity to Oblivion: Running in the Congressional Primary* (Knoxville: University of Tennessee Press, 1982), 34.

69. Alan Ehrenhalt, *The United States of Ambition* (New York: Random House, 1991), 17.

70. The four Capitol Hill campaign committees are the National Republican Senatorial Committee (NRSC), Democratic Senatorial Campaign Committee (DSCC), National Republican Congressional Committee (NRCC), and Democratic Congressional Campaign Committee (DCCC). See Paul S. Herrnson, *Congressional Elections: Campaigning at Home and in Washington,* 4th ed. (Washington, DC: CQ Press, 2004), 90–94.

71. Jennifer L. Lawless, *Becoming a Candidate: Political Ambition and the Decision to Run for Office* (New York: Cambridge University Press, 2012), 137. See also David E. Broockman, "Mobilizing Candidates: A Field Experiment and a Review," *Journal's of Experimental Political Science,* 1 (Winter 2014): 104–119.

72. Edward Walsh, "To Every Campaign, There Is a Recruiting Season," *Washington Post,* November 12, 1985, A1.

73. Abby Livingston, "Democrats Eyeing Five House Race Rematches in 2016," At the Races, *Roll Call* weblog, November 13, 2014, http://atr.rollcall.com/house-democrats-eyeing-five-rematches/.

74. C. Douglas Swearingen and Walt Jatkowski III, "Is Timing Everything? Retirement and Seat Maintenance in the U.S. House of Representatives," *Legislative Studies Quarterly* 36 (May 2011): 309–330.

75. David T. Canon, *Actors, Athletes, and Astronauts: Political Amateurs in the United States Congress* (Chicago: University of Chicago Press, 1990), 2–3, 25–31.

76. "New Members of the 114th Congress," *National Journal's,* December 7, 2014, http://www.nationaljournal.com/almanac/114th-congress-new-members.

77. Michael Janofsky, "Two Congressional Candidates Know They'll Lose, But It's Still Fun," *New York Times,* October 31, 1992, 27.

78. Maisel, *From Obscurity to Oblivion,* 23.

79. This conceptualization is a combination of insights derived from a broad-based, pioneering study of House candidate recruitment by a team of scholars: Cherie D. Maestas, Sara Fulton, L. Sandy Maisel, and Walter J. Stone, "When to Risk It? Institutions, Ambitions, and the Decision to Run for the U.S. House," *American Political Science Review* 100 (May 2006): 195–208; and Stone and Maisel, "The Not-So-Simple Calculus of Winning: U.S. House Candidates' Nomination and General Election Prospects," *Journal's of Politics* 65 (November 2003): 951–977.

80. Danielle M. Thomsen, "Ideological Moderates Won't Run: How Party Fit Matters for Partisan Polarization in Congress," *Journal's of Politics* 76 (3, 2014): 786-797.

81. Paul Kane, "Senate Headed for Record Number of Former House Members in Its Lineup," *Washington Post,* July 23, 2014, http://www.washingtonpost.com/politics/senate-headed-for-record-number-of-former-house-members-in-its-lineup/2014/07/23/31c88518-11e4-11e4-9285-4243a40ddc97_story.html.

82. The seminal work on strategic politician theory is Gary C. Jacobson and Samuel Kernell, *Strategy and Choice in Congressional Elections*, 2d ed. (New Haven, CT: Yale University Press, 1983).

83. Shira Toeplitz, "Ohio's Limits Tip Races," *Roll Call*, November 20, 2008, 15.

84. Jacobson and Kernell, *Strategy and Choice in Congressional Elections*, chap. 3.

85. L. Sandy Maisel, Cherie D. Maestas, and Walter J. Stone, "The Party Role in Congressional Competition," in *The Parties Respond*, ed. Paul S. Herrnson (Boulder, CO: Westview Press, 2002), 129.

86. Brian D. Feinstein, "The Dynasty Advantage: Family Ties in Congressional Elections," *Legislative Studies Quarterly* 35 (November 2010): 571–598.

87. Linda L. Fowler and Robert D. McClure, *Political Ambition: Who Decides to Run for Congress* (New Haven, CT: Yale University Press, 1989).

88. Quoted in Burt Solomon, "A Daunting Task: Running for House," *National Journal's*, March 21, 1992, 712.

89. Jacobson, *Politics of Congressional Elections*, 23.

90. Clark Mindock, "30 Members, 1 Senator Running Unopposed," At the Races, *Roll Call* weblog, November 3, 2014, http://atr.rollcall.com/elections-2014-running-unopposed-congress/.

91. Catalina Camia, "Tenn. Democrats Disavow Party's Senate Nominee," On Politics, *USA Today*, August 4, 2012, http://content.usatoday.com/communities/onpolitics/post/2012/08/mark-clayton-tennessee-senate-bob-corker-hate-group/1#.UOYpoKzjNGo.

92. Jacobson, *Politics of Congressional Elections*, 38.

93. See Walter J. Stone, Sarah A. Fulton, Cherie D. Maestas, and L. Sandy Maisel, "Incumbency Reconsidered: Prospects, Strategic Retirement, and Incumbent Quality in U.S. House Elections," *Journal's of Politics* 72 (January 2010): 178–190.

94. Ibid.

95. Maisel, Maestas, and Stone, "Party Role in Congressional Competition," 129.

96. Lawless, *Becoming a Candidate*, 171–172.

97. Jennifer L. Lawless and Richard L. Fox, *It Still Takes a Candidate: Why Women Don't Run for Office*, rev. ed. (New York: Cambridge University Press, 2010).

98. Jacobson, *Politics of Congressional Elections*, 19.

99. Stephen Ansolabehere, John Mark Hansen, Shigeo Hirano, and James M. Snyder Jr., "The Decline of Competition in U.S. Primary Elections, 1908–2004," in *The Marketplace of Democracy*, ed. Michael P. McDonald and John Samples (Washington, DC: Cato Institute and Brookings, 2006), 74–101.

100. Robert G. Boatright, *Getting Primaried: The Changing Politics of Congressional Primary Challenges* (Ann Arbor: University of Michigan Press, 2013).

101. Harvey L. Schantz, "Contested and Uncontested Primaries for the U.S. House," *Legislative Studies Quarterly* 5 (November 1980): 559. The linkage between interparty and intraparty competition is sometimes referred to as Key's Law. See V. O. Key Jr., *Parties, Politics, and Pressure Groups*, 5th ed. (New York: Crowell, 1964), 438, 447.

102. Ansolabehere et al., "Decline of Competition in U.S. Primary Elections," 81.

103. L. Sandy Maisel, Cary T. Gibson, and Elizabeth J. Ivry, "The Continuing Importance of the Rules of the Game: Subpresidential Nominations in 1994 and 1996," in *The Parties Respond: Changes in American Parties and Campaigns*, 3d ed., ed. L. Sandy Maisel (Boulder, CO: Westview Press, 1998), 162–164.

104. Maisel, Maestas, and Stone, "Party Role in Congressional Competition," 132.

105. Ed O'Keefe and Sean Sullivan, "The Fix's Top 10 House Race Rematches of 2014," The Fix, *Washington Post* weblog, January 24, 2014, http://www.washingtonpost.com/blogs/the-fix/wp/2014/01/24/the-fixs-top-10-house-race-rematches/.

106. Austin Ranney, "Parties in State Politics," in *Politics in the American States*, ed. Herbert Jacob and Kenneth Vines (Boston: Little, Brown, 1976), 61–99.

107. John F. Bibby, "State Party Organizations," in *The Parties Respond*, 3d ed., ed. L. Sandy Maisel (Boulder, CO: Westview Press, 1998), 20.

CHAPTER 4

1. See Philip Rucker and Dan Balz, "How Joni Ernst's ad about 'castrating hogs' transformed Iowa's U.S. Senate Race," May 11, 2014, http://www.washingtonpost.com/politics/how-joni-ernsts-ad-about-castrating-hogs-transformed-iowas-us-senate-race/2014/05/11/c02d1804-d85b-11e3-95d3-3bcd77cd4e11_story.html.

2. See Realclearpolitics summary of polling, http://www.realclearpolitics.com/epolls/2014/senate/ia/iowa_senate_ernst_vs_braley-3990.html#polls.

3. Emily Shultheis, "Bruce Braley on Chuck Grassley: A 'farmer' with no law degree." *Politico*, March 25, 2014, http://www.politico.com/story/2014/03/bruce-braley-chuck-grassley-farmer-with-no-law-degree-105010.html.

4. See Greg Sargent, "Joni Ernst Tries to Cover Her Tracks on 'Personhood,'" *Washington Post*, October 3, 2014, http://www.washingtonpost.com/blogs/plum-line/wp/2014/10/03/joni-ernst-tries-to-cover-her-tracks-on-personhood/.

5. Jennifer Steinhauer, "Endurance Test of a Race, for Candidates and Voters in Iowa," *New York Times*, November 1, 2014, http://www.nytimes.com/2014/11/02/us/politics/endurance-test-of-a-race-for-candidates-and-voters-in-iowa.html.

6. See Rick Corasaniti, "99 Counties, 24 Hours, 2 Candidates, 1 State (Iowa)," *New York Times*, November 3, 2014, http://www.nytimes.com/politics/first-draft/2014/11/03/?entry=4233&_r=0; and Sheryl Gay Stolberg, "Joni Ernst's Playbook, for Women to Win Men's Vote," *New York Times*, October 28, 2014, http://www.nytimes.com/2014/10/29/us/iowans-playbook-for-women-to-win-mens-vote.html.

7. See Dena Levy and Peverill Squire, "Television Markets and the Competitiveness of U.S. House Elections," *Legislative Studies Quarterly* 25 (May 2000): 313–325; and James M. Snyder Jr. and David Stromberg, "Press Coverage and Political Accountability," *Journal's of Political Economy* 118 (April 2010): 355–408.

8. Theodore E. Jackson Jr., "Brand Marketing in Today's Cluttered Political Marketplace," *Campaigns and Elections* 24 (April 2003): 30.

9. Allison Stevens, "House Candidates in Maryland Striving to Hone Their Messages," *The Hill*, May 8, 2002, 31–32.

10. Quoted in Robin Toner, "In a Cynical Election Season, the Ads Tell an Angry Tale," *New York Times*, October 24, 1994, A1.

11. Parke Skelton, quoted in Mary Clare Jalonick, "How to 'Primary' an Incumbent," *Campaigns and Elections* 22 (May 2001): 35.

12. See Paul S. Herrnson, *Congressional Elections: Campaigning at Home and in Washington*, 6th ed. (Washington, DC: CQ Press, 2012), 174.

13. The figures cited in this chapter for the 2013–2014 cycle were taken from the website of the Center for Responsive Politics, www.opensecrets.org.

14. Norman J. Ornstein, Thomas E. Mann, and Michael J. Malbin, *Vital Statistics on Congress, 2008* (Washington, DC: American Enterprise Institute, 2008), 75–76.

15. Quoted in Ryan Grim and Sabrina Siddiqui, "Call Time for Congress Shows How Fundraising Dominates Bleak Work," *Huffington Post*, politics blog, January 8, 2013, www.huffingtonpost.com/2013/01/08/call-time-congressional-fundraising_n_2427291.html?ncid=edlinkusaolp00000003.

16. A survey of members by the Congressional Management Foundation suggests that less time is spent on fund-raising than the DCCC recommends. Members report that they spend roughly 18 percent of their work time on campaign activities, with much of this time devoted to fund-raising (see Ezra Klein, "Congress spends too much time fundraising, but it's less time than you think," *Washington Post*, July 29, 2013, http://www.washingtonpost.com/blogs/wonkblog/wp/2013/07/29/congress-spends-too-much-time-fundraising-but-its-less-time-than-you-think/).

17. *Buckley v. Valeo*, 424 U.S. 1 (1976).

18. Robert Barnes, "Supreme Court Strikes Down Limits on Federal Campaign Donations," *Washington Post*, April 2, 2014.

19. *Citizens United v. Federal Election Commission*, 558 U.S. 310 (2010), slip op. at 44.

20. *Speechnow.org v. Federal Election Commission*, 99 F.3d 686 (2010).

21. Ibid., at 55.

22. David G. Savage, "Corporate Campaign Ads Haven't Followed Supreme Court's Prediction," *Los Angeles Times*, October 27, 2010 (online edition).

23. Michael Luo and Stephanie Strom, "Donor Names Remain Secret as Rules Shift," *New York Times*, September 20, 2010 (online edition).

24. Ray LaRaja, "Why Super PACs: How the American Party System Outgrew the Campaign Finance System," *The Forum* 10, no. 4 (2012): 91–104.

25. Ray LaRaja, "Money in the 2014 Congressional Elections: Institutionalizing a Broken Regulatory System," *The Forum*, 12 (2014): 713–728.

26. Under the BCRA, individuals could donate $32,400 to national party committees per calendar year during the 2014 election cycle and $10,000 as a combined limit on contributions to state, district, and local party committees. These amounts are adjusted annually for inflation.

27. LaRaja, "Money in the 2014 Congressional Elections."

28. In December 2013, Sen. Mitch McConnell succeeded in adding a provision to a massive spending bill that further loosened the limitations on party fund-raising. The new rules allow party organizations to raise up to $97,200 per year from individuals to go into each of three separate accounts. See ibid.

29. Ibid.

30. Ibid.

31. Quoted in Luo and Strom, "Donor Names Remain Secret as Rules Shift."

32. Campaign data are drawn from the Federal Elections Commission data compiled by the Center for Responsive Politics, www.opensecrets.org/overview/incumbs.php, and by the Campaign Finance Institute http://www.cfinst.org/.

33. Gary C. Jacobson, *The Politics of Congressional Elections*, 8th ed. (New York: Pearson Education, 2013), 54.

34. For a recent study documenting the fund-raising advantage of majority party members, see Erik J. Engstrom and William Ewell, "The Impact of Unified Party Government on Campaign Contributions," *Legislative Studies Quarterly* 35 (2010): 543–569.

35. Thomas B. Edsall, "In Tight Races, Early Cash Means Staying Competitive," *Washington Post*, July 14, 1998, A6.

36. Gary C. Jacobson, "The Effects of Campaign Spending on Congressional Elections," *American Political Science Review* 72 (June 1978): 469–491.

37. Gary C. Jacobson, "Money in the 1980 and 1982 Congressional Elections," in *Money and Politics in the United States: Financing Elections in the 1980s*, ed. Michael J. Malbin (Chatham, NJ: Chatham House, 1984), 57.

38. Gary C. Jacobson, *The Politics of Congressional Elections*, 6th ed. (New York: Pearson Longman, 2004), 98.

39. Carl Hulse and Adam Nagourney, "Specter Switches Parties: More Heft for Democrats," *New York Times,* April 29, 2009, A1; Kathleen Hunter and Bart Jansen, "Specter's Defection Has Consequences for Balance of Power on Committees," *CQ Today,* April 30, 2009, 8, 12.

40. David Hinckley, "Average American Watches 5 Hours of TV per Day, Report Shows," *New York Daily News,* March 5, 2014, http://www.nydailynews.com/life-style/average-american-watches-5-hours-tv-day-article-1.1711954.

41. Erika Franklin Fowler and Travis N. Ridout, "Political Advertising in 2014: The Year of the Outside Group," *The Forum,* 12, no. 4 (2014): 663–684.

42. Robin Toner, "In Final Rounds, Both Sides Whip Out Bare-Knuckle Ads," *New York Times,* October 21, 1996, B7.

43. James A. Thurber and Carolyn Long, "Brian Baird's 'Ring of Fire': The Quest for Funds and Votes in Washington's Third District," in *The Battle for Congress,* ed. James A. Thurber (Washington, DC: Brookings, 2001), 188.

44. Andrew Mayerson, "Campaign Spending Habits: Democrats v. Republicans," Center for Responsive Politics, October 23, 2013, http://www.opensecrets.org/news/2013/10/campaign-spending-habits-democrats-v-republicans/.

45. Tom Rosenstiel and Amy Mitchell, "As General Election Nears, Internet Gains Most as Campaign News Source but Cable TV Still Leads," Pew Research Center's Project for Excellence in Journalism, October 25, 2012, www.journalism.org/commentary_backgrounder/social_media_doubles_remains_limited.

46. Erika Franklin Fowler generously provided this data. See also Erika Franklin Fowler, "Making the News: Is Local News Coverage Really That Bad?" in Travis N. Ridout, ed., *New Directions in Media and Politics* (New York: Routledge, 2012).

47. Larry J. Sabato and Glenn R. Simpson, *Dirty Little Secrets: The Persistence of Corruption in American Politics* (New York: Times Books, 1996), 156.

48. Joshua Miller, "Three Takeaways for 2014 from the RNC Autopsy Report," *Roll Call,* March 19, 2013, 11.

49. Quoted in Janet Hook, "Negative Ads a Positive in GOP Strategy," *Los Angeles Times,* September 26, 2006, A10.

50. Stephen Ansolabehere and Shanto Iyengar, *Going Negative: How Attack Ads Shrink and Polarize the Electorate* (New York: Free Press, 1996), 128.

51. Quoted in David S. Broder, "Death by Negative Ads," *Washington Post,* November 3, 2002, B7.

52. Katharine Q. Seelye, "Kentucky G.O.P. Candidate, Livid over Opponent's Ad, Lashes Out," *New York Times,* October 22, 2010, www.nytimes.com/2010/10/23/us/politics/23kentucky.html.

53. Frank Newport, "State of the States: Importance of Religion," Gallup press release, January 28, 2009, www.gallup.com/poll/114022/State-States-Importance-Religion.aspx.

54. Manu Raju, "'Aqua Buddha' Ad Backfires on Jack Conway," *Politico,* October 26, 2010, www.politico.com/news/stories/1010/44222.html.

55. See Howard Kurtz, "Hearing 'Foul,' Stations Pull Political Ads," *Washington Post,* September 20, 2002, A14.

56. Pew Research Center for the People and the Press, "In Changing News Landscape, Even Television Is Vulnerable," September 27, 2012, www.people-press.org/files/legacy-pdf/2012%20News%20Consumption%20Report.pdf.

57. Rosenstiel and Mitchell, "As General Election Nears."

58. Dan Morain, "Undercover Campaigning on the Web," *Los Angeles Times,* March 21, 2007, A11.

59. Ibid.

60. Merle Miller, *Lyndon: An Oral Biography* (New York: Putnam, 1980), 120.

61. "Lessons from Recent GOTV Experiments," GOTV, Yale University, Institution for Social and Policy Studies, http://gotv.research.yale.edu/?q=node/10.

62. Donald P. Green and Alan S. Gerber, *Get Out the Vote!* (Washington, DC: Brookings, 2004), 93–96.

63. Ibid., 40.

64. Dan Glickman, as told to Amy Zipkin, "Landing the Job He Wanted," *New York Times,* April 17, 2005, C10.

65. Paul Houston, "TV and High Tech Send Campaign Costs Soaring," *Los Angeles Times,* October 2, 1986, 121.

66. Jamie Stiehm, "Ben and Jerry's State Offers a Choice of Three Flavors," *The Hill,* November 22, 1995, 26.

67. Glenn R. Simpson, "In Rhode Island, Everyone Goes to Bristol Parade," *Roll Call,* July 9, 1990, 1; Glenn R. Simpson, "Judging from July 4th Bristol Parade in R.I., Chafee Looks Well-Positioned for November," *Roll Call,* July 11, 1994, 21.

68. Leslie Wayne, "Democrats Take Page from Their Rival's Playbook," *New York Times,* November 1, 2008, A15.

69. "Unions on the March," *The Economist,* November 3, 2014, http://www.economist.com/blogs/democracyinamerica/2014/11/politics-and-labour.

70. Reid Wilson, "Candidates Become Partisan Stereotypes in Super PAC Era," *National Journal's,* November 4, 2012.

71. Michael P. McDonald, "2014 November General Election Turnout Rates," accessed January 15, 2015, http://www.electproject.org/2014g.

72. Michael P. McDonald, "2014 November General Election Turnout Rates," *United States Elections Project,* accessed January 5, 2015, http://www.electproject.org/2012g.

73. M. Margaret Conway, "Political Participation in Midterm Congressional Elections," *American Politics Quarterly* 9 (April 1981): 221–244.

74. International turnout figures from the Institute for Social Research, University of Michigan, reported in Pippa Norris, *Electoral Engineering: Voting Rules and Political Behavior* (Cambridge, UK: Cambridge University Press, 2004). A sensible review of the question is found in Martin P. Wattenberg, *Where Have All the Voters Gone?* (Cambridge, MA: Harvard University Press, 2002).

75. Pew Research Center for the People and the Press, "Who Votes, Who Doesn't, and Why," October 18, 2006, 4.

76. "New CIRCLE Estimate: 2014 Youth Turnout Was 22.2%," CIRCLE: The Center for Information and Research on Civic Learning and Engagement, Jonathan M. Tisch College of Citizenship and Public Service, Tufts University, December 10, 2014, http://www.civicyouth.org/new-circle-estimate-2014-youth-turnout-was-22-2/.

77. Data on the results of the act are distressingly incomplete. See Raymond E. Wolfinger and Jonathan Hoffman, "Registering and Voting with Motor Voter," *PS* 34 (March 2001): 85–92.

78. Nina Totenberg, "Supreme Court Weighs Voter ID Requirements," *Morning Edition,* January 9, 2008, www.npr.org/templates/story/story.php?storyId=17942818.

79. Joseph D. Rich, "Playing Politics with Justice," *Los Angeles Times,* March 29, 2007, A23. Rich is former chief (1999–2005) of the voting section in the Department of Justice's Civil Rights Division.

80. *Crawford v. Marion County Election Board,* 553 U.S. 181 (2008).

81. Michael Cooper, "After Ruling, States Rush to Enact Voting Laws," *New York Times,* July 5, 2013, http://www.nytimes.com/2013/07/06/us/politics/after-Supreme-Court-ruling-states-rush-to-enact-voting-laws.html?pagewanted=all&_r=0.

82. David Damron and Scott Powers, "Researcher: Long Lines at Polls Caused 49,000 Not to Vote," *Orlando Sentinel,* December 29, 2012, http://articles.orlandosentinel.com/2012-12-29/news/os-discouraged-voters-20121229_1_long-lines-higher-turnout-election-day.

83. Richard Morin and Claudia Deane, "As Turnout Falls, Apathy Emerges as Driving Force," *Washington Post,* November 4, 2000, A1; Michael Waldman and Justin Levin, "The Myth of Voter Fraud," *Washington Post,* March 29, 2007, A19.

84. Sidney Verba, Kay Lehman Schlozman, and Henry E. Brady, *Voice and Equality: Civic Voluntarism in American Politics* (Cambridge, MA: Harvard University Press, 1995).

85. Samuel L. Popkin, *The Reasoning Voter* (Chicago: University of Chicago Press, 1994), 7.

86. Exit polls, November 2, 2004, and November 7, 2006, reported in *New York Times,* November 9, 2006, P7; and by Ronald Brownstein, "Democrats' Losses Go Far beyond One Defeat," *Los Angeles Times,* November 4, 2004, A1, A17.

87. National House exit poll, *Washington Post,* http://www.washingtonpost.com/wp-srv/special/politics/2014-midterms/exit-polls/.

88. Quoted in Richard Morin and Claudia Deane, "How Independent Are Independents?" *Washington Post,* August 2, 2002, A1.

89. Gary C. Jacobson, *The Politics of Congressional Elections,* 5th ed. (New York: Addison, Wesley, Longman, 2001), 108.

90. Martin P. Wattenberg, *The Rise of Candidate-Centered Politics* (Cambridge, MA: Harvard University Press, 1991), 36–39.

91. See Bernard Grofman, William Koetzle, Michael P. McDonald, and Thomas L. Brunell, "A New Look at Split-Ticket Outcomes for House and President: The Comparative Midpoints Model," *Journal's of Politics* 62 (February 2000): 34–50.

92. Cited in Jeffrey McMurray, "Conservative Southern Dems Disappearing," *Washington Post,* April 25, 2005, A1.

93. Jacobson, *Politics of Congressional Elections,* 8th ed., 176.

94. Ibid., 175.

95. James E. Campbell, "The Midterm Landslide of 2010: A Triple Wave Election," *The Forum* 8 (2010): art. 3.

96. Angus Campbell, "Surge and Decline: A Study of Electoral Change," in *Elections and the Political Order,* ed. Angus Campbell, Phillip E. Converse, Warren E. Miller, and Donald E. Stokes (New York: Wiley, 1966), 40–62; Raymond E. Wolfinger, Steven J. Rosenstone, and Richard A. McIntosh, "Presidential and Congressional Voters Compared," *American Politics Quarterly* 9 (April 1981): 245–255.

97. Eric M. Uslaner and M. Margaret Conway, "The Responsible Electorate: Watergate, the Economy, and Vote Choice in 1974," *American Political Science Review* 79 (September 1985): 788–803; Samuel Kernell, "Presidential Popularity and Negative Voting: An Alternative Explanation of the Midterm Congressional Decline of the President's Party," *American Political Science Review* 71 (March 1977): 44–46.

98. Roberto Alesina and Howard Rosenthal, *Partisan Politics, Divided Government, and the Economy* (New York: Cambridge University Press, 1995).

99. Joseph Bafumi, Robert S. Erikson, and Christopher Wlezien, "Balancing, Generic Polls and Midterm Congressional Elections," *Journal's of Politics* 72 (2010): 705–719.

100. Quoted in Dale Russakoff, "In Tight Arkansas Senate Race, Family Matters," *Washington Post,* August 3, 2002, A1.

101. Jacobson, *Politics of Congressional Elections,* 8th ed., 35.

102. Ibid., 27–28. See Gary C. Jacobson, "Barack Obama and Nationalized Electoral Politics in the 2014 Midterm," *Political Science Quarterly* 130 (Spring 2015): 1–25.

103. David R. Mayhew, *Congress: The Electoral Connection,* 2d ed. (New Haven, CT: Yale University Press, 2004).

104. National Election Studies (now called the American National Election Studies, or ANES), 1980–2002, summarized in Jacobson, *Politics of Congressional Elections,* 122–126; Thomas E.

Mann and Raymond E. Wolfinger, "Candidates and Parties in Congressional Elections," *American Political Science Review* 74 (September 1980): 623.

105. On the first view mentioned in this paragraph, see Morris P. Fiorina, *Congress: Keystone of the Washington Establishment,* 2d ed. (New Haven, CT: Yale University Press, 1989); and Bruce Cain, John Ferejohn, and Morris Fiorina, *The Personal Vote: Constituency Service and Electoral Independence* (Cambridge, MA: Harvard University Press, 1987), esp. chaps. 6–7. For more on the second view, see Glenn R. Parker and Roger H. Davidson, "Why Do Americans Love Their Congressmen So Much More Than Their Congress?" *Legislative Studies Quarterly* 4 (February 1979): 53–61. On the question of whether incumbents' resources are directly tied to votes, see John R. Johannes, *To Serve the People: Congress and Constituency Service* (Lincoln: University of Nebraska Press, 1984), esp. chap. 8.

106. Michael J. Robinson, "Three Faces of Congressional Media," in *The New Congress,* ed. Thomas E. Mann and Norman J. Ornstein (Washington, DC: American Enterprise Institute, 1981), 91.

107. Frances E. Lee and Bruce I. Oppenheimer, *Sizing Up the Senate: The Unequal Consequences of Equal Representation* (Chicago: University of Chicago Press, 1999), chap. 4.

108. Gary C. Jacobson, "Incumbents' Advantages in the 1978 U.S. Congressional Elections," *Legislative Studies Quarterly* 6 (May 1981): 198.

109. Owen G. Abbe, Jay Goodliffe, Paul S. Herrnson, and Kelly D. Patterson, "Agenda Setting in Congressional Elections: The Impact of Issues and Campaigns on Voting Behavior," *Political Research Quarterly* 56 (December 2003): 419.

110. John B. Bader, *Taking the Initiative: Leadership Agendas in Congress and the "Contract with America"* (Washington, DC: Georgetown University Press, 1996).

111. Edward Epstein, "The Search Is on for a Takeover Manifesto," *CQ Weekly,* February 8, 2010, 318.

112. Quoted in Judy Newman, "Do Women Vote for Women?" *Public Perspective* 7 (February–March 1996): 10.

113. Karen M. Kaufmann and John R. Petrocik, "The Changing Politics of American Men: Understanding the Sources of the Gender Gap," *American Journal's of Political Science* 43 (July 1999): 864–887.

114. Quoted in Barbara Vobejda, "Fragmentation of Society Formidable Challenge to Candidates, Report Says," *Washington Post,* March 7, 1996, A15.

115. For a discussion of these reversals, see Gary Miller and Norman Schofield, "Activists and Partisan Realignment in the United States," *American Political Science Review* 97 (May 2003): 245–260.

116. Jacobson, *Politics of Congressional Elections,* 6th ed., 249–253.

117. Delegates to the parties' national conventions were analyzed in a classic study by Herbert McCloskey, Paul Hoffman, and Rosemary O'Hara, "Issue Conflict and Consensus among Party Leaders and Followers," *American Political Science Review* 54 (1960): 406–427.

118. The "middlingness" of the citizenry is vigorously argued in Morris P. Fiorina, with Samuel J. Abrams and Jeremy C. Pope, *Culture War? The Myth of a Polarized America* (New York: Pearson-Longman, 2005).

119. Alan I. Abramowitz, *The Disappearing Center: Engaged Citizens, Polarization, and American Democracy* (New Haven, CT: Yale University Press, 2010). See also Pew Research Center for the People and the Press, "The 2004 Political Landscape: Evenly Divided and Increasingly Polarized," survey report, November 5, 2003, www.people-press.org/reports/.

120. David W. Brady, "Electoral Realignments in the U.S. House of Representatives," in *Congress and Policy Change,* ed. Gerald C. Wright Jr., Leroy N. Reiselbach, and Lawrence C. Dodd (New York: Agathon Press, 1986), 46–69.

121. Campbell, "Midterm Landslide of 2010."

122. Jennifer E. Manning, "Membership of the 114th Congress: A Profile," Congressional Research Service, January 2015.

123. Warren E. Miller and Donald E. Stokes, "Constituency Influence in Congress," *American Political Science Review* 57 (March 1963): 45–57.
124. Tracy Sulkin, *Issue Politics in Congress* (New York: Cambridge University Press, 2005), 2.
125. Ibid., 177.

CHAPTER 5

1. Eric Russell, "Sen. Collins Tours Alzheimer's Unit, Pushes for More Funds," *Portland Press Herald*, January 22, 2014.
2. Jen Lynds, "Collins Touts Success in Securing White Potatoes for Federal Food Assistance Program," *Bangor Daily News*, December 10, 2014.
3. Abby Smith, "Dem Goes grassroots on Centrist Dealmaker Collins," *The Hill*, July 31, 2014.
4. Kirk Victor, "Still an Old Boys' Club?" *National Journal's*, March 12, 2005, 750, 752.
5. Maite Jullian, "Snowe, Collins Key Players across Senate Aisle," *Bangor Daily News*, November 7, 2008.
6. Carl Hulse, "Maine Senators Break with Republican Party on Stimulus," *New York Times*, February 10, 2009.
7. Rachel Huggins, "Sen. Collins Endorses Same-Sex Marriage," *The Hill*, June 25, 2014.
8. Ida Brudnick, "Congressional Salaries and Allowances," Congressional Research Service Report No. RL30064, January 15, 2013.
9. Open Secrets Blog, Center for Responsive Politics, January 9, 2014, http://www.opensecrets.org/news/2014/01/millionaires-club-for-first-time-most-lawmakers-are-worth-1-million-plus/.
10. John Stuart Mill, *Considerations on Representative Government* (London: Longmans, Green, 1967 [1861]), quoted in Lisa Schwindt-Bayer and William Mishler, "An Integrated Model of Women's Representation," *Journal's of Politics* 67 (2005): 413.
11. Hannah Finichel Pitkin, *The Concept of Representation* (Berkeley: University of California Press, 1967), 166.
12. See David T. Canon, *Race, Redistricting, and Representation: The Unintended Consequences of Black Majority Districts* (Chicago: University of Chicago Press, 1999); Brinck Kerr and Will Miller, "Latino Representation, It's Direct and Indirect," *American Journal's of Political Science* 41 (1997): 1066–1071; Michele L. Swers, *The Difference Women Make* (Chicago: University of Chicago Press, 2002); and Sue Thomas, *How Women Legislate* (New York: Oxford University Press, 1994).
13. See Claudine Gay, "Spirals of Trust? The Effect of Descriptive Representation on the Relationship between Citizens and Their Government," *American Journal's of Political Science* 46 (2002): 717–732; John D. Griffin and Michael Keane, "Descriptive Representation and the Composition of African American Turnout," *American Journal's of Political Science* 50 (2006): 998–1012; and Katherine Tate, "The Political Representation of Blacks in Congress: Does Race Matter?" *Legislative Studies Quarterly* 26 (2001): 623–638.
14. Data on characteristics of members are found in Jennifer E. Manning, "Membership of the 114th Congress: A Profile," Congressional Research Service Report No. R43869, 2015.
15. Alan Ehrenhalt, *The United States of Ambition: Politicians, Power, and the Pursuit of Office* (New York: Times Books, 1992), 16.
16. William T. Bianco, "Last Post for 'The Greatest Generation': The Policy Implications of the Decline of Military Experience in the U.S. Congress," *Legislative Studies Quarterly* 30 (February 2005): 85–102.
17. Nicholas Carnes, "Does the Numerical Underrepresentation of the Working Class in Congress Matter?" *Legislative Studies Quarterly* 37, no. 1 (2012): 5–34.

18. Ibid. See also Nicholas Carnes, *White-Collar Government: The Hidden Role of Class in Economic Policy Making* (Chicago: University of Chicago Press, 2013).

19. Betsy Rothstein, "Congresswomen Press Women's Health Issues," *The Hill*, February 24, 1999, 19; Maureen Dowd, "Growing Sorority in Congress Edges into the Ol' Boys' Club," *New York Times*, March 5, 1993, A1, A18.

20. Kerry L. Haynie, "African Americans and the New Politics of Inclusion: A Representational Dilemma?" in *Congress Reconsidered*, 8th ed., ed. Lawrence C. Dodd and Bruce I. Oppenheimer (Washington, DC: CQ Press, 2005).

21. Thomas L. Brunell, Christopher J. Anderson, and Rachel K. Cremona, "Descriptive Representation, District Demography, and Attitudes toward Congress among African Americans," *Legislative Studies Quarterly* 33 (2008): 223–242.

22. Tate, "The Political Representation of Blacks in Congress," 631.

23. Janet M. Box-Steffensmeier, David C. Kimball, Scott R. Meinke, and Katherine Tate, "The Effects of Political Representation on the Electoral Advantages of Incumbents," *Political Research Quarterly* 56 (September 2003): 264.

24. See Canon, *Race, Redistricting, and Representation*; and Kerry L. Haynie, *African American Legislators in the American States* (New York: Columbia University Press, 2001); Katrina L. Gamble, "Black Political Representation: An Examination of Legislative Activity within U.S. House Committees," *Legislative Studies Quarterly* 32 (2007): 421–448; Michael D. Minta, "Legislative Oversight and the Substantive Representation of Black and Latino Interests in Congress," *Legislative Studies Quarterly* 34 (2009): 193–218.

25. Inter-Parliamentary Union, "Women in National Parliaments," November 1, 2014, www.ipu. org/wmn-e/classif.htm.

26. The pioneering study of this subject is Irwin N. Gertzog, *Congressional Women: Their Recruitment, Treatment, and Behavior* (New York: Praeger, 1984). Two more recent studies are Barbara C. Burrell, *A Woman's Place Is in the House* (Ann Arbor: University of Michigan Press, 1994); and Richard Logan Fox, *Gender Dynamics in Congressional Elections* (Thousand Oaks, CA: Sage, 1997).

27. Quoted in Sheryl Gay Stolberg, "Working Mothers Swaying Senate Debate, as Senators," *New York Times*, June 7, 2003, A3.

28. Jamie Stiehm, "In Senate, Sisterhood Can Override Party," *The Hill*, November 22, 1995, 16.

29. Arturo Vega and Juanita Firestone, "The Effects of Gender on Congressional Behavior and the Substantive Representation of Women," *Legislative Studies Quarterly* 20 (May 1995): 213–222.

30. Jeremy Peters, "Objections by Women Open Rift in G.O.P.," *New York Times*, January 22, 2015, http://www.nytimes.com/2015/01/23/us/politics/house-gop-discards-bill-banning-abortion-at-20-weeks-but-passes-another-restriction.html?_r=0.

31. Kris Kitto, "Moms in Congress, Part I," *The Hill*, May 3, 2011.

32. Quoted in ibid., 19.

33. See Kathleen A. Dolan, *Voting for Women: How the Public Evaluates Women Candidates* (Boulder, CO: Westview Press, 2003); Leonie Huddy and Nayda Terkildsen, "Gender Stereotypes and the Perception of Male and Female Candidates," *American Journal's of Political Science* 37 (1993): 119–147.

34. Michele Swers, "Building a Reputation on National Security: The Impact of Stereotypes Related to Gender and Military Experience," *Legislative Studies Quarterly* 32 (2007): 559–595.

35. Kirk Victor, "Still an Old Boys' Club?" *National Journal's*, March 12, 2005, 750, 752.

36. Niels Lesniewski, "Feinstein Unveils CIA Torture Report," *Roll Call*, December 9, 2014.

37. Donald P. Haider-Markel, Mark R. Joslyn, and Chad J. Kniss, "Minority Group Interests and Political Representation: Gay Elected Officials in the Policy Process," *Journal's of Politics* 62 (2000): 568–577.

38. Quoted in Erika Niedowski, "Four Walk Out of the Closet and toward the House," *CQ Weekly,* April 25, 1998, 1051.

39. Pew Charitable Trusts, Religion and Public Life Project, "Faith on the Hill," January 5, 2015, http://www.pewforum.org/2015/01/05/faith-on-the-hill/.

40. Ibid.

41. Peter Sullivan, "Most Diverse Congress in History Poised to Take Power," *The Hill,* January 5, 2015.

42. Ibid., 6. For tenure figures, see Table 2-1.

43. Charles S. Bullock and Burdett A. Loomis, "The Changing Congressional Career," in *Congress Reconsidered,* 3d ed., ed. Lawrence C. Dodd and Bruce I. Oppenheimer (Washington, DC: CQ Press, 1985), 66–69, 80–82.

44. Jennifer Wolak, "Strategic Retirements: The Influence of Public Preferences on Voluntary Departures from Congress," *Legislative Studies Quarterly* 32 (May 2007): 285–308.

45. Quoted in Shailagh Murray, "GOP Lawmakers Gird for Rowdy Tea Party," *Washington Post,* July 18, 2010, A3.

46. Frances E. Lee and Bruce I. Oppenheimer, *Sizing Up the Senate: The Unequal Consequences of Equal Representation* (Chicago: University of Chicago Press, 1999), 20–23. Also see Robert A. Dahl, *A Preface to Democratic Theory* (New Haven, CT: Yale University Press, 1956).

47. John D. Griffin, "Senate Apportionment as a Source of Political Inequality," *Legislative Studies Quarterly* 31 (2006): 405–432.

48. Bruce I. Oppenheimer, "The Representational Experience: The Effect of State Population on Senator-Constituency Linkages," *American Journal's of Political Science* 40 (1996): 1280–1299.

49. Frances E. Lee, "Representation and Public Policy: The Consequences of Senate Apportionment for the Geographic Distribution of Federal Funds," *Journal's of Politics* 60 (1998): 34–64. Also see Stephen Ansolabehere, Alan Gerber, and James M. Snyder Jr., "Equal Votes: Equal Money: Court-Ordered Redistricting and the Distribution of Public Expenditures in the American States," *American Political Science Review* 96 (2002): 767–777.

50. Robert Weissberg, "Collective vs. Dyadic Representation in Congress," *American Political Science Review* 72 (1978): 535–547.

51. Jane Mansbridge, "Rethinking Representation," *American Political Science Review* 97 (November 2003): 515–528.

52. Barry C. Burden, *Personal Roots of Representation* (Princeton, NJ: Princeton University Press, 2007).

53. Richard F. Fenno Jr., *The Making of a Senator: Dan Quayle* (Washington, DC: CQ Press, 1989), 119.

54. Quoted in Adam Nagourney, "Upbeat Schumer Battles Polls, Low Turnouts, and His Image," *New York Times,* May 16, 1998, A14.

55. Frank E. Smith, *Congressman from Mississippi* (New York: Pantheon, 1964), 129–130.

56. Donald R. Matthews, *U.S. Senators and Their World* (Chapel Hill: University of North Carolina Press, 1960), chap. 5; Ross K. Baker, *House and Senate,* 3d ed. (New York: Norton, 2001), chap. 2.

57. Barbara Sinclair, *The Transformation of the U.S. Senate* (Baltimore: Johns Hopkins University Press, 1989).

58. Herbert B. Asher, "The Learning of Legislative Norms," *American Political Science Review* 67 (June 1973): 499–513.

59. "Political Incivility: A Weekend of Ugly Discourse Preceded Historic Health Vote," *Cleveland Plain Dealer,* March 22, 2010, www.cleveland.com/nation/index.ssf/2010/03/political_incivility_a_weekend.html.

60. Quoted in Thomas E. Cavanagh, "The Two Arenas of Congress," in *The House at Work,* ed. Joseph Cooper and G. Calvin Mackenzie (Austin: University of Texas Press, 1981), 65.

61. Daniel M. Butler, Christopher F. Karpowitz, and Jeremy C. Pope, "A Field Experiment on Legislators' Home Styles: Service versus Policy," *Journal's of Politics* 74 (April 2012): 474–486.

62. David C. W. Parker and Craig Goodman, "Making a Good Impression: Resource Allocation, Home Styles, and Washington Work," *Legislative Studies Quarterly* 34 (November 2009): 493–524. See also Justin Grimmer, Sean Westwood, and Solomon Messing, *The Impression of Influence: Legislator Communication, Representation, and Democratic Accountability* (Princeton, NJ: Princeton University Press, 2014).

63. Box-Steffensmeier et al., "Effects of Political Representation," 266.

64. Kenneth M. Bickers and Robert M. Stein, "The Electoral Dynamics of the Federal Pork Barrel," *American Journal's of Political Science* 40 (November 1996): 1300–1326.

65. Robert M. Stein and Kenneth M. Bickers, "Congressional Elections and the Pork Barrel," *Journal's of Politics* 56 (May 1994): 377–399.

66. Quoted in Louis Jacobson, "For Arkansas, No Abundance of Clout," *National Journal's,* February 20, 1999, 475.

67. Quoted in Scott MacKay, "Chafee's New Book Is Tough on Pro-War Democrats, Republicans, President Bush," *Providence Journal's,* January 27, 2008.

68. Marian Currinder, *Money in the House: Campaign Funds and Congressional Party Politics* (Boulder, CO: Westview Press, 2009); Eric S. Heberlig, "Congressional Parties, Fundraising, and Committee Ambition," *Political Research Quarterly* 56 (2003): 151–161; Anne H. Bedlington and Michael J. Malbin, "The Party as Extended Network: Members Giving to Each Other and to Their Parties," in *Life after Reform,* ed. Michael J. Malbin (Lanham, MD: Rowman and Littlefield, 2003), 121–140.

69. Patrick Sellers, ~~Cycles of Spin: Strategic Communication in the U.S. Congress~~ (New York: Cambridge University Press, 2010).

70. Roger H. Davidson, The *Role of the Congressman,* (New York: Pegasus, 1969), 98; U.S. Congress, Senate Commission on the Operation of the Senate, *Toward a Modern Senate,* S. Doc. 94–278, 94th Cong., 2d sess., committee print, 1997, 27; U.S. Congress, House Commission on Administrative Review, *Final Report,* 2 vols., H. Doc. 95–272, 95th Cong., 1st sess., December 31, 1977, 2: 874–875.

71. Richard L. Hall, *Participation in Congress* (New Haven, CT: Yale University Press, 1998).

72. Ross A. Webber, "U.S. Senators: See How They Run," *Wharton Magazine* (Winter 1980–1981): 38.

73. Quoted in Richard E. Cohen, "Member Moms," *National Journal's,* April 7, 2007, 17, 21.

74. U.S. Congress, Senate Commission on the Operation of the Senate, *Toward a Modern Senate.*

75. Quoted in Lindsay Sobel, "Former Lawmakers Find Trade Association Gold," *The Hill,* November 26, 1997, 14.

76. Center for Responsive Politics, *Congressional Operations: Congress Speaks—A Survey of the 100th Congress* (Washington, DC: Center for Responsive Politics, 1988), 47–49. See also Congressional Management Foundation, *Life in Congress: The Member Perspective* (Washington, DC: Congressional Management Foundation, 2013).

77. Quoted in *Washington Post,* October 18, 1994, B3.

78. U.S. Congress, Joint Committee on the Organization of Congress, *Organization of Congress* 2 (December 1993): 281–287; Luke Rosiak, "AWOL on Hill: Fundraising Trumps Voting," *Washington Times,* February 20, 2013, A1.

79. Quoted in Vernon Louviere, "For Retiring Congressmen, Enough Is Enough," *Nation's Business,* May 1980, 32.

80. John R. Hibbing, *Congressional Careers: Contours of Life in the U.S. House of Representatives* (Chapel Hill: University of North Carolina Press, 1991), 117.

81. Craig Volden and Alan E. Wiseman, *Legislative Effectiveness in the United States Congress* (Cambridge, UK: Cambridge University Press, 2014).

82. Ibid., 126, 128.
83. Gerard Padro I. Miquel and James M. Snyder Jr., "Legislative Effectiveness and Legislative Careers," *Legislative Studies Quarterly* 31 (August 2006): 348.
84. Ibid.
85. Gary W. Cox and William C. Terry, "Legislative Productivity in the 93rd–105th Congresses," *Legislative Studies Quarterly* 33 (2008): 613. See also Volden and Wiseman, *Legislative Effectiveness in the United States Congress*, 2014.
86. William H. Riker, *The Theory of Political Coalitions* (New Haven, CT: Yale University Press, 1962), 24-38.
87. Pitkin, *Concept of Representation*, 166.
88. Steven Kull, *Expecting More Say: The American Public on Its Role in Government Decision-making* (Washington, DC: Center on Policy Attitudes, 1999), 13–14.
89. Henry J. Hyde, "Advice to Freshmen: 'There Are Things Worth Losing For,'" *Roll Call,* December 3, 1990, 5.
90. Quoted in Jamie Stiehm, "Ex-Rep Mike Synar, Who Fought Lobbyists, Succumbs to Brain Tumor," *The Hill,* January 10, 1996, 5.
91. Thomas E. Cavanagh, "The Calculus of Representation: A Congressional Perspective," *Western Political Quarterly* 35 (March 1982): 120–129.
92. John W. Kingdon, *Congressmen's Voting Decisions,* 3d ed. (Ann Arbor: University of Michigan Press, 1989), 47–54.
93. Lawrence N. Hansen, *Our Turn: Politicians Talk about Themselves, Politics, the Public, the Press, and Reform,* part 2 (Washington, DC: Centel Public Accountability Project, 1992), 9.
94. Richard F. Fenno Jr., *Home Style: House Members in Their Districts* (New York: Pearson Longman, 2003), 1.
95. See the discussion of senators' varied constituencies in Lee and Oppenheimer, *Sizing Up the Senate,* chap. 3.
96. Fenno, *Home Style,* 4–8.
97. John F. Bibby and Thomas M. Holbrook, "Parties and Elections," in *Politics in the American States: A Comparative Analysis,* 7th ed., ed. Virginia Gray, Russell L. Hanson, and Herbert Jacob (Washington, DC: CQ Press, 1999), 66–112. Also see Thomas L. Brunell, *Redistricting and Representation: Why Competitive Elections Are Bad for America* (New York: Routledge, 2008).
98. James L. Payne, "The Personal Electoral Advantage of House Incumbents, 1936–1976," *American Politics Quarterly* 8 (October 1980): 465–482; Robert S. Erikson, "Is There Such a Thing as a Safe Seat?" *Polity* 8 (Summer 1976): 623–632.
99. We classify a winning incumbent as having received a warning sign if he or she received 55 percent or less of the two-party vote.
100. Thomas E. Mann, *Unsafe at Any Margin: Interpreting Congressional Elections* (Washington, DC: American Enterprise Institute, 1978).
101. Fenno, *Home Style,* 8–27.
102. Thomas P. O'Neill Jr., with William Novak, *Man of the House* (New York: St. Martin's Press, 1987), 25.
103. Nancy Bocskor, "Fundraising Lessons Candidates Can Learn from Tom Sawyer . . . and Other Great American Salesmen," *Campaigns and Elections* 24 (April 2003): 33.
104. Richard F. Fenno Jr., *Senators on the Campaign Trail* (Norman: University of Oklahoma Press, 1996), 131–132.
105. David E. Price, *The Congressional Experience,* 3d ed. (Boulder, CO: Westview Press, 2004), 10.
106. Fenno, *Home Style,* 153.
107. Ibid., 56.

108. Anthony Champagne, *Congressman Sam Rayburn* (New Brunswick, NJ: Rutgers University Press, 1984), 28.

109. Parker and Goodman, "Making a Good Impression," 517.

110. See Justin Grimmer, *Representational Style in Congress* (Cambridge and New York: Cambridge University Press, 2014).

111. Kingdon, *Congressmen's Voting Decisions.*

112. Brian J. Fogarty, "The Strategy of the Story: Media Monitoring Legislative Activity," *Legislative Studies Quarterly* 33 (August 2008): 445–469.

113. Quoted in Jim Wright, *You and Your Congressman* (New York: Coward-McCann, 1965), 35.

114. Betsy Rothstein, "Hey, Congressman! Someone Is Blocking My Driveway!" *The Hill,* June 9, 2004, 18–19.

115. Lee and Oppenheimer, *Sizing Up the Senate,* 56.

116. The National Election Study is now the American National Election Study (ANES). Warren E. Miller, Donald R. Kinder, Steven J. Rosenstone, and the National Election Study, *American National Election Study, 1990: Post-Election Survey,* 2d ed. (Ann Arbor, MI: Inter-University Consortium for Political and Social Research, January 1992), 166–170.

117. Ida A. Brudnick, "Congressional Salaries and Allowances," Congressional Research Service Report RL30064, December 30, 2014. Also see Congressional Management Foundation, *1999 Senate Staff Employment Study* (Washington, DC: Congressional Management Foundation, 1999), 82ff; and Congressional Management Foundation, *2000 House Staff Employment Study* (Washington, DC: Congressional Management Foundation, 2000), 48–49.

118. Congressional Management Foundation, *2004 House Staff Employment Study*; and Congressional Management Foundation, *2001 Senate Staff Employment Study.* See also Emily Goodin, "Congressional Staffers Say Low Pay, Long Hours Has Them Eying New Jobs," *The Hill,* September 9, 2013.

119. Cited in C. Simon Davidson, "Congressional Office Off-Limits for Members' Campaigns," *Roll Call,* April 16, 2007, 8.

120. Brian Wingfield, "The Latest Initiative in Congress: Blogging," *New York Times,* February 24, 2005, E4; Jennifer Bendery, "Social Media Goes Viral on Capitol Hill," *Roll Call,* February 7, 2011, 1; Michael D. Shear, "G.O.P. to Open House to Electronic Devices," *New York Times,* December 25, 2010, A16.

121. E. Scott Adler, Chariti E. Gent, and Cary B. Overmeyer, "The Home Style Homepage: Legislator Use of the World Wide Web for Constituency Contact," *Legislative Studies Quarterly* 23 (November 1998): 585–595.

122. Jacob R. Straus and Matthew E. Glassman, "Congressional Adoption of Vine," In Focus, Congressional Research Service, April 10, 2014.

123. Dana Milbank, "A Tale of 140 Characters, Plus the Ones in Congress," *Washington Post,* February 25, 2009, A3; Jacob R. Strauss, Matthew Eric Glassman, Colleen J. Shogan, and Susan Navarro Smelcer, "Communicating in 140 Characters or Less: Congressional Adoption of Twitter in the 111th Congress," *PS, Political Science & Politics,* January 2013, 60–66; and Emily Cahn, "More Members Are Using Social Media to Interact with Their Constituents," *Roll Call,* January 4, 2013, 7.

124. Charles Bosley, "Senate Communications with the Public," in U.S. Senate, Commission on the Operation of the Senate, *Senate Communications with the Public,* 94th Cong., 2d sess., 1977, 17.

125. See Michael J. Robinson, "Three Faces of Congressional Media," in *The New Congress,* ed. Thomas E. Mann and Norman J. Ornstein (Washington, DC: American Enterprise Institute, 1981), 80–81.

126. R. Douglas Arnold, *Congress, the Press, and Political Accountability* (Princeton, NJ: Princeton University Press, 2004).

127. For descriptions of the studios, see Michael J. Robinson, "Three Faces of Congressional Media," in *The New Congress*, ed. Thomas E. Mann and Norman J. Ornstein (Washington, DC: American Enterprise Institute, 1981), 62–63; and Martin Tolchin, "TV Studio Serves Congress," *New York Times*, March 7, 1984, C22.

128. Tolchin, "TV Studio Serves Congress."

129. Cokie Roberts, "Leadership and the Media in the 101st Congress," in *Leading Congress: New Styles, New Strategies*, ed. John J. Kornacki (Washington, DC: CQ Press, 1990), 94.

130. Markus Prior, "The Incumbent in the Living Room: The Rise of Television and the Incumbency Advantage in U.S. House Elections," *Journal's of Politics* 68 (August 2006): 657–673. See also Brian F. Schaffner, "Local News Coverage and the Incumbency Advantage in the U.S. House," *Legislative Studies Quarterly* 31 (November 2006): 491–511.

131. Bob Benenson and Jonathan Allen, "It's Looking Like Blue Skies All Over Again," *CQ Weekly Report*, November 26, 2007, 3541.

132. Fenno, *Home Style*, 99.

CHAPTER 6

1. Quoted in Lauren Fox, "Mitch McConnell: 'The First Thing I Need to Do Is Get the Senate Back to Normal,'" *National Journal's*, November 5, 2014.

2. Quoted in Boyer, "House Rule."

3. Francine Kiefer, "Trent Lott's advice to Mitch McConnell: 'Deal Sternly' with GOP Obstructionists," *Christian Science Monitor*, December 4, 2014.

4. *Wall Street Journal's*, January 30, 1985, 5.

5. The seminal work on the collective action problem is by Mancur Olson, *The Logic of Collective Action, Public Goods, and the Theory of Groups* (Cambridge, MA: Harvard University Press, 1965).

6. Matthew N. Green, *The Speaker of the House: A Study of Leadership* (New Haven, CT: Yale University Press, 2010), 4.

7. Aaron Blake, "John Boehner Just Endured the Biggest Revolt against a House Speaker in More than 100 Years," The Fix, *Washington Post* weblog, January 6, 2016, http://www.washingtonpost.com/blogs/the-fix/wp/2015/01/06/boehner-could-face-biggest-speaker-defection-since-1923/.

8. Michael Teitelbaum, "You're Off to a Great Start, but Can You Keep It Up," *CQ Today*, February 2, 2007, 1.

9. See Graeme Browning, "The Steward," *National Journal's*, August 5, 1995, 2004–2007.

10. For an excellent discussion of this era, see Gregory Koger, *Filibustering: A Political History of Obstruction in the House and Senate* (Chicago: University of Chicago Press, 2010).

11. Quoted in *U.S. News and World Report*, October 13, 1950, 30.

12. See, for example, Barbara Sinclair, *Majority Leadership in the U.S. House* (Baltimore: Johns Hopkins University Press, 1983).

13. Tom Kenworthy, "House GOP Signals It's in a Fighting Mood," *Washington Post*, December 26, 1988, A8.

14. See Barbara Sinclair, *Unorthodox Lawmaking: New Legislative Processes in the U.S. Congress*, 3d ed. (Washington, DC: CQ Press, 2007), Table 6.4, 123.

15. The GOP had wandered in the "wilderness of the minority" for forty years. A. B. Stoddard, "Rejuvenated Gingrich Mounts Media Offensive," *The Hill*, July 10, 1996, 24.

16. Ibid., 165–176.

17. Quoted in Cannon Centenary Conference, *The Changing Nature of the Speakership*, H. Doc. 108–204 (Washington, DC: Government Printing Office, 2004), 62.

18. Ben Pershing, "Smith Spars with Leaders," *Roll Call*, March 26, 2003, 13.

19. Sarah A. Binder, Thomas E. Mann, Norman J. Ornstein, and Molly Reynolds, *Mending the Broken Branch: Assessing the 110th Congress, Anticipating the 111th*, Brookings, January 2009, www.brookings.edu/papers/2009/0108_broken_branch_binder_mann.aspx.

20. Major Garrett, "A Politician's Politician," *National Journal's*, January 7, 2011.

21. Molly K. Hooper, "Boehner to Members: Leadership Is Watching Your Voting Patterns," *The Hill*, December 6, 2012.

22. Jonathan Allen, "The A—hole Factor," *Politico*, December 13, 2012.

23. "Boehner's First Remarks as House Speaker," *New York Times*, January 5, 2011, www.nytimes.com/2011/01/06/us/politics/06cong-text.html?pagewanted=all.

24. Ashley Parker and Jonathan Weisman, "After Deriding GOP on Immigration Bill, Boehner Shifts His Aim to Obama," *New York Times*, April 30, 2014, A16.

25. See, for example, John H. Aldrich and David W. Rohde, "The Transition to Republican Rule in the House: Implications for Theories of Congressional Politics," *Political Science Quarterly* 112 (Winter 1997–1998): 541–567.

26. John H. Aldrich and David Rohde, "The Logic of Conditional Party Government: Revisiting the Electoral Connection," in *Congress Reconsidered*, 7th ed., ed. Lawrence Dodd and Bruce Oppenheimer (Washington, DC: CQ Press, 2001), 275–276.

27. See "The House in Sam Rayburn's Time," in Nelson W. Polsby, *How Congress Evolves: Social Bases of Institutional Change* (New York: Oxford University Press, 2003).

28. See Keith Krehbiel, *Pivotal Politics: A Theory of U.S. Lawmaking* (Chicago: University of Chicago Press, 1998).

29. Randall Strahan, *Leading Representatives: The Agency of Leaders in the Politics of the U.S. House* (Baltimore: Johns Hopkins University Press, 2007), xii.

30. See, for example, Green, *Speaker of the House*; Ronald M. Peters Jr., *The American Speakership: The Office in Historical Perspective*, 2d ed. (Baltimore: Johns Hopkins University Press, 1997); and D. B. Hardeman and Donald C. Bacon, *Rayburn: A Biography* (Austin: Texas Monthly Press, 1987).

31. Quoted in Jonathan Kaplan, "Hastert, DeLay: Political Pros Get Along to Go Along," *The Hill*, July 22, 2003, 8.

32. Eric Cantor, Paul Ryan, and Kevin McCarthy, *Young Guns: A New Generation of Conservative Leaders* (New York: Threshold Editions, 2010).

33. Quoted in Michelle Cottle, "McCarthyism," *New Republic*, October 26, 2010, 17.

34. Sometimes exceptions are made to the general norm that top party leaders do not chair committees. During the 107th Congress (2001–2003), Majority Leader Dick Armey, R-Tex., chaired the Select Committee on Homeland Security, which reported the bill signed into law by President George W. Bush creating the Department of Homeland Security.

35. Christopher Madison, "Message Bearer," *National Journal's*, December 1, 1990, 2906.

36. Floyd M. Riddick, *Congressional Procedure* (Boston: Chapman and Grimes, 1941), 345–346.

37. Philip Rucker and Paul Kane, "No Looking Back for Pelosi in House," *Washington Post*, December 22, 2010, A3.

38. Anna Palmer and John Bresnahan, "Nancy Pelosi the Money Juggernaut," *Politico*, September 9, 2014.

39. Carl Hulse, "Fractured Democrats Keep Pelosi as Leader," *New York Times*, November 18, 2010, A22.

40. Richard E. Cohen, "GOP's Dilemma: Substance Versus Spin," *National Journal's*, March 7, 2009.

41. See Charles O. Jones, *The Minority Party in Congress* (Boston: Little, Brown, 1970), 23.

42. See Frances E. Lee, "Presidents and Party Teams," *Presidential Studies Quarterly* 43, no. 4 (2013): 775–791.

43. Quoted in Jackie Kucinich, "New Whips Work in Tag Team," *Roll Call*, December 6, 2010.

44. Quoted in Jennifer Yachnin, "No 'Sharp Elbows' for Whip Clyburn," *Roll Call,* December 11, 2006, 36. Also see Richard Cohen, "A Different Kind of Whip," *National Journal's,* January 20, 2007, 42–44.

45. Alan K. Ota, "Eye of the Tiger," *CQ Weekly,* September 8, 2014, 1134–1138.

46. Jonathan Kaplan, "New GOP Whip, Roy Blunt Offers Different Style," *The Hill,* November 20, 2002, 4.

47. Michael Doyle, "House GOP's Vote-Getter Off to a Rough Start," McClatchy Washington Bureau, February 11, 2011.

48. Woodrow Wilson, *Congressional Government* (Boston: Houghton Mifflin, 1885), 223.

49. David J. Rothman, *Politics and Power: The United States Senate, 1869–1901* (Cambridge, MA: Harvard University Press, 1966), 5–7.

50. See Gerald Gamm and Steven S. Smith, "Emergence of Senate Leadership: 1833–1946," in *U.S. Senate Exceptionalism,* ed. Bruce I. Oppenheimer (Columbus: Ohio State University Press, 2002), 212–238.

51. Margaret Munk, "Origin and Development of the Party Floor Leadership in the United States Senate," *Capital Studies* 2 (Winter 1974): 23–41; Richard A. Baker and Roger H. Davidson, eds., *First among Equals: Outstanding Senate Leaders of the Twentieth Century* (Washington, DC: Congressional Quarterly, 1991).

52. See Robert Caro, *Master of the Senate* (New York: Random House, 2002).

53. Rowland Evans and Robert Novak, *Lyndon B. Johnson: The Exercise of Power* (New York: New American Library, 1966), 104.

54. See John G. Stewart, "Two Strategies of Leadership: Johnson and Mansfield," in *Congressional Behavior,* ed. Nelson W. Polsby (New York: Random House, 1971), 61–92; William S. White, *Citadel: The Story of the United States Senate* (New York: Harper and Bros., 1956); Joseph S. Clark, *The Senate Establishment* (New York: Hill and Wang, 1963); and Randall B. Ripley, *Power in the Senate* (New York: St. Martin's Press, 1969).

55. *Congressional Record,* 96th Cong., 2d sess., April 18, 1980, S3294.

56. Quoted in Kathleen Hunter, "Zen and the Art of Walking Softly," *CQ Weekly,* June 29, 2009, 1504.

57. See Frances E. Lee, *Beyond Ideology: Politics, Principles, and Partisanship in the U.S. Senate* (Chicago: University of Chicago Press, 2009).

58. Kirk Victor, "Deconstructing Daschle," *National Journal's,* June 1, 2002, 610.

59. Kirk Victor, "Getting to 60," *National Journal's,* January 13, 2007, 37.

60. Quoted in William Welch, "In Reid, Bush Faces a Tenacious Force in the Senate," *USA Today,* December 12, 2006, 13A.

61. Quoted in Carl Hulse and Adam Nagourney, "Senate G.O.P. Leader Finds Weapon in Unity," *New York Times,* March 16, 2010.

62. Kirk Victor, "Short on Surprises," *National Journal's,* October 28, 2006, 37.

63. Quoted in Jill Zuckman, "Dick Durbin's Passion Ignites Foes' Ire," *Chicago Tribune,* June 17, 2005 (online edition).

64. *New York Times,* December 6, 1988, B13.

65. David Truman, *The Congressional Party* (New York: Wiley, 1959).

66. Stephen Jessee and Neil Malholtra, "Are Congressional Leaders Middlepersons or Extremists? Yes." *Legislative Studies Quarterly,* 35 (2010): 361–392.

67. David S. Joachim, "Louisianan Extends His Rapid Rise in the House G.O.P.," *New York Times,* June 19, 2014.

68. David Grant, "Women Step Up in House GOP Leadership. Why That's Just a Start," DC Decoder Wire, *Christian Science Monitor,* November 15, 2012, www.csmonitor.com/USA/DC-Decoder/Decoder-Wire/2012/1115/Women-step-up-in-House-GOP-leadership.-Why-that-s-just-a-start.

69. Sinclair, *Majority Leadership in the U.S. House.*

70. *Congressional Record,* 98th Cong., 1st sess., November 15, 1983, H9856.

71. Quoted in Thomas B. Rosenstiel and Edith Stanley, "For Gingrich, It's 'Mr. Speaker!'" *Los Angeles Times,* November 9, 1994, A2.

72. *Congressional Record,* 94th Cong., 1st sess., January 26, 1973, S2301.

73. Richard E. Cohen, Jake Sherman, and Simmi Aujla, "GOP Taps Freshmen for Prime Spots," *Politico,* December 9, 2010, www.politico.com/news/stories/1210/46216.html.

74. Paul Kane, "Harry Reid Endorses Chuck Schumer to Succeed Him as Senate Democratic Leader," *Washington Post,* March 27, 2015, http://www.washingtonpost.com/blogs/post-politics/wp/2015/03/27/harry-reid-endorses-chuck-schumer-to-succeed-him-as-senate-minority-leader/.

75. S. A. Miller, "Warren Gets Top Democratic Leadership Job," *Washington Times,* November 14, 2014, A1.

76. Matt Canham, "Sen Mike Lee Joins Republican Leadership Team He Has Often Defied," *Salt Lake Tribune,* January 23, 2015, http://www.sltrib.com/news/2026476-155/sen-mike-lee-joins-republican-leadership.

77. Neil MacNeil, *Dirksen: Portrait of a Public Man* (New York: World, 1970), 168–169.

78. Mark Preston, "Daschle May Write Book Chronicling His Times as Leader," *Roll Call Daily Issue,* e-newsletter, May 20, 2002, 3.

79. Sidney Waldman, "Majority Leadership in the House of Representatives," *Political Science Quarterly* 95 (Fall 1980): 377.

80. Patrick Sellers, *Cycles of Spin: Strategic Communication in the U.S. Congress* (New York: Cambridge University Press, 2010).

81. *New York Times,* June 7, 1984, B16.

82. Noelle Straub and Melanie Fonder, "GOP Shifts Strategy for New Minority Status," *The Hill,* July 18, 2001, 6.

83. Ed O'Keefe, "Boehner to Report Record Fundraising Numbers," Post Politics, *Washington Post* weblog, October 15, 2014, http://www.washingtonpost.com/blogs/post-politics/wp/2014/10/15/boehner-to-report-record-fundraising-numbers/.

84. Mark Preston, "Lott Showcases Senators Facing Re-election," *Roll Call,* March 15, 2001, 3.

85. Eric Heberlig, Marc Hetherington, and Bruce Larson, "The Price of Leadership: Campaign Money and the Polarization of Congressional Parties," *Journal's of Politics* 68 (2006): 992–1005. See also Eric Heberlig and Bruce Larson, *Congressional Parties, Institutional Ambition, and the Financing of Majority Control* (Ann Arbor: University of Michigan Press, 2012), esp. 159–196.

86. Stephen Gettinger, "Potential Senate Leaders Flex Money Muscles," *Congressional Quarterly Weekly Report,* October 8, 1988, 2776.

87. Sinclair, *Majority Leadership in the U.S. House,* 96–97.

88. Gail Russell Chaddock, "Two House Health Care Reform Votes," *Christian Science Monitor,* March 20, 2010.

89. House Democrats disbanded their policy committee at Pelosi's direction. In its place, she established a revamped Steering Committee, which has a policy component (headed by George Miller of California) and a committee assignment component (chaired by Rosa DeLauro of Connecticut). See Erin Billings, "Pelosi Revamps the Steering Committee," *Roll Call,* March 13, 2003, 3.

90. Quoted in Fred Barnes, "Raging Representatives," *New Republic,* June 3, 1985, 9.

91. See Logan Dancey and Geoffrey Sheagley, "Heuristics Behaving Badly: Party Cues and Voter Knowledge," *American Journal's of Political Science,* 52, no. 2 (2013): 312–325; and Marc J. Hetherington, "Resurgent Mass Partisanship: The Role of Elite Polarization," *American Political Science Review* 95, no. 3 (2001): 619–631.

92. Jim Hoagland, "The Price of Polarization," *Washington Post,* May 5, 2005, A25.

93. Gail Russell Chaddock, "Obama Wins His Economic Stimulus Package, but without the Bipartisanship He Sought," *Christian Science Monitor,* February 14, 2009.

94. Quoted in Elizabeth Shogren, "Will Welfare Go Way of Health Reform?" *Los Angeles Times,* August 10, 1995, A18.

95. See V. O. Key Jr., *Politics, Parties, and Pressure Groups,* 5th ed. (New York: Crowell, 1964); and Austin Ranney and Willmoore Kendall, *Democracy and the American Party System* (New York: Harcourt Brace, 1956).

96. See Harold W. Stanley and Richard G. Niemi, *Vital Statistics on American Politics, 2007–2008* (Washington, DC: CQ Press, 2007), Tables 1-10 and 1-11.

97. Quoted in Jackie Kucinich and Anna Palmer, "House GOP Bulks Up Outreach Operation," *Roll Call,* January 7, 2009.

98. Quoted in Ben Weyl, "The Tables Have Turned," *CQ Weekly,* November 6, 2014, 7.

99. *Congressional Record,* 104th Cong., 1st sess., October 11, 1995, E1926. Rep. Lee H. Hamilton, D-Ind., who made the comment, strongly opposed the overuse of omnibus bills.

100. Lee H. Hamilton, with Jordan Tama, *A Creative Tension: The Foreign Policy Roles of the President and Congress* (Washington, DC: Woodrow Wilson Center Press, 2002), 33.

101. Quoted in Richard E. Cohen, "Byrd of West Virginia: A New Job, a New Image," *National Journal's,* August 20, 1977, 1294.

102. Quoted in Emma Dumain, "Democrats Irrelevant? Don't Be So Sure, Pelosi Promises," 218, *Roll Call* weblog, December 7, 2014, http://blogs.rollcall.com/218/nancy-pelosi-democrats-irrelevant-just-watch/?dcz=.

103. Peter Sullivan, "Boehner: 'I Have a Few Knuckleheads in My Conference,' Briefing Room, *The Hill* weblog, September 16, 2014, http://thehill.com/blogs/blog-briefing-room/217934-boehner-i-have-a-few-knuckleheads-in-my-conference.

104. Ed O'Keefe, "Boehner Appearing on Leno: GOP Is to Blame for Shutdown," Post Politics, Washington *Post* weblog, January 24, 2014, http://www.washingtonpost.com/blogs/post-politics/wp/2014/01/24/john-boehner-appears-on-the-tonight-show-with-jay-leno/.

CHAPTER 7

1. *Washington Post,* May 14, 1987, A23.

2. *Congressional Record,* 100th Cong., 1st sess., June 25, 1987, H5564.

3. Woodrow Wilson coined the term *little legislatures* in *Congressional Government* (Boston: Houghton Mifflin, 1885), 79.

4. The House has five delegates (American Samoa, District of Columbia, Guam, Northern Mariana Islands, and Virgin Islands) and one resident commissioner (Puerto Rico).

5. Quoted in *New York Times,* July 11, 1988, A14.

6. See, for example, Kenneth A. Shepsle and Barry R. Weingast, "The Institutional Foundations of Committee Power," *American Political Science Review* (March 1987): 85–104.

7. See Keith Krehbiel, *Information and Legislative Organization* (Ann Arbor: University of Michigan Press, 1991); and Bruce Bimber, "Information as a Factor in Congressional Politics," *Legislative Studies Quarterly* (1991): 585–606.

8. John W. Ellwood, "The Great Exception: The Congressional Budget Process in an Age of Decentralization," in *Congress Reconsidered,* 3d ed., ed. Lawrence C. Dodd and Bruce I. Oppenheimer (Washington, DC: CQ Press, 1985), 329. For the classic discussion of committee and member roles, see Richard F. Fenno Jr., *Congressmen in Committees* (Boston: Little, Brown, 1973).

9. Roy Swanstrom, *The United States Senate, 1787–1801,* S. Doc. 87–64, 87th Cong., 1st sess., 1962, 224.

10. Lauros G. McConachie, *Congressional Committees* (New York: Crowell, 1898), 124.

11. DeAlva Stanwood Alexander, *History and Procedure of the House of Representatives* (Boston: Houghton Mifflin, 1916), 228; George H. Haynes, *The Senate of the United States: Its History and Practice,* vol. 1 (Boston: Houghton Mifflin, 1938), 272; Ralph V. Harlow, *The History of Legislative Methods in the Period before 1825* (New Haven, CT: Yale University Press, 1917), 157–158.

12. *Cannon's Procedures in the House of Representatives,* H. Doc. 80–122, 80th Cong., 1st sess., 1959, 83.

13. Quoted in *Wall Street Journal's,* May 3, 1979, 1.

14. Alan K. Ota, "Reid's New Panel Ratios Meet GOP Resistance," *Roll Call,* November 14, 2012, online edition. Sens. Angus King of Maine and Bernie Sanders of Vermont, neither of whom ran as Democrats, are considered Democrats because they caucus with that party.

15. Ibid.

16. Marc Heller, "Reps. Meehan, Noem to Join House Panel; Republicans Gain Slot on Ways and Means," *Daily Report for Executives,* November 24, 2014, 226.

17. Other exceptions to the five-subcommittee limit include Armed Services (seven), Foreign Affairs (seven), Transportation and Infrastructure (six), and Agriculture (six). Various reasons account for these deviations: long-standing custom, acquisition of additional jurisdiction, accommodations of lawmakers, bicameral, and workload concerns.

18. *Congressional Record,* 104th Cong., 1st sess., January 4, 1995, H33.

19. The rules also specify that the chair "shall formalize in writing for the other Republican Members of the Committee the procedures to be followed in selecting Subcommittee Chairmen and individual subcommittee assignments and shall do so in advance of the Committee's organization. The procedures may be modified by a majority vote of the Republican Members of the full Committee."

20. Theo Emery, "Controversial King Denied Top Immigration Slot," *CQ Today,* January 10, 2011, 5.

21. Deb Reichmann, "House Reauthorizes Special Committee Probing Benghazi Attack," *Washington Times,* January 7, 2015, A6. Also see Shawn Zeller, "Probe to Nowhere," *CQ Weekly,* May 19, 2014, 704–712; and Ed O'Keefe, "House GOP Not Finished Investigating Benghazi," *Washington Post,* November 25, 2014, A2.

22. Greg Miller, "Democrats: Benghazi Panel Out of Bounds," *Washington Post,* February 6, 2015, A3. Also see Connor O'Brien, "Benghazi Committee Democrat Says His Party Should Bolt 'Partisan' Panel," *CQ News,* January 15, 2015, online edition; and Jonathan Weisman and Jennifer Steinhauer, "Democrats Wary of Benghazi Inquiry Stretching into '16 Election Season," *New York Times,* August 29, 2014, A14.

23. Keith Krehbiel, Kenneth A. Shepsle, and Barry R. Weingast, "Why Are Congressional Committees Powerful?" *American Political Science Review* 81 (September 1987): 935.

24. Roderick Kiewiet and Mathew McCubbins, *The Logic of Delegation: Congressional Parties and the Appropriations Process* (Chicago: University of Chicago Press, 1991).

25. Humberto Sanchez and Niels Lesniewski, "Spending Panel Loses Its Luster," *Roll Call,* December 21, 2012, 1.

26. Brian Faier, "Appropriations Loses Allure in Tight-Budget Congress," *Washington Examiner,* January 31, 2011, 13.

27. Carl Hulse, "3 Republicans in Race to Lead Appropriations Committee," *New York Times,* December 7, 2010, A5.

28. Tamar Hallerman, "Conservatives' Goal Is a 'Disappropriations' Panel," *Roll Call,* February 3, 2014, 4.

29. Tamar Hallerman, "GOP Names Four Freshmen to Senate Appropriations," *CQ News*, December 15, 2014, online edition.

30. Alex Isenstadt, "The Lucre of Landing a Key Committee," *Politico*, January 19, 2011, 20.

31. David Hawkings, "Take a Seat! The Opaque World of Committee Assignments," *Roll Call*, December 1, 2014, 12.

32. James Bornemeier, "Berman Accepts Seat on House Ethics Panel," *Los Angeles Times*, February 5, 1997, B1; *CQ Daily Monitor*, December 11, 1999, 1. Also see Hannah Hess, "House Ethics: An Isolating Gavel to Hold," *Roll Call*, December 9, 2014, 3.

33. Fenno, *Congressmen in Committees*. Also see Heinz Eulau, "Legislative Committee Assignments," *Legislative Studies Quarterly* (November 1984): 587–633.

34. Christopher J. Deering and Steven S. Smith, *Committees in Congress*, 3d ed. (Washington, DC: CQ Press, 1997), 61–62, 78.

35. Shirley Chisholm, *Unbought and Unbossed* (Boston: Houghton Mifflin, 1970), 84, 86.

36. Daniel Newhauser, "House Republicans Just Picked 21 Committee Chairs. 20 Are Men," *National Journal's Daily*, November 19, 2014, online edition.

37. Quoted in Ethan Wallison, "Freshman Democrats Get Panel Waivers," *Roll Call*, June 21, 1999, 20.

38. Reid Wilson, "McConnell Promises Boozman Ag Seat," *National Journal's Hotline*, July 7, 2010, online edition.

39. Andrew Beadle, "First Lady's Résumé Won't Impress Seniority System," *CQ Daily Monitor*, November 20, 2000, 9.

40. Pelosi and Hoyer's quotes are from Mike Lillis, "Pelosi's Pick Wins Round 1 for Energy Panel," *The Hill*, November 19, 2014, 10.

41. Both quotations in the paragraph are from Lauren French and Anna Palmer, "More House Dems Want Term Limits," *Politico*, January 12, 2015, 14.

42. Katie Glueck and Jonathan Topaz, "Ryan Rules Out 2016 White House Run to Focus on Ways and Means," *Politico*, January 13, 2015, 3.

43. The four who were removed were Justin Amash, Mich., and Tim Huelskamp, Kan., from the Budget Committee; David Schweikert, Ariz., from Financial Services; and Walter Jones, N.C., from Foreign Affairs.

44. Jake Sherman and John Bresnahan, "Boehner Takes Revenge: Foes Find Themselves Losing Plum Committee Posts," *Politico*, January 6, 2015, http://www.politico.com/story/2015/01/boehner-allies-out-for-revenge-114007.html.

45. Jonathan Strong, "Speak Softly or Carry a Big Stick," *CQ Weekly*, January 24, 2013, 63.

46. Paul Gigot, "Mack Uses Knife on Old Senate Order," *Wall Street Journal's*, July 14, 1995, A12.

47. Paul Kane, "Immigration Strategy Infuses GOP Choice for Budget Panel," *Washington Post*, November 27, 2014, A1; Burgess Everett and Seung Min Kim, "Budget Brawl," *Politico*, December 4, 2014, 1; and Jonathan Nicholson, "Sen. Enzi to Head Budget Panel; Sessions to Focus on Welfare, Wasteful Spending," *Daily Report for Executives* December 18, 2014, A-13.

48. Margaret Kriz, "Gavels Turn Green," *National Journal's*, November 18, 2006, 62.

49. Chris Frates, "Trust Fall," *National Journal's*, February 2, 2013, 35.

50. Quoted in *Washington Post*, November 20, 1983, A9.

51. Amy Fagan, "Thomas Takes Reins on Social Security," *Washington Times*, February 6, 2005, A3.

52. Of course, there is no guarantee that GOP control of the House and Senate would produce smooth going. After all, the two chambers are fundamentally unlike in many respects: size, rules, constituency, and so on. See, for example, Paul Kane, "McConnell Quickly Boxed in on Shutdown," *Washington Post*, February 14, 2014, A1.

53. Anna Palmer, "Cummings Bypasses Issa in Fight over Access to Letters," *Roll Call*, January 31, 2011, online edition.

54. Michelle Cottle, "The Media's Best Friend," *National Journal's*, January 24, 2015, 27.

55. See David King, *Turf Wars* (Chicago: University of Chicago Press, 1997).

56. Allison Stevens, "No Ordinary Power Grab: Chairman Complains of 'Bold' Power Grab," *CQ Today,* June 23, 2004, 1, 9.

57. Darren Samuelsohn and Robin Bravender, "GOP Takeover Prompts Committee Turf Wars," *Politico,* November 11, 2010, 21.

58. Rep. Fred Upton, "Don't Dilute Energy and Commerce Clout," *Roll Call,* November 3, 2010, 5.

59. *CQ Today,* December 10, 2010, 10.

60. Quoted in Bob Pool, "Survivors Take Stock of Gains against Cancer," *Los Angeles Times,* May 30, 1997, B1.

61. Ralph Vartabedian, "Senate Panel Is Ready to Take IRS to Task," *Los Angeles Times,* September 22, 1997, A1.

62. "Dodd-Frank" refers to Sen. Christopher Dodd, D-Conn., who chaired the Banking, Housing, and Urban Affairs Committee, and Rep. Barney Frank, D-Mass., who headed the Financial Services Committee. Senator Dodd retired at the end of the 111th Congress. Frank served as the ranking member on Financial Services because of GOP control of the House in the 112th Congress; he retired at the end of that Congress.

63. Darlene Superville, "Congressional Panels Seek 'Real People,'" *Los Angeles Times,* March 25, 2007, online edition.

64. Elizabeth Brotherton, "Webcasting Goes Mainstream among House Committees," *Roll Call,* March 7, 2007, 3.

65. Ashley Halsey III, "On Hill, a Bipartisan Twitter Push for Transportation Bill," *Washington Post,* February 9, 2015, A2.

66. Sean Piccoli, "Hill Samples 'Third Wave,'" *Washington Times,* June 13, 1995, A8.

67. Warren Leary, "When Astronauts Brief Congress, a Little Levity Goes a Long Way," *New York Times,* June 15, 2005, A16.

68. *Congressional Record,* 107th Cong., 2d sess., July 16, 2002, S6849.

69. Quoted in *Washington Post,* November 25, 1985, A4. Also see Richard L. Hall, *Participation in Congress* (New Haven, CT: Yale University Press, 1998).

70. Quoted in "CQ Midday Update Email," December 14, 2004, 1, www.cq.com.

71. Eric Redman, *The Dance of Legislation* (New York: Simon and Schuster, 1973), 140.

72. Hugh Heclo, "Issue Networks in the Executive Establishment," in *The New American Political System,* ed. Anthony King (Washington, DC: American Enterprise Institute, 1978), 87–124. Also see David E. Price, "Policy Making in Congressional Committees: The Impact of 'Environmental Factors,'" *American Political Science Review* (Fall 1978): 548–574.

73. Molly Hopper, "House Judiciary Committee Seeks Bipartisan Touch," *The Hill,* January 18, 2011, 8.

74. Norris Cotton, *In the Senate* (New York: Dodd, Mead, 1978), 65.

75. *Washington Post,* March 20, 1977, E9.

76. David Whiteman, *Communication in Congress: Members, Staff, and the Search for Information* (Lawrence: University Press of Kansas, 1995). A good article on the role of staff is Steven T. Dennis, "Nabors Is the 'Glue' Between WH, Congress," *Roll Call,* May 10, 2012, 1.

77. Siobhan Gorman and Richard Cohen, "Hurtling toward an Intelligence Overhaul," *National Journal's,* September 18, 2004, 2808.

78. Quoted in *Washington Post,* November 20, 1983, A13.

79. Brett Pulley, "Black Clerics Criticize Torricelli on Minority Hiring for His Staff," *New York Times,* March 21, 1997, A25.

80. Josephine Hearn, "House Staffers Follow Bosses' Footsteps on the Campaign Trail," *The Hill,* October 18, 2006, 4.

81. Quoted in Andrew Taylor, "Security Plan Changes Committee Name, Little Else," *CQ Today,* October 8, 2004, 1.

82. Ibid., 4.

83. *Congressional Record,* 109th Cong., 1st sess., January 4, 2005, H25–H26.

84. *CQ Weekly,* December 27, 2010, 2901.

85. Quoted in Roger H. Davidson and Walter J. Oleszek, *Congress against Itself* (Bloomington: Indiana University Press, 1977), 263.

86. E. Scott Adler, *Why Congressional Reforms Fail* (Chicago: University of Chicago Press, 2002), 11.

87. Richard Cohen and Marilyn Serfina, "Taxing Times," *National Journal's,* December 23, 2000, 39–61.

88. Quoted in Peter Kaplan and David Mark, "With Election Day Over, the Campaign Begins in the House," *CQ Daily Monitor,* November 20, 2000, 3.

89. David Firestone, "G.O.P.'s 'Cardinals of Spending' Are Reined In by House Leaders," *New York Times,* December 2, 2002, A16.

90. Alexander Bolton, "House GOP Puts Taylor on Warning," *The Hill,* February 15, 2005, 1.

91. Quoted in Josephine Hearn, "Pelosi Riles Old Guard Chairmen," *Politico,* January 23, 2007, 4.

92. John Boehner, "What the Next Speaker Must Do," *Wall Street Journal's,* November 5, 2010, A19.

93. Derek Willis, "A Do-Nothing Congress? Well, Pretty Close," *New York Times,* May 29, 2014, A3.

94. Lauren French and Jake Sherman, "House GOP Leaders to Subcommittee Chairs: Vote with Us or Step Down," *Politico,* February 13, 2015, online edition.

95. David Drucker and Emily Pierce, "Reid to Baucus: Stop Chasing GOP Votes on Health Care," *Roll Call,* July 7, 2009, online edition.

96. David Nather, "Daschle's Soft Touch Lost in Tough Senate Arena," *CQ Weekly,* July 20, 2002, 1922.

97. *Congressional Record,* January 7, 2015, S28.

98. Sarah Mimms, "Reid Didn't Deliver on His Promises. Will McConnell?" *National Journal's Daily,* January 4, 2015, online edition.

99. Alexander Bolton, "McConnell Grabs the Wheel in the Senate," *The Hill,* January 6, 2015, 6.

100. Susan Davis, "Pelosi, Boehner Name Eight Members to Ethics Task Force," *Roll Call,* February 1, 2007, 3.

101. Jonathan Weisman, "House Creates New Panel on Ethics," *Washington Post,* March 12, 2008, A1.

102. Alan Ota, "Republicans Look for Input from House High-Tech Team," *CQ Today,* January 25, 2011, 1.

103. *National Journal's CongressDaily AM,* January 30, 2007, 15.

104. Both quotations in this paragraph are from Ronald Brownstein, "Gangmen Style," *National Journal's,* May 11, 2013, 9.

105. Meredith Shiner, "'Gang of Eight' Takes on Gang of 'No,'" *Roll Call,* June 12, 2013, 8.

106. The information in this paragraph is largely from Emma Dumian, "Diaz-Balart and the Art of an Immigration Deal Undone," *Roll Call,* January 14, 2015, 1.

107. *Congressional Record,* 108th Cong., 2d sess., February 14, 2004, S1496.

108. Nather, "Daschle's Soft Touch Lost."

109. Paul Kane, "Committee Chairs Seek to Reassert Power in Congress," *Washington Post,* February 17, 2013, A4.

110. *Committee Structure,* Hearings before the Joint Committee on the Organization of Congress (Washington, DC: Government Printing Office, 1993), 779.

111. Curt Suplee, "The Science Chairman's Unpredictable Approach," *Washington Post,* October 15, 1991, A21.

CHAPTER 8

1. *Constitution, Jefferson's Manual, and Rules of the House of Representatives,* H. Doc. 111–157, 111th Cong., 2011, 129. The rules of the Senate are contained in *Senate Manual,* S. Doc. 107–1, 107th Cong., 2002.

2. Donald R. Matthews, *U.S. Senators and Their World* (Chapel Hill: University of North Carolina Press, 1960), chap. 5.

3. *Congressional Record*, January 16, 2014, S385.

4. *Congressional Record*, January 5, 2011, H21.

5. See Barry C. Burden, *Personal Roots of Representation* (Princeton, NJ: Princeton University Press, 2007).

6. Quoted in John Solomon, "Family Crisis Shifts Politics," *USA Today*, August 16, 2001, 15A.

7. Deborah Sontag, "When Politics Is Personal," *New York Times Magazine*, September 15, 2002, 92.

8. Matt Fuller, "Members Offer Rare Display of Emotion with ABLE Act," *Roll Call*, December 4, 2014; see http://blogs.rollcall.com/218/disability. ABLE stands for "Achieving a Better Life Experience." It allows individuals with disabilities to create tax-exempt savings accounts that will allow them to prepare for future financial needs.

9. *National Journal's*, April 10, 1982, 632.

10. Reid Wilson, "Partisan Roles Don't Keep Van Hollen, Sessions from Reaching across the Aisle," *The Hill*, March 12, 2009, 3.

11. Quoted in Julie Rovner, "Senate Committee Approves Health Warnings on Alcohol," *Congressional Quarterly Weekly Report*, May 24, 1986, 1175.

12. Woodrow Wilson, *Congressional Government* (Boston: Houghton Mifflin, 1885), 320.

13. Theodore Sorensen, *Kennedy* (New York: Harper and Row, 1965), 184.

14. *Wall Street Journal's*, June 2, 1988, 56.

15. David A. Fahrenthold, "Rep. Andrews, Leaving with No Laws, Cites Successes," *Washington Post*, February 5, 2014, A6.

16. *Congressional Record*, 95th Cong., 1st sess., May 17, 1977, E3076.

17. Richard Simon, "Congress Turns Bill Titles into Acts of Exaggeration," *Los Angeles Times*, June 19, 2011, online edition.

18. Ibid.

19. For information on the drafting process, see Lawrence E. Filson, *The Legislative Drafter's Desk Reference* (Washington, DC: Congressional Quarterly, 1992).

20. *CQ Monitor*, July 24, 1998, 5.

21. Lawrence J. Haas, "Unauthorized Action," *National Journal's*, January 2, 1988, 20.

22. See Peter Hanson, *Too Weak to Govern: Majority Party Power and Appropriations in the U.S. Senate* (New York: Cambridge University Press), 2014.

23. Stacy Kaper, "Bob Corker Charts Leadership Course," *National Journal's Daily*, April 13, 2013, 5.

24. T. R. Reid, *Congressional Odyssey: The Saga of a Senate Bill* (San Francisco: W. H. Freeman, 1980), 17.

25. Paul Singer, "More Bills, More Lawyers for Leg. Offices," *Roll Call*, March 28, 2007, 22.

26. Carroll J. Doherty, "Lots of Inertia, Little Lawmaking as Election '98 Approaches," *CQ Weekly*, July 18, 1998, 1925.

27. Quoted in Margaret Kriz, "Still Charging," *National Journal's*, December 6, 1997, 2462.

28. Christopher M. Davis, "How Legislation Is Brought to the House Floor: A Snapshot of Parliamentary Practice in the 113th Congress (2013–2014)," Congressional Research Service Report, February 13, 2015, 4.

29. Martin Gold et al., *The Book on Congress* (Washington, DC: Big Eagle Publishing, 1992), 124.

30. Donald R. Wolfensberger, "Suspended Partisanship in the House: How Most Laws Are Really Made" (paper prepared for the annual meeting of the American Political Science Association, Boston, August 29–September 1, 2002), 11.

31. *Congressional Record*, 112th Cong., 1st sess., January 5, 2011, H29.

32. Davis, "How Legislation Is Brought to the House Floor," 6.

33. Privileged business under House rules includes such items as committee assignment resolutions, adjournment resolutions, or "rules" from the Rules Committee.

34. Quoted in Jonathan Salant, "Under Open Rules, Discord Rules," *Congressional Quarterly Weekly Report,* January 28, 1995, 277.

35. *National Journal's,* January 21, 1995, 183.

36. Lizette Alvarez, "Campaign Finance Measure Soundly Rejected by House," *New York Times,* June 18, 1998, A26.

37. "Switched Votes for Gas Bill," *Congressional Quarterly Weekly Report,* February 14, 1976, 313.

38. Mary Lynn F. Jones, "The Republican Railroad," *American Prospect,* April 2003, 16.

39. *Congressional Record,* 110th Cong., 1st sess., March 20, 2007, H2682.

40. *Congressional Record,* 112th Cong., 1st sess., January 5, 2011, H5.

41. Ibid., January 15, 2011, H805.

42. *Survey of Activities of the House Committee on Rules for the 113th Congress,* House Report 113-726, January 2, 2015 (Washington, DC: U.S. Government Printing Office, 2015), 106. 110.

43. Molly Hooper, "Leaders Push Back on Farm Bill Vote," *The Hill,* September 19, 2012, 8.

44. Lindsay Sobel, "Democrats Weigh Discharge Petition Barrage," *The Hill,* July 1, 1998, 2.

45. Alexander Bolton, "House Leaders Tighten Grip, Anger Centrists," *The Hill,* January 15, 2003, 23.

46. Information courtesy of Richard Beth, specialist in legislative process, Congressional Research Service, Library of Congress.

47. *National Journal's CongressDaily PM,* January 13, 1995, 4.

48. Robert S. Walker, "Why House Republicans Need a Watchdog," *Roll Call,* January 19, 1987, 10.

49. John F. Bibby, ed., *Congress Off the Record* (Washington, DC: American Enterprise Institute, 1983), 2.

50. *Congressional Record,* 111th Cong., 2d sess., May 20, 2010, H3683.

51. Sen. J. Bennett Johnston, D-La. (1972–1997), quoted in *New York Times,* November 22, 1985, B8.

52. Quoted in "Democrats to Forgo Control in Brief Edge," *Washington Times,* November 29, 2000, A4.

53. *Congressional Record,* 101st Cong., 2d sess., July 20, 1990, S10183.

54. Susan F. Rasky, "With Few Bills Passed or Ready for Action, Congress Seems Sluggish," *New York Times,* May 14, 1989, 24.

55. *Congressional Record,* 98th Cong., 2d sess., January 27, 1984, S328–S329.

56. Walter J. Oleszek, *Congressional Procedures and the Policy Process,* 9th ed. (Washington, DC: CQ Press, 2014), 319–325. Also see Lewis A. Froman Jr., *The Congressional Process* (Boston: Little, Brown, 1967); and Terry Sullivan, *Procedural Structure: Success and Influence in Congress* (New York: Praeger, 1984).

57. *Congressional Record,* 111th Cong., 2d sess., September 21, 2010, S7251.

58. Elizabeth Drew, *Senator* (New York: Simon and Schuster, 1979), 158.

59. *Congressional Record,* 97th Cong., 2d sess., May 20, 1982, S5648.

60. Mary Dalrymple, "Democrats Say They Are Unified in Opposition Platform," *CQ Today,* January 29, 2002, 5.

61. Christopher M. Davis, "Filling the Amendment Tree in the Senate," *CRS Report RS22854,* February 2, 2011, 2.

62. *Congressional Record,* January 22, 2015, S405.

63. Ross K. Baker, "Beware the Bipartisan Spring," *USA Today,* April 24, 2015, online edition. Also see Michael Barone, "Bipartisanship Is Busting Out All Over," WashingtonExaminer.com, April 27, 2015, 16.

64. *Congressional Record,* 107th Cong., 2d sess., April 17, 2002, S2850.

65. Gail Russell Chaddock, "Limits on Filibusters Are Already Pervasive," *Christian Science Monitor,* May 24, 2005, 2.

66. See comments by Alan Cranston of California, then Senate Democratic whip, in *New York Times,* July 17, 1986, A3.

67. David Herszenhorn, "Thrust and Parry on the Senate Floor," *New York Times*, November 22, 2009, E3.

68. U.S. Congress, *Operations of the Congress: Testimony of House and Senate Leaders,* hearing before the Joint Committee on the Organization of Congress (Washington, DC: Government Printing Office, 1993), 50.

69. Doug Obey, "Alaska," *The Hill,* July 10, 1996, 27.

70. Sixteen additional cloture motions were filed but not voted upon. Two of the sixteen, however, were agreed to by unanimous consent. Information for the 109th Congress compiled by the U.S. Senate Library.

71. Data compiled by the Senate Library.

72. *Congressional Record,* 111th Cong., 2d sess., September 15, 2010, S7120.

73. *Congressional Record,* 112th Cong., 1st sess., January 27, 2011, S322.

74. Steven S. Smith, *The Senate Syndrome* (Norman, OK: University of Oklahoma Press, 2014), 265.

75. Valerie Heitshusen, "Majority Cloture for Nominations: Implications and the 'Nuclear' Option," Congressional Research Service Report, R43331, 5. For the procedural details associated with establishment of the new precedent, see *Congressional Record*, November 21, 2013, S8416-S8418.

76. *Congressional Record*, November 21, 2013, S8420.

77. Shawn Zeller, "Rule Here To Stay?" *CQ Weekly*, October 13, 2014, 1286.

78. See Barbara Sinclair, "Ping Pong and Other Congressional Pursuits: Party Leaders and Post-Passage Procedural Choice," in Jacob Strauss, ed., *Party and Procedure in the United States Congress* (Lanham, MD: Rowman and Littlefield, 2012), 231–252.

79. Jonathan Allen and John Cochran, "The Might of the Right," *CQ Weekly,* November 8, 2003, 2762.

80. Randall B. Ripley, *Power in the Senate* (New York: St. Martin's Press, 1969), 128.

81. Barbara Sinclair, *Unorthodox Lawmaking: New Legislative Processes in the U.S. Congress*, 4th ed. (Washington, DC: CQ Press, 2012).

82. Barber B. Conable, "Weaving Webs: Lobbying by Charities," *Tax Notes,* November 10, 1975, 27–28.

CHAPTER 9

1. Justin Sink, "Obama Signs Short-Term Funding Measure," *The Hill*, December 12, 2014, http://thehill.com/policy/finance/226912-obama-signs-short-term-funding-measure.

2. Gail Collins, "Dinner Party Political Primer," *New York Times* December 12, 2014, p. A19.

3. "Pelosi: Members 'Blackmailed' on 'Cromnibus,'" *Roll Call*, http://www.rollcall.com/multimedia/-238656-1.html.

4. Ed O'Keefe, "House Passes $1.1 Trillion Spending Bill," *Washington Post*, December 11, 2014, http://www.washingtonpost.com/politics/house-poised-to-narrowly-approve-101-trillion-spending-bill/2014/12/11/820d8974-8147-11e4-81fd-8c4814dfa9d7_story.html.

5. Scott Wong, Justin Sink, and Mike Lillis, "How the $1.1 Trillion Funding Bill Survived," *The Hill*, December 12, 2104, http://thehill.com/homenews/house/226995-how-the-house-approved-the-11-trillion-government-funding-bill.

6. Ashley Parker and Robert Pear, "Ending Days of Chaos at the Capitol, Senate Passes $1.1 Trillion Spending Bill," *New York Times*, December 14, 2014, p. A28.

7. Humberto Sanchez and Niels Lesniewski, "Senate Avoids Shutdown, Passes Cromnibus in Bipartisan Vote," *Roll Call*, December 13, 2014, http://blogs.rollcall.com/wgdb/senate-schedule-shutdown-possible/?dcz=.

8. Rebecca Shabad, "Obama Backs 'Cromnibus' ahead of Vote," *The Hill*, December 11, 2014, http://thehill.com/policy/finance/226817-white-house-signals-support-for-cromnibus-ahead-of-critical-vote.

9. Richard L. Hall, *Participation in Congress* (New Haven, CT: Yale University Press, 1998), 27–30.

10. Amanda H. Allen and Stacy Goers, "Obscure Caucus: The Quiet Men of Congress," September 6, 2013. The listing omits senators: "Senators are by definition not obscure, although there are several who seem to strive for it." To be listed in the Obscure Caucus, House members must have served at least two full terms.

11. See Craig Volden and Alan E. Wiseman, *Legislative Effectiveness in the United States Congress* (Cambridge, UK: Cambridge University Press, 2014).

12. Quoted in *The Hill*, November 15, 2000, 16.

13. David Price, *Who Makes the Laws?* (Cambridge, MA: Schenkman Publishing, 1972), 297; David E. Price, *The Congressional Experience*, 3d ed. (Boulder, CO: Westview Press, 2004), chap. 6.

14. Quoted in Bernard Asbell, *The Senate Nobody Knows* (Garden City, NY: Doubleday, 1978), 210.

15. Richard F. Fenno Jr., "Observation, Context, and Sequence in the Study of Politics," *American Political Science Review* 80 (March 1976): 3–15.

16. Lindsay Sobel, "Early Fast-Track Support Cost Members Leverage," *The Hill*, November 12, 1997, 33.

17. Matthew Daly, "Indians Benefited in 111th Congress," *Washington Times*, December 30, 2010, A4.

18. Cited in Philippe Shepnick, "Moynihan Is Champion Bill Writer," *The Hill*, March 10, 1999, 6.

19. These data are from the 109th Congress (2005–2006) and were calculated by Laurel Harbridge. For a valuable analysis of cosponsorship dynamics in recent decades see Harbridge, *Is Bipartisanship Dead? Policy Agreement and Agenda-Setting in the House of Representatives* (New York: Cambridge University Press, 2015).

20. Jacob R. Straus, "Dear Colleague Letters in the House of Representatives: The Tracking of Internal House Communications" (paper presented at the annual meeting of the Midwest Political Science Association, Chicago, April 2–5, 2009), fig. 1.

21. T. R. Reid, *Congressional Odyssey: The Saga of a Senate Bill* (San Francisco: W. H. Freeman, 1980), 15.

22. Hall, *Participation in Congress*, 139; also see 119.

23. Ibid., 126–127.

24. Ibid., 102.

25. Gary Mucchiaroni and Paul J. Quirk, *Deliberative Choices: Debating Public Policy in Congress* (Chicago: University of Chicago Press, 2006), 197.

26. "Final Word," NationalJournal.com, June 5, 2012, 4.

27. *Congressional Record*, August 2, 2012, H5660, H5662.

28. *Congressional Record*, 103d Cong., 1st sess., June 23, 1993, H3941–H3973.

29. John D. Wilkerson, "'Killer' Amendments in Congress," *American Political Science Review* 93 (September 1999): 535–552. See also Charles J. Finocchiaro and Jeffery A. Jenkins, "In Search of Killer Amendments in the Modern U.S. House," *Legislative Studies Quarterly* 33, no. 2 (2008): 263–294, which identifies five successful killer amendments in the House from 1953 to 2004.

30. Quoted in Peter Gosselin, "Paulson Will Have No Peer under Bailout Deal," *Los Angeles Times*, September 29, 2008, online edition.

31. Dave Cook, "'Brutal Vote' Ahead on Whether to Raise the National Debt Ceiling," *Christian Science Monitor*, November 19, 2010, online edition.

32. 2013 *CQ Almanac*, "Voting Participation History," B-27.

33. Niels Lesniewski and Stacey Skotzko, "Members Go to Great Lengths for Voting Stats," *Roll Call*, July 16, 2012, 5.

34. Dan Friedman, "A Rare 'Present' Vote for Schumer," NationalJournal.com, July 16, 2012.
35. John B. Gilmour, *Strategic Disagreement: Stalemate in American Politics* (Pittsburgh: University of Pittsburgh Press, 1995), 41.
36. Quoted in Ramesh Ponnuru, "Division on the Right," *National Review,* November 21, 2003.
37. David C. King and Richard J. Zeckhauser, "Congressional Vote Options," *Legislative Studies Quarterly* 28 (August 2003): 400–401.
38. Quoted in Eric Schmitt, "House Votes to Bar Religious Abuse Abroad," *New York Times,* May 15, 1998, A1.
39. Albert R. Hunt, "Balanced-Budget Measure Is Likely to Pass Senate Next Week, Faces Battle in House," *Wall Street Journal's,* July 30, 1982, 2.
40. Ben Weyl, "2013 Vote Studies: Party Unity," *CQ Weekly*, February 3, 2014, 183.
41. Ibid.
42. Ibid.
43. Ibid.
44. Shankar Vedantam, "My Team vs. Your Team: The Political Arena Lives Up to Its Name," *Washington Post,* September 29, 2008, A6.
45. For an extended analysis of partisan interests as a source of party cohesion and conflict, see Frances E. Lee, *Beyond Ideology: Politics, Principles, and Partisanship in the U.S. Senate* (Chicago: University of Chicago Press, 2009).
46. Gary C. Jacobson, *The Politics of Congressional Elections,* 7th ed. (New York: Pearson Longman, 2009), 135–144.
47. John Breaux, "Congress's Lost Art of Compromise," *Roll Call,* April 19, 2005, 17.
48. Quoted in ibid.
49. Gary W. Cox and Mathew D. McCubbins, *Setting the Agenda: Responsible Party Government in the U.S. House of Representatives* (New York: Cambridge University Press, 2005), 18.
50. See John W. Kingdon, *Congressmen's Voting Decisions* (New York: Harper and Row, 1981); and Randall B. Ripley, *Party Leaders in the House of Representatives* (Washington, DC: Brookings, 1967), 139–159.
51. Donald R. Matthews and James A. Stimson, *Yeas and Nays: Normal Decisionmaking in the U.S. House of Representatives* (New York: John Wiley, 1975), 95.
52. Quoted in Morton Kondracke, "Who's Running the House? GOP Freshmen or Newt?" *Roll Call,* December 18, 1995, 5.
53. See Gary W. Cox and Mathew D. McCubbins, *Legislative Leviathan: Party Government in the House* (Berkeley: University of California Press, 1993); Gary W. Cox and Keith T. Poole, "On Measuring Partisanship in Roll-Call Voting: The U.S. House of Representatives, 1877–1999," *American Journal's of Political Science* 46, no. 3 (2002): 477–489; and Sean M. Theriault, *Party Polarization in Congress* (New York: Cambridge University Press, 2008).
54. *Congressional Record,* 100th Cong., 1st sess., June 23, 1987, S8438.
55. David Fahrenthold, "In Political Gamble, Reid Holds Senate Votes He Knows He'll Lose," *Washington Post,* December 9, 2010, A3.
56. Helmut Norpoth, "Explaining Party Cohesion in Congress: The Case of Shared Policy Attitudes," *American Political Science Review* 70 (December 1976): 1171.
57. Major Garrett, "The $100 Billion Cave," *National Journal's,* February 19, 2011, 48.
58. Robert Costa, David Fahrenthold, and Sean Sullivan, "Boehner Survives Leadership Challenge from Conservative Members," *Washington Post,* January 6, 2015.
59. Seung Min Kim, "New Democrats Try to Redefine 'Moderate,'" *Politico,* May 11, 2012, 15.
60. For discussion of the "creative class," see Richard Florida, "The Rise of the Creative Class," *Washington Monthly,* May 2002. For extended treatment of these different sources of electoral support for the Democratic Party, see John B. Judis and Ruy Teixeira, *The Emerging Democratic Majority* (New York: Simon and Schuster, 2004).

61. John F. Manley, "The Conservative Coalition in Congress," *American Behavioral Scientist* 17 (December 1973): 223–247; Barbara Sinclair, *Congressional Realignment: 1925–1978* (Austin: University of Texas Press, 1982); and Mack C. Shelley, *The Permanent Majority: The Conservative Coalition in the United States Congress* (Tuscaloosa: University of Alabama Press, 1983).

62. See, for example, William A. Galston, "Can a Polarized American Party System Be 'Healthy'?" *Issues in Governance Studies* (Brookings), April 20, 2010, 1; and Thomas E. Mann and Norman J. Ornstein, *It's Even Worse Than It Looks: How the American Constitutional System Collided with the New Politics of Extremism* (New York: Basic Books, 2012), 51–58.

63. Stephen Gettinger, "R.I.P. to a Conservative Force," *CQ Weekly,* January 9, 1999, 82–83.

64. Sarah A. Binder, "The Disappearing Political Center," *Brookings Review* 15 (Fall 1996): 36–39. An extended analysis of the problem and its results is found in Sarah A. Binder, *Stalemate: Causes and Consequences of Legislative Gridlock* (Washington, DC: Brookings, 2003).

65. Keith T. Poole and Howard Rosenthal, "Patterns of Congressional Voting," *American Journal's of Political Science* 35 (February 1991): 228–278; Keith T. Poole and Howard Rosenthal, *Congress: A Political-Economic History of Roll-Call Voting* (New York: Oxford University Press, 1997). See Norman J. Ornstein, Thomas E. Mann, and Michael J. Malbin, *Vital Statistics on Congress, 2008* (Washington, DC: Brookings, 2008), 160–161.

66. Using different measures of similar data, the same point is made in Morris P. Fiorina, with Samuel J. Adams and Jeremy C. Pope, *Culture War? The Myth of a Polarized America,* 2d ed. (New York: Pearson Longman, 2006), 16–21, and fig. 2-2.

67. Sean M. Theriault, "The Case of the Vanishing Moderates: Party Polarization in the Modern Congress" (paper presented at the 2003 annual meeting of the Western Political Science Association, Denver), fig. 1. Ideology scores from similar years (1969–1970 and 1999–2000) yield virtually the same results. Binder, *Stalemate,* 23–26.

68. Quoted by E. J. Dionne Jr., "The Real Pelosi," *Washington Post,* April 9, 2009, A17.

69. Binder, "Disappearing Political Center," 37. Binder defines centrists as those members who are closer to the ideological midpoint between the two parties than to the ideological center of their own party.

70. These estimates are based on Professor Keith Poole's DW-NOMINATE scores for senators and House members provided on his website, http://voteview.com/dwnomin.htm.

71. The South includes the eleven states of the Confederacy.

72. David W. Rohde, "Electoral Forces," in *Parties and Leaders in the Postreform House* (Chicago: University of Chicago Press, 1991), esp. 34–40.

73. Jeffrey M. Stonecash, Mark D. Brewer, and Mack Mariani, *Diverging Parties* (Boulder, CO: Westview Press, 2002).

74. David Wasserman, "The Bittersweet Mosaic," *National Journal's,* April 14, 2012, 27.

75. Ibid., 30. Also see Naftali Bendavid, "Southern White Democrats Face End of Era in Congress," *Wall Street Journal's,* August 9, 2012, A1; and Ed O'Keefe, "White Democratic Congressmen in the South Are Becoming an Endangered Species," *Washington Post,* September 7, 2012, A9.

76. See Sunlight Foundation, OpenCongress, "Voting with Party," https://www.opencongress.org/people/votes_with_party, accessed February 23, 2015.

77. Ibid.

78. R. Douglas Arnold, *The Logic of Congressional Action* (New Haven, CT: Yale University Press, 1990).

79. Ibid., 68.

80. Ibid., 84.

81. It is worth noting that recent presidents have taken stands on fewer issues. See Ornstein, Mann, and Malbin, *Vital Statistics on Congress, 2008,* 144–145.

82. Joseph Schatz, "Legislative Success, Political Peril," *CQ Weekly,* January 3, 2011 19.

83. Shawn Zeller, "Victory from Defeat," *CQ Weekly,* January 21, 2013, 120.

84. John W. Kingdon, *Congressmen's Voting Decisions,* 3d ed. (Ann Arbor: University of Michigan Press, 1989).

85. Quoted in John F. Bibby, ed., *Congress Off the Record* (Washington, DC: American Enterprise Institute, 1983), 22.

86. Roger H. Davidson, *The Role of the Congressman* (Indianapolis: Bobbs-Merrill, 1969), 22–23.

87. Robert L. Peabody, "Organization Theory and Legislative Behavior: Bargaining, Hierarchy, and Change in the U.S. House of Representatives" (paper presented at the 1963 annual meeting of the American Political Science Association, New York).

88. Carl J. Friedrich, *Constitutional Government and Democracy,* 4th ed. (Waltham, MA: Blaisdell Publishing, 1967), 269–270.

89. Quoted in Claudia Dreifus, "Exit Reasonable Right," *New York Times Magazine,* June 2, 1996, 26.

90. It is worth noting that a fall 2010 poll found that nearly "half of America—including nearly two-thirds of Republicans and 53 percent of independents—admires political leaders who refuse to compromise." But governing means bargaining. If half of Americans "admire political leaders who stick to their positions without compromising," then they are endorsing a formula for policy gridlock and polarized partisanship. Major Garrett, "Poll: Americans Want Their Leaders to Stand and Fight," *National Journal's CongressDaily AM,* September 21, 2010, 1.

91. Meredith Shiner, "The Speaker of the Unruly," *CQ Weekly,* September 10, 2012, 1834.

92. Edward J. Derwinski, "The Art of Negotiation within the Congress," in *International Negotiation: Art and Science,* ed. Diane B. Bendahmane and John W. McDonald Jr. (Washington, DC: U.S. Department of State, Foreign Service Institute, 1984), 11.

93. Elliott Abrams, "Unforgettable Scoop Jackson," *Reader's Digest,* February 1985. Quotation cited in *Congressional Record,* 99th Cong., 1st sess., February 20, 1985, E478.

94. Quoted in David E. Rosenbaum, "The Favors of Rostenkowski: Tax Revision's Quid Pro Quo," *New York Times,* November 27, 1985, B6.

95. Quoted in John Sawyer, "Prescription Drug Vote Came Down to Emerson, Push for Reimportation; Missouri Republican Believes Measure Could Save Billions in Drug Costs," *St. Louis Post-Dispatch,* June 29, 2003, A5.

96. Ibid.

97. Lynn Sweet, "House OKs Foreign Drug Imports," *Chicago Sun-Times,* July 26, 2003, 3.

98. Quotes from Jonathan Allen, "Effective House Leadership Makes the Most of Majority," *CQ Weekly,* March 29, 2003, 751.

99. See, for example, Chris Frates, "Payoffs for States Get Reid to 60," *Politico,* December 19, 2010, online edition.

100. Gilmour, *Strategic Disagreement,* 4.

101. Gary W. Cox and Jonathan N. Katz, "Gerrymandering Roll Calls in Congress, 1879–2000," *American Journal's of Political Science* 51 (January 2007): 117.

102. See William H. Riker, *The Theory of Political Coalitions* (New Haven, CT: Yale University Press, 1962), 32. Theorists define legislative bargaining situations formally as *n*-person, zero-sum games in which side payments are permitted—that is, a sizable number of participants are involved; when some participants win, others must lose; and participants can trade items outside the substantive issues under consideration.

103. John G. Stewart, "Two Strategies of Leadership: Johnson and Mansfield," in *Congressional Behavior,* ed. Nelson W. Polsby (New York: Random House, 1971), 67.

104. Russell Hardin, "Hollow Victory: The Minimum Winning Coalition," *American Political Science Review* 79 (December 1976): 1202–1214.

105. Breaux, "Congress's Lost Art of Compromise," 17.

106. Binder, *Stalemate,* 127.

107. Robert J. Dole, quoting Dirksen, in remarks to the Senate, March 29, 2000. Dole quoted in *The Hill,* April 5, 2000, 32.

108. Clinton T. Brass, "Shutdown of the Federal Government: Causes, Processes, and Effects," Congressional Research Service Report RL34680, September 27, 2011. Note that "funding gaps" occur when there is a lag between the expiration of a continuing resolution (CR) and the enactment of a new one. In the absence of a CR, agencies begin their shutdown, even if it is only for a few days. For further information about funding gaps, see Jessica Tollestrup, "Federal Funding Gaps: A Brief Overview," Congressional Research Service Report RS20348, January 19, 2012. A summary of the controversial 1995–1996 shutdowns can be found in the *Congressional Quarterly Almanac, 1995* (Washington, DC: Congressional Quarterly, 1996), 11-3–11-6.

CHAPTER 10

1. Dave Boyer, "Obama's Year-End Low Polls a Gift Horse for Republicans," *Washington Times*, December 19, 2014, A1.

2. Peter Baker, "A Bold Call to Action, Even if No Action Is Likely," *New York Times*, January 21, 2015, A1.

3. *Congressional Record*, December 12, 2014, S6764.

4. Emma Roller, "A Portrait of Two Presidents, Reconciling Their Political Struggles," *National Journal's Daily*, November 10, 2014, online edition.

5. Karen Tumulty and Juliet Eilperin, "On a Host of Issues, Obama Opts to Fight Rather Than Retreat," *Washington Post*, November 14, 2014, A4.

6. *Congressional Record*, January 7, 2015, S41.

7. Ibid., January 8, 2015, H118.

8. Jeremy W. Peters and Emmarie Huetteman, "Republicans Have One Word for President's Proposals and Veto Threats: 'No," *New York Times*, January 21, 2015, A15.

9. Ruth Marcus, "A Moderates' Revolt?" *Washington Post*, January 25, 2015, A23.

10. Gerald F. Seib, "Will Obama, Republicans Find a Way to Work?" *Wall Street Journal's*, November 5, 2014, A8.

11. Len Bracken, "Hatch Pledges to Move Quickly on TPA; Hoyer, Pelosi Seek Assurances on TPP," *Daily Report for Executives*, January 21, 2015, A-19.

12. Carol E. Lee, "Obama Pivots to Lawmakers," *Wall Street Journal's*, January 2, 2015, A1.

13. Quoted in Michael Memoli, "Mitch McConnell's Remarks on 2012 Draw White House Ire," *Los Angeles Times*, October 27, 2012, online edition.

14. Juliet Eilperin and David Nakamura, "What Went Wrong for President Obama?" *Washington Post*, November 4, 2014, A7.

15. For detail on this episode, see Bob Woodward, *The Price of Politics* (New York: Simon and Schuster, 2012).

16. Rosalind S. Helderman, "Outgoing Congress Remains Unproductive to the End," *Washington Post*, December 30, 2012, A11.

17. See Stephen Wayne, *The Legislative Presidency* (New York: Harper and Row, 1978).

18. Charles O. Jones, *Separate but Equal Branches: Congress and the Presidency* (Chatham, NJ: Chatham House, 1995), 138–157.

19. See Norman J. Ornstein, "Theories of the Presidency," in *Encyclopedia of the American Presidency,* vol. 4, ed. Leonard Levy and Louis Fisher (New York: Simon and Schuster, 1994), 1458–1462.

20. Richard E. Neustadt, *Presidential Power* (New York: John Wiley, 1960), 23.

21. Ibid., 16.

22. Leonard D. White, *The Federalists* (New York: Macmillan, 1948), 55.

23. Leonard D. White, *The Jeffersonians* (New York: Macmillan, 1951), 35.

24. Paul C. Light, *The President's Agenda* (Baltimore: Johns Hopkins University Press, 1982), 230–231.

25. John A. Farrell, *Tip O'Neill and the Democratic Century* (Boston: Little, Brown, 2001), 553.

26. Karen Tumulty, "Obama Looks to Last Two Years of Presidency with Resolve," *Washington Post*, November 6, 2014, A13.

27. Juliet Eilperin, "Obama Reaches Out to His Party," *Washington Post*, December 4, 2014, A6.

28. Lyndon B. Johnson, *The Vantage Point* (New York: Popular Library, 1971), 448.

29. Jack Valenti, "Some Advice on the Care and Feeding of Congressional Egos," *Los Angeles Times*, April 23, 1978, 3.

30. See, e.g., Carl Hulse, Jeremy Peters, and Michael Shear, "Obama Is Seen as Frustrating His Own Party," *New York Times*, August 18, 2014, http://www.nytimes.com/2014/08/19/us/aloof-obama-is-frustrating-his-own-party.html.

31. Richard Berke, "Courting Congress Nonstop, Clinton Looks for an Alliance," *New York Times*, March 8, 1993, A1.

32. Roy P. Basler, ed., *The Collected Works of Abraham Lincoln*, vol. 3 (New Brunswick: Rutgers University Press, 1953), 27.

33. Samuel Kernell, *Going Public: New Strategies of Presidential Leadership*, 3d ed. (Washington, DC: CQ Press, 1997), 2. Also see James Ceaser et al., "The Rise of the Rhetorical Presidency," *Presidential Studies Quarterly* 21 (Spring 1981): 158–171.

34. Richard M. Pious, *The American Presidency* (New York: Basic Books, 1979), 194. Also see George C. Edwards III, *The Public Presidency* (New York: St. Martin's Press, 1983).

35. George C. Edwards III, *On Deaf Ears: The Limits of the Bully Pulpit* (New Haven, CT: Yale University Press, 2003); *Governing by Campaigning: The Politics of the Bush Presidency* (New York: Pearson Longman, 2008); and *The Strategic President: Persuasion and Opportunity in Presidential Leadership* (Princeton, NJ: Princeton University Press, 2009).

36. Farrell, *Tip O'Neill and the Democratic Century*, 553.

37. *Wall Street Journal's*, December 4, 1987, 8D.

38. George Hager, "For GOP, a New Song—Same Ending," *Congressional Quarterly Weekly Report*, June 14, 1997, 1406.

39. Paul Bedard, "Living, Dying by the Polls," *Washington Times*, April 30, 1993, A1.

40. David S. Broder, "The Reticent President," *Washington Post*, April 22, 2001, B7. Also see Mike Allen, "Bush on Stage: Deft or Just Lacking Depth?" *Washington Post*, February 19, 2001, A8–A9.

41. Ibid., A20.

42. Quoted in Jeff Eller, "It's Time to Rewrite the Bully Pulpit," *Politico*, November 18, 2008, 29.

43. Peter Baker, "President Sticks to the Script, with a Little Help," *New York Times*, March 6, 2009, A16. President Obama uses a teleprompter regularly for both major addresses and routine announcements.

44. Christi Parsona and Mark Z. Barabak, "Obama to Sit Down with Leno on *The Tonight Show*," *Los Angeles Times*, March 17, 2009, online edition.

45. Jonathan Martin, "Obama Wants Filter-Free News," *Politico*, March 24, 2009, 17.

46. Sheryl Gay Stolberg, "Obama Makes History in Live Internet Video Chat," *New York Times*, March 27, 2009, A15.

47. Cecilia Kang, "Obama to Hold First Twitter Town Hall," *Washington Post*, July 6, 2011, A4; and Hayley Peterson, "Obama to Field 'Tweets' on Jobs, Economy," *Washington Examiner*, July 6, 2011, 12.

48. Darlene Superville, "Obama Sets Up Web Page for Citizen Petitions," *Washington Times*, September 2, 2011, A4.

49. Tal Kopan, "101,000 Petitioners Turn Their Lonely Eyes to W.H.," *Politico*, March 25, 2014, 21; and Andrea Drusch, "Petition: Opening Day Should Be National Holiday," *Politico*, February 26, 2014, 20. An especially informative analysis of the White House's petition process is Stephen Dinan, "We the People Petition Site Slows to a Trickle," *Washington Times*, January 29, 2014, A1.

50. Chris Cillizza, "Three Lessons for Obama from His First Four Years," *Washington Post*, January 21, 2013, A2.

51. Alan Lichtman, "State of the Union: A Trending Topic?" *Los Angeles Times*, January 18, 2015, online edition.

52. James Oliphant, "Obama's First Line of Defense," *National Journal's*, May 10, 2014, 22.

53. Juliet Eilperin, "To Get His Message Out, Obama Can Reach for the Stars," *Washington Post*, September 21, 2014, A4. Also see Zachary A. Goldfarb and Juliet Eilperin, "Obama Tries to Tap Polarized News Media," *Washington Post*, May 7, 2014, A6; and Ashley Parker, "With Social Media's Rise, the Pulpit Isn't Just the President's Anymore," *New York Times*, January 29, 2014, A12.

54. Michael Gerson, "The Lost Communicator," *Washington Post,* September 10, 2010, A27.

55. John Harwood, "After 15 Months in Office, Policy vs. Politics for Obama," *New York Times*, April 26, 2010, A13.

56. Emma Roller, "A Portrait of Two Presidents, Reconciling Their Political Struggles," *National Journal's Daily*, November 9, 2014, online edition.

57. The figures for both the informal and formal press sessions are cited in Donovan Slack, "Obama Lags in First-Term Press Conferences," *Politico*, January 16, 2013, 11. On the other hand, the president has given numerous TV interviews. See George E. Condon Jr., "Tuned Out," *National Journal's*, November 5, 2011, 26–33.

58. Quoted in Walter Pincus, "More from Nixon the Political Scientist," *Washington Post,* January 26, 2010, A13.

59. Gerald F. Seib, "The Transformation of Presidential Power," *Wall Street Journal's*, February 14, 2014, A4.

60. Ibid.

61. See, for example, Richard P. Nathan, *The Administrative Presidency* (New York: John Wiley, 1983); and Robert R. Durant, *The Administrative Presidency Revisited* (Albany: State University of New York Press, 1992).

62. William G. Howell and David E. Lewis, "Agencies by Presidential Design," *Journal's of Politics*, November 2002, 1096.

63. Ibid., 1100.

64. William G. Howell, *Power without Persuasion: The Politics of Direct Presidential Action* (Princeton, NJ: Princeton University Press, 2003). The Obama administration has abandoned the term *enemy combatant* for those held at Guantánamo Bay, Cuba. See David Savage, "No More 'Enemy Combatants' at Guantánamo Bay," *Los Angeles Times*, March 14, 2009, online edition.

65. John M. Donnelly, "Obama Spoils for Fight over Gitmo," *CQ News*, January 7, 2015, online edition. Also see Charles Hoskinson, "Obama Sidesteps Congress in Releasing Gitmo Prisoners," *WashingtonExaminer.com*, January 12, 2015, 8. When Gitmo opened in 2002, it held 779 prisoners.

66. See Kenneth Mayer, *With the Stroke of a Pen: Executive Orders and Presidential Power* (Princeton, NJ: Princeton University Press, 2001). Presidents also justify their issuance of executive orders and memorandums by citing their constitutional "executive Power" authority, role as "Commander in Chief," and right to "take Care That the Laws be faithfully executed." For a review of the difference between executive orders and presidential memorandums, see

Gregory Korte, "How Obama Became the GO-It-Alone President," *USA Today*, December 17, 2013, online edition; Glenn Kessler, "Claims About Obama's Use of Executive Orders and Presidential Memorandums," *Washington Post*, January 4, 2015, A4; and Kenneth S. Lowande, "After the Orders: Presidential Memoranda and Unilateral Action," *Presidential Studies Quarterly*, December 2014, 724–741.

67. Elizabeth Shogren, "President Plans Blitz of Executive Orders Soon," *Los Angeles Times,* July 5, 1998, A11.

68. Linda Feldmann, "Faith-Based Initiatives Quietly Lunge Forward," *Christian Science Monitor,* February 6, 2003, 2.

69. Gregg Carlstrom, "Midnight Rule-Making Bonanza," *Federal Times,* November 3, 2008, 19.

70. Ceci Connolly and R. Jeffrey Smith, "Obama Positioned to Quickly Reverse Bush Actions," *Washington Post,* November 9, 2008, A16.

71. Charlie Savage, "Shift on Executive Power Lets Obama Bypass Rivals," *New York Times*, April 23, 2012, A1. See Andrew Rudalevige, "Executive Orders and Presidential Unilateralism," *Presidential Studies Quarterly*, March 2012, 138–160.

72. Carrie Budoff Brown and Jennifer Epstein, 'Pen and Phone' Strategy Gets Mixed Results," *Politico*, October 8, 2014, 1.

73. Lyndsey Layton, "Education Overhaul Largely Bypasses Congress," *Washington Post*, September 21, 2012, A1.

74. See, for example, *Congressional Record*, November 19, 2014, S6169; Sen. Ted Cruz, "A Monarch in President's Clothing," *Wall Street Journal's*, November 20, 2014, 4; S. A. Miller, "Republicans: Move Sets 'Monarch' Precedent," *Washington Times*, November 21, 2014, A1; and Peter H. Schuck, "Why Congress Can Impeach Obama," *New York Times*, November 22, 2014, A19. It is worth noting that the immigration order provoked Republicans to call him a tyrant, yet they also call the president too weak in certain areas, such as foreign policy. See Julia Azari, "Tyrant or Weakling? Obama's Critics Can't Make Up Their Minds," *Politico*, June 9, 2014, 21.

75. Michael D. Shear and Julia Preston, "Obama Pushed 'Fullest Extent' of His Powers," *New York Times*, November 29, 2014, A1; and Warren Richy, "Is Obama's Immigration Action Legal," *Christian Science Monitor*, December 8, 2014, 13.

76. David Nakamura, "Obama Acts to Overhaul Immigration," *Washington Post*, November 21, 2014, A8.

77. Aaron Wildavsky, "The Two Presidencies Thesis Revisited at a Time of Political Dissensus," in *The Beleaguered Presidency,* ed. Aaron Wildavsky (Brunswick, NJ: Transaction Publishers, 1991), 29. Wildavsky's article originally appeared in the December 1966 issue of *Transaction* magazine.

78. Ibid., 47–65.

79. Paul Richter, "Ballot Results Follow Obama Abroad," *Los Angeles Times*, November 10, 2014, online edition.

80. Dan Balz, "Bush Lays Out Ambitious Plan for Long Term," *Washington Post,* May 6, 2001, A10.

81. Ronald Brownstein, "Strategies Shift as Bush Drops in Polls," *Los Angeles Times,* July 5, 2001, A9.

82. John Harwood and Jeanne Cummings, "Bush's Approval Rating Slips to 50%, a 5-Year Presidential Low," *Wall Street Journal's,* June 28, 2001, A18.

83. Ron Faucheux, "Presidential Popularity: A History of Highs and Lows," *CQ Daily Monitor,* February 7, 2002, 14.

84. "Bush's Big Regret," *Los Angeles Times,* December 4, 2008, online edition.

85. Woodrow Wilson, *Congressional Government* (Boston: Houghton Mifflin, 1885), 52.

86. Kevin R. Kosar, "Regular Vetoes and Pocket Vetoes: An Overview," Congressional Research Service Report RS22188, January 26, 2009, 1.

87. The Senate maintains a public list of presidential veto counts: see http://www.senate.gov/ reference. The American Presidency Project at the University of California, Santa Barbara, also tracks presidential vetoes as well as signing statements, executive orders, and many other data and documents. See http://www.presidency.ucsb.edu.

88. Alexis Simendinger, "The Veto-Free Zone," *National Journal's,* December 17, 2005, 3888.

89. Tim Groseclose and Nolan McCarty, "The Politics of Blame: Bargaining before an Audience," *American Journal's of Political Science* 45, no. 1 (2001): 100–119.

90. Ethan Wallison, "Can President Bush Stay Veto-Free for Four More Years?" *Roll Call,* January 24, 2005, 10. See Patrick T. Hickey, "Beyond Pivotal Politics: Constituencies, Electoral Incentives, and Veto Override Attempts in the House," *Presidential Studies Quarterly,* December 2014, 577–601.

91. Jill Barshay, "Popularity Not Required," *CQ Weekly,* January 1, 2007, 45.

92. Nancy Ognanovich, "Obama Veto Threat Said to Doom Spending Earmarks for Next Two Years," *Daily Report for Executives,* January 27, 2011, A-22. Also see Sam Youngman, "Obama Promises That He'll Veto All Earmarks," *The Hill,* January 26, 2011, 1.

93. Dave Boyer, "For Obama, Veto Isn't Overriding Concern," *Washington Times,* December 26, 2012, A1.

94. Andrew Restuccia and Jennifer Epstein, "White House Issues Keystone Veto Threat," *Politico Pro Report,* January 6, 2015, 5.

95. Julie Hirschfeld Davis, "When Picking a Fight Can Start a Conversation," *New York Times,* January 13, 2015, A16.

96. Ibid.

97. *Los Angeles Times,* March 18, 1988, part I, 4.

98. See T. J. Halstead, "Presidential Signing Statements: Constitutional and Institutional Implications," Congressional Research Service Report RL33667, April 13, 2007.

99. Charles Savage, "Bush Challenges Hundreds of Laws; President Cites Powers of His Office," *Boston Globe,* April 30, 2006, A1. Also see Phillip J. Cooper, "George W. Bush, Edgar Allan Poe, and the Use and Abuse of Presidential Signing Statements," *Presidential Studies Quarterly* (September 2005): 515–532.

100. Dan Friedman, "On the Other Hand," *National Journal's,* March 28, 2009, 54.

101. Laurence H. Tribe, "'Signing Statements' Are a Phantom Target," *Boston Globe,* August 9, 2006, A9. Also see Joshua B. Kennedy, "Signing Statements, Gridlock, and Presidential Strategy," *Presidential Studies Quarterly,* December 2014, 602–622.

102. Michael D. Shear, "Obama Pledges to Limit Use of Signing Statements," *Washington Post,* March 10, 2009, A4.

103. Charlie Savage, "Obama Says He Can Ignore Some Parts of Spending Bill," *New York Times,* March 12, 2009, A18.

104. David Nather, "Grassley Blows Whistle on Obama for Signing Statement," *CQ Today,* March 16, 2009, 10.

105. Aaron Lorenzo, "Obama Review of Past Signing Statements Does Not Signal End of Presidential Practice," *Daily Report for Executives,* March 10, 2009, A-25.

106. Charlie Savage, "Obama Disputes Detainee Limits in Defense Bill," *New York Times,* January 4, 2013, A14.

107. Laura Meckler, "Obama Shifts View of Executive Power," *Wall Street Journal's,* March 30, 2012, A12.

108. *Congressional Record,* 110th Cong., 2d sess., October 2, 2008, E2197.

109. Louis Fisher, "The Pocket Veto: Its Current Status," Congressional Research Service Report RL30909, March 30, 2001, summary.

110. Erika Niedowski, "GOP to Skirt Line-Item Veto," *The Hill,* February 12, 1997, 24.

111. Helen Dewar and Joan Biskupic, "Line-Item Vote Struck Down: Backers Push for Alternative," *Washington Post,* June 26, 1998, A1.

112. Neustadt, *Presidential Power,* 187.

113. Glenn Thrush, "With the 111th, the Age of Pelosi Dawns," *Politico,* January 6, 2009, 16.

114. See Frances E. Lee, "How Party Polarization Affects Governance," *Annual Review of Political Science* 18 (2015).

115. Doyle McManus, "The Death of the Moderate Republican," *Los Angeles Times*, November 18, 2012, online edition.

116. Johnson, *Vantage Point,* 448.

117. Burgess Everett and Lauren French, "Coburn Leaves Brasher Bomb-Throwers in Wake," *Politico*, July 9, 2014, 14.

118. Carrie Budoff Brown and Jennifer Epstein, "The Obama Paradox," June 2, 2014, 15.

119. Niels Lesniewski and Steven T. Dennis, "Schmoozer in Chief Helps to Save the Day," *CQ Weekly*, January 7, 2013, 14.

120. Peter Baker, "Washington Worries about Its New Power Couple," *New York Times,* November 10, 2010, A18.

121. See Joseph P. Harris, *The Advice and Consent of the Senate* (Berkeley: University of California Press, 1953); and G. Calvin Mackenzie, *The Politics of Presidential Appointments* (New York: Free Press, 1981).

122. James MacGregor Burns, *Presidential Government* (Boston: Houghton Mifflin, 1966), 284.

123. See, for example, Stephen J. Wayne, "Great Expectations: What People Want from Presidents," in *Rethinking the Presidency,* ed. Thomas E. Cronin (Boston: Little, Brown, 1982), 185–199.

124. Dean Scott, "Next President Likely to Have Limited Chance for Passage of Emission Caps, Senator Says," *Daily Report for Executives,* August 4, 2008, A-15.

125. Arthur M. Schlesinger Jr. and Alfred De Grazia, *Congress and the Presidency: Their Role in Modern Times* (Washington, DC: American Enterprise Institute, 1967), 1.

126. Wilson, *Congressional Government;* Burns, *Presidential Government.*

127. See Joseph S. Clark, *Congress: The Sapless Branch* (New York: Harper and Row, 1964); and Arthur Schlesinger Jr., *The Imperial Presidency* (Boston: Houghton Mifflin, 1973).

128. Andrew Restuccia, "Cantor Assails Obama's 'Imperial Presidency,'" *Politico*, October 24, 2012, 28.

129. David Mayhew, *Divided We Govern* (New Haven, CT: Yale University Press, 1991), 198.

CHAPTER 11

1. Bill Bishop, "Don't Trust Government? It's a Global Phenomenon," *Politico*, April 29, 2010, 26. Also see James A. Barnes, "The Great Distrust," *National Journal's*, March 26, 2011, 24–28.

2. Michael Walzer, "The Popular Patron," *New Republic*, April 9, 1984, 35.

3. David S. Broder, "So, Now Bigger Is Better?" *Washington Post,* January 12, 2003, B1.

4. Janet Hook, "Obama's Budget Is the End of an Era," *Los Angeles Times,* February 27, 2009, online edition.

5. "Transcript: Obama on Taxes, Economy, and START," interview, National Public Radio, December 10, 2010, 5.

6. Lee H. Hamilton, "We'll Never Agree on the Role of Government . . . and That's Fine," *Newsletter,* Center on Congress, Indiana University, September 12, 2012, 2–3.

7. Quoted in E. J. Dionne Jr., "Back from the Dead: Neoprogressivism in the '90s," *American Prospect,* September–October 1996, 25.

8. Richard E. Neustadt, "Politicians and Bureaucrats," in *The Congress and America's Future,* 2d ed., ed. David B. Truman (Englewood Cliffs, NJ: Prentice-Hall, 1973), 199. See also Louis

Fisher, *The Politics of Shared Power: Congress and the Executive,* 3d ed. (Washington, DC: CQ Press, 1993).

9. See Harold Relyea, "Executive Branch Reorganization and Management Initiatives: A Brief Overview," Congressional Research Service Report RL33441, May 30, 2006.

10. *Congressional Record,* 109th Cong., 1st sess., February 15, 2005, S1437.

11. Keith Koffler, "Confirmation Wars Could Be Thing of the Past," *Roll Call,* November 21, 2008, 10.

12. Steven V. Roberts, "In Confirmation Process, Hearings Offer a Stage," *New York Times,* February 8, 1989, B7.

13. "*Noel Canning* Would Have Nixed Hundreds," *Daily Report for Executives,* February 6, 2013, A-10.

14. See Vivian S. Chu, "Recess Appointments: A Legal Overview," Congressional Research Report RL33009, August 29, 2014.

15. See Henry Hogue, *Temporarily Filling Presidentially Appointed, Senate-Confirmed Positions,* Congressional Research Service Report RS21412, January 25, 2008.

16. See, for example, Will Englund, "Czar Wars," *National Journal's,* February 14, 2009, 16–24.

17. Jim Puzzanghera and Peter Nicholas, "Obama Decision to Avoid Confirmation Battle for Elizabeth Warren Is Hailed and Criticized," *Los Angeles Times,* September 18, 2010, online edition. Also see John Maggs, "Warring over Warren," *National Journal's,* July 1, 2010, 41–42.

18. Bruce Ackerman, "A Role for Congress to Reclaim," *Washington Post,* March 11, 2009, A15.

19. Ibid.; William Schneider, "New Rules for the Game of Politics," *National Journal's,* April 1, 1989, 830.

20. See Dennis Thompson, *Ethics in Congress* (Washington, DC: Brookings, 1995).

21. Norman Ornstein, "Confirmation Process Leaves Government in Serious Gridlock," *Roll Call,* March 25, 2009, 6.

22. Edward Luce and Krishna Guha, "Appointments Bottleneck at Treasury Tightens," *Financial Times,* March 19, 2009, 4.

23. Philip Rucker, "Potential Obama Appointees Face Extensive Vetting," *Washington Post,* November 18, 2008, A12.

24. Nancy Kassebaum Baker and Franklin Raines, "Uncle Sam Wants a Few Good Appointees," *Los Angeles Times,* April 5, 2001, A17. Baker and Raines were cochairs of the Presidential Appointee Initiative Advisory Board, a project of the Brookings Institution. Its basic goal was to propose improvements in the presidential appointment process. See *To Form a Government: A Bipartisan Plan to Improve the Presidential Appointments Process* (Washington, DC: Brookings, April 2001).

25. G. Calvin Mackenzie, "Hung Out to Dry," *Washington Post,* April 1, 2001, B5.

26. Alan K. Ota, "A Capital's Empty Chairs," *CQ Weekly,* July 5, 2010, 1604.

27. See Clay Johnson and Mack McLarty, "A Better Way to Govern," *The Aspen Idea* (Summer 2012): 64–66.

28. Paul C. Light, "Big Bureaucracy," *Washington Times,* May 10, 2001, A17.

29. Christopher Lee, "Agencies Getting Heavier on Top," *Washington Times,* July 23, 2004, A27.

30. Fareed Zakaria, "Be More Like Ike," *Newsweek,* August 28 and 30, 2010, 18.

31. Stephen Barr, "Title Creep Reported at Agencies," *Washington Post,* March 8, 1999, A17.

32. Jim Rutenberg, "Secret Donors Finance Fight against Hagel," *New York Times,* January 27, 2013, 1.

33. Doyle McManus and Robert Shogun, "Acrid Tone Reflects Long-Term Trend for Nominations," *Los Angeles Times,* March 9, 1997, A6.

34. Stephen Barr, "Plum Book Counts Political Jobs in Executive, Legislative Branches," *Washington Post,* December 15, 2004, B2.

35. See Henry Hogue, "Statutory Qualifications for Executive Branch Positions," Congressional Research Service Report RL33886, February 20, 2007.

36. *Congressional Record,* 105th Cong., 1st sess., September 12, 1996, S10367.

37. Shankar Vedantam, "Who Are the Better Managers—Political Appointees or Career Bureaucrats?" *Washington Post,* November 24, 2008, A6.

38. Joe Davidson, "The Do's and Don'ts on Political Activity," *Washington Post*, October 31, 2013, A17.

39. Alyssa Rosenberg, "Minding the Hatch Act," *Government Executive,* October 2008, 76.

40. Joe Davidson, "Guidelines on Hatch Act and Social Media Are 'Rules of the Road' for Upcoming Elections," *Washington Post,* August 24, 2010, B3.

41. Bart Jansen, "Details of the Lobbying Rules Law," *CQ Weekly,* September 17, 2007, 2693.

42. Zachary A. Goldfarb, "Regulators See Chance to Cash In," *Washington Post,* December 30, 2010, A11.

43. Kenneth P. Vogel, "Not Even Obama Can Halt the Hill's Revolving Door," *Politico,* January 18, 2011, 6.

44. Quoted in Vic Hallard, "In Defense of Legislatures," *The Council of State Governments,* February 1, 1996, 9.

45. See the three-part series on the post-9/11 explosion of the intelligence community in Dana Priest and William Arkin, "A Hidden World, Growing Beyond Control," *Washington Post,* July 19, 2010, A1; "National Security, Inc.," July 20, 2010, A1; and "The Secrets Next Door," July 21, 2010, A1.

46. Jackie Calmes, "Cuts to Achieve Goal for Deficit, but Toll Is High," *New York Times*, March 3, 2013, 26.

47. Stephen Dinan and Dave Boyer, "Obama Taxes Set Off Budget War with GOP," *Washington Times,* February 3, 2015, A1.

48. Fawn Johnson and Daniel Newhauser, "Obama's Budget Is Done. Now It's the GOP's Turn," *National Journal's Daily,* February 3, 2015, 9.

49. Craig Whitlock, "Thousands of Defense Jobs to Be Eliminated," *Washington Post,* August 10, 2010, A4.

50. Ellen Nakashima, "Pentagon Hires Out More Than In," *Washington Post,* April 3, 2001, A19.

51. Ibid.

52. Paul C. Light, "The True Size of Government," *Government Executive,* January 1999, 20. Also see Light, *The True Size of Government.* (Washington, DC: Brookings, 1990). Periodically, Light updates the number of contract workers. In his August 2006 revision, he compares the number of contract workers in 1999 (6.968 million) to 2005 (10.526 million), a 51.1 percent increase.

53. Joe Davidson, "Defining 'Inherently Governmental' and Role of Contractors in War," *Washington Post,* June 22, 2010, B3.

54. *Congressional Record,* 100th Cong., 1st sess., July 29, 1987, S10850.

55. Richard S. Beth, "The Congressional Review Act and Possible Consolidation into a Single Measure of Resolutions Disapproving Regulations," Congressional Research Service Report R40163, January 26, 2009, 8. Worth noting is that since the start of 2012, the "Obama administration, either because of bureaucratic oversight or because they were considered too minor to be reported" has failed to report many rules to the House and Senate and to the Government Accountability Office (GAO). About 1,800 regulations have not been reported to Congress or the GAO as the law requires. See Juliet Eilperin, "Study: Hundreds of Rules Passed by Obama Administration Are Technically Illegal," *Washington Post,* July 30, 2014, online edition.

56. Tim Devaney, "GOP Finds Secret Weapon versus Obama Regulations," *The Hill,* January 20, 2015, 6.

57. Rebecca Adams, "Republicans Dust Off a Little-Used Tool to Go after Overhaul Rules," *CQ Today,* November 29, 2010, 3.

58. Devaney, "GOP Finds Secret Weapon versus Obama Regulations," 6.

59. Gautham Nagesh, "Agencies Flooded by Comments on New Rules," *Wall Street Journal's,* September 4, 2014, A4.

60. Matthew Wald, "Court Voids a Bush Move on Energy," *New York Times,* January 14, 2004, A12.

61. Cyril Zaneski, "Escape Artist," *Government Executive,* March 2001, 29. The U.S. Supreme Court is also considering whether agency "guidance" documents are being employed to reinterpret and implement statutory requirements. At issue is "whether federal agencies increasingly preferred to issue interpretive rules instead of regulations to avoid the drawn-out process that includes public notice and comment periods," as required by the Administrative Procedures Act. See Erica Martinson, "Justices Probe Basis of Some Regulatory Efforts," *Politico,* December 2, 2014, 13.

62. Susan Dudley, "Government Regulations: Rhetoric vs. Reality," *Politico,* September 13, 2012, 28. Also see Jia Lynn Yang, "Do Federal Regulations Really Kill Jobs?" *Washington Post,* November 14, 2011, A1.

63. Larry Margasak, "GOP Agenda: Major Impact May Be on 2012 Election," *Washington Examiner,* January 3, 2011, 13.

64. "A Coming Assault on the E.P.A.," *New York Times,* December 25, 2010, A20.

65. Timothy Cama, "Rep. Chaffetz Takes Aim at EPA," *The Hill,* February 3, 2015, 7.

66. Amy Harder, "House GOP Push on EPA Running out of Steam," *National Journal's Daily,* December 6, 2012, 8.

67. Benjamin Goad, "GOP: We Will Gain from Backlash on Regulation," *The Hill,* September 29, 2014, 8.

68. Frank Ackerman, Lisa Heinzerling, James K. Hammitt, and Milton C. Weinstein, "Balancing Lives against Lucre," *Los Angeles Times,* February 25, 2004, A17. Ackerman and Heinzerling are economists, and Hammitt and Weinstein are risk analysis experts.

69. *Congressional Record,* July 11, 1995, S9705.

70. Ibid., S9697.

71. Joseph S. Clark, *Congress: The Sapless Branch* (New York: Harper and Row, 1964), 63–64.

72. David B. Frohnmayer, "The Separation of Powers: An Essay on the Vitality of a Constitutional Idea," *Oregon Law Review* (Spring 1973): 330.

73. David B. Truman, *The Governmental Process,* rev. ed. (New York: Knopf, 1971), 439.

74. Woodrow Wilson, *Congressional Government* (Boston: Houghton Mifflin, 1885), 297.

75. Lisa Rein, "Conversations: Gene L. Dorado," *Washington Post,* December 30, 2010, B3.

76. David Rogers, "Sen. Lott Becomes GOP's New Standard-Bearer, but His Style Will Be Tested in the Next Congress," *Wall Street Journal's,* November 15, 1996, A16.

77. Jennifer Steinhauer and Robert Pear, "Republicans, Sensing Weakness in Health Law Rollout, Switch Tactics," *New York Times,* October 24, 2013, A19.

78. Wilson, *Congressional Government,* 303.

79. Rochelle Stanfield, "Plotting Every Move," *National Journal's,* March 26, 1988, 796.

80. *Watkins v. United States,* 354 U.S. 178 (1957). See also James Hamilton, *The Power to Probe* (New York: Vantage Books, 1976).

81. William S. Cohen and George J. Mitchell, *Men of Zeal: A Candid Inside Story of the Iran-Contra Hearings* (New York: Viking Penguin, 1988), 305.

82. *Immigration and Naturalization Service v. Chadha,* 462 U.S. 919 (1983).

83. Louis Fisher, in *Extensions* (Carl Albert Congressional Research and Studies Center newsletter) (Spring 1984): 2.

84. John R. Johannes, "Study and Recommend: Statutory Reporting Requirements as a Technique of Legislative Initiative—A Research Note," *Western Political Quarterly* (December 1976): 589–596.

85. Guy Gugliotta, "Reporting on a Practice That's Ripe for Reform," *Washington Post,* February 11, 1997, A19.

86. John T. Bennett, "Fewer Reports to Congress? DoD Move Could Backfire, Experts Warn," *Federal Times,* October 18, 2010, 11.

87. Ibid.

88. Michael W. Kirst, *Government without Passing Laws* (Chapel Hill: University of North Carolina Press, 1969).

89. Joseph A. Davis, "War Declared over Report-Language Issue," *Congressional Quarterly Weekly Report,* June 25, 1988, 1752–1753; David Rapp, "OMB's Miller Backs Away from Report-Language Battle," *Congressional Quarterly Weekly Report,* July 9, 1988, 1928.

90. Sen. Chuck Grassley, "The Federal Government Needs an IG in Chief," *Politico,* July 22, 2009, 30. Also see Charles S. Clark, "Into the Limelight," *Government Executive,* March 2011, 17–24. There are instances when IGs fail to do their job. According to one account, the IG at the Department of Veterans Affairs "did not sound the alarm that a 'systemic' nationwide fraud was being perpetrated against veterans seeking medical care until [2014], despite finding the schemes at multiple facilities since 2005." See Mark Flatten, "Inspector General Missed Warning Signs for a Decade," *WashingtonExaminer.Com,* October 6, 2014, 30, and Peter H. Schuck, "The VA's Problem? Congress," *Washington Post,* May 30, 2014, A15.

91. R. Jeffrey Smith, "Initiative on Worker Safety Gets Poor Marks," *Washington Post,* April 2, 2009, A6.

92. Otto Kreisher, "Pentagon IG Details Waste in Military Contractor Spending," *National Journal's CongressDaily AM,* February 27, 2009, 8.

93. Jared Allen, "'Personal Pain' Is Teed Up for Head of HUD," *The Hill,* July 30, 2010, 8.

94. Greta Wodele, "DHS Facing Appropriators' Wrath for Missing Deadlines," *National Journal's CongressDaily PM,* February 17, 2005, 2.

95. Nancy Ognanovich, "Rogers Says Panel to Target Duplication While Preserving Core Federal Programs," *Daily Report for Executives,* January 29, 2015, A-4.

96. Slade Gorton and Larry Craig, "Congress's Call to Accounting," *Washington Post,* July 27, 1998, A23.

97. Jason A. MacDonald, "Limitation Riders and Congressional Influence over Bureaucratic Policy Decisions," *American Political Science Review,* November 2010, 781. Also see Jessica Tollestrup, "The Appropriations Process and Limitation Amendments: A Case Study of Party Politics on the House Floor," in Jacob Strauss, ed., *Party and Procedure in the United States Congress* (Lanham, MD.: Rowman and Littlefield, 2012), 61–99.

98. *Congressional Record,* 95th Cong., 1st sess., April 30, 1975, E2080.

99. Alan Baron and Michael Gerhardt, "Porteous Impeachment: A First," *National Law Journal's,* January 17, 2011, 34.

100. See Peter Baker, *The Breach: Inside the Impeachment and Trial of William Jefferson Clinton* (New York: Scribner, 2000).

101. See Joel D. Aberbach, *Keeping a Watchful Eye: The Politics of Congressional Oversight* (Washington, DC: Brookings, 1990); and James Q. Wilson, *Bureaucracy: What Governmental Agencies Do and Why They Do It* (New York: Basic Books, 1991).

102. Matt Fuller, "McCarthy Offers Glimpse of GOP's 2015 Priority: 'Government Reform,'" *CQ News,* October 22, 2014, online edition.

103. Richard Cohen, "King of Oversight," *Government Executive,* September 1988, 17.

104. David Nather, "Congress as Watchdog: Asleep on the Job?" *CQ Weekly,* May 22, 2004, 1190.

105. *Congressional Record*, 111th Cong., 2d sess., September 29, 2010, S7705.

106. Joel D. Aberbach, "The Congressional Committee Intelligence System: Information, Oversight, and Change," *Congress and the Presidency* 14 (Spring 1987): 51–76; Mathew McCubbins and Thomas Schwartz, "Congressional Oversight Overlooked: Police Patrol versus Fire Alarm," *American Journal's of Political Science* (February 1984): 165–177.

107. Bill Myers, "'Google Your Government' Database Bill Signed into Law," *Examiner,* September 29, 2006, 17.

108. Jennifer Martinez, "GOP to Public: We Want to Know What You'd Cut," *Politico*, January 20, 2011, 6.

109. Stephen Dinan, "Coburn Issues His Final Wastebook," *Washington Times*, October 22, 2014, A5.

110. Lyndsey Layton, "'Citizen Regulators' Take Toy Safety Testing into Their Own Hands," *Washington Post*, December 26, 2010, A3.

111. Louis Fisher, "Micromanagement by Congress: Reality and Mythology" (paper presented at a conference sponsored by the American Enterprise Institute, Washington, D.C., April 8–9, 1988), 8. See also David S. Broder and Stephen Barr, "Hill's Micromanagement of Cabinet Blurs Separation of Powers," *Washington Post,* July 25, 1993, A1.

CHAPTER 12

1. Alexis de Tocqueville, *Democracy in America* (New York: American Library, 1956), 72.

2. 567 U.S. ____ (2012).

3. 759 F. 3rd 358 (2014).

4. *Marbury v. Madison,* 5 U.S. (1 Cranch) 137 (1803).

5. *United States v. Nixon,* 418 U.S. 683 (1974).

6. See Dexter Perkins and Glyndon Van Deusen, *The United States of America: A History,* vol. 2 (New York: Macmillan, 1962), 560–566.

7. Alexander Bickel, *The Least Dangerous Branch* (Indianapolis, IN: Bobbs-Merrill, 1962), 1.

8. *National Federation of Independent Business v. Sebelius,* 567 U.S. ____ (2012).

9. Jamin Raskin, "Courts v. Citizens," *American Prospect* 14 (March 2003): A25.

10. Charles Gardner Geyh, *When Courts and Congress Collide: The Struggle for Control of America's Judicial System* (Ann Arbor: University of Michigan Press, 2006), 229.

11. *District of Columbia v. Heller,* 554 U.S. 570 (2008).

12. See, for example, Robert Schlesinger, "Sotomayor Hearings Remind Us the Republicans Can Be Judicial Activists, Too," *U.S. News and World Report*, July 22, 2009, www.usnews.com.

13. *Kelo v. City of New London,* 545 U.S. 469 (2005). See, for example, an editorial in the July 11, 2005, *New Republic* praising the *Kelo* decision as one that "defenders of judicial constraint, particularly liberals, should applaud" (p. 7).

14. For example, Sen. John McCain singled out *Kelo* as an example of judicial activism in a speech at Wake Forest University on May 6, 2008. Sen. Jeff Sessions made the same point in a *Washington Post* op-ed on May 7, 2010, A25.

15. Sandra Day O'Connor, "The Threat to Judicial Independence," *Wall Street Journal's,* September 27, 2006, A18.

16. See, for example, the House debate on the Lilly Ledbetter case, *Congressional Record,* 111th Cong., 1st sess., January 9, 2009, H113–H138.

17. Ashley Parker, "House G.O.P. Files Lawsuit in Battling Health Law," *New York Times*, November 21, 2014, http://www.nytimes.com/2014/11/22/us/politics/obamacare-lawsuit-filed-by-republicans.html.

18. Louis Fisher, "The Law: Litigating the War Power with *Campbell v. Clinton*," *Presidential Studies Quarterly* (September 2000): 568.

19. *National Federation of Independent Business v. Sebelius*, 567 U.S. _____ (2012).

20. *Carr v. United States*, 130 S. Ct. 2229, 2236 (2010).

21. See Robert A. Katzmann, ed., *Judges and Legislators* (Washington, DC: Brookings, 1988); and Robert A. Katzmann, *Courts and Congress* (Washington, DC: Brookings, 1997).

22. *New York Times*, May 12, 1983, B8.

23. Dan Eggen, "Record Shows Senators' 'Debate' That Wasn't," *Washington Post*, March 29, 2006, A6.

24. Emily Bazelon, "Invisible Men: Did Lindsey Graham and Jon Kyl Mislead the Supreme Court?" *Slate*, March 27, 2006.

25. Eggen, "Record Shows Senators' 'Debate' That Wasn't," A6.

26. See, for example, Antonin Scalia, *A Matter of Interpretation* (Princeton, NJ: Princeton University Press, 1997).

27. Quoted in Joan Biskupic, "Scalia Sees No Justice in Trying to Judge Intent of Congress on a Law," *Washington Post*, May 11, 1993, A4.

28. Jonathan Kaplan, "High Court to Congress," *The Hill*, February 5, 2003, 21.

29. 759 F. 3rd 358 (2014).

30. Stanley I. Kutler, *Judicial Power and Reconstruction Politics* (Chicago: University of Chicago Press, 1968).

31. Howard Gillman, "How Political Parties Can Use the Courts to Advance Their Agendas: Federal Courts in the United States, 1875–1891," *American Political Science Review* 96 (September 2002): 511–524.

32. Quoted in Stephen Dinan, "DeLay Threatens to Curb Courts' Jurisdiction," *Washington Times*, March 6, 2003, A4.

33. Tom S. Clark, "The Separation of Powers, Court Curbing, and Judicial Legitimacy," *American Journal's of Political Science* 53 (October 2009): 971–989.

34. Joan Biskupic and Elder Witt, *Guide to the U.S. Supreme Court*, 3d ed., vol. 2 (Washington, DC: CQ Press, 1997), 720.

35. William H. Rehnquist, *Grand Inquests: The Historic Impeachment of Justice Samuel Chase and President Andrew Johnson* (New York: William Morrow, 1992), 132.

36. Russell R. Wheeler and Robert A. Katzmann, "A Primer on Interbranch Relations," *Georgetown Law Journal's* (April 2007): 1172.

37. Rehnquist, *Grand Inquests*, 114.

38. "History of the Federal Judiciary: Impeachments of Federal Judges," Federal Judicial Center, www.fjc.gov/history/home.nsf/page/judges_impeachments.html.

39. Biskupic and Witt, *Guide to the U.S. Supreme Court*, 717.

40. Ibid., 718.

41. Carol Leonning, "New Rules for Judges Are Weaker, Critics Say," *Washington Post*, December 17, 2004, A31; David Von Drehle, "Scalia Rejects Pleas for Recusal in Cheney Case," *Washington Post*, February 12, 2004, A35; Eileen Sullivan, "Courts Order Review of Judges' Security," *Federal Times*, March 21, 2005, 12.

42. Tony Mauro, "Kennedy Talks Tough on Salaries, Cameras," *Legal Times*, February 19, 2007, 14.

43. Nathan Koppel, "Kagan Says 'Yes' to Cameras in the Courtroom," Law Blog, *Wall Street Journal's*, June 29, 2010, http://blogs.wsj.com/law/2010/06/29/kagan-says-yes-to-cameras-in-the-courtroom/.

44. Tony Mauro, "As Judiciary Chair, Grassley Likely to Push for Cameras in the Supreme Court," *National Law Journal's*, November 12, 2014, http://www.nationallawjournal.com/supreme-courtbrief/id=1202676220755/As-Judiciary-Chair-Grassley-Likely-to-Push-for-Cameras-in-Supreme-Court#ixzz3LtwsxfVk.

45. Seth Stern, "A Career as Federal Judge Isn't What It Used to Be," *Christian Science Monitor,* January 22, 2002, 1.

46. American Bar Association, "Federal Judicial Pay, an Update on the Urgent Need for Action," May 2003, 4.

47. Several federal judges had filed cases challenging Congress's withholding of cost-of-living increases from Article III judges. The cost-of-living adjustments went back as far as 1995. In December 2013, the Justice Department essentially gave up contesting the matter in the Court of Federal Claims, clearing the way for a pay increase to take effect.

48. Mark Sherman, "Big Money Depletes Judges' Ranks," *Washington Times,* December 30, 2008, B3. Also see Adam Liptak, "The State of Courts, and a Plea for a Raise," *New York Times,* January 1, 2009, A13. The current (and past) salary figures are available at http://www.uscourts.gov/ JudgesAndJudgeships/JudicialCompensation/judicial-salaries-since-1968.aspx#1.

49. Linda Greenhouse, "Chief Justice Advocates Higher Pay for Judiciary," A14. Also see editorial, "There Oughta Be a Law," *USA Today,* January 9, 2007, 12A.

50. Adam Liptak, "On the Subject of Judicial Salaries, a Sharp Difference of Opinion," *New York Times,* January 20, 2009, A14.

51. *Chisholm v. Georgia,* 2 U.S. 419 (1793).

52. *Dred Scott v. Sandford,* 60 U.S. 393 (1857).

53. See Louis Fisher, *American Constitutional Law,* 6th ed. (Durham, NC: Carolina Academic Press, 2005), 1072.

54. Jennifer Dlouhy, "Congress Reluctant to Change Constitution," *CQ Today,* February 11, 2003, 9.

55. Norman Ornstein, "To Break the Stalemate, Give Judges Less Than Life," *Washington Post,* November 28, 2004, B3.

56. Tony Mauro, "Profs Pitch Plan for Limits on Supreme Court Service," *Legal Times,* January 3, 2005, 1. Also see Robert Barnes, "Legal Experts Propose Limiting Justices' Powers, Terms," *Washington Post,* February 23, 2009, A15.

57. Jeff Zeleny, "A Premium on Secrecy in Vetting of Court Pick," *New York Times,* May 13, 2009.

58. Alpheus Thomas Mason, *Harlan Fiske Stone: Pillar of the Law* (New York: Viking, 1959), chap. 12.

59. Dennis Steven Rutkus and Lorraine H. Tong, "The Chief Justice of the United States: Responsibilities of the Office and Process for Appointment," Congressional Research Service Report RL32831, September 12, 2005, 30.

60. Ibid. The four occasions where cloture has been moved on Supreme Court nominations were: in 1968, on Abe Fortas's nomination to be chief justice; in 1971, on William Rehnquist's nomination to be an associate justice; in 1986, on Rehnquist's nomination to be chief justice; and in 2006, on Samuel A. Alito's nomination.

61. Brannon Denning, "The 'Blue Slip': Enforcing the Norms of the Judicial Confirmation Process," *William and Mary Bill of Rights Journal's* 10 (December 2001): 92.

62. Sheldon Goldman, Elliot Slotnick, and Sara Schiavoni, "Obama's Judiciary at Midterm," *Judicature* 94, no. 6 (2011): 267.

63. Quoted in ibid., 268.

64. Quoted in Keith Perine, "As Judiciary Battles Loom, Leahy Revives Senate 'Blue Slip' Tradition," *CQ Today,* January 4, 2007, 3.

65. Ralph Neas, "United States Needs More Discussion of Judicial Philosophy," *Roll Call,* May 9, 2002, 10.

66. Seth Stern, "Senate Shows Supreme Decline in Deference," *CQ Weekly,* July 12, 2010, 1635.

67. Quoted in ibid.

68. Terri L. Peretti, "Where Have All the Politicians Gone? Recruiting for the Modern Supreme Court," *Judicature* (November–December 2007): 120. Also see Paul A. Sracic, "Politician on Court Isn't a Bad Thing," *USA Today,* March 30, 2005, 13A.

69. Charles E. Schumer, "Judging by Ideology," *New York Times,* June 26, 2001.

70. Lee Epstein, René Lindstädt, Jeffrey A. Segal, and Chad Westerland, "The Changing Dynamics of Senate Voting on Supreme Court Nominees," *Journal's of Politics* 68 (May 2006): 306.

71. James Robertson, "A Cure for What Ails the Judiciary," *Washington Post,* May 27, 2003, A19.

72. Linda Greenhouse, "Case of the Dwindling Docket Mystifies the Supreme Court," *New York Times,* December 7, 2006, A1.

73. Elizabeth Palmer, "Appellate Courts at Center of Fight for Control of Judiciary," *CQ Weekly,* February 23, 2002, 534.

74. Ibid.

75. John Stanton, "GOP Begins Judge Blockade," *Roll Call,* June 14, 2012.

76. See, for example, Sen. Mike Lee in the *Congressional Record,* June 25, 2012, S4438.

77. Sarah Binder, "Advice and Consent for Judicial Nominations" (paper prepared for delivery at the seminar "Presidential Nominations and the Senate Confirmation Process," Woodrow Wilson International Center for Scholars, Washington, DC, March 16, 2009), 16.

78. Neil A. Lewis, "New Democratic Majority Throws Bush's Judicial Nominations into Uncertainty," *New York Times,* November 12, 2006, 22.

79. R. Jeffrey Smith, "Judge's Fate Could Turn on 1994 Case," *Washington Post,* May 27, 2003, A8.

80. E. J. Dionne Jr., "They Started It," *Washington Post,* February 21, 2003, A27.

81. John Sides, "Obama's Judicial Appointments: Liberal, but Not That Liberal," April 14, 2014, http://www.washingtonpost.com/blogs/monkey-cage/wp/2014/04/14/obamas-judicial-appointments-liberal-but-not-that-liberal/.

82. Charlie Savage, "Obama Lags on Judicial Picks, Limiting His Mark on Courts," *New York Times, August 17, 2012.*

83. Goldman et al., "Obama's Judiciary at Midterm," 263.

84. Sarah A. Binder and Forrest Maltzman, *Advice and Dissent: The Struggle to Shape the Federal Judiciary* (Washington, DC: Brookings, 2009), 75.

85. Emily Bazelon, "Obama's Fight Song (Finally)," *Slate,* June 4, 2013, http://www.slate.com/articles/news_and_politics/jurisprudence/2013/06/barack_obama_judicial_nominees_the_president_named_three_people_to_the_u.html

86. Sen. Orrin Hatch, "Don't Change the Filibuster Again," *Politico,* December 8, 2014, http://www.politico.com/magazine/story/2014/12/orrin-hatch-filibuster-113388.html#.VI3ghSda9FU.

87. Niels Lesniewski, "How the Nuclear Option Changed the Judiciary," *Roll Call,* December 19, 2014, http://blogs.rollcall.com/wgdb/nuclear-option-judiciary-nominations/.

88. Ibid.

89. Francine Keifer, "One Year Later, the 'Nuclear Option' Has Worked. Is That Good?" *Christian Science Monitor,* December 9, 2014, http://www.csmonitor.com/USA/DC-Decoder/2014/1209/One-year-later-Senate-s-nuclear-option-has-worked.-Is-that-good-video.

90. Timothy M. Phelps, *Los Angeles Times,* November 3, 2014, online edition.

91. Ibid.

92. Joyce Russell, "Grassley to Oversee Obama Judgeships," Iowa Public Radio, November 11, 2014, http://iowapublicradio.org/post/grassley-oversee-obama-judgeships.

93. Louis Fisher, "Congressional Checks on the Judiciary," in *Congress Confronts the Court,* ed. Colton C. Campbell and John F. Stack Jr. (Lanham, MD: Rowman and Littlefield, 2001), 35.

CHAPTER 13

1. Peter Dreier, "Lessons from the Health-Care Wars," *American Prospect* (May 2010): 29.

2. Dan Eggen, "Interest Groups Rally for a Big Finish on Health-Care Reform," *Washington Post,* February 28, 2010, A3.

3. Michael D. Shear, "Health Bill Foes Solicit Funds for Economic Study," *Washington Post,* November 16, 2009, A1.

4. Bennett Roth and Alex Knott, "Medical Interests Spend $876 Million on Reform," *Roll Call,* May 3, 2010, 6. For an analysis of the battle over President Clinton's health care plan, see Haynes Johnson and David S. Broder, *The System* (Boston: Little, Brown, 1996).

5. See John R. Hibbing and Elizabeth Theiss-Morse, *Congress as Public Enemy: Public Attitudes toward American Political Institutions* (New York: Cambridge University Press, 1995).

6. Joel Jankowsky and Thomas Goldstein, "In Defense of Lobbying," *Wall Street Journal's,* September 4, 2009, A15.

7. Kate Ackley, "'Kick the Lobbyist' Is Still a Favorite Pastime," *Roll Call,* May 10, 2010, 10.

8. Bill Swindell, "Industry's Increased D.C. Presence Reflects New Reality," *National Journal's CongressDaily AM,* July 28, 2010, 1, 14. *CongressDaily* is published by *National Journal's,* a Washington-based Journal's.

9. Ibid., 14.

10. Baa Vaida, "Brisk Business for K Street in 2010," *National Journal's,* July 24, 2010, 44. Many lobbying groups have their offices on K Street in the District of Columbia.

11. "Waning Influence?" OpenSecrets.org Reports, Center for Responsive Politics, March 18, 2014, https://www.opensecrets.org/news/reports/. See also Lee Drutman, *The Business of America Is Lobbying: How Corporations Became Politicized and Politics Became More Corporate* (New York: Oxford University Press, 2015).

12. Alexander Becker, "Spending on Lobbying Is Actually Falling. Or Is It?" Post Politics, *Washington Post* weblog, August 19, 2014, http://www.washingtonpost.com/blogs/post-politics/wp/2014/08/19/spending-on-lobbying-is-actually-falling-or-is-it/.

13. Anna Palmer, "K Street's Continuing Slump," *Politico,* July 23, 2012, 4.

14. Alexis de Tocqueville, *Democracy in America,* ed. Phillips Bradley (New York: Knopf, 1951), 119.

15. Janny Scott, "Medicine's Big Dose of Politics," *Los Angeles Times,* September 25, 1991, A15.

16. Robert Putnam, "The Strange Disappearance of Civic America," *American Prospect* (Winter 1996): 35.

17. Quoted in Suzi Parker, "Civic Clubs: Elks, Lions May Go Way of the Dodo," *Christian Science Monitor,* August 24, 1998, 1.

18. Theda Skocpol, *Diminished Democracy: From Membership to Management in American Civic Life* (Norman: University of Oklahoma Press, 2003).

19. Everett Carll Ladd, "The American Way—Civic Engagement—Thrives," *Christian Science Monitor,* March 1, 1999, 9.

20. Fawn Johnson, "Why Are Political Scientists Studying Ice Bucket Challenges?" *National Journal's Daily,* October 17, 2014, online edition, http://www.nationaljournal.com/next-economy/big-questions/why-political-scientists-now-study-ice-bucket-challenges-20141016.

21. Mancur Olson Jr., *The Logic of Collective Action: Public Goods and the Theory of Groups* (Cambridge, MA: Harvard University Press, 1965).

22. Kay L. Schlozman and John T. Tierney, *Organized Interests and American Democracy* (New York: Harper and Row, 1986).

23. E. E. Schattschneider, *The Semi-Sovereign People* (New York: Holt, Rinehart and Winston, 1960), 35.

24. Melinda Burns, "K Street and the Status Quo," *Miller-McCune,* September–October 2010, 65. Also see Frank R. Baumgartner et al., *Lobbying and Policy Change: Who Wins, Who Loses, and Why* (Chicago: University of Chicago Press, 2009).

25. Kristina C. Miler, "The View from the Hill: Legislative Perceptions of the District," *Legislative Studies Quarterly* 32 (November 2007): 597–628.

26. Sidney Verba, Kay Lehman Schlozman, and Henry Brady, "The Big Tilt: Participatory Inequality in America," *American Prospect* (May/June 1997): 78.

27. Greg Sargent, "Democrats' Sequester Conundrum," *Washington Post*, April 30, 2013, A13. Also see Darren Samuelsohn, "Sequester Exemptions as Earmarks," *Politico*, April 23, 2013, 1.

28. Elise D. Garcia, "Money in Politics," *Common Cause*, February 1981, 11.

29. Jeffrey H. Birnbaum, "Lobbyists: Why the Bad Rap?" *American Enterprise*, November/December 1992, 74. Also see also Jeffrey H. Birnbaum, *The Lobbyists* (New York: Times Books, 1992).

30. David Karol, "Party Activists, Interest Groups, and Polarization in American Politics," *American Gridlock: The Sources, Character, and Impact of Political Polarization*, ed., James Thurber and Antoine Yoshinaka (New York: Cambridge University Press, forthcoming 2015).

31. "NRA Threats Fail to Sway Senators on Sotomayor," *Washington Times*, August 2, 2009, http://www.washingtontimes.com/news/2009/aug/2/nra-threats-fail-to-sway-senators-on-sotomayor/?page=all.

32. Tory Newmyer, "Majority Formalizes K St. Ties," *Roll Call*, February 15, 2007, 23.

33. Alexander Bolton, "Dems Enlist Help to Push Their Agenda," *The Hill*, February 14, 2007, 1.

34. Emily Pierce, "GOP Taps Thune to Get Cozy with K St.," *Roll Call*, January 22, 2009.

35. Anna Palmer, "K Street Prepares for Televised Rendezvous with GOP Leaders," *Roll Call*, July 15, 2010, online edition.

36. Jeffrey Birnbaum, "The Thursday Group," *Time*, March 27, 1995, 30–31.

37. Quoted in Hedrick Smith, *The Power Game* (New York: Random House, 1988), 232.

38. Ronald J. Hrebenar and Ruth K. Scott, *Interest Group Politics in America* (Englewood Cliffs, NJ: Prentice-Hall, 1982), 63.

39. Quoted in Alan K. Ota, "Democratic Foot in Revolving Door," *CQ Weekly*, June 25, 2007, 1900.

40. Mark Preston, "Ex-GOP Senators Get Special Access," *Roll Call*, April 3, 2003, 1, 24.

41. Quoted in Alan K. Ota, "Democratic Foot in the Revolving Door," *CQ Weekly*, June 25, 2007, 1900.

42. Chris Frates, "Hill Experience Gives Lobbyists a Leg Up," *Politico*, May 17, 2007.

43. Fredreka Schouten, "Ex-Lawmakers Go to Lobbying-Related Jobs," *USA Today*, March 25, 2013, http://www.usatoday.com/story/news/politics/2013/03/25/former-lawmakers-lobbying-jobs/2011325/.

44. R. Jeffrey Smith and Dan Eggen, "More Former Lobbyists Flocking to Jobs on Hill," *Washington Post*, March 18, 2011, A1.

45. Anna Palmer, "Help Wanted: Lobbyists Who Can Raise Cash," *Politico*, May 21, 2012, 15.

46. Quoted in Sam Walker, "Who's In and Who's Out among Capitol Lobbyists," *Christian Science Monitor*, November 8, 1995, 3.

47. Quoted in *National Journal's CongressDaily PM*, March 15, 2002, 8.

48. Steven Brill, "On Sale: Your Government," *Time*, July 12, 2010, 32.

49. Bertram J. Levine, *The Art of Lobbying: Building Trust and Selling Policy* (Washington, DC: CQ Press, 2008).

50. Adam Graham-Silverman, "Travel Decreases as Ethics Rules Complicate Privately Funded Trips," *CQ Weekly*, December 1, 2008, 3178.

51. John Cochran and Martin Kady II, "The New Laws of the Lobby," *CQ Weekly*, February 26, 2007, 594.

52. Eliza Newlin Carney and Bara Vaida, "Shifting Ground," *National Journal's*, March 31, 2007, 27.

53. Quoted in Cochran and Kady, "New Laws of the Lobby," 594.

54. Joseph Curl, "Big Money Buys Seats at Lawmakers' Dinner Tables," *Washington Times*, November 3, 2009, A1.

55. David Kirkpatrick, "Congress Finds Ways of Avoiding Lobbyist Limit," *New York Times*, February 11, 2007, 1. The political action committee of Finance chair Max Baucus, D-Mont., often sponsors fund-raising events at the Big Sky Resort in Montana that feature "fly-fishing

and golf in the summer and skiing in the winter." See Kate Ackley, "Baucus' Network in High Demand," *Roll Call*, June 19, 2012, 21.

56. Ibid.
57. John Breaux, "Effective Coalitions for Coalitions," *The Hill*, March 21, 2007, 18.
58. Kate Ackley, "Defense, Other Sectors Band Together to Fight Sequester," *Roll Call*, February 8, 2013, online edition.
59. Dan Eggen, "Investments Can Yield More on K Street, Study Indicates," *Washington Post*, April 12, 2009, A8.
60. Ernest Wittenberg, "How Lobbying Helps Make Democracy Work," *Vital Speeches of the Day*, November 1, 1982, 47.
61. Ellyn Ferguson, "An Unexpected Alliance Fights Ethanol Expansion," *CQ Today*, July 26, 2010, 7. Also see Anna Palmer, "Lobbying Coalition Calls for Congressional Hearing on Ethanol," *Roll Call*, August 25, 2010, online edition.
62. Martin Kady II, "Keeping Grass-Roots Lobbying under Wraps," *CQ Weekly*, March 26, 2007, 877.
63. Rosalind S. Helderman, "Uber's Aggressive Tactics Push Change," *Washington Post*, December 14, 2014, p. A1.
64. Edward T. Walker, "Grass-Roots Mobilization, by Corporate America," *New York Times*, August 10, 2012, http://www.nytimes.com/2012/08/11/opinion/grass-roots-mobilization-by-corporate-america.html?_r=0.
65. John T. Tierney and Kay Lehman Schlozman, "Congress and Organized Interests," in *Congressional Politics,* ed. Christopher J. Deering (Chicago: Dorsey, 1989), 212.
66. Kady, "Keeping Grass-Roots Lobbying under Wraps," 877.
67. Alison Mitchell, "A New Form of Lobbying Puts Public Face on Private Interest," *New York Times,* September 30, 1998, A14. Also see Ken Kollman, *Outside Lobbying: Public Opinion and Interest Group Strategies* (Princeton, NJ: Princeton University Press, 1998).
68. David Gelles, "Lobbying Scuttles U.S. Piracy Laws," *Financial Times*, January 21–22, 2012, 1.
69. Justin Cox, "Trading Bullhorns for Blog Posts," *The Hill*, June 23, 2010, 42.
70. Cecilia Kane, "Twitter: A Live Megaphone for Lobbying Groups, Firms," *Washington Post*, February 14, 2013, A12.
71. Matea Gold, Joseph Tanfani, and Lisa Mascaro, "NRA Clout Rooted More in Its Tactics Than Its Election Spending," *Los Angeles Times*, July 29, 2012, online edition.
72. Jeffrey Birnbaum, "The Forces That Set the Agenda," *Washington Post*, April 24, 2005, B5.
73. Tom Hamburger, "U.S. Chamber of Commerce Grows into a Political Force," *Los Angeles Times*, March 8, 2010, online edition.
74. Paul S. Herrnson, "Party Organizations, Party-Connected Committees, Party Allies, and the Financing of Federal Elections," *Journal's of Politics* (November 2009).
75. Brody Mullins, "Growing Role for Lobbyists: Raising Funds for Lawmakers," *Wall Street Journal's*, January 27, 2006, A1.
76. Philip M. Stern, "The Tin Cup Congress," *Washington Monthly*, May 1988, 24.
77. *Congressional Record*, 100th Cong., 1st sess., August 5, 1987, S11292.
78. "Fundamentals of Fund-raising," *Washington Post*, December 5, 1990, A23.
79. Fredreka Schouten, "Polled PAC Donations Add $33M Punch to Races," *USA Today*, August 17, 2010, 5A.
80. Manu Raju, "Members Get Bundles of Lobbyist Cash," *Politico*, February 16, 2010, 1.
81. Jack Maskell, "Lobbying Law and Ethics Rules Changes in the 110th Congress," Congressional Research Service Report RL 33836, September 18, 2007.
82. Tom McGinty and Brody Mullins, "Political Spending by Unions Far Exceeds Direct Donations," *Wall Street Journal's*, July 10, 2012, A1, A7.

83. "Overall Spending Inches Up in 2014: Megadonors Equip Outside Groups to Capture a Bigger Share of the Pie," Open Secrets Blog, Center for Responsive Politics, October 29, 2014, http://www.opensecrets.org/news/2014/10/overall-spending-inches-up-in-2014-mega-donors-equip-outside-groups-to-capture-a-bigger-share-of-the-pie/.

84. John Brinkley, "Members of Congress Perform under Judging Eyes of Lobbyists," *Washington Times,* March 16, 1994, A16. Also see John Cochran, "Interest Groups Make Sure Lawmakers Know the 'Score,'" *CQ Weekly,* April 19, 2003, 924–929.

85. See Robert L. Reynolds, "A Pledge to End All Pledges," *Wall Street Journal's,* December 24, 2012, A13; and Grover Norquist, "The Case for the Tax Pledge: Political Accountability," *USA Today,* December 13, 2012, 8A.

86. Bill Whalen, "Rating Lawmakers' Politics by Looking into Their Eyes," *Insight,* October 20, 1986, 21. Also see Cochran, "Interest Groups Make Sure Lawmakers Know the 'Score.'"

87. Eliza Newlin Carney, "Keeping Score," *CQ Weekly,* January 21, 2013, 118–119.

88. *CQ Monitor,* April 13, 1998, 4.

89. "Environment," *National Journal's CongressDaily PM,* February 21, 2006, 10.

90. Hibbing and Theiss-Morse, *Congress as Public Enemy,* 63–65.

91. Frank R. Baumgartner and Beth L. Leech, *Basic Interests: The Importance of Groups in Politics and in Political Science* (Princeton, NJ: Princeton University Press, 1998), 13.

92. Burns, "K Street and the Status Quo," 64; and Baumgartner et al., *Lobbying and Policy Change.*

93. Interview with Prof. Marie Elizabeth Hojnacki, *CQ Weekly,* September 6, 2010, 2005.

94. Janet M. Gretzke, "PACs and the Congressional Supermarket: The Currency Is Complex," *American Journal's of Political Science* 33 (1989): 1–24; Lawrence S. Rothenberg, *Linking Citizens to Government: Interest Group Politics at Common Cause* (New York: Cambridge University Press, 1992); John R. Wright, "Contributions, Lobbying, and Committee Voting in the U.S. House of Representatives," *American Political Science Review* 84 (1990): 417–438.

95. Gary J. Andres, *Lobbying Reconsidered* (New York: Pearson Longman, 2009), 159. Worth noting is that the House Office of Congressional Ethics has investigated the "propriety of [lawmakers] using a vote as a fundraising opportunity by hosting events in close proximity to a major vote." See Edward Epstein, "Outside Panel in for Insider Criticism," *CQ Weekly,* August 9, 2010, 1911.

96. See the labor union profile at the Center for Responsive Politics, www.opensecrets.org/. The center is a nonprofit research organization that tracks the role of money in politics.

97. James G. Gimpel, Frances E. Lee, and Michael Parrott, "Business Interests and the Party Coalitions: Industry Sector Contributions to U.S. Congressional Candidates," *American Politics Research* 42 (2014): 1034–1076; and Karol, "Party Activists, Interest Groups, and Polarization."

98. Richard L. Hall and Frank W. Wayman, "Buying Time: Moneyed Interests and the Mobilization of Bias in Congressional Committees," *American Political Science Review* 84 (September 1990): 800. See also their review of the literature on patterns in campaign contributions on pages 799–800.

99. Quoted in Claudia Dreifus, "And Then There Was Frank," *New York Times Magazine,* February 4, 1996, 25.

100. Don Van Natta Jr., "$250,000 Buys Donors 'Best Access to Congress,'" *New York Times,* January 27, 1997, A1.

101. See Richard A. Smith, "Advocacy, Interpretation, and Influence in the U.S. Congress," *American Political Science Review* 78 (1984): 44–63; and Hall and Wayman, "Buying Time." Also see Eric Lipton and Kevin Sack, "Fiscal Footnote: Big Senate Gift to Drug Maker," *New York Times,* January 20, 2013, A1.

102. Marie Hojnacki and David C. Kimball, "Organized Interests and the Decision of Whom to Lobby in Congress," *American Political Science Review* (December 1998): 775–790.

103. *Washington Star,* May 22, 1978, A1.
104. Elizabeth Brotherton, "A Recycled Idea," *Roll Call,* June 13, 2006, 3.
105. See Eric Lipton and Eric Lichtblau, "In Black Caucus, a Fund-Raising Powerhouse," *New York Times,* February 14, 2010, 1; Paul Singer, "The Tax-Payer-Funded Caucus Is Still Thriving," *Roll Call,* May 18, 2010, 4; Fredreka Schouten, "Lobbyists Get Power Access Via Caucuses," *USA Today,* July 24–26, 2009, 1A.
106. Richard L. Hall and Alan V. Deardorff, "Lobbying as Legislative Subsidy," *American Political Science Review* (February 2006): 69–84.
107. *Wall Street Journal's,* October 5, 1987, 54.
108. Mary Lynn Jones, "Survey Says Lobbyists Find Information Rules the Hill," *The Hill,* November 18, 1998, 8. A recent study of congressional lobbying suggests that lobbyists' political connections to lawmakers are more important than their issue expertise. The president of the American League of Lobbyists, however, disputes this judgment. See Jeremy Hainsworth, "Study Finds Who You Know Counts Most Among Congressional Lobbyists," *Daily Report for Executives,* March 25, 2011, A-8.
109. Kirk Victor, "New Kids on the Block," *National Journal's,* October 31, 1987, 2727.
110. Burns, "K Street and the Status Quo," 66. As an example, see Patrice Hill, "Facts Spin on Small-Business Tax," *Washington Times,* August 31, 2010, A1.
111. E. Scott Adler and John S. Lapinski, "Demand-side theory and congressional committee composition: A constituency characteristics approach," *American Journal's of Political Science* 41 (1997): 895–918; and E. Scott Adler, "Constituency Characteristics and the 'Guardian' Model of Appropriations Subcommittees, 1959–1998," *American Journal's of Political Science* 44 (2000): 104–114.
112. *Congressional Record,* December 15, 2011, S8629. See also Rebecca U. Thorpe, *The American Warfare State: The Domestic Politics of Military Spending* (Chicago: University of Chicago Press, 2014).
113. *Congressional Record,* December 15, 2011, S8629.
114. The "Guide to the Lobbying Disclosure Act" can be found on the website of the clerk of the U.S. House of Representatives: http://clerk.house.gov.
115. William Luneburg and Thomas Susman, *The Lobbying Manual,* 3d ed. (Washington, DC: American Bar Association, 2005), 7.
116. U.S. Congress, *Organization of the Congress,* H. Rept. 1675, 79th Cong., 2d sess., 1946, 26.
117. *United States v. Harriss,* 347 U.S. 612 (1954).
118. Francesca Contiguaglia, "GAO Finds That Lobbyist Registration Has Soared," *Roll Call,* May 14, 1998, 14.
119. Data from Opensecrets.org, Center for Responsive Politics, October 27, 2014, https://www.opensecrets.org/lobby/.
120. Lee Fang, "Where Have All the Lobbyists Gone?" *The Nation,* February 19, 2014, http://www.thenation.com/article/178460/shadow-lobbying-complex#.
121. Sam Fulwood, "Lobbying Reform Passes House on Unanimous Vote," *Los Angeles Times,* November 30, 1995, A9.
122. Alex Knott, *Special Report: Industry of Influence Nets Almost $13 Billion* (Washington, DC: Center for Public Integrity, 2005), 1–4.
123. Lee H. Hamilton, "Lobbying Murkiness Undermines Our Trust in Congress," Center on Congress at Indiana University, April 11, 2005, 2, http://congress.indiana.edu.
124. Deirdre Shesgreen, "Shining a Dim Light," *Legal Times,* December 21 and 28, 1998, 26, 27.
125. See John D. McKinnon and Brody Mullins, "Lawmakers Face Ethics Probe," *Wall Street Journal's,* September 1, 2010, A4.
126. Kate Ackley, "Unlobbyists Give Real Lobbyists a Bad Name," *Roll Call,* February 13, 2012, 1.

127. Chris Frates, "When a Lobbyist Isn't a Lobbyist," *Politico*, July 26, 2010, 1, 12.

128. Megan R. Wilson, "Bombshell: Ethics Office Alleges Illegal Lobbying," *The Hill*, July 25, 2014, http://thehill.com/business-a-lobbying/business-a-lobbying/213394-bombshell-ethics-office-alleges-illegal-lobbying#ixzz38nBcr66y.

129. Janie Lorber and Kate Ackley, "Tracking Lobbyists for Other Countries," *Roll Call*, October 2, 2012, 3. Also see Arnd Jurgensen and Renan Levine, "Foreign Lobbying," in Burdett Loomis, ed., *Guide to Interest Groups and Lobbying in the United States* (Washington, DC: CQ Press, 2012), 321–332.

130. T. W. Farnam, "Trips Fly through Hole in Rules," *Washington Post*, February 18, 2013, A6. The material in this paragraph is drawn from the detailed analysis of these cultural exchange trips conducted by the *Post*.

131. Kevin Bogardus, "Korea Bulks Up on K Street as Obama Presses Trade Deal," *The Hill*, July 16, 2010, 9.

132. Kevin Bogardus, "First DC Firm to Sign with Libyan Rebels Is Rewarded with Contract," *The Hill*, April 4, 2012, 20.

133. See Ken Silverstein, "Oil Adds Sheen to Kazakh Regime," *Los Angeles Times*, May 12, 2004, A1.

134. Ibid.

135. See Adam Hochschild, "Into the Light from the Heart of Darkness," *Los Angeles Times*, December 6, 1998, M1; and Katharine Seeyle, "National Rifle Association Is Turning to World Stage to Fight Gun Control," *New York Times*, April 2, 1997, A12.

136. Julian Pecquet, "NRA Draws Red Line on Civilian Weapons in UN's Arms Treaty," *The Hill*, July 12, 2012, 9.

137. Alan Ohnsman and Gopal Ratnam, "Toyota to Boost Lobbying Efforts as U.S. Operations Expand," *Washington Examiner*, March 7, 2007, 21.

138. Edgar Lane, *Lobbying and the Law* (Berkeley: University of California Press, 1964), 18.

139. Brill, "On Sale: Your Government," 32.

CHAPTER 14

1. Cristina Marcos and Paul M. Krawzak, "Battle Over, but 'War' Continues," *CQ Weekly*, October 21, 2013, 1756.

2. Paul M. Krawzak, "2013 Legislative Summary: Fiscal 2014 Budget Resolution and Budget Agreement," *CQ Weekly*, January 6, 2014, 36.

3. Ian Katz, "Lew Tells Congress Treasury to Hit Debt Limit in Mid-October," *Bloomberg*, August 26, 2013, http://www.bloomberg.com/news/2013-08-26/lew-tells-congress-treasury-will-hit-debt-limit-in-mid-october.html.

4. Daniel Newhauser and Emily Ethridge, "Shutdown Showdown," *CQ Weekly*, September 23, 2013, 1550.

5. Ibid.

6. Jonathan Weisman, "Pressed from His Right, Speaker Yields on a Budget Showdown," *New York Times*, September 18, 2013. See also Jonathan Martin, "G.O.P. Governors Warn Party Members in Congress Not to Shut Government," *New York Times*, August 4, 2013.

7. Jonathan Weisman, "Senator Persists Battling Health Law, Irking Even Many in His Own Party," *New York Times*, September 24, 2013.

8. Adriel Bettelheim, "GOP Looks beyond Shutdown," *CQ Weekly*, October 7, 2013, 1654.

9. Jake Sherman, John Bresnahan, and Seung Min Kim, "House Pulls Back on Boehner Plan," *Politico*, October 15, 2013, http://www.politico.com/story/2013/10/government-shutdown-debt-ceiling-default-update-98317.html.

10. Cristina Marcos and Paul M. Krawzak, "Battle Over, but 'War' Continues," *CQ Weekly*, October 21, 2013, 1756.

11. Matea Gold, "Tea Party Activists Call Bipartisan Deal a Capitulation, Say They Are Unbowed," *Washington Post*, October 16, 2013.

12. Marcos and Krawzak, "Battle Over, but 'War' Continues."

13. Jonathan Weisman, "Capitol Leaders Agree to a Deal on the Budget," *New York Times*, December 10, 2013.

14. Randall B. Ripley and Grace A. Franklin, *Congress, the Bureaucracy, and Public Policy*, 5th ed. (Pacific Grove, CA: Brooks/Cole, 1991).

15. John W. Kingdon, *Agendas, Alternatives, and Public Policies* (Boston: Little, Brown, 1984), 3.

16. Ibid., 17–19.

17. Ibid., chap. 2.

18. Rand Paul, "We Must Demilitarize the Police," *Time*, August 14, 2014, http://time.com/3111474/rand-paul-ferguson-police/?utm_source=twitterfeed&utm_medium=twitter.

19. See Justin Gillis, "U.N. Panel Issues Its Starkest Warning Yet on Global Warming," *New York Times*, November 2, 2014, http://www.nytimes.com/2014/11/03/world/europe/global-warming-un-intergovernmental-panel-on-climate-change.html; and William Nordhaus, *The Climate Casino* (New Haven: Yale University Press), 2013.

20. Nelson W. Polsby, "Strengthening Congress in National Policymaking," *Yale Review* (Summer 1970): 481–497.

21. James L. Sundquist, *Politics and Policy: The Eisenhower, Kennedy, and Johnson Years* (Washington, DC: Brookings, 1968).

22. Elizabeth Wehr, "Numerous Factors Favoring Good Relationship between Reagan and New Congress," *Congressional Quarterly Weekly Report*, January 24, 1981, 173.

23. Kingdon, *Agendas, Alternatives, and Public Policies*, 148–149.

24. American Enterprise Institute, *The State of the Congress: Tomorrow's Challenges?* (Washington, DC: AEI, 1981), 8.

25. Theodore Lowi, "American Business, Public Policy, Case Studies, and Political Theory," *World Politics* (July 1964): 677–715; Theodore Lowi, "Four Systems of Policy, Politics, and Choice," *Public Administration Review* (July–August 1972): 298–310; Samuel P. Huntington, *The Common Defense* (New York: Columbia University Press, 1961); Ripley and Franklin, *Congress, the Bureaucracy, and Public Policy*.

26. Mary Russell, "'Park-Barrel Bill' Clears House Panel," *Washington Post*, June 22, 1978, A3.

27. George E. Condon Jr., "Bending Congress's Ear(marks)," *National Journal's CongressDaily*, February 11, 2011, 5.

28. Stephen Dinan, "Earmarks End for One Year, but Perk Still Potent on Hill," *Washington Times*, February 10, 2011, A6.

29. Ibid.

30. *Congressional Record*, 111th Cong., 1st sess., May 6, 2009, H5279.

31. Frank Oliveri, "McKeon Lays Out Rules for Keeping Earmarks Out of Defense Authorization Bill," *CQ Today*, March 28, 2011, 2.

32. Raymond Hernandez, "A House District Liked Its Earmarks, and Then Elected Someone Who Didn't," *New York Times*, February 5, 2011, A16.

33. Humberto Sanchez, "Senators Line Up to Endorse Earmark Moratorium," *National Journal's CongressDaily*, February 2, 2011, 7.

34. Eliza Newlin Carney, "The Earmarks Paradox," *National Journal's CongressDaily*, February 14, 2011, 5.

35. Humberto Sanchez, "Senators Want to Clarify What Makes an Earmark," *National Journal's CongressDaily*, March 3, 2011, 11.

36. Ron Nixon, "Earmarks Ban May Loom, but Lawmakers Find Ways to Finance Pet Projects," *New York Times,* December 28, 2010, A11.

37. Kevin Bogardus, "Keep the Earmark Requests Coming, Say Some Lawmakers to Constituents," *The Hill,* March 17, 2011, 12.

38. Diana Evans, *Greasing the Wheels: Using Pork Barrel Projects to Build Majority Coalitions in Congress* (New York: Cambridge University Press, 2004).

39. Jonathan Rauch, "The Case for Corruption: Why Washington Needs More Honest Graft," *Atlantic,* February 19, 2014, http://www.theatlantic.com/magazine/archive/2014/03/the-case-for-corruption/357568/.

40. Condon, "Bending Congress's Ear(marks)," 5.

41. See, for example, Margaret Kriz, "Heavy Breathing," *National Journal's,* January 4, 1997, 8–12.

42. Joby Warrick, "White House Taking a Hands-on Role in Writing New Clean Air Standards," *Washington Post,* May 22, 1997, A10.

43. Alan Charles Raul, "Obama Review of Regulatory Burden to Be Weighed in Cost-Benefit Analysis," *Daily Report for Executives,* February 9, 2011, B-1.

44. See, for example, Kenneth A. Shepsle, Robert P. Van Houweling, Samuel J. Abrams, and Peter C. Hanson, "The Senate Electoral Cycle and Bicameral Appropriation Politics," *American Journal's of Political Science* 53 (2009): 343–359; Jeffrey Lazarus and Amy Steigerwalt, "Different Houses: The Distribution of Earmarks in the U.S. House and Senate," *Legislative Studies Quarterly* 34 (2009): 347–373; and Robert A. Bernstein, Gerald C. Wright Jr., and Michael B. Berkman, "Do U.S. Senators Moderate Strategically?" *American Political Science Review* 82 (1988): 237–245.

45. Donald Lambro, "Steady GOP Rebound Strategy," *Washington Times,* June 7, 2001, A17.

46. Judy Sarasohn, "Money for Lat. 40 N, Long. 73 W," *Congressional Quarterly Weekly Report,* May 12, 1979, 916.

47. See Maggie Severns, "The Plot to Overhaul No Child Left Behind," *Politico,* January 2, 2015, http://www.politico.com/story/2015/01/the-plot-to-overhaul-no-child-left-behind-113857.html.

48. "Don't Just Do Something, Sit There," *Economist,* December 23, 1995–January 5, 1996, 11–12.

49. "Feel-good Legislation: Congress's Symbolic Energy Bills," *Houston Chronicle,* May 15, 2008, www.chron.com/opinion/editorials/article/Feel-good-legislation-Congress-symbolic-energy-1772616.php.

50. Barber Conable, "Government Is Working," *Roll Call,* April 19, 1984, 3. Congress has initiated change many times. A classic example is the Thirty-seventh Congress (1861–1863), which drafted "the blueprint for modern America" by enacting measures to finance the Civil War, build the transcontinental railroad, eradicate slavery, promote the land-grant college movement, provide settlers with homestead land, and create the Department of Agriculture. See James M. McPherson, *Battle Cry of Freedom: The Civil War Era* (New York: Ballantine, 1988), 452.

51. *Congressional Record,* 110th Cong., 2d sess., September 22, 2008, S9173.

52. Robert Luce, *Legislative Problems* (Boston: Houghton Mifflin, 1935), 426. Also see Louis Fisher, "The Authorization-Appropriation Process in Congress: Formal Rules and Informal Practices," *Catholic University Law Review* (Fall 1979): 51–105; Richard F. Fenno Jr., *The Power of the Purse* (Boston: Little, Brown, 1966).

53. John Cranford, "Just Say Maybe," *CQ Weekly,* March 7, 2011, 542.

54. Richard Munson, *The Cardinals of Capitol Hill* (New York: Grove Press, 1993), 6.

55. See Louis Fisher, "Annual Authorizations: Durable Roadblocks to Biennial Budgeting," *Public Budgeting and Finance* (Spring 1983): 23–40.

56. Chris Strohm, "Tensions Arise over Revised Intel Measure," *National Journal's's CongressDaily*, March 16, 2011, 16.

57. Quoted in Alan Ota, "Spending Bills May Be Democrats' Plan B," *CQ Today*, April 27, 2007, 8.

58. Jason A. MacDonald, "Limitation Riders and Congressional Influence over Bureaucratic Policy Decisions," *American Political Science Review* 104, no. 4 (2010): 766–782.

59. See Elana Shor and Jackie Kucinich, "GOP Plots Blue-Slip Attack," *The Hill*, May 30, 2007, 1.

60. See Peter Hanson, *Too Weak to Govern: Majority Party Power and Appropriations in the U.S. Senate* (Cambridge, UK: Cambridge University Press, 2014).

61. Major Garrett, "Extreme Makeover," *National Journal's*, March 12, 2011, 20.

62. Ibid., 18.

63. Susan Davis, "Yellow Lights," *National Journal's*, February 5, 2011, 47.

64. Sarah Barr, "House Republicans Plan Legislation to Make Defunding Reform Law Easier," *Daily Report for Executives*, March 4, 2011, A-15.

65. Jason DeParle, "U.S. Welfare System Dies as State Programs Emerge," *New York Times*, June 30, 1997, A1.

66. Quoted in Jonathan Weisman and Michael Fletcher, "GOP May Be Splintering on Social Security," *Washington Post*, April 27, 2005, A4.

67. Social Security Administration, "A Summary of the 2014 Annual Reports," www.ssa.gov/oact/trsum/index.html.

68. Ibid.

69. *Congressional Record*, 109th Cong., 1st sess., February 28, 2005, S1784.

70. David R. Francis, "Social Security: A Contrarian View," *Christian Science Monitor*, February 26, 2007, 17.

71. Billy House, "Dems Ramp Up Criticism of GOP on Social Security Cuts," *National Journal's CongressDaily*, March 10, 2011, 12.

72. Neil King Jr. and Scott Greenberg, "Poll Shows Budget-Cuts Dilemma," *Wall Street Journal's*, March 3, 2011, A5.

73. Alex Roarty, "Senior Moment," *National Journal's*, February 26, 2001, 76.

74. David Cook, "Rising Healthcare Costs Pose Fundamental Risk to U.S.," *Christian Science Monitor*, September 18, 2007, online edition.

75. 75. Social Security Administration, "A Summary of the 2014 Annual Reports," www.ssa.gov/oact/trsum/index.html.

76. William Welch, "Medicare: The Next Riddle for the Ages," *USA Today*, March 17, 2005, 10A.

77. Quoted in Julie Rovner, "The Real Budget Buster," *National Journal's CongressDaily AM*, April 5, 2001, 5.

78. Donald Kettl, "Looking for a Real Crisis: Try Medicaid," *Governing*, April 2005, 20.

79. Matthew Miller, "The Big Federal Freeze," *New York Times Magazine*, October 15, 2000, 94.

80. Jonathan Nicholson, "Do Tax Expenditures Really Work? Experts Say Not Enough Data to Tell," *Daily Report for Executives*, October 25, 2010, J-1.

81. Ibid.

82. Robert A. Green, "Limiting Deductions Could Be the New Tax Hike in Fiscal Cliff Avoidance," *Forbes*, November, 12, 2012.

83. Floyd Norris, "Republican's Tax Plan Awkwardly Aims at Rich," *New York Times*, March 6, 2014, http://www.nytimes.com/2014/03/07/business/economy/from-an-unexpected-source-a-tax-proposal-that-targets-the-rich.html?_r=0.

84. N. Gregory Mankiw, "The Blur between Spending and Taxes," *New York Times*, November 21, 2010, B5. Also see Nicholson, "Do Tax Expenditures Really Work?" J-1.

85. See Suzanne Mettler, *The Submerged State: How Invisible Government Policies Undermine American Democracy* (Chicago: University of Chicago Press, 2011); and Christopher

Howard, *The Hidden Welfare State: Tax Expenditures and Social Policy in the United States* (Princeton, NJ: Princeton University Press, 1997).

86. Gerald F. Seib, "As Budget Battle Rages On, a Quiet Cancer Grows," *Wall Street Journal's*, March 8, 2011, A4.

87. Congressional Budget Office, "CBO's Projection of Federal Interest Payments," September 3, 2014, https://www.cbo.gov/publication/45684.

88. Congressional Budget Office. "CBO's Projections of Federal Spending over the Next Decade," February 14, 2014, http://www.cbo.gov/publication/45087.

89. *Congressional Record,* 106th Cong., 2d sess., March 2, 2000, S1050.

90. Stephanie Kirchgaessner, "Republicans' Rising Start Takes Risk on Medicare," *Financial Times,* April 6, 2011, 4. Also see Paul D. Ryan, "The GOP Path to Prosperity," *Wall Street Journal's,* April 5, 2011, A15.

91. Mark Preston, "'Vote-a-Rama' Keeps Wearing Senate Down," *Roll Call,* March 26, 2003, 1.

92. *Congressional Record,* 107th Cong., 1st sess., February 15, 2001, S1532.

93. John Ellwood, "Budget Control in a Redistributive Environment," in *Making Economic Policy in Congress,* ed. Allen Schick (Washington, DC: American Enterprise Institute, 1983), 93. Data on the number of times reconciliation has been employed were provided by budget expert Robert Keith, Congressional Research Service.

94. Testimony of Sen. Robert C. Byrd, Senate Budget Committee, *Senate Procedures for Consideration of the Budget Resolution/Reconciliation,* February 12, 2009, 3.

95. David Rosenbaum, "Democratic Filibuster Hopes Fade," *New York Times,* November 18, 2002, A15; David Baumann, "The Octopus That Might Eat Congress," *National Journal's,* May 14, 2005, 1470–1475.

96. The election was to fill the vacancy due to the death of Democrat Ted Kennedy.

97. William Dauster, "Budget Process Issues for 1993," *Journal's of Law and Politics* 9 (1992): 26.

98. Quoted in ibid., 27.

99. Lori Montgomery, "House GOP Passes New Rules on Tax and Spending Legislation," *Washington Post,* January 6, 2011, A7.

100. Cristina Marcos, "House Adopts 'Dynamic Scoring' Rule," *The Hill,* January 6, 2015, http://thehill.com/blogs/floor-action/house/228684-house-adopts-dynamic-scoring-rule.

101. Congressional Budget Office, "An Update to the Budget and Economic Outlook: 2014 to 2024," August 27, 2014, https://www.cbo.gov/publication/45653.

102. Matt Bai, "Sure Recipe for Decline: Neglect and Gluttony," *New York Times,* February 17, 2011, A17.

103. *Congressional Record,* 107th Cong., 2d sess., July 16, 2002, H4749.

CHAPTER 15

1. Jay Solomon and Carol E. Lee, "An Arc of Instability Unseen since the '70s," *Wall Street Journal's,* July 14, 2014, A1.

2. Ronald Brownstein, "World of Hurt," *National Journal,* July 26, 2014, 14.

3. Mark Landler, "A White House Position That Stands on a Narrow Definition of War," *New York Times,* September 19, 2014, A9.

4. James Kitfield, "Balance of Power," *Government Executive,* July/August 2014, 41.

5. Michael Crowley, "The War over President Obama's New War in Iraq," *Politico,* November 10, 2014, 1, online edition.

6. Quoted in Samuel Eliot Morison, *The Oxford History of the American People* (New York: Oxford University Press, 1965), 346.

7. Edward S. Corwin, *The President: Office and Powers, 1787–1957*, 4th ed. (New York: New York University Press, 1957), 171. Also see Cecil V. Crabb Jr. and Pat M. Holt, *Invitation to Struggle: Congress, the President, and Foreign Policy*, 4th ed. (Washington, DC: CQ Press, 1992).

8. Corwin, *The President*, 171 (emphasis in the original).

9. Alexander Hamilton, James Madison, and John Jay, *The Federalist Papers*, ed. Clinton Rossiter (New York: Mentor Books, 1961), 391–393.

10. On how the growth of the security state has affected interbranch relationships, see Rebecca U. Thorpe, *The American Warfare State: The Domestic Politics of Military Spending* (Chicago: University of Chicago Press, 2014).

11. Testimony before the House International Relations Committee, January 12, 1995. Reported by Maureen Dowd, *New York Times*, January 13, 1995, A1.

12. Corwin, *The President*, 171 (emphasis in the original).

13. Louis Fisher, *The Politics of Shared Power: Congress and the Executive*, 4th ed. (College Station, TX: Texas A&M University Press, 1998), 177.

14. *Youngstown Sheet and Tube Co. v. Sawyer*, 343 U.S. 636 (1952).

15. Rajiv Chandrasekaran, "Battle Looms over Pace of Afghanistan Pullout," *Washington Post*, March 31, 2011, A11.

16. Karen DeYoung and Missy Ryan, "U.S. Expands Scope of Future Operations in Afghanistan," *Washington Post*, November 23, 2014, A18; and Mark Mazzetti and Eric Schmitt, "In Secret, Obama Extends U.S. Role in Afghan Combat," *New York Times*, November 22, 2014, A1.

17. Cecil V. Crabb Jr., Glenn J. Antizzo, and Leila E. Sarieddine, *Congress and the Foreign Policy Process* (Baton Rouge: Louisiana State University Press, 2000), 4.

18. Ibid., 163.

19. Bryan Bender, "Kerry Poised to Cap Long Journey," *Boston Globe*, November 20, 2008, online edition.

20. Jonathan Broder, "Foreign Relations," *CQ Weekly*, November 6, 2014, 74.

21. Martin Matishak, "Chairman Emerges as Top Obama Critic," *The Hill*, September 17, 2014, 6.

22. Amy B. Zegart, "The Domestic Politics of Irrational Intelligence Oversight, *Political Science Quarterly* (Spring 2011): 25.

23. Henry A. Kissinger, "Implementing Bush's Vision," *Washington Post*, May 16, 2005, A17.

24. *Congressional Record*, 105th Cong., 2d sess., March 2, 1998, E252.

25. Kevin Baron, "Panetta Says Washington 'Dysfunction' Now a Security Threat," *NationalJournal.com*, June 22, 2012, online edition. Also see Coral Davenport, "Pentagon Signals Security Risks of Climate Change," *New York Times*, October 14, 2014, A14.

26. Quoted in George E. Condon, "Selling Foreign Policy," *National Journal's*, March 1, 2014, 35.

27. Chris Strohm, "A Secure Role," *National Journal's CongressDaily*, February 28, 2011, 3.

28. Fareed Zakaria, "A Pentagon Out of Control," *Washington Post*, December 5, 2014, A17.

29. Christopher J. Deering, "Congress, the President, and Military Policy," in *Congress and the Presidency: Invitation to Struggle*, ed. Roger H. Davidson, *The Annals* 499 (September 1988): 136–147.

30. Dion Nissenbaum, "Fighting Islamic State Strains the Budget," *Wall Street Journal*, October 1, 2014, A4.

31. William D. Hartung, "The Pentagon's Mystery Money," *Los Angeles Times*, August 15, 2014, online edition.

32. *Congressional Record*, September 17, 2014, E1444.

33. Walter Pincus, "The Military's New Metrics: Smaller, Leaner, More Agile," *Washington Post*, February 7, 2012, A25.

34. Quoted in Matt Richtel, "Trade Investors Cull Start-Ups for Pentagon," *New York Times*, May 7, 2007, C8.

35. *Budget of the United States Government, Fiscal Year 2006,* Historical Tables (Washington, DC: Government Printing Office, 2005), table 3.2.

36. Quoted in Thomas Shanker, "Defense Secretary Urges More Spending for U.S. Diplomacy," *New York Times,* November 27, 2007, A6.

37. Christopher Dickey, "The Surveillance-Industrial Complex," *New York Times Book Review,* January 11, 2009, 11.

38. Tim Smart, "Getting the F-22 off the Ground," *Washington Post,* April 20, 1998, 12; Tim Weiner, "Air Superiority at $258 Million a Pop," *New York Times,* October 27, 2004, C1.

39. Christian Davenport, "The Warthog Still Has Its Wingmen," *Washington Post,* November 19, 2014, A12.

40. Rowan Scarborough, "Firestorm after 'Friendly Fire,'" *Washington Times,* October 30, 2014, A13.

41. Ibid.

42. *Congressional Record,* June 18, 2014, H5485.

43. Charles Hoskinson, "Unloved Warthog Lives On to Fight Another Day," *WashingtonExaminer.Com,* December 8, 2014, 4.

44. Rowan Scarborough, "Prices Soar, Enthusiasm Dives for F-35 Lightning," *Washington Times,* March 7, 2013, A1. The items quoted in this paragraph are taken from this source.

45. Patrick Tucker, "Five Things You Can Buy for an F-35," *Government Executive,* November/December 2014, 35.

46. Rajiv Chandrasekaran, "Too Big to Bail," *Washington Post,* March 10, 2013, A8, A9. Also see Tony Capaccio, "Pentagon Cuts Plan for F-35 Jet Order," February 17, 2014, A17.

47. Quoted in Kevin Sack, "For the South, GOP Secures Defense Bounty," *New York Times,* November 18, 1997, A1.

48. *Congressional Record,* 100th Cong., 2d sess., July 7, 1988, 17072.

49. Karl Viox, "It's Closing Time for Base Commission," *Washington Post,* December 29, 1995, A21. Scholars regard this as an intriguing example of blame-avoidance politics. See, for example, Christopher J. Deering, "Congress, the President, and Automatic Government: The Case of Military Base Closures," in *Rivals for Power: Presidential-Congressional Relations,* ed. James A. Thurber (Washington, DC: CQ Press, 1996).

50. Megan Scully, "Military Plan Hits BRAC Wall," *CQ Weekly,* February 6, 2012, 235.

51. Megan Scully, "Lawmakers Give Pentagon Green Light for BRAC-Related Study," *Roll Call,* December 3, 2014, online edition. A Pentagon official made clear that the BRAC-related study "would simply provide an overview of how much excess capacity exists—not where it exists, which would be a politically sensitive issue that could make convincing Congress of the need for another BRAC round even more difficult than it already is."

52. William H. Cooper, "The Future of U.S. Trade Policy: An Analysis of Issues and Options for the 112th Congress," Congressional Research Service Report R41145, January 4, 2011.

53. U.S. Trade Representative Ron Kirk, "The Monitor Breakfast," *Christian Science Monitor,* March 28, 2011, 19.

54. Rep. David Dreier, "Parties Can Work Together to Revive Trade Agenda," *Politico,* January 5, 2011, 35.

55. Quoted in John Stanton, "Sessions Continues Blockade of Trade Bill over Sleeping Bags," *Roll Call,* February 9, 2011, online edition.

56. Len Bracken, "Obama to Discuss Trade Promotion Authority with Congressional Leaders of Both Parties," *Daily Report for Executives,* December 4, 2014, A-32.

57. Both quotations in the paragraph are found in Kate Ackley, "Fast-Track Issue Drives Debate on Trade Pacts," *CQ Weekly,* November 17, 2014, 1366.

58. Richard G. Lugar and Thomas A. Daschle, "Defeating a Global Enemy—Hunger," *Washington Times,* May 1, 2013, B4. Also see Ellyn Ferguson, "Despite Tug-of-War, USAID Gains Leeway

on Food Aid," *Roll Call*, March 3, 2014, 4; and Philip Brasher, "Fragile Future for Food Aid," *CQ Weekly*, December 8, 2014, 1458–1461.

59. Thom Shanker, "U.S. Arms Sales Make Up Most of Global Market," *New York Times*, August 27, 2012, A6.

60. Leslie Wayne, "Foreign Sales by U.S. Arms Makers Doubled in a Year," *New York Times*, November 11, 2006, B3.

61. Charles McC. Mathias Jr., "Ethnic Groups and Foreign Policy," *Foreign Affairs* 59 (Summer 1981): 975–998.

62. Joseph J. Schatz, "Has Congress Given Bush Too Free a Spending Hand?" *CQ Weekly*, April 12, 2002, 859.

63. James Kitfield, "The Indispensable, Unaffordable Nation," *National Journal's*, September 11, 2010, 35.

64. Marian L. Lawson and Curt Tarnoff, "U.S. Foreign Assistance," *In Focus* (Congressional Research Service), October 22, 2014, 1. This section on foreign assistance draws heavily on the CRS report.

65. Reps. Howard I. Berman and Gerald E. Connolly, "Overhaul of U.S. Foreign Aid Is Overdue," *The Hill*, December 21, 2012, 16.

66. Ibid.

67. Ibid.

68. Lawson and Tarnoff, "U.S. Foreign Assistance," 1.

69. David P. Auerswald, "Advice and Consent: The Forgotten Power," in *Congress and the Politics of Foreign Policy,* ed. Colton C. Campbell, Nicol C. Rae, and John Stack (Upper Saddle River, NJ: Prentice Hall, 2003), 47–48.

70. Peter Baker, "Gamble by Obama Pays Off with Final Approval of Arms Control Pact," *New York Times,* December 23, 2010, A6.

71. Quoted in Gail Russell Chaddock, "Off-Radar Tax Breaks Draw New Scrutiny," *Christian Science Monitor,* March 9, 2005, 11.

72. Michael John Garcia, "International Law and Agreements: Their Effect upon U.S. Law," Congressional Research Service Report RL32528, January 23, 2014, 5.

73. Glen S. Krutz and Jeffrey S. Peake, *Treaty Politics and the Rise of Executive Agreements: International Commitments in a System of Shared Powers* (Ann Arbor: University of Michigan Press, 2009), 10.

74. Jeanne J. Grimmett, "Why Certain Trade Agreements Are Approved as Congressional–Executive Agreements Rather Than as Treaties," Congressional Research Service Report 97-896, February 17, 2009, 5.

75. This section draws on the invaluable summary of congressional policy initiation in Ellen C. Collier, "Foreign Policy Roles of the President and Congress," Congressional Research Service Report 93–20F, January 6, 1993, 11–17.

76. The classic account of this incident is Chalmers M. Roberts, "The Day We Didn't Go to War," *Reporter,* September 14, 1954, 31–35.

77. *Congressional Record*, July 22, 2014, S4767.

78. William G. Howell and Jon C. Pevehouse, *When Danger Lurks: Congressional Checks on Presidential War Powers* (Princeton, NJ: Princeton University Press, 2007), 223.

79. Ellen C. Collier, "Foreign Policy by Reporting Requirement," *Washington Quarterly* 11 (Winter 1988): 75.

80. Bruce J. Schulman, "Congress' Wartime Quandary," *Los Angeles Times,* April 27, 2003, M2.

81. Matt Hansen, "Investigating Benghazi," *Los Angeles Times*, December 4, 2014, online edition.

82. Ibid.

83. Michael S. Schmidt, "G.O.P.-Led Benghazi Panel Bolsters Administration," *New York Times*, November 23, 2014, 12. Also see Michael S. Schmidt, "Benghazi Panel Leader Defends Inquiry," *New York Times*, December 11, 2014, A20.
84. Jonathan Weisman and Jennifer Steinhauer, "Democrats Wary of Benghazi Inquiry Stretching into '16 Election Season," *Washington Post*, August 29, 2014, A2.
85. Guy Taylor, "Carter Hearings May Hit Obama," *Washington Times*, December 8, 2014, A4.
86. Stacy Kaper, "Hold on Nominees Useful Leverage for Senate Hawks," *National Journal's Daily*, January 15, 2013, 8.
87. James M. Lindsay, "Congress, Foreign Policy, and the New Institutionalism," *International Studies Quarterly* 38 (June 1994): 281–304.
88. An early influential analysis of this phenomenon is John E. Mueller, *War, Presidents, and Public Opinion* (New York: Wiley, 1973), 208–213.
89. Richard F. Grimmett, "Instances of Use of United States Armed Forces Abroad, 1798–2006," Congressional Research Service Report RL32170, January 8, 2007.
90. Quotes from Helen Dewar, "Congress's Reaction to TV Coverage Shows Ambivalence on Foreign Policy," *Washington Post*, October 9, 1993, A14; and Helen Dewar, "Clinton, Congress at Brink of Foreign Policy Dispute," *Washington Post*, May 16, 1994, A1.
91. Douglas L. Kriner, *After the Rubicon: Congress, Presidents, and the Politics of Waging War* (Chicago: University of Chicago Press, 2010).
92. Richard F. Grimmett, "War Powers Resolution: Presidential Compliance," Congressional Research Service Report RL33532, March 25, 2011. Also see Richard Grimmett, "The War Powers Resolution after Thirty-Six Years," Congressional Research Service Report R4119, April 22, 2010.
93. See David A. Fahrenthold, "Obama Misses Deadline for Approval of Libya Operations," *Washington Post*, May 21, 2011, A3; and John C. Yoo and Robert J. Delahunty, "Libya and the War Powers Resolution," *Wall Street Journal's*, May 20, 2011, A15.
94. Jacqueline Klimas, "Impasse May Doom War Vote," *Washington Times*, December 5, 2014, A3.
95. Charlie Savage, "Congress's Inaction Could Be Legal Basis for Stronger Executive War Powers," *New York Times*, September 19, 2014, A10.
96. Congress is providing in 2015 over $700 million "to recruit, train and equip a rebel army in Syria." This type of support is intended for "appropriately vetted elements of the Syrian opposition and other appropriately vetted Syrian groups or individuals." Furthermore, "Syria now has the largest concentration of Islamist terror groups, all fighting to overthrow the Assad regime. Some experts estimate the number of these groups at more than 1,000, with many consisting of just a few members." See John M. Donnelly, *CQ News*, December 12, 2014, 1–6.
97. *Congressional Record*, September 17, 2014, H7623.
98. Jeremy Herb, "Q&A with Retiring Armed Services Chairman Levin," *Politico*, December 9, 2014, 6.
99. Carol Morello, "Kerry: Don't Bind President's Hands," *Washington Post*, December 10, 2014, A19.
100. Jacqueline Klimas, "Congress Still Not Calling Islamic State Battle a War," *Washington Times*, April 28, 2015, A4.
101. David E. Sanger, David Barboza, and Nicole Perlroth, "China's Army Seen as Tied to Hacking against U.S.," *New York Times*, February 19, 2013, A1.
102. Nicole Perlroth, "Report Says Cyberattacks Originated Inside Iran," *New York Times*, December 3, 2014, A14.
103. Rob Margetta, "Defense Authorization Bill Ramps Up Cyber-Security," *Roll Call*, December 3, 2013, online edition.

104. Tom Kean and Lee Hamilton, "A New Threat Grows amid Shades of 9/11," *Wall Street Journal's*, September 11, 2014, A13. Former New Jersey governor Thomas Kean and former House member Lee Hamilton headed the 9/11 Commission created shortly after the 2001 terrorist attack on the United States.

105. "The Spy Inside," *Washington Post*, December 4, 2014, A16. See Ellen Nakashima, "NSA Chief: Foreign Powers Are Penetrating U.S. Infrastructure," *Washington Post*, November 21, 2014, A6.

106. David E. Sanger, "Syria War Stirs New U.S. Debate on Cyberattacks," *New York Times*, February 25, 2014, A1.

107. Jack Goldsmith, "Stealth Wars Require Rules, Too," *Washington Post*, February 6, 2013, A17. Goldsmith also includes covert action, special forces, drone surveillance and targeting, and other stealthy means within his call for new rules for a new type of war. Also see David E. Sanger, "In Cyberspace, New Cold War," *New York Times*, February 25, 2013 A1.

108. "Drones Will Change War—and More," *The Economist*, March 29, 2014, 11.

109. See, for example, Mark Mazzetti, "Use of Drones for Killings Risks a War without End, Panel Concludes in Report," *New York Times*, June 26, 2014, A9; Doyle McManus, "The Coming Backlash against Drones," *Los Angeles Times*, July 6, 2014, online edition; Sam Jones, "Drone Strikes on ISIS Loom Large in Allies' Strategy," *Financial Times*, October 13, 2014, 4; and Greg Miller, "Payouts after U.S. Drone Strike Top $1 Million," *Washington Post*, August 19, 2014, A7.

110. Sam Leith, "Saying Nothing Is Not an Option," *Financial Times*, October 10–11, 2014, 19.

111. David Ignatius, "Hemmed in by a Limited War," *Washington Post*, October 10, 2014, A21.

112. James Kitfield, "Patterns of Death," *National Journal's*, March 10, 2012, 24.

113. Daniel Dombey, James Blitz, and Peter Spiegel, "An Advancing Front," *Financial Times*, May 20, 2011, 9.

114. James Mann, "On Realism, Old and New," *The American Prospect* (Fall 2014): 30.

115. James M. Lindsay, "Congress and Foreign Policy: Why the Hill Matters," *Political Science Quarterly* 107 (Winter 1992–1993): 626–627.

116. Robert C. Byrd, *Losing America* (New York: Norton, 2005), 23.

CHAPTER 16

1. Quoted in Carl Hulse and David M. Herszenhorn, "Behind Closed Doors, Warnings of Calamity," *New York Times*, September 20, 2008, C5.

2. Jonathan Weisman, David Cho, and Paul Kane, "With No Plan B, House Reluctantly Passes Politically Risky Measure," *Washington Post*, October 4, 2008, A1.

3. Quoted in ibid.

4. David M. Herszenhorn, "Administration Is Seeking $700 Billion for Wall Street in Possible Record Bailout," *New York Times*, September 21, 2008, A1.

5. Quoted in Hulse and Herszenhorn, "Behind Closed Doors," C5.

6. Quoted in Joe Nocera, "36 Hours of Alarm and Action as Crisis Spread," *New York Times*, October 2, 2008, A1.

7. Jackie Calmes, "Dazed Capital Feels Its Way, Eyes on Nov. 4," *Washington Post*, September 20, 2008, A1.

8. Quoted in Lori Montgomery, Paul Kane, and Neil Irwin, "Bailout Proposal Meets Bipartisan Outrage; Lawmakers Balk as Officials Press Case for Quick Action," *Washington Post*, September 24, 2008, A1.

9. David M. Herszenhorn, "Word Reaches Congress: As the Market Goes Down, So Goes the Electorate," *New York Times*, October 2, 2008, C10.

10. Jonathan Weisman, "House Rejects Financial Rescue, Sending Stocks Plummeting," *Washington Post*, September 30, 2008, A1.

11. "Bailout Breakdown," *New York Times*, September 25, 2008, A18; David S. Broder, "Credibility Test for Congress," September 25, 2008, A19.

12. For a more detailed account of these events, see Robert G. Kaiser, *Act of Congress: How America's Essential Institution Works, and How It Doesn't* (New York: Knopf, 2013), 13–26.

13. Sarah A. Binder, Thomas E. Mann, Norman J. Ornstein, and Molly Reynolds, "Mending the Broken Branch: Assessing the 110th Congress, Anticipating the 111th," Brookings Institution Report, January 2009, www.brookings.edu/papers/2009/0108_broken_branch_binder_mann .aspx, 33.

14. Andrew Kohut, "Pessimistic Public Doubts Effectiveness of Stimulus, TARP," Pew Research Center for the People and the Press, April 28, 2010, http://people-press.org/reports/pdf/608. pdf.

15. Paul Kiel and Dan Nguyen, "Bailout Tracker," ProPublica (updated January 23, 2015), http:// projects.propublica.org/bailout/.

16. Tim Massad, "The Response to the Financial Crisis—in Charts," *Treasury Notes*, U.S. Department of the Treasury, April 13, 2012, www.treasury.gov/connect/blog/Pages/financial-crisis-response-in-charts.aspx.

17. Steven Pearlstein, "Unfairly Rewarding Greedy Bankers, and Why It Works," *Washington Post*, January 14, 2009, D1.

18. See Charles O. Jones, *The Presidency in a Separated System* (Washington, DC: Brookings, 1994).

19. *Congressional Record*, 105th Cong., 1st sess., May 21, 1997, H3072.

20. Glenn R. Parker and Roger H. Davidson, "Why Do Americans Love Their Congressmen So Much More Than Their Congress?" *Legislative Studies Quarterly* 4 (February 1979): 53–61.

21. See Roger H. Davidson, "The House of Representatives: Managing Legislative Complexity," in *Workways of Governance: Monitoring Our Government's Health*, ed. Roger H. Davidson (Washington, DC: Governance Institute and Brookings, 2003), 24–46; and Sarah A. Binder, "The Senate: Does It Deliberate? Can It Act?" in Davidson, *Workways of Governance*, 47–64.

22. Michael Leahy, "House Rules: Freshman Congressman Joe Courtney, Elected by a Margin of 83 Votes, Is Learning That the First Requirement of Power Is Self-Preservation," *Washington Post Magazine*, June 10, 2007, W12.

23. Congressional Management Foundation and the Society for Human Resource Management, *Life in Congress: The Member Perspective*, 2013, http://www.congressfoundation.org/storage/ documents/CMF_Pubs/life-in-congress-the-member-perspective.pdf.

24. Quoted in Mary Lynn F. Jones, "Family Concerns Prompt Early Hill Retirements," *The Hill*, March 20, 2002, 12.

25. Quoted in ibid.

26. Quoted in Leahy, "House Rules," W12.

27. Philip Edward Jones, "Which Buck Stops Here? Accountability for Policy Positions and Policy Outcomes in Congress," *Journal's of Politics*, 73 (2011): 764–782.

28. Quoted in ibid.

29. Bob Benenson, "Savvy 'Stars' Making Local TV a Potent Tool," *Congressional Quarterly Weekly Report*, July 18, 1987, 1551–1555.

30. Timothy Cook, *Making Laws and Making News: Media Strategies in the U.S. House of Representatives* (Washington, DC: Brookings, 1989), 82–83.

31. Rebecca Rifkin, "Americans Rate Nurses Highest on Honesty, Ethical Standards," Gallup, Inc., news release, December 18, 2014, http://www.gallup.com/poll/180260/americans-rate-nurses-highest-honesty-ethical-standards.aspx.

32. Gallup, Congress and the Public, http://www.gallup.com/poll/1600/congress-public.aspx.

33. Lee H. Hamilton, "Ten Things I Wish Political Scientists Would Teach about Congress," Pi Sigma Alpha Lecture, American Political Science Association, August 31, 2000, 7. Also see Hamilton's thoughtful book, *How Congress Works and Why You Should Care* (Bloomington: Indiana University Press, 2004).

34. Quoted in T. R. Goldman, "The Influence Industry's Senior Class," *Legal Times,* June 16, 1997, 4.

35. Robert Costa, "Rep. Michael Grimm to Resign," *Washington Post,* December 29, 2014, http://www.washingtonpost.com/blogs/post-politics/wp/2014/12/29/rep-grimm-expected-to-resign/.

36. Susan Schmidt and James V. Grimaldi, "Abramoff Pleads Guilty to 3 Counts," *Washington Post,* January 4, 2006, A1.

37. Paul Blumenthal, "Abramoff Investigation Continues Apace," Sunlight Foundation weblog, February 2, 2009, http://sunlightfoundation.com/blog/2009/02/02/abramoff-investigation-continues-apace/.

38. Scott Higham, "Congressional Ethics Committees Protect Legislators, Critics Say," *Washington Post*, October 7, 2012, www.washingtonpost.com/investigations/congressional-ethics-committees-protect-legislators-critics-say/2012/10/07/a313e59c-e251-11e1-ae7f-d2a13e249eb2_story.html.

39. Ethics Committee, U.S. House of Representatives, "Summary of Activities One Hundred Thirteenth Congress," H. Rept. 113–727, https://www.congress.gov/113/crpt/hrpt727/CRPT-113hrpt727.pdf.

40. Rifkin, "Americans Rate Nurses Highest."

41. Cass R. Sunstein, "Unchecked and Unbalanced," *American Prospect* 38 (May–June 1998): 23. Sunstein served as head of the Office of Information and Regulatory Affairs in the Office of Management and Budget during President Obama's first term.

42. Ashley Parker, "Congressman in Drug Case Resigns Seat in Florida," *New York Times,* January 27, 2014, http://www.nytimes.com/2014/01/28/us/politics/florida-congressman-facing-pressure-after-cocaine-charge-to-resign.html?_r=0.

43. John Bresnahan and Jake Sherman, "Report: Video Shows Vance McAllister Kissing Staffer," *Politico,* April 7, 2014, http://www.politico.com/story/2014/04/vance-mcallister-video-kissing-staffer-105435.html.

44. This list includes Rep. Bob Livingston, R-La. (1977–1999); Rep. Gary A. Condit, D-Calif. (1989–2003); Rep. Mark Foley, R-Fla. (1995–2006); Rep. Tim Mahoney, D-Fla. (2007–2008); Rep. Mark Souder, R-Ind. (1995–2010); Rep. Chris Lee, R-N.Y. (2009–2011); Sen. John Ensign, R-Nev. (2001–2011); Rep. Anthony Weiner, D-N.Y. (1999–2011); and Rep. Vito Fossella, R-N.Y. (1997–2009).

45. John M. Barry, *The Ambition and the Power: The Fall of Jim Wright* (New York: Viking, 1989).

46. Edward Epstein, "GOP Makes Much Ado about the Size of Pelosi's Plane; the House Speaker Has Had the Use of a Government Jet since the September 11 Attacks," *San Francisco Chronicle,* February 8, 2007, A3.

47. G. Calvin Mackenzie with Michael Hafken, *Scandal Proof: Do Ethics Laws Make Government Ethical?* (Washington, DC: Brookings, 2002), 158.

48. Benjamin Ginsberg and Martin Shefter, *Politics by Other Means: Politicians, Prosecutors, and the Press from Watergate to Whitewater,* 3d ed. (New York: Norton, 2002).

49. Jennifer L. Lawless and Richard L. Fox, *Running from Office: Why Young Americans Are Turned Off to Politics* (New York: Oxford University Press, 2015). See also Paul C. Light, "Measuring the Health of the Public Service," in Davidson, *Workways of Governance,* 96–97.

50. Jennifer L. Lawless and Richard Logan Fox, *It Still Takes a Candidate: Why Women Don't Run for Office* (New York: Cambridge University Press, 2010).

51. Jennifer L. Lawless, *Becoming a Candidate: Political Ambition and the Decision to Run for Office* (New York: Cambridge University Press), 166–170.

52. Gary C. Jacobson, "The Misallocation of Resources in House Campaigns," *Congress Reconsidered*, 5th ed., ed. Lawrence C. Dodd and Bruce I. Oppenheimer (Washington, DC: CQ Press, 1993), 153–182.

53. Diane Hollern Harvey, "Who Should Govern? Public Preferences for Congressional and Presidential Power," Ph.D. dissertation, University of Maryland, 1998.

54. Hamilton, "Ten Things I Wish Political Scientists Would Teach about Congress," 3.

55. Paul C. Light, *Government's Greatest Achievements: From Civil Rights to Homeland Security* (Washington, DC: Brookings, 2002).

56. Ibid., 63.

57. See, for example, the collection of essays in Nathaniel Persily, ed., *Solutions to Political Polarization in America* (New York: Cambridge University Press, 2015).

58. Richard Hall, *Participation in Congress* (New Haven, CT: Yale University Press, 1996), 2.

59. Binder et al., "Mending the Broken Branch," 7.

60. Barbara Sinclair, *Unorthodox Lawmaking: New Legislative Processes in the U.S. Congress*, 4th ed. (Washington, DC: CQ Press, 2011).

61. Ibid.

62. James M. Curry, *Legislating in the Dark: Information and Power in the House of Representatives* (Chicago: University of Chicago Press, 2015).

63. Bridget Bowman, "After Years of Cuts, Committees Hope to Bolster Budgets," *Roll Call*, February 11, 2015, 1.

64. Norman J. Ornstein, Thomas E. Mann, Michael J. Malbin, Andrew Rugg, and Raffaela Wakeman, *Vital Statistics on Congress—a Joint Effort from Brookings and the American Enterprise Institute*, http://www.brookings.edu/research/reports/2013/07/vital-statistics-congress-mann-ornstein, Table 5-5.

65. R. Eric Petersen and Ida A. Brudnick, "Legislative Branch: FY2015 Appropriations," CRS Report for Congress, R43557, November 13, 2014.

66. Matthew Rumsey, "Continued Cuts to Legislative Branch Budget Hurt Transparency, Accountability, and Capacity," The Sunlight Foundation, July 9, 2013, http://sunlightfoundation.com/blog/2013/07/09/continued-cuts-to-legislative-branch-budget-hurt-transparency-accountability-and-capacity/.

67. Thomas E. Mann and Norman J. Ornstein, *The Broken Branch: How Congress Is Failing America and How to Get It Back on Track* (New York: Oxford University Press, 2006), 216.

68. Commission on Political Reform, "Governing in a Polarized America: A Bipartisan Blueprint to Strengthen Our Democracy," Bipartisan Policy Center, June 24, 2014, http://bipartisanpolicy.org/wp-content/uploads/sites/default/files/files/BPC%20CPR%20Governing%20in%20a%20Polarized%20America.pdf.

69. Lee Hamilton, "We Can't Wait Much Longer to Fix Congress," *Comments on Congress*, December 15, 2005.

70. Nelson W. Polsby, *How Congress Evolves: Social Bases of Institutional Change* (New York: Oxford University Press, 2004), 130–137.

71. Mickey Edwards, "Wanted: A Congress with a Backbone," *Los Angeles Times*, August 29, 2006, B13.

72. Binder et al., "Mending the Broken Branch," 7.

73. Quoted by David S. Broder, "Role Models, Now More Than Ever," *Washington Post*, July 13, 2003, B7.

74. Laurel Harbridge and Neil Malhotra, "Electoral Incentives and Partisan Conflict in Congress: Evidence from Survey Experiments," *American Journal's of Political Science* 55 (July 2011): 494–510.

75. Mark D. Ramirez, "The Dynamics of Partisan Conflict on Congressional Approval," *American Journal's of Political Science* 53 (July 2009): 683.

76. Sinclair, *Unorthodox Lawmaking.*

77. Alexander Burns, "VP: Constitution 'On Its Head,'" Politico44: A Living Diary of the Obama Presidency, *Politico* weblog, January 18, 2010, www.politico.com/politico44/perm/0110/biden_slams_filibuster_fe40df44-9045-4c26-a715-51c427035eae.html.

78. Sinclair, *Unorthodox Lawmaking*, 282.

79. Ian Millhiser, "The Tyranny of the Timepiece: Senate Rules Obstruct Voting to a Degree That Wounds Our Government," Center for American Progress Report, September 28, 2010, www.americanprogress.org/issues/2010/09/tyranny_of_the_timepiece.html.

80. Peter C. Hanson, "Abandoning the Regular Order: Majority Party Influence on Appropriations in the U.S. Senate." *Political Research Quarterly* 67 (2014): 519–532.

81. Frances E. Lee and Sarah A. Binder, "Making Deals in Congress" in *Solutions to Political Polarization in America*, Nathaniel Persily, ed. (New York: Cambridge University Press, 2015), 240–261.

82. For an extended analysis of these dilemmas, see John B. Gilmour, *Strategic Disagreement: Stalemate in American Politics* (Pittsburgh: University of Pittsburgh Press, 1995).

83. C-SPAN began gavel-to-gavel telecasting of House proceedings in 1979 and Senate proceedings in 1986.

84. Joseph J. Schatz, "Tune a New Channel into the Senate," *CQ Weekly*, April 19, 2010, 956.

85. E. Scott Adler, *Why Congressional Reforms Fail: Reelection and the House Committee System* (Chicago: University of Chicago Press, 2002), 11.

86. Eric Schickler, *Disjointed Pluralism: Institutional Innovation and the Development of the U.S. Congress* (Princeton, NJ: Princeton University Press, 2001), 268.

87. Bob Schieffer, *This Just In: What I Couldn't Tell You on TV* (New York: Putnam, 2003).

88. See Martin P. Wattenburg, *Is Voting for Young People?* 2d ed. (New York: Pearson Longman, 2007), esp. chaps. 1–2.

89. Bill Moyers, "Journalism and Democracy," *Nation*, May 7, 2001, 12.

90. Media critic Neal Gabler's commentaries are especially incisive. See "The Media Bias Myth," *Los Angeles Times*, December 22, 2002, M1.

91. Jessica C. Gerrity, "Understanding Congressional Approval: Public Opinion from 1974 to 2014," in *The Evolving Congress*, U.S. Senate Committee on Rules and Administration, S. Prt. 113-30, 189–216.

92. Lydia Saad, "Congress Approval at 18%, Stuck in Long-Term Low Streak," Gallup, Inc., news release, November 26, 2012, www.gallup.com/poll/158948/congress-approval-stuck-long-term-low-streak.aspx.

93. John R. Hibbing and Elizabeth Theiss-Morse, *Congress as Public Enemy* (Cambridge, UK: Cambridge University Press, 1995), 147.

94. Gerrity, "Understanding Congressional Approval," 210.

95. See Louis Fisher, *Presidential War Power*, 2d ed. (Lawrence: University Press of Kansas, 2004).

96. Josh Rogin, "How Obama Turned on a Dime toward War," The Cable, *Foreign Policy* weblog, March 18, 2011, http://thecable.foreignpolicy.com/posts/2011/03/18/how_obama_turned_on_a_dime_toward_war.

97. Quoted in Kirk Victor, "Congress in Eclipse," *National Journal's*, April 5, 2003, 1068.

98. John Bresnahan and Seung Min Kim, "Attorney General Eric Holder Held in Contempt of Congress," *Politico*, June 28, 2012, http://www.politico.com/news/stories/0612/77988.html.

99. Jake Sherman and John Bresnahan, "White House Met Twice with Congress Aides on ISIL," *Politico*, September 29, 2014, http://www.politico.com/story/2014/09/white-house-aumf-islamic-state-111442.html; and Stephanie Condon, "Can Congress Keep Putting Off a Vote on the War on ISIS?" CBS News, December 10, 2014, http://www.cbsnews.com/news/can-congress-keep-putting-off-a-vote-on-the-war-on-isis/.

100. Hamilton, "We Can't Wait Much Longer to Fix Congress:" David Nather, "Congress as Watchdog: Asleep on the Job?" *CQ Weekly*, May 22, 2004, 1190.

101. Richard L. Hasen, "End of the Dialogue? Political Polarization, the Supreme Court, and Congress," *Southern California Law Review*, 86, no. 2 (2013): 2012–265.

102. Ibid., 139.

103. James L. Sundquist, *The Decline and Resurgence of Congress* (Washington, DC: Brookings, 1981), 482–483.

104. Andrew Rudalevige, *The New Imperial Presidency: Renewing Presidential Power after Watergate* (Ann Arbor: University of Michigan Press, 2005), 261.

CONGRESSIONAL TIME LINE: **1789–1932**

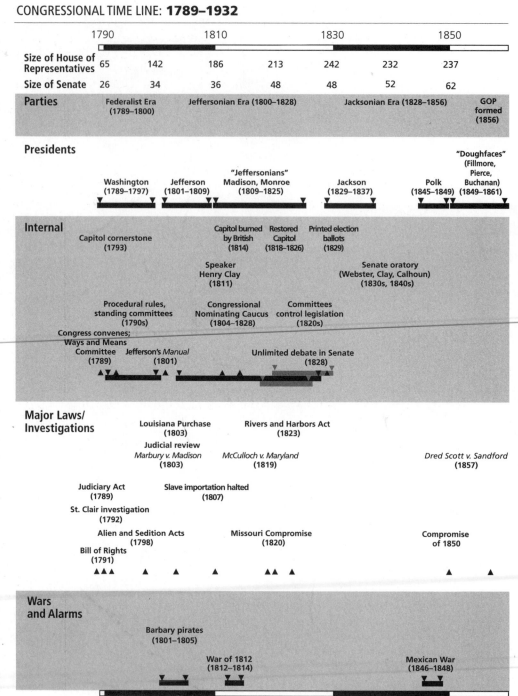

	1790		1810		1830		1850	
Size of House of Representatives	65	142	186	213	242	232	237	
Size of Senate	26	34	36	48	48	52	62	

Parties

Federalist Era (1789–1800) | Jeffersonian Era (1800–1828) | Jacksonian Era (1828–1856) | GOP formed (1856)

Presidents

Washington (1789–1797) | Jefferson (1801–1809) | "Jeffersonians" Madison, Monroe (1809–1825) | Jackson (1829–1837) | Polk (1845–1849) | "Doughfaces" (Fillmore, Pierce, Buchanan) (1849–1861)

Internal

Capitol cornerstone (1793)

Capitol burned by British (1814) | Restored Capitol (1818–1826) | Printed election ballots (1829)

Speaker Henry Clay (1811)

Senate oratory (Webster, Clay, Calhoun) (1830s, 1840s)

Procedural rules, standing committees (1790s)

Congressional Nominating Caucus (1804–1828)

Committees control legislation (1820s)

Congress convenes; Ways and Means Committee (1789) | Jefferson's *Manual* (1801)

Unlimited debate in Senate (1828)

Major Laws/Investigations

Louisiana Purchase (1803)

Rivers and Harbors Act (1823)

Judicial review *Marbury v. Madison* (1803)

McCulloch v. Maryland (1819)

Dred Scott v. Sandford (1857)

Judiciary Act (1789)

Slave importation halted (1807)

St. Clair investigation (1792)

Alien and Sedition Acts (1798)

Missouri Compromise (1820)

Compromise of 1850

Bill of Rights (1791)

Wars and Alarms

Barbary pirates (1801–1805)

War of 1812 (1812–1814)

Mexican War (1846–1848)

| 1790 | 1810 | 1830 | 1850 |